Available for students to use with this text:

Study Guide—Includes a detailed outline, questions with answers, problems with answers, and computer exercises tied in to the investment software.

Two investment software floppy disks—Featuring portfolio optimization through Markowitz and the Single Index Model, term structure analysis, bond immunization, Black-Scholes option pricing, option pricing through binomial approximation, option position analysis, and the dividend discount model.

Complimentary copies of the software are made available to the instructor upon adoption of the text.

Permission is granted for students to copy the software from the instructor's disks.

If these items are not present in your bookstore, please ask the instructor to place an order for them through the bookstore.

INTRODUCTORY INVESTMENT THEORY

ROBERT A. HAUGEN

Bailey Professor of Finance
University of Illinois
Urbana/Champaign

Prentice-Hall, Inc., Englewood Cliffs, New Jersey 07632

Library of Congress Cataloging-in-Publication Data

Haugen, Robert A.
  Introductory investment theory.

  Includes bibliographies and index.
  1. Investment analysis. 2. Portfolio management.
I. Title.
HG4529.H378 1987   332.6   86–25373
ISBN 0–13–501933–8

Editorial/production supervision: Barbara Grasso
Interior design: Jules Perlmutter
Cover design: Suzanne Behnke
Manufacturing buyer: Ed O'Dougherty

Printed in the United States of America

10 9 8 7 6 5 4 3 2 1

ISBN 0-13-501933-8 01

Prentice-Hall International (UK) Limited, *London*
Prentice-Hall of Australia Pty. Limited, *Sydney*
Prentice-Hall Canada Inc., *Toronto*
Prentice-Hall Hispanoamericana, S.A., *Mexico*
Prentice-Hall of India Private Limited, *New Delhi*
Prentice-Hall of Japan, Inc., *Tokyo*
Prentice-Hall of Southeast Asia Pte. Ltd., *Singapore*
Editora Prentice-Hall do Brasil, Ltda., *Rio de Janeiro*

*This book is dedicated
to the three women in my life:
Wendy, Sally, and Tiffany*

CONTENTS

PART TWO   PORTFOLIO MANAGEMENT

14 Financial Forward and Futures Contracts   353

PART SIX   ISSUES IN INVESTMENT MANAGEMENT

15 The Effect of Taxes on Investment Strategy and Securities Prices   381

20 Market Efficiency: The Evidence   467

PREFACE

This book is intended for the first course in investment management. In an intuitively simple manner, it presents the developments in investment theory over the past twenty years, stressing applications of the models and techniques in the real investment community. A complete understanding of the presentation requires minimal training in mathematics and statistics. All the statistical concepts required for an understanding of the text are provided in a review in the appendices to Chapters 3 and 4. The book differentiates itself in the following respects. The coverage of portfolio theory is complete, discussed in three chapters. The properties of the minimum variance set are used extensively throughout the book to gain an easy but deeper understanding of theories such as the Capital Asset Pricing Model and the Arbitrage Pricing Theory. The coverage given to single and multi-index models reflects the growing use of these models in the industry, and, at the same time, paves the way for an easy grasp of the assumptions underlying the Arbitrage Pricing Theory.

Second, extensive coverage is given to the controversial issues related to capital asset pricing. The Capital Asset Pricing Model is discussed in great detail. Emphasis is given to discriminating between the properties of the model that derive from economics and the properties that derive from definitional identities. Rather than skirt the Roll critique, it is discussed in depth, as befits the prominence of the issue in academics and the securities industry. The coverage of the Arbitrage Pricing Theory is both complete and up to date. The issues involved in testing the APT are also explored in detail. Emphasis is given to the flaws in both the CAPM and the APT. It is my feeling that we no longer need to convince the student that a study of modern finance will increase their human capital.

Most of the theories and models in this book are widely employed in the real world. Rather than trying to convince them of their merits, I believe that students should thoroughly understand their weaknesses as well as their strengths, so they will know which models to lean on, and how hard, in making their investment decisions.

Third, the book presents three chapters on interest rates and bond management. It is no secret that in recent years interest rates have become increasingly volatile, increasing both the complexity and excitement of bond portfolio management. Two chapters are devoted to the economic forces that push both the general level and term structure of interest rates around. A third chapter is devoted to aggressive and defensive bond portfolio management. The students learn how to make the most out of their forecasts of future interest rates. They also learn how to immunize their portfolio against the threat of changing interest rates. There is a growing interest in immunization among pension funds and other financial institutions. A knowledge of interest immunization has become an essential weapon in the modern portfolio manager's arsenal.

Fourth, as befitting the increasing popularity of these contracts, the coverage of options and forward and futures contracts is very extensive. Two chapters are devoted to options pricing. In the first chapter, as the students are taken through simplified valuation frameworks, they learn the behavioral characteristics of options prices, the concept of pricing an option to provide those who hedge with the risk-free rate of return, and the Black-Scholes options pricing model. In the second chapter they learn put-call parity, why American options may be exercised early, and biases that may exist in the Black-Scholes Model. In the chapter on forward and futures contracts, emphasis is given to the pricing of these contracts. A simplified discussion is presented of the latest consumption-based models of forward and futures pricing, as well as hedging strategies employing forward and futures contracts.

Finally, two chapters are devoted to the efficient markets controversy. The presentation is balanced, and there is a complete and up-to-date discussion of the interesting anomalies that have been published in the recent literature.

In addition to these distinctions in coverage, the book presents many mini-case studies that show students how the techniques explored in the book are actually used in the real world. The individuals and firms discussed in these case studies are real. In addition to motivating the student to learn the material, they are likely to provoke in-class discussion of the material.

Importantly, adopters of this book may receive complimentary computer software covering many of the topics addressed in the book by writing to the publisher, Prentice-Hall, Inc. The software may then be copied and put on reserve for individual student use.

Completion of a book of this size is a considerable task involving the participation of many people. I would like to thank my secretaries, Ruth Dresen, Kathy Halpin, and Angie Patard, for editing the first draft. A special thanks also goes to my editor at Prentice-Hall, Linda Frascino, for her help and encouragement. Rick Green and Jay Shanken were of great help in the chapters on asset pricing. I take full responsibility, however, for any remaining errors. I should also say that the final tone of the chapters reflects my own views and not necessarily those of Green or Shanken.

I thank Ravi Jagannathan for helpful comments on the chapters on the pricing of complex securities. Bill Lepley, who was my teaching assistant in the course for several years, participated extensively in writing the end-of-chapter questions. Others who made important contributions to the manuscript include David Cho, Jim Johannes, Charles Kroncke, Jay Lee, Sreenivasa Ramachandran, and Leigh Reddick. Finally, a special thanks goes to all the professionals who participated in the "Out on the Street" segments of the book. These people devoted their time freely to the project, and their time is very much appreciated. It is hoped that their stories will be a source of inspiration to the students who will follow in their footsteps.

1 INTRODUC...
TO INVESTM...
THEORY

Introduction

This is a book about the theory of securities pricing, the management of investment portfolios, and the measurement of investment performance. After you learn the various theories and concepts in this book, you will, among other things, be able to manage investment risk, detect mispriced securities, forecast interest rates, avoid taxes, and measure the performance of investment managers.

Perhaps in no other area of business education have theories and techniques that have been developed in economics departments and business schools had such a profound effect on professional behavior and practice in the real world. Modern investment theory is widely employed throughout the investment community by investment and portfolio analysts, who are becoming increasingly sophisticated. Admittedly, many of the models and techniques are complex and difficult to master, but many of them are effective. They can help you capture extra returns beyond those that are available without their use. They can create new products and land new accounts. A thorough understanding of these models and techniques can conceivably mean the difference between success and failure in your investment career.

An understanding of investment theory will help you learn how to accomplish goals in portfolio management. You will learn how to set up a hedged position that eliminates part or all of the risk associated with an investment by using options or futures contracts. You will learn how to guarantee that pensioners will be assured of getting all their promised

etirement benefits no matter how variable the returns are on the portfolio that is invested to pay these benefits. You will also learn how to squeeze the most return out of a portfolio, given the level of risk, or how to make the returns on one portfolio mimic the returns on another.

In addition, as you master investment theory, you will gain a deeper understanding of the way securities are priced by the market. You will understand the forces that push interest rates up and down, or why short-term rates may be above or below the level of long-term rates. You will understand how to measure the risk of an investment and the influence that this risk has on securities prices and expected rates of return. You will see how options behave in relation to the stocks they are written on and gain some insight into the factors that influence the agreed-upon price in a futures contract. The more knowledge you have about the nature of securities pricing, the easier it will be for you to detect deviations from a pricing structure and thereby capture superior returns on your investments.

THE DEVELOPMENT OF MODERN INVESTMENT THEORY

The beginnings of modern portfolio theory date back to 1952, when Harry Markowitz published a paper entitled ''Portfolio Selection.'' In it, he showed how to create a ''frontier'' of investment portfolios by combining available securities investments such that each investment had the greatest possible expected rate of return, given its level of risk. The technique was computationally very complex, especially given the technology of the time. A student of Markowitz, William Sharpe (1963), developed a simplified version of the technique that is now referred to as the Single Index Model. The simplified version made portfolio theory practical, even when managing large numbers of securities. In the 1970s, after techniques for estimating the required inputs to the model were perfected and were packaged and marketed as computer software, modern portfolio theory took off in terms of practical application in the real world. Now the Single Index Model is employed to allocate investments in a portfolio among individual securities, and the original, more general model of Markowitz is widely used to allocate investments among types of securities, such as bonds, stock, venture capital, and real estate.

Prior to the dissemination of portfolio theory into the real world, three individuals simultaneously and independently asked themselves the question: Suppose *everyone* managed his or her investments using Markowitz portfolio theory and invested in the most desirable portfolios on the frontier. How would this affect the pricing of securities? In answering this question, Sharpe (1964), Lintner (1965), and Mossin (1966) developed what became known as the Capital Asset Pricing Model. This model was premier in the field of finance for nearly

fifteen years. In addition to finding its way into elementary finance textbooks, it became a popular benchmark to specify the appropriate expected rate of return on an investment, given its level of risk. In the real world it was used to measure portfolio performance, value securities, make capital budgeting decisions, and even regulate public utilities. In 1976, however, the model was called into question by Richard Roll (1977, 1978), who argued that it should be discarded because it was impossible to verify empirically its single economic prediction, that the aggregate portfolio of all available investments, the market portfolio, was itself positioned on the efficient frontier. This controversial issue is still the subject of heated debate.

At the same time, an alternative to the Capital Asset Pricing Model was being developed by Steve Ross (1976), the Arbitrage Pricing Theory. This theory argued that expected return must be related to risk in such a way that no single investor could create unlimited wealth through arbitrage. The theory was argued to be less demanding in terms of its assumptions, and both Roll and Ross (1984) argued that it was testable, at least in principle. These points have also been the subject of much debate.

At this point, although it is being questioned, the Capital Asset Pricing Model is still widely used in the real world. The Arbitrage Pricing Theory, however, seems to be gaining momentum, at least in academic circles.

The question of how to price options contracts to buy and sell securities long puzzled researchers in finance until a paper by Fisher Black and Myron Scholes was published in 1973. They argued that you can create a riskless hedged position with an option by taking a position in both the option and the stock that it is written on. It will cost you money to set up the hedge, and because the hedge is riskless, the option must be priced relative to the stock so that you get the riskless rate of return on your hedged investment. They developed a model that would price the option so as to produce this result. The Black-Scholes Model has become extremely popular in the investment community. Options have literally exploded in terms of variety and volume of trading, and options traders have become extremely sophisticated. The Black-Scholes Model remains the most widely used, but since 1973 many alternatives have been developed. Some of these more sophisticated approaches to valuing options are beginning to affect behavior and prices on the floors of the options exchanges.

Even as researchers were attempting to determine the nature of the pricing structure in the securities markets, the issue of how efficient the market was in pricing to its structure was called into question. In 1965 the Ph.D. dissertation of Eugene Fama was published in the *Journal of Business*. In it, he made a compelling argument: There are literally thousands of intelligent, well-informed professional investors actively searching for mispriced securities. Because, upon finding them, these professionals trade and thereby affect prices, it is quite possible that securities prices, at any given time, reflect the collective wisdom of these professional traders. If information rapidly and efficiently becomes impounded into the prices of securities through the trading activities of professional investors, then it becomes impossible to "beat" the market through any form of security analysis.

Terminal Investing

The bright glow of the computer terminal seemed to turn everything it touched in the dimly lit office a pale green, including the face and hands of Terry Langetieg.

It was 10:00 P.M., and Terry was finding it difficult to think. He had arrived at his Salomon Brothers office at 9:00 A.M. that morning. Thirteen-hour days were new to him, after spending the last decade as a finance professor at the University of Southern California. They were new, but they weren't that uncommon in the four months that he had been working for the firm.

Terry was only one of several academics in finance who had recently made the switch from the classroom to the real world of investment analysis. New faces seemed to be popping up all over, and these weren't the traditional pin-striped M.B.A. investment types you'd normally expect to see. These people had Ph.D. degrees, and not just in finance or economics either. Increasingly, you'd see new colleagues with terminal degrees in mathematics, statistics, and even physics. The feeling was that these people would pick up the finance they'd need to know on the job during their first few months with the firm. The important thing was that they had the advanced quantitative skills to contribute to the highly sophisticated investment analysis that Salomon Brothers was using to create new financial products and new securities and to detect and take advantage of arbitrage opportunities.

The computer age in investments was definitely here. Terry normally spends six hours of his working day before a computer terminal. The models and valuation techniques that were developed by professors like Terry over the last twenty years are about to be applied by the practitioners in a big way. Students desiring to enter the world of investment analysis would be advised to prepare by expanding their programming abilities in the various computer languages.

Terry himself has been spending the past four months applying modern investment theory in building bond portfolios that track and beat, in the sense of earning fifty or more annual basis points, the Broad Investment Grade Bond Index recently developed by Salomon Brothers. The main index is divided into three subindices, one consisting of treasury and government agency securities, a second consisting of corporate bonds rated BBB or better and having total market values of $25 million or more, and a third consisting of generic mortgage-backed securities, like Ginnie Mae passthroughs. Surprisingly, the size of the market for mortgage-backed securities now rivals the market for tradeable corporate bonds. The broad index consists of $1.4 trillion worth of securities.

Terry tries to *track* movements in the index by using a measure of the average maturity of the payments associated with a bond issue called "duration" (which we will learn more about in Chapter 19). Roughly speaking, he tries to build bond portfolios that have the same duration as the duration of the index. One way he tries to *beat* the return produced by the index is by analyzing spreads between the yields on individual bonds and the yields on nearly identical treasury issues that have comparable durations.

During the course of the past four months, Terry has developed a feel for the efficiency of the bond market. He sees a bond market consisting of thousands of traders who expect instant access to information and analysis of any security in any tradeable market. They are hooked into sophisticated systems that compute yields based on a multiplicity of reinvestment assumptions and then compute duration-based yield spreads matched to the treasury yield curve. Some systems, based on a forecast of interest rates over some time horizon, determine the impact of the forecasted change in rates on the outlook for the bonds being called by the issuing firms at their call prices. This analysis is used to develop a rate of return profile for any menu of bonds over the time horizon. Some, more sophisticated programs use Monte Carlo techniques to simulate the effects of different interest rate patterns on bond returns in order to develop probability distributions for returns on the bonds over the horizon period.

Terry has come to believe that, given the number of analysts employing sophisticated technology, the market has achieved a tremendous degree of efficiency. Yes, opportunities for arbitrage do exist, but they certainly don't last long. Terry doubts very much the viability of the so-called market segmentation theory of the term structure (which we will learn about in Chapter 10). There is little scientific evidence supporting the theory, and he sees many, many traders arbitraging across the entire term structure. Although there are clienteles for bonds of specific maturity ranges, even banks are somewhat heterogeneous in terms of their desired maturities.

Which bonds, long or short, are viewed as being riskier? In Terry's view, it's the long bonds for sure. Yes, some institutions have long-term liabilities, but the performance of most money managers is still evaluated on an annual basis, and given that this is so, they will be concerned about their returns during the course of a year. Long-term bonds contribute the most to the variability of these returns.

It's possible, however, that the new bond indices may change this perception. The broad index has a duration of approximately five years. To the extent that performance is measured in terms of the deviation of a manager's return from the return on the index, bonds with average maturities greater or less than five years may be viewed as comparatively risky.

The day is finally done! As Terry makes his way to the elevator, he notices many lights still on in many offices. It's 11:00 P.M. No question about it, this is definitely not USC.

This controversial issue became known as the efficient market hypothesis, and it still remains to be settled to this day. The debate spawned an extremely large number of empirical studies directed at determining the quantity and quality of information reflected in securities prices. Initially, the weight of the evidence clearly favored the view that the market was highly efficient. The results of these studies had their effect in the real world. Mutual funds were established that made no attempt to beat the market. Their philosophy was that this was a waste of time and money, and they would only attempt to match the market's performance. Gradually, however, as better data became available and statistical techniques were refined, some holes were punched through the efficient market hypothesis. At this point, the prevailing view is that although the market appears to be clearly more efficient than was thought prior to the publication of Fama's dissertation, securities prices reflect less than the complete set of information available to the diligent investor.

WHY SHOULD YOU LEARN
MODERN INVESTMENT THEORY?

Rapid advances in computer technology have revolutionized professional investment management. Managers can sit at terminals and access detailed data relating to myriad companies in all sectors of the market. This has had two important implications.

First, information is channeled more rapidly from its source to the analysts and traders who process and act on it. The probable effect is to reduce the lag between the occurrence of an event and its effect on securities prices. In discussions with professional traders, I have come away with the distinct impression that the efficiency of the markets in processing information has increased significantly in the last few years. This seems especially true in the options markets. Second, the explosive growth in personal computers and computer software has made possible the everyday use of extremely sophisticated financial models. Hundreds of services have appeared that specialize in writing software based on stock, bond, or options valuation models, routines that optimize portfolio composition, and sophisticated statistical procedures to obtain estimates of the required inputs for techniques like the Single Index Model and the Black-Scholes options pricing model.

The computer age has had a dramatic impact on both the speed and sophistication of investment management, and there is no reason to think that the process won't continue to move in this direction.

There are plenty of people out there who are more than willing to take your job, your money, or both, if you choose to make them available. To survive in tomorrow's market, you have to be both alert and sophisticated in your techniques of analysis. If you don't believe that a deep understanding of modern investment theory is important to your survival, read a copy of the latest Chartered Financial Analysts examination, or talk to a sophisticated floor trader on the Chicago Board Options Exchange.

As you learn investment theory, it is important to concentrate on the weaknesses and biases of the various models. Although widely used, these models are by no means perfect. If you understand their strengths as well as their weaknesses, you will know when and how hard to lean on them. You will be in the best position to critique the presentations made by the representatives of the financial software companies. You will be in a position to lead your firm in new directions. You may even want to start your own investment management firm, or you may want to design and market your own computer software.

The techniques of modern investment theory will enable you to do some things that may surprise you and that many other investors may find very attractive. Here are some examples:

1. You will learn how to obtain a forecast of the market's estimate of the future direction of interest rates from the current structure of securities prices.

2. You will learn how to estimate the market's estimate of the future variability of a stock price based on the price of an option written on the stock.

3. The return on a common stock is the sum of dividend income and price appreciation. You will learn how to separate a stock into two securities, one paying off only dividends, the other paying off only capital gains. You can then market the two securities to two separate clients, who, for tax or other reasons, want one but not the other.

4. You will learn how to provide clients with the following service. For a small fee you will insure their portfolios in the sense that if their portfolios go up in value they will capture the appreciation. On the other hand, if their portfolios go down in value they need not participate in the depreciation. The values of their portfolios can increase but cannot decrease. Aside from payment of the "insurance premium," the clients face the attractive prospect of the possibility of dramatic gains but no losses. This is called portfolio insurance, and it is only one of many things that can be done with options pricing models. This product has only recently appeared, but already billions of dollars are insured in this way.

Products like these aren't hard to create. You can create them, and others like them, by applying the techniques of modern investment theory and your own imagination.

Throughout this book you will find stories about individuals like Dennis Tito, Michelle Clayman, Jack Reynoldson, Peter Thayer, and Larry Davanzo, who are trading in the markets and marketing products. These people are real and their stories are true. Investment management is an exciting industry, populated by intelligent, dynamic, determined individuals. You can become one of them. You can make money, *if* you are well informed.

OUT ON THE STREET

Making a Mark

Dennis Tito sips his coffee and then lowers the cup to the saucer on the coffee table. His hand shakes, spilling a few drops to the floor. Dennis is a little nervous, but his concern is justified. Dennis has been working for a shot at this account for months.

The account is the Public Employees Retirement System of the state of California—a pension fund with $23 billion in assets! Dennis is president of Wilshire Associates, based in Santa Monica, California. Wilshire employs approximately 100 people and has approximately 250 clients, including big money management funds and banks in New York, big pension funds such as Texaco and Goodyear, and more recently, public pension funds such as this one in California.

Wilshire is a consulting firm to the sponsors of pension plans and to investment managers. It specializes in the application of modern portfolio management techniques to solving the problems of investors. In addition to estimating risk and expected return for individual investments, the company advises clients on how much of their portfolios to invest in various types of securities, what individual securities to buy of each type, and how to monitor the ongoing performance of the managers.

Dennis is sitting in the mezzanine lobby of the Sir Francis Drake Hotel in San Francisco. Next to him sit Larry Davanzo, a partner in the firm, Jim Blanchard, and Allan Emkin. It was Allan who worked with the California State Teachers account, which itself is a $12 billion account. Through Allan's contacts, Wilshire has earned a shot at the remaining $23 billion Public Employees Retirement System. Together, the combined $35 billion account represents the largest pension fund in the country and one of the largest in the world.

Across from them is a large door, and behind the door sits the entire investment board of the state of California. Wilshire has one hour to convince the board that it is right for the job. If Wilshire succeeds, it will be the biggest moment ever for the rapidly growing firm. The four men enter the room, and Dennis begins his presentation.

Wilshire proposes to do a complete evaluation of the retirement system's investment program, including

1. Advising the system on the optimal allocation of its investments among the various types of assets, such as stocks, bonds, and real estate.
2. Helping the system establish a planning statement of investment objectives and policies.
3. Advising the system on the relative

BIBLIOGRAPHY

BLACK, F., and M. SCHOLES, "The Pricing of Options and Corporate Liabilities," *Journal of Political Economy* (May–June 1973).

merits of using external versus internal managers for investments.

4. Establishing a performance objective that will serve as the basis for the bonus paid to the system's chief of investments.

5. Helping the system draw on the various techniques of modern portfolio theory that Wilshire has available on its computers.

To illustrate its techniques, Wilshire has taken the largest membership population in the $23 billion plan and has modeled it to show the effects of various investment strategies on investment values and required future contributions that the state must make to the plan.

Midway through the presentation a pertinent question is raised: "But we've got a problem in California. Unlike your private plans, we are restricted by law with regard to the types of investments we can make. For example, we can buy only common stocks that have paid dividends in eight of the last ten years, and the dividends paid in each of the past three years must have been earned in the year paid. Given this law, we can't invest in stocks like General Motors, Texas Instruments, and Chrysler, even though these stocks have performed quite well of late. In the face of these severe restrictions, how can we expect to benefit

from your techniques, which require considerable flexibility?"

Another board member elaborates: "On top of that, it's a constitutional law. That means that in order to remove it, you would need a statewide ballot."

Dennis ponders a choice between a conservative and a risky response. He chooses risk to maximize return. "Then we'll change the law. The law is antiquated in any case. These arbitrary restrictions make no sense in the context of modern investment theory. We'll help you launch a campaign to get a constitutional amendment on the ballot. Given that the present law is obviously suboptimal, I think we can succeed."

The account is won, and the campaign is launched.

On June 5, 1984, Proposition 21 is put before the voters of the state of California. It passes, despite the fact that a similar proposition had been defeated two years previously. The earlier version was written in such a manner that it focused only on the potential increased risk that might result from eliminating a 25 percent maximum equity investment constraint. Wilshire advised that the new proposition stress that all investments made by the state of California would be judged against the expert prudent person rule, rather than on the basis of an arbitrary set of restrictions.

FAMA, E. F., "The Behavior of Stock Prices," *Journal of Business* (January 1965).

———, "Efficient Capital Markets: A Review of Theory and Empirical Work," *Journal of Finance* (May 1970).

LINTNER, J., "The Valuation of Risk Assets and the Selection of Risky Investments in

Stock Portfolios and Capital Budgets," *Review of Economics and Statistics* (February 1965).

MARKOWITZ, H. M., "Portfolio Selection," *Journal of Finance* (December 1952).

MOSSIN, J., "Equilibrium in a Capital Market," *Econometrica* (October 1966).

ROLL, R., "A Critique of the Asset Pricing Theory's Tests: Part I: On the Past and Potential Testability of the Theory," *Journal of Financial Economics* (March 1977).

———, "Ambiguity When Performance Is Measured by the Security Market Line," *Journal of Finance* (September 1978).

ROLL, R., and S. ROSS, "A Critical Reexamination of the Empirical Evidence on the Arbitrage Pricing Theory: A Reply," *Journal of Finance* (June 1984).

ROSS, S. A., "The Arbitrage Theory of Capital Asset Pricing," *Journal of Economic Theory* (December 1976).

SHARPE, W. F., "A Simplified Model of Portfolio Analysis," *Management Science* (January 1963).

———, "Capital Asset Prices: A Theory of Market Equilibrium Under Conditions of Risk," *Journal of Finance* (September 1964).

2 SECURITIES AND MARKETS

Introduction

Before we explore the principles of portfolio management and the economics of pricing in the financial markets, we will spend some time reviewing the characteristics of the different securities traded and the nature and mechanics of the markets themselves.

Ultimately, we want to learn how to construct an optimal portfolio of investments. We want to understand the determinants of the general level of interest rates, and how one security is priced relative to another, given the characteristics of the stream of income it offers to investors. To gain this understanding, we need to be aware of the various investment alternatives available, and be able to discern the nature of the cash flows an investor might expect to gain from a given investment, as well as the risks associated with making the commitment.

Because each security is a claim on the wealth of an individual, firm, or government, in making these estimates we need to understand the contractual provisions of the claims. In executing a decision to invest in various securities, we also need to know where they are traded and the procedures through which the trades can be consummated.

Fixed-income securities, like bonds, have a defined, limited dollar claim. The dollar receipts from these investments will never exceed this promised claim, although they can fall short of the promise in the case of default. *Variable-income securities,* like common stock, have a residual claim to the earnings of a company. Claimants are entitled to whatever is left after all other security holders have exercised their claims to the firm's earnings. While stockholders' claims to the earnings are residual, they are also unlimited in amount. If the firm proves to be a huge success, the stockholders may reap huge gains, whereas the bondholders receive only their fixed claim. On the other hand, if the firm doesn't do too well, the stockholders are the first to feel the pinch, in the form of a reduction in their income.

Primary securities are issued by firms. They obligate the firm to the payment of some part of its income. *Secondary securities* are issued by individual traders rather than firms. An example of a secondary security is an options contract, giving its holder the right to buy or sell a primary security at a certain price. For every trader buying a secondary security as an asset, there is another trader selling the security as a liability. If we were to add up all the positive and negative positions in secondary securities, we would find that their total value sums to zero. On the other hand, if we were to add up the total value of all the primary securities, we would find that their total value sums to the total value of the assets of all the firms and governments issuing them.

Securities are usually issued by governments and private firms. Governments issue securities to finance deficits in their budgets when revenues fall short of expenditures. Government securities are almost invariably bond issues of various types and are issued by governments at all levels—federal, state, and municipality. Because the federal government can print money, its securities are not subject to default. The securities of state and municipal governments, however, are only as sound as the ability of these governments to raise revenue through taxation and other means. Private firms issue a wide variety of different types of securities, from bonds to common stock. The quality of these issues is based on the quality of the earning power of the firms issuing them.

Government Bonds

Securities issued by the federal government include U.S. savings bonds, treasury bills, treasury notes, treasury bonds, and the bonds issued by the various agencies of the U.S. government.

U.S. savings bonds are usually sold to individual investors. They can be redeemed at any time at specified amounts that gradually increase from the original purchase price to the maximum redemption value at their maturity. Series EE bonds pay no periodic cash interest payments to their investors. Interest received is based on the difference between the original purchase price and the value of the bond when redeemed. The redemption values are usually structured to provide an incentive to hold the bond until maturity. Series HH bonds pay interest semiannually and mature in ten years with the payment of principal.

Treasury bills have very short maturities, the maximum being one year. These securities can be redeemed only at maturity. Unlike savings bonds, there is a very active market for these issues, and they can be easily sold at prices that reflect prevailing interest rates prior to maturity. You buy a treasury bill at a discount from its promised payment at maturity. Your interest on the investment is represented by the difference between the promised payment and your purchase price. There are no other periodic cash interest payments associated with a treasury bill. These securities are usually issued in denominations of $10,000 in terms of their promised payments.

The annual rates of return produced by treasury bills in the years 1926 through 1983 are presented in Figure 2-1a; the frequency distribution for these returns is presented in Figure 2-1b. Notice that treasury bill returns have been fairly stable over the years, but also quite modest. These returns tend to go up and down with the expected rate of inflation. Thus, many analysts consider treasury bills to be the best hedge against inflation currently available in the U.S. securities markets.

Treasury notes have maturities of up to seven years. They are issued in denominations of $1000 or more. Unlike treasury bills, notes pay cash interest payments on a semiannual basis. As with all U.S. government securities, aside from savings bonds, these securities are traded in an active market, so investment in them can be easily liquidated at any time. As with any bond, when you buy a treasury note you must pay the seller of the bond not only the prevailing market price but also any interest that has accrued. For example, suppose you are buying a treasury note that has a semiannual interest payment of $100. It has been exactly 60 days since the last interest payment, and it will be 120 days until the next payment. The seller has accrued interest on the bond of $33.33 = (60/180) × $100. You must pay the seller the accrued interest, in addition to the market price, when you buy the bond.

There is no maximum maturity for a *treasury bond*. These securities are identical to treasury notes in form, with two possible distinguishing features. These bonds are sometimes issued with call provisions attached. The call provision gives the government the option to retire the issue at a stated call price prior to maturity. The call option does not become active until a stated date, perhaps five years prior to actual maturity. Also, certain designated treasury bonds can be used to pay federal estate taxes, dollar for dollar, on the basis of their principal values. These bonds were originally issued when interest rates were much lower than they are today. Because of their very small interest payments, the bonds sell at prices that are discounted below their principal values, making them advantageous for paying inheritance taxes. Unless a purchaser is planning to use them for this purpose, however, these bonds are unattractive investments because their yields are usually well below those of conventional treasury bonds.

Annual rates of return to a portfolio of long-term U.S. government treasury bonds and their frequency distribution are presented in Figures 2-2a and 2-2b. Note that their returns are considerably more variable than are treasury bill re-

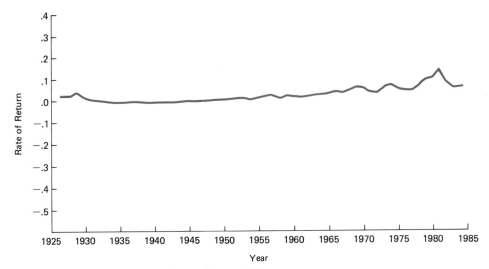

Figure 2-1a Yearly Rates of Return on Treasury Bills

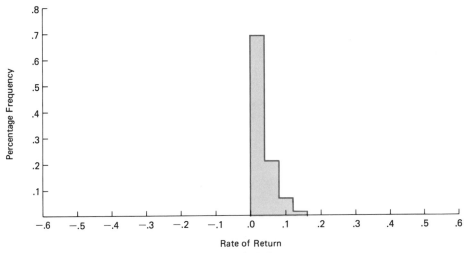

Figure 2-1b Frequency Distribution for Treasury Bill Returns

turns. These returns reflect both annual interest payments and capital gains or losses. In the years in which the total return was negative, the capital loss has been large enough to more than offset the annual interest payment. The capital losses are the result of increases in the rate of interest, which drives down the market value of these bonds. Interest rates go up in times of high inflation; thus, these bonds produce their lowest returns when the inflation rate is unexpectedly high. Therefore, treasury bonds have been a poor inflation hedge in the past.

The various agencies of the federal government also issue bonds that, with some exceptions, are backed with the full faith and credit of the U.S. government. Among others, these agencies include the Federal Housing Administration, the Federal Land Banks, and the Federal National Mortgage Association.

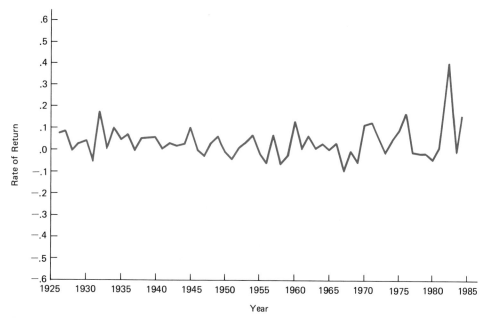

Figure 2-2a Yearly Rates of Return on Long-Term Treasury Bonds

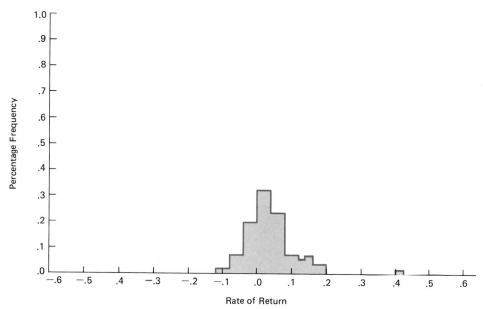

Figure 2-2b Frequency Distribution for Treasury Bond Returns

CHAPTER 2   **Securities and Markets**   15

Tax-Exempt Bonds

Thursday, May 1, 1986

Here are current prices of several active tax-exempt revenue bonds issued by toll roads and other public authorities.

Agency	Coupon	Mat	Bid	Asked	Chg.
Alabama G.O.	8⅜s	'01	107	110	....
Bat Park City Auth NY	6⅜s	'14	84	89	– ½
Chelan Cnty PU Dist	5s	'13	83½	85½	....
Clark Cnty Arpt Rev	10½s	'07	111	114	....
Columbia St Pwr Exch	3⅞s	'03	93	95	....
Dela River Port Auth	6½s	'11	93½	96½	....
Douglas Cnty PU Dist	4s	'18	61½	64½	+ ½
Ga Mun El Auth Pwr Rev	8s	'15	97	100	....
Intermountain Pwr	7½s	'18	93	97	....
Intermountain Pwr	10½s	'18	123	127	....
Intermountain Pwr	14s	'21	136	141	....
Jacksonville Elec Rev	9¼s	'13	107	111	....
Loop	6½s	'08	76	79	....
MAC	7½s	'92	100½	104½	....
MAC	7½s	'95	102	106	....
MAC	8s	'86	99	103	....
MAC	8s	'91	100	104	....
MAC	9.7s	'08	111½	115½	....
MAC	9¾s	'92	102	106	....
MAC	10¼s	'93	107	111	....
Mass Port Auth Rev	6s	'11	88	92	....
Massachusetts G.O.	6½s	'00	97	100	....
Mass Wholesale	6⅜s	'15	73	76	....
Mass Wholesale	13⅜s	'17	121	124	....
Metro Transit Auth	9¼s	'15	106	125	....
Michigan Public Pwr	10⅝s	'18	120	125	....
Nebraska Pub Pwr Dist	7.1s	'17	91	95	....
NJ Turnpike Auth	4¾s	'06	80	83	....
NJ Turnpike Auth	5.7s	'13	85½	88½	....
NJ Turnpike Auth	6s	'14	90	93	....
NY Mtge Agency Rev	9½s	'13	102	107	....
NY State Pwr Escr	5½s	'10	83	88	– ½
NY State Pwr	6⅝s	'10	90	95	– ½
NY State Pwr Escr	9½s	'01	109	114	– ½
NY State Pwr	9⅞s	'20	109	114	– ½
NY State Thruway Rev	3.1s	'94	82	85	....
NY State Urban Dev Corp	6s	'13	77½	82½	....
NY State Urban Dev Corp	7s	'14	88½	93½	....
NC East Mun Pwr Agcy	11¼s	'18	122	126	....
Okla Tpke Auth Rev	4.7s	'06	80	82	....
Port of NY & NJ	4¾s	'03	75	80	– ½
Port of NY & NJ	6s	'06	86	90	– ½
Port of NY & NJ	7s	'11	97	102	– ½
Port of NY-Delta	10½s	'08	114	119	....
Salt River-Arizona	9¼s	'20	103	108	....
SC Pub Svc Auth	10¼s	'20	115	118	....
Texas Munic Pwr Agcy	9½s	'12	107	111	....
Valdez (Exxon)	5½s	'07	79½	82½	....
Valdez (Sohio)	6s	'07	80	83	....
Wshngtn PPSS #4-5	f6s	'15	9	12	....
Wshngtn PPSS #4-5	f7¾s	'18	9½	12½	....
Wshngtn PPSS #4-5	f9⅞s	'12	10	13	....
Wshngtn PPSS #4-5	f12½s	'10	11	13½	....
Wshngtn PPSS #2	6s	'12	69	72	....
Wshngtn PPSS #1	7¾s	'17	85	87	....
Wshngtn PPSS #2	9¼s	'11	99	103	....
Wshngtn PPSS #3	13⅞s	'18	121	124	....
Wshngtn PPSS #2	14¾s	'12	127	130	....
Wshngtn PPSS #1	15s	'17	136	140	....

f-Trades flat without payment of current interest.

Figure 2-3 Quotations for Tax-Exempt Bonds

SOURCE: *Wall Street Journal,* May 2, 1986, p. 36. Reprinted by permission of *Wall Street Journal,* © Dow Jones & Company, Inc. 1986. All rights reserved.

Although backed by the U.S. government, these bonds usually sell at slightly higher interest rates than do the direct obligations of the government (for instance, treasury bills). Most of the bonds issued by these agencies are conventional in form. However, some, such as those issued by the Federal National Mortgage Association, are participation certificates. These particular securities are called *Ginnie Mae passthroughs*. A group of residential mortgages is pooled, and certificates are issued, the payments of which are based on the payments associated with the individual mortgages. Default on the payments of the pass-throughs themselves is no problem because the payments are guaranteed by the association and backed by the federal government. The holder of the pass-throughs receives a monthly annuity until maturity.

State and municipal governments also issue debt to finance their expenditures. *General obligation bonds* are backed by the full faith and credit of the issuing government or agency. The interest and principal payments for these bonds may be paid from any source of revenue of the particular government. The interest and principal payments on *revenue bonds,* on the other hand, may be paid only from the revenues associated with a particular project, such as a toll bridge. If the project fails to produce sufficient revenue to make the scheduled payments, the bondholders have no access to the other sources of revenue of the issuing government or agency. When seeking to finance short-term expenditures, governments may frequently issue *tax-anticipation notes,* which are secured by taxes already due but not yet paid.

Some quotations for tax-exempt bond issues of local governments and agencies are given in Figure 2-3. The column labeled "Coupon" lists the annual interest payment as a percentage of the face or principal payment. The next column (Mat) lists the year in which the bond matures. The Bid and Asked columns list what dealers are willing to buy and sell the individual bonds for. This price is expressed as a percentage of face or principal value. The last column (Chg) lists the change in the price of the bond from the preceding trading day.

Corporate Fixed-Income Securities

Debt issued by business firms comes in a wide variety of forms. *Mortgage bonds* are backed by the pledge of specific property as security. Should the firm be unable to fulfill its pledge to make the scheduled payments on the bond, the bondholders are entitled to sell the property and retain the proceeds. Typically, however, the property pledged is illiquid, and the real protection behind the bonds is the earning power of the assets and not their liquidating value.

On the other hand, *equipment trust certificates* are usually backed by a particular piece of equipment, like a railroad car, that is both readily transportable and marketable. In some cases, title to the equipment resides with the creditors through a trustee. The corporation receives title to the equipment only when all the scheduled payments are made.

Debenture bonds are unsecured by real property. Their claim is fixed, but based only on the firm's ability to generate cash flow. Given the illiquid status of the security backing most mortgage bonds, however, the unsecured status of debenture bonds should not be a source of concern. One meaningful difference between mortgage and debenture bonds occurs in technical default, where the firm is profitable but has insufficient cash to make the scheduled payments on its debt issues. In this case, the claim of the mortgage bondholder takes priority over the government's claim to the corporate income tax. The government's claim, on the other hand, takes priority over the claim of the debenture bondholder.

The interest payments on *income bonds* need only be paid if the income of the firm is sufficient to make payment. Failure to pay when earnings are insufficient does not result in bankruptcy. Failure to pay principal at maturity, however, does result in bankruptcy, irrespective of the level of the firm's income.

Convertible bonds give holders the option of exchanging their bonds for the common stock of the firm. The ratio of the number of shares of stock that may be acquired for each bond surrendered is called the conversion ratio. The bonds may be convertible as of a certain future date, and there is frequently a provision for the conversion ratio to fall as the bonds approach maturity.

Corporate bonds are backed by an *indenture* in which the firm promises the bond trustee that it will comply with certain provisions. Among these is the payment of scheduled interest and principal. There may also be restrictions on the amounts of dividends that can be paid to stockholders, as well as restrictions on the use of the proceeds of the bond issue, guarantees on the acquisition of insurance, and investments by the firm in the capital market.

The vast majority of corporate bonds are *callable*. As with treasury bonds, this gives the issuing firm the option to retire the bonds at a stated call price. The call option usually becomes operative after a stated period of call protection, which is usually either five or ten years after original issuance. The call price usually begins at a value close to the sum of the principal plus one annual interest payment, and it steadily declines to the value of the principal at maturity.

Corporate bonds may also contain *sinking fund provisions*. The sinking fund provision requires the firm to retire a stated fraction of the issue each year. In complying with this provision, the firm can usually exercise one of three options: It can (1) retire the bonds at a stated sinking fund call price. If this action is taken, the bonds retired will be determined by lottery. It can also (2) purchase the required quantity of bonds in the open market. Many sinking funds give the firm a third option of (3) acquiring bonds of other firms of similar quality in the market. This third option is designed to prevent financial institutions from buying large blocks of the bonds in an effort to force a firm to exercise option 1 when it would be more advantageous for the firm to exercise option 2. This strategy is called "cornering the sinking fund," and it enables the financial institution to sell the bonds to the firm for considerably more than they are worth, based on prevailing interest rates.

Commercial paper is a short-term promissory note issued by a corporation. The maximum maturity of commercial paper is 270 days, and it is issued in denominations of $100,000 or more. The quality of commercial paper can vary, depending on the quality of the issuing firm and its access to other forms of credit.

Corporate bonds are rated for quality by two major rating agencies, Standard & Poor's Corporation and Moody's. The ratings are based on an analysis of a firm's financial statements and other factors, such as the nature of its industry and its position in the industry. Of major concern is the extent to which the firm can be expected to weather economic adversity, such as a major recession. A sample of the ratings by each agency is given in Tables 2-1 and 2-2.

Table 2–1 Moody's Rating System

Aaa
Bonds which are rated Aaa are judged to be of the best quality. They carry the smallest degree of investment risk and are generally referred to as "gilt edge." Interest payments are protected by a large or by an exceptionally stable margin and principal is secure. While the various protective elements are likely to change, such changes as can be visualized are most unlikely to impair the fundamentally strong position of such issues.

Aa
Bonds which are rated Aa are judged to be of high quality by all standards. Together with the Aaa group, they comprise what are generally known as high-grade bonds. They are rated lower than the best bonds because margins of protection may not be as large as in Aaa securities or fluctuation of protective elements may be of greater amplitude, or there may be other elements present which make the long-term risks appear somewhat larger than in Aaa securities.

A
Bonds which are rated A possess many favorable investment attributes and are to be considered as upper-medium-grade obligations. Factors giving security to principal and interest are considered adequate, but elements may be present which suggest a susceptibility to impairment sometime in the future.

Baa
Bonds which are rated Baa are considered as medium-grade obligations; i.e., they are neither highly protected nor poorly secured. Interest payments and principal security appear adequate for the present, but certain protective elements may be lacking or may be characteristically unreliable over any great length of time. Such bonds lack outstanding investment characteristics, and in fact have speculative characteristics as well.

Ba
Bonds which are rated Ba are judged to have speculative elements; their future cannot be considered as well assured. Often the protection of interest and principal payments may be very moderate and thereby not well safeguarded during both good and bad times over the future. Uncertainty of position characterizes bonds of this class.

B
Bonds which are rated B generally lack characteristics of the desirable investment. Assurance of interest and principal payments or of maintenance of other terms of the contract over any long period of time may be small.

Caa
Bonds which are rated Caa are of poor standing. Such issues may be in default, or there may be present elements of danger with respect to principal or interest.

Ca
Bonds which are rated Ca represent obligations which are speculative in a high degree. Such issues are often in default or have other marked shortcomings.

C
Bonds which are rated C are the lowest-rated class of bonds, and issues so rated can be regarded as having extremely poor prospects of ever attaining any real investment standing.

SOURCE: *Moody's Bond Record,* July 1984, p. 1.

Table 2–2 Standard & Poor's Rating System

AAA
Debt rated AAA has the highest rating assigned by Standard & Poor's. Capacity to pay interest and repay principal is extremely strong.
AA
Debt rated AA has a very strong capacity to pay interest and repay principal and differs from the higher rated issues only in small degree.
A
Debt rated A has a strong capacity to pay interest and repay principal, although it is somewhat more susceptible to the adverse effects of changes in circumstances and economic conditions than debt in higher rated categories.
BBB
Debt rated BBB is regarded as having an adequate capacity to pay interest and repay principal. Whereas it normally exhibits adequate protection parameters, adverse economic conditions or changing circumstances are more likely to lead to a weakened capacity to pay interest and repay principal for debt in this category than in higher rated categories
BB, B, CCC, CC
Debt rated BB, B, CCC, and CC is regarded, on balance, as predominantly speculative with respect to capacity to pay interest and repay principal in accordance with the terms of the obligation. BB indicates the lowest degree of speculation and CC the highest degree of speculation. While such debt will likely have some quality and protective characteristics these are outweighed by large uncertainties or major risk exposures to adverse conditions.
C
The rating C is reserved for income bonds on which no interest is being paid.
D
Debt rated D is in default, and payment of interest and/or repayment of principal is in arrears.

SOURCE: *Standard & Poor's Bond Guide,* April 1986, pp. 10–11.

Figure 2-4 is a partial listing of quotations for corporate bonds. The first column identifies the issuer of the bonds, the annual interest payment as a percentage of face or principal, and the year of maturity. The second column (Cur Yld) lists the bond's current yield or the ratio of the annual interest payment to the current market value of the bond. The next three columns list the highest traded price, the lowest traded price, and the closing price for the day. The final column lists the change in the closing price from the previous day.

Annual rates of return and the frequency distribution of returns to a portfolio of long-term corporate bonds are given in Figures 2-5a and 2-5b. These returns are affected, for the most part, by fluctuations in prevailing interest rates, although changes in the anticipated probabilities for default also play a role.

CORPORATION BONDS
Volume, $39,120,000

Bonds	Cur Yld	Vol	High	Low	Close	Net Chg.
AMR 10¼06	10.4	2	99	99	99	...
Advst 9s08	cv	225	115	113	114¾	– 1¼
AetnLf 8⅛07	8.6	10	95	95	95	+ 1¾
AlaP 9s2000	9.3	7	97¾	96⅞	96⅞	+ ½
AlaP 7¾s02	8.9	20	87¼	87⅛	87⅛	...
AlaP 8⅞s03	9.3	20	95¾	95¾	95¾	+ ⅜
AlaP 10⅞05	10.6	4	103	103	103	...
AlaP 10½05	10.2	9	103⅜	103⅜	103⅜	+ ½
AlaP 8¾07	9.3	17	94⅜	94⅛	94⅜	+ 1⅜
AlaP 9¼07	9.3	12	99	99	99	+ ⅛
AlaP 9½08	9.5	40	99¾	97⅛	99¾	+ 1⅛
AlaP 9⅝08	9.7	11	98¾	98¾	98¾	– ¼
AlaP 12⅝10	11.6	6	109¼	109¼	109¼	– ¼
AlaP 15¼10	13.6	96	112¼	112¼	112¼	...
AlaP 18¼89	16.9	42	108	107½	108	+ 1
AlskA 9s03	cv	10	114	114	114	– 3
AlskH 16¼99	14.4	13	113	113	113	...
AlskH 17¾91	14.8	13	119¾	119¾	119¾	– 1¼
AlskH 18⅜01	16.4	190	115	110⅜	111⅞	– 3⅛
AlskH 15¼92	14.5	28	105	105	105	...
AlskH 12⅞93	12.3	10	105	105	105	+ 1
Alco 8½10	cv	10	113	113	113	– 1½
AllgWt 4s98	6.8	3	59⅛	59⅛	59⅛	+ ⅝
Allgl 10.4s02	12.5	27	83⅞	83¼	83¼	– ⅝
Allgl 9s89	9.8	4	91⅜	91⅜	91⅜	+ ⅞
AlldC 6.6s93	7.3	1	90¼	90¼	90¼	...
AlldC 7⅞96	8.2	25	96½	96½	96½	– 1½
AlldC zr87	...	30	90⅞	90⅞	90⅞	...
AlldC zr92	...	16	58⅝	58⅜	58⅜	– ⅝
AlldC zr96	...	40	43½	43	43	– 1⅜
AlldC zr98	...	3	33½	33½	33½	+ ⅛
AlldC zr2000	...	45	27¾	27⅜	27¾	+ ⅛
AlldC d6s88	6.3	5	94⅞	94¾	94⅞	+ ⅛
AlldC d6s90	6.5	8	92½	92½	92½	+ 1¾
AlldC zr91	...	50	64	64	64	– 1
AlldC zr95	...	50	44⅛	44⅛	44⅛	+ ⅛
AlldC zr05	...	5	17¾	17¾	17¾	+ ¼
AlldC zr09	...	65	13	13	13	+ ⅛
AlsCha 16s91	14.3	27	111½	111½	111½	...
Alcoa 7.45s96	8.2	1	91⅜	91⅜	91⅜	– ⅛
AMAX 8½96	10.3	20	82⅝	82⅝	82⅝	...
AMAX 14¼90	13.3	60	107⅝	107⅜	107⅜	– ¼
AMAX 14½94	13.2	46	110⅛	110	110	– ⅝
AAirl 4¼92	5.6	4	76⅛	76	76	+ ¾
ABrnd 4⅝90	5.2	1	88⅛	88⅛	88⅛	+ ⅛
ABrnd 5⅞92	6.6	2	89⅜	89⅜	89⅜	+ ⅜
ACan 6s97	7.6	6	79⅛	79	79	– ½
ACan 11⅜10	10.5	4	108	108	108	+ 1
ACan 13¼93	12.0	25	110½	110½	110½	+ ½
ACeM 6¾91	cv	10	67½	67½	67½	– 2⅞
AExC 14¾92	12.4	17	119	119	119	...
AmGn 11s07	cv	3	210	210	210	+ 1
AHoist 5½93	cv	38	73	73	73	...
AmMed 9½01	cv	170	106	105	105	– 1
AmMed 8¼08	cv	37	96¾	96½	96¾	...
AmMot 6s88	cv	4	89½	89¼	89½	+ ⅛

Figure 2-4 Quotations for Corporate Bonds

SOURCE: *Wall Street Journal,* May 2, 1986, p. 38. Reprinted by permission of *Wall Street Journal,* Dow Jones & Company, Inc. 1986. All rights reserved.

Corporate Stock

Preferred stock is a hybrid of sorts between a fixed- and a variable-income security. Its claim isn't really fixed and definite, in the sense that it can force the firm into bankruptcy if it isn't paid in full. On the other hand, its claim is limited in size to a specified amount. In general, the only leverage that a preferred

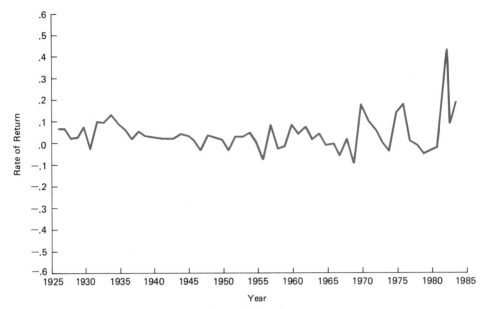

Figure 2-5a   Yearly Rates of Return on Corporate Bonds

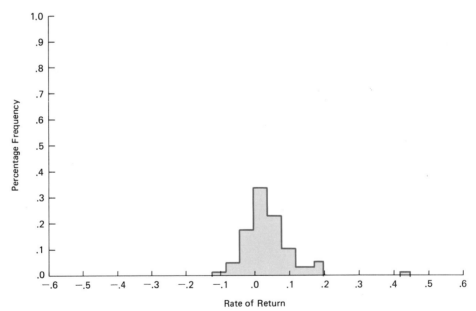

Figure 2-5b   Frequency Distribution for Corporate Bond Returns

stockholder has over the firm is that no dividends can be paid on the common stock until the specified dividends have been paid on the preferred stock. Preferred stocks are usually perpetual securities having no maturity date, although there are exceptions to this general rule. Preferred stocks are commonly callable, however.

There are two basic types of preferred stocks, cumulative and noncumulative. In the case of *cumulative preferred,* if the firm skips its dividend in any given year, no dividend can be paid on the common stock until that dividend, and any other arreared dividends on the preferred, have been paid in full. In the case of *noncumulative preferred,* if the firm skips the dividend on the preferred in any given year, it can pay dividends on the common as long as it pays the dividends on the preferred in the same year. As you may surmise, a noncumulative preferred has a very weak claim on the earnings of the firm.

Standing last in line, *common stock* is the residual claimant to the earnings of the firm. Common stockholders receive whatever is left after all other claimants have taken their rightful share. Payment of the common dividend is purely discretionary on the part of management. If earnings are retained rather than distributed, stockholders do benefit, in the sense that if the retained earnings are invested profitably, the firm will grow in size, and being the residual claim, the stockholders will eventually capture the growth.

Thus, stockholders can expect to receive their income in the form of capital gains as well as dividends. Management controls the distribution of income between dividends and capital gains through its control over the fraction of earnings distributed as dividends. Firms that pay out a smaller fraction of their earnings as dividends can be expected to grow at a faster rate than firms that pay out a larger fraction.

A partial listing of common stock price quotations from the New York Stock Exchange is provided in Figure 2-6. The first two columns list the highest and lowest traded prices for each stock over the past fifty-two weeks. The stock is identified in the third column. The anticipated annual dividend is given in the fourth column, and the ratio of this dividend to the current market price is given in the fifth. The sixth column shows the ratio of the current market price to current earnings per share available for distribution to common stockholders. The seventh column lists the volume of trading in the stock in hundreds of shares. Finally listed are the highest, lowest, and closing prices for the day, as well as the change from the close on the previous day.

Annual rates of return and the frequency distribution of returns to a large, well-diversified portfolio of common stocks are presented in Figures 2-7a and 2-7b. These returns reflect both dividends and capital gains. Over the years, stock returns have been much more variable than bond returns. The average returns to investors have also been much higher in the stock market.

As volatile as stocks are, they aren't the most volatile securities traded in the markets. That dubious honor is reserved for the securities discussed in the next section.

52 Weeks High	52 Weeks Low	Stock	Div.	Yld %	P-E Ratio	Sales 100s	High	Low	Close	Net Chg.
		– A – A – A –								
24	10¾	AAR s	.44	2.0	20	108	22¼	21⅞	21⅞	– ⅝
28½	11½	AFG s		...	16	1024	25½	24⅝	24¾	– 1
25⅜	12¾	AGS		...	17	85	22⅝	22¼	22½	+ ¼
15	9⅞	AMCA		...	...	31	12⅞	12⅜	12⅞	+ ⅜
60⅝	37½	AMR		...	12	3474	58¾	57⅞	58¼	+ ¼
25¾	18⅝	AMR pf	2.18	8.6	...	15	25½	25⅜	25⅜	– ⅛
12½	7⅝	APL		...	7	18	12	12	12	...
16¾	10⅜	ARX		...	14	150	15¾	15½	15½	– ⅛
53⅜	32¾	ASA	2.00a	5.6	...	250	36¾	35⅞	36	– ⅝
18⅜	10½	AVX		2.2	...	1561	14⅜	14⅛	14¼	– ⅛
32	22½	AZP	2.72	9.8	7	15158	27⅞	25⅞	27¾	– ½
91⅞	49½	AbtLab	1.68	2.0	21	1950	86⅜	84⅜	85¾	– ½
45⅞	24¾	AbtLb wi		...	...	12	43½	43	43⅜	– ⅝
31⅞	19⅝	AccoWd	.50	1.7	21	202	29	28⅞	29	– ⅜
24¾	10	AcmeC	.40	3.1	...	245	13	12¾	12⅞	– ¼
9¼	7	AcmeE	.32b	3.9	20	17	8¼	8⅛	8¼	– ⅛
20	16⅜	AdaEx	1.90e	9.6	...	136	19⅞	19⅜	19¾	+ ⅛
29	14	AdmMl	.40	1.5	12	84	26½	26	26¼	– ⅜
20⅜	8⅞	AdvSys	.83t	4.8	16	107	17⅞	17⅛	17⅛	– ½
32⅞	22⅛	AMD		...	...	4024	29⅛	28	28⅞	+ ⅜
12⅝	8¼	Adobe n		...	...	68	8¾	8⅝	8⅝	+ ⅛
18⅜	14⅝	Adob pf	1.84	11.3	...	22	16⅜	16¼	16¼	+ ⅛
20¼	15¼	Adob pf	2.40	12.5	...	7	19⅛	19⅛	19⅛	– ¼
19½	8⅛	Advest	.12a	.7	13	531	17⅞	16⅞	17½	+ ⅛
66¼	41⅞	AetnLf	2.64	4.4	11	5516	60½	59	60	– ⅝
57½	52⅛	AetL pf	4.97e	9.2	...	24	53⅞	53⅞	53⅞	+ ⅛
69¼	29	Ahmns	1.38	2.3	7	3067	60⅝	59	59¾	– 1⅜
4¾	2½	Aileen		...	75	9	3¾	3¾	3¾	...
83⅜	47½	AirPrd	1.48	1.9	16	607	79⅝	78⅝	79⅝	...
27¾	17½	AirbFrt	.60	2.8	19	71	22½	21⅝	21⅝	– ¾
2⅛	⅜	AlMoan	1.50c	...	...	50	½	15/32	½	+ 1/32
10¼	7¼	AlaP dpf	.87	8.9	...	35	9⅞	9¾	9¾	– ⅛
101	66⅞	AlaP pf	8.16	8.2	...	z60	99	99	99	– 1
90¾	66½	AlaP pf	8.28	9.4	...	z110	89	88	88	– ¾
26⅜	15¼	AlskAir	.16	.9	12	703	18⅞	18¼	18½	– ¼
25	7⅞	Albrto s	.21	1.0	28	171	21	20⅝	20⅞	– ⅝
39	26⅞	Albtsns	.84	2.4	14	310	35½	35	35¼	– ⅛
34⅝	22¾	Alcan	.80	2.6	...	3058	30½	30⅛	30¼	– ¼
46¾	32	AlcoStd	1.24	3.1	19	443	40½	39⅞	40⅜	+ ¼
38¾	26	AlexAlx	1.00	2.7	31	1618	36¾	36	36⅜	...
43	21¾	Alexdr		...	71	21	36⅞	36⅝	36⅞	...
101	75½	AllgCp	1.54t	1.6	21	31	95⅞	95	95¼	– ⅞
28¼	25⅝	AlgCp pf	2.86	10.2	...	3	28⅛	28⅛	28⅛	+ ⅛
28¾	16½	AlgInt	.35j	1.6	...	10349	22	21	21¾	– ⅛
20¾	15⅛	AlgIn pf	2.19	11.7	...	21	18⅞	18¾	18¾	– ⅛

Figure 2-6 Quotations for Common Stock on the New York Stock Exchange

SOURCE: *Wall Street Journal,* May 2, 1986, p. 48. Reprinted by permission of *Wall Street Journal,* © Dow Jones & Company, Inc. 1986. All rights reserved.

Options and Warrants

An *option* gives its holder the right to buy or sell a particular asset at a particular price, on (or possibly before) a particular expiration date. Options are written on stocks, U.S. treasury bonds, and even stock market indices.

A *call option* gives its holder the right to *buy* a share of stock at a particular price called the "exercise" or "strike" price. A *put option* gives its holder the right to *sell* at a particular price. As you might expect, as the price of the underlying stock rises, the price of a call written on it goes up, while the price of a put goes down. The opposite happens when the stock goes down in price.

Put and call options are examples of secondary securities. They are not issued by firms, and the net supply of these securities is zero. Options are written and sold by individual investors. If you sell an option, you have given someone the right to buy a share of stock from you at a stated price. You receive cash upon its sale and you carry the obligation as a liability. If you buy an option, you have

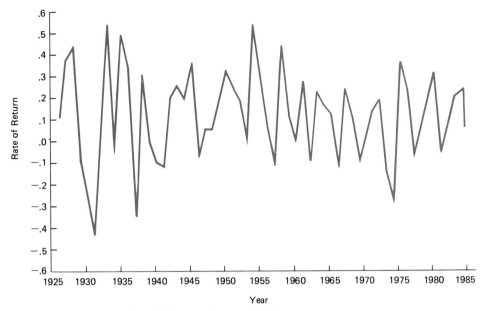

Figure 2-7a Yearly Rates of Return on Common Stocks

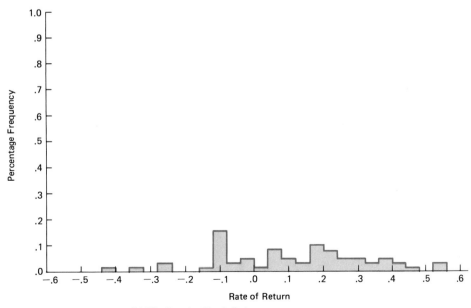

Figure 2-7b Frequency Distribution for Stock Returns

CHAPTER 2   **Securities and Markets**

purchased the right to buy the stock. You pay cash upon purchase, and you carry the option as an asset. If we were to add up the values of all the assets and liabilities, they would sum to zero.

A partial listing of option prices from the Chicago Board Option Exchange is

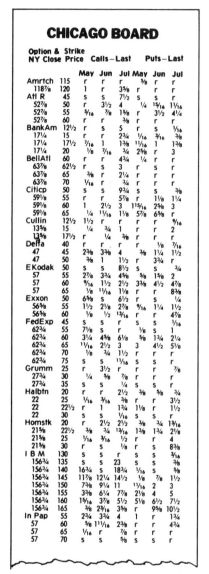

Figure 2-8 Quotations for Put and Call Options

SOURCE: *Wall Street Journal,* May 2, 1986, p. 42. Reprinted by permission of *Wall Street Journal,* © Dow Jones & Company, Inc. 1986. All rights reserved.

provided in Figure 2-8. The first column identifies the common stock the options are written on, as well as current market price for the stock. The second column lists the exercise or strike price for the option. Then the closing market prices for three different call options, all with the given exercise price but expiring in the months of May, June, and July, are given. The symbol "r" indicates that the option was not traded on the previous day. Closing market prices for put options are provided in the final three columns.

A *warrant,* on the other hand, is a primary security. It is issued by a firm, and it is a claim on the assets of the firm. A warrant is, in all other respects, identical to a call option, although warrants usually have longer lives than call options. A warrant gives its holder the right to purchase shares of stock in the firm at a particular price before a particular date. If the warrant is exercised, the firm must issue new shares of common stock to the holder of the warrant. Thus, the effect of exercise is to dilute the per-share value of the stock. Warrants are often given to executives as part of their compensation. They are also frequently attached to other securities, like bonds, when originally issued to make the issue more attractive to investors.

Forward and Futures Contracts

Forward and futures contracts obligate you to buy or sell a particular commodity at a particular price on a particular day. They are distinguished from options in that they don't give you the *right* but rather the *obligation* to buy or sell. If you buy a forward or futures contract, you have obligated yourself to buy the commodity at the stated price. On the other hand, if you sell such a contract, you have obligated yourself to sell the commodity at the stated price. Because of these qualifications, forward contracts can do something that none of the other contracts discussed can do: Their values can become negative. If you have obligated yourself to buy a commodity at a price of $100 and the commodity is currently selling at $70, the value of your forward contract to buy is negative. You are actually paying someone to take it off your hands.

When originally issued, the exercise price you must later buy or sell for is set such that the buyer and seller will exchange the contract with no associated cash payment. That is, the exercise price is set to make the current market value of the contract equal to zero. The market value of a *forward* contract subsequently is allowed to become positive or negative as the commodity price goes up or down. In the case of a *futures* contract, however, one aspect of the contract is changed each day to keep the market value of the contract at zero. The aspect of the contract that is revised is the exercise price, in a process called "marking to market."

The process of marking to market is one of the main features that differentiates a futures from a forward contract. To see how it works, consider the following example. Suppose you buy a futures contract on June 1 to buy wheat in September at $10 a bushel. On June 2 other futures contracts are being negotiated at $11 a bushel. The terms of your contract would now be revised to $11 and you would have the difference of $1 added to your account. If, instead, the negotiated price went down to $9, you would have to make up the difference and $1 would be subtracted from your account. This process continues on a daily basis.

Futures contracts are written on such commodities as gold, silver, and agricultural products, as well as on various financial contracts, such as treasury bills, treasury bonds, Ginnie Mae passthroughs, and even stock market indices. In fact, the market for financial futures is currently exploding in terms of types of contracts traded, volume of trading, and investor interest.

The Shares of Investment Companies and Mutual Funds

The investments described so far are individual securities. You would normally not invest in these one at a time. Rather, you would combine many of them into a well-diversified portfolio to reduce the risk of your overall investment. It may be possible, however, that you don't have the funds to spread over many individual investments, or the time to manage such a portfolio. If this is the case, you may want to consider investing in a closed-end investment company or in a mutual fund. Both of these institutions manage a diversified portfolio for you. When you invest with these institutions, you, in effect, buy into a piece of the portfolio. The difference between them is in the way this is accomplished.

A *closed-end investment company* makes an initial sale of shares to investors in much the same way any corporation does when it commences operations or finances a new investment project. The investment company invests the proceeds of the sale of shares in a diversified portfolio of securities. To buy into the portfolio, you must buy shares of the portfolio from individual investors who already own them. These shares are traded in the financial markets, and you must pay the same types of brokerage commissions that you would pay to buy any stock. Closed-end investment companies are conceptually identical to nonfinancial corporations, except that they make financial investments, whereas nonfinancial corporations make real, economic investments in such tangibles as plant and equipment.

Closed-end investment companies have an interesting feature that at times can make them attractive investments. From time to time, these companies publish the total market value of the securities in their portfolios. Comparing these total market values with the total market value of the shares in the closed-end investment company, you will at times find big differences. More often than not, the market value of the shares in the investment company is less than the market value of the securities in the company's portfolio. In fact, sometimes the market value of the shares can be as little as 60 percent of the market value of the securities. This means that if you invest in the investment company, you acquire the securities at bargain prices. Thompson (1978) has shown that the shares of these deeply discounted investment companies produce abnormally large rates of return to their investors *after* the discounts have been established. It seems to be an investment opportunity worth watching.

There are many more *mutual funds* than there are closed-end investment companies. You buy shares in the mutual fund directly from the fund itself. The price you pay for each share is equal to the total market value of the securities in the fund divided by the number of shares currently outstanding. As a consequence, there are no opportunities for bargains in mutual fund shares. Some mutual funds charge a sales fee, or a "load," in order to buy into the fund; for many others there is no such fee. All mutual funds, however, charge a management fee to cover the expenses incurred for analysis and administration. Management fees can range from 2 percent of the total market value of the portfolio per year to as little as 0.5 percent.

Different mutual funds can have different investment objectives. Money market funds invest in short-term, high-quality, fixed-income securities. The market value of these funds is quite stable, but their yields fluctuate daily. There are also mutual funds that invest in long-term U.S. government bonds, corporate bonds, municipal bonds, and bonds and stock and common stock of different types.

As an investor in a money market mutual fund, you can usually arrange to write checks on your account with the fund. Many mutual funds manage several different types of portfolios. If you wish to transfer some or all of your funds from the money market portfolio to the long-term U.S. government bond portfolio, or any of the other portfolios run by the fund, you can arrange to do this simply by making a telephone call to the fund.

Mutual funds are a very convenient way to manage your money. If you are a small investor, they provide for an economical way to broadly diversify your portfolio. To the extent that the fund's investment decisions are made by skillful analysts who can spot undervalued securities, they may also be able to provide additional, abnormal returns for you. This latter point is the subject of much controversy, and we will talk about this more in Chapter 20.

A partial listing of some quotations for mutual funds is provided in Figure 2-9. At the top of each list the organization is identified in boldface type. The individual types of funds sponsored by the organization are provided below. For example, the AARP Invest Program has a capital growth stock fund, a general bond fund, a fund that invests in Ginnie Mae passthroughs, a growth-income fund that invests in bonds as well as stocks, a state and municipal bond fund, and a fund that invests in short-term tax-exempt securities. The column labeled "NAV" (net asset value) lists the total market value of the securities owned by the fund divided by the number of outstanding shares in the fund. The offer price includes this net asset value plus the maximum charge required to buy the fund, if any is so assessed on the investor.

```
                    Offer NAV
               NAV  Price Chg.
AARP Invest Program:
  Cap  Grw   22.34 N.L. − .06
  Gen  Bnd   16.05 N.L. − .02
  Ginnie M   16.11 N.L.   ...
  Gro   Inc  21.39 N.L. − .13
  TxFr  Bd   16.21 N.L. − .02
  TxF Shrt   15.51 N.L. + .01
ABT Midwest Funds: .....
  Emrg Gr     9.38 10.25 − .04
  Growth I   13.48 14.73 − .03
  Int  Govt  10.73 10.74 − .01
  LG  Govt   10.79 11.24 − .02
  Sec   Inc  10.98 12.00 − .05
  Util   Inc 14.36' 15.69 + .04
  Acorn Fnd  41.01 N.L. − .04
  Adtek   Fd 12.02 N.L. − .05
Advest Advantage: ........
  Govt       10.08 N.L. − .02
  Growth     10.55 N.L. − .03
  Income     10.32 N.L. + .02
  Specl      10.33 N.L. − .02
  Afuture Fd 14.98 N.L. − .04
AIM  Funds:
  Conv Yld   12.90 13.80 − .05
  Grnway     10.48 11.21 − .05
  HiYld Sc   10.08 10.78 + .01
  Summit      7.08 (z) − .03
Alliance  Capital:
  Alli  Gov   9.33  9.87 − .04
  Alli  HiY  10.58 11.20 − .02
  Alli  Intl 21.77 23.79 − .46
  Alli Mtge   9.78 10.35   ...
  Alli Tech  23.88 26.10 − .18
  Chem Fd     9.15 10.00 − .05
  Surveyr    16.75 18.31 − .06
```

Figure 2-9 Quotations for Mutual Funds

SOURCE: *Wall Street Journal,* May 2, 1986, p. 40. Reprinted by permission of *Wall Street Journal,* © Dow Jones & Company, Inc. 1986. All rights reserved.

THE FINANCIAL MARKETS

The Difference Between Primary and Secondary Markets

When securities are initially offered to the public, they are said to be sold in the *primary market*. In the primary market, the proceeds of the sale are used by the seller, perhaps a corporation, to make investments in real capital goods.

Investment banking firms are important institutions in the primary market. They stand between the corporation and its potential security holders and provide the corporation with a number of important services in marketing its securities. They have a knowledge of the current state of the market, and they provide the firm with information about how much money can be currently raised and what types of securities would be most effective in raising it. They prepare a prospectus, which is a brochure disclosing information that is relevant to the valuation of the securities by potential investors. They may also organize a group of individual investment bankers to work together on the actual distribution, or sale, of the securities and the collection of the proceeds. If, after the initial offering some securities remain unsold, the investment bankers are allowed to maintain an order in the market for the securities for up to ten days after the initial offering.

Investment bankers are compensated either through a fixed fee or through an arrangement in which they promise the firm a fixed amount of proceeds from the sale and they receive the difference between this fixed amount and what they actually are able to raise.

Frequently, securities are *privately placed* in the primary market. If the investment bankers contact as few as twenty-five potential buyers for the offering, many of the costly disclosure requirements of the Securities and Exchange Commission, such as the prospectus, are waived. Also, the issue can frequently be better tailored to meet the needs of the issuing firm and the investors who make final purchase. Private placements are usually made to financial institutions, and in the vast majority of cases they involve bond issues.

Financial institutions, such as commercial banks and savings and loans, also participate in the primary market when they make loans to business firms and even to individuals for home construction. These institutions stand as an intermediary between individual savers and the borrowers of the funds. The intermediaries act as agencies that collect information (which might not otherwise be publicly disclosed) from borrowers, analyze information (using techniques and skills that might not be available to the general public), and repackage investments (such as loans and mortgages) into forms (checking and savings deposits) that are more attractive to individual investors.

After securities are initially offered in the primary market, they are then traded from investor to investor in the *secondary market*. The role of the secondary market is to provide investors with liquidity for their investments, enabling them to move quickly, and without substantial loss in market value, from security to cash and from one security to another. In buying or selling in the secondary market, you will either trade in an organized exchange or in the over-the-counter market. Organized exchanges are centralized auction-type markets, whereas the over-the-counter market is an intricate network of security dealers who take positions in various securities and buy and sell from their own portfolios.

Organized Exchanges for Common Stock and Bonds

There are several organized stock exchanges in the United States and Canada. Far and away the largest is the New York Stock Exchange (NYSE) in which the shares of approximately 1600 companies are traded. The second largest stock exchange is the American Stock Exchange (AMEX). The other exchanges are much smaller and are called regional exchanges. Most of the exchanges deal in a variety of securities in addition to common stock. You can buy or sell corporate bonds as well as warrants on the NYSE. In addition to these, you can trade in options on the AMEX and on some of the regional exchanges, such as the Pacific Coast Stock Exchange.

Suppose you want to buy 100 shares of IBM stock. You would first call a brokerage house in your town. This will probably be a branch of a large firm like the Milwaukee Company. If you don't have an account, you will be asked to open one. You will fill out a form disclosing information about your personal income and finances. You will deal with a broker or account executive who will probably be your connection with the market for some time to come. The broker will provide you with information about the company you are interested in, about general economic trends, and about other investments of interest. The brokerage house may also have attractive investment packages like tax shelters of various forms and will provide you with information about these.

It is important for you to understand that brokers are, for the most part, salespeople. They are a very heterogeneous group in terms of their training in finance and investments. If you are going to rely on a broker for investment advice, as opposed merely to a link between you and the market, it is important that you determine the broker's formal training and experience before you act on his or her recommendations.

From the brokerage house, your order will be called to the floor of the exchange to a person called a *floor broker*. Floor brokers actually buy and sell securities on the floor of the exchange. The floor broker will usually buy your 100 shares of IBM from a person called a *specialist*. The specialist keeps an inventory in one or more stocks and buys and sells out of that inventory. The specialists publicize prices at which they are willing to buy a stock *(bid prices)* and prices at which they are willing to sell *(asked prices)*. These prices are based on the orders to buy and sell the stock *at specific prices* that other traders have made before you, or the price the specialists are ready to buy or sell the stock for from their own accounts. In any case, the specialist must trade on the basis of the price that is most advantageous to you.

After seeing the bid and asked prices, the floor broker will call out a price he or she is willing to pay for the stock. The stock may be bought from the specialist or, for that matter, anyone else on the floor of the exchange who is willing to sell the stock at that price. If the trade is consummated, you get the shares for that price.

To execute the trade for you, the brokerage house will charge you a commission of anywhere from 1 to 10 percent of the total market value of the transaction, depending on the price per share and the number of shares you buy. In general, the smaller the transaction, the larger the commission. If you buy or sell in less than a round lot (100 shares), you will be charged an additional fee. To minimize your commissions, you may want to deal with a *discount broker* as opposed to a *full service broker*. Full service brokers provide you with investment advice and investment packages like tax shelters and they are willing to hold your securities in safekeeping until you are ready to trade again. Discount brokers provide none of these services. They just execute your trade, but they do it at a lower price.

You can make your trade by employing any one of a number of different orders. If you use a *market order,* the broker will buy or sell the number of securities directed at the best available price. If you use a *limit order,* the trade will be executed only at a price at least as advantageous as a stated price. If the trade cannot be completed at that price, it is delayed until it can be executed under those conditions. A *stop loss order,* on the other hand, is an order to sell a stock you already own as soon as its price falls to a specified level. Orders can also be differentiated on the basis of allowable time for completion. An order is *good until canceled* if it remains in effect indefinitely. A *day order* must be executed by the end of the day, or it is canceled. A *fill or kill* order must be executed immediately or canceled.

Organized Exchanges for Options

Options are traded on four organized exchanges in the United States: the Chicago Board Options Exchange, the American Stock Exchange, the Philadelphia Stock Exchange, and the Pacific Coast Stock Exchange.

As you recall, an option is a contract to buy or sell a stock at a stated exercise price. Normally, when you acquire an option to buy something like a house, you are dealing with a particular individual. If you decide to exercise your option, you will buy the house from that particular individual. When you buy or sell options through an organized options exchange, however, an *exchange clearinghouse* stands between you and the other party to the contract. If you decide to sell the option that you have acquired, the clearinghouse will randomly match you with someone who wants to buy the option. If you wish to exercise your option, the clearinghouse will match you with someone who has sold an identical option.

This matching process requires that the options be standardized with respect to their characteristics. For any given stock the options outstanding on the stock will have a few specific exercise prices, usually differentiated by $10 amounts, and a few specific expiration dates, usually approximately three months apart, with the maximum being nine months off.

The clearinghouse guarantees to the buyer of an option that the terms of the contract will be honored if it is exercised. The clearinghouse backs the contract with its own financial resources. It also requires the sellers of the option to escrow the proceeds of sale and to put up an additional amount of money as a margin to guarantee that they will be able to honor the contracts if they are exercised.

Organized Exchanges for Futures Contracts

Among the organized exchanges that trade in futures contracts are the Chicago Mercantile Exchange, the Chicago Board of Trade, and the New York Futures Exchange.

As with the options exchanges, a clearinghouse stands between the buyers and sellers of futures contracts. Because of the presence of the clearing corporation, buyers of the contracts need not be concerned about the creditworthiness

OUT ON THE STREET

Getting Started

Lightning in a snowstorm. Tom Dumphy knew what that meant from past experience. At least six inches of snow would fall tonight. The first real snow of the winter. Just in time, this, the start of the holiday season.

Tom stared out his window, which was really part of the outer wall of the glass-enclosed First Wisconsin Bank Building in Madison, Wisconsin. Directly across the street was the State Capitol building, an almost exact replica of the Capitol in Washington D.C. Floodlights illuminated the building from four sides. It was eerie. The floodlights, the lightning, and the snow created a scene that Tom would remember for some time to come.

From outside, the light in Tom's room was a single beacon on the northern wall of the building. It was 6 P.M., and nearly everyone had already left for home. Tom was about to leave as well.

For Tom, life was good. He lived comfortably, felt secure and fulfilled. Over the years as a broker for the Milwaukee Company, he had built up a solid clientele. But it hadn't always been this way.

Tom started in the business in January 1973, after graduating with a bachelor's degree in finance from the state university.

After four or five months of training and correspondence courses, and passing two exams, Tom received his license, and officially entered the business.

Many people have the conception that stockbrokers become rich overnight. Not true. Tom found himself at ground zero. Although he was guaranteed a salary for his first year, after that he was going to be strictly on his own, receiving 40 percent of all the commissions he could generate. At ground zero he had *no* customers, and he needed a "system" to generate some.

There are many different "systems." You can "cold call" people on the telephone. You can walk the streets and introduce yourself to likely prospects. You can use mass mailings or even seminars. As one of Tom's colleagues is fond of saying, "The name of this game is exposure. Expose yourself any way you can, short of indecent." Tom's system was to go through the city directory, looking for the names of executives of the major corporations. Even before he got his license, he compiled an extensive list of names and addresses. Then he would send out ten to fifteen pieces of mail a day, containing some research information and a letter introducing himself and saying he'd be calling in the future. The future was the next day.

Landing clients wasn't easy. Tom

of sellers, and vice versa. However, because buyers and sellers once again are randomly matched, the terms of the contract must be standardized—this time with respect to expiration date, as the exercise price is the same for all futures contracts after marking to market.

Membership in the exchange itself can be divided between *commission bro-*

remembers contacting one person eight times. Each time the guy showed interest, but Tom would never get an order. Finally, Tom convinced him to invest in Westinghouse Electric stock, and he became Tom's first customer. The next week Westinghouse announced some really bad news, and the price of the stock fell by half. After picking his heart up from the floor, Tom bit the bullet, picked up the phone, and explained the situation to the client. The client was impressed with Tom's sincerity; he realized that the situation couldn't be anticipated in advance and has stayed on to this very day. Honesty is very important in this business. If something is going wrong, don't try to hide it. Tell them!

In January 1973 the Dow hit 1050. It wouldn't see that level again for many years. These were rough times in the business. Of the eight young brokers Tom started with, all have left the business. Tom stuck it out, and he's glad he did.

The best thing about being a broker is that you are your own person. You have the freedom of basically running your own business. You can work when you want and as hard as you want. Some brokers make as little as $30,000. But others make ten times that much, even in a relatively small community like Madison. In larger cities the big producers make $600,000, with a few exceptions in the $1 million to $2 million range.

The worst things are the uncertainty of the market and the stress that comes with it. No matter how hard you try to do a good job, no matter how sound your advice is, the market may always turn on you. You must then watch your clients lose money and know it's beyond your control. It affects your personal relationship with them. You lose sleep. It's difficult to shake that feeling, but you keep going because you know it's the long-term result that's really important.

Tom has long passed the initial building stage of his career, but the building never really stops. He now builds on referrals and looks toward bigger accounts like pension and profit-sharing plans. You never really do stop cold calling, however. In fact, Tom spent the entire morning introducing himself to people who hopefully had some holiday spirit.

Now it's time for Tom to have some holiday spirit. He rises from his desk and kills the light. The northern glass wall of the building is now a solid mirror reflecting the spectacle of the lights, the lightning, and the snow falling on the Capitol.

kers, who execute trades for customers who may not be members of the exchange, and *locals*, who trade for their own accounts.

Locals are typically classified on the basis of their trading horizon. Those with the shortest trading horizons are called *scalpers*. Scalpers operate on the basis of a heavy volume of trading and try to take advantage of the smallest trade-to-trade fluctuations in the price of the commodity. *Day traders* look to wider price swings that occur during the course of a day, but they rarely carry a position overnight. *Position traders* hold a position over the course of days or even weeks. They are concerned with extended price movements that result from fundamental changes in supply and demand relationships for the commodity. A *spreader,* on the other hand, watches the shifting relationships between prices for different delivery dates for the same commodity. When these relationships move away from their typical patterns, spreaders move in and sell the high market and buy the low market.

Futures contracts are seldom actually executed. Normally, buyers and sellers liquidate their positions through the clearing corporation before the expiration date. If you are a buyer and choose to execute the contract, you must notify the clearing corporation two business days before the first day allowed for deliveries. Sellers of the contract must also notify the clearinghouse if they intend to deliver. The clearinghouse then matches buyers and sellers and notifies both parties of their identities. The sellers then acquire the commodity for delivery and make delivery, and title passes from seller to buyer.

The sellers actually have a choice of commodities they can deliver. Thus, if you are going to deliver for a treasury bond futures contract, you don't have to deliver a particular bond. Rather, you have a choice of delivering any treasury bond that has fifteen years or more to maturity or earliest call date. If a particular bond is called for, the seller may find that the market for the bond is cornered on the delivery date. To avoid this risk, the seller is given a choice of deliverable bonds.

The Over-the-Counter Market

Securities that aren't traded on organized exchanges are traded in the over-the-counter (OTC) market. The OTC market consists of a network of thousands of dealers in particular securities. Each dealer maintains inventories of one or more securities and has a bid price for which she or he is willing to buy the stock to add to inventory and an asked price at which she or he is willing to sell the stock from inventory. The dealer's profit, of course, derives from the difference between the two prices.

There are two levels of prices, wholesale and retail. *Retail* prices are offered to individual investors who are usually executing orders through brokers. *Wholesale* prices are offered to other dealers who wish to make changes in their inventory positions.

Whereas the organized exchanges are auction markets, the prices on the OTC are set on the basis of negotiation between the individual dealers and their customers. It is also the case that while a limited number of securities are traded on the organized exchanges, virtually any registered security may be traded on the OTC.

The terms of trade are communicated throughout the market system through the National Association of Security Dealers Automated Quotations System. Members may subscribe to the system at three different levels, which can be differentiated on the basis of the nature of the price quotations and the ability to enter quotations into the system. The quotations system allows all dealers and brokers in the network to know the terms being offered by all dealers in a given stock at any given point in time. Actual trades are subject to negotiation between brokers and dealers, but the system does report completed transactions.

Summary

In this chapter some institutional background on financial securities and their markets has been provided. Securities can be categorized into fixed income, stock, options, and forward and futures contracts. Fixed-income securities, or bonds, are issued by the federal government, state and municipal governments, and corporations. The two major types of stock are preferred and common, with preferred offering a prior but limited claim, and common taking whatever remains after all other security holders have taken their rightful share.

Options are contracts to buy or sell a particular commodity on or before a particular date. A put option gives you the right to sell, and a call option gives you the right to buy. Neither has to be exercised. You do so only if it is in your interest. Otherwise, the contract may be discarded.

Forward and futures contracts obligate you to buy or sell a commodity at a specified price on a particular date. The buyer of the contract is obligated to buy, and the seller is obligated to sell, the commodity. The difference between a forward and a futures contract is in the way your account is handled. The exercise price of a futures contract is changed each day to the value being used for contemporary contracts. To make up for the change in the contract, your account is credited or debited in a process called marking to market.

Investment companies and mutual funds invest in diversified portfolios of securities. You can buy shares in either type of fund and thereby obtain diversification with a small amount of capital. In the case of a closed-end investment company, you buy shares from another investor who holds them. In the case of a mutual fund, you buy shares from the fund itself.

Securities are traded in the primary and secondary markets. When originally issued to finance capital investment, securities are marketed through investment banking firms in the primary market. The primary market, therefore, connects the users of capital with the suppliers or savers. Securities are traded from one investor to another in the secondary market. The secondary market serves as a source of liquidity for securities that already exist. The secondary market consists of organized exchanges and the over-the-counter market. The organized exchanges are centralized auction markets; the OTC market is a nationwide network of dealers who make markets by taking positions in individual securities.

QUESTIONS AND PROBLEMS

1. Why is the return associated with common stock referred to as a "residual claim"? Contrast this kind of claim with a "fixed claim."
2. How do investors in a U.S. treasury bill receive their returns?
3. Why are U.S. government securities viewed differently from state and local government securities in terms of default risk?
4. Why might the general obligation bonds of a state yield a different return than revenue bonds issued by the same state?
5. Explain the meaning of a call provision on a bond.
6. What is the priority of claims on the corporation's earnings held by (a) common stockholders, (b) bondholders, and (c) preferred stockholders?
7. Contrast an option with a futures contract. Could either or both of these contracts have *negative* value to you?
8. What is the basic difference between a forward contract and a futures contract?
9. What is a mutual fund? Why might a person buy shares in a mutual fund rather than shares of individual corporations?
10. Define the following: (a) limit order, (b) stop loss order, and (c) day order.
11. What apparatus facilitates purchases and sales of futures contracts?
12. What is a "private placement"? What are its potential advantages for the firm issuing securities?

BIBLIOGRAPHY

AMLING, F., *Investments: An Introduction to Analysis and Management*. Englewood Cliffs, N.J.: Prentice-Hall, 1984.

CAMPBELL, T. S., *Financial Institutions, Markets, and Economic Activity*. New York: McGraw-Hill, 1982.

POLAKOFF, M. E., and T. A. DURKIN, *Financial Institutions and Markets*. Boston: Houghton Mifflin, 1981.

STEVENSON, R. A., and E. H. JENNINGS, *Fundamentals of Investments*. St. Paul, Minn.: West, 1984.

THOMPSON, R., "The Information Content of Discount and Premiums on Closed-End Investment Fund Shares," *Journal of Financial Economics* (September 1978).

3

COMBINING INDIVIDUAL SECURITIES INTO PORTFOLIOS

Introduction

Suppose you have two securities with probability distributions like those in Figures 3-1 and 3-2.

In the figures we are plotting the probability of getting particular rates of return (perhaps in the course of the next month) on the vertical axis. The possible returns, themselves, are plotted horizontally. The symbol h_i denotes the *probability* of the stock producing rate of return i. The symbol $r_{A,i}$ denotes the ith possible rate of return for stock A, and $E(r_A)$ denotes the *expected* rate of return for the stock. The expected rate of return is found by multiplying each possible return, $r_{A,i}$, by its associated probability, h_i, and summing the products.

Now construct a portfolio by investing some of your money in one security and the rest of it in the other. The issue addressed in this chapter is: What would the probability distribution of returns to the *portfolio* look like if it were drawn in Figure 3-3? Actually, we are going to restrict the question to just two properties of the distribution: the expected rate of return and the variance or standard deviation. As its name implies, the expected rate of return tells you what you can expect to get from the investment, while variance (or the square root of variance, the standard deviation) tells you about the investment's propensity to produce actual returns that *deviate* from the expected. *Variance is actually the expected value of the squared deviations from E(r).* In this book the variance of a portfolio will be used as the primary measure of the risk of the portfolio.

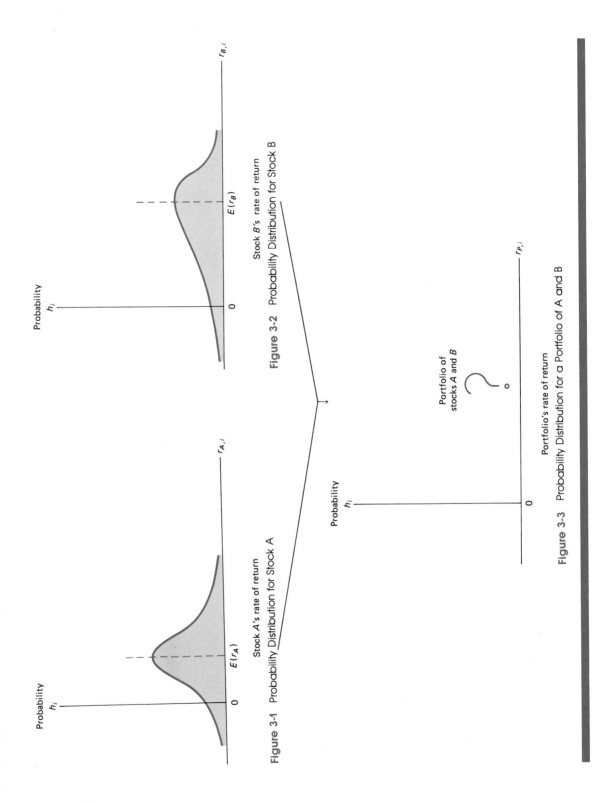

Figure 3-1 Probability Distribution for Stock A

Figure 3-2 Probability Distribution for Stock B

Figure 3-3 Probability Distribution for a Portfolio of A and B

40

Taking variance as our measure of the risk of a portfolio, we're going to find out how to predict the risk and expected rate of return of a portfolio, based on the characteristics of the securities we put into it.

THE RISK AND EXPECTED RETURN OF A PORTFOLIO

The Portfolio's Expected Rate of Return

Suppose we consider a given time period, say a month. If the individual securities in the portfolio have various expected rates of return for the month, what will be the expected return to the portfolio as a whole?

Let's consider a portfolio of two stocks, and first compute the expected *dollar* return to the portfolio. We'll assume that we have $1000 to invest at the beginning of the month, and we invest $400 in stock A and $600 in stock B. In the course of the month, A is expected to produce a rate of return of 10 percent (a dollar return of $40), and B a rate of return of 6 percent ($36). What is the expected *dollar* rate of return to the portfolio? The total expected dollar return to the portfolio is obviously the sum of the dollar returns to the two stocks:

$$\$76 = (\$400 \times .10) + (\$600 \times .06)$$
$$\$76 = \quad \$40 \quad + \quad \$36$$

The expected *percentage rate* of return to the portfolio is given by the dollar return divided by the amount invested, which in this case is $1000, at the beginning of each month. Dividing both sides of the above equation by $1000, we get

$$7.6\% = \$76/\$1000 = (\$400/\$1000) \times .10 + (\$600/\$1000) \times .06$$
$$E(r_P) \quad = \quad x_A \quad \times E(r_A) + \quad x_B \quad \times E(r_B)$$

The term x is the fraction of the money you are investing in each security. Thus, the expected rate of return to the portfolio is a weighted average of the expected rates of return produced by the securities in the portfolio, where we are weighting by the fraction of our own money that we are investing in each security.

These fractions are also called *portfolio weights*. When summed, they add up to 100 percent, and they are computed as follows:

$$x_A = \frac{\text{Dollar amount of security A bought (sold short)}}{\text{Total equity investment in the portfolio}}$$

A portfolio weight can be either positive or negative. A positive weight means that you are buying the stock; we also refer to this as taking a "long" position in the stock. The opposite of taking a long position is taking a short position, or "selling short." In this case the portfolio weight is negative, because the numerator is negative. We are selling the stock rather than buying it.

Selling a stock short isn't quite the same as selling some stock that you happen to own. When you sell short you borrow shares of stock from someone (usually your broker). After a certain period of time, you are obligated to return to this person the same number of shares you borrowed. Suppose, for example, you borrow 100 shares of a stock from your broker. Then you sell the stock for $10 per share, collecting $1000. After a period of time the stock falls to $5 per share. You then go back into the market and buy back the 100 shares for a total of $500. You then return the 100 shares that you borrowed from your broker, and the short sale is completed. You have made a profit of $500 on this short sale, the difference between the $1000 you got for the borrowed stock when you sold it and the $500 it took to buy the stock back later in the market. Incidentally, if the stock paid any dividends between the time you sold it and the time you bought it back, you would have to pay cash, in the amount of these dividends, to the person from whom you borrowed the stock.

You might ask, "What can be done with the $1000 proceeds of the short sale between the time I short sell and the time I buy the stock back?" If you or I, as individuals, were to sell short, we would be unable to reinvest the proceeds. In addition, we would have to let the person from whom we borrowed the shares hold some of our own money (typically 30 percent, or $300 in this case) as a margin on the transaction. This insures that we will have the financial resources to repurchase the stock when the time comes to close the short sale. Large financial institutions, however, don't suffer from the same limitations on the use of proceeds of short sales. Because financial institutions are the principal users of portfolio techniques, we will assume, for purposes of discussion, that when we sell short we are free to use the proceeds to invest in other securities, and no margin is required on the transaction.

How do you compute the portfolio weight associated with a short position in a security? Suppose you have $1000 of your own money and you sell short $600 of stock C and use this money, in addition to your own money, to buy $1600 of stock A. Let's find the portfolio weights.

You are buying $1600 of stock A, which is 160 percent of your $1000 equity investment. Thus, x_A is 1.6. At the same time you're *selling* $600 of stock C, which is -60 percent of your equity investment. The sign is negative because you are doing the opposite of buying the stock—you are selling it. Note that the two portfolio weights still add up to 100 percent.

Now suppose that in the period of time you're holding this position, stock A is expected to produce a 20 percent rate of return, and stock C is expected to produce a 10 percent rate of return. What is the expected rate of return on the portfolio of the two stocks?

$$E(r_P) = [x_A \times E(r_A)] + [x_C \times E(r_C)]$$
$$.26 = (1.6 \times .20) + (-.6 \times .10)$$

To verify this, consider that we've got an expected profit on our long position of $320 (.20 × $1600). We've also got a $60 expected loss on the short sale. Our net profit, therefore, is $260. Because we initially invested $1000 of our own money, this represents a 26 percent expected rate of return on our investment.

To summarize, we can say that in any given period of time, the expected rate of return on our portfolio is a weighted average of the expected rates of return on the stocks in the portfolio. In taking the average, the weights are given by the fraction of our own money that we are investing in each stock. If we are buying the stock in question, the weight assigned to the stock is positive; if we are short selling the stock, the weight is negative. In any case, the sum of the weights is always 100 percent.

The Portfolio's Variance

To compute the variance of a portfolio of securities, you need to know the co-variances among the securities in the portfolio. In any given period securities may produce returns that *deviate* from their expected values. For any pair of securities we can take the deviations that are occurring and multiply them together to get a product. *The covariance is the expected value of this product.* If, when one security produces a return *above* its expected value, the other tends to do so also, the covariance between them is positive. The covariance is negative if, when one is above its expected value, the other tends to be below. Co-variance is discussed further in the appendix to this chapter. The *covariance matrix* gives the covariances among all the securities that are in the portfolio. The covariance matrix among three stocks, A, B, and C, is written as

Stock	A	B	C
A	$Cov(r_A, r_A)$	$Cov(r_B, r_A)$	$Cov(r_C, r_A)$
B	$Cov(r_A, r_B)$	$Cov(r_B, r_B)$	$Cov(r_C, r_B)$
C	$Cov(r_A, r_C)$	$Cov(r_B, r_C)$	$Cov(r_C, r_C)$

Each element of the matrix tells you the covariance between the returns to the security given at the top of the columns and the returns to the security given at the left of the row(s). To illustrate, as we go down the diagonal of the matrix from the extreme northwest corner to the extreme southeast corner, we are looking at the covariance between each security and *itself*. This may seem strange at first, but if you consider what the variance and covariance are, you will realize that the covariance between a security and itself is simply its own variance.

In general, to compute the covariance between two securities, in each period take the deviation from the mean for one security and multiply it by the deviation from the mean that is occurring for the other security. In computing the covariance between a security and itself, each deviation is multiplied by itself, or squared, as it is in computing the variance. Thus, all the numbers going down the diagonal of the matrix represent the variances for the individual securities.

It is also true that, for each number above the diagonal, there is a corresponding and equal number below the diagonal. This is true because the covariance between securities A and B is the same as the covariance between securities B and A.

To determine the variance of a portfolio, we need to know the portfolio weights for each stock, and we need to have estimates for the numbers in the covariance matrix. We then set up the matrix in the following way:

	Stock	x_A A	x_B B	x_C C
x_A	A	$\sigma^2 r_A$	$Cov(r_B, r_A)$	$Cov(r_C, r_A)$
x_B	B	$Cov(r_A, r_B)$	$\sigma^2 r_B$	$Cov(r_C, r_B)$
x_C	C	$Cov(r_A, r_C)$	$Cov(r_B, r_C)$	$\sigma^2 r_C$

where $\sigma^2 r_A$ is the variance of stock A.

Computing the variance is now a comparatively simple operation: Take each of the variances and covariances in the matrix and multiply it by the portfolio weight at the top of the column and then again by the portfolio weight at the left side of the row. For example, in the case of $Cov(r_A, r_B)$ you would compute the following product:

$$Cov(r_A, r_B) \times x_A \times x_B$$

After obtaining such a product for each element of the matrix, you add up all the products, and the resulting sum is the variance of the portfolio. Obviously, to compute the standard deviation of the portfolio, you need only take the square root of the sum.

COMBINATION LINES

A combination line is drawn on a graph when you are plotting expected return against the square root of variance or standard deviation. Each point on the combination line shows the expected rate of return and standard deviation of a portfolio of two stocks with given portfolio weights. Each point on the line represents a different set of portfolio weights in the two stocks. Thus, the combination line tells us how the expected return and risk of a two-stock portfolio changes as we change the weights in the two stocks.

Recognizing that in a portfolio of two stocks $x_B = (1 - x_A)$, we have the equations for expected return and standard deviation:

$$E(r_P) = x_A E(r_A) + (1 - x_A)E(r_B)$$

and

$$\sigma r_P = [x_A^2 \, \sigma^2 r_A + (1 - x_A)^2 \, \sigma^2 r_B + 2x_A (1 - x_A) \, \text{Cov} \, (r_A, r_B)]^{1/2}$$

The equation for the standard deviation reflects the operation of summing the products obtained from the two-by-two covariance matrix. The sum of the three terms inside the brackets, [ ], on the right-hand side represents the variance of the portfolio. The first two terms are the products obtained by going down the diagonal of the matrix. In each case you multiply the variance of the stock by its own portfolio weight twice—once for the weight at the top of the column and again for the same weight at the side of the row. You will also obtain two products from either side of the diagonal. These products are identical, and are represented by the third term in brackets. The three terms sum to the variance of the portfolio.

As shown in the appendix to this chapter

$$\text{Cov}(r_A, r_B) = \rho_{A,B} \, \sigma r_A \, \sigma r_B$$

where $\rho_{A,B}$ is the correlation coefficient between the two securities.

Therefore, we can rewrite the equation for the standard deviation as

$$\sigma r_P = [x_A^2 \, \sigma^2 r_A + (1 - x_A)^2 \, \sigma^2 r_B + 2 \, x_A (1 - x_A) \, \rho_{A,B} \, \sigma r_A \, \sigma r_B]^{1/2} \quad (3\text{-}1)$$

To illustrate the concept of a combination line, suppose we have two stocks with the following characteristics:

Stock	A	B
Expected return	.10	.04
Standard deviation	.05	.10

To construct a combination line for the two stocks, we need to make an assumption about the degree to which they are correlated. Let's assume that the correlation coefficient between the two stocks is zero. Filling in the above numbers for the corresponding values in the equations for expected return and standard deviation gives

$$E(r_P) = x_A \, .10 + (1 - x_A) \, .04$$
$$\sigma r_P = [x_A^2 \, .05^2 + (1 - x_A)^2 \, .10^2]^{1/2}$$

Note that the covariance term has disappeared from the formula for standard deviation, because the correlation is presumed to be zero.

Assume that you have $1000 to invest, and you short sell $500 of stock B and use the proceeds, in addition to your equity, to invest $1500 in stock A. Your portfolio weight in A is, thus, 1.5. Substituting this value into the formulas, we get the following values for the expected rate of return and standard deviation:

$$E(r_P) = 1.50 \times .10 - .5 \times .04 = .13$$
$$\sigma r_P = [1.50^2 \times .05^2 + (-.50)^2 \times .10^2]^{1/2} = .09$$

By making the same computations for other values for x_A, we obtain the following schedule:

Portfolio Weight for Security A	Portfolio Expected Return	Portfolio Standard Deviation
1.50	.130	.090
.75	.085	.045
.50	.070	.056
.25	.055	.076
−.50	.010	.152

The points in the schedule are plotted in Figure 3–4a. If still more such points
were plotted for different values for the portfolio weight in security A, they
would trace out the bullet-shaped curve seen in the figure. This curve is called
the *combination line* for the two stocks. It shows what happens to the risk and

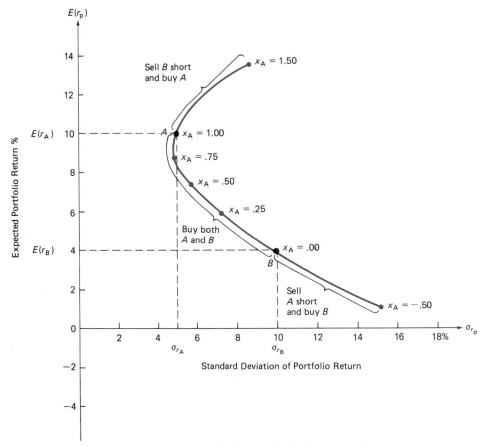

Figure 3-4a   Combination Line Between Stocks A and B for the Case of Zero Correlation

expected return to a portfolio of the two stocks as the portfolio weights are shifted from one value to another.

The two stocks themselves are positioned at points A and B. At these points, the portfolio weight in A is equal to 1.00 and .00, respectively. For points along the curve to the northeast of point A, we are short selling stock B and investing in stock A. For points on the curve between points A and B, we are taking positive positions in both stocks. For points to the southeast of B, we are short selling A and investing in stock B. Although these points represent unattractive portfolios, in the sense that risk is high and expected return is low, nevertheless, they are available, given the assumed position of the two stocks.

You also should understand that the combination line extends indefinitely toward the northeast and toward the southeast. The more we short sell of stock B, the farther we move on the curve to the northeast, and the more we short sell of A, the farther we move to the southeast.

To see what is happening as we move along the combination line, consider Figure 3–4b. In this figure probability distributions for rates of return are shown

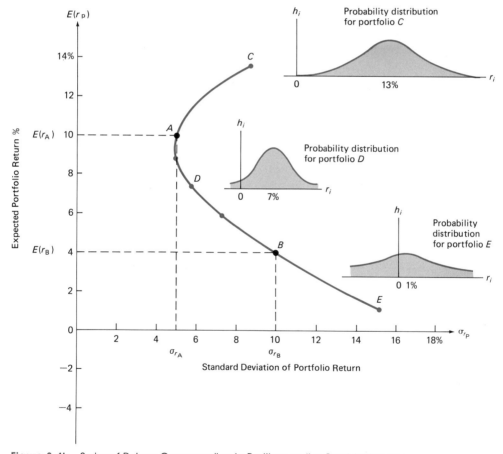

Figure 3-4b Series of Returns Corresponding to Positions on the Combination Line

for three portfolios along the combination line—portfolios C, D, and E. Note that as you move from C to D to E, the expected rate of return becomes smaller and smaller. The variance of the portfolio returns grows smaller as you move from portfolio C to D, but then it increases in magnitude as you go from portfolio D to E.

The Cases of Perfect
Positive and Negative Correlation

The combination line of Figure 3–4a is drawn for a *particular* assumed value for the correlation coefficient between the two stocks A and B, 0.0. If we assume a different value for the correlation coefficient for A with B, the schedule of values for the standard deviation would change, and we would obtain a different combination line. In fact, there is a family of different combination lines, one line for each assumed value for the correlation coefficient.

Suppose, for example, that the two stocks A and B are perfectly positively correlated. The following pairs of returns on the two stocks are consistent with the expected returns and standard deviations given above and perfect positive correlation:

Month	1	2	3
Return to stock A	15%	10%	5%
Return to stock B	14%	4%	−6%

These pairs of returns are plotted in Figure 3–5. Notice that all the returns plot on a straight line with a positive slope. This is consistent with perfect positive correlation.

Now consider the standard deviation of a two-stock portfolio as given by Equation (3–1). When the correlation coefficient is assumed to be 1.00, the terms in brackets become a perfect square in the sense that $(x_A \, \sigma r_A + (1 - x_A) \, \sigma r_B)$ multiplied by itself produces the expression in brackets. Thus, for the case of perfect positive correlation, we can say that the standard deviation of a portfolio is a simple weighted average of the standard deviations of the stocks we are putting in the portfolio.

$$\sigma r_P = x_A \, \sigma r_A + (1 - x_A) \, \sigma r_B$$

Technically speaking, because the standard deviation is always a positive number (it is the square root of the variance), the portfolio's standard deviation is equal to the absolute value of the right-hand side of the equation.

Given the above expression and the previous values for expected return and standard deviation for A and B, we can again develop a schedule of values for portfolio expected return and standard deviation, given different values for the portfolio weight in security A.

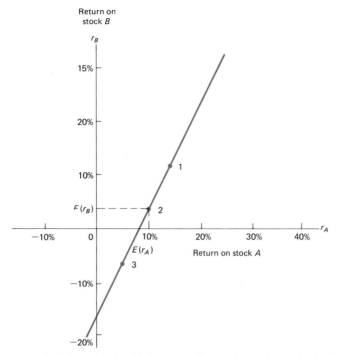

Figure 3-5   The Relationship Between Stocks A and B with Perfect
Positive Correlation

Portfolio Weight for Security A	Portfolio Expected Return	Portfolio Standard Deviation
3.00	.220	.0500
2.00	.160	.0000
1.50	.130	.0250
.75	.085	.0625
.50	.070	.0750
.25	.055	.0875
− .50	.010	.1250

These points are plotted on the broken combination line of Figure 3–6. Note
that you can achieve a riskless portfolio by selling B short in an amount equal
to 100 percent of your equity investment and using the proceeds to add to your
equity investment in A. To see this, consider the three pairs of returns in Figure
3–5, which are presumed to be observed in three successive months.

Now consider the corresponding returns to a portfolio with weights that are
adjusted to $x_A = 2.00$ and $x_B = -1.00$ at the beginning of each month:

$$.16 = 2.00 \times .15 + (-1.00) \times \quad .14$$

$$.16 = 2.00 \times .10 + (-1.00) \times \quad .04$$

$$.16 = 2.00 \times .05 + (-1.00) \times \quad -.06$$

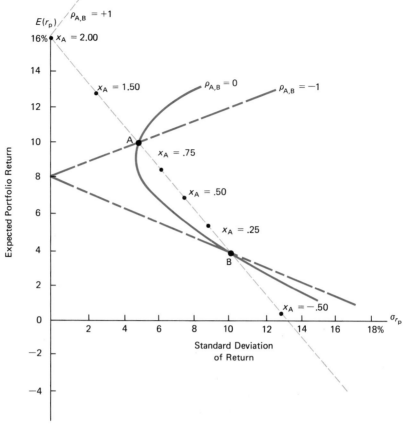

Figure 3-6 Combination Lines for the Cases of Perfect Positive, Perfect Negative, and Zero Correlation

The portfolio's return is perfectly stable at 16 percent. This is true no matter what pairs of returns we take from the line of Figure 3–5. With these weights we have created a riskless portfolio. We can always do this by selling one of the two stocks short to some degree, provided the stock's standard deviations are not equal and the stocks are perfectly positively correlated.

Now suppose, instead, the two stocks are perfectly *negatively* correlated. The following pairs of returns are consistent with the average rates of return and standard deviations of stocks and the assumed condition of perfect negative correlation:

Month	1	2	3
Return to stock A	15%	10%	5%
Return to stock B	−6%	4%	14%

These pairs of returns are plotted in Figure 3–7. Note that each pair falls on a straight line with a negative slope. This again satisfies the condition of perfect negative correlation.

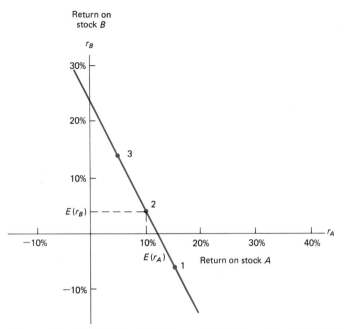

Figure 3-7 The Relationship Between Stocks A and B with Perfect Negative Correlation

Consider again Equation (3–1) for the standard deviation of a two-stock portfolio. If we assume a value of -1.00 for the correlation coefficient, the terms in brackets again become a perfect square in the sense that the term $[x_A \sigma r_A - (1 - x_A) \sigma r_B]$, when multiplied by itself, produces the bracketed expression. Thus, in this case, the formula for the standard deviation of a two-stock portfolio reduces to

$$r_P = x_A \sigma r_A - (1 - x_A) \sigma r_B$$

This expression is almost the same as that for the case of perfect positive correlation, except that a negative sign now separates the two terms on the right side. The standard deviation is again equal to the absolute value of the right side of the expression.

We can again derive a schedule showing expected portfolio return and portfolio standard deviation values corresponding to various values for the portfolio weight in security A:

Portfolio Weight for Security A	Expected Portfolio Return	Portfolio Standard Deviation
3.000	.220	.3500
2.000	.160	.2000
1.500	.130	.1250
.667	.080	.0000
.250	.055	.0875
$-.500$	.010	.1750

Estimating Risk and Return

"Would you like something to drink, Mr. Davanzo?"

"No, thanks, but I would like a copy of *Business Week* or *Forbes,* if you have one please."

Larry Davanzo settles back into the relatively comfortable first-class seat of the DC-10. He is flying from Chicago to Los Angeles after having stopped in Washington, D.C., and New York City. Larry is the director of consulting to public and private pension plans at Wilshire Associates, Inc., a consulting firm specializing in the application of modern portfolio techniques.

This has been a successful trip. This time it has pretty much been a case of helping clients allocate their assets among basic investment types. Each pension client has an associated stream of projected benefit liabilities. Larry shows the client the impact that different asset mixes will have on asset values, benefits, and future required contributions by the plan's sponsor, usually a corporation, and in some cases a state or municipality.

Using Wilshire's computer programs, Larry can specify any arbitrary mix of portfolio investments. Estimates of risk and expected rates of return for each mix are then produced for the client, given certain minimum and maximum amounts of investments in different types of assets. The programs can consider up to twenty basic asset categories, including stocks, bonds, real estate, venture capital, options, international stocks and bonds, and any other quantifiable asset. In making the asset allocation decision, the objective is not to determine the specific stock investments but rather to determine how much money to invest in one asset category as opposed to another.

To run the programs, Larry must come up with estimates of the expected rate of return on each asset category, the standard deviation of returns to each category, and the coefficient of correlation between the categories.

The estimates of expected return are made in consultation with each client. Larry tries to get a feel for the individual client's expectation for the rate of inflation over the client's horizon period. On this particular trip, expectations ranged from 4 percent to as high as 7 percent for the next three to five years. Then, using Wilshire's data base, an estimate is made of the real, inflation-adjusted, expected rate of return in each asset category. These estimates are based, to a considerable extent, on the historical

With perfect negative correlation, we can create a riskless portfolio by taking positive positions in both stocks. Whenever the return on stock B increases, the return on stock A decreases. Thus, if we invest positive amounts in both stocks, movement in their returns will tend to offset each other. Note, however, that when the return on A changes by a given amount, the return on B changes by

record. For example, over the last fifty years or so, the real rate of return to stock investments has been slightly greater than 6 percent. However, in the last decade, it has dropped to about 2 percent. Thus, Wilshire may project about 4 to 5 percent, depending on the economic outlook. Based on current interest rates, fixed-income securities have a real rate of interest of nearly 9 percent, but to obtain a forecast consistent with its stock forecast, Wilshire will project this to fall to 3 percent over the next three years or so. In any case, all these projections are developed jointly with the client.

The projections for standard deviation are also based, to a great extent, on historical returns. For example, over the last fifty years the standard deviation of rates of return to long-term bonds has been 7 to 8 percent. However, in the last ten years it has been 15 to 16 percent. Wilshire assumes a movement back toward the historical norm and usually forecasts in the neighborhood of 10 to 12 percent.

Turning to correlation coefficients, the long-term correlation coefficient between stocks and bonds has been about 16 percent, but in the last ten years it has been up to 40 percent. In each case, Wilshire looks at the history and then imposes some kind of subjective correction where it thinks the past doesn't adequately reflect the best estimate of prospects for the future. Investment categories like venture capital present special problems because no decent data exist on the past rates of return to these types of investments. The correlation with stocks is probably positive. Wilshire feels it is more positive for more aggressive stock portfolios because these are usually invested in smaller stocks, which themselves resemble venture operations.

Larry ascertains his clients' tolerance for risk by showing them the results of computerized projections. He might say, "Here's an asset mix that's conservative, and here's another that's aggressive. If you follow the conservative strategy, here's what might happen to the required contributions to the pension fund on a best and worst case basis." Then he does the same thing with the aggressive strategy. A client might react by saying, "I could never live with the possibility of my contribution rate doubling in five years if something goes wrong with that aggressive policy." Thus, Larry gains an understanding of his clients' risk objectives by presenting them with alternatives that they can understand.

twice the amount. Consequently, to make the canceling complete, we must invest twice as much in A as we do in B. This is the case when the portfolio weights are $x_A = .667$ and $x_B = .333$.

To see this, consider the three pairs of returns plotted in Figure 3–7. If, at the beginning of each month, we adjust to portfolio weights equal to $x_A = .667$ and

$x_B = .333$, the portfolio will produce an 8 percent return in each of the three periods:

$$.08 = .667 \times .15 \times .333 \times -.06$$
$$.08 = .667 \times .10 + .333 \times .04$$
$$.08 = .667 \times .05 + .333 \times .14$$

Contrast the risk associated with short selling under conditions of perfect positive and negative correlation. If we are short in either stock, the risk of the portfolio is higher if the correlation is negative. Remember, if you are short, it is better for the return to be low rather than high. With perfect negative correlation, when the return on one stock is high, the return on the other stock is invariably relatively low. If you are short in the high stock and long in the low, both parts of your portfolio are suffering. On the other hand, if you're long in the high and short in the low, both parts are prospering. Because both parts of your portfolio tend to suffer and prosper at the same time, the portfolio exhibits greater variability over time.

The opposite situation occurs with perfect positive correlation. Here, when the return on one stock is high, the other will be also. You will prosper from your long position but suffer from your short. Moreover, when the returns on both stocks are low, you will suffer from your long but prosper from your short. The returns from your long and short positions will cancel, and the return to your overall position will be stabilized.

Borrowing and Lending at a Risk-Free Rate

Consider Figure 3–8, where two investments are plotted. A risky security is plotted at point A, with an expected return of 8 percent and a standard deviation of 6 percent, and a risk-free security (perhaps a bond with a return guaranteed by the government) is plotted at point B. Only one return is possible on the bond investment. The probability of getting a 4 percent rate of return on the bond is 100 percent. The standard deviation of the returns on the bond is, therefore, equal to 0 percent. Now consider Equation (3–1) for the standard deviation of a portfolio of two stocks. If we set $\sigma r_B = 0$, the second and third terms in the brackets drop out, leaving

$$\sigma r_P = (x_A{}^2 \, \sigma^2 r_A)^{1/2}$$

This reduces to

$$\sigma r_P = x_A \, \sigma r_A$$

Given the above expression, we can again produce a schedule showing the risk and average return to our portfolio, given various values for x_A.

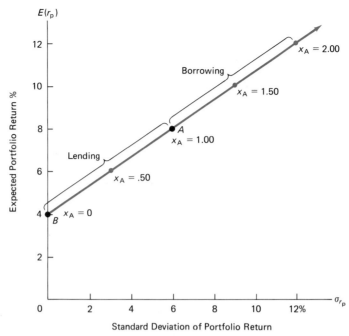

Figure 3-8   The Effect of Borrowing and Lending on Risk and Expected Rate of Return

Portfolio Weight for Security A	Portfolio Expected Return	Portfolio Standard Deviation
.00	.040	.000
.50	.060	.030
1.00	.080	.060
1.50	.100	.090
2.00	.120	.120

These points are plotted in Figure 3–8 on the combination line between the two investments. When one of the two investments is risk free, as it is here, the combination line is always a straight line. Correlation is obviously meaningless when one of the investments has no variability in its return.

If you take a position between points *A* and *B,* you are investing positive amounts in both the stock and the risk-free bond. In this case, you are *lending* to the person from whom you bought the bond. When you take positions on the combination line to the northeast of point *A,* you are *borrowing,* because you are selling the bond to raise money to add to your investment in stock A. The more you borrow, the farther out on the combination line you go, increasing your risk as well as your expected rate of return.

Remember that, if a risk-free borrowing and lending opportunity exists, such as the one in Figure 3–8, you can attain any position on a straight line extending out from the risk-free rate through any investment opportunity that exists in expected return-standard deviation space.

WOULD HAVE BEEN AND WILL BE

Suppose you observe the twelve monthly rates of return for two stocks over the preceding year. Based on the observed returns, you compute the average return and variance for each stock and the covariance between them. Now decide on the portfolio weights for each stock. Insert your estimates of average returns, variances and covariances, and assumed portfolio weights into the formulas for the average return and variance of a portfolio. Solving the formulas, you come up with numbers for the portfolio's variance and average return. How do you interpret these numbers?

The numbers tell you exactly what the average return and variance of a portfolio with your selected weights *would have been* if you had rebalanced the portfolio at the end of each year, by selling some of one stock and investing the proceeds in the other, so as to return to the originally selected portfolio weights. That is, if you compute what the individual monthly returns to this portfolio would have been and then compute the mean and variance of these returns, they would correspond exactly to the numbers given by the formulas for the average return and variance of a portfolio.

In practice, however, you are not usually interested in what would have been. Rather you are interested in what *will be* if you choose to adopt a given investment strategy. You are usually not interested in what the average return to the portfolio would have been over some past period, but rather what you can expect it will be in the future.

As discussed above, you compute the *expected return* to an investment by multiplying each possible return by its associated probability of appearance and then adding up the products. For example, if there is a 60 percent chance of a stock producing a 10 percent return and a 40 percent chance of it producing a 20 percent return, the expected return is 14 percent.

$$14\% = .60 \times 10\% + .40 \times 20\%$$

You may want to employ sample mean returns from past periods as estimates of expected rates of return. Usually, however, more subjective procedures are employed. For example, suppose your investment horizon extends over the next quarter. You might ask your analysts to estimate the intrinsic market value of a given stock under three different market scenarios: pessimistic, unchanged, and optimistic. You also ask for estimates of the quarterly dividend payment in each scenario. The rate of return under each scenario is given by the following formula:

$$r = \frac{\text{Dividend} + \text{Estimated market price (end of quarter)}}{\text{Current market price}} - 1$$

To compute the stock's expected return, assign probabilities to each scenario, multiply the probabilities by the returns, and add up the products.

It is also true that you are not usually interested in what a portfolio's variance would have been in some past period. Rather, you are interested in what it will be in the future. If you are confident that the past will repeat itself, you may want to employ sample estimates of variances and covariances in the formula for portfolio variance. If, instead, you believe that the future will depart from the past in some predictable way, you may want to modify your sample estimates of variances and covariances to account for this. If you employ your modified estimates in the formula for portfolio variance, you will get an inaccurate estimate of what the portfolio's variance would have been in the past, but perhaps a more accurate estimate of what the portfolio's variance will be in the future.

Summary

In this chapter we examined how individual securities combine to form a portfolio. We concentrated on determining the expected rate of return and variance of a portfolio, based on the characteristics of the stocks in the portfolio.

The expected portfolio return is simply a weighted average of the expected rates of return of the individual securities in it. The weights are the fractions of the equity investment we commit to each security in our portfolio. If you buy (go long) a security, the weight for the security is positive; if you sell the security short, the weight is negative.

The portfolio variance is determined on the basis of the covariances for the individual stocks in the portfolio. For each covariance element in the covariance matrix, we multiply the covariance by the two portfolio weights for the associated stocks. Then the products are summed to obtain the variance of the portfolio.

A combination line shows what happens to the expected return and standard deviation of a two-security portfolio as the portfolio weights in the two securities are changed from one value to another. Given two investments with particular expected returns and standard deviations, a family of combination lines exists, one for each value for the coefficient of correlation between the returns on the two stocks. When one of the two investments is risk free, the combination line is a straight line extending out from the risk-free rate and passing through the position of the other risky investment.

To this point we have learned only how to determine the positions of portfolio opportunities available to us, given a selection of stock investments. We haven't learned how to determine the most desirable opportunities. That is the subject of Chapter 4.

APPENDIX: REVIEWING SOME STATISTICAL CONCEPTS

STATISTICS DESCRIBING THE PROPERTIES OF A SINGLE SECURITY

Suppose we are looking across some period of time in the future, say, over the next month, and are contemplating the potential for getting various rates of return on our investment. We might ask, "What is the probability of getting a rate of return in the next month that is less than zero?" If we explore questions like this thoroughly, we might be able to see in our minds what is called a "simple probability distribution" for the investment. The simple probability distribution shows the probabilities of getting various rates of return over the course of the month.

The distribution might look like the one in Figure A3–1. Horizontally, we are plotting the rates of return that might develop on the investment, which we will presume is a common stock. The symbol r is the rate of return that stock J might produce in some possible state of the world i.

The rate of return is the percentage increase in your wealth associated with holding the stock for the period. The dollar increase is equal to cash dividends received during the period plus any change in the value of the stock that occurs during the period. Your percentage rate of return is equal to the dollar increase divided by the market value of the stock at the beginning of the period.

$$r = \frac{\text{Dividends + Change in market value}}{\text{Beginning market value}}$$

On the vertical axis of Figure A3–1 we are measuring the probability of getting any particular rate of return. The graph is drawn as if the returns were continu-

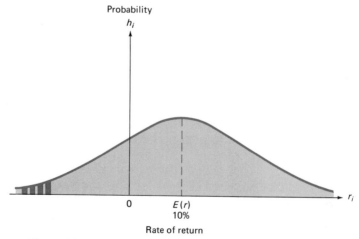

Figure A3-1 Marginal Probability Distribution for Rates of Return

ous along the horizontal axis. Actually, assume that there are a series of discrete possible rates of return, each associated with one of the vertical bars drawn on the graph. The length of each bar represents the probability of getting the particular rate of return represented below the bar. If you summed the probabilities represented by all the bars, the sum would equal 1, or 100 percent, because the returns plotted on the horizontal axis constitute everything that can happen to the stock in the next month.

The Sample Mean or Average Rate of Return

Suppose you can't see the actual probability distributions that represent the likelihood of getting the various returns for individual securities. Is there any way to infer what the underlying distributions look like, if you can't actually see them? This is an important question, because in the real world you can't see the probability distributions for investments. We cannot see the probabilities as they exist in the example depicted in Figure A3–1. Consequently, you usually have to estimate the properties of the distribution by sampling.

In taking sample estimates, you assume that the underlying probability distribution for the returns remains constant as time goes by. If you are dealing with a probability distribution for monthly rates of return, you assume that the distribution doesn't change from month to month. You then observe the rates of return that are supposedly drawn from this distribution month after month.

In Figure A3–2 we have plotted a time series of such returns for a security. Rates of return are plotted vertically, and time is plotted horizontally, for six months. To illustrate, note that the security produces a positive return equal to 6 percent in period 1. Given the returns produced in the six months, you can get

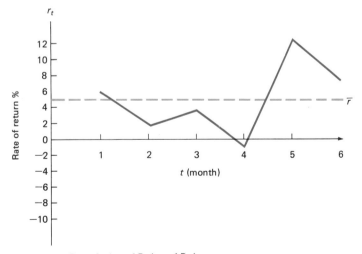

Figure A3-2   Time Series of Rates of Return

an estimate of the central location of the underlying distribution by taking the sample mean of the returns:

$$\text{Sample mean} = \bar{r} = \frac{\text{Sum of individual returns}}{\text{Number of sampled returns}}$$

In this example, the number of returns is equal to 6, and the sample mean is computed as the average of 6, 2, 4, -1, 12, and 7 percent, for a mean value of 5 percent. The sample mean gives you an idea of what you can expect to get as a return from the stock in any given month.

The Variance and Standard Deviation

What about the possibility of getting returns that deviate from the sample mean or average rage of return? The *variance* of return describes the propensity of the security to produce returns that are above or below the sample mean. To estimate the variance, you must once again resort to a sampling procedure. The sample variance is computed using the following formula:

$$\text{Variance} = \sigma^2_r = \frac{\text{Sum of squared deviations from sample mean}}{\text{Number of sampled returns less 1}}$$

where the squared deviation for a particular period, say, a month, is the square of the difference between the return for the month and the sample mean return.

To compute the variance, again observe the stock's returns over a number of periods. In each period you subtract, from the return produced, the sample mean rate of return. You square the differences and sum them up. Then you divide the sum by the number of returns observed, less 1. You subtract 1 because you are using an *estimate* in the computation of the variance. The estimate is the sample mean. Subtracting 1 from the denominator gives an unbiased estimate for the variance when you are dealing with a relatively small sample. In our example, the variance is computed as follows:

$$
\begin{aligned}
(\ \ .06 - .05)^2 &= .0001 \\
(\ \ .02 - .05)^2 &= .0009 \\
(\ \ .04 - .05)^2 &= .0001 \\
(-.01 - .05)^2 &= .0036 \\
(\ \ .12 - .05)^2 &= .0049 \\
(\ \ .07 - .05)^2 &= \underline{.0004} \\
\text{Total} &= .0100 \\
.0103/(6 - 1) &= .0020 = \text{variance}
\end{aligned}
$$

The propensity to deviate from the average rate of return can also be measured with another statistic called the "standard deviation." The standard deviation is computed merely by taking the square root of the variance.

$$\text{Standard deviation} = \sigma_r = \text{Square root of variance}$$

In our example, the standard deviation is given by

$$.04 = (.002)^{1/2}$$

STATISTICS DESCRIBING THE INTERRELATIONSHIPS AMONG SECURITIES

The average rate of return and the variance, or standard deviation, provide us with information about the probabilities for returns to a single security or for a portfolio of securities. However these numbers tell us nothing about the way the returns on securities *interrelate*. Suppose in some given month one security produces a rate of return that is above its average return. If we know that this has happened, what does it do to our expectation for the rate of return produced on some other stock in the same period? When one stock produces a rate of return above its average value, do other stocks have a propensity to do so as well? A statistic that provides us with some information about this question is the covariance between the two stocks.

The Covariance

To illustrate what the covariance is, suppose we have two securities, A and B. In a period of five months they produce the following rates of return:

Month	1	2	3	4	5	Mean
Stock A	.04	− .02	.08	− .04	.04	.02
Stock B	.02	.03	.06	− .04	.08	.03

The five pairs of monthly returns are plotted against one another in Figure A3–3. The mean rates of return on the two stocks are represented by the broken horizontal and vertical lines.

To compute the sample covariance based on these five monthly rates of return, we compute the deviation that is occurring from the mean return for each of the stocks in each of the months. Then in each month we multiply together the deviations for each of the stocks to get a product. Then we use the following formula:

$$\text{Covariance} = \text{Cov}(r_A, r_B) = \frac{\text{Sum of the products of the deviations}}{\text{Number of sampled returns less 1}} \quad (A3\text{--}1)$$

Thus, we start with the first pair of monthly returns marked 1 in the graph. In this month stock A is producing 4 percent, and stock B is producing 2 percent. We first compute the deviation that these returns represent from the mean returns of each stock. Note that stock A is 2 percent above its mean of 2 percent,

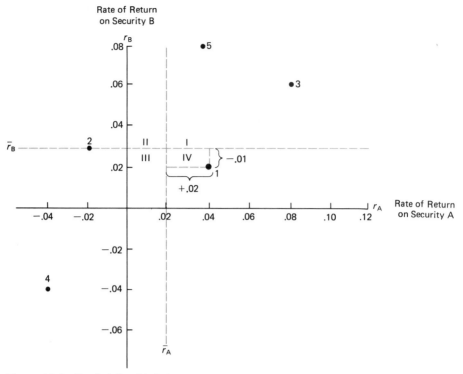

Figure A3-3 The Relationship Between the Returns on Two Stocks Over Time

and stock B is 1 percent below its mean of 3 percent. After expressing the two deviations as decimals, we multiply them to get a product of $-.0002$. We now do the same for each of the other four return pairs and sum them up as follows:

$$
\begin{aligned}
(\ .04 - .02)(\ .02 - .03) &= -.0002 \\
(-.02 - .02)(\ .03 - .03) &= \ \ .0000 \\
(\ .08 - .02)(\ .06 - .03) &= \ \ .0018 \\
(-.04 - .02)(-.04 - .03) &= \ \ .0042 \\
(\ .04 - .02)(\ .08 - .03) &= \ \ \underline{.0010} \\
\text{Total} &= \ \ .0068
\end{aligned}
$$

We then divide the total by the number of sampled returns, less 1, to obtain the covariance.

$$.0068/(5 - 1) = .0017$$

As a number, the covariance doesn't provide much detail about the relationship between the returns on the two stocks. In this case, because it is a positive number, the covariance tells you that when one security produces a return above its average return, the other security has a propensity to do the same thing.

Figure A3–3 can be divided into four quadrants on the basis of the mean returns on the two stocks. In quadrant I, both stocks are above their mean returns;

in III, both are below. In II, stock A is below and B is above. In IV, B is below and A is above. Note that in quadrants I and III the deviations from the mean for both stocks have the same sign: In I the deviations are positive and in III they are negative. In these two quadrants, when we take the products of the deviations, we get positive numbers. Contrast this with quadrants II and IV, where the deviations are of opposite sign, and we get negative products.

If the majority of the observations are in quadrants I and III, as they are in this case, the sum of the products will tend to be positive, as will the covariance. To see this, consider Figures A3–4 and A3–5. The covariance between the stocks in Figure A3–4 is negative. In this case the observations of quadrants II and IV dominate those of I and III. When one stock is above its mean, the other tends to be below, and vice versa. On the other hand, the covariance between the stocks in Figure A3–5 is approximately zero. The observations are scattered uniformly throughout the four quadrants, and the negative products offset the positive products in the sum. Thus, the products of the deviations sum to approximately zero.

The covariance number is important because it is a critical input in determining the variance of a portfolio of securities. However, as we said earlier, it doesn't describe very fully the nature of the relationship between the two investments. Nevertheless, we can standardize the covariance to obtain a better descriptor called the correlation coefficient.

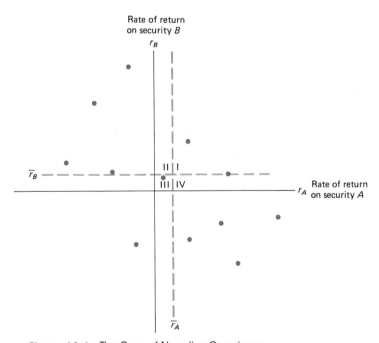

Figure A3-4   The Case of Negative Covariance

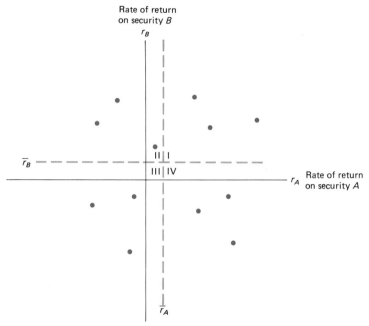

Figure A3-5 The Case of Zero Covariance

The Correlation Coefficient

Theoretically, the possible range for the covariance extends all the way from minus to plus infinity. We can bound it, however, by dividing it by the product of the standard deviations for the two investments:

$$\text{Correlation coefficient} = \rho_{A,B} = \frac{\text{Covariance}}{\text{Product of standard deviations}} \quad (A3\text{--}2)$$

The resulting number is called the correlation coefficient, and it falls within the range of -1 to $+1$. In our example, the standard deviation of the five returns to security A is equal to 4.9 percent and the standard deviation for B is equal to 4.6 percent. The correlation coefficient is thus

$$\text{Correlation coefficient} = \frac{.0017}{.049 \times .046} = .76$$

Figures A3–6 through A3–10 represent samples of paired returns taken from stocks. The correlation coefficients for the stocks of Figures A3–6 and A3–7 are both equal to $+1$. Notice that in both cases you can pass a straight line through every observation. This is the unique characteristic of perfect positive $(+1)$ or perfect negative (-1) correlation. If the slope of the line passing through all the observations is positive, the correlation coefficient is equal to $+1.00$; if it is negative, the correlation coefficient is equal to -1.00. Other than its sign, the

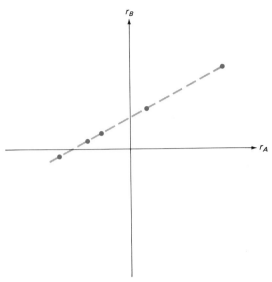

Figure A3-6   Perfect Positive Correlation

magnitude of the slope is immaterial. Thus, Figures A3–6 and A3–7 represent cases of perfect positive correlation. Figure A3–8, however, represents perfect negative correlation.

If you can't pass a straight line through all the observations, the correlation is imperfect, falling between −1 and +1. You can still pass a line through the scatter of observations that is called "the line of best fit." This line minimizes

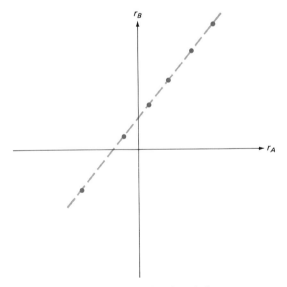

Figure A3-7   Perfect Positive Correlation

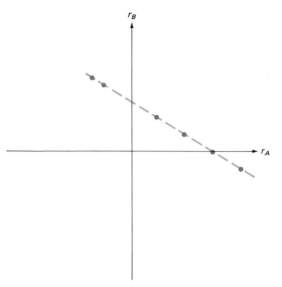

Figure A3-8 Perfect Negative Correlation

the sum of the squared vertical distances from each individual observation to the line. The distance labeled ϵ in Figure A3–9 is one of these vertical distances, and the line drawn through the scatter is the line of best fit. If this line has a positive slope, the correlation is again positive, but if the individual observations are scattered about the line, the correlation coefficient falls between 0 and $+1$. In the case of Figure A3–9, the correlation coefficient is approximately .90. The correlation coefficient approaches 1.00 as the fit about the line becomes tighter and tighter. If the line of best fit has a slope of zero, the correlation coefficient is also equal to zero. This is the case of Figure A3–10.

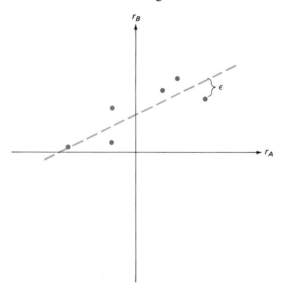

Figure A3-9 Imperfect Positive Correlation

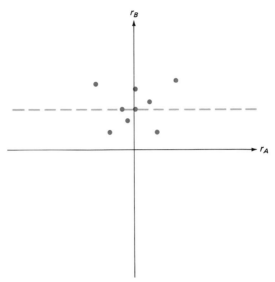

Figure A3-10   Zero Correlation

Before moving on, note that given the definition for the correlation coefficient in Equation (A3–2), we can write the covariance as the product of the correlation coefficient and the standard deviations of the two securities:

Covariance = Correlation coefficient × Product of standard deviations

The Coefficient of Determination

If we square the correlation coefficient, we obtain the coefficient of determination. This is the percentage of the variability in the returns on one investment that can be associated with variability in the returns on some other. For example, because the correlation coefficient for Figure A3–9 is +.90, we can say that approximately 81 percent of the variability in the returns on security A can be associated with, or explained by, the returns on security B. Note that the coefficient of determination for the cases represented by Figures A3–6 through A3–8 is 100 percent. Thus, if we somehow knew what the return on one of the securities was going to be in the next month, we could predict the return on the other security with perfect accuracy.

QUESTIONS AND PROBLEMS

1. Explain the concept of short selling.
2. Suppose you purchase $1000 of stock A, purchase $500 of stock B, and borrow $500. If these transactions constitute your entire portfolio, what are the "portfolio weights" for each component of the portfolio?

3. Compute the variance and expected return of the portfolio in question 2, given the following additional information:

	A	B
Variance	.25	.49
E(r)	.10	.16

The correlation of A with B is .7. Borrowing takes place at a certain interest rate of .05.

4. Write the formula that would be required to compute the variance on a five-stock portfolio.

Assume the following information for questions 5 through 7:

Stock	E(r)	Standard Deviation	Correlation Coefficients
1	.05	.20	1 with 2 = −.2
2	.10	.10	1 with 3 = .3
3	.20	.15	1 with 4 = .5
4	.15	.30	2 with 3 = .2
			2 with 4 = −.5
			3 with 4 = 0

A portfolio is formed as follows: Sell short $2000 of stock 1 and buy $3000 of stock 2, $2000 of stock 3, and $3000 of stock 4. The cash provided by the owner of the portfolio is $2000, and any additional funds required to finance the portfolio are borrowed at an interest rate of 5 percent. There are no restrictions on the use of short sale proceeds.

5. Compute the portfolio weights for each component of the portfolio.
6. Compute the expected return of the portfolio.
7. Compute the standard deviation of the portfolio.
8. Consider two securities, A and B, which have the following characteristics:

	A	B
E(r)	.12	.06
Standard deviation	.12	.06

Correlation coefficient of A with B = −1.0. Compute the expected returns and standard deviations of each of the following portfolios of A and B. Also, plot securities and the portfolios of A and B on a graph with expected return and standard deviation on the axes.

Portfolio 1	$x_A = 2$	$x_B = -1$
Portfolio 2	$x_A = .5$	$x_B = .5$
Portfolio 3	$x_A = 1/3$	$x_B = 2/3$
Portfolio 4	$x_A = -.5$	$x_B = 1.5$

9. Consider two stocks with the following characteristics:

	Stock X	Stock Y
Expected return	.10	.14
Standard deviation	.25	.30

Suppose you build a portfolio with equal dollar amounts in the two stocks. Compute the expected return and variance of the portfolio under each of the following assumptions about the correlation between returns on X and Y: (a) correlation = 1, (b) correlation = 0, (c) correlation = −1.

10. Assume that two stocks have a correlation coefficient of −1.0.

   a. What would be the lowest possible standard deviation that could be achieved by constructing a portfolio of these two stocks?

   b. Use your answer to part a and Equation (3–1) to derive an expression for the lowest standard deviation portfolio weights for the stocks. (The weights for the stocks will be a function of the standard deviations of the two stocks.)

11. Two stocks, L and M, are perfectly negatively correlated. The standard deviation of L is .6 and that of M is .8. Find the portfolio of L and M that will result in the lowest possible standard deviation.

12. What does a combination line for two stocks tell you?

13. Suppose you construct a combination line for two assets, with one of the assets having a zero standard deviation. What is a feature of this particular combination line that is not true for any arbitrary combination line?

14. If two stocks were perfectly positively correlated, would it be possible to construct a portfolio of the two stocks with zero standard deviation? Explain.

BIBLIOGRAPHY

BREALEY, R. A., and S. D. HODGES, "Playing with Portfolios," *Financial Analysts Journal* (March 1974).

CLARKSON, G. P., *Portfolio Selection: A Simulation of Trust Investment.* Englewood Cliffs, N.J.: Prentice-Hall, 1962.

HESTER, D. D., and J. TOBIN, *Risk Aversion and Portfolio Choice.* New York: Wiley, 1967.

LEVY, H., "Does Diversification Always Pay?" *TIMS Studies in Management Science* (1979).

RENSHAW, E. F., "Portfolio Balance Models in Perspective: Some Generalizations That Can Be Derived from the Two-Asset Case," *Journal of Financial and Quantitative Analysis* (June 1967).

SHARPE, W. F., "Portfolio Analysis," *Journal of Financial and Quantitative Analysis* (June 1967).

WAGNER, W., and S. LAU, "The Effect of Diversification on Risk," *Financial Analysts Journal* (November–December 1971).

4

MAXIMIZING RETURN WHILE MINIMIZING RISK

Introduction

In the previous chapter we learned how securities combine into portfolios in terms of expected return and standard deviation. In this chapter we will learn how to find the *best* ways to combine securities. What is best? We will take best to mean those combinations which provide the greatest possible expected return given the risk, or standard deviation, that we are exposing ourselves to. The portfolios that are best, for different levels of risk exposure, are the portfolios in the efficient set.

THE MINIMUM VARIANCE AND EFFICIENT SETS

In Figure 4–1 we are plotting expected return against standard deviation of return. The points in the figure represent individual securities. For example, the security denoted by point *A* has an average rate of return of 10 percent and a standard deviation of 15 percent. These individual securities can be combined

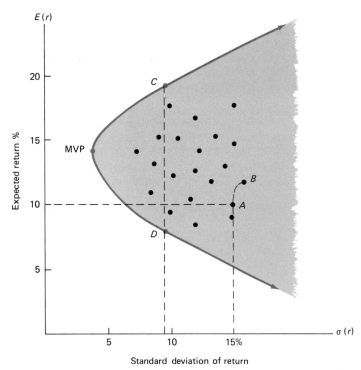

Figure 4-1 The Minimum Variance Set

into portfolios. For example, we can invest in securities A and B and attain positions anywhere on the broken combination line.

As you might imagine, by taking positive positions in some of the securities and short positions in others, we can form a wide variety of portfolios that would be positioned at various points on the graph. This constitutes the set of investment opportunities available to us. We would, of course, prefer some of these positions to others. Given the level of risk, or standard deviation, we prefer positions with higher expected rates of return; given the level of expected return, we prefer positions of lower risk. In any case, given the characteristics of the available population of securities, the investment opportunity set has a perimeter that is represented by the bullet-shaped curve. From now on, we will refer to this perimeter as the *minimum variance set*.

Each point on the minimum variance set represents a portfolio, with portfolio weights allocated to each of the securities in the population. Each of the portfolios in the minimum variance set meets the following criterion: *Given a particular level of expected rate of return, the portfolios have the lowest standard deviation (or variance) achievable with the available population of stocks.* As befitting its shape, from time to time we shall refer to the minimum variance set as the "bullet," irrespective of whether standard deviation or variance is being measured along the horizontal axis. Because the portfolios that minimize *variance,* given expected return, are identical to the portfolios that minimize *stan-*

Allocating Assets

Jeff Diermeier, a vice president at First National Bank of Chicago, walks into the office of his boss, Gary Brinson. Gary is president of First Chicago Investment Advisors, a wholly owned subsidiary of the First Chicago Corporation. First Chicago is at the forefront of the application of sophisticated techniques of modern portfolio analysis to investment management. First Chicago's reputation in this area is due, in large part, to the leadership of Gary Brinson. It was Gary who initially steered First Chicago away from the traditional techniques of security analysis toward the more quantitative approach that now guides most of the firm's investment decisions.

Jeff begins his discussion of the results of his latest computer run. The output indicates recommended fractions of portfolios that are invested in various types of investments. Given various risk levels, the computer has calculated overall portfolio weights in each type of asset. The weights are determined on the basis of the efficient set found through the Markowitz portfolio technique. The computer is constrained to avoid short selling, and in some cases it is constrained to limit the total amount in any one type of investment.

Nine classes of investments are used in the analysis:

1. The common stocks of large companies

2. The common stocks of small companies

3. Venture capital investments

4. Foreign common stocks

5. Domestic fixed-income securities, including corporate bonds, government and agency securities, and mortgages

6. Eurodollar investments—international bonds denominated in dollars but issued by or in non-U.S. provinces

dard deviation, the terms *minimum variance set* and *minimum standard deviation set* can be used interchangeably.

The minimum variance set can be divided into two halves, a top and a bottom. The halves are separated at point *MVP*. Point *MVP* represents the single portfolio with the lowest possible level of standard deviation, the *global minimum variance portfolio*. The most desirable portfolios for us to hold are those in the top half of the bullet; the least desirable are those in the bottom half.

The top half of the bullet is called the *efficient set*. All the portfolios in the efficient set meet the following criterion: *Given a particular level of standard deviation, the portfolios have the highest attainable expected rate of return.* Thus, whereas in Figure 4–1 both portfolios C and D meet the criterion for the minimum variance set (lowest standard deviation, given expected return), only

7. Nondollar bond investments, for example, bonds issued by a German manufacturer, denominated in a nondollar currency such as Swiss francs. This classification would also include straight foreign bonds
8. Real estate investments
9. Money market investments

Jeff and his staff estimate the expected rates of return on each class of investments on the basis of historical rates of return, current yields to maturity, forecasts of the future direction of interest rates, and forecasts of general economic conditions currently being made by the firm.

The covariance matrix is estimated on the basis of sample estimates taken from historical returns associated with portfolios of securities in each investment class. Some of the classes, such as venture capital, are problematic in this respect. In the case of venture capital, Jeff uses the returns from a venture capital fund that is managed by the bank itself.

The expected returns and covariances are supposedly representative of the reward and risk associated with each general investment classification. At this point in time, interest rates are expected to decline. The estimates of the expected rates of return on domestic bonds and common stocks are consequently quite high. As a result, the computer's recommended portfolio weights in money market instruments, real estate, venture capital, and foreign securities are lower than usual, especially for the relatively high-risk portfolios. Because Jeff is in charge of asset allocation at the bank, the weights help him to determine the general structure of the portfolios managed by the bank at each level of desired risk. After the general asset allocation decisions have been made, the analysis becomes more micro in nature as individual investments within each classification are selected.

C meets the criterion for the efficient set (highest expected return, given standard deviation). Portfolio D actually has the lowest expected return, given the standard deviation level.

FINDING THE EFFICIENT SET

In practice, you will find the efficient set using a computer. To illustrate the process employed by the computer, we shall consider an example where we build portfolios from three available stocks—A, Acme Steel; B, Brown Drug;

and C, Consolidated Electric. The three stocks have the following expected rates of return:[1]

Acme Steel	$E(r_A)$ =	5%
Brown Drug	$E(r_B)$ =	10%
Consolidated Electric	$E(r_C)$ =	15%

The covariance matrix for the stocks is given by

Stock	A	B	C
A	.25	.15	.17
B	.15	.21	.09
C	.17	.09	.28

By taking the square root of the variances going down the diagonal of the matrix, we can compute the standard deviations of the stocks as follows:

Acme Steel	σr_A =	.50
Brown Drug	σr_B =	.46
Consolidated Electric	σr_C =	.53

The expected returns and standard deviations of the three stocks are plotted in Figure 4–2. The minimum variance set of portfolios of the three stocks is plotted as the solid curve. Combination lines between the stocks are plotted inside the curve.

We shall now examine a procedure for finding the portfolios in the minimum variance set.

In Figure 4–3 we are plotting the *portfolio weights* in Acme Steel and Brown Drug. The portfolio weight in Consolidated Electric is not represented on the diagram, but it is implied by the values for the weights in Acme and Brown. For example, if we are at point U, the portfolio weight in Brown is equal to .30, and the portfolio weight in Acme is given by .00. Because there are only three stocks, the portfolio weight in Consolidated is always equal to $(1 - x_A - x_B)$ and is therefore .70. Each point in Figure 4–3 thus represents a portfolio with particular weights allocated to each of the three stocks.

Now consider the triangle drawn in Figure 4–3. The points of the triangle are given by A, B, and C. All positions *inside* the triangle represent portfolios where we have invested positive amounts of money in each of the three stocks. To illustrate, consider point L. This point represents a portfolio where we are investing 50 percent of our money in Acme, 45 percent in Brown, and the remaining 5 percent in Consolidated. For portfolios on the *perimeter* of the triangle, we are investing a combined total of 100 percent of our money in two of the stocks, and we aren't taking any position at all in the third. At point Q on perimeter BC,

---

[1]The process of finding the minimum variance set described in this chapter was originally developed by Harry Markowitz (1952).

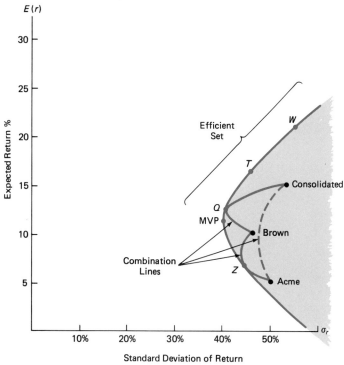

Figure 4-2   The Minimum Variance Set for Consolidated, Brown, and Acme

we are investing 60 percent in Brown, 40 percent in Consolidated, and nothing in Acme. On perimeter *BA,* we are taking no position in Consolidated; on *CA* we have no position in Brown.

If we are *outside* the triangle, at any point to the northeast of the line labeled *Y'X,* we are selling Consolidated short. If we are positioned to the west of the figure's vertical axis, we are selling Acme short, and if we are anywhere to the south of the horizontal axis we are selling Brown short. To illustrate, at point *Y',* we are selling Acme short and adding the proceeds to our equity to invest in Brown.

The Expected Return Plane

The expected rate of return to a portfolio is a simple weighted average of the expected rates of return to the securities we are putting in the portfolio. Thus, securities combine in a linear fashion in terms of their expected rates of return.

Return to Figure 4–3. This is a two-dimensional diagram. Now think of adding a third dimension that comes directly out from the page. We will plot expected portfolio return on this dimension. We now have three axes. On the floor or base of the diagram (which is actually Figure 4–3) we have our two horizontal

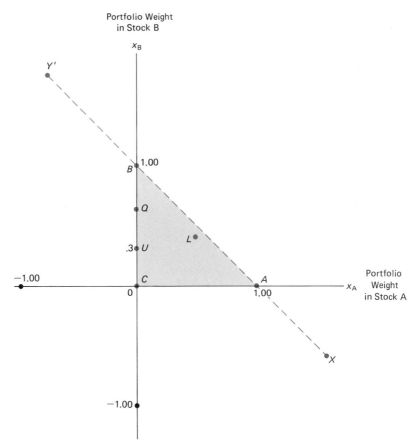

Figure 4-3 Portfolio Weights in the Three-Stock Portfolio

axes, which show the portfolio weights in Acme and Brown. On the vertical axis we are plotting the expected portfolio return, which corresponds to each combination of portfolio weights plotted on the base.

This three-dimensional diagram is depicted in Figure 4–4. The plane depicted in the diagram is situated directly above the triangle covering positive positions in the three stocks. It is a flat surface sloping down toward you. The plane shows you the expected return to portfolios of Acme, Brown, and Consolidated, which are plotted on the base of the diagram.

Let's first consider the three points of the triangular plane. Consider point A on the base of the diagram. At A, you are investing all of your money in Acme and nothing in the other two stocks. Because you have formed a portfolio that is actually Acme and nothing else, it will have an expected return that is equal to 5 percent, the expected return for Acme. To find the expected portfolio return corresponding to point A, move directly up from the base at point A. You will hit the plane at a 5 percent rate of return relative to the vertical axis. Similarly, at point C, where you are investing everything in Consolidated, moving directly

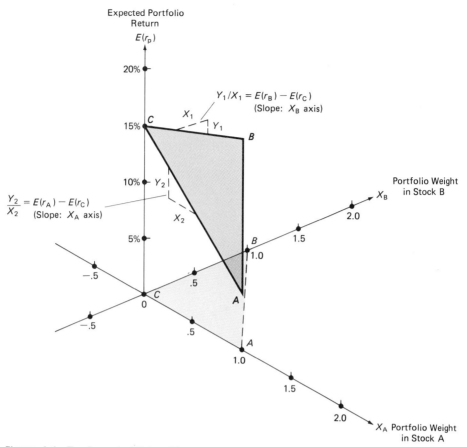

Figure 4-4 The Expected Return Plane

up from the base you hit the plane at a 15 percent expected return, the expected return to Consolidated. Moving up from *B*, where you are investing everything in Brown, you hit the plane at Brown's 10 percent expected return. Moving up from a point inside the triangle, where you are combining an investment in all three of the stocks, you find that the portfolio's expected rate of return is a linear combination of the expected returns to the three stocks. Remember that the expected return to a portfolio is a simple weighted average of the expected returns to the stocks in the portfolio.

You should be able to see that the plane is sloping down toward you only because Acme has the lowest expected rate of return. If Acme's expected return were, instead, the highest, the plane would then be sloping in an upward direction.

The plane actually extends indefinitely north, south, east, and west. For convenience, however, we have drawn only that segment positioned directly over the triangle, representing positive positions in each of the stocks.

Iso-Standard Deviation Ellipses

A similar diagram can be constructed showing the standard deviation of various portfolios of the three stocks. Figure 4–5a is similar to Figure 4–4, the only difference being that we are now plotting portfolio standard deviation on the vertical axis instead of expected return. For any given combination of portfolio weights, the standard deviation of the portfolio is computed by (a) taking each number in the covariance matrix and multiplying it by the portfolio weights for

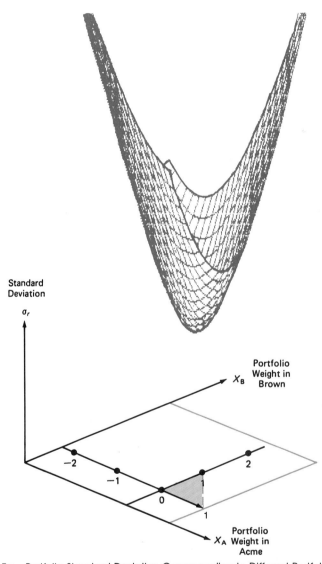

Figure 4-5a Portfolio Standard Deviation Corresponding to Different Portfolio Weights

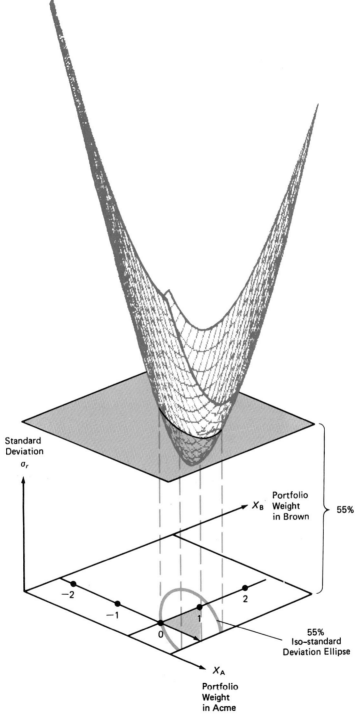

Standard
Deviation

σ_r

Portfolio
Weight
in Brown

X_B

55%

−2

−1

0

1

2

55%
Iso-standard
Deviation Ellipse

X_A

Portfolio
Weight
in Acme

Figure 4-5b   Drawing an Iso-Standard Deviation Ellipse

CHAPTER 4   Maximizing Return While Minimizing Risk

79

the two stocks associated with the covariance, (b) adding up the products, and (c) taking the square root of the sum. This is not, as in the case of the expected portfolio return, a simple linear process. Therefore, it shouldn't surprise us that the surface depicting the standard deviation of the portfolios represented on the base isn't flat either.

If portfolio standard deviation is repeatedly calculated for the various combinations of portfolio weights on the base of the diagram, a plot of the resulting portfolio standard deviations would produce the three-dimensional surface of Figure 4–5a. This surface looks like an artillery shell (that has somewhat of an elliptical shape) pointed directly down toward the base of the diagram.

If you pick a point on the base of the diagram representing a particular set of portfolio weights for the three stocks, the distance you would have to move directly upward to hit the three-dimensional shell would correspond to the standard deviation of a portfolio with the selected weights.

In Figure 4–5b we have sliced the shell with a horizontal plane at a particular level of portfolio standard deviation (55 percent). The points of intersection between the shell and the horizontal plane trace out as a portion of an ellipse. When the ellipse is superimposed on the base of the diagram, as in Figure 4–5b, it indicates those combinations of portfolio weights, all of which represent portfolios with 55 percent standard deviations. This ellipse is called an *iso-standard deviation ellipse*. If we sliced the surface of Figure 4–5b with another horizontal plane at a different level of portfolio standard deviation, we would get another iso-standard deviation ellipse representing a different portfolio standard deviation.

Two members of the family of iso-standard deviation ellipses for Acme, Brown, and Consolidated are drawn in Figure 4–6. The ellipses are centered about point *MVP*. The larger ellipse represents a larger portfolio standard deviation. Point *MVP* represents the one set of portfolio weights that produces the smallest possible portfolio standard deviation or variance. We have called this portfolio the *global minimum variance portfolio*. It is positioned at the lowest point of the shell of Figure 4–5a at point *MVP*. Drop a marble into the shell, and it will settle at a position directly over *MVP*.

The Critical Line

Now consider Figure 4–7. In this figure we are again plotting expected portfolio return on the vertical axis, as in Figure 4–4. In this figure the iso-standard deviation ellipses of Figure 4–6 have been superimposed on the expected return plane of Figure 4–4. For reasons that will become obvious, the plane has now been drawn to extend farther out toward the northwest.

Our objective is to find the portfolio with the highest expected return, given the level of standard deviation. Suppose we want the standard deviation of our portfolio to be 45 percent. Given this constraint, we want the expected return on the portfolio to be as high as possible. If we want a 45 percent portfolio standard deviation, we must position ourselves somewhere on the 45 percent

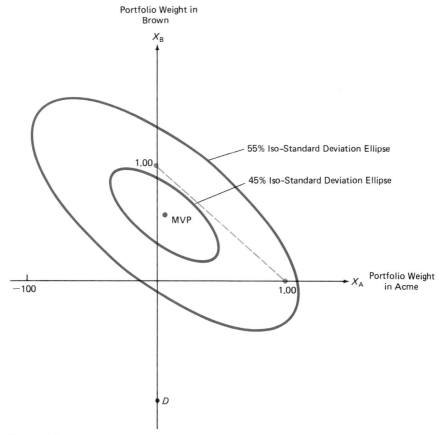

Figure 4-6 Two Iso-Standard Deviation Ellipses

iso-standard deviation ellipse. Given the location of the ellipse on the plane, we reach the highest possible point on the plane at point *T*. This is the portfolio with the highest possible expected return, given a 45 percent standard deviation. To construct this portfolio we must short sell Acme and invest the proceeds in Brown and Consolidated. We know that this is the case because point *T* is positioned over a point on the base of the diagram that represents a negative weight in Acme and a weight between 0.00 and 1.00 in Brown. The remaining portfolio position consists of a positive investment in Consolidated.

Because this portfolio provides the highest possible expected return, given a 45 percent standard deviation, it can be found on the efficient set of Figure 4–2 at point *T*. If we want a portfolio with a larger standard deviation, say, 55 percent, we move to the 55 percent ellipse. Moving along the ellipse, we reach the highest point on the plane at point *W*. We are now selling additional amounts of Acme short, using the proceeds to increase our long position in both Brown and Consolidated. This portfolio can be found on the efficient set of Figure 4–2 at point *W*.

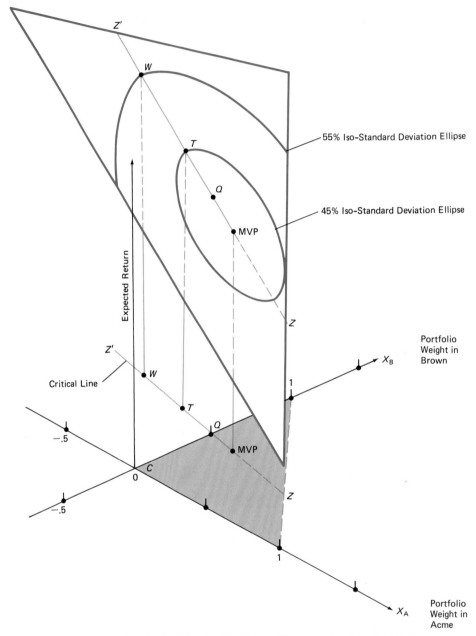

Figure 4-7 Superimposing the Iso-Standard Deviation Ellipses on the Expected Return Plane

Because the expected return plane is flat, and the iso-standard deviation ellipses are concentric about point *MVP*, we can pass a straight line through the points on each ellipse representing the highest possible expected return. This is line *Z'Z* in Figure 4–7. This line, called the *critical line,* is superimposed on the base of the diagram and then plotted in two dimensions in Figure 4–8. The portfolios in the efficient set (highest expected return, given standard deviation) are represented by the solid portion of the critical line. The broken portion of the line represents the remaining portfolios in the minimum variance set. These portfolios have the lowest possible expected return, given their standard deviation. Remember that each point in Figure 4–8 represents the portfolio weights for a given portfolio. The points on the critical line represent the portfolio weights for all the portfolios in the minimum variance set.

Consider point *Q* on the solid portion of the critical line representing the efficient set. This point is on the western edge of the triangle, representing a portfolio with positive positions in Brown and Consolidated and nothing in Acme. As such, this portfolio must be on the combination line between Brown and Consolidated. In fact, this portfolio is positioned at point *Q* in Figure 4–2.

Moving beyond point *Q* into the triangle of Figure 4–8, we move past the global minimum variance portfolio at point *MVP*. We are now taking positive positions in all three stocks. When we reach point *Z*, we are investing all of our money in Acme and Brown and nothing in Consolidated. As such, we are at point *Z* in Figure 4–2, on the combination line between Acme and Brown.

Note that the critical line doesn't pass through the southern edge of the triangle, so the combination line between Acme and Consolidated isn't tangent to

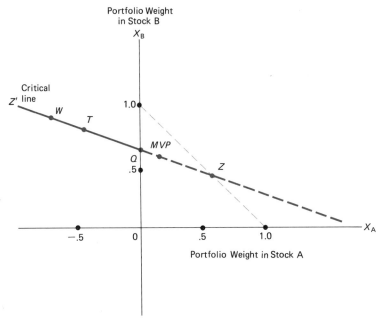

Figure 4-8 The Critical Line

the minimum variance set. So in Figure 4–2, we know that the broken combination line between A and C doesn't touch the minimum variance set as drawn.

As we move past point Z on the critical line, we begin selling Consolidated short and investing positive amounts in Acme and Brown. Eventually, where the critical line passes through the horizontal axis, we begin to sell both Consolidated and Brown short and use their proceeds to invest in Acme.

TWO KEY PROPERTIES OF
THE MINIMUM VARIANCE SET

Property I: If we combine two or more portfolios on the minimum variance set, we get another portfolio on the minimum variance set.

This important property follows directly from the fact that the critical line is a straight line. Recall that the critical line traces out the points of highest expected return on the iso-standard deviation ellipses. The critical line is linear because the iso-standard deviation ellipses are all symmetric about a common point (the minimum variance portfolio). As a result, when we trace out the points of highest expected return, we trace out a straight line.

To illustrate property I, consider portfolios I and III in Figure 4–9, where the portfolio weights for Acme and Brown are plotted on the horizontal and vertical axes, respectively. Suppose we combine these two portfolios by investing $1000 in each. The portfolio weights for the two portfolios are given by

	x_A	x_B	x_C
Portfolio I	-1.50	1.20	1.30
Portfolio III	.00	.70	.30

Given a $1000 investment in each portfolio, these portfolio weights are consistent with the following dollar commitments:

	Acme	*Brown*	*Consolidated*
Portfolio I	$-$1500	$1200	$1300
Portfolio III	$0	$700	$300
Combined portfolio II	$-$1500	$1900	$1600

Because we are investing a total of $2000 in the combined portfolio, the dollar positions in the three stocks are consistent with the following portfolio weights for the three stocks:

	A	B	C
Portfolio II	$-.75$	.95	.80

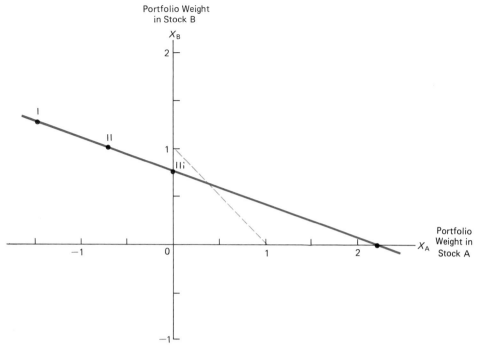

Figure 4-9 Portfolio Weights in Acme and Brown

If we plot the combined portfolio in Figure 4–9, it plots at point II. Note that this point is on the critical line, so the combined portfolio is also a member of the minimum variance set. This same thing will happen no matter which, or how many, of the minimum variance portfolios are combined. We can, in fact, sell short some of the portfolios and use the proceeds to invest in others. As long as all the portfolios are in the minimum variance set, the combined portfolio will also be on the bullet.

As we will see in Chapter 6, the central prediction of the Capital Asset Pricing Model (CAPM) is that the market portfolio is positioned on the efficient set. The CAPM is a theory that assumes that everyone can short sell without restriction and predicts the way securities would be priced if everyone used portfolio theory and invested in efficient portfolios. Keep in mind that the market portfolio is a combination of all the portfolios of every investor in the economy. Given property I, we know that if each investor holds an efficient portfolio, the combination of all of them will be efficient as well. In this sense, property I drives the central prediction of the CAPM.

The *beta factor* of a security describes the response of the security's returns to changes in the rates of return to the market portfolio, which is a portfolio composed of all risky (e.g., having positive standard deviations) investments in the economic system. To illustrate the concept of a beta factor, suppose we expect the return to the market portfolio to be 6 percent greater next month than it was last. If this causes us to revise upward our expectation for the rate of return on an individual stock by 12 percent, we can say that the stock has a beta factor of 2.00. If, instead, our expectation for the stock increased by only 3 percent, the stock would have a beta of only .50. (The concepts of beta and market portfolio are discussed in more detail in the appendix to this chapter.)

Property II: Given a population of securities, there will be a simple linear relationship between the beta factors of different securities and their expected (or average) returns if and only if the betas are computed using a minimum variance market index portfolio.[2]

Property II says that if we estimate betas by using a minimum variance portfolio as a proxy for the market portfolio, the relationship between our estimated betas for individual stocks and their average rates of return will be exactly linear. To see this, suppose we sample the returns to Acme, Brown, and Consolidated over a six-year period and find that the stocks produce the following rates of return:

Year	Acme	Brown	Consolidated
1	36%	35%	53%
2	−11%	−8%	−37%
3	−18%	−20%	69%
4	70%	28%	50%
5	25%	76%	16%
6	−72%	−51%	−61%
Mean	5%	10%	15%
Standard deviation	49.6%	45.3%	53.0%

The sample covariance matrix for the three stocks for the six-year period can be computed from these returns as

Stock	Acme	Brown	Consolidated
Acme	.246	.179	.178
Brown	.179	.205	.112
Consolidated	.178	.112	.281

Based on these numbers we can now compute the minimum variance set. The minimum variance set and the positions of the three stocks are plotted on the left-hand side of Figure 4–10.

Now suppose we want to compute beta factors, with reference to some index portfolio, for the three stocks. Assume that we select, as such an index portfolio, one of the portfolios in the minimum variance set, say, portfolio M in Figure 4–10. Portfolio M is represented by a set of portfolio weights, one weight for each of the three stocks:

[2]This property was originally discovered by Sharpe (1964). Its implications were not fully appreciated, however, until the publication of an important paper by Roll (1977).

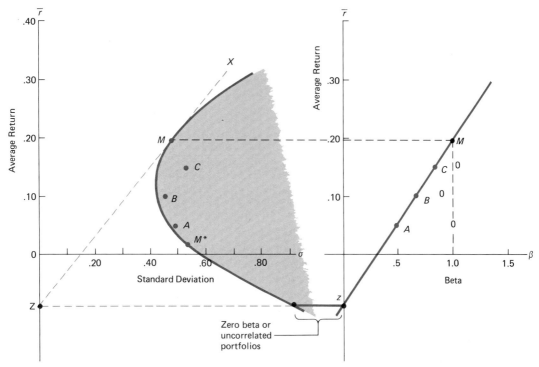

Figure 4-10 The Positioning of Stocks in Average Return-Beta Space

Portfolio Weights in Portfolio M	
Acme	−1.000
Brown	1.139
Consolidated	.861

Because we have six yearly returns for each of the three stocks, we can compute the corresponding six yearly returns to portfolio M. For each year we multiply the return to each stock by its portfolio weight and sum up the products. For example, the portfolio's return in the first year can be computed as

$$49.5\% = -1.00 \times 36\% + 1.139 \times 35\% + .861 \times 53\%$$

In this way the six portfolio returns can be computed as

Year	Return to Portfolio M
1	49.5%
2	−29.9%
3	54.6%
4	4.9%
5	75.3%
6	−38.6%
Mean	19.3%
Standard deviation	47.3%

Now we can compute the beta factor for each stock by relating the individual stock's returns to portfolio M's returns, as we do for Acme, Brown, and Consolidated in Figures 4–11a, 4–11b, and 4–11c. The broken line in each figure is our estimate of the characteristic line for the stock. The slope of these lines is our estimate of the beta factor (computed as indicated in the Appendix, as the ratio of each stock's sample covariance with portfolio M to portfolio M's sample variance). The betas are given by

	Beta Factor
Acme	.493
Brown	.670
Consolidated	.848

At this point we plot the betas against the average rates of return for each stock. Given the position of the three stocks and portfolio M, as drawn in the left side of Figure 4–10, the plot *must* look like that of the right side of Figure 4–10. Note that we can draw a straight line through the positions of each of the three stocks on the right side. This will always be the case, no matter how many stocks we are dealing with, as long as the market index we select is in the minimum variance set for the stocks considered. In fact, we don't even have to go through the trouble of computing the betas for each of the stocks and then plotting them to find the line. The position of the line on a graph relating average or expected return to beta can be found directly.

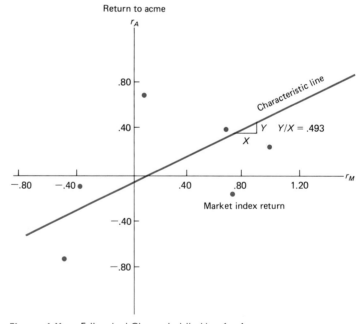

Figure 4-11a Estimated Characteristic Line for Acme

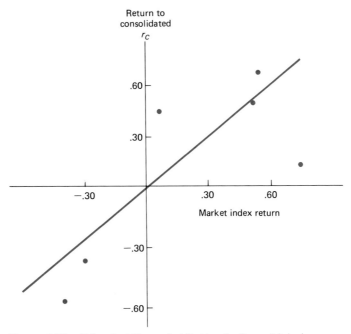

Figure 4-11b Estimated Characteristic Line for Consolidated

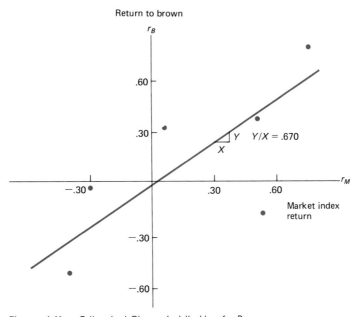

Figure 4-11c Estimated Characteristic Line for Brown

To find the line relating average return to beta, first draw a line tangent to the bullet at the position of the index portfolio you have selected. The broken line *ZX* in Figure 4–10 is such a line. Now consider point *Z*, where the line of tangency intersects the vertical axis. Plot this same level of average return on the vertical axis of the right-hand graph of Figure 4–10 at *z*. Now plot the index portfolio on the right-hand side. To do this, think of a plot like those in Figures 4–11a through 4–11c for the market index itself.

Because, in this case, we are plotting the same returns on both the horizontal and vertical axes, all points will fall on a 45-degree line extending from the origin of the graph. The slope of this line, of course, would be equal to 1. The index portfolio, therefore, has a beta equal to 1 and is plotted at point *M* in the right side of Figure 4–10.

The relationship between beta and average return for all securities can now be found by drawing a straight line through points *Z* and *M*. *Every* security in the population considered will be positioned on this line. The position of each security on the line (and, therefore, the beta factor for each stock) is determined completely by the average return for the security in the time period observed.

Note that all securities with an average return equal to *Z* will have a beta equal to 0. Given that beta is equal to security covariance with the index portfolio divided by the index portfolio's variance, we know that all securities positioned on the solid segment of the horizontal line passing through the bullet are completely uncorrelated with the index portfolio. One of these portfolios has the lowest variance and is therefore positioned on the bullet. We shall refer to this portfolio as the *minimum variance, zero beta portfolio*.

You should be able to see that if the index portfolio is positioned on the bullet above the minimum variance portfolio, the line on the right side of Figure 4–10 will be positively sloped. If it is positioned below the minimum variance portfolio, the line will be negatively sloped. With a market index like *M*, Consolidated has the largest beta because it has the largest average return. On the other hand, if we selected an index portfolio like *M**, Acme would have the largest beta, because it has the smallest average return.

The relationship of property II stems from the fact that the combination lines between each of the individual securities and the index portfolio must be tangent to the bullet at the position of the index portfolio, as in Figure 4–12a. If the combination lines didn't reflect *off* the bullet at this point but rather went *through* it, the bullet couldn't be efficient or minimum variance, as we have defined it.

In Figure 4–12b we are dealing with an index portfolio that is *inefficient*. Now the combination lines for the various stocks can move through the position of the portfolio at various angles relative to one another. It is no longer true that, for changes in the weight assigned to each individual stock, the average return and variance of the portfolio change in the same proportion.

If the index portfolio is minimum variance, however, the combination line for all the securities must have the same slope at the position of the index portfolio on the bullet. This means that if we slightly change the portfolio weight assigned to *any* security, the standard deviation and average return of the index portfolio

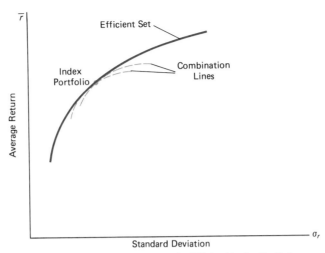

Figure 4-12a Combination Lines for Efficient Index Portfolio

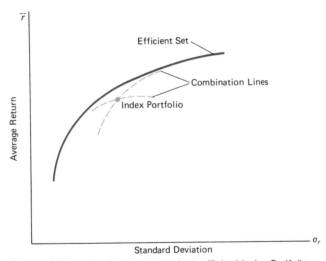

Figure 4-12b Combination Lines for Inefficient Index Portfolio

will change in the same proportions relative to one another for each and every security. Suppose, for example, I slightly change the weight in the index portfolio assigned to Acme, and suppose I find that the change in the average return to the index portfolio is twice as great as the change in its standard deviation. I will find that this is also the case when I change the weights assigned to Brown and Consolidated.

Consider, first, what determines the extent to which the portfolio's expected return changes as we change the portfolio weight. The magnitude of the change increases with the difference between the expected return to the stock and the index. At the extreme, where they have the same expected return, there would be no change as we change the weight.

Now consider the effect of a change in the weight assignment on the index portfolio's *standard deviation*. In this case the larger the covariance between the stock and the index portfolio, the larger will be the impact of a change in weight assignment on the portfolio's standard deviation. Because, as we show in the appendix, beta is computed as the ratio of this covariance to the variance of the market index, we can also say that the effect on the portfolio's standard deviation is directly related to beta.

Thus, as we change the portfolio weight, the impact on portfolio expected return depends on the expected return to the stock (relative to the index, which is a constant across all the stocks). The impact on portfolio standard deviation increases with the beta of the stock. If the index is minimum variance, the change in expected return is in the same proportion to the change in standard deviation as we make slight changes in the portfolio weights assigned to each and every stock in the population. This can be true only if security betas are linearly related to security expected rates of return. This relationship exists under property II.

Property II is extremely important and will be referred to many times throughout this book. To appreciate the importance of this property, consider the fact that, armed with properties I and II, we can get a sneak preview of the essential characteristics of the Capital Asset Pricing Model, which is more completely discussed in Chapter 6.[3]

The Capital Asset Pricing Model describes the way expected returns on different securities will relate to their risks if everyone in the economy used portfolio theory, as we have described it, to determine his or her investment positions. In such an event, we all would take positions scattered along the efficient set. If I am more aggressive than you, my position would be higher on the bullet than yours, but we would both be positioned somewhere on the bullet. The market portfolio is a portfolio containing all the capital investments in the economic system. It is, therefore, the aggregate of everyone's portfolio. On the basis of property I, we know that combinations of efficient portfolios are also efficient. This means that when we aggregate the efficient portfolios of all investors to obtain the market portfolio, it too will be efficient. The market portfolio will be sitting on the skin of the bullet.

In the Capital Asset Pricing Model, beta is taken to be the appropriate measure of risk of an individual security or investment. Betas are obtained by relating individual security returns to the returns of the market portfolio. We know, on the basis of property II, that because the market portfolio is efficient, there will be a simple linear relationship between the beta of any security and its expected rate of return. In the context of the CAPM, this relationship is referred to as the security market line. Thus, if index portfolio M on the left-hand side of Figure 4–10 is the market portfolio, we have the CAPM, and the solid line on the right-hand side is the security market line.

---

[3]For a formal proof of property II, see the appendix to Chapter 6 in Haugen (1986).

Summary

Given a plot of portfolio investment opportunities in expected return-standard deviation space, the bullet-shaped minimum variance set represents those portfolios that have the lowest possible variance, given a particular level of expected return. The portfolio in the minimum variance set with the lowest variance, or standard deviation, is called the minimum variance portfolio. All portfolios in the minimum variance set that have expected returns equal to or greater than the minimum variance portfolio are in the efficient set. Portfolios in the efficient set have the highest possible expected return, given their level of standard deviation.

The critical line provides the portfolio weights for the portfolios in the minimum variance set. In cases where short selling is allowed without limitation, the critical line is linear. If short selling is allowed, and we select as a market index a portfolio from the minimum variance set, and we compute beta factors for the stocks in the available population by relating the returns on the stocks to the returns on the index, a linear, deterministic relationship will exist between the expected returns on the stocks and their betas. If the index portfolio is not in the minimum variance set, then the relationship between beta and average return is no longer linear, except for portfolios that are themselves members of the minimum variance set.

It should be stressed that there is no economic or behavioral content in the two properties discussed in this chapter. We made no assumptions regarding the investment behavior of human beings, nor did we learn anything about such behavior. The properties follow strictly and exactly from the statistical definitions of expected value, variance, covariance, and beta.

APPENDIX: THE RELATIONSHIP BETWEEN A STOCK AND THE MARKET PORTFOLIO

We are going to consider some statistics that describe the relationship between the returns on an individual security and a portfolio of securities that we shall call the market portfolio. The market portfolio is composed of every risky asset in the international economic system. The amount invested in any one asset is proportional to the total market value of the asset relative to the total value of all other assets. A portfolio weighted in this way is commonly called a *value weighted portfolio*. In the market portfolio, General Motors will be a much bigger fraction of the total than will be a smaller company like American Motors.

Suppose you want to construct an index of the market portfolio. You can do it by investing in some arbitrary percentage, perhaps 1/100 of 1 percent, of the total market value of every single risky asset in existence. While you own the same fraction of the total value of each company, your dollar holdings of General Motors are much larger than your dollar holdings of American Motors, because GM is a much larger company. Moreover, the proportion of your total investment that you have invested in GM is larger than the proportion of your money that is invested in AMC.

The market portfolio can be thought of as the "ultimate market index." Think about the relationship that might exist between an individual security and the market portfolio. Designate the rates of return on security J as r_J and the rates of return to the market portfolio as r_M. Suppose that you observe the returns to security J and to the market portfolio over five months, and you see the following series:

Month	1	2	3	4	5
Stock J	2%	3%	6%	−4%	8%
Market portfolio	4%	−2%	8%	−4%	4%

For convenience these are the same pairs of returns that we looked at in the appendix to Chapter 3 for securities A and B.

The Characteristic Line

The pairs of returns are plotted in Figure A4–1, with the broken line of best fit passing through the series of paired returns. This line helps describe the relationship between the security and the market portfolio, or the "market." When you relate an individual security to the market in this way, the line of best fit is also referred to as the security's "characteristic line." The characteristic line shows the return that you expect the stock to produce, given that a particular rate of return appears for the market. For example, as we see in Figure A4–1, if the market produces a 2 percent rate of return, we expect stock J to produce a 3 percent rate of return, given the position of its characteristic line.

The Beta Factor

Because the characteristic line is a straight line, we can draw it if we are told its slope and the point where it passes through the vertical axis, or its intercept. The slope of the characteristic line is commonly referred to as the stock's beta factor, or β. We shall refer to the intercept by the symbol A.

The beta factor and the intercept can be computed directly using the following formulas:

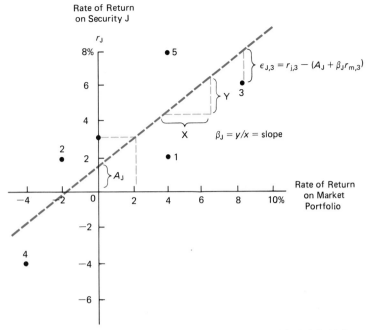

Figure A4-1 The Relationship Between Stock J and the Market Portfolio

$$\text{Beta factor} = \beta = \frac{\text{Covariance between security and market returns}}{\text{Variance of market returns}}$$

$$\text{Intercept} = A = \text{Security mean return} - \text{Beta factor} \times \text{Market mean return}$$

In our example using stock J, the sample variance of the five rates of return to the market portfolio is computed by first summing the deviations from the market's mean return:

$$
\begin{aligned}
(\ .04 - .02)^2 &= .0004 \\
(-.02 - .02)^2 &= .0016 \\
(\ .08 - .02)^2 &= .0036 \\
(-.04 - .02)^2 &= .0036 \\
(\ .04 - .02)^2 &= \underline{.0004} \\
\text{Total} \quad\; &= .0096
\end{aligned}
$$

and then dividing the total by the number of observations, less 1:

$$.0096/(5 - 1) = .0024 = \text{Variance of market returns}$$

Thus, the beta factor and intercept can be computed as

$$\text{Beta factor} = .0017/.0024 = .708$$
$$\text{Intercept} \quad = .0300 - .708 \times .0200 = .0158$$

The beta factor of the stock is an indicator of the degree to which the stock responds to changes in the return produced by the market. For stock J, the beta factor is .708. This would indicate that, if we knew the return for the market was going to be higher by 1 percent next month, we would increase our expectation for stock J's return by .708 percent. The intercept serves only as a convenient reference point to fix the position of the line. It should be interpreted only as our expected rate of return to the stock, should the market happen to produce a zero rate of return in any given month.

The characteristic line we draw, based on the computed slope and intercept, is identical to the line of best fit that minimizes the sum of the squared vertical distances from the line for each of the five pairs of returns.

Residual Variance

Another dimension of the relationship between the stock and the market is the propensity of the stock to produce returns that deviate from the characteristic line. The statistic describing this propensity is called the *residual variance*. Whereas the stock's variance describes the stock's propensity to produce returns that deviate from its expected value, the residual variance describes the stock's propensity to produce returns that deviate from its characteristic line.

Residual variance describes the potential for variability in the stock's residuals, or shock terms. A *residual,* or shock term, is the vertical distance between the pair of returns and the characteristic line. To compute a residual, use the following formula:

Residual = ϵ = Actual security return − Conditional security return

The conditional security return is what you would expect the security to produce, given what the market has produced as a return for the period:

Conditional security return = Intercept + Beta factor × Market return

To illustrate, consider the third month in our example. In this month the stock produces a 6 percent rate of return, and the market produces a return of 8 percent. Based on the stock's characteristic line, the residual for security J in month 3 is computed as

$$\epsilon_{J,3} = .06 - (.0158 + .708 \times .08)$$
$$\epsilon_{J,3} = .06 - .0724 = -.0124$$

In month 3 the security is producing a return that is lower than expected, given the performance of the market in the month. Perhaps some negative information about the company that issued the security has been released during the month and it has had a depressing effect on the market price of the security. Given a market return of 8 percent and the stock's characteristic line, we would expect the stock to produce a return of 7.24 percent. Instead, the return is only 6 percent. The difference of −1.24 percent is the residual for the third month. The residuals for the other months are computed in the same way:

Month		Residual
1	.02 − (.0158 + .708 × .04) =	− .0241
2	.03 − (.0158 + .708 × − .02) =	.0284
3	.06 − (.0158 + .708 × .08) =	− .0124
4	− .04 − (.0158 + .708 × − .04) =	− .0275
5	.08 − (.0158 + .708 × .04) =	.0359

Just as the stock's variance is computed by squaring the deviations from the expected value, the residual variance is computed by squaring the residuals or the deviations from the stock's characteristic line:

$$\text{Residual variance} = \sigma_{\epsilon,J}^2 = \frac{\text{Sum of squared residuals}}{\text{Number of observations less 2}}$$

We subtract 2 from the number of observations this time because we are employing two estimates instead of one in making the computation. When we compute the sample variance, we employ one estimate, the sample mean. Here we employ estimates of both the intercept and the slope of the characteristic line in order to compute the residuals.

In our example, the residual variance is computed as follows:

Month	Squared Residual
1	$(-.0241)^2$ = .00058
2	$(\ .0284)^2$ = .00081
3	$(-.0124)^2$ = .00015
4	$(-.0275)^2$ = .00076
5	$(\ .0359)^2$ = .00129
	Total = .00359

$$.00359/(5 - 2) = .0012 = \sigma_{\epsilon,J}^2$$

Recall the discussion of the correlation coefficient from Chapter 3 and note that as the residual variance of a stock approaches zero, the correlation coefficient approaches either plus or minus 1, depending on whether the characteristic line has a positive or negative slope.

In Figures A4–2 and A4–3 we are plotting the relationship between two stocks, American Telephone and Telegraph and United Airlines, and a portfolio that is supposed to represent the market portfolio. This portfolio is a value weighted portfolio of 500 stocks called the Standard and Poor's 500 Stock Index.

Each observation plotted represents the pair of returns for each stock and the 500 for a particular month. The broken lines going through both figures are the lines of best fit or the characteristic lines for the two stocks. These lines were drawn based on sample estimates of the covariances, market (500) variances, and mean returns for the two stocks and the 500. Note that AT&T has a beta factor of about .5 and an intercept of approximately 0. The intercept for United Airlines is also approximately 0, but its beta factor is much larger at 1.5. In fact, the great majority of stocks have betas between these two rather extreme values.

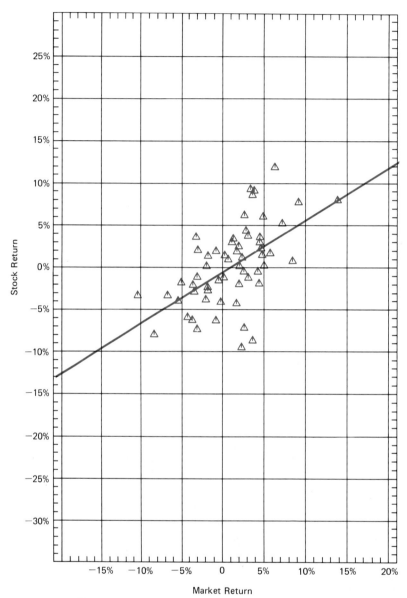

Figure A4-2 Estimate of the Characteristic Line for AT&T

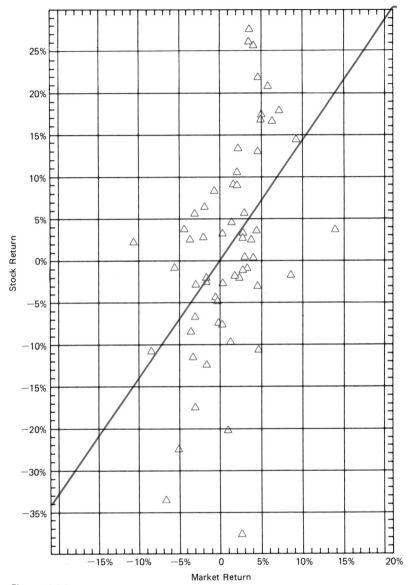

Figure A4-3 Estimate of the Characteristic Line for United Airlines

1. What criterion must a portfolio meet in order to be in the minimum variance set?

2. Contrast the minimum variance set with the efficient set.

3. Referring to Figure 4–6:

   a. What part of the figure corresponds to portfolios having negative weight for stock C?

   b. What are the portfolio weights corresponding to point *D?*

   c. Could a portfolio standard deviation of 50 percent be achieved if short selling were not permitted?

4. Suppose the expected returns on three stocks are as follows:

	X	Y	Z
E(r)	.07	.11	.16

   If the weight on stock Y were restricted to zero, what weights for stocks X and Z would result in a portfolio expected return of .15?

5. What criterion must a portfolio meet to be located on the critical line?

6. Refer to Figure 4–8. What would the critical line for stocks A, B, and C look like if you were restricted from selling A and B short but were permitted to sell C short?

7. Refer to Figure 4–6 and the data that are the basis for that figure.

   a. Find the portfolios that have a standard deviation of 45 percent and that have zero weight for stock A.

   b. Which, if any, of the portfolios you find in part a would constitute possible investments if short selling were not allowed?

8. Which points on the minimum variance set depicted in Figure 4–2 correspond to portfolios in which all three of the stocks are used? Also, which points on the critical line depicted in Figure 4–8 correspond to these same portfolios?

9. Suppose there were two portfolios known to be in the minimum variance set for a universe of three stocks. There are no restrictions on short sales. The weights for each of the two portfolios are as follows:

	X_A	X_B	X_C
Portfolio 1	− .5	.5	1.0
Portfolio 2	1.25	.25	− .5

   a. What would the stock weights be for a portfolio constructed by investing $3000 in portfolio 1 and $1000 in portfolio 2?

b. Would the new portfolio in part a be in the minimum variance set?

c. Suppose you combined the portfolio in part a with portfolio 1 to form yet another portfolio. Would this new portfolio be in the minimum variance set?

Refer to the following diagram for questions 10 through 12. The figure represents the minimum variance set for a set of stocks.

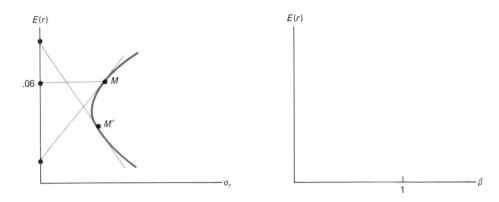

10. Assuming that short selling is allowed and that betas of stocks and portfolios are computed with reference to M, draw the implied relationship between beta values and mean returns.

11. Given the assumptions of question 10, what would the implied beta value be for an asset having a mean return of .06?

12. Assume now that short selling is allowed, but that the betas are computed with reference to M'. Draw the implied relationship between beta values and mean returns.

13. Consider the following statement: "Given a population of stocks, the only asset that would have a beta value equal to 1.0 would be the market index that was used to compute the betas." Is this statement true or false? Explain.

BIBLIOGRAPHY

BAWA, V. S., E. J. ELTON, and M. J. GRUBER, "Simple Rules for Optimal Portfolio Selection in a Stable Paretian Market," *Journal of Finance* (September 1979).

BRITO, N. O., "Portfolio Selection in an Economy with Marketability and Short Sales Restrictions," *Journal of Finance* (May 1978).

COHEN, K. J., and E. J. ELTON, "Inter-Temporal Portfolio Analysis Based on Simulation of Joint Returns," *Management Science* (September 1967).

ELTON, E. J., and M. J. GRUBER, "Simple Criteria for Optimal Portfolio Selection," *Journal of Finance* (December 1976).

————, "Simple Criteria for Optimal Portfolio Selection: Tracing Out the Efficient Frontier," *Journal of Finance* (March 1978).

FAMA, E. F., *Foundations of Finance*. New York: Basic Books, 1976.

GREEN, R. C., "Benchmark Portfolio Inefficiency and Deviations from the Security Market Line," Working Paper. Carnegie-Mellon University, 1984.

HAUGEN, R., *Modern Investment Theory*. Englewood Cliffs, N.J.: Prentice-Hall, 1986.

HOGAN, W., and J. M. WARREN, "Computation of the Efficient Boundary in the E-S Portfolio Selection Model," *Journal of Financial and Quantitative Analysis* (September 1972).

JONES-LEE, M. W., "Some Portfolio Adjustment Theorems for the Use of Non-Negativity Constraints on Security Holdings," *Journal of Finance* (June 1971).

MAO, J. C. T., "Essentials of Portfolio Diversification Strategy," *Journal of Finance* (December 1970).

MARKOWITZ, H. M., "Portfolio Selection," *Journal of Finance* (December 1952).

PORTER, R. B., and R. BEY, "An Evaluation of the Empirical Significance of Optimal Seeking Algorithms in Portfolio Selection," *Journal of Finance* (December 1974).

ROLL, R., "A Critique of the Asset Pricing Theory's Tests: Part I: On the Past and Potential Testability of the Theory," *Journal of Financial Economics* (March 1977).

SHARPE, W. F., "Capital Asset Prices: A Theory of Market Equilibrium Under Conditions of Risk," *Journal of Finance* (September 1964).

5 INDEX MODELS

Introduction

The technique we have been using to construct the efficient set is called the Markowitz Model, named after the individual who introduced it in 1952. Markowitz showed how to squeeze the maximum amount of expected return from our portfolio, given our level of risk exposure.

Remember that the Markowitz Model uses a matrix of covariances to compute the variance of a portfolio of securities. Each element of the matrix represents the covariance between the rates of return for two of the securities. To compute the variance of a portfolio of the securities, you multiply the covariance number by the fraction of the money that you are investing in each of the two securities. You obtain a similar product for each element in the matrix and add them up to obtain the variance of the portfolio.

This procedure is perfectly accurate, given the accuracy of the covariance estimates. Suppose, for example, that the covariance numbers are sample estimates, taken from the returns on the stocks over the last twelve months. This being the case, the portfolio variance that we get is the actual variance of the portfolio for the twelve months of the preceding year. While it may not be an accurate prediction of what the variance is going to be in the coming year—that depends on the stability of the covariance numbers over time—it is a perfectly accurate estimate of the variance in the year in which the sample estimates of the covariance are taken.

However, there is a problem in computing portfolio variance in this way.

The problem becomes apparent when the number of securities in the population becomes large. When this happens, the number of elements in the covariance matrix becomes extremely large. Suppose, for example, we tried to determine the efficient set for the approximately 1600 stocks on the New York Stock Exchange. The matrix would be 1600 by 1600, and it would contain more than 2.5 million covariance numbers. Granted, for each covariance on one side of the diagonal, there is a matching number on the other side of the diagonal, but we still would have to estimate nearly 1.3 million variances and covariances.

Even if we went to the trouble of making that many estimates, our problems are just beginning. Think of the process a computer goes through in finding the efficient set. Every time it needs to compute the variance of a portfolio, it must add more than 2.5 million products. Even if we use the fastest computers and the most efficient computer programs, the problem exceeds the practical capacity of the machine.

This is the problem with the Markowitz Model.[1] It employs an equation for portfolio variance that is perfectly accurate, but also *intractable,* when we are dealing with a large number of securities. What we need is an alternative formula for portfolio variance that is capable of dealing with large populations of stocks. We get such a capability with index models.

THE SINGLE INDEX MODEL

Although the Single Index Model gives a simple formula for portfolio variance, it also makes an assumption about the process generating security returns. The accuracy of the Single Index Model's formula for portfolio variance is as good as the accuracy of its assumption.

The Assumption of the Single Index Model

Essentially, the Single Index Model assumes that security returns are correlated for only one reason. Each security is assumed to respond, in some cases more and in other cases less, to the pull of the market portfolio. As the market portfolio makes a significant movement upward, nearly all stocks go up with it. Some stocks rise in price more than others, but as we observe the movement of stock prices over time, it is assumed that variability in the market portfolio accounts

[1] Actually, this may not be the only problem with the Markowitz Model. In order to estimate the covariance matrix needed to calculate portfolio variance, the number of observations in the time series of sample rates of return must be greater than the number of securities represented in the matrix. This can present data problems when the number of securities being considered is very large.

for all of the co-movement that we see among the stocks. This is, in fact, the assumption of the Single Index Model: The model assumes that all the numbers in the covariance matrix can be accounted for by the fact that all of the stocks are responding to the pull of this single, common force.

To state the assumption of the Single Index Model more precisely, consider Figure 5–1, where we have related the returns on an arbitrarily selected stock to the returns on the market portfolio. The broken line running through the scatter is the line of best fit (minimizing the sum of the squared vertical deviations of each observation from the line), or an estimate of the stock's characteristic line. The intercept of the characteristic line is given by A, and the slope by the beta factor, β. As defined in the appendix to Chapter 4, the vertical deviations from the characteristic line are called residuals or shock terms, ϵ.

The rate of return for the stock in any one month can be written as

$$r_t = A + \beta r_{M,t} + \epsilon_t$$

where r_t is the rate of return to a security or portfolio, and $r_{M,t}$ is the rate of return to the market portfolio.

The Single Index Model assumes that two types of events produce the period-to-period variability in a stock's rate of return. We refer to the first type of event as a *macro event*. Examples might include an unexpected change in the rate of inflation, a change in the Federal Reserve discount rate, or a change in the prime rate of interest. In any case, macro events are broad or sweeping in their impact. They affect nearly all firms to one degree or another, and they may have an

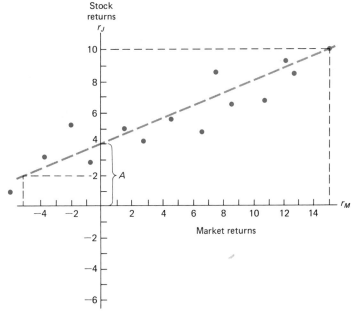

Figure 5-1 Relationship Between the Returns on an Individual Investment and the Returns on the Market Portfolio

effect on the general level of stock prices. They produce a change in the rate of return to the market portfolio, and through the pull of the market, they induce changes in the rates of return on individual securities. Thus, in Figure 5–1, if the return to the market portfolio in a given period was equal to −5 percent, we would expect the return to the stock to be 2 percent. If the market's return was, instead, 15 percent, we would expect the stock's return to be 10 percent. The difference in the stock's expected return can be attributed to the difference in the pull of the market from one period to the other.

The second type of event that produces variability in a security's return in the Single Index Model is micro in nature. *Micro events* have impact on individual firms but no generalized impact on other firms. Examples include the discovery of a new product or the sudden obsolescence of an old one. They might also include a local labor strike, a fire, or the resignation or death of a key person in the firm. These events affect the individual firm alone. They are assumed to have no effect on other firms, and they have no impact on the value of the market portfolio or its rate of return. Micro events do affect the rate of return on the individual security affected, however. They cause the stock to produce a rate of return that might be higher or lower than normal, given the rate of return produced by the market portfolio in the period. Micro events, therefore, are presumed to cause the appearance of the residuals or deviations from the characteristic line.

A third type of event has been assumed away by the model. This might be referred to as an *industry event,* an event that has a generalized impact on many of the firms in a given industry but is not broad or important enough to have a significant impact on the general economy or the value of the market portfolio. Events of this nature also may, conceivably, cause the appearance of a residual, but the Single Index Model assumes that residuals are always caused by micro events.

The above scenario is consistent with the assumption that the residuals or shock terms for different companies are uncorrelated with one another, as is depicted in Figure 5–2. The residuals will be uncorrelated if they are caused by micro events that have impact on the individual firm alone but none on other firms.

As noted, the Single Index Model assumes that all the numbers in the covariance matrix for the returns on securities can be accounted for by the fact that each of the stocks responds, to its own degree, to the pull of a single common factor, the market. In fact, given the assumption of the Single Index Model, we can write the covariance between any two securities, J and K, as

$$\text{Covariance} = \text{Beta(J)} \times \text{Beta(K)} \times \text{Market Variance}$$

The right-hand side of this equation is the product of three terms. The third, which is the variance of the rate of return to the market, specifies the magnitude of the market's movement or the strength of its pull; the first two, which are the beta factors for the two securities, specify the extent to which each of the two securities responds to the pull.

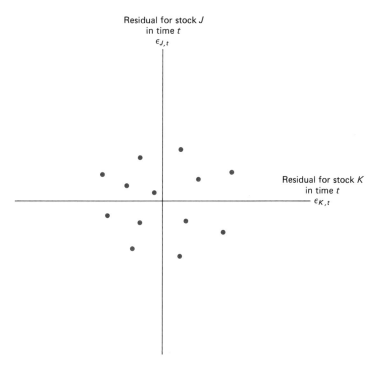

Figure 5-2   Relationship Between Residuals on Stocks J and K

The Single Index Model's
Simplified Formula for Portfolio Variance

Based on the above assumptions and conditions, we can derive an alternative formula for the variance of a portfolio that is much less demanding in terms of estimation and computation time. We begin by noting that, after passing a line of best fit through points representing pairs of returns between security or portfolio returns and market returns, as in Figure 5–1, we can always split the variance of the return on a security or portfolio into two parts:

$$\sigma^2 r \quad = \quad \beta^2 \, \sigma^2 r_{\mathrm{M}} \quad + \quad \sigma_\epsilon^2$$
$$\text{Total variance} = \text{Systematic risk} + \text{Residual variance}$$

$(5\text{--}1)$

The first term on the right-hand side of Equation (5-1) is called the systematic risk of the investment. Under the assumptions of the Single Index Model, it accounts for that part of the security's variance that cannot be diversified away. This part of the variance is contributed to the variance of a well-diversified portfolio of many different stocks. The second term is called residual variance or unsystematic risk. It represents that part of a security's total variance that disappears as we diversify. It is mainly because of residual variance that the variance of a portfolio is less than the weighted average of the variances of the securities in the portfolio.

We can see from the equation that variability in return is accounted for by two things. The systematic risk accounts for that part of the total variability that is due to market movement pulling the security *along* its characteristic line. Note that systematic risk itself is the product of two terms. The first term involves the security's beta, which tells us the extent to which the security responds to the up and down pull of the market. The second term is the market's variance, which tells us the extent to which the market is pulling up and down. The second part of a security's variance is the residual variance. This accounts for that part of the variability that is due to deviations *from* the characteristic line. Thus, when we think of the total variability in a security's returns under the Single Index Model, part of it is due to movement by the security along its characteristic line and part of it is due to deviations from the characteristic line.

Equation (5-1) holds for an individual security and for a portfolio as well. Rewriting the equation for the case of a portfolio, we get

$$\sigma^2 r_P = \beta_P{}^2 \sigma^2 r_M + \sigma_{\epsilon,P}{}^2 \qquad (5\text{--}2)$$

At this point, we need equations for the beta factor and residual variance of a portfolio as functions of the characteristics of the securities we put in the portfolio. Once we have these equations, we can substitute them for portfolio beta and residual variance and obtain a more simple, alternative expression for portfolio variance to use in finding the minimum variance set.

The beta factor for a portfolio of M securities is a simple weighted average of the betas of the stocks in the portfolio, where the weights are the relative amounts invested in each security.

$$\beta_P \quad = \quad \sum_{J=1}^{M} x_J \beta_J$$

Portfolio beta = Weighted average of security betas

Thus, if we have two stocks, one with a beta of 1.00 and the other with a beta of 0.00, and we invest 75 percent of our money in the stock with the larger beta and 25 percent in the other stock, the portfolio would have a beta of .75.

Now consider the formula for the residual variance of a portfolio. To determine what the residual variance is, we can, if we wish, use the same procedure we used to determine the variance of the portfolio's returns (as opposed to its residuals) in the Markowitz Model. That is, we could employ the covariance matrix for the residuals on the various stocks. For the case of a three-security portfolio, the matrix would look like this:

	Security	x_A A	x_B B	x_C C
x_A	A	$\sigma_{\epsilon,A}^2$	$Cov(\epsilon_B,\epsilon_A)$	$Cov(\epsilon_C,\epsilon_A)$
x_B	B	$Cov(\epsilon_A,\epsilon_B)$	$\sigma_{\epsilon,B}^2$	$Cov(\epsilon_C,\epsilon_B)$
x_C	C	$Cov(\epsilon_A,\epsilon_C)$	$Cov(\epsilon_B,\epsilon_C)$	$\sigma_{\epsilon,C}^2$

You might object at this point and say, "Wait a minute! I thought the whole idea of the Single Index Model was to get away from this matrix. Why are we bringing it back in to compute residual variance?" This is where the assumption of the Single Index Model comes into play. The covariance between the residuals on any two securities is assumed to be equal to zero. Given this assumption, all the covariances in the above matrix that are *off* the diagonal are equal to zero. This means that to compute the residual variance of a portfolio, we need only go down the diagonal of the matrix, taking each security's residual variance and multiplying it by the portfolio weight at the top of the column and again by the portfolio weight at the left-hand side of the row. Because both these two weights are equal to the portfolio weight for the security itself, we have the following relationship:

$$\sigma^2_{\epsilon,P} \qquad = \qquad \sum_{J=1}^{M} x_J^2 \sigma^2_{\epsilon,J}$$

Portfolio residual = "Weighted average" of security residual variances where
    variance   portfolio weights are squared

Thus, the residual variance of a portfolio is also a weighted average (of sorts) of the residual variances of the securities in the portfolio. However, this time, in taking the average, we square the portfolio weights.

Given the assumption of uncorrelated residuals among securities, the residual variance of a portfolio begins to disappear as the number of securities in the portfolio is increased. Consider the residual variance formula, and suppose we have a large number of securities, each with a residual variance equal to 10 percent. If we invest half our money equally in two of the securities, the residual variance of the two-security portfolio is 5 percent according to the above formula.

$$\sigma^2_{\epsilon,P} = (.50^2 \times .10) + (.50^2 \times .10) = .05$$

In the same sense, if we invest a third of our money in each of three of the securities, the residual variance of the portfolio would be 3.33 percent and so on, as shown by the solid curve in Figure 5-3.

As we diversify, the residual variance of the equally weighted portfolio approaches, but never quite reaches, zero. This is because the residuals in the portfolio are presumed to be uncorrelated, and the good things that are happening to some of the securities are being offset by the bad things that are happening to others. Some are above their characteristic lines, but others are below; the residual of the portfolio, being the average of the residuals of the individual securities, is always quite small if the number of securities is large. In fact, when we are dealing with a portfolio that is weighted *equally* among the various securities, the residual variance of the portfolio is equal to the average residual variance of the stocks, divided by the number of securities in the portfolio. Of course, as the residual variance of the portfolio gets smaller and smaller, the correlation of the portfolio's returns with the market gets larger and larger, as shown in Figure 5-4.

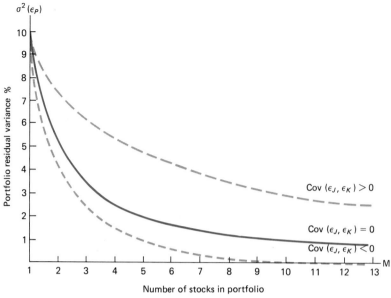

Figure 5-3 The Effect of Diversification on the Residual Variance of a Portfolio

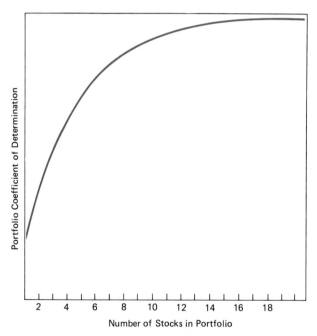

Figure 5-4 Relationship Between the Coefficient of Determination and the Number of Stocks in the Portfolio in the Single Index Model

These relationships depend crucially on our assumption that the residuals for different securities are uncorrelated. Suppose that this is an invalid assumption. Suppose that industry-type events frequently occur, and the covariance between the residuals for different securities is typically *positive* and not zero. In this case, the off-diagonal elements of the matrix for residual covariances will be predominantly positive numbers. If we follow the Single Index Model formula for portfolio residual variance and simply go down the diagonal of the matrix, we will underestimate the true residual variance of the portfolio. The actual residual variance will be larger than the Single Index Model tells us it is, based on its assumption, because it is ignoring the positive elements in the sum that are off the diagonal. The relationship between the true residual variance and the number of securities in the portfolio may really look like the upper broken line of Figure 5-3.

Suppose, on the other hand, that the covariances between the residuals for the securities in the population are typically *negative*. This might be the case for two stocks issued by companies that are competitors. In this case, any event that has a positive impact on one of the companies is negative for the other. If the numbers off the diagonal in the covariance matrix for the residuals are predominantly negative, the Single Index Model gives an overestimate of the true residual variance of the portfolio. The actual residual variance, obtained by summing the products obtained for each element in the matrix, would be smaller than the sum obtained by simply going down the diagonal. The actual relationship between residual variance and the number of securities in the portfolio might then look like the lower dotted line of Figure 5-3.

To summarize, the beta factor of a portfolio is equal to a weighted average of the betas of the securities in the portfolio, where the weights are equal to the fractions of the money that we invest in each security. The residual variance under the Single Index Model is assumed to be given by a similar weighted average, but this time, in taking the average, we square the portfolio weights.

We know that in the context of the Single Index Model we can split the variance of any investment, including a portfolio, into two components, systematic risk and residual variance, as in Equation (5-2). Substituting the expressions we have derived for the portfolio's beta and residual variance, we obtain the Single Index Model's simplified formula for portfolio variance:

$$\sigma r_P{}^2 \quad = \quad \underbrace{\left[\sum_{J=1}^{M} (\beta_J x_J) \right]^2}_{\substack{\text{Portfolio} \\ \text{beta}}} \underbrace{\sigma^2 r_M}_{\substack{\text{Market} \\ \text{variance}}} \quad + \quad \sum_{J=1}^{M} x_J{}^2 \sigma_{\epsilon,J}{}^2$$

$$\underset{\substack{\text{Total portfolio} \\ \text{variance}}}{} = \underset{\substack{\text{Portfolio systematic} \\ \text{risk}}}{} + \underset{\substack{\text{Portfolio residual} \\ \text{variance}}}{}$$

Contrast this expression with the procedure for computing portfolio variance under the Markowitz Model. For 1600 stocks, we need approximately 1.3 million variance and covariance estimates under Markowitz. Under the Single Index Model, we need only 1600 estimates of beta for each stock, 1600 estimates of residual variance, and one estimate for the variance of the market portfolio. In addition, the computation time required to compute the variance is dramatically reduced.

However, the reduction in the complexity of the model comes at a price. As we said before, the variance number obtained from the Markowitz formula is perfectly accurate, given the accuracy of the covariance estimates. The model makes no assumptions regarding the process generating security returns. The Single Index Model, on the other hand, assumes that the residuals, or deviations from the characteristic line, are uncorrelated across different companies. The variance number obtained from the Single Index Model, therefore, is only an approximation of the true variance. Even if the estimates of beta and residual variance that we feed into the model are perfectly accurate, the estimate of portfolio variance that we obtain from the model is only as accurate as our assumption regarding the residuals.

It is obvious that the assumption isn't strictly accurate. After all, suppose that something good happens to General Motors. This has an immediate impact not only on General Motors itself but also on the company's suppliers and competitors. Many companies would be affected simultaneously, some positively and others negatively. The residuals that appear for these firms would not be independent, but rather would be generated by a common event. We know, therefore, that the residuals are correlated to some degree. We hope, however, that the degree of correlation is small enough that the inaccuracy of the Single Index Model's portfolio variance equation doesn't transcend its relative efficiency.

An Example in Which the Single Index Model Works

Consider two hypothetical stocks, Blue Steel and Black Rubber companies. In Table 5-1 are the rates of return for these companies, for the market portfolio, and for an equally weighted portfolio of the two stocks for five periods of time. The two-stock portfolio is assumed to be rebalanced to equal weights at the beginning of each period. Given this, the return for the portfolio is a simple average of the returns to the stocks in each period.

The returns for each stock and for the portfolio are plotted against the returns for the market in Figures 5-5, 5-6, and 5-7. Note that the beta factor for Blue Steel is equal to 1.00, the beta for Black Rubber is equal to .50, and the beta for

Table 5-1 Rates of Return to the Market, Two Stocks, and a Portfolio

Period	Market Portfolio r_M	Blue Steel r_S	Black Rubber r_R	Two-Stock Portfolio r_P
1	30%	30%	55%	42.5%
2	40	60	40	50
3	20	50	30	40
4	35	45	27.5	36.25
5	25	15	22.5	18.75

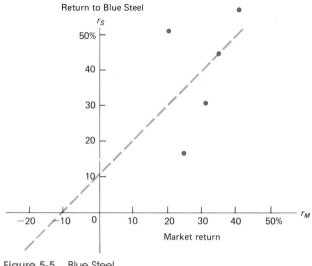

Figure 5-5 Blue Steel

the portfolio is the average of the two, or .75. The intercept of the portfolio (15 percent) is also the weighted average of the intercepts on Blue Steel (10 percent) and Black Rubber (20 percent).

Recall that the general statistical procedure for computing residual variance is first to compute the differences between the actual rates of return to the investment and the rates of return you expect the investment to produce, given its

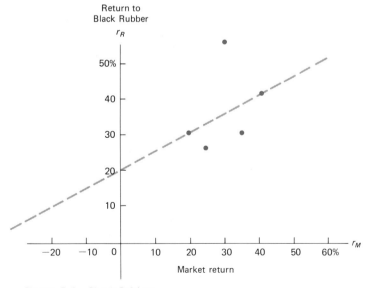

Figure 5-6 Black Rubber

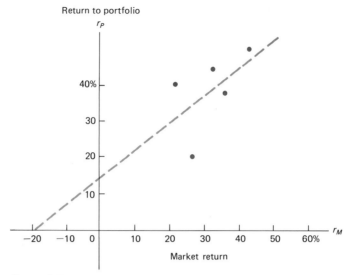

Return to portfolio
r_P

Market return

Figure 5-7 Two-Stock Portfolio

characteristic line and the market return for the period. The difference for any one period would be equal to

$$r_t - (A + \beta r_{M,t})$$

The differences for each period are then squared and the squared differences summed. The sum is divided by the number of periods observed, less 2. Therefore, the residual variance of Blue Steel can be computed as

$$
\begin{array}{l}
[.30 - (.10 + 1.00 \times .30)]^2 \\
+ [.60 - (.10 + 1.00 \times .40)]^2 \\
+ [.50 - (.10 + 1.00 \times .20)]^2 \\
+ [.45 - (.10 + 1.00 \times .35)]^2 \\
+ [.15 - (.10 + 1.00 \times .25)]^2 \\
\hline
.1000
\end{array}
$$

$$.1000/(5 - 2) = .0333$$

And the residual variance for Black Rubber as

$$
\begin{array}{l}
[.55 \quad - (.20 + 0.50 \times .30)]^2 \\
+ [.40 \quad - (.20 + 0.50 \times .40)]^2 \\
+ [.30 \quad - (.20 + 0.50 \times .20)]^2 \\
+ [.275 - (.20 + 0.50 \times .35)]^2 \\
+ [.225 - (.20 + 0.50 \times .25)]^2 \\
\hline
.0600
\end{array}
$$

$$.0600/(5 - 2) = .0200$$

The residual variance for the portfolio is given by

$$
\frac{
\begin{aligned}
& [.425 \ - (.15 + 0.75 \times .30)]^2 \\
+ \ & [.500 \ - (.15 + 0.75 \times .40)]^2 \\
+ \ & [.400 \ - (.15 + 0.75 \times .20)]^2 \\
+ \ & [.3625 - (.15 + 0.75 \times .35)]^2 \\
+ \ & [.1875 - (.15 + 0.75 \times .25)]^2
\end{aligned}
}{.0399}
$$

$$.0399/(5 - 2) = .0133$$

The portfolio's residual variance conforms to the value predicted by the Single Index Model, a weighted average of the residual variances of each stock, where we square the portfolio weights.

$$.0133 = (.50)^2 \times .0333 + (.50)^2 \times .0200$$

This is true because the example was constructed so the correlation coefficient between the residuals was equal to zero.

An Example of a Potential Problem with the Single Index Model

To illustrate the potential problem with the Single Index Model, consider the following example. Suppose we have two stocks, Unitech (U) and Birite (B). The stocks have the following characteristics:

	Beta	Residual Variance
Unitech	0.50	.0732
Birite	1.50	.0548
Market index variance:	.0600	

Given this information, the variance of the two stocks can be written as the sum of their respective systematic risks and residual variances:

$$\sigma r_J^2 \ = \ \beta_J^2 \sigma^2 r_M \ \ \ \ \ + \ \sigma^2_{\epsilon,J}$$

Unitech $\ \ .0882 = \ \ .50^2 \times .060 + .0732$

Birite $\ \ \ \ .1898 = 1.50^2 \times .060 + .0548$

The covariance matrix for the *rates of return* to the two stocks is assumed to be given by

Stocks	Unitech	Birite
Unitech	.0882	.0594
Birite	.0594	.1898

Under the assumption of the Single Index Model, the covariance between the *returns* on the two stocks is equal to the product of their betas and the variance of the market index.

$$\text{Covariance (returns)} = \text{Beta (U)} \times \text{Beta (B)} \times \text{Market variance}$$
$$.0450 = 0.50 \times 1.50 \times .060$$

The actual covariance between the rates of return is greater than this number, which means that the residuals for the two stocks are positively correlated. The covariance matrix for the *residuals* is in fact assumed to be given by

Stock	Unitech	Birite
Unitech	.0732	.0144
Birite	.0144	.0548

Now suppose we form an equally weighted portfolio of the two stocks. The beta factor of the portfolio is given by

$$\beta_P = x_U \times \beta_U + x_B \times \beta_B$$
$$1.00 = .50 \times .50 + .50 \times 1.50$$

Under the assumption of the Single Index Model, the residual variance can be *estimated* by going down the diagonal of the covariance matrix for the residuals.

$$\sigma^2_{\epsilon,P} = x^2_U \times \sigma^2_{\epsilon,U} + x^2_B \times \sigma_{\epsilon,B}^2$$
$$.032 = .25 \times .0732 + .25 \times .0548$$

To compute the *true* residual variance of the portfolio, we would have to add to this number the two products from the two off-diagonal elements of the covariance matrix for the residuals.

$$\sigma^2_{\epsilon,P} = .032 + 2 \times .50 \times .50 \times .0144$$

Under the assumption of the Single Index Model, we would estimate the variance of the equally weighted portfolio as

$$\sigma^2 r_P = \beta^2_P \times \sigma^2 r_M + \sigma^2_{\epsilon,P}$$
$$.092 = 1.00 \times .060 + .032$$

This is really an underestimate of the true portfolio variance. To find the true variance, we use the Markowitz technique, multiplying each element in the covariance matrix of returns by the portfolio weights for the two stocks.

$$
\begin{array}{r}
.50 \times .50 \times .0882 \\
+\ .50 \times .50 \times .0594 \\
+\ .50 \times .50 \times .0594 \\
+\ .50 \times .50 \times .1898 \\
\hline
.0992
\end{array}
$$

The difference between the actual portfolio variance and our estimate using the Single Index Model is equal to our underestimate of the residual variance.

$$\text{Markowitz variance} - \text{SIM variance}$$
$$.0992 \qquad - \qquad .0920 \qquad = .0072$$

$$\text{Actual residual variance} - \text{SIM residual variance}$$
$$.0392 \qquad - \qquad .032 \qquad = .0072$$

In actual practice, portfolio managers employ the Single Index Model in determining which individual securities to buy and how much to invest in them. They tend to use the more general Markowitz Model for the problem of asset allocation—that is, allocating investments in the portfolio to various classes of assets, such as bonds, stocks, real estate, venture capital, and the like. Usually for this problem up to ten classes of assets are considered, so the covariance matrix is of manageable size. Once the Markowitz Model dictates a percentage allocation of the portfolio to stocks, then the managers must deal with a stock population that is much larger in terms of the number of members. At this point, the Single Index Model is used to optimize the stock portfolio.

This approach can be criticized, however. In estimating the covariance matrix for the various classes of assets, samples of rates or return on various indices, such as Standard and Poor's 500, are employed. These indices are not themselves optimal portfolios. Thus, the final ending portfolio resulting from the two-stage application of the Markowitz and Single Index models is inferior to what would have been obtained under a general application of the Markowitz Model.

WHAT IS THE CORRELATION BETWEEN THE RESIDUALS OF DIFFERENT COMPANIES?

Firms are interconnected through either customer/supplier or competitive relationships. This being the case, it cannot be strictly true that the unique events that affect one firm have absolutely no effect on any of the others. The interesting question is whether we can account for a sufficient fraction of the covariances between the returns with the single market index, so as to make the Single Index Model's formula for portfolio variance a useful approximation.

Fisher Black, Michael Jensen, and Myron Scholes (BJS) conducted an empirical investigation (1972) of the properties of stock returns that sheds some light on the question of residual correlation. BJS began their study by computing beta factors, using monthly rates of return, for every stock on the New York Stock Exchange (NYSE) from 1926 through 1930. They then ranked all the stocks by their betas and separated the stocks into ten groups or portfolios. Each portfolio was equally weighted between each of the stocks. Portfolio 1 contained the 10 percent of the stocks with the highest beta factors. Portfolio 2 contained all the stocks ranked in the second decile. Finally, portfolio 10 contained the 10 percent of the stocks with the lowest beta factors.

They then recorded the rates of return on each of the portfolios in each of the next twelve months of 1931. At the end of the year they recomputed the beta factors for each of the stocks, reranked on the basis of beta, and re-formed the ten portfolios, getting twelve more rates of return for 1932. They continued this process through 1965, obtaining a series of monthly returns on each of the portfolios from 1931 through 1965. From these monthly returns, they then computed the beta factor for each of the portfolios by relating its returns to their market index, an equally weighted portfolio of all stocks on the NYSE.

In the process of computing the beta for each portfolio, BJS also computed the coefficient of determination for each portfolio, or the percentage of the variability in each portfolio's return that could be accounted for by variability in the return to the market. The relationship between the beta factors for the ten portfolios and their coefficients of determination are plotted in Figure 5-8.

The number of stocks in each portfolio changed as time went by and the number of stocks listed on the NYSE increased. At any given point in time, each portfolio contained a number of stocks equal to somewhat less than 10 percent of the total number of stocks on the exchange. (The number is somewhat less, because to qualify for entry into a portfolio, a stock had to be listed on the exchange during the preceding five years to obtain an estimate of its beta.) Thus, the number of stocks in each portfolio is quite large. In fact, it is large enough so that if the assumption of the Single Index Model were strictly accurate, the residual variance of each portfolio would be close to zero. We see from Figure 5-8, however, that a substantial amount of residual variance remains for many of the portfolios. We know this is true, because if the residual variance were approximately equal to 0, the coefficient of determination would be approximately equal to 1. That is, virtually all of the variability in the portfolio's return could be accounted for by variability in the market's return.

The residual variance for all the portfolios is larger than we would expect,

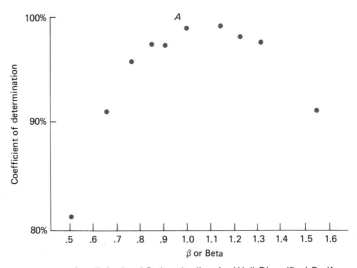

Figure 5-8 Coefficients of Determination for Well Diversified Portfolios with Different Beta Factors

given the formula for residual variance under the Single Index Model. Considering our discussion of Figure 5-3, it must be the case that the covariances between the residuals for stocks are predominantly positive numbers. If the numbers off the diagonal in the covariance matrix are generally positive, you get a larger total by summing all the products associated with each element of the matrix than by summing the products associated with only those elements going down the diagonal. The equation for residual variance under the Single Index Model tells us to sum only those products going down the diagonal. To obtain the *actual* residual variance, we sum all the products, *including* those off the diagonal. Thus, if the off-diagonal covariances are positive, the actual portfolio residual variance is greater than that estimated by the Single Index Model.

Note from Figure 5-8 that the problem of correlated residuals is severer for portfolios of very low and very high degrees of beta risk. This result is confirmed in a number of other, unrelated studies conducted by other researchers. This finding is probably due in part to the fact that the portfolios at the extremes of risk are concentrated heavily in companies from the same industry. The low beta portfolios are probably heavily invested in the utility industry, and the high beta portfolios are probably heavily invested in industries like the airline industry. The returns to the stocks within each of these industries are probably responsive to common factors that are distinct from the market factor.[2]

MULTI-INDEX MODELS

The Assumption of Multi-Index Models

In the Single Index Model, we attribute the covariances between the returns on stocks to a single factor, the market. In a multi-index model, we attribute the covariances to two or more factors, usually including the market. Suppose, for example, we assume that stocks tend to move up and down together because they are simultaneously responding to two factors, movement in the rate of return to the market portfolio and movement in the economy-wide growth rate in industrial production. The rate of return to any stock J in any period t is given by

$$r_{J,t} = A_J + \beta_{M,J}\, r_{M,t} + \beta_{g,J} g_t + \epsilon_{J,t}$$

where $\beta_{M,J}$ is the stock's market beta. It measures the response of the stock to changes in the market portfolio's rate of return. The term g_t is the unexpected growth rate in industrial production in any given period, and $\beta_{g,J}$ measures the stock's response to unexpected changes in the growth rate in industrial production. We say *unexpected* changes because the price of the stock is likely to be affected only by changes in industrial production that were not already anticipated by investors and discounted into the price of the stock. Just as in the

---

[2]The presence of an industry factor in stock returns was first investigated by B. King in 1966.

context of the Single Index Model the beta factor is estimated by relating the returns to the stock to the returns to the market index over a number of previous periods, so in a multi-index model the betas can be estimated by relating the stock's returns to both the market's returns and to the unexpected growth rate in industrial production. One way of obtaining numbers for the latter series is to take the difference between the actual growth rate in industrial production and the average growth rate that was forecasted by some group of professional economists.

In the context of a Single Index Model, we slide a line of best fit through the data (stock returns versus market returns). Similarly, in the context of a double index model, like the one above, we slide a plane of best fit through the data (stock returns versus market returns and unexpected changes in industrial production). If the plane is drawn to minimize the sum of the squared deviations from it, the residuals, or vertical deviations from the plane, will be uncorrelated with both the market returns and industrial production.

The Equation for Portfolio Variance Under the Multi-Index Model

If we assume, in addition, that the rate of return to the market and the unexpected growth rate in industrial production are also uncorrelated with each other, we can write the variance of a portfolio of M stocks as

$$\underset{\substack{\text{Total}\\\text{variance}}}{\sigma^2 r_P} = \underset{\substack{\text{Systematic risk}\\\text{(market)}}}{\beta^2_{M,P}\sigma^2 r_M} + \underset{\substack{\text{Systematic risk}\\\text{(industrial production)}}}{\beta^2_{g,P}\sigma^2 g} + \underset{\substack{\text{Residual}\\\text{variance}}}{\sigma^2_{\epsilon,P}}$$

The market beta for the portfolio is again a weighted average of the market betas of the stocks in the portfolio. This is also true of the portfolio's beta with respect to unexpected changes in industrial production.

If we now assume that the residuals on any two stocks are also uncorrelated with each other, as with the Single Index Model, we can write the residual variance of a portfolio as

$$\sigma^2_{\epsilon,P} = \sum_{J=1}^{M} x_J^2 \sigma^2_{\epsilon,J}$$

The final equation for residual variance is based on the presumption that we have now fully considered all the factors that account for the interrelationships among the returns on stocks. This being the case, the residuals for different companies will now be uncorrelated. If we should find, to our dismay, that the covariances between the residuals are still significantly different from zero, we haven't taken into account all the relevant factors. We need to move to a tri-index model or beyond. The search for such factors is now a matter of intense interest among researchers in finance. The best evidence to date seems to indicate that the covariances among stock returns can be explained by at least as many as four or five factors.

Using the Multi-Index Model

Whenever you employ a multi-index model to find the minimum variance set, you supply the computer with an equation for portfolio variance similar to the one given above. You also supply the computer with estimates of each of the factor betas for each of the companies and with estimates of residual variance for each company. The computer then attempts to minimize portfolio variance, given a target expected rate of return.

Another alternative use for a multi-index model is to construct optimal portfolios, given forecasts of the performance of your indices. For example, suppose that among your indices you had factors like changes in the real price of oil, changes in the rate of growth in the money supply, or changes in the rate of inflation. Suppose, in addition, you feel that in the coming months the real (inflation-adjusted) price of oil will be down, but the rate of growth of the money supply will be up, as will be the rate of inflation. To take an optimal portfolio posture relative to this forecast, you will want to construct a portfolio of stocks with relatively small "oil betas" and relatively large "money and inflation betas." If your forecast for these variables materializes, the return on your portfolio should be substantial, especially if you have adequately diversified to minimize unexpected shocks coming from residual variance.

Estimating Portfolio Variance
Using a Multi-Index Model: An Example

Recall our earlier discussion of Unitech (U) and Birite (B) corporations. In the example, we estimated the variance of an equally weighted portfolio of the two stocks using the Single Index Model. The Single Index Model underestimated the actual variance of the portfolio because the residuals for the two stocks were positively correlated. A single index was apparently inadequate in terms of explaining the covariance between these two stocks. The actual covariance between the two stocks was .0594, greater than the covariance predicted by the Single Index Model.

$$\text{Cov}(r_U, r_B) > \beta_U \times \beta_B \times \sigma^2 r_M$$
$$.0594 > .50 \times 1.50 \times .06$$

Suppose the covariance between the residuals is caused by the presence of a second index, say, unanticipated changes in the rate of inflation. The betas for the two stocks with respect to the market and inflation and the true residual variances are assumed to be given by

	Market Beta	Inflation Beta	Residual Variance
Unitech	.50	1.20	.030
Birite	1.50	.40	.050

The variance of the market index remains at 6 percent. The variance of the index of unanticipated inflation is assumed to be 3 percent.

The variance of each stock can be expressed as

$$\text{Total variance} = \underbrace{\text{(market)}}_{\beta^2_M \sigma^2 r_M} + \underbrace{\text{(inflation)}}_{\beta_i^2 \sigma_i^2} + \text{Residual variance}$$

		Systematic Risk	
Unitech	.0882	$= .25 \times .06 + 1.44 \times .03 +$	.03
Birite	.1898	$= 2.25 \times .06 + .16 \times .03 +$	.05

Suppose we again form an equally weighted portfolio of these two stocks. The portfolio's betas with respect to the two indices is given by

$$\text{Market beta} \quad 1.00 = .50 \times .50 + .50 \times 1.50$$

$$\text{Inflation beta} \quad .80 = .50 \times 1.20 + .50 \times .40$$

Given the assumption that the residuals are now truly uncorrelated, the residual variance of the portfolio can be computed as the weighted average of the true residual variances of the two stocks, where we square the portfolio weights.

$$\text{Portfolio residual variance} = .50^2 \times .03 + .50^2 \times .05 = .02$$

The total variance of the portfolio is estimated as the sum of the two systematic risk terms and the residual variance.

$$\text{Total variance} = \underbrace{\text{(market)}}_{\beta^2_M \sigma^2 r_M} + \underbrace{\text{(inflation)}}_{\beta_i^2 \sigma_i^2} + \text{Residual variance}$$

$$.0992 = 1.00^2 \times .06 + .80^2 \times .03 + .02$$

If you recall, this is the answer we got when we computed the variance using the Markowitz technique. We get the correct answer this time, because the example has been constructed assuming a double index framework.

ESTIMATING BETAS AND RESIDUAL VARIANCES FOR INDEX MODELS

In actual practice, most investors who use modern portfolio theory find that the Single Index Model is acceptable for their purposes. To operationalize the model, however, they need to have accurate estimates of the required inputs into the model.

Consider the time frame depicted in Figure 5-9. Assume that we are at the end of year t. Our investment planning horizon is the month of January for year $t + 1$. We are attempting to find the minimum variance set for rates of return on stocks over this month. Because our time horizon is one month, we will want to sample using rates of return that are also measured over a single month. Keep in mind that we want to estimate the population values for the variances of the

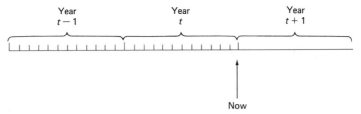

Figure 5-9 Time Frame for Estimating Beta

returns for different portfolios in the next month. We are using the Single Index Model, so we will need estimates of population values for betas and residual variances for the next month.

Sample Estimates for Population Values

The most straightforward approach to obtaining estimates of these inputs is to take sample estimates over some past period of time. The *Value Line Investment Survey* uses this approach in obtaining the beta estimates for the stocks it reviews in its weekly publication. *Value Line* uses weekly rates of return and estimates beta by relating each stock's returns to the New York Stock Exchange Index over the preceding five-year period, if that much data are available on the company. Thus, it computes a sample covariance and then divides this number by the sample variance of returns to the New York Stock Exchange Index. To be technically correct, dividends in the rates of return should be included. However, because the preponderance of the variability in the series is due to the capital gain or loss component of the return, it really makes little difference to the estimate whether or not dividends are included.

Suppose we decide to sample the twelve returns for each stock in year *t;* we compute the sample covariance of the returns to each stock with our market index and divide this by the sample estimate of the variance of our market index to obtain our sample estimates of beta. Based on this straightforward approach, our estimate of the population value, β_{t+1}, is simply equal to the unadjusted sample estimate:

$$\beta_{t+1} = \hat{\beta}_t$$

Modified Sample Estimates

There may be a systematic relationship between the value for beta, as computed in a given period, and its value in the next. If this is true, you may want to take the relationship into account as, in fact, *Value Line* does in your estimate of beta in the future period.[3] To do this, of course, you must first estimate the

---

[3]See Blume (1971) for an early example of estimating such a relationship.

OUT ON THE STREET

Selling Fundamental Betas

"Ms. Sawyer will see you now, Mr. Stevens."

Tom Stevens opened the door and walked into the impressively large office of June Sawyer, the newly appointed president of the trust division of one of the nation's largest banks. Behind June's desk was a spectacular view of the skyline of the city of Chicago. In fact, just two floors above them a low-level cloud was floating by.

"How do you do, Tom; I've been looking forward to your call. As you know, I've been president of this division for only three weeks. I want to make some changes, major changes. You see, I don't particularly like our image—it's too traditional, too antiquated. We're sitting right in the middle of banks like First Chicago, Harris Trust, and Northern Trust— some of the premier institutions in the use of modern quantitative techniques of investment analysis. In this group we stick out like a sore thumb. Most of our analysts haven't seen a beta since their fraternity days, which, in most cases, are a long time past. I want to change direction, and you may be the one to help me change. Now what can you do for me?"

Tom hadn't had an opening like this in years. "Well, as you know, I represent Wilshire Associates. Our firm has a broad array of services spanning both quantitative and computer-assisted more traditional tools of investment management like income and balance sheet analysis. Perhaps I should begin with my own area of specialization. One of the services we offer is a quantitative assessment of the risk of individual stocks and portfolios. We call this the fundamental beta."

"I know what a beta is, but what on earth is a fundamental beta?"

"It's an estimate of beta that's not only based on the stock's past relationship with the market but also on the characteristics of the company behind the stock. We look at forty-eight factors, such as variability in earnings per share, company size, and financial leverage, and relate these factors to company betas in the past to find the relationship between them. In the case of balance sheet and income statement items, we use up to five years of past ratios. In the case of market value items, we use up to sixty past monthly prices. After modeling the relationship, we estimate the company's current beta by plugging the company's forty-eight characteristics into the model."

"What advantage do fundamental betas have over straight historical beta estimates?"

"They have greater predictability. Now they're far from being perfectly accurate,

relationship between beta factors for stocks in successive periods of time. We can do this, in the context of the time frame of Figure 5-9, by taking sample estimates of the betas for our stocks in the twelve months of year $t - 1$ and relating them to the sample estimates in year t. The relationship might look like that of Figure 5-10.

Each observation point in the figure represents one of the stocks in the sambut they do a better job than the straight historical model alone."

"What do I do with them?"

"Well, when averaged to obtain the fundamental portfolio beta, they are becoming increasingly accepted as a measure helpful in describing the character of the portfolio. For example, a growth manager may wish to demonstrate to clients just how much orientation his or her portfolios have had toward growth. The fundamental beta of the portfolio may be useful in a comparison against the market or against other managers. In another situation, suppose you think you're approaching a major bull market, and you want to check the posture of your portfolio to see how responsive your investments will be to the general price level increase. The fundamental beta of your portfolio gives you useful information in this regard. By keying on a certain market index and moving toward a portfolio beta equal to 1.00, you can create a portfolio that will track the index. Overall, I think I can honestly say that fundamental beta has grown to become one of the *basic* parameters describing a portfolio's orientation. Today, it's regarded on a par with the price-earnings ratio and the dividend yield."

"What are the weaknesses of these fundamental betas?"

"Well, I think they're more useful in capturing the character of a portfolio as a whole than they are for individual companies. Just like any model, depending on how they are picked up by the model, a certain stock's characteristics can interact to create a beta estimate that's clearly out of line. Because of this, some people have been known to get frustrated when using beta to estimate things like discount rates that are to be applied to income streams. Currently, we are stressing its use in portfolios rather than individual stock application. To give you another example, we use fundamental betas in the assessment of the performance of portfolio managers."

"To your knowledge, does First Chicago employ fundamental betas in its quantitative investment analysis?"

"As a matter of fact, one of the key people in First Chicago's trust department is a friend of mine. They've not only employed fundamental betas for many years now but they've been highly successful with them."

As Tom watches the cloud move away toward the Sears Tower and the First National Bank of Chicago Plaza, he feels his confidence growing. His story is far from over, but Wilshire will have one more account by the end of the day.

ple. For example, the stock at point A has a beta of .60 in period $t - 1$ and .90 in period t. If, for every stock, the sample estimate of beta was the same in each period, then every observation would fall on the broken 45-degree line. Because the observations are scattered, we know we obtain different sample estimates of beta as we go from one period to the next. To obtain an estimate of the relationship between beta values in successive periods, we slide a line of best fit through

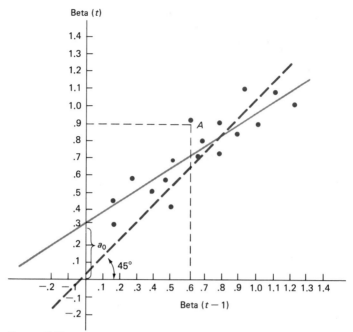

Figure 5-10 Relationship Between Betas for Different Stocks in Successive Periods

the observations. Because the line can be described by its slope and its intercept, we have

$$\hat{\beta}_t = a_0 + a_1 \hat{\beta}_{t-1}$$

If we assume that the relationship between betas in successive periods remains constant over time, we can use the coefficients a_0 and a_1 to modify our sample estimate of beta in period t to obtain an estimate of its population value in period $t + 1$.

$$\beta_{t+1} = a_0 + a_1 \hat{\beta}_t$$

For example, in Figure 5-10, $a_0 = .25$ and $a_1 = .75$; so if our sample estimate for the beta of a stock was 1.50 in period t, we would estimate its population value to be 1.38 for the next period.

$$1.38 = .25 + .75 \times 1.50$$

Employing Firm
Characteristics to Estimate Population Values

In the two methods just described, we used only the past series of rates of return on the stock to estimate its beta. Presumably, however, the beta factor and residual variance of a stock are fundamentally determined by the characteristics of the company behind the stock. Given this, we should take these characteristics into consideration in estimating the population values. Before we can do this, however, we need to estimate the relationship between different company characteristics and the values for beta and residual variance.

To illustrate the procedure, suppose we feel that the size of a company is an important determinant of the risk of the company. We want to include this consideration in estimating the beta factors for our stocks. To do this, we estimate the relationship between the size of each company at the end of period $t - 1$ and the sample estimate of beta in period t, much in the same way as we estimated the relationship between betas in successive periods. We can, in fact, estimate the relationship for both variables (company size and beta in the previous period) at the same time. Rather than slide a line through a scatter of observations in two dimensions ($\hat{\beta}_t$ and $\hat{\beta}_{t-1}$) as we did before, we now slide a plane through a scatter of points in three dimensions ($\hat{\beta}_t$, $\hat{\beta}_{t-1}$, and SIZE). The equation for the plane is given by

$$\hat{\beta}_t = a_0 + a_1\hat{\beta}_{t-1} + a_2 \text{ SIZE}_{t-1}$$

As before, if we assume that this relationship remains constant over time, we can estimate the population value for beta in the next period through the following equation:

$$\beta_{t+1} = a_0 + a_1\hat{\beta}_t + a_2 \text{ SIZE}_t$$

Size isn't, of course, the only company characteristic that may have an effect on stock risk. Stability of earnings, financial leverage, and the liquidity position of the company are only a few of the many variables we may wish to take into account in making our estimates. Thus, the size of the final equation may become very large. Commercial services are available that estimate beta factors for stocks in nearly this same way. These services employ a wide variety of firm characteristics in their beta estimates.

Although the above equation is used to estimate the beta factor for a given stock, nearly identical procedures can be employed to estimate residual variances.[4]

Summary

The Markowitz and index models are both used in constructing the minimum variance set. The difference between the two methods is the formulas used in each to determine the variance of a portfolio. The formula used by Markowitz is perfectly accurate; the formulas used by the index models are approximations that are as accurate as is their assumption that the residuals for different stocks are perfectly uncorrelated with each other.

[4]This procedure to estimate fundamental beta and residual variance estimates was originally developed by Barr Rosenberg (1974).

The Markowitz Model makes no assumptions regarding the source of the covariances between stocks in the covariance matrix. They could be due to any number or kind of interrelationships that exist between the stocks. The index models, however, assume that all the covariances can be accounted for by the relative responses of each stock to common forces, such as the movement in the market itself. If this is true, then the residuals, or deviations from the characteristic lines, will indeed be uncorrelated with each other.

In using the Markowitz Model to find the efficient set, you provide the computer with estimates of the covariances among all of the stocks in the population from which you want to choose. If this population is large, you have an extremely large number of covariances to estimate, and a large amount of computation time is required to compute the variance of any given portfolio. This is the problem with the Markowitz Model.

If you are trying to find the minimum variance set using the Single Index Model, you provide the computer with the model's alternative formula for portfolio variance. You also supply it with estimates of the beta factor for each stock, the residual variance for each stock, and the variance of the market portfolio. With a large population of stocks from which to choose, the number of required estimates has been greatly reduced, and the time required to compute the variance has been similarly reduced. It must be recognized, however, that the minimum variance set you obtain is not likely to be the *true* minimum variance set. Unless the residuals are truly uncorrelated, if you recomputed the variance of your portfolios using the *correct* formula as given by the Markowitz Model, you would find that these portfolios lie inside the true bullet, as found with the Markowitz Model.

Empirical evidence seems to indicate that the covariances between the residuals for different companies are predominantly positive. This means that the residual variance of a portfolio is likely to be larger than one might predict it to be on the basis of the equation of the Single Index Model. This appears to be especially true for portfolios that have unusually low or high beta factors.

If correlation between the residuals is a problem, you can attempt to overcome it by using multi-index models. The Single Index Model assumes that the correlations between the rates of return on different stocks can all be accounted for by the fact that all stocks respond to some degree to variability in the returns to the market. Multi-index models bring in factors in addition to the market to account for the correlations. The covariances that may exist between the residuals in the Single Index Model can presumably be accounted for by the presence of these other factors. Once these factors are accounted for, in the context of a multi-index model, the remaining residuals will be uncorrelated. In any case, the problem of residual correlation hasn't been sufficiently severe to prevent the widespread use of the Single Index Model by practicing portfolio analysts.

In estimating the inputs for index models, you can simply use sample estimates, or you can employ more sophisticated procedures that take into account the relationship between beta and residual variance and the fundamental characteristics of the company behind the stock.

QUESTIONS AND PROBLEMS

1. What assumption serves as the foundation of the Single Index Model?
2. Given the following information and the assumption of the Single Index Model, what is the covariance between stocks 1 and 2?

$$\beta_1 = .85$$
$$\beta_2 = 1.30$$
Variance of the market index $= .09$

3. Assume the following:

	Residual Variance	
Stock X	.02	$Cov(\epsilon_X, \epsilon_Y) = .01$
Stock Y	.06	

Also assume that a portfolio of X and Y is constructed, with a 2/3 weight for X and a 1/3 weight for Y.

a. What is the residual variance of the portfolio if the Single Index Model is assumed?
b. What is the residual variance of the portfolio without the Single Index Model assumption?

4. Suppose you had estimated the following relationship for firm J's return as a function of the return on a market index.

$$r_J = .03 + 1.3 \, r_M + \epsilon_J$$

a. If the return on the market index should fall by two percentage points, what is the expected change in firm J's return?
b. What is the name given to the graphic representation of the above equation?
c. What might account for J's *actual* return being different from that expected on the basis of the first two terms of the equation?

Refer to the following data for questions 5 through 8.

Security	Beta	Residual Variance	σ^2_r
A	.5	.04	.0625
B	1.5	.08	.2825

Suppose an equally weighted portfolio of A and B is formed.

5. What is the beta coefficient for the portfolio?
6. Compute the residual variance of the portfolio, assuming the Single Index Model.
7. Compute the variance of the portfolio, assuming the Single Index Model.
8. Fill in the missing columns in the following table. Assume the variance of the market index (M) to be .0016.

Security i	Variance of i	Correlation of i with M	Beta	Systematic Risk	Unsystematic Risk
i = 1	.006	.9			
i = 2	.006	.3			
i = 3	.006	0			

9. What is the meaning of "unsystematic risk"?

Refer to the following data for questions 10 through 15.

Correlation coefficient between stocks A and B = .50

Standard deviation of the market index (M)   = .10

	Correlation of Stock with M	Standard Deviation
Stock A	0	.10
Stock B	.5	.20

10. What are the beta values for A and B?
11. What is the covariance between A and B, assuming the Single Index Model?
12. What is the true covariance between A and B?
13. Suppose a portfolio was constructed, with weights of .40 for A and .60 for B. What is the beta of this portfolio?
14. Compute the variance of the portfolio in question 13, assuming the Markowitz Model.
15. Compute the variance of the portfolio in question 13, assuming the Single Index Model.
16. What is an index model (either a single index or multi-index) supposed to accomplish? What is the potential advantage of the multi-index approach, in comparison with the Single Index Model?

17. What kind of systematic relationship between market betas and residual variance of well-diversified portfolios was discovered in the work of Black, Jensen, and Scholes?

18. Suppose you employed a two-index model to estimate the following relationship for the percentage return on stock K:

$$r_K = .5 + .8\ r_M + .2\ g + \epsilon_K$$

where r_M represents the percentage return on the market index and g represents the unexpected growth rate of industrial production.

   a. If the market index's return is 5 percent and the unexpected growth of industrial production is 2 percent, what return would you expect for stock K?

   b. What kind of *change* in stock K's return would you expect if there were to be no change in g and a two-percentage-point decrease in r_M?

19. Write the formula for the variance of a portfolio, assuming that a two-factor model has been used to explain returns and that the covariance between the factors is zero. Also, write the *general* expression for the portfolio's residual variance. If the two-factor model is really appropriate to account for the interrelationships among returns on individual stocks, what simplification occurs in the general expression for the portfolio's residual variance?

20. Compute the variance of stock X using the expression derived from the two-index model and the following information. The two factors consist of the return on a market index and an index of unexpected growth in industrial production.

Stock X's market beta	= .75
Stock X's growth beta	= .40
Growth index variance	= .10
Market index variance	= .08
Stock X's residual variance	= .03

Refer to the following data for questions 21 through 25. A two-factor model is being employed, one being a market index (M) and the other being an index of unexpected changes in the growth of industrial production (*g*).

	Market Beta	Growth Beta	Residual Variance
Stock 1	.6	.2	.05
Stock 2	.9	.1	.02

Variance of the market index	= .12
Variance of the growth index	= .10
Covariance between residuals of stocks 1 and 2 =	.02
Covariance between M and *g*	= 0

21. Compute the variance of stock 1.

22. Assume you had constructed an equally weighted portfolio of stocks 1 and 2. Compute the residual variance of this portfolio in two ways:

 a. Making the simplifying assumption of the two-index model about residual covariance.

 b. Without making the simplifying assumption about residual covariance.

23. Compute the market beta and the growth beta for an equally weighted portfolio of stocks 1 and 2.

24. For an equally weighted portfolio of stocks 1 and 2, compute the variance of the portfolio in two ways:

 a. Making the simplifying assumption of the two-index model about residual covariance.

 b. Without making the simplifying assumption about residual covariance.

25. Why would you want to compute portfolio variance by a single or multi-index model rather than by the Markowitz Model?

26. Discuss how we would arrive at an estimated beta value for a stock based on historical information. Further, try to speculate on potential difficulties in using historical information to estimate beta.

27. For a given stock, you have estimated the following time series relationship for market betas:

$$\beta_t = .20 + .85 \, \beta_{t-1}$$

where t indicates the year of interest.

 a. If you relied on this relationship for prediction purposes, and the beta in 1987 was 1.2, what would your predicted beta be for 1988?

 b. What are you implicitly assuming in using this relationship for predictive purposes?

28. Question 27 discussed a relationship between betas at different points in time. What other variables might be used in an attempt to predict future beta values for a stock?

BIBLIOGRAPHY

BLACK, F., M. C. JENSEN, and M. SCHOLES, "The Capital Asset Pricing Model: Some Empirical Tests," in *Studies in Theory of Capital Markets,* ed. M. C. Jensen. New York: Praeger, 1972.

BLUME, M. E., "On the Assessment of Risk," *Journal of Finance* (March 1971).

BRENNER, M., and S. SMIDT, "Asset Characteristics and Systematic Risk," *Financial Management* (Winter 1978).

CHEN, S., "Beta Non-Stationarity, Portfolio Residual Risk and Diversification," *Journal of Financial and Quantitative Analysis* (March 1981).

COHEN, K., and J. POGUE, "An Empirical Evaluation of Alternative Portfolio Selection Models," *Journal of Business* (April 1967).

CORNELL, B., and J. K. DIETRICH, "Mean-Absolute-Deviation Versus Least-Squares Regression Estimation of Beta Coefficients," *Journal of Financial and Quantitative Analysis* (March 1978).

EUBANK, A. A., and J. K. ZUMWALT, "How to Determine the Stability of Beta Values," *Journal of Portfolio Management* (Winter 1979).

FAMA, E. F., "A Note on the Market Model and the Two Parameter Model," *Journal of Finance* (December 1973).

FRABOZZI, F. J., and J. C. FRANCIS, "Beta as a Random Coefficient," *Journal of Financial and Quantitative Analysis* (March 1978).

FRANKFURTER, G. M., "The Effect of 'Market Indices' on the Ex-Post Performance of the Sharpe Portfolio Selection Model," *Journal of Finance* (June 1976).

HILL, N. C., and B. K. STONE, "Accounting Betas, Systematic Operating Risk, and Financial Leverage: A Risk Composition Approach to the Determinants of Systematic Risk," *Journal of Financial and Quantitative Analysis* (September 1980).

KING, B. F., "Market and Industry Factors in Stock Price Behavior," *Journal of Business* (January 1966).

KLEMKOSKY, R. C., and J. D. MARTIN, "The Adjustment of Beta Forecasts," *Journal of Finance* (September 1975).

LINDAHL-STEVENS, M., "Some Popular Uses and Abuses of Beta," *Journal of Portfolio Management* (Winter 1978).

MCCLAY, M., "The Penalties of Incurring Unsystematic Risk," *Journal of Portfolio Management* (Spring 1978).

ROBICHEK, A. A., and R. A. COHN, "The Economic Determinants of Systematic Risk," *Journal of Finance* (May 1974).

ROENFELDT, R. L., G. L. GRIEPENTROF, and C. C. PFLAUM, "Further Evidence on the Stationarity of Beta Coefficients," *Journal of Financial and Quantitative Analysis* (March 1978).

ROSENBERG, B, "Extra-Market Components of Covariance Among Security Returns," *Journal of Financial and Quantitative Analysis* (March 1974).

ROSENBERG, B., and J. GUY, "Beta and Investment Fundamentals—II," *Financial Analysts Journal* (July–August 1976).

SCHOLES, M., and J. WILLIAMS, "Estimating Beta from Nonsynchronous Data," *Journal of Financial Economics* (December 1977).

SHARPE, W. F., "A Simplified Model of Portfolio Analysis," *Management Science* (January 1963).

THEOBALD, M., "Beta Stationarity and Estimation Period: Some Analytical Results," *Journal of Financial and Quantitative Analysis* (December 1981).

UMSTEAD, D. A., and G. L. BERGSTROM, "Dynamic Estimation of Portfolio Betas," *Journal of Financial and Quantitative Analysis* (September 1979).

WEINSTEIN, M., "The Systematic Risk of Corporate Bonds," *Journal of Financial and Quantitative Analysis* (September 1981).

6

THE CAPITAL ASSET PRICING MODEL

Introduction

The previous three chapters were devoted to techniques for managing portfolios. Our objective was to find the portfolios in the efficient set. Here, we are going to talk about theories concerning the way securities are priced by the market, or the *structure* of stock prices. In particular, we are asking about the pricing structure as it relates to risk. If two securities are identical in every way except for their risk, how will they differ in terms of the price investors are willing to pay for them? How will they differ in terms of the rate of return investors expect to get from them?

In this chapter we will discuss the Capital Asset Pricing Model.[1] Essentially, the CAPM is based on the following premise: Suppose *all* investors employed Markowitz portfolio theory to find the portfolios in the efficient set, and then, based on their individual risk aversion, each of them invested in one of the portfolios in the efficient set. How, then, would we measure the relevant risk of an individual security, and what, then, would be the relationship between risk and the returns investors expect and require from their investments?

---

[1]The Capital Asset Pricing Model was simultaneously and independently discovered by John Lintner (1965), Jan Mossin (1966), and William Sharpe (1964).

134

THE ASSUMPTIONS OF THE
CAPITAL ASSET PRICING MODEL

Assumption I: Investors can choose between portfolios on the basis of expected return and variance.

In Figure 6-1 we have drawn the probability distributions for two portfolios. The distributions are obviously very different. Portfolio A has a higher expected value. It has a higher variance, and its distribution is skewed to the left instead of to the right. Assumption I states that if you had to choose between these two portfolios as an investment, the only things you would have to know about the portfolios are their expected returns and variances.

Investors *can* choose on the basis of expected return and variance if all the probability distributions for portfolio returns are *normally distributed*.[2] This means that they all look something like the bell-shaped distribution of Figure 6-2. Normal distributions can be completely described by their expected value and variance. If you tell me the expected value, the variance, *and* that the distribution is normal, I know everything I need to know to describe the distribution accurately. All normal distributions are identical in every respect other than their expected value and variance. They are all, for example, perfectly symmetric, having no skewness in either direction. Thus, even if we had a preference

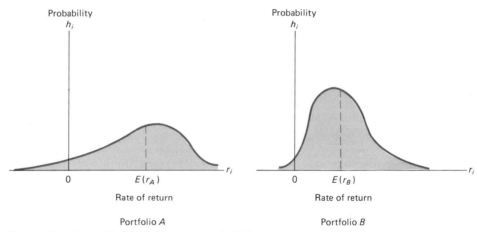

Figure 6-1 Probability Distributions for Two Portfolios

---

[2]This was first proven by Tobin (1958). A second condition, which allows you to choose between portfolios solely on the basis of expected return and variance, is that the relationship between utility, u, and the value of your portfolio, V, is *quadratic* in form. If this is true, then the utility associated with any ith value for your portfolio is given by the following equation:

$$u_i = a_0 + a_1 V_i + a_2 V_i^2$$

where $a_1 > 0$, and $a_2 < 0$.

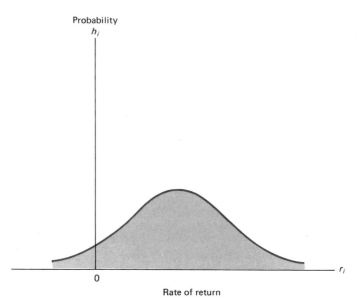

Probability
h_i

0

Rate of return

r_i

Figure 6-2 A Normal Probability Distribution

for distributions that were skewed to the right, it would be immaterial, because none of the distributions would be skewed in either direction.

The assumption of normality isn't unreasonable in some cases. Although the possible range for the rate of return is truncated at the lower end (the lowest possible return is -100 percent, but there is no bound on the highest possible return), this is of no *practical* consequence if the time horizon is relatively short, say, a month. Rarely do stocks more than double in price or fall by more than 50 percent in such a short period of time. As a consequence, if you were to observe the monthly returns on a typical stock over a period of time where there was no change in the underlying variance of the series, the frequency distribution for the returns would not depart significantly from that of a normal distribution.[3]

For longer intervals, such as for yearly returns, the distribution of returns for individual stocks does tend to be skewed to the right. However, keep in mind that the assumption relates to portfolios rather than individual stocks. Even if the distributions for individual stocks are not normal, when we combine many of these stocks into a well-diversified portfolio, we know, from the central limit theorem, that the distribution for the portfolio itself will be *approximately* normal.[4]

In fact, given that the distribution of portfolio returns is normal, we can plot points of indifference for you on an expected return-standard deviation graph

[3]See, for example, Hsu, Miller, and Wichern (1974). There is some evidence of the existence of skewness in the distribution of daily and weekly returns.

[4]This argument is weakened when one recognizes that the strong form of the central limit theorem requires that the objects being combined be uncorrelated. Security returns are, of course, correlated to some degree.

like that in Figure 6-3. In the figure you are indifferent to portfolio A and portfolio B. Although B has a higher level of standard deviation, it has just enough additional expected return to make you indifferent between investing in it or portfolio A. In fact, you would be indifferent toward investing in any portfolio that was positioned on the curve going through the two points. This circle is called an *indifference curve*. Each indifference curve represents a given level of expected utility. As you move to the northwest on the graph, you are moving to more desirable positions.

Assumption II: All investors are in agreement regarding the planning horizon and the distributions of security returns.

We are going to assume that all investors plan their investments over a single period of time that is the same for all. Furthermore, we all agree on the numbers required as inputs to our Markowitz portfolio model. We all agree on the expected rates of return for each security. We all agree on the numbers in the covariance matrix for all the securities in the market. To some extent, this assumption is consistent with assumption III, that information about securities flows freely throughout the capital market.

Assumption III: There are no frictions in the capital market.

Frictions are defined as impediments to the free flow of capital and information throughout the market. Thus, we will assume that there are no transactions costs

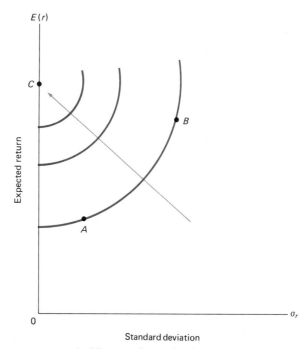

Figure 6-3   Indifference Curves in $E(r)$, σ_r Space

associated with buying or selling securities. We will also assume that no taxes are imposed on dividends, interest income, or capital gains. Moreover, we assume that information flows freely to everyone in the marketplace, and there are no restrictions on short selling.

In general, these assumptions are made so that we can obtain a definitive picture of the relationship between risk and expected return in the market. We want to see the effect of risk on expected return. We don't want expected return to be affected by the costs of transacting, and we don't want expected return to be influenced by the degree to which the income from a security is exposed to taxes. Also, we don't want the picture to be clouded by market inefficiencies caused by impediments in the flow and processing of information. In the presence of these assumptions we will get a "clean" picture of the risk-return relationship.

Many of the assumptions of the CAPM are admittedly unrealistic. However, it should be stressed that the model can be derived without the need to make many of these assumptions. For example, the model has been derived in the presence of transactions costs, taxes, and differing beliefs regarding probability distributions.[5] In each case, the final form of the model is essentially similar to the form we obtain on the basis of the assumptions made here. We are making the assumptions because the model is easier to derive on this basis.

THE CAPITAL ASSET PRICING MODEL WITH A RISK-FREE ASSET

The Capital Market Line

We will derive the Capital Asset Pricing Model first by assuming that a risk-free bond exists. You can assume that it is a bond that matures at the end of the planning horizon, and that its payment is guaranteed by the government. Its rate of interest is equal to r_F. Also assume that all investors can buy or sell as much of the bond as they desire. If you sell the bond, you are free to use the proceeds to invest in other securities. This is consistent with our general assumption that investors are free to short sell any security without restriction.

Consider first the portfolio opportunities available to investors. On the basis of assumption I, we can represent them in terms of their expected return and standard deviation. The points in Figure 6–4 represent individual securities. The solid curve represents the minimum variance set based on the population of securities. On the basis of assumption II, we know that all investors see this same picture of portfolio opportunities. They all make their investment decisions based on the *same* minimum variance set.

---

[5]See Chen, Kim, and Kon (1975) for a derivation of the CAPM under transactions costs, Brennan (1973) for a derivation under personal income taxes, and Lintner (1970) for a derivation under heterogeneous expectations.

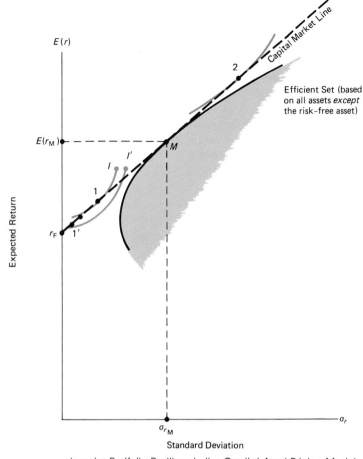

$E(r)$

$E(r_M)$

Expected Return

r_F

2

Capital Market Line

Efficient Set (based
on all assets *except*
the risk-free asset)

M

I'

I

1

1'

σ_{r_M}

Standard Deviation

σ_r

Figure 6-4   Investor Portfolio Positions in the Capital Asset Pricing Model

If a risk-free asset didn't exist, investors would take positions at various points on the efficient set.[6] The composition of each portfolio, held by each investor, would be different. If a risk-free bond exists, however, it makes sense for everybody in the market to hold the same portfolio of risky assets. This portfolio is the one portfolio in the efficient set that has the highest value for the ratio of (a) the difference between the portfolio's expected return and the risk-free rate to (b) the standard deviation of the portfolio's rate of return.

In Figure 6–4, the portfolio with the highest value for the above ratio is portfolio M. To find this portfolio, extend a straight line vertically from r_F and gradually tilt it to the right until it touches the bullet. The portfolio at the point where

---

[6]A no borrowing form of the Capital Asset Pricing Model was independently derived by Black (1972) and Vasicek (1971).

it touches the bullet is the best portfolio on the efficient set for everyone to hold, regardless of his or her relative risk preferences. The efficient set now becomes the straight line extending from r_F through portfolio M. You can attain positions between r_F and M by investing some of your money in portfolio M and the rest of it in the risk-free bond. For these positions you are *buying* the risk-free bond. You can attain positions on the line beyond point *M* by selling the risk-free bond and using the proceeds of sale, in addition to your own funds, to buy portfolio M.

If you are highly risk averse, you will have indifference curves that look like *I* and *I'*. To maximize your utility, attain a position on an indifference curve as far to the northwest as possible. You can do this if you take a position where the line between r_F and *M* is tangent to your indifference curve. This position is labeled point 1 on the graph. Notice that if you move away from point 1 in either direction along the line, you move to an indifference curve representing a lower amount of utility, such as point 1'. If you have a lower degree of risk aversion, the point of tangency with the new linear efficient set may be one where you are selling the risk-free bond or *borrowing* to invest in portfolio M, as with point *2* in Figure 6–4.

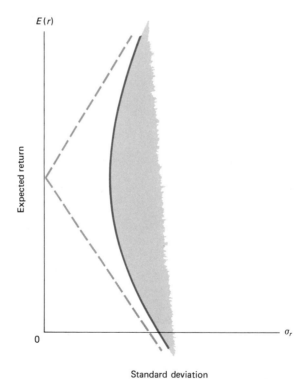

Standard deviation

Figure 6-5   Minimum Variance Set with High Risk Aversion

In equilibrium, the prices for all assets must adjust so that there is as much buying of the risk-free bond as there is selling. This means that the risk-free rate and the shape of the bullet must adjust to one another so that the points of tangency between investors' indifference curves and the linear efficient set are distributed uniformly on both sides of point *M*. If investors in the market are, in general, highly risk averse, the bullet will be as drawn in Figure 6–5. If investors are less risk averse on average, the differences between expected rates of return on different securities will be smaller, and the bullet will appear as drawn in Figure 6–6. In any case, prices will adjust until the market clears for all assets, including the risk-free bond.

In Figure 6–4, the straight line extending from r_F through portfolio M is called the *capital market line*. All investors take portfolio positions on this line by borrowing or lending. However, as explained above, regardless of our positions on the capital market line, all of us are investing in portfolio M. The ratio of the market value of stock X to stock Y in my portfolio is exactly the same as in yours. We are all holding the same portfolio of *risky* assets, portfolio M.

We know that whenever we aggregate the portfolio holdings of everyone in the market, we get the market portfolio. Given this, because we are all holding the same portfolio of risky assets, the portfolio weights in this portfolio must be identical to those of the market portfolio. When you can buy or sell a risk-free asset, everyone in the market holds the same portfolio of risky assets, and that portfolio is the market portfolio.

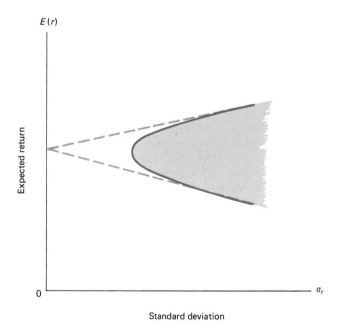

Figure 6-6 Minimum Variance Set with Low Risk Aversion

Measuring the Risk of an Individual Security

Because, as an investor, your ultimate concern is your final portfolio position, you will assess the risk of an individual security on the basis of its contribution to the variance of your portfolio. Because we are all holding the market portfolio, a security's risk can be measured on the basis of its contribution to the variance of the market.

We know that the beta factor of a portfolio is a simple weighted average of the betas for the securities contained in the portfolio.

$$\beta_P = \sum_{J=1}^{M} X_J \beta_J$$

Since beta is the covariance between the security and the market divided by the market's variance, if we multiply both sides of the above expression by the variance of the market, we find that the covariance of any portfolio with the market is also a simple weighted average of the covariances of the securities in the portfolio with the market.

$$Cov(r_P, r_M) = \sum_{J=1}^{M} x_J Cov(r_J, r_M)$$

Portfolio = Weighted average of
covariance   security covariances
with portfolio

(6–1)

This equation holds for any portfolio, including the market itself. Thus, we can write it as

$$Cov(r_M, r_M) = \sigma^2 r_M \qquad = \sum_{J=1}^{M} x_J Cov(r_J, r_M)$$

Covariance of = Market = Weighted average of
market with   variance   security covariances
itself   with market

(6–2)

It is obvious from Equation (6–2) that the contribution an individual security makes to the variance of the market portfolio is measured by the covariance between the security and the market. In this form of the Capital Asset Pricing Model, *all* investors hold the market portfolio as their investment in risk-bearing securities. Thus, covariance with the market is perceived by all to be the relevant measure of the risk of an individual security. Because the beta factor of a security is equal to this covariance divided by the market's variance, and because the market's variance is the same for all securities, we can measure the risk of a security by either its covariance with the market or by its beta. Beta is more intuitively appealing, so we shall use it as the measure of security risk in the majority of cases.

Thus, in the Capital Asset Pricing Model, the risk of an investor's portfolio is measured in terms of its variance, and the risk of an individual security in terms of its beta. Only a fraction of a security's variance is of concern to a portfolio investor. If you will recall in our discussion of the market model, the variance of any security can be split into two parts, systematic risk (the product of beta squared and market variance) and residual variance. The part of the variance that concerns investors is systematic risk, because only that part is contributed to the variance of the portfolio they all hold. Residual variance disappears under diversification. It is of no concern to investors, and under the CAPM, it has no effect on the price of a security or its expected rate of return.

The Relationship Between the Risk of a Security and Its Expected Rate of Return

If beta is the appropriate measure of the risk of a security, what is the relationship between beta and expected rate of return? Based on property II of the minimum variance set (discussed in Chapter 4), it is easy to answer this question. We know that the market portfolio is positioned at point M in Figure 6–7 on the skin of the bullet. If the market portfolio is efficient, then a perfect linear relationship should exist between the beta factors for securities and their expected rates of return.

Given property II, the relationship can be found by drawing a line tangent to the bullet at M. The line of tangency is, in fact, the capital market line, and it intercepts the vertical axis at r_F. The line relating betas to expected rates of returns, therefore, will also intercept the vertical axis at r_F, as in Figure 6–8. Given that the market portfolio is on the efficient set, every security in the market must be positioned on this line.

The relationship of Figure 6–8 is called the *security market line*. The security market line is drawn in expected return-beta space, and it shows the relationship between a security's risk and its expected rate of return. Whereas only the portfolios that are candidates for those to be held by investors are positioned on the capital market line (drawn in expected return-standard deviation space), all portfolios and individual securities are positioned on the security market line.

Because the security market line is linear, it can be expressed in terms of its intercept and its slope. The intercept of the line is, of course, the risk-free rate. The slope is the vertical distance required to return to the line, divided by the horizontal distance you have moved away from the line. In Figure 6–8, if we move horizontally from 0 to 1.00 in terms of beta, we must move vertically by a distance equal to $E(r_M) - r_F$ in order to return to the line. Thus, the slope is equal to $[E(r_M) - r_F]/1.00$, or $E(r_M) - r_F$. The equation for the security market line relating expected return to beta, therefore, is

$$E(r_J) \quad = \quad r_F \quad + \quad [E(r_M) - r_F] \quad \times \quad \beta_J \qquad (6\text{--}3)$$

Expected $=$ Risk-free $+$ Market risk premium $\times$ Security
return   rate   risk

Security Risk Premium

OUT ON THE STREET

Hunting for Bargains

Jeff Diermeier sits at his desk on the ninth floor of Three First National Plaza in downtown Chicago. Jeff is a vice president at First Chicago Investment Advisors, which is a division of First National Bank of Chicago's holding company.

Jeff is carefully studying some computer output in which the market prices of various stocks are compared with estimates of their intrinsic values. He is looking for "bargain" stocks with market prices considerably below the computer's estimate of intrinsic value. The intrinsic value estimate is based on the discounted value of a stream of future dividends. Dividends are projected to grow at three distinct rates in three distinct future periods. The projected future dividends are then discounted to a present value, using a discount rate that reflects the risk of each individual stock.

First Chicago uses the Capital Asset Pricing Model to determine the proper discount rate for each stock. To estimate the discount rate, Jeff uses the equation for the security market line. He employs the current yield to maturity on long-term government bonds as an estimate of the risk-free rate. The bank subscribes to a service that provides it with estimates of beta factors on a wide variety of different stocks. This service estimates betas on the basis of past stock returns as well as a large number of other company characteristics, such as earnings volatility and financial leverage, in the manner described in Chapter 8.

The remaining estimate required for the security market line equation is the expected rate of return to the common stock market portfolio. This estimate evolves from a more comprehensive index made up of several different types of investments. Included are common stocks, real estate, treasury bills and other government bonds, corporate bonds, and even venture capital. Their proxy is a value weighted portfolio of all these investments.

To estimate the expected rate of return on this portfolio, Jeff employs the following equation:

The equation states that the expected rate of return on a security is equal to the risk-free rate (compensating investors for delaying consumption over the planning horizon), plus a risk premium (compensating them for taking on the risk associated with the investment). The risk premium itself can be broken into two parts. The term in brackets, on the right-hand side of the equation, is the risk premium for the market portfolio. It can also be thought of as the risk premium for an average, or representative, security. To get the risk premium for security J, we multiply the risk premium for an average security by the other term, the risk measure for security J.

The weighted average beta factor for all securities in the market is equal to 1. Given the equation for the security market line, if a security is of average risk,

$$E(r_M) = d + [E(g) - e(n)] + E(f)$$

The equation breaks down the expected return into three basic components— current income, real growth, and the expected rate of inflation. The first term, d, on the left side of the equation, is the ratio of current income to current market value. This is computed as a weighted average of the various types of investments in the portfolio. The term in brackets represents the expected real (inflation-adjusted) growth in long-term income that will accrue to a current investor in the portfolio. This is broken down into the difference between the overall real growth in income, $E(g)$, less that which stems from the sale of new securities to outside investors, $E(n)$. $E(g)$ is estimated by the firm's expectation of the real rate of growth in gross national product. The estimate of $E(n)$ is obtained by observing the financing behavior of firms in the past. The final term in the equation, $E(f)$, is the bank's estimate of the long-run rate of inflation.

Jeff feels that it's easier to use this methodology to estimate the expected rate of return to the market as a whole than it would be on a firm by firm basis.

After estimating the expected return to the market, this, along with estimates of the risk-free rate and the stock's beta, is substituted into the security market line equation to estimate each stock's discount rate.

$$E(r_J) = \hat{r}_F + [E(\hat{r}_M) - \hat{r}_F]\hat{\beta}_J$$

The discount rates are then used to capitalize the projected flows of dividends into present, intrinsic values for each of the stocks. If the estimate of intrinsic value is considerably above the current stock price, the stock is screened out as a potentially attractive candidate for investment in the accounts managed by the company.

Jeff has a lot of confidence in the procedure. It is well founded in theory, and it has worked well for him in the past in identifying issues that have subsequently produced some remarkable rates of return.

having a beta equal to 1, it will carry the average risk premium. If it is twice the average risk, it will carry twice the average risk premium.

In Figure 6–8, security A has a beta of 1.5. The risk-free rate is assumed to be 10 percent, and the expected rate of return to the market portfolio is assumed to be 15 percent. Given this, the expected rate of return to security A is equal to

$$17.5\% = 10\% + (15\% - 10\%) \times 1.50$$

Note that securities that are negatively correlated with the market, and therefore have negative betas, sell at expected rates of return that are below the risk-free rate. Conceivably, their expected rates of return could even be negative.

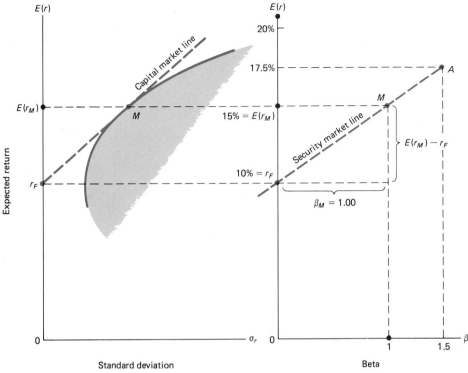

Figure 6-7 The Capital Market Line

Figure 6-8 The Security Market Line

You might find it hard to believe that anyone would be willing to invest in a security that had a negative expected rate of return. However, you might be surprised to know that you probably regularly invest in a security of sorts that has an expected rate of return that is as low as −50 percent—your automobile insurance! In some cases, for every dollar that you pay the insurance company, you can *expect* to get back fifty cents in benefits. The remainder goes to pay company expenses and underwriting profits. Why do you engage in such a transaction? Because it reduces the risk of your overall portfolio of assets. The returns on your insurance policy are negatively correlated with the value of one of the other assets in your portfolio, your car. As you drive down the road, your car is worth a lot, and your policy pays off nothing. Drive off the road and into a tree, and your car is now worth little, but your insurance policy pays off a lot.

Investors are willing to invest in low-return securities that are negatively correlated with other securities at low expected returns for the same reason. Because they are negatively correlated, they reduce the overall risk level of their portfolios. This is the central message of the Capital Asset Pricing Model. In assessing risk, in order to price stocks, investors consider more than the expected return and variance of the individual security itself. They also consider the *interrelationships* that exist between the returns on different securities.

The Positions of Individual Securities
in Expected Return-Standard Deviation Space

As discussed, individual investors take their ultimate portfolio positions on the capital market line by borrowing or lending and investing in the market portfolio. Although the portfolios held by investors are all positioned on the capital market line, individual securities are positioned to the right of the line. The distance of each security from the line is related to the magnitude of the security's residual variance.

To see this, consider Figure 6–9. We have retained our assumption that the risk-free rate is 10 percent, and the expected rate of return to the market portfolio is 15 percent. The market's standard deviation is also assumed to be 15 percent. Its variance, therefore, is 2.25 percent. Now consider stock A. Its beta is 1.00, so we know, based on the security market line, that its expected rate of return must be 15 percent. The standard deviation of stock A is 15 percent, and its variance is 2.25 percent.

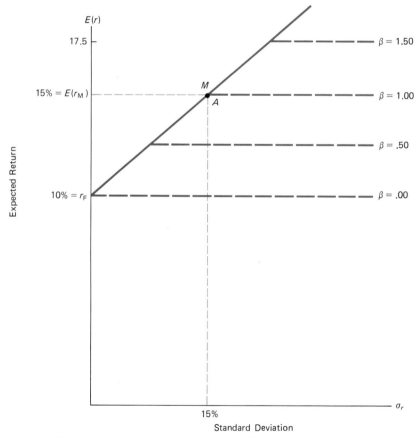

Figure 6-9 The Positions of Individual Stocks in $E(r)$, σ_r Space

Based on its beta, the systematic risk of this stock (the product of its beta squared and the variance of the market) is 2.25 percent. Because the stock's systematic risk is equal to its total variance, the residual variance of stock A must be zero. Thus, it must be perfectly correlated with the market. This will be true for any security positioned on the security market line. If we were to increase the residual variance of stock A, but leave its beta unchanged, we would not change its expected rate of return (which is based on beta alone), but we would increase its total variance and standard deviation. The stock would move to the right in Figure 6–9. In general, the more residual variance in a security's return, the farther to the right of the capital market line it is positioned.

Thus, there is a series of horizontal iso-beta lines, each representing a given level of beta. Any security, for example, with a beta of .50 must be positioned on the line labeled $\beta = .50$. The greater the level of residual variance for the security, the farther to the right on the line it is positioned.

THE CAPITAL ASSET PRICING MODEL WITH NO RISK-FREE ASSET

It is important to realize that much of the structure of the Capital Asset Pricing Model derives from the two properties of the minimum variance set. Remember that these properties are merely mathematical identities, and they do not reflect or predict the behavior of portfolio investors. As a consequence, although, on the surface, the CAPM appears to be rich in economic content and predictive power, it really makes only one interesting economic prediction: *All* investors hold portfolios that are on the efficient set, and as a result the market portfolio is itself on the efficient set.

We can see this most easily in the context of a version of the model where we assume that there is no risk-free bond available to buy or sell. We will assume that all the other assumptions of the model are intact.

The minimum variance set available to all investors is depicted in Figure 6–10a. On the basis of the assumption that all investors choose between portfolios on the basis of expected return and variance, or standard deviation, they all take positions on the efficient set above the minimum variance portfolio. Surprising as it may seem, we have now completed the economic analysis of the model! Everything we say from here on follows on the basis of identity relationships.

From property I we know that the market portfolio is efficient because it is the aggregate of all portfolios, held by all investors, all of which are efficient. From property II we know that if the market portfolio is efficient, there will be a deterministic, linear relationship among the beta factors of individual stocks and their expected returns, as in Figure 6–10b. This relationship (the security market line) has a positive slope (the market portfolio is not only on the minimum variance set; it is efficient), and it intercepts the expected return axis at the point labeled $E(r_Z)$, which is the expected return at which a line drawn tan-

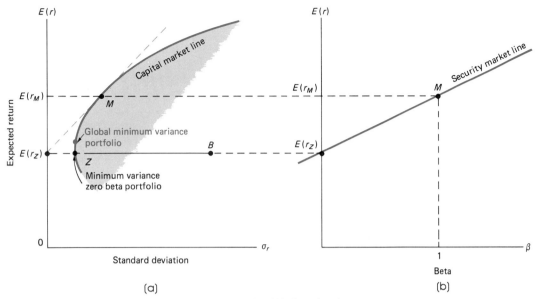

Figure 6-10 The Capital Asset Pricing Model with No Risk-Free Asset

gent to the bullet at *M* intersects the vertical axis. On the basis of our discussion of property II, we know that all the investments inside the bullet falling on the solid line beginning at Point *Z* and passing through point *B* will always be perfectly *uncorrelated* with the index portfolio taken from the bullet. In this case, the index portfolio is the market portfolio. Of those portfolios that are uncorrelated, the portfolio having the lowest variance is portfolio Z. This portfolio is called the *minimum variance, zero beta portfolio*. Its beta is zero, of course, because its correlation with the market is zero. In this version of the model, the security market line intersects the expected return axis at the expected return to the minimum variance, zero beta portfolio.

As you can see, the structure of the entire model automatically falls into place as soon as we specify that all investors are holding efficient portfolios. This is the only real prediction of the Capital Asset Pricing Model.

AN EMPIRICAL TEST OF THE CAPITAL ASSET PRICING MODEL

Rather than test the central prediction of the CAPM directly, initial testing of the model centered on the properties of the security market line. We know from property II that if the market portfolio is efficient, there will be a linear, positive relationship between the beta of any security and the security's expected rate of return. This relationship is called the security market line.

In testing the theory, the initial tests used a two-stage technique. The betas of securities or portfolios were estimated in the first stage. Security or portfolio returns were related to the returns to a market index. The line of best fit passing through the pairs of returns from each period serves as an estimate of the investment's characteristic line, and the slope of the characteristic line is the estimate of the investment's beta. The second stage of the test was cross-sectional in nature. Each observation was an individual security or portfolio. In the second pass, betas estimated in the first pass were related to average returns earned by the investments. The line of best fit through the observations in this pass is an estimate of the security market line. The researchers then tried to determine whether the properties of this estimate were in accord with the CAPM predictions.

A classic test of the Capital Asset Pricing Model was conducted by Black, Jensen, and Scholes (1972). Black, Jensen, and Scholes (BJS) did not directly test the prediction that the market portfolio is on the efficient set. They concentrated, instead, on the security market line.

BJS restricted their initial sample to all stocks traded on the New York Stock Exchange (NYSE) during the period 1926 to 1965, starting their study with the subperiod 1926 through 1930. They computed betas for all stocks that were on the exchange throughout this period, using as a market index an equally weighted portfolio of all stocks on the NYSE. They then ranked the stocks on the basis of beta and formed ten portfolios. The 10 percent of the stocks with the highest betas went into portfolio 1, and so on, through portfolio 10.

They then computed the rates of return to each of the portfolios in each of the twelve months of 1931. At the end of that year, they again computed the betas for every stock on the exchange in the period 1927 through 1931, and they reformed the ten portfolios. They repeated this process in each of the years 1931 through 1965, obtaining a series of monthly rates of return for each of the ten portfolios. They then attempted to estimate the expected rates of return and beta factors for each of the portfolios by taking sample estimates from the rates of return.

The sample estimate of the expected value is, of course, the arithmetic mean rate of return. This is the unbiased estimator of the expected rate of return at the beginning of each month. BJS estimated the beta of each portfolio by relating the portfolio returns to their market index. Although they took sample estimates of beta and average return for the portfolios over various subintervals in the period, we will concentrate on their sample estimates for the overall period 1931 through 1965.

The relationship BJS found between beta and average rate of return is depicted in Figure 6–11. The fit is remarkably good for a cross-sectional relationship, The graphing can be interpreted as an estimate of the security market line for the overall period.

Recall that if investors can borrow and lend at a risk-free rate, the security market line is given by

$$E(r_J) = r_F + [E(r_M) - r_F] \beta_J$$

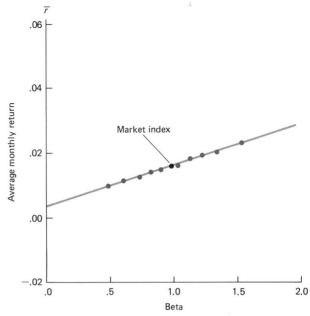

Figure 6-11 Estimate of the Security Market Line by Black, Jensen, and Scholes

where $E(r_J)$ is the expected return to stock J, r_F is the risk-free rate, $E(r_M)$ is the expected rate of return to the market portfolio, and β_J is the beta factor of stock J.

On the other hand, if investors can't borrow at a risk-free rate, the equation for the security market line is given by

$$E(r_J) = E(r_Z) + [E(r_M) - E(r_Z)] \beta_J$$

where $E(r_Z)$ is the expected rate of return on the minimum variance, zero beta portfolio.

The slope of the security market line is equal to the expected risk premium on the market portfolio. The slope of the BJS–estimated security market line is .01081, reflecting a market risk premium of 1.081 percent per month, or 12.972 percent per year.

The intercept is supposed to be equal to the rate of return on a risk-free bond or the expected rate of return on a zero beta portfolio. The intercept of the estimated security market line is .00519, reflecting a rate of return of .519 percent per month, or 6.225 percent per year. This number is significantly greater than the average interest rate on riskless bonds during the overall period. BJS concluded that their results are consistent with the form of the CAPM that disallows for riskless borrowing.

Overall, their results *appear* to offer strong support for the CAPM. There is little or no evidence of nonlinearity in their estimated security market line; the slope is highly significant and positive. Moreover, nearly 100 percent of the

Doubts About CAPM

"Do you swear to tell the truth, the whole truth, and nothing but the truth, so help you God?" Bob Malko, the chief economist of the Public Service Commission for the state of Wisconsin responds, "I do." Bob is sitting in a large room that looks much like a courtroom, but Bob isn't in court today. Instead, he is testifying before the Public Service Commission in regard to the matter of the appropriate cost of capital for the Wisconsin Electric Power Company, the largest regulated electric utility in Wisconsin.

Bob sits before a panel of three commissioners and a judge. Behind him, sitting at a table, are the lawyers representing consumer groups as well as the company. As chief economist for the commission, Bob is philosophically positioned between these groups, as an advocate of the rights of the general public as well as the rights of the security holders in Wisconsin Electric Power. There are literally hundreds of millions of dollars at stake in these hearings, and both sides will try to rip Bob's testimony apart if they feel it's in their interest to do so. This is a pressure cooker!

As the first lawyer approaches the witness stand, Bob tries to relax and collect his thoughts. He thinks back to the past few months and recalls the events that brought him here.

Bob was asked by the Public Service Commission to review the alternative methods of estimating the cost of equity capital for an electric utility and then do a specific application using the CAPM. The CAPM is used as the principal method for computing the cost of capital by at least two state regulatory agencies, Oregon and South Carolina. The Public Service Commission was interested in its usefulness for the regulatory process in Wisconsin.

Bob and his research assistant, Greg Enholm, prepared some estimates of the beta factor for the company being reviewed, Wisconsin Electric Power. They were surprised to find that, in the period subsequent to 1980, the beta factor for the utility was actually negative. These results, in addition to Bob's knowledge of Richard Roll's criticisms of the CAPM, made him skeptical of the model's usefulness in the regulatory process.

Bob's estimate of the cost of equity capital, based on the security market line, ranged from 11.9 to 14.7 percent. This was quite low based on prevailing capital

cross-sectional differences in the average returns on the portfolios can be explained by differences in beta factors. On the surface, at least, there appears to be little room for other risk variables to explain differences in expected rates of return. Recall that in the CAPM, beta should be the *only* determinant of differences in expected rates of return. However, as we shall see in the next section, these results are not really as supportive of the model as they appear to be on the surface.

market rates and was far short of what the company was requesting. Bob had little confidence in these estimates, in large part because of the instability in the estimates of the beta factor.

It was Bob's feeling that the approach of adding a risk premium to a riskless rate of return taken from the bond market was basically sound. The Capital Asset Pricing Model could be thought of as a refinement of this approach. But the theory isn't testable. In addition, there was the question of the adequacy of beta as a risk measure. In the case of a utility there are other nonmarket risks like regulatory risk and, among other things, the risk that the regulators won't grant rate increases that are timed and matched to increases in the cost of operations.

Bob wished there was a more sophisticated risk premium model that would not be open to as much theoretical debate as the CAPM. As things stood now, a witness advocating the CAPM was open to severe cross-examination. Attorneys would pick and pick away at the various uncertain issues raised by Roll.

The examination of Dr. J. Robert Malko begins. After a few preliminaries, the attorney for the Public Service Commission asks, "What are your conclusions regarding the application of the CAPM methodology in this case?"

Bob replies, "The commission should place no weight on the estimates of WEPCo's cost of equity developed using the CAPM methodology. There are too many unanswered questions. It appears that Roll's concerns regarding the choice of a market proxy are valid in Mr. Enholm's application, especially in the 1980s."

Several months later, in December 1983, the commission released its findings of fact and order in the matter (DN6630-ER-18). The findings of fact stated: "The Commission concludes that the Capital Asset Pricing Model (CAPM) is a sophisticated extension of the risk premium method for estimating cost of equity. CAPM provides several useful concepts including systematic risk. However, the Commission recognizes there are significant inadequacies and unresolved issues concerning the use of CAPM in a regulatory proceeding, which include selecting the appropriate market portfolio, testing CAPM predictions, and considering risk factors in addition to market risk" (pp. 13–14).

The commission granted a return of 14.75 percent on equity capital.

ROLL'S CRITIQUE OF TESTS OF THE CAPITAL ASSET PRICING MODEL

In 1976 Richard Roll wrote an extensive paper in which he criticized empirical testing of the Capital Asset Pricing Model. Roll's critique can be divided into two parts. First, he claims that the results of tests like those of BJS are *tautological*. By this he means that it is not improbable that we would obtain results like these no matter how stocks were priced in relation to risk in the real world. If this is true, we have learned little or nothing about the structure of stock prices from these tests, and the CAPM has never really been tested. Second, he claims that because the only real prediction of the CAPM is that the market portfolio is efficient, *this* is the prediction that has to be confirmed. However, the market portfolio contains every asset in the economic system. It is simply impossible to determine if such a portfolio is efficient in expected return-standard deviation space. If this is true, it follows that the Capital Asset Pricing Model can never be tested.

The Inadequacy of Previous Tests

Suppose we have a hat and many small pieces of paper. On each piece we write a number that represents a rate of return over a period of time, let's say a month. We put all the pieces into the hat and mix them up. Now pull twelve pieces of paper from the hat. The number on each piece will represent the rate of return on a stock in each of twelve months. Call this first stock 1, and put the pieces of paper back into the hat. Now do the same thing for another stock called 2, repeating the process through stock 100. You now have 100 series of monthly returns, one for each stock. The series might look like Table 6-1.

Because we have pulled only twelve returns from the hat for each security, the sample mean returns for the individual securities may differ considerably, even though their expected rates of return are all the same. The mean monthly return represents the rate of return to our market index, an equally weighted portfolio of the 100 stocks. This index is constructed in the same way as the index used by BJS.

Now we will compute beta factors for each of the 100 stocks. We relate the returns of each stock to the twelve returns of our market index. The line of best fit passing through the relationship is our estimate of the stock's characteristic line, and the slope of the line is our estimate of the stock's beta. We will find that the average beta for all of the stocks is exactly equal to 1.00, and the betas for the individual stocks are scattered above and below 1.00, just as in the real world. They might look like the beta factors listed in Table 6-1. The average

TABLE 6-1   An Example Pulled from a Hat

Month: Stock	1	2	3	· · ·	12	Stock Beta	Average Return
1	12%	5%	20%		−14%	1.30	7%
2	8%	16%	2%		3%	.70	2%
·	·	·	·		·	·	·
·	·	·	·		·	·	·
·	·	·	·		·	·	·
100	20%	1%	7%		10%	1.05	10%
Mean monthly return	8%	3%	7%		4%		

returns to the right of the beta factors are obtained by simply totaling the monthly returns on each stock and dividing by twelve.

At this point we form ten portfolios in the manner of BJS. We rank the stocks by beta, and put the 10 percent of the stocks with the highest beta into the first portfolio, and so on. As with BJS, the portfolios are equally weighted, so the return on each portfolio, in each month, is the average of the returns on its ten stocks. We also compute the beta for each portfolio by relating their returns to the returns of our market index. The schedule of betas and average rates of return to the portfolios might look like Table 6–2.

Suppose we now test the CAPM by examining the properties of the security market line. We estimate the security market line by relating beta to average return, first across the 100 individual stocks and then across the ten portfolios. The nature of our results depends on the position of our market index relative to the minimum variance set for our sample of stocks. Even though our stocks were pulled from a hat, they still have an associated minimum variance set. Based on the numbers in Table 6–1, we can compute a covariance matrix for the 100-stock population. Given the covariance matrix and the average returns for the stocks, we can construct the minimum variance set. It might look like the one depicted in Figure 6–12.

Suppose our market index portfolio happens to be one of the portfolios in the minimum variance set, positioned at point *M* in Figure 6–12. It is extremely unlikely that this would happen, but suppose that it did. This being the case, we know, on the basis of property II, that a perfect relationship will exist between beta factors and average returns for both individual stocks and for portfolios. Given that our market index is positioned at *M*, the relationship will look like that of Figure 6–13. Each point in Figure 6–13 represents the position of a stock or portfolio. Note that the security market line intercepts the vertical axis at the average rate of return of portfolio Z, positioned on the minimum variance set of Figure 6–12. We will find (on the basis of property II) that this portfolio is perfectly uncorrelated with our market index, and we will call this portfolio the minimum variance, zero beta portfolio.

The results of our test are consistent with the CAPM even though the returns were pulled from a hat—and *this* is the problem. The results of tests such as these can well be consistent with the CAPM no matter what the actual pricing structure looks like in the market!

Table 6–2 Betas and Average Returns to the Ten Portfolios

Portfolio	Beta	Average Return
A	1.30	12%
B	1.25	10%
.	.	.
.	.	.
.	.	.
J	.40	3%

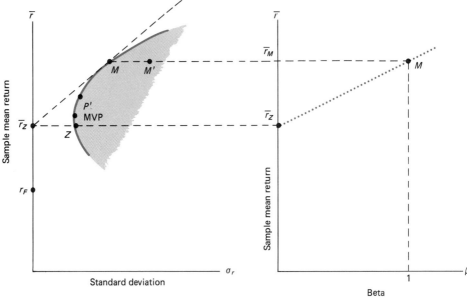

Figure 6-12 Minimum Variance Set for Stocks Drawn from the Hat

Figure 6-13 Security Market Line Corresponding to Market Index "M"

At this point you might object and say, "But you have assumed that the market index is on the efficient set, and this is extremely unlikely to happen." True enough, but if we look at our portfolios, we will obtain results that are consistent with the CAPM as long as our market index has an average return that is greater than the average return to the global minimum variance portfolio, positioned at point *MVP* in Figure 6–12.

Suppose, for example, that our market index is positioned at point *M'* in Figure 6–12. Because the index is inside the bullet, we know that the relationship between beta and average return for the individual stocks will look something like the scatter in Figure 6–14. Each point in the scatter represents one of the 100 stocks in our example. The broken line running through the scatter is the line of best fit. It will have a positive slope, provided that the market index has an average return greater than that of the global minimum variance portfolio.

BJS did not look at individual stocks; they looked at portfolios. The x's in Figure 6–14 represent the ten stocks with the highest betas, all of which we put into portfolio A. Note that some of the stocks are above the line of best fit and some are below. This, of course, will tend to be true, given the properties of a line of best fit. Because the return on the portfolio is the average of the returns on the component stocks, the portfolio itself will be positioned very close to the line of best fit in Figure 6–15. This also will be true of the other portfolios like B, C, and so on. Thus, even though the market index is well inside the bullet, the relationship between *portfolio* beta and average rate of return may

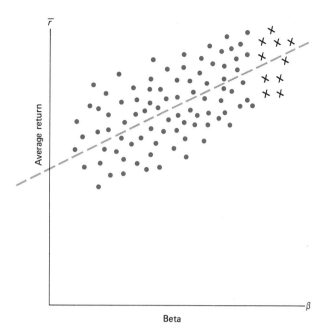

Figure 6-14 Relationship Between Beta and Average Return for Stocks Drawn from the Hat

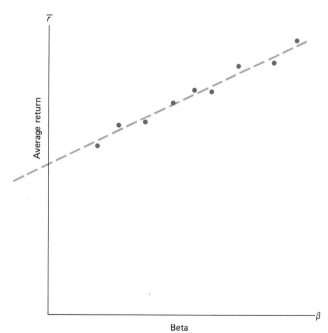

Figure 6-15 Relationship Between Beta and Average Return for Portfolios Drawn from the Hat

well be *approximately* consistent with the prediction of the Capital Asset Pricing Model.

Just as the test failed to indicate that the returns on the stocks were pulled from a hat, the tests conducted on real data tell us little about the properties of the pricing structure in the securities market. Although they indicate that the market indices employed were positioned above the minimum variance portfolio, in terms of expected return, they tell us little about the relative efficiency of the index used as a proxy for the market portfolio.

Can the Capital Asset Pricing Model Ever Be Tested?

Roll's second point is that the CAPM is, in principle, an untestable theory. To see this, suppose that you recognize the problem with the earlier tests of the model, and you seek instead to determine directly whether your market index is efficient. Assume that you restrict yourself to the NYSE. You construct a value weighted portfolio of all the stocks on the exchange. You compute its average return and its standard deviation over some past period of time, and then position the index relative to the minimum variance set. Because there are well over a thousand stocks on the exchange, to compute the minimum variance set you are going to be dealing with a huge covariance matrix. However, assume that you somehow are able to find the set. Your next job is to determine whether the degree of inefficiency exhibited by your index is statistically significant.

Assume that your index plots inside the bullet, as in Figure 6–16. Given the risk of your index, if it were efficient, its average return would be $\bar{r}_M{}'$; instead, it is $\bar{r}_M$. What is the probability that the difference is due to chance? Suppose you run a statistical test and conclude that the probability is remote. You come to me and say, "I can reject the CAPM on the basis of this test." My response would be, "No you can't, because you haven't tested the prediction of the CAPM." You see, the CAPM predicts that the *market portfolio* is efficient. It doesn't predict that the NYSE index will be efficient relative to the minimum variance set based on NYSE stocks alone.

Suppose the market portfolio is, in fact, efficient relative to the bullet based on the population of all assets. Even given this it is highly unlikely that a value weighted portfolio of a subset of these assets will be efficient relative to a bullet based on the subset. This will be true even if the subset is a fairly large percentage of the total population. Thus, even if the true market portfolio is efficient, it is highly unlikely that the NYSE index is going to be efficient relative to a minimum variance set based on NYSE stocks alone. So you can't reject the CAPM on the basis of your finding.

To reject the CAPM, you have to reject the efficiency of the true market portfolio. This is going to be extremely difficult, if not impossible, to do. You will have to expand your study to include stocks on all other exchanges, as well as in the over-the-counter markets. You will also have to include bonds, preferred stocks, and other types of securities. Many bonds are held privately by

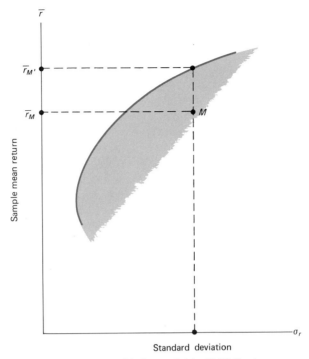

Figure 6-16 Minimum Variance Set for NYSE Stocks

firms and are consequently never traded. You won't be able to observe the returns for these securities. You also won't be able to observe the returns on many other assets you will have to include, such as farms and proprietorships. Remember, also, that portfolio investors can diversify internationally, so you must include in your market portfolio all the capital assets of every country in the world. You indeed face an impossible task!

There are two important points to remember here. First, there is no reason to believe that a market portfolio containing even a large fraction of the total assets in the economic system is going to be efficient based on the minimum variance set for the fraction, even if the CAPM is the true underlying model. Second, given available information, we can observe the returns on only a tiny fraction of the total number of capital assets in existence.

Based on these arguments, many in the profession have concluded that no one has ever come close to constructing a valid test of the Capital Asset Pricing Model, and no one ever will. They feel that the CAPM is simply not a testable theory. Work on deriving alternatives to the CAPM is under way. The Arbitrage Pricing Theory is an alternative that captures the appealing intuition of the CAPM, while purporting, at least by some, to be testable at the empirical level. We will examine this model in Chapter 7.

Summary

The portfolio models discussed in previous chapters can be viewed as *tools* to find the efficient set in expected return-standard deviation space. The Capital Asset Pricing Model can be viewed as a *theory* of the way stocks would be priced if everyone in the market used these tools and took positions on the efficient set. Because, in a world where short selling is permitted, when we aggregate everyone's efficient portfolio to obtain the market portfolio, we will find that the market portfolio itself is on the efficient set. This then automatically implies a linear, positively sloped relationship between expected stock return and beta.

In the Capital Asset Pricing Model, the risk of a portfolio that is held by an investor is measured in terms of its standard deviation or variance. On the other hand, the risk of an individual security is measured in terms of the contribution that the security makes to the variances of the portfolios that investors hold. This contribution can be measured by the beta factor for the stock.

The capital market line is drawn in expected return-standard deviation space. When investors are permitted to borrow and lend at a risk-free rate, the capital market line is linear and positively sloped. The portfolios held by investors are positioned on this line. Unless a stock happens to be perfectly positively correlated with the market, it is positioned to the right of the capital market line. The greater a stock's residual variance, the farther to the right of the capital market line it is positioned.

The security market line is drawn in expected return-beta space. It is linear and positively sloped, irrespective of whether investors can borrow or lend at a risk-free rate. All individual securities and portfolios are positioned on the security market line.

The greater the degree of risk aversion of investors in the market, the greater are the slopes of both the capital market line and the security market line. At the extreme, if investors have zero risk aversion or are risk neutral, the slope of both lines will be zero, and all securities will sell at prices to produce the same expected rate of return.

To test the CAPM you must directly test whether the market portfolio is on the efficient set. The most recent tests of the CAPM are directed at answering this question. It must be said, however, that these tests are not likely to provide convincing empirical support for the model. The inherent problem with the CAPM is that the market portfolio contains every capital asset in the economic system. There is no possible way to determine whether such a portfolio is efficient relative to the minimum variance set for the entire capital asset population. The observable market portfolio is only a tiny fraction of the true market portfolio. Moreover, even if the true market portfolio *is* efficient with respect to the total population, there is no reason to believe that a submarket portfolio is going to be efficient with respect to a subpopulation of assets, even though the subpopulation is a large fraction of the total. Because of this, we shall never be able to test empirically the single economic prediction of the Capital Asset Pricing Model.

This is not to say that the CAPM is defective on a theoretical level. The model follows logically from its assumptions, and it comes to a conclusion that is intuitively appealing. It makes sense that investors will price securities according to the contribution that each makes to the risk of their overall portfolios. Thirty years ago we believed that the risk of an individual security could be measured on the basis of the properties of its simple or marginal probability distribution, without regard to its relationships with other securities. The insight provided by the CAPM was a major step forward in our understanding of the way securities are priced in the marketplace. In fact, it may be possible that the CAPM may be the true underlying structure for securities prices, but we are simply having a difficult, even impossible, time proving it.

It is also true that the CAPM is accepted in the securities industry. It is used by firms to make capital budgeting and other decisions. It is used by some regulatory authorities to regulate utility rates. It is used by rating agencies to measure the performance of investment managers. The model would not be so widely used if it were not regarded as a useful benchmark. It is, therefore, extremely important for you to understand the CAPM in terms of both its strengths and weaknesses.

QUESTIONS AND PROBLEMS

1. What is the assumption covered in the chapter that would allow us to claim that investment choices can be evaluated solely on the basis of expected return and variance?

2. In the context of the CAPM with unlimited borrowing and lending at the risk-free rate of interest, explain the meaning of the capital market line.

3. If the risk-free rate of interest is 6 percent and the return on the market portfolio is 10 percent, what is the equilibrium return on an asset having a beta of 1.4, according to the CAPM (with no constraints on riskless borrowing and lending)?

Questions 4 through 7 refer to the following information:

Stock i	Correlation Coefficient i with M	Standard Deviation of i
1	.3	.4
2	.8	.3

$E(r_M) = .11$

$r_F = .06$

Variance of market portfolio's return $= .25$

4. Compute betas for

   a. Stock 1

   b. Stock 2

   c. A portfolio consisting of 60 percent invested in stock 1 and 40 percent invested in stock 2.

   According to the CAPM, how would you rank these securities according to risk?

5. Compute the equilibrium expected return according to the CAPM for

   a. Stock 1

   b. Stock 2

   c. The portfolio indicated in question 4c.

6. Sketch the security market line and indicate the positions of stock 1, stock 2, and the portfolio in question 4c.

7. Sketch the characteristic lines for stock 1, stock 2, and the portfolio in question 4c.

Questions 8 through 11 refer to the following diagram:

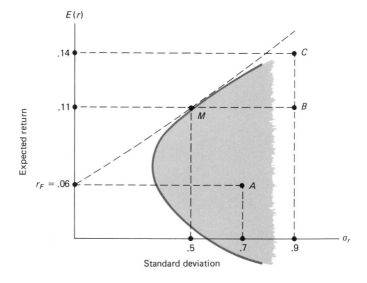

8. What are the beta values of stocks A, B, and C?

9. What are the residual variances of stocks A, B, and C?

10. Consider a portfolio consisting of 20 percent invested in A and 80 percent invested in C.

   a. What is the beta of this portfolio?

   b. According to the CAPM, what should the portfolio's equilibrium return be?

11. Evaluate the following statement: "Stocks B and C should be viewed as equally risky because they have the same standard deviation."

12. Suppose that the relevant equilibrium model is the CAPM with unlimited borrowing and lending at a riskless rate of interest. Suppose, further, that you discovered a security that was located *below* the security market line.

   a. What would you conclude about the pricing of this particular security?

   b. Describe any changes you would expect to occur in its price.

13. Suppose that the relevant equilibrium model is the CAPM with unlimited borrowing and lending at a riskless rate of interest. Complete the blanks in the following table.

Asset	Expected Return	Standard Deviation	Beta	Residual Variance
A	.08	.10	——	0
B	.12	——	2	.49
C	——	——	1	0
D	.05	——	0	.36

14. Assume the CAPM with *no* riskless asset.

   a. Contrast the capital market line in this model with the capital market line when there *is* a riskless asset that can be bought or sold.

   b. What is the interpretation of the market portfolio in this model?

15. a. What does it mean to say that "the market portfolio is efficient"?

   b. What approach have studies like that of Black, Jensen, and Scholes taken to test whether the market portfolio is efficient?

16. The CAPM conclusions are couched in terms of *expectations* of the future. How can we then proceed to test the theory with historical data?

BIBLIOGRAPHY

BLACK, F., "Capital Market Equilibrium with Restricted Borrowing," *Journal of Business* (July 1972).

BLACK, F., M. C. JENSEN, and M. SCHOLES, "The Capital Asset Pricing Model: Some Empirical Tests," *Studies in Theory of Capital Markets*. New York: Praeger, 1972.

BRENNAN, M. J., "Capital Market Equilibrium with Divergent Borrowing and Lending Rates," *Journal of Financial and Quantitative Analysis* (December 1971).

———, "Taxes, Market Valuation and Corporate Finance Policy," *National Tax Journal* (December 1973).

CHEN, A. H., E. H. KIM, and S. J. KON, "Cash Demand, Liquidation Costs and Capital Market Equilibrium Under Uncertainty," *Journal of Financial Economics* (September 1975).

CONSTANTINIDES, G. M., "Intertemporal Asset Pricing with Heterogeneous Consumers and Without Demand Aggregation," *Journal of Business* (April 1982).

FAMA, E. F., "Risk, Return and Equilibrium: Some Clarifying Comments," *Journal of Finance* (March 1968).

FAMA, E. F., and J. MACBETH, "Tests of Multiperiod Two Parameter Model," *Journal of Political Economy* (May 1974).

FRIEND, I., and R. WESTERFIELD, "Co-Skewedness and Capital Asset Pricing," *Journal of Finance* (September 1980).

FRIEND, I., R. WESTERFIELD, and M. GRANITO, "New Evidence on the Capital Asset Pricing Model," *Journal of Finance* (June 1978).

HAGGERMAN, R. L., and E. H. KIM, "Capital Asset Pricing with Price Level Changes," *Journal of Financial and Quantitative Analysis* (September 1960).

HARRINGTON, D., "Trends in Capital Asset Pricing Model Use," *Public Utilities* (August 1981).

————, "Whose Beta Is Best?" *Financial Analysts Journal* (July/August 1983).

HECKERMAN, D. G., "Portfolio Selection and the Structure of Capital Asset Prices When the Prices of Consumption Goods May Change," *Journal of Finance* (March 1972).

HOGAN, W. W., and J. M. WARREN, "Toward the Development of an Equilibrium Capital-Market Model Based on Semi-Variance," *Journal of Financial and Quantitative Analysis* (January 1974).

HSU, D., R. MILLER, and D. WICHERN, "On the Stable Paretian Character of Stock Market Prices," *Journal of the American Statistical Association* (March 1974).

JARROW, R., "Heterogeneous Expectations, Restrictions on Short Sales, and Equilibrium Asset Prices," *Journal of Finance* (December 1980).

JENSEN, M. C., *Studies in the Theory of Capital Markets*. New York: Praeger, 1972a.

————, "Capital Markets: Theory and Evidence," *Bell Journal of Economics and Management Science* (Autumn 1972b).

KRAUS, A., and R. H. LITZENBERGER, "Market Equilibrium in a Multiperiod State Preference Model with Logarithmic Utility," *Journal of Finance* (December 1975).

————, "Skewedness Preference and the Valuation of Risk Assets," *Journal of Finance* (September 1976).

LEE, C. F., "Investment Horizon and the Functional Form of the Capital Asset Pricing Model," *Review of Economics and Statistics* (August 1976).

LEROY, S. F., "Expectations Models of Asset Prices: A Survey of Theory," *Journal of Finance* (March 1982).

LEVY, H., "The Capital Asset Pricing Model: Theory and Empiricism," *Economic Journal* (March 1983).

LINTNER, J., "The Valuation of Risk Assets and the Selection of Risky Investments in Stock Portfolios and Capital Budgets," *Review of Economics and Statistics* (February 1965a).

————, "Security Prices, Risk, and Maximal Gains from Diversification," *Journal of Finance* (December 1965b).

————, "The Aggregation of Investors' Diverse Judgments and Preferences in Purely

Competitive Security Markets," *Journal of Financial and Quantitative Analysis* (December 1970).

MOSSIN, J., "Equilibrium in a Capital Market," *Econometrica* (October 1966).

MULLINS, D. W., "Does the Capital Asset Pricing Model Work?" *Harvard Business Review* (January/February 1982).

REINGANUM, M. R., "A New Empirical Perspective on the Capital Asset Pricing Model," *Journal of Financial and Quantitative Analysis* (November 1981).

ROLL, R., "A Critique of the Asset Pricing Theory's Tests: Part I: On the Past and Potential Testability of the Theory," *Journal of Financial Economics* (March 1977).

———, "Ambiguity When Performance Is Measured by the Security Market Line," *Journal of Finance* (September 1978).

ROSS, S. A., "The Capital Asset Pricing Model (CAPM), Short Sale Restrictions and Related Issues," *Journal of Finance* (March 1977).

———, "The Current Status of the Capital Asset Pricing Model (CAPM)," *Journal of Finance* (June 1978).

SHARPE, W. F., "Capital Asset Prices: A Theory of Market Equilibrium," *Journal of Finance* (September 1964).

STAMBOUGH, R., "On the Exclusion of Assets from Tests of the Two-Parameter Model," *Journal of Financial Economics* (November 1982).

TOBIN, J., "Liquidity Preference as Behavior Towards Risk," *Review of Economic Studies* (February 1958).

TREYNOR, J. L., "Toward a Theory of Market Value of Risky Assets," unpublished manuscript, 1961.

VASICEK, O., "Capital Asset Pricing Model with No Riskless Borrowing," unpublished manuscript, Wells Fargo Bank, March 1971.

WESTON, J. F., "Investment Decisions Using the Capital Asset Pricing Model," *Financial Management* (Spring 1973).

WILLIAMS, J. T., "Capital Asset Prices with Heterogeneous Beliefs," *Journal of Financial Economics* (November 1977).

7

THE ARBITRAGE PRICING THEORY

Introduction

The empirical problems with the Capital Asset Pricing Model have stimulated interest in an alternative model of asset pricing called the Arbitrage Pricing Theory (APT), which was first introduced by Ross (1976). Proponents of the APT argue that it has two major advantages over the CAPM. First, it makes assumptions regarding investors' preferences toward risk and return that some would argue are less restrictive. Recall that one of the assumptions of the CAPM is that investors can choose between alternative portfolio investments only on the basis of expected return and standard deviation. While the APT does place some restrictions on the preferences of investors, they are less restrictive. Second, APT proponents argue that the model can be refuted or verified empirically. As we shall see, this point of view has been the subject of much dispute, but to many the testability of APT is still an open question.

DERIVING THE ARBITRAGE PRICING THEORY

The fundamental assumption of the APT is that security returns are generated by a process identical to the index models discussed in Chapter 5. We assume that the correlations between security returns can be attributed to the securities' response, to one degree or another, to the pull of one or more factors. We don't have to specify exactly what these factors are, but we do assume that the relationship between the security returns and the factors is linear, as in the case of a multi-index model. Thus, the rate of return to stock J in any given period t is assumed to be given by

$$r_{J,t} = A_J + \beta_{1,J}I_{1,t} + \beta_{2,J}I_{2,t} + \ldots + \beta_{n,J}I_{n,t} + \epsilon_{J,t} \qquad (7\text{--}1)$$

where I represents the value of any one of the factors that affect the rate of return to the stock. The number of factors is equal to n. Actually, the number of factors is unimportant to the theory (except we need to assume that there are many more securities than there are factors), although it may be important to empirical implementation of the theory. The intercept term, A, should be interpreted as it was before, in the context of the multi-index model. It is the expected rate of return on the stock, conditioned on the fact that all of the indices take on a zero value (have no impact on the stock) during the period. The individual betas, β, measure the responsiveness of security return to changes in the indices. The betas can be positive or negative from factor to factor and from stock to stock. The term ϵ is a residual or shock term that is induced by the incidence of an event that affects only the individual firm.

Because it is assumed that all of the covariances between the rates of return to the securities are attributable to the effect of the factors, the residual term, ϵ, will be uncorrelated between companies. Given this, the residual variance for any portfolio of individual securities is given by the familiar expression

$$\sigma^2_{\epsilon,P} = \sum_{J=1}^{M} x_J^2 \, \sigma^2_{\epsilon,J} \qquad (7\text{--}2)$$

Moreover, the variance of portfolio return is given by the formula for portfolio variance under the multi-index model,[1] where $\sigma^2 I$ is the index variance:

$$\sigma^2 r_P = \beta^2_{1,P} \, \sigma^2 I_1 + \beta^2_{2,P} \, \sigma^2 I_2 + \ldots + \beta^2_{n,P} \, \sigma^2 I_n + \sigma^2_{\epsilon,P} \qquad (7\text{--}3)$$

| Total portfolio variance | = | Portfolio factor systematic risks | + | Portfolio residual variance |

And, as with the multi-index model, the portfolio's beta with respect to any one of the factors is a simple weighted average of the betas of the securities in the portfolio:

$$\beta_{1,P} = \sum_{J=1}^{M} x_J \, \beta_{1,J}$$

In addition to imposing the above constraints on the process generating security returns, we will make the additional assumptions that the number of secu-

---

[1]Actually, this equation assumes that the covariance among the factors is equal to zero. This is not a necessary assumption for the APT. Even with nonzero covariances among the factors, although the equation below will have some additional terms relating to factor covariances, these terms will all drop out for zero beta portfolios, leaving the variance of the portfolios equal to the residual variance.

rities in the market is infinite and that there are no restrictions on short selling. Given these assumptions, we can derive the approximate relationship between expected return and risk under the APT.

To derive the APT risk-return relationship, suppose, first, that a single factor can explain all the covariances that exist among stocks. What will the relationship between the expected rate of return to stocks and their responsiveness, β, to the factor look like? Suppose it looks like the nonlinear relationship in Figure 7–1. It is easy to show that such a nonlinear relationship is infeasible, given the assumptions made thus far. If the relationship looked like that in Figure 7–1, all of us could make unlimited sums of money with no required investment and no assumed risk.

There are an infinite number of securities scattered along the curved line in Figure 7–1. Six of these securities are labeled at points A, B, C, D, E, and F. Because both portfolio beta and expected portfolio return are simple weighted averages of the betas and expected rates of return of the securities in the portfolio, combination lines can be drawn as straight lines passing through the points on the graph. Thus, the combination line for stocks C and E is given by the line passing through points $E(r_Z')$, C, and E. Positions between C and E are taken by investing positive amounts of money in both stocks. Positions between $E(r_Z')$ and C are taken by selling short stock E and using the proceeds to invest in stock C.

Note that by selling short stock E and investing in C, I can construct a portfolio positioned on the graph at point $E(r_Z')$. The beta of this portfolio is equal to zero. I have assumed the position at $E(r_Z')$ by using two stocks, C and E, but

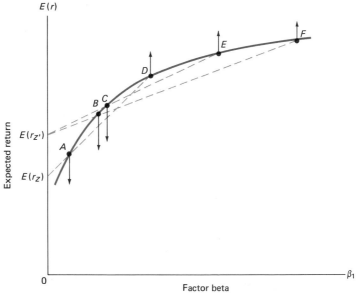

Figure 7-1 An Infeasible Relationship Between $E(r_J)$ and β_1 in a One-Factor Model

I could have also assumed it by using four, shorting stocks E and F and using the proceeds to invest in stocks C and B. In fact, I can assume a position at $E(r_Z')$ by using as many pairs of stocks as I want. Because there is an infinite number of securities scattered along the line, I can use an infinite number of pairs to assume the position. If I do, the portfolio will have a zero variance. This is true because its beta is zero by construction, and its residual variance is zero on the basis of Equation (7–2). Because M is equal to infinity, the individual portfolio weights are so small that when we square them, in taking the weighted average, the residual variance sums to zero.

The portfolio has no systematic risk and no residual variance, but it has a (riskless) expected rate of return equal to $E(r_Z')$.

Note that I can construct still another portfolio positioned at $E(r_Z)$ by selling short stock D and investing in stock A. Again, by employing an infinite number of pairs of stocks, I can construct a portfolio positioned at $E(r_Z)$ with no systematic risk or residual variance.

I have constructed two zero variance, or riskless, portfolios with two different expected rates of return. A position in either portfolio requires a positive capital commitment, but we can take a position in both portfolios with no capital commitment at all. We can do this by selling short a given amount of the portfolio positioned at $E(r_Z)$ and using the proceeds (with no equity investment of our own) to invest in the portfolio positioned at $E(r_Z')$.

Assume that $E(r_Z) = 10$ percent and $E(r_Z') = 14$ percent; we sell short \$1 million of the 10 percent portfolio and use the proceeds to invest in the 14 percent portfolio. The certain loss in the short sale of the 10 percent portfolio is

$$10\% \times -\$1,000,000 = -\$100,000$$

and the certain gain on the investment in the 14 percent portfolio is

$$14\% \times \$1,000,000 = \$140,000$$

The difference of \$40,000 is a pure and riskless profit, which is available to us all. Because there are no assumed restrictions on short sales, we can become as rich as we please!

Needless to say, we'll all be trying to take advantage of this opportunity, selling short stocks like D, E, and F and buying stocks like A, B, and C. In our attempts to make money, we will drive down the prices of stocks D, E, and F and drive up their expected rates of return. In the same sense, our buying activity will drive up the prices of stocks A, B, and C and drive down their expected rates of return in the direction indicated by the arrows in Figure 7–1.

The effect of all this will be to ''unbend'' the line until the general relationship between expected return and factor risk becomes linear, as in Figure 7–2. Given this particular relationship, any riskless portfolio we construct with any of the stocks will always have the same expected return, $E(r_Z)$. Pure, riskless arbitrage opportunities are unavailable when the general relationship between expected return and factor risk is linear, as it is in Figure 7–2.

Thus, in a single factor APT the relationship between factor risk and expected rates of return is given by

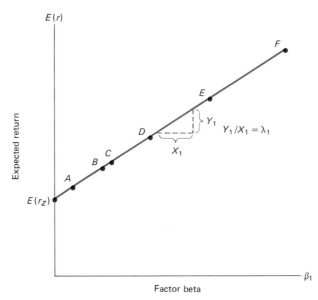

Figure 7-2 The Feasible Relationship Between $E(r_J)$ and β_j

$$
\begin{array}{ccccccc}
E(r_J) & \approx & E(r_Z) & + & \lambda_1 & \times & \beta_{1,J} \\
\text{Expected return} & \approx & \text{Risk-free} & + & \text{Factor} & \times & \text{Factor} \\
 & & \text{rate} & & \text{price} & & \text{beta}
\end{array}
$$

$$\underbrace{\text{Risk premium}}$$

The expression is written as an approximation, because, although the general relationship between factor risk and expected return will be linear, there still may be individual deviations, as long as there aren't a sufficient number of them to open up riskless arbitrage opportunities.

In the approximation, λ_1 is the slope of the relationship between factor risk and expected return. The magnitude of the slope depends on how risk averse investors are and how important they regard the factor as a source of stock variability. If there is more than one factor, some factors may not be priced, and in this case the slope will be zero. From time to time we will refer to the slope of the relationship between the factor beta and the expected rate of return as the factor price.

Let's add a second factor to the model, assuming that the covariances between the returns on securities are attributable to the fact that the returns respond to two factors. Again, what will be the feasible relationship between factor risk and expected rates of return?

Suppose the relationship is given by the curved, three-dimensional surface of Figure 7–3. Again, we assume that an infinite number of securities are distributed over the surface. In the figure expected return increases with the degree of responsiveness of a security's return to each of the two factors. However, ex-

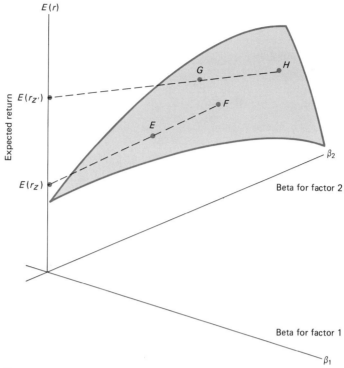

Figure 7-3 An Infeasible Relationship Between $E(r_j)$ and $\beta_{1,J}$ and $\beta_{2,J}$ in a Two-Factor Model

pected return increases at a decreasing rate. Given this nonlinear relationship between factor risk and expected return, we can again create riskless arbitrage opportunities that promise unlimited wealth. By selling short securities like H and using the proceeds to invest in securities like G, we can create a zero beta position for *both* factors with an expected return equal to $E(r_z')$. By doing this with an infinite number of pairs of securities, we can drive the variance of our zero beta portfolio to zero.

To see this, imagine yourself sitting at $E(r_z')$ with a laser gun. By pointing the gun in different directions, you can fire beams such that they pass through two points on the curved surface. The securities positioned at the two points can be combined to achieve a position at $E(r_z')$. At the same time, by short selling securities like F and investing in securities like E, we can construct a zero beta, zero variance portfolio with an expected return equal to $E(r_z)$. We then short sell the portfolio with the lower expected return and use the proceeds to invest in the higher return portfolio. Our arbitrage profit is equal to the difference in expected return multiplied by the dollar amount we sold short. Because it is assumed that we can short sell in unlimited amounts, we can create unlimited amounts of wealth for ourselves in this manner.

In short selling securities like F and H and buying securities like E and G, investors will affect prices and expected rates of return, thus unbending the surface and making it into a linear plane like that in Figure 7–4. Given a linear relationship between expected return and the factor risks, no arbitrage opportunities are available. All zero beta portfolios have the same expected rate of return, $E(r_Z)$.

The equation for the risk-expected return relationship is now given by the approximation for the plane:

$$E(r_J) \approx E(r_Z) + \lambda_1 \times \beta_{1,J} + \lambda_2 \times \beta_{2,J} \qquad (7\text{–}4)$$

| Expected return | $\approx$ Risk-free rate | + Factor 1 price | × Factor 1 beta | + Factor 2 price | × Factor 2 beta |

$$\underbrace{\hspace{7cm}}_{\text{Risk premium}}$$

In the approximation the coefficients λ_1 and λ_2 represent the factor prices, given in Figure 7–4 by

$$\lambda_1 = Y_1/X_1$$
$$\lambda_2 = Y_2/X_2$$

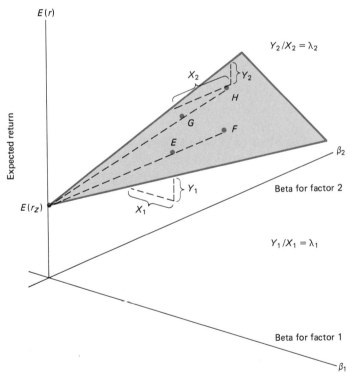

Figure 7-4 A Feasible Relationship Between Expected Return and Factor Risk in a Two-Factor Model

In the figure both coefficients are positive, but they need not be. In a multifactor model many of the coefficients can be negative as well as positive.

Beyond two factors are the multidimensional hyperplanes, which are impossible to visualize. Nevertheless, it is still the case that, unless the relationship between factor risks and expected returns is approximately linear, unlimited arbitrage opportunities may become available. This is the central message of the APT. If security returns are generated by a process equivalent to that of a linear multifactor model, the relationship between expected return and factor risk must be approximately linear.

In the context of the APT, it is impossible to construct two different portfolios, both having zero variance, with two different expected rates of return. This will be the case if the relationship between the factor betas and the expected rates of return is linear. It will not be the case if the relationship is generally nonlinear—as in the examples cited above. As we have stressed, the absence of arbitrage opportunities doesn't ensure *exact* linear pricing, however. We may have a few securities positioned above and below the plane of Figure 7–4, for example. Because their number is fewer than required to drive the residual variance of the portfolio to zero, we no longer have a riskless arbitrage opportunity. Although the linear relationship prices most assets with negligible error, it can be highly inaccurate in pricing some of them.

EMPIRICAL TESTS OF THE APT

Initial Empirical Tests

An initial empirical test of the APT was conducted by Roll and Ross (RR) (1980). Their methodology was, in a sense, similar to that used by Black, Jensen, and Scholes (BJS) in testing the CAPM. They estimated first the factor betas for securities and then the cross-sectional relationship between security betas and average rates of return.

RR estimated the factor betas using a statistical technique called factor analysis. The input to factor analysis is the covariance matrix among the returns to the securities in the sample. Factor analysis determines the set of factor betas that best explains the covariances among the securities in the sample.

In a single factor model, the covariance between the rates of return on any two stocks is assumed to be given by the product of (a) the factor beta for the first stock, (b) the factor beta for the second stock, and (c) the variance of the factor. In a multifactor model the covariance is assumed to be given by the sum of a series of such products, one for each of the factors.

$$\text{Cov}(r_J, r_K) = \beta_{1,J}\beta_{1,K}\sigma^2 I_1 + \beta_{2,J}\beta_{2,K}\sigma^2 I_2 + \ldots + \beta_{n,J}\beta_{n,K}\sigma^2 I_n$$

Factor analysis makes the working assumption that the individual factor variances are equal to 1.00, and then it finds that set of factor betas for each stock

OUT ON THE STREET

A "Defensive" Strategy

"Yes, as indicated in the report, our analysis is telling us that these are the stocks and this is the portfolio that will maximize your performance, given your projected increase in defense spending. On the basis of our model, these stocks show great sensitivity to unanticipated changes in real, inflation-adjusted, defense spending. If, as you project, defense spending increases rapidly during the next four years, these stocks should, as a group, produce very attractive rates of return."

Michelle Clayman is talking on the phone to one of Salomon Brothers' many institutional clients. Michelle is a vice president in the stock research department of Saloman Brothers. She works in an area called Strategy Systems, which is a quantitative research group consisting of five people.

Michelle's office is on the fortieth floor of a building located at the southernmost tip of Manhattan. The view from her office is spectacular, overlooking Governors Island and the Statue of Liberty. Michelle spends much of her time talking to the many investors across the country who manage literally billions of dollars with the aid of quantitative models developed by the Strategy Systems group.

This morning she is discussing the Fundamental Factor Model with a client on the West Coast. The model works in the context of the multifactor process that generates returns in the Arbitrage Pricing Model. The model breaks the systematic risk of a stock into components deriving from five basic factors. The five factors are unexpected changes in

1. The rate of growth in real gross national product
2. The rate of inflation
3. The real rate of interest
4. The rate of change in real oil prices
5. The rate of growth in real defense spending

Salomon Brothers has an interesting and unique method of determining the responsiveness of stocks to these factors. Rather than estimate the factor betas through factor analysis or time series regression, it employs a type of sensitivity analysis. The sensitivity analysis is based on a sophisticated input-output model of the U.S. economy. Given inputs relating to housing starts or retail automobile sales, for example, the input-output model is capable of estimating intermediate demands for such products as plastics, glass, aluminum, and steel. In fact, given what is called a "base case forecast" for the general economy provided by Salomon Brothers' economists, the input-output model can provide disaggregated forecasts for different sectors of the economy over the next five years. Based on the model, estimates can be obtained of the impact of various macroeconomic changes on accounting statements at the individual firm level.

The factor betas are estimated as the product of two elasticities. The first measures the expected change in the rate of growth in earnings per share accompanying a given change in one of the factors. This elasticity is estimated through the input-output model by observing the estimated change in the earnings per share for a given firm accompanying a change in one of the factors. The second elasticity measures the expected change in the price accompanying a given change in the rate of growth in earnings per share. This second elasticity is estimated on the basis of the *duration* of the dividend stream for the stock. Duration will be discussed in more detail later in the book. You can think of it as a measure of the average period of time before the dividends in the stream are expected to be paid. Under certain assumptions, duration also serves as a measure of the expected response of the stock price to changes in either the rate at which dividends are capitalized to a present value or the rate at which they are expected to grow.

When the two elasticities—response of earnings growth to the factor and response of the stock price to the change in earnings growth—are multiplied together, the product can be taken as the factor beta, depicting the expected change in the stock price accompanying a change in the factor.

Salomon Brothers has back-tested the model and has found that in periods where there are large, unanticipated changes in the factors, relative rates of return on individual stocks can be successfully predicted on the basis of the estimated factor betas.

Salomon Brothers uses a Fundamental Factor Model for three types of applications. First, the model is useful for the managers of index-type funds. These managers try to build a portfolio that mimics as closely as possible the performance of a stock index, like the Standard and Poor's 500. In using the model, the first step is to estimate the factor betas for the component stocks in the 500 and then set up an indexed portfolio that has a factor beta structure that is as close as possible to that of the 500. In this way the indexed portfolio will mimic the responses of the 500 to changes in the factors that occur over time.

Second, the model can be used to position clients best to take advantage of their forecasts for changes in the macroeconomic climate. Suppose, for example, a portfolio manager is predicting a sharp increase in gross national product. The model can isolate those stocks that can be expected to show the greatest price appreciation, should the prediction regarding the growth in GNP materialize. At this moment, Michelle is using the model in this very way to advise her client on the optimal strategy to take advantage of a forecast of a rapid increase in defense spending.

Finally, Michelle's group is currently developing a portfolio optimizer that will estimate an efficient set of portfolios, based on the multi-index model. The variances and covariances among individual securities can be estimated on the basis of the factor betas and the estimates of the factor variances. Expected rates of return on individual securities can be estimated on the basis of joint forecasts of changes in the various factors made by Saloman Brothers and the clients themselves. Given expected rates of return and the covariance matrix, the efficient set can be easily calculated.

that will make the covariances among the stocks correspond as closely as possible to the sample covariances, as computed directly from the returns. The program continues to add additional factors until the probability that the next portfolio explains a significant fraction of the covariances between stocks goes below some predetermined level.

After estimates of the factor betas are obtained, the next step is to estimate the value of the factor price, λ, associated with each factor. This is done by cross-sectionally relating the factor betas to average returns, using a procedure similar to that used by BJS for market betas.

Because of its complexity, factor analysis can only be employed on a relatively small number of stocks at a time. RR applied the analysis to forty-two groups of thirty stocks in the period July 1962 through December 1972. They found that four or possibly five different factors have significant explanatory power. Moreover, they found that the residual variance of securities is unrelated to average returns.

The APT would predict that the estimates of the intercept term, $E(r_Z)$, and the values for the λ's should be the same for each sample tested. In a later study, Brown and Weinstein (1983) tested this prediction and found ambiguous results. At this point, it is safe to say empirical testing of the APT is at an early stage of development, and there is no conclusive evidence either supporting or contradicting the model.

Is APT Testable in Principle?

Several authors have raised the issue of the testability of the APT. One problem is the necessity of conducting the factor analysis on relatively small samples of firms. Dhrymes, Friend, and Gultekin (DFG) (1984) found that as the number of securities in the factor analysis increases from fifteen to sixty, the number of significant factors increases from three to seven. As Roll and Ross (1984) point out, however, there are many reasons why we should expect this to happen. In any group, say, thirty stocks, there may be only one cosmetics company. You would not likely find a "cosmetics factor" until you expanded your sample to include more cosmetics companies. They argue that this does not necessarily mean that conducting the tests on small samples is inappropriate, because, unless the factors are pervasive they can be diversified away, and they will not be priced. As such, they are not of interest in testing the theory.

DFG also found that the conclusion as to whether the intercept term is the same or different across different samples depends on the way you group the stocks. In a later paper Dhrymes, Friend, Gultekin, and Gultekin (1984) found that the number of "priced" factors is also dependent on the number of observations in the time series, and the number of "priced" factors increases with the number of securities factor analyzed.

Overall, these initial empirical results indicate that the APT may be difficult to test by factor analysis.

As an alternative to using factor analysis to test the APT, you can hypothesize that a given set of *specified* factors explain the covariance matrix among securities. In this approach, you can use large samples to estimate the factor betas and the factor prices (the λ's). In employing this procedure, Chen, Roll, and Ross (1983) have determined that a large fraction of the covariances among securities can be explained on the basis of unanticipated changes in four specified factors:

1. The difference between the yield on a long-term and a short-term treasury bond.

2. The rate of inflation

3. The difference between the yields on BB rated corporate bonds and treasury bonds

4. The growth rate in industrial production

Shanken (1982) has raised an even more serious issue about the testability of the APT. He argues that the shares of stock traded in the marketplace are actually portfolios of the individual units of production in the economy. These portfolios were created through merger and by the adoption of multiple capital budgeting projects by individual firms. Consequently, given a factor structure that explains the covariances among the returns to the individual units of production, we may not be able to recognize it on the basis of the portfolios (the stocks traded in the marketplace).

His point is easy to understand if we suppose a double factor APT is in effect, and both factors are priced. Assume that the stocks in our example are issued by firms that put together portfolios of capital budgeting projects. They may have even merged with other firms in the past. Conceivably, they could disassemble themselves by spinning off divisions or by merging in whole or in part with other firms. They could even reorganize themselves into "portfolios" such that their factor betas were all zero. What would happen to our test of the APT if the firms assembled themselves in this way? We know, in truth, that there are two factors and they are priced, in the sense that they affect expected rates of return. However, if we do a factor analysis on the reorganized firms in our example, we will find their returns are totally uncorrelated, and conclude falsely that there are no factors that are priced. It appears we cannot reject the APT on the basis of such a test, because we can never observe the covariance matrix for the basic units of production in the economy. We can only observe "portfolios" of production units put together on the basis of capital budgeting and merger decisions.

The fact that we can only observe such portfolios may lead us falsely to reject the APT. Suppose, again, that we have a two-factor structure with two different factor prices. We test the theory by doing a factor analysis with two separate samples. In the first sample the firms have combined in such a way that their betas with respect to the *first* factor are zero. The firms in the second sample have combined to make their *second* factor betas equal to zero. In running a factor analysis in each sample, you will conclude that there is only one factor. Moreover, when you relate factor betas to average returns, you will conclude that the pricing of the factor is different as between the two samples. You will incorrectly reject the APT because you, unknowingly, are observing two different factors at work in each of the two samples.

The testability of APT can be called into question in another sense. As was mentioned above, as the number of companies factor analyzed is increased, the number of factors that you find explaining the covariance matrix of returns increases as well. Suppose you take two groups of fifty stocks, factor analyze each one, find four factors in each, and then look at the cross-sectional relationships between average return and factor betas in each. You find that the risk-free rates are different in each. You then announce that you have evidence rejecting the APT. I can now object by saying that there are missing variables in your cross-sectional regressions. The missing variables are the betas for the factors that you have failed to capture due to your relatively small sample size of fifty. The variables that are missing may well differ, as between the two samples, accounting for the different risk-free rates of return in the two samples.

You react to my criticism by obtaining more variables by increasing the sample size to 100. You find more factors, but still different risk-free rates of return. You claim you have rejected the APT, and I again object, claiming missing variables. We are in a bind similar to the one we were in with the CAPM. With the CAPM even the best proxies are only a small fraction of the true market portfolio. With the APT, even if you increase the sample size to the limits imposed by computing technology, given the requirements of factor analysis, your sample is only a small fraction of the total number of production units in the international economic system. Differences in factor prices and intercepts among samples can always be attributed to missing factors not captured because of small sample size. Moreover, this theory doesn't tell us the number of factors we should expect to see or the names for any of the factors. Consequently, I can always say that the number of factors priced by the market is greater than the number you have estimated.

You may feel more comfortable if you find that the number of priced factors increases at a decreasing rate as the sample size increases. This might imply that there may be a point beyond which increasing the sample size will have little impact on your empirical results. Keep in mind, however, that just as any market proxy falls far short of the true market portfolio, any sample size you can factor analyze falls far short of the total international population of production units. The number of priced factors may increase at a decreasing rate over the first hundred units, but you won't be able to tell what happens over the next thousand units.

Summary

The Capital Asset Pricing Model is intuitively pleasing, but it isn't testable. The Arbitrage Pricing Theory has been suggested as a testable alternative. It captures some of the intuition of the CAPM (that only nondiversifiable risk affects expected security returns); but, although testing it may be an extremely hazardous business at best, its testability, at least in principle, is still an open question.

The APT assumes that security returns are produced by a process identical to a linear single or multi-index model. In the presence of such a return-generating process, the relationship between expected return and factor risk(s) must be approximately linear.

Thus far, empirical tests of the APT have produced inconclusive results. It appears that an extensive number of factors account for the covariances that exist among securities. There is some evidence that these factors affect the prices that investors are willing to pay for securities. In some studies pricing seems to be consistent across different samples; in others, it is not. The empirical results appear to be highly dependent on the methodology employed in the tests.

In one important respect both models exhibit a similar vulnerability. With both models we are looking for a benchmark for purposes of comparing the *ex-post* performance of portfolio managers and the *ex-anti* returns on real and financial investments. In the case of CAPM we can never determine the extent to which deviations from the securities market line benchmark are due to something real or are due to the obvious inadequacies in our proxies for the market portfolio. In the case of APT, because the theory gives us no direction as to the choice of factors, we cannot determine whether deviations from an APT benchmark are due to something real or are merely due to inadequacies in our choice of factors.

QUESTIONS AND PROBLEMS

1. Suppose that three factors were sufficient to account for the covariances between stock returns. A large portfolio (with n stocks) has been formed. You have already computed the factor betas for each of the component stocks in the portfolio.

   a. How would you use the above information to compute the factor betas for the portfolio?

   b. How would you represent the portfolio variance (using the factor betas for the portfolio), assuming that (i) the residual variance of the portfolio has been "diversified" to zero and that (ii) the covariance between any pair of factors is zero?

2. What do we mean by a "riskless arbitrage opportunity"?

3.

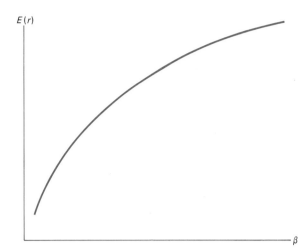

Suppose asset returns were described by the relationship in the accompanying figure (from a one-factor model).

a. Why would such a relationship open up the possibility of riskless arbitrage?

b. What qualifications to part a are required?

4. Assume that a two-factor APT model is appropriate and that there are an infinite number of assets in the economy. The cross-sectional relationship between expected return and factor betas indicates that the price of factor 1 is .15 and the price of factor 2 is − .2. You have estimated factor betas for stocks X and Y as follows:

	β_1	β_2
Stock X	1.4	.4
Stock Y	.9	.2

Also, the expected return on an asset having zero betas (with respect to both factors) is .05. According to the APT, what are the approximate equilibrium returns on each of the two stocks?

5. You have concluded that a two-factor APT model is appropriate and the cross-sectional relationship between return and each factor is as indicated in the accompanying figures.

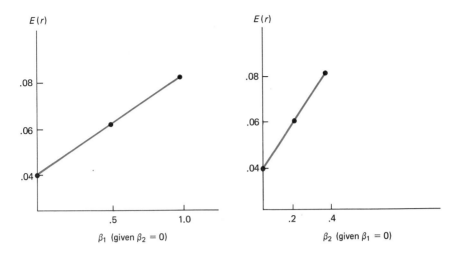

What should the equilibrium return be on an asset having $\beta_1 = .75$ and $\beta_2 = .5$?

6. Assume a three-factor APT model and that there are an infinite number of assets. The expected return on a portfolio with zero beta values is 5 percent. You are interested in an equally weighted portfolio of two stocks, A and B. The factor prices are indicated below, along with the factor betas for A and B. Compute the approximate expected return of the portfolio.

Factor i	β_{iA}	β_{iB}	Factor Prices
1	.3	.5	.07
2	.2	.6	.09
3	1.0	.7	.02

7. What was the finding of Dhrymes, Friend, and Gultekin concerning the number of factors that were significant in explaining returns?

8. The APT expected return relationship looks much like the security market line that was derived in the Capital Asset Pricing Model. How would one discriminate between the APT and the CAPM?

9. With regard to the number of different factors that are priced:

a. What do the *theoretical* results in the APT say about the number of factors?

b. What did the empirical evidence of Roll and Ross indicate about the number of factors?

10. Suppose that two factors have been deemed appropriate to "explain" returns on stocks and that the covariance between the factors is zero. Based on the information in the table on two stocks, X and Y, and the two factors, 1 and 2, what is the variance of a portfolio consisting of $1000 invested in X and $2000 invested in Y?

	Beta (factor 1)	Beta (factor 2)	Residual Variance
Stock X	1.1	.5	.02
Stock Y	.2	.8	.05

Variance of factor 1 = .15
Variance of factor 2 = .10

11. Assume a one-factor APT model having the expected return-beta relationship shown in the accompanying figure.

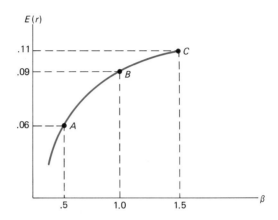

a. Find a portfolio of A and C that would result in a beta of zero. What is the expected return on this portfolio?

b. Find a portfolio of B and C that would result in a beta of zero. What is the return on this portfolio?

c. What action would be suggested by your answers to parts a and b?

BIBLIOGRAPHY

BROWN, S. J., and M. I. WEINSTEIN, "A New Approach to Testing Asset Pricing Models: The Bilinear Paradigm," *Journal of Finance* (June 1983).

CHEN, N. F., "Some Empirical Tests of the Theory of Arbitrage Pricing," *Journal of Finance* (December 1983).

CHEN, N. F., R. ROLL, and S. ROSS, "Economic Forces and the Stock Market," unpublished manuscript, Yale University, 1983.

CHO, D. C., E. J. ELTON, and M. J. GRUBER, "On the Robustness of the Roll and Ross APT Methodology," *Journal of Financial and Quantitative Analysis* (March 1984).

CONNOR, G., "A Factor Pricing Theory for Capital Assets," Working Paper, Northwestern University, 1983.

DHRYMES, P., I. FRIEND, and N. GULTEKIN, "A Critical Reexamination of the Empirical Evidence on the Arbitrage Pricing Theory," *Journal of Finance* (June 1984).

DHRYMES, P., I. FRIEND, N. GULTEKIN, and M. GULTEKIN, "New Tests of the APT and Their Implications," Working Paper, Wharton School of Finance, July 1984.

JOBSON, J. D., "A Multivariate Linear Regression Test for the Arbitrage Pricing Theory," *Journal of Finance* (September 1982).

KRYZANOWSKI, L., and T. CHAU, "General Factor Models and the Structure of Security Returns," *Journal of Financial and Quantitative Analysis* (March 1983).

MORRISON, D. F., *Multivariate Statistical Methods*. New York: McGraw-Hill, 1976.

REINGANUM, M. R., "The Arbitrage Pricing Theory: Some Empirical Results," *Journal of Finance* (May 1981).

ROLL, R., and S. A. ROSS, "An Empirical Investigation of the Arbitrage Pricing Theory," *Journal of Finance* (December 1980).

———, "A Critical Reexamination of the Empirical Evidence on the Arbitrage Pricing Theory: A Reply," *Journal of Finance* (June 1984).

ROSS, S. A., "The Arbitrage Theory of Capital Asset Pricing," *Journal of Economic Theory* (December 1976).

———, "Return, Risk and Arbitrage," in *Risk and Return in Finance,* vol. 1, ed. Irwin Friend and James L. Bicksler. Cambridge, Mass.: Ballinger, 1977.

SHANKEN, J., "The Arbitrage Pricing Theory: Is It Testable?" *Journal of Finance* (December 1982).

8

MEASURING PORTFOLIO PERFORMANCE

Introduction

In this chapter we will learn how to measure the performance of a portfolio manager. Presumably, skillful managers have access to information that the public at large doesn't have. They get this information by probing private sources, or they may create private information by analyzing public information using proprietary models and techniques. In any case, they know more than the average investor, and on the basis of their knowledge, they can find the most profitable investments.

Skillful managers should tend to produce relatively high rates of return for their portfolios. However, how do we discriminate between a manager who is truly skillful and one who has been merely lucky? How do we discriminate between skillful managers and ones who produce high returns merely because they capture the expected risk premiums in the equilibrium returns on their high-risk investments?

The performance measures discussed in this chapter will help us discriminate among those who have skill, those who are lucky, and those who earn higher returns merely because they take risks. These measures are widely used in the securities market. Billions of dollars are actually shifted from investment firm to investment firm, because some get higher marks on the basis of these measures than do others. Someday you may win or lose accounts on the basis of *your* marks. You may even be promoted or demoted because of them. Thus, it is imperative that you understand how the performance measures work and their relative strengths and weaknesses.

Why can't we measure performance on the basis of the rate of return produced by a portfolio? Perhaps you have seen rankings of mutual funds in financial magazines. The rankings are usually based on the rates of return produced by the funds in the preceding year. Sometimes the funds are ranked on the basis of their average rate of return over several preceding years. You have to be very careful in interpreting rankings based purely on the rate of return for a single year, or even average rate of return over a number of different years. The funds may be ranked by their rate of return, but it is highly unlikely that these rankings even roughly correspond to rankings based on the skill level of the portfolio managers. In fact, the position of a portfolio in a ranking based on rate of return is more likely to depend on (a) the target risk level of the portfolio and (b) the performance of the market than it does on (c) the skill level of the portfolio manager.

To understand this, consider the two mutual funds in Table 8–1. In each of the eleven years the two funds are ranked by their rate of return. Note how the rankings flip-flop from year to year. Surely the relative skill of the funds' management isn't changing in such a volatile way. The real reason behind the instability in the rankings is because the beta factors for the two funds are very different, and the performance of the market is changing dramatically from year to year, causing them to respond differently to changes in the return to the market portfolio. If one has a higher than average beta and the other a lower than average beta, their characteristic lines may plot as in Figure 8–1.

Assume, for simplicity, that investors are risk neutral, and the two characteristic lines intersect at a point on the graph that is positioned directly over the expected return to the market. This being the case, both mutual funds will have the same expected rate of return, $E(r_P)$. Although their *expected* returns are the same, their *realized* returns will nearly always be different. In a bear market—when the market produces a rate of return that is less than expected, like r_M—the fund with the lower beta will produce the greater rate of return and will rank first. In a bull market—when the market's return is greater than expected, like $r_M{}^*$—the higher beta fund will rank on top. The relative returns, and the rankings based on them, are highly dependent on market performance and relative beta. In fact, they are so dependent on these factors that they are almost useless for judging the relative skill of the managers.

We need a measure of performance that is insensitive to relative risk and the

Table 8–1 Rankings of Two Mutual Funds Based on Rate of Return in Each Year

	1984	83	82	81	80	Year 79	78	77	76	75	74
Nicholas Fund	1	2	1	1	2	2	1	1	2	1	2
Omega Fund	2	1	2	2	1	1	2	2	1	2	1

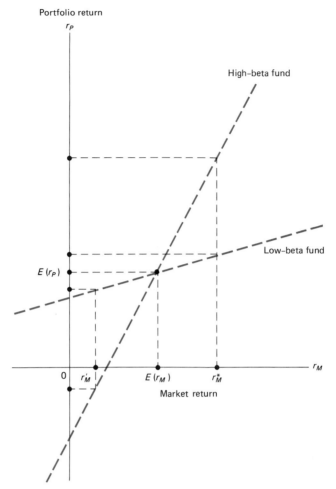

Portfolio return

r_P

High–beta fund

Low–beta fund

$E(r_P)$

r_M' 0 $E(r_M)$ r_M^* r_M

Market return

Figure 8-1   Characteristic Lines of a High and Low Beta Fund

strength of the market. Such a measure will adjust the portfolio's return by the amount that is attributable to the relative risk of the portfolio, given the strength of the market in the period that performance is evaluated. A risk-adjusted measure of performance should be insensitive to the risk of a portfolio. That is, in using such a measure, there should be no propensity for portfolios with unusually high or low levels of risk to earn unusually high or low marks, irrespective of the performance of the market.

In constructing a risk-adjusted performance measure, you have to make assumptions about the nature of risk and the relationship between return and risk. You have to assume that stocks are priced according to some asset pricing model, such as the CAPM and the APT.

RISK-ADJUSTED PERFORMANCE MEASURES
BASED ON THE CAPITAL ASSET PRICING MODEL

Let's assume that for the set of information relevant to the valuation of any given stock, we can divide the information into two parts, public information, which is freely available to everyone, and private information, which is available to only select individuals, possibly at some cost. Assume, also, that stock prices are established only on the basis of publicly available information and that the pricing structure is that of the standard CAPM where both borrowing and lending at a risk-free rate are permitted. This implies that if we were to estimate expected returns, variances, and covariances, based on a thorough analysis of publicly available information alone, we would see every stock and portfolio positioned on the securities market line, as in Figure 8–3, and the market portfolio would be positioned on the capital market line, as in Figure 8–2.

Now consider two professionally managed portfolios, Alpha Fund and Omega Fund. The managers of Alpha Fund have acquired private information relating to a *single* company. The information is favorable in the sense that the expected rate of return to the stock is higher than one would think based on public information alone. The managers of Alpha Fund know that the stock's expected rate of return is 10 percent, and analysis based on publicly available information

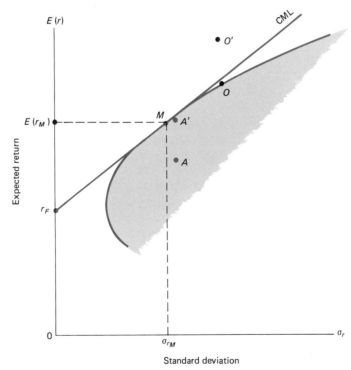

Figure 8-2 Position of Alpha and Omega Relative to Capital Market Line

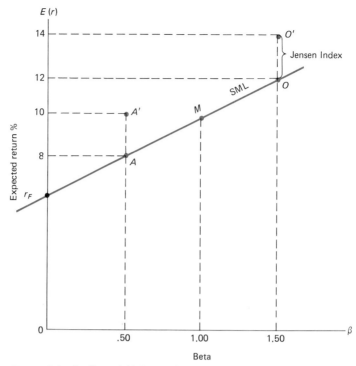

Figure 8-3   Position of Alpha and Omega Relative to Security Market Line

alone would lead you to conclude that the expected return is only 8 percent. The private information is assumed to have no bearing on your assessment of the risk of the stock. The stock's beta factor is .50 and its residual variance is positive.

The managers of Alpha Fund have invested 100 percent of the money in their portfolio in this single stock. If you were to plot the portfolio's position, based on public information *alone,* it would plot at point A in Figures 8–2 and 8–3. Note that although the portfolio is positioned on the security market line (as is everything else), it is positioned well inside the efficient set due to the large amount of residual variance remaining in the (undiversified) portfolio. Based on *both* public and private information, Alpha plots at the point A' in the two figures. It is positioned above the security market line. However, even with the additional increment of 2 percent in its expected rate of return, it is still positioned inside the efficient set.

The managers of Omega Fund are either more skillful or better endowed, in the sense that they have been able to acquire private information on many more companies. It is assumed that, in this case also, the private information affects only estimates of expected return and not estimates of risk. In any case, the managers of Omega have put together a well-diversified portfolio, taking appropriate positions in the various stocks. As it turns out, the expected rate of return on the portfolio, based on private as well as public information, is 14 percent.

However, as naive investors possessing public information alone, if you or I were to estimate the portfolio's expected return, we would think it was only 12 percent. Omega's beta is 1.50, and we will assume that, because it is broadly diversified, its residual variance has been driven to a negligible level. Omega is positioned in Figures 8–2 and 8–3 at points O and O', based, respectively, on public information alone and both public and private information.

Note that Omega is not only positioned above the security market line but, because it has only a minimal level of residual variance, the 2 percent increment in extra expected return is sufficient to lift it to a position outside the efficient set. Remember that only those with private information see it at this position. Omega doesn't look very special to those of us who only have public information to make our estimates.

We are looking for a yardstick by which we can rank the funds on the basis of the skill of their managers. We know that the managers of Omega are more skillful than the managers of Alpha. We hope that our yardstick will tell us this. Three risk-adjusted performance measures are in widespread use. All three are based on the Capital Asset Pricing Model. The measures are named after those who introduced them—the Jensen Index, the Treynor Index, and the Sharpe Index.

The Jensen Index

The Jensen Index (1969) uses the security market line as a benchmark. The index is actually the difference between the expected rate of return on the portfolio and what its expected return would be if the portfolio were on the security market line at a position corresponding to the portfolio's risk.

If we were to analyze the ability of the managers, based on the total of both public and private information, we would conclude that both Alpha and Omega are managed by individuals with equal skill levels, since they both have Jensen indices of 2 percent.

Jensen Index = Fund expected return −   SML expected return
(risk-free rate + CAPM risk premium)

Alpha	.02	=	.10	− [.06 + (.10 − .06) × .50]
Omega	.02	=	.14	− [.06 + (.10 − .06) × 1.50]

In Figure 8–3, the Jensen Index is given by the vertical distance of each fund from the security market line. If the fund has a positive Jensen Index, it is positioned above the security market line, and it is considered to have good performance. A negative Jensen Index indicates bad performance, and a position below the security market line.

In actual practice, of course, we wouldn't know the expected returns or betas for the funds. We would, therefore, have to compute sample estimates by observing the rates of return produced by the portfolios over a successive number of periods in relation to the returns to a portfolio we select as a proxy for the market portfolio. We need estimates of each portfolio's beta and expected rate of return. Because 10 and 14 percent are the "true" expected returns on Alpha and Omega, based on the market values of their stocks and the full set of available information relating to their future returns, the sample estimates should serve as unbiased estimates of these true expected returns.

Similar estimates are required for the expected return to our market proxy and the risk-free rate. If we are observing monthly returns on the portfolios over the preceding year, we might employ the mean monthly rate of return to the market proxy and the mean rate of return to one-month treasury bills over the preceding year.

The simple rate of return is defective as a performance index because rankings based on this measure depend more on the risk of the fund and the performance of the market than they do on the skill of the fund's managers. In theory at least, rankings based on the Jensen Index should be insensitive to fund risk and market performance. To see this, suppose we have a bull market where realized returns are unexpectedly high. In this case we would expect that high beta funds should have much greater rates of return than low beta funds. After all, beta measures the responsiveness of a fund to the pull of the market, and in a bull market, the market is pulling hard. However, although the rate of return to high beta stocks should be larger than that of low beta stocks, there's no reason to expect the same to be true of *excess returns*.

In Figure 8–4 is a sample estimate for the security market line (SML) for a bull market period. The return to the market index is very high, so the slope of the security market line is very large. However, although the rate of return to low beta fund C is lower than its high beta counterpart D, the Jensen Index for C is actually greater than that for D. The ranking of the two funds remains the same as we go to the bear market condition of Figure 8–5. Here the return to the market index is low, the market is pulling down, and the slope of the *estimated* security market line is negative, but fund C still has the larger Jensen Index. In theory, the magnitude of the Jensen Index should be insensitive to either the risk of the fund or the performance of the market.

Although the Jensen Index is insensitive to risk and market performance, even if our sample estimates are perfectly accurate, if we are asking the question, "Which fund has the more skillful managers?" the Jensen Index gives us the wrong answer. It tells us that the managers of Alpha and Omega are equally skillful. They are not.

We can think of a portfolio manager's performance in terms of depth and breadth. Depth relates to the magnitude of the excess return captured by the manager. Breadth relates to the number of different securities for which a manager can capture excess returns. The Jensen Index is sensitive only to depth and not breadth. The managers of Alpha have less breadth than those of Omega, but they get the same marks under Jensen because they have the same depth.[1] How-

[1]The Jensen Index can be used to detect breadth of performance if you are willing to go to the trouble of computing the index separately for each of the fund's individual investments. Then you can note the number and proportion of the investments that have significantly positive indices.

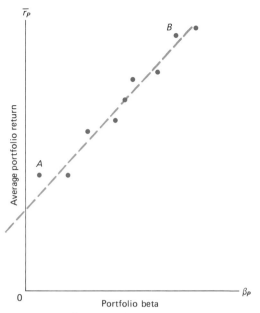

Figure 8-4 Estimated SML (Bull Market)

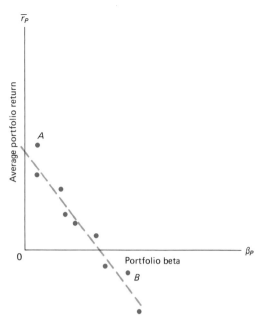

Figure 8-5 Estimated SML (Bear Market)

ever, if you are asking a different question, "Which fund is the best investment?" it may be desirable to ignore breadth and look only at depth, because your investment in the fund is only one of many potential investments you might make. Given that you yourself are diversifying, you might well be most attracted to the funds with the greatest depth, irrespective of their breadth. But if you are ranking managers on the basis of their ability, you will want to consider both breadth and depth in assessing their skills.

The Treynor Index

The Treynor Index (1965) is also insensitive to the breadth dimension of performance, but it has an advantage over the Jensen Index. Alpha and Omega are plotted relative to the security market line in Figure 8–6. Although both funds have the same excess rate of return (2 percent), Alpha has a greater rate of return per unit of risk exposure. Given that we can borrow at the risk-free rate, r_F, we can lever a position in Alpha Fund by selling the risk-free bond and using the funds to invest in Alpha to attain a position at point A^*. This position has the same beta as Omega Fund, but it has a higher expected rate of return. We can, therefore, dominate Omega Fund by levering our position in Alpha Fund. In this sense, Alpha is a more desirable portfolio investment.

The Treynor Index takes the opportunity to lever excess return into account in ranking. The Treynor Index is, in fact, the risk premium earned per unit of risk taken. Risk is measured in terms of the beta factor of the portfolio. On a

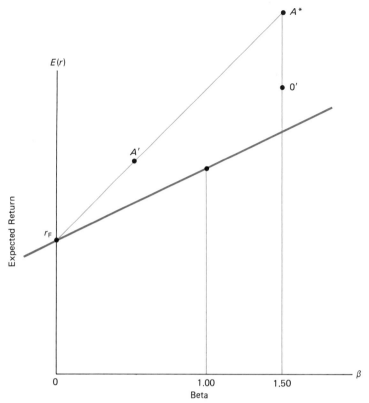

Figure 8-6 Levering Alpha to Dominate Omega

graph like that of Figure 8–6, the Treynor Index is equal to the slope of a straight line connecting the position of the fund with the risk-free rate. Obviously, although both Alpha and Omega have the same Jensen Index, Alpha Fund has the greater Treynor Index. Alpha can be viewed as providing a superior position for portfolio investors because it gives them the opportunity to lever the position by borrowing at the risk-free rate.

Note, however, that we are again getting the wrong answer to the question as to which group of managers has the greater ability. Treynor gives us the wrong answer because it, too, measures risk in terms of the beta factor. The beta factor of a portfolio is a simple weighted average of the securities in the portfolio. There is no propensity for beta to grow smaller as the number of securities in the portfolio increases. So there is no propensity for the Treynor Index to grow larger as we increase the number of securities in the portfolio, given a fixed value for the excess rate of return. The Treynor Index, therefore, is also insensitive to the breadth dimension of portfolio performance.

To obtain a risk-adjusted measure that is sensitive to breadth, we need to employ a risk measure that is sensitive to breadth. This brings us to the Sharpe Index.

The Sharpe Index

The Sharpe Index (1966) uses the capital market line as a benchmark. The index is computed by dividing the risk premium for the portfolio (the difference between the portfolio's expected rate of return and the risk-free rate) by its standard deviation. It measures the risk premium earned per unit of risk exposure.

Consider Alpha and Omega positioned relative to the capital market line in Figure 8–7. The Sharpe Index is equal to the slope of a straight line connecting the position of the fund with the risk-free rate. To determine the quality of performance, compare the Sharpe Index for the manager's portfolio with the Sharpe Index for the market. A higher Sharpe Index would indicate that the manager has outperformed the market; a lower Sharpe Index would indicate underperformance.

Note that any portfolio that is positioned on the capital market line has a Sharpe Index equal to that of the market and, therefore, is characterized by neutral performance. This makes sense under the CAPM because, on the basis of public information alone, any investor can construct a portfolio that is positioned on the capital market line.

Omega Fund ranks higher than Alpha under the Sharpe Index, so we get the correct answer to our question regarding relative management skills. On the other hand, it would be a mistake to conclude that because Alpha has a Sharpe

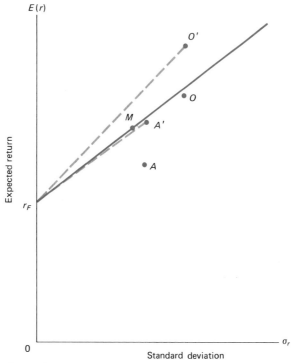

Figure 8-7 Performance of Alpha and Omega According to Sharpe Index

OUT ON THE STREET

Assigning a Grade

Peter Dietz sits at his desk in Tacoma, Washington, trying to make a unified picture out of the mass of data before him. Peter is senior vice president and director of research and development at the Frank Russell Company. Among other things, the Frank Russell Company evaluates the performance of the managers of some forty pension funds throughout the United States. Included in its accounts are the pension funds of American Telephone and Telegraph and General Motors Corporation. Its bigger accounts typically average approximately $2.5 billion in assets.

Peter has a Ph.D. from Columbia University and was a professor at Northwestern University and the University of Oregon before joining Frank Russell. He has written several articles on portfolio evaluation in such publications as the *Journal of Finance,* the *Journal of Portfolio Management,* and the *Financial Analysts Journal.* Now he puts into practice what he previously wrote about and taught.

This morning he is preparing an assessment of a management team for one of the firm's clients. The Frank Russell Company segregates common stock portfolio managers into five basic styles:

1. Aggressive growth managers would hold at least 70 percent of their invested assets in companies with less than $1 billion in total market value and portfolio betas greater than 1.20.
2. Quality growth managers hold relatively low payout, larger, technology-oriented stocks with betas ranging from 1.05 to 1.2.
3. Broadly diversified managers participate in all sectors of the market and have betas ranging from .95 to 1.05.
4. Rotating managers shift from one style to another depending on their assessment of economic conditions. Their portfolios display high turnover, and the beta factors tend to be unstable.
5. Defensive yield managers invest in stocks in stable industries with high payouts and lesser growth. Their portfolio betas are typically .95 or less.

Peter has classified this morning's management team as mostly quality growth.

Ranked with all other managers on the basis of the Jensen or Treynor Index, the team falls in the lowest quartile. To compute the indices, Peter uses the treasury bill rate for the period of assessment as the risk-free rate. Beta is measured on the basis of a sampling of historical returns going back various periods into the past. Various indices are also employed for the market, including the Standard and Poor's Composite Index of 500 Stocks, the New York Stock Exchange Index, and the Wilshire 5000 Index.

Peter is well aware of Roll's contention that performance rankings can be influenced by the analyst's choice of a market index. In fact, he is planning to participate in a major seminar to discuss potential problems associated with a methodology developed to get around the "Roll problem." The methodology was developed by a firm called Barra Associates. Barra attempts to define the natural habitat of a portfolio manager, and from this it constructs a normal "market" portfolio to serve as a benchmark for the manager. For example, if a manager normally chooses investments from a population of 300 quality growth stocks, his or her performance will be judged relative to the performance of this universe. The actual benchmark will be the manager's expected return based on a multifactor APT-type model, but the factor loadings are estimated on the basis of the manager's peer group universe of investments.

Peter is troubled by the fourth quartile ranking for the management team. In the first place, quality growth managers who aren't currently ranked in the fourth quartile are rare. The market hasn't been very kind to the types of issues that quality growth managers invest in as of late. Second, Peter and his staff have been impressed with this manager's team on the basis of numerous on-site visits, and a detailed analysis of their trading history. This analysis takes into account, among other things, a consideration of value added to the portfolio as they moved from one transaction to another and from one position in an industry to another. They also feel that the team's trades were generally consistent with the overall objectives set by the portfolio. Nevertheless, it's difficult to sell the virtues of a fourth quartile management team, no matter how strongly you try to sell them on a qualitative basis.

Peter's *quantitative* evaluation of the management is quite sophisticated. He performs a statistical evaluation to determine whether the portfolio is positioned at a statistically significant distance above or below the security market line. In the case of this particular management team, Peter can say with greater than 90 percent confidence that the portfolio is positioned below his estimate of the security market line. However, based on his qualitative analysis of the situation, Peter feels that, for the most part, this is because the market has recently treated badly the type of stock favored by these managers.

In addition, Peter knows that this management team typically invests in the stocks of very large companies. Based on his own experience and what he has read in academic journals, the stocks of large companies are typically positioned below the security market line. Peter makes no specific quantitative adjustment for this. The phenomenon appears to be an inadequacy in the Capital Asset Pricing Model, and until a well-founded substitute becomes available, any adjustment made is qualitative rather than quantitative.

In any case, all these considerations and more go into the final report. In spite of the fourth quartile ranking, the overall assessment of the management team is favorable. However, Peter has his doubts whether the client is going to be able to overlook the ranking itself and recognize the other, more favorable aspects of the team's performance.

Index less than that of the market, the managers of this fund have no skill or are, in fact, even doing something systematically wrong. The managers of Alpha do have some (limited) skill. The Sharpe Index is sensitive to both breadth and depth. In this case its sensitivity to Alpha's lack of breadth is overcoming its sensitivity to Alpha's (limited) ability to capture excess return.

We can see the Sharpe Index's sensitivity to breadth by asking what would happen to Alpha's index if the managers acquired private information for many more stocks. Suppose each additional stock has a 2 percent excess return and a beta identical to the one it already holds in its portfolio. In this case, the expected rate of return to the portfolio would remain at 10 percent, but the portfolio's standard deviation would become smaller. This is because the residual variance of the portfolio becomes smaller with diversification. The portfolio's position moves to the west on the graph and the Sharpe Index increases.

PITFALLS IN MEASURING PERFORMANCE WITH THE JENSEN, TREYNOR, AND SHARPE INDICES

Misspecifying the Market Pricing Structure

The three risk-adjusted performance measures are based on the standard form of the CAPM where a risk-free asset exists and you can buy or sell it. When you use the measures, you must assume that securities are priced in accord with this model. If your assumption is wrong, rankings based on the measures are likely to be biased.

Suppose, for example, that securities are actually priced in accord with the form of the CAPM where investors can't lend or borrow, at the risk-free rate. Under this form of the model the security market line is like that in Figure 8–8. Note that the line is assumed to intercept the vertical axis above the risk-free rate at the expected rate of return to the minimum variance, zero beta portfolio, $E(r_Z)$. If we use the standard form of the Jensen Index, we will measure performance on the basis of deviations from a "security market line," which we will assume runs along the broken line between the risk-free rate and the position of the market portfolio. A fund like A will have a positive Jensen Index, even though it is positioned directly on the true security market line. The managers of the fund have no skill. They receive good marks under Jensen merely because they are low risk. In the same sense, a high-risk fund like B receives low marks merely because it is high risk. Under these conditions neither the Jensen nor the Treynor Index is truly risk adjusted.

This problem can be corrected if we use as a benchmark a security market line anchored at the expected rate of return to the zero beta portfolio, rather than at the risk-free rate. The problem is that we have to estimate the expected return to the zero beta portfolio. One method commonly employed is to follow

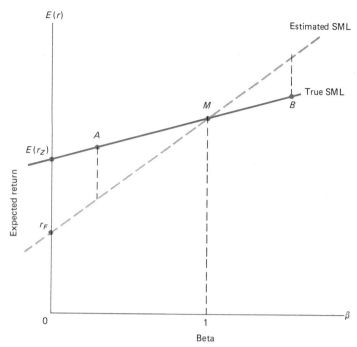

Figure 8-8 Bias in the Jensen Index Due to Misspecification of Pricing Structure

an approach similar to that in the Black, Jensen, and Scholes (1972) study. For the period over which you are measuring performance, construct several non-managed portfolios with widely divergent beta factors. Next, relate beta to average portfolio return by sliding a line of best fit through the scatter of portfolio positions in average return, beta space, as in Figure 8–9. The vertical intercept of the line of best fit serves as the estimate of the average return to the zero beta portfolio. In fact, in the case of the Jensen Index, the line of best fit can actually serve as your benchmark from which to measure performance.

The Sharpe Index can also give biased measures of performance if we misspecify the pricing structure. The Sharpe Index assumes that the capital market line is straight, which it is under the standard form of the CAPM. Suppose, however, that a risk-free security exists and investors can buy this security, but they can't sell it to raise additional funds. In this case the capital market line extends from the position of the risk-free bond to the efficient set and then bends back along the minimum variance set, as it does in Figure 8–10.

Recall that the Sharpe Index is equal to the slope of a straight line connecting the position of the fund or portfolio with the risk-free rate. Consider various portfolios all of which are positioned on the capital market line. Because anyone can achieve a position on the capital market line, the managers of none of the portfolios have exhibited any real skill. In spite of this, all the funds positioned between the risk-free rate and portfolio P' in Figure 8–10 will have the same

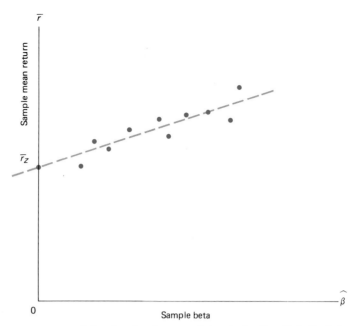

Figure 8-9 Estimating the Average Return to the Zero Beta Portfolio

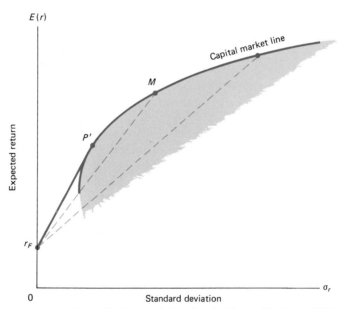

Figure 8-10 Bias in the Sharpe Index Due to Misspecification of Pricing Structure

Sharpe Index, and it will be greater than that of the market. As we move from P' to M on the graph, the Sharpe Index becomes smaller, gradually approaching that of the market. As we move beyond M on the capital market line, the Sharpe Index continues to grow smaller, and it is now less than that of the market. Under these conditions, the index gives an upward biased indication of the performance of low-risk portfolios and a downward biased indication of the performance of high-risk portfolios.

There is no easy way to correct the measure for this problem, as there was with the Jensen and Treynor indices. A simple measure really requires a linear benchmark. The capital market line is only linear under the standard form of the CAPM. In other versions, expected return is a rather complicated function of standard deviation, which doesn't lend itself to the application of a simple index.

Suppose You Select the Wrong Market Index

In addition to his critique of empirical tests of the CAPM, Richard Roll (1978) also criticized the Jensen (and implicitly the Treynor) measure of portfolio performance. It can be argued that an assessment of performance under the Jensen Index is related more to the character of the market index and its position relative to the efficient set than it is to the quality of the managers running the portfolio.

To see this, consider Figures 8–11 and 8–12. Figure 8–11 presents the minimum variance set for a population of assets. Points *A* and *B* denote the positions of two mutual funds having the same expected rate of return but different standard deviations. Suppose portfolio M is selected as the market index. Because it is on the efficient set, based on property II (see Chapter 4), all portfolios and securities will be positioned on the security market line in Figure 8–12. Because funds A and B have the same expected rate of return as the market portfolio, they both must have a beta of 1.00, and they are positioned at point *AMB*. The Jensen Index for both funds is, of course, zero.

Suppose, instead, we had selected portfolio M' in Figure 8–11 as the market index. This portfolio is slightly inside the bullet, so we know on the basis of property II that individual securities and portfolios will be positioned *off* the security market line in Figure 8–12. Positions will change in Figure 8–12, not because of changes in expected return (expected return will not change just because we go from one index to another) but rather because of changes in *beta* factors. It can be shown that dramatic changes in beta can result from slight changes in the composition of the market index selected. Consequently, in going from M to M' the beta of fund A can decrease dramatically, moving the fund to point *A* in Figure 8–12, and the beta for fund B can, at the same time, increase, moving the fund to point *B*.

If we select M as our market index, we conclude that neither fund outperformed the market. If we select M' instead, we give high marks to A and low

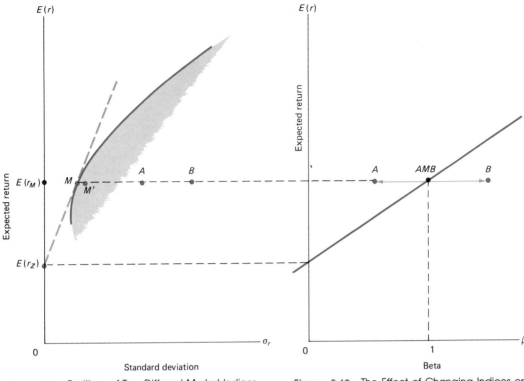

Figure 8-11 Positions of Two Different Market Indices

Figure 8-12 The Effect of Changing Indices on Beta

marks to B. We could easily reverse our rankings if we select still another index. Performance evaluation seems to be highly dependent on the choice of a market index. How are we to decide which index is the most appropriate?

Ambiguity of ranking based on choice of market index is really the same as the problem we had in testing the CAPM. In choosing the Jensen Index, we have assumed that securities are priced in accord with the CAPM. The CAPM tells us that betas should be computed with reference to the true market portfolio. Our choice of a market index with respect to measuring performance is *unambiguous*. We should use the index that most closely approximates the true market portfolio. Our prior opinion should be that this would be the portfolio that includes the largest number of available securities and investments. Ambiguity in performance measurement is not the real problem. The real problem is, once again, that we can never employ a market index that comes even close to the true market portfolio. As a consequence, we can never know whether our relative performance indices are due to relative skill or, instead, to the fact that our index, even though it is the best available, is still a very poor approximation for the market portfolio. Finally, because the problem results from the sensitivity of beta to the choice of a market index, rankings under the Sharpe Index (which employs standard deviation as opposed to beta) are insensitive to this problem. The problem works its way in through the back door, however, when you select market proxy as a basis of comparison.

MEASURING PERFORMANCE USING THE ARBITRAGE PRICING THEORY

The Jensen Index uses the linear relationship of the security market line as a benchmark to measure performance. In the Arbitrage Pricing Theory there is a similar linear relationship between the factor betas and the expected rates of return on securities and portfolios. The relationship for any given portfolio, P, is given by

$$E(r_\mathrm{P}) \quad = \quad E(r_\mathrm{Z}) \; + \; \lambda_1\beta_{1,\mathrm{P}} \; + \; \lambda_2\beta_{2,\mathrm{P}} \; + \; \cdots \; + \; \lambda_n\beta_{n,\mathrm{P}}$$

$$\begin{matrix} \text{Expected} & \text{Risk-} & \\ \text{portfolio} = \text{free} & + \text{ Sum of factor risk premiums} \\ \text{return} & \text{rate} & \end{matrix}$$

Once we have estimates of $E(r_\mathrm{Z})$ and the various factor prices, λ, we can use this relationship as a benchmark, measuring performance as the difference between a portfolio's rate of return in a given period and what we would expect it to be, based on the APT equation for expected return. Although there are several ways to do this, we might proceed as follows. The first step is to decide on the number of factors needed to account for the covariances between stocks. Suppose that your prior opinion with respect to this question is that there are two, and that the factors are unexpected changes in the rate of inflation and the real rate of interest.

The next step is to estimate the factor betas for a cross section of securities. This is done by relating the returns on each security to the unexpected percentage changes in each of the two factors. We are dealing with a three-dimensional space, where we are plotting the security's rates of return on the vertical axis and the unexpected percentage changes in each of the two factors on the two horizontal axes. We slide a plane of best fit through the scatter of points, as in Figure 8–13, each point representing the rates of return to the security and the unexpected percentage changes in each of the two factors in a particular period of time, say, a month. The slopes of the plane going down each axis represent the sensitivity of the security's return to changes in the two factors. These slopes serve as estimates of the two factor betas.

The next step is to estimate the factor prices. This can be done cross sectionally by relating the estimated factor betas to the average rates of return on each stock for the total period examined, in the manner of Black, Jensen, and Scholes. Here, again, we are sliding a plane of best fit through a scatter of points in three dimensions. On the vertical axis we have average return, and on the

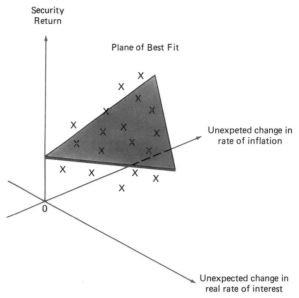

Figure 8-13 Relationship Between Security Return and Portfolio Return

two horizontal axes we have the factor betas for each stock. Each point in the scatter represents one of the stocks in the population. The plane is depicted in Figure 8–14. The point where the plane intercepts the vertical axis is our estimate of the average rate of return to a stock or portfolio with zero factor risk, r_Z. The slope of the plane relative to each horizontal axis serves as the estimates of the two factor prices.

We now have a benchmark to measure performance. The risk-adjusted performance measure is the difference between the portfolio's actual average rate of return for the period and the rate of return given by the position of the portfolio on the plane, given estimates of its factor betas. In Figure 8–14, point X represents a portfolio with superior performance relative to this benchmark. Given the estimated factor betas for the portfolio and the portfolio's average rate of return, it is positioned above the plane.

Note that this performance measure is subject to one of the criticisms leveled at the Jensen Index. It reflects only depth and not breadth of performance. Performance measures based on the APT are also subject to the same types of criticisms that are levied at CAPM-based performance measures. As we know, the APT really makes no predictions about what the factors are. Given the freedom to select factors (or, alternatively, portfolios that represent factors) without restriction, it can be argued that you can literally make the performance of a portfolio anything you want it to be. In the case of the CAPM, you can never know whether portfolio performance is due to management skill or to the fact that you have an inaccurate index of the true market portfolio. In the case of

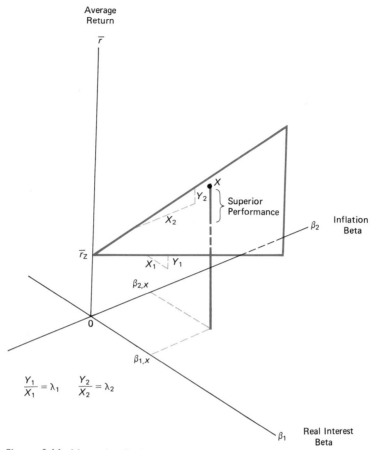

Figure 8-14 Measuring Performance with APT

APT-based measures, you have similar questions with regard to the selection of the appropriate factors.

Summary

A portfolio's rate of return is an inadequate measure of performance. It is more dependent on the risk of the portfolio and the performance of the market than it is on the quality of the portfolio's managers. Because of this, we use risk-adjusted measures of performance that remove from the portfolio's return the component due to relative risk, given market performance.

Three risk-adjusted measures of performance based on the CAPM have been suggested. The Jensen and Treynor indices use the security market line as a benchmark. Both focus on management's ability to generate excess returns (depth of performance) and ignore management's ability to generate excess returns on more than one security (breadth of performance). The Treynor Index recognizes the opportunity for portfolio investors to lever excess returns. It is in that sense a better measure of the attractiveness of a given portfolio as an investment opportunity. The Sharpe Index uses the capital market line as a benchmark. It is a composite measure of the depth and breadth of performance.

All three measures suffer from potential problems. If, in estimating the measures, you assume the wrong form of the CAPM holds in the marketplace, you get biased measures of performance, usually in favor of low-risk portfolios. This problem is easily corrected in the case of the Jensen and Treynor measures, but the problem is not so easily handled in the case of Sharpe. The Jensen and Treynor measures also suffer from the problem of possible misspecification of the market portfolio. In constructing the measures, you clearly want to use the broadest market indices that most closely approximate the market portfolio. However, because even the broadest market indices are very distant cousins of the true market portfolio, you never know whether the number you get for the index is related to the quality of the portfolio's management or the inadequacy of the index you used.

Performance can also be measured in terms of the APT. In using an APT-based performance measure, you must first estimate the factor structure and then the factor prices and the risk-free rate. Because we know very little about the factor structure at this point, performance measurement based on the APT is in its early stages of development.

To sum up, based on the current state of the art, you may well have a right to scream and yell if you ever get fired on the basis of poor portfolio performance. It is hoped that what you have learned in this chapter will provide you with some effective arguments to enable you to retain your job.

QUESTIONS AND PROBLEMS

1. In selecting a measure of managerial performance, why do we want a measure that is insensitive to the risk of the investment?

Refer to the following information for questions 2 through 4.

Suppose the returns and corresponding beta values for two assets (A and B) were as indicated in the accompanying figure.

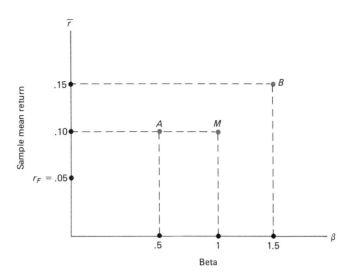

2. a. Compute the Treynor Index for A and B.
   b. Interpret the results.

3. a. Compute the Jensen Index for A and B.
   b. Interpret the results.

4. Suppose one manager had selected a portfolio represented by A and another manager had selected a portfolio represented by B. Would you feel confident in evaluating the managers' relative performance with the Treynor or Jensen results? Explain.

Refer to the accompanying figure for questions 5 through 8.

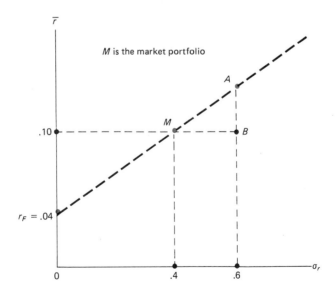

5. Compute the Sharpe Index for B. How would you interpret this result?

6. Compute the Sharpe Index for A. How would you interpret this result?

7. Suppose you decided that the "no-borrowing at a risk-free rate" version of the CAPM was the appropriate model. How would your interpretation of A's performance (question 6) be affected?

8. Suppose you were presented with an asset with a beta of .5 and an expected return of 7.5 percent. What could you conclude about the Jensen Index of this asset?

Refer to the following information for questions 9 through 12.

	Observed $\bar{r}$	Beta	Residual Variance	
Portfolio 1	.15	1.3	0	$\bar{r}_F = .05$
Portfolio 2	.09	.9	.04	$\bar{r}_M = .10$
				Standard Deviation of Market = .3

9. Compute the Jensen Index for portfolios 1 and 2. Interpret the results.

10. Compute the Treynor Index for portfolios 1 and 2. Interpret the results.

11. Compute the Sharpe Index for the market portfolio.

12. Compute the Sharpe Index for portfolios 1 and 2. Interpret the results.

BIBLIOGRAPHY

ANG, J. S., and J. H. CHUA, "Composite Measures for the Evaluation of Investment Performance," *Journal of Financial and Quantitative Analysis* (June 1979).

ARDITTI, F. D., "Another Look at Mutual Fund Performance," *Journal of Financial and Quantitative Analysis* (June 1971).

BLACK, F., M. C. JENSEN, and M. SCHOLES, "The Capital Asset Pricing Model: Some Empirical Tests," *Studies in Theory of Capital Markets.* New York: Praeger, 1972.

BOWER, R. S., and R. F. WIPPERN, "Risk-Return Measurement in Portfolio Selection and Performance Appraisal Models: Progress Report," *Journal of Financial and Quantitative Analysis* (December 1969).

CARLSON, S., "Aggregate Performance of Mutual Funds: 1948–1967," *Journal of Financial and Quantitative Analysis* (March 1970).

DIETS, P. O., "Measurement of Performance of Security Portfolios Components of a Measurement Model, Rate of Return, Risk and Timing," *Journal of Finance* (May 1968).

FAMA, E. F., "Components of Investment Performance," *Journal of Finance* (June 1970).

FRIEND, I., and M. BLUME, "Measurement of Portfolio Performance Under Uncertainty," *American Economic Review* (September 1970).

HENDRIKSSON, R. D., and R. C. MERTON, "On Market Timing and Investment Performance: II. Statistical Procedures for Evaluating Forecasting Skills," *Journal of Business* (October 1981).

JENSEN, M. C., "Problems in Selection of Security Portfolios: The Performance of Mutual Funds in the Period 1945–1964," *Journal of Business* (May 1968).

———, "Risk, the Pricing of Capital Assets, and the Evaluation of Investment Portfolios," *Journal of Finance* (April 1969).

JOY, M. O., and R. B. PORTER, "Stochastic Dominance and Mutual Fund Performance," *Journal of Financial and Quantitative Analysis* (January 1974).

KLEMKOSKY, R. C., "The Bias in Composite Performance Measures," *Journal of Financial and Quantitative Analysis* (June 1973).

KON, S. J., and F. C. JEN, "The Investment Performance of Mutual Funds: An Empirical Investigation of Timing, Selectivity and Market Efficiency," *Journal of Business* (April 1979).

ROLL, R., "Ambiguity When Performance Is Measured by the Security Market Line," *Journal of Finance* (September 1978).

SCHLARBAUM, G. G., "The Investment Performance of the Common Stock Portfolios of Property-Liability Insurance Companies," *Journal of Financial and Quantitative Analysis* (January 1974).

SCHLARBAUM, G. G., W. G. LEWELLEN, and R. C. LEASE, "The Common Stock Portfolio Performance Record of Individual Investors: 1964–1970," *Journal of Finance* (May 1978).

SHARPE, W. F., "Mutual Fund Performance," *Journal of Business* (January 1966).

TREYNOR, J. L., "How to Rate Management Investment Funds," *Harvard Business Review* (January–February 1965).

TREYNOR, J. L., and K. MAZUY, "Can Mutual Funds Outguess the Market?" *Harvard Business Review* (July–August 1966).

WILLIAMSON, P. F., "Measuring Mutual Fund Performance," *Financial Analysts Journal* (November–December 1972).

9

WHAT DETERMINES THE LEVEL OF REAL AND NOMINAL INTEREST RATES?

Introduction

In the chapters on asset pricing we discussed the determinants of differences in expected rates of return to securities that differed in terms of their risk. In this chapter we shift our attention from the *structure* of expected rates of return to the determinants of the *average level* of these returns. What forces determine the average level of interest rates in the economy?

There is increasing concern about the effect of fluctuations in interest rates on the returns to investments. This concern can be attributed to the fact that interest rates have become much more variable in recent years. This increased volatility may be due in part to the fact that in October 1979, the Federal Reserve Board changed its main target from the level of interest rates to the rate of growth in the money supply. Prior to October, the Fed adjusted the rate of growth in the money supply to achieve a targeted level for the rate of interest. In the next two or three years after October 1979 the money supply was adjusted so as to achieve target levels in *its* rate of growth. The Fed selected a range of acceptable growth rates in the money supply for the quarter of the year and then tried to adjust the money supply to keep its growth rate in the acceptable range.

As you can see from Figure 9–1, the probable result of the shift in policy was to increase the volatility of interest rates. Interest rates have now become an extremely important factor not only in the management of

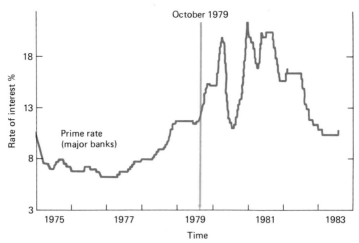

Figure 9-1 Increased Volatility of Interest Rates Since October 1979
source: *Federal Reserve Chart Book,* August 1983.

portfolios of fixed-income securities but for portfolios of common stocks as well. As a result, it is important for you to understand why interest rates move up and down over time. Once you understand this, it will help you not only to forecast the future direction of rates but also to intelligently explain to your clients and superiors why your forecasts may have gone wrong.

THE REAL AND NOMINAL RATES OF INTEREST

If you looked up the rate of interest on thirty-day treasury bills in the financial section of a newspaper, you would find the nominal, thirty-day, risk-free interest rate. The *nominal rate* can be divided into two parts, the real rate of interest and the inflation premium.

The *real rate of interest* compensates investors for delaying consumption for the next thirty days. Most people want to fulfill their desires now rather than later. If they invest in treasury bills, they have to wait. To induce them to wait, investment in a treasury bill must offer the prospect of greater consumption in the future. The real rate of interest represents the expected percentage increase in your consumption of goods and services associated with making an investment in a riskless security.

The *inflation premium* compensates investors for the loss in the purchasing power of the dollar that is expected to occur over the life of the security. With a thirty-day treasury bill, the inflation premium is the expected rate of inflation over the next thirty days. The inflation premium in a ten-year government bond is the average expected rate of inflation over the next ten years.

The nominal rate of interest is, therefore, the sum of the real rate of interest plus the inflation premium.

INTEREST RATES AND THE SUPPLY AND DEMAND FOR MONEY

The money supply is a crucial determinant of the level of interest rates in the economy. The equilibrium interest rate is determined when the quantity of money demanded is equal to the quantity of money supplied. The *supply* of money is determined by the central bank or, in the case of the United States, the Federal Reserve System. We shall segment the *demand* for money into two parts, the transactions demand and the speculative demand.[1]

The Transactions Demand for Money

Transactions demand is the demand for money as a medium of exchange. Money serves as an efficient alternative to barter. We need it to trade goods and services. If you assume money can be held in two forms, checking accounts and savings accounts, you can consider the transactions demand for money is that which we hold in checking accounts so that we can buy things as needed.

What determines the total demand for checking account balances? To answer this question, think about what determines the amount of money you keep in your checking account. Suppose you get paid $1000 once a month. You deposit your check in your checking account at the beginning of the month and spend it at a uniform rate throughout the month. This being the case, your average checking account balance for the month as a whole is obviously $500. Now suppose your income increases to $1500 per month. If you continue to spend all of your money at a stable rate each month, your average checking account balance increases to $750.

Because the aggregate transactions demand for money is found by summing across all in the economy, we can say that the overall demand for checking accounts increases with the aggregate level of income in the economy. One possible relationship between the level of income and transactions demand for money is depicted in Figure 9–2. The relationship is assumed to be linear, but it need not be. The slope of the relationship of Figure 9–2 is equal to .50. If we take the inverse of this number, we get the "velocity of money," or the number

---

[1]A third component of the demand for money is sometimes referred to as precautionary demand. To simplify the discussion, we will assume that precautionary demand is part of the speculative demand for money.

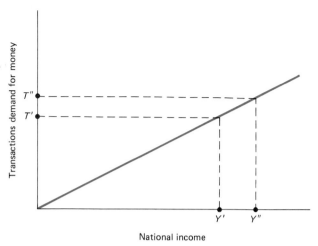

Figure 9-2   The Transactions Demand for Money

of dollars of income supported by each dollar of money (in checking accounts) in the economy. The velocity of money in the example is 2.00.

The velocity of money can change over time. Suppose that your monthly income is $1000, but you are paid twice rather than once per month. In this case your required average checking account balance falls from $500 to $250. If this happens to many people in the economy, the slope of the relationship between transactions demand and income falls, and the velocity of money rises. As Figure 9–3 indicates, the actual velocity of money in the U.S. economy has been steadily rising over time.

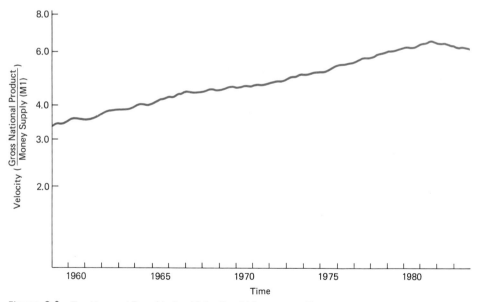

Figure 9-3   The Upward Trend in the Velocity of Money over Time

CHAPTER 9   **What Determines the Level of Real and Nominal Interest Rates?**   211

To summarize, the transactions demand for money is assumed to increase with the level of national income, and the relationship between income and transactions demand can change with changes in the payments system in the economy. Over time the payments system has become more efficient, increasing the velocity of money.

The Speculative Demand for Money

Money is also demanded as an alternative form of investment. We shall assume a very simple economy with two forms of investments, savings accounts and a perpetual bond, or consol, the payments on which are guaranteed by the government. The consols are issued by business firms to raise money to finance their investments on plant and equipment and by government to finance deficit spending. The consols represent the many different securities that are available in the actual economy. The expected rate of interest on the consols represents the average expected rate of return on all securities. We want to find the forces that determine that expected rate of return.

Assume that all investors look forward over a common horizon period, say, a month. The nominal rate of interest on the savings accounts is assumed to be fixed over the month. On the other hand, in any given period, the realized nominal rate of return on the consols is given by

$$\frac{\text{Interest payment } + \text{ Change in market price}}{\text{Current market price}} \qquad (9\text{--}1)$$

The realized real rate of return on the consol or the savings account can be obtained by subtracting the rate of inflation for the period from the realized nominal rate of return. The dollar interest payments on both the consol and the savings account are assumed to be guaranteed by the government, but the market price of the consol at the end of the month is given by the present value of its future interest payments, discounted at rates expected to prevail in the future. As interest rates go up, the market value of the consol falls; as rates go down, the market value rises. In short, even though the interest payments are guaranteed, the monthly nominal and real rates of return for the consol are uncertain because both the future level of interest rates and the rate of inflation are uncertain. There is an interest rate risk and an inflation risk associated with investing in the consol. In the case of the savings account, there is only an inflation risk, and the overall risk associated with the savings account is presumed to be less than that of the consol.

The probability distributions for the monthly real rates of return on the consol and the savings account are given in Figure 9–4. If we assume that investors are risk averse, the expected rate of return on the consol will be higher than that on the savings account. This is because the variance of the rate of return on the consol is greater than that of the savings account.

When we speak of the real rate of interest in the economy, we are referring to the *expected real* rate of return to the consol over the next month. Given this, if the real rate of interest on the consol increases, what will happen to the spec-

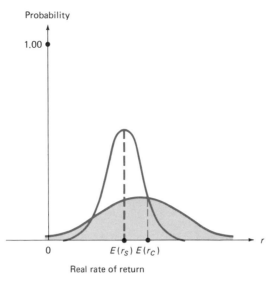

Figure 9-4 Probability Distributions for the Consol and the Savings Account

ulative demand for money or the demand for savings accounts? You can think of the consols as having an advantage and a disadvantage relative to the savings accounts. They have the advantage of having a higher expected real rate of return, but they also have the disadvantage of having greater risk. If the expected real rate of return on the consols goes up, and nothing happens to relative risk or the expected real rate of return on savings accounts, the advantage is enhanced, but nothing happens to the disadvantage. Given this, we would expect that investors would want to invest a greater percentage of their money in consols and a lesser percentage in savings accounts. Given the *dollar* inventory of consols and money in the economy, this translates into a decrease in the dollar demand for savings accounts.

The total demand for savings accounts thus falls as the real rate of interest on consols goes up. In Figure 9–5 we have drawn the dollar speculative demand for money as a decreasing function (the solid line) of the real rate of interest on the other form of investment, consols. Remember that we are plotting dollars on the horizontal axis of the graph, but the dollar demand derives from the percentage allocation to consols and savings accounts in the portfolios of investors. Investors assess the risk and expected rates of return on the two forms of investments and then assign portfolio weights. Given the existing inventories of the investments in the economy, the portfolio weights translate into dollar demands.

The Total Demand for Money

Given a level for national income and the real rate of interest, we can find the total demand for money by summing the two component demands, transactions demand and speculative demand. In Figure 9–6 we have drawn the two compo-

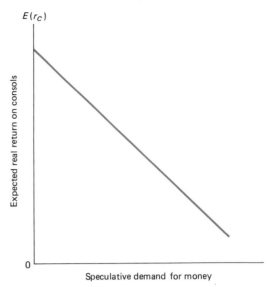

Figure 9-5 The Speculative Demand for Money

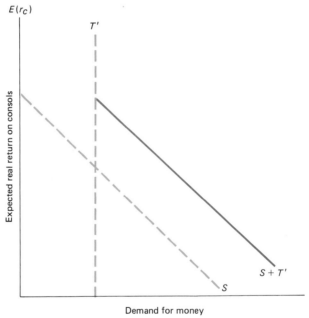

Figure 9-6 The Total Demand for Money

nents and the total demand as they relate to the level of the real rate of interest. We have assumed a given level of national income in Figure 9–2 equal to Y', which is consistent with a transactions demand for money of T'. The transactions demand for money is drawn as a constant at a level equal to T' in Figure 9–6 because it is assumed to be unrelated to the real rate of interest. The speculative demand for money schedule is merely repeated from Figure 9–5. To get the total demand at each rate of interest, we merely add T' to the speculative demand at each interest rate. This produces the schedule $T' + S$.

Remember, if we change the level of national income, we change the transactions demand and move to a new total demand for money schedule.

The Supply of Money and the Equilibrium Interest Rate

The supply of money is determined by the Federal Reserve Board. The Fed can change the money supply by changing the interest rate on the loans it makes to the banking system or by changing the amount of idle reserves that banks are required to keep to back up their deposits. However, the Fed's principal tool to change the money supply is open market operations. In *open market operations,* the Fed buys and sells government bonds (in our simple economy, consols) from its own account. If it buys consols, there are fewer consols in the system and more money. If it sells consols there are more consols but less money.

We will assume that the Fed is not using an interest rate target, so the quantity of money in the system is not causally related to the level of the real rate of interest. Thus, the schedule relating the supply of money to the real rate of interest is perfectly inelastic, as in Figure 9–7.

We have equilibrium in the economy when the interest rate is such that the quantity of money supplied by the Fed is equal to the quantity of money demanded. This will be true in Figure 9–7 when the interest rate is equal to $E(r_c^*)$.

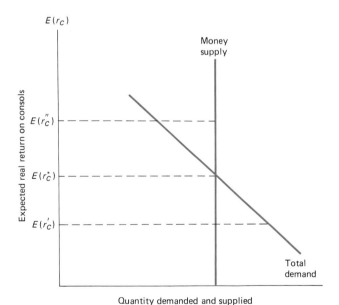

Figure 9-7 The Equilibrium Real Interest Rate

To show this, suppose we are in a state of *disequilibrium,* and the rate of interest is too high, at $E(r_c'')$. In this case the total demand for money is less than the supply. There is surplus liquidity. Individuals will attempt to get rid of it by buying consols in the securities market. (I say "attempt," because only the Fed can really get rid of money in the economy; individuals can merely pass it from one to another through trading.) However, in the process of attempting to get rid of it by buying consols, they will raise the current price of consols and lower the expected real rate of interest. This will continue to happen until the interest rate has reached its equilibrium level. At the equilibrium level, the supply of money is the same as it was before. However, the demand for money has now increased to equal the supply because the demand for savings accounts has increased due to the lower rate of interest on consols.

In the same sense, if the rate of interest was below its equilibrium level, at $E(r_c')$, the supply of money would be less than the demand. There would be a shortage of liquidity. People would attempt to increase liquidity by selling consols in the securities market. This would drive down the current market price of consols and the expected real rate of interest up to the equilibrium level.

Thus, the real interest rate settles at the intersection of supply and demand. Interest rates may change with a change in the supply of money. They may change with a change in the perceived risk of consols, which would shift the schedules for the speculative and total demand for money. They may also change with a change in the level of national income, which would change transactions demand and the schedule for the total demand for money. To gain a deeper understanding of the forces controlling interest rates, we move now to an examination of the forces controlling the level of national income.

INVESTMENT, SAVINGS, AND NATIONAL INCOME

Business firms are on the other side of the consol market. They issue consols to finance their investments. The consols, of course, are perpetual bonds, and therefore don't mature. To retire them, the firm must repurchase the consols in the securities market at prevailing market prices. Over the planning horizon, the real cost of capital to the firm is equal to the expected real rate of return to the consol. In making its investment decisions, the firm compares its estimates of the real rates of return on its capital investment projects with the real cost of capital. If the project return is greater than the cost of acquiring capital to finance, the project is profitable and will increase the value of the firm.

Given the set of expected real rates of return on the firm's investment opportunities, if the real rate of interest falls, the firm will find that more projects can be profitably undertaken. Now, as all firms attempt to increase their spending on plant and equipment, the relative prices of capital goods should begin to rise. This will curb to some extent the increase in capital spending, because it brings down estimates of the rates of return on these investments. Nevertheless, a reduction in the real rate of interest should be accompanied by a net increase in the level of investment spending on plant and equipment by business firms. Conversely, an increase in the real rate should be accompanied by a reduction in the level of spending on plant and equipment.

Thus, there is a connection between the level of interest rates and the level of economic investment on the part of business firms. Noting this, we now move to the link between economic investment and the level of national income.

Consider Figure 9–8. We start at the top with a given level of national income ($10 billion). We will initially assume a simple economy, with no government. Consumers divide up the income between consumption and savings. We assume that for each dollar earned 20¢ is saved and 80¢ is spent on consumption goods. In the next year, business firms make their production and investment decisions. Production of consumption goods in year $t + 1$ is assumed to be determined by the following rule of thumb: The amount produced this year is equal to total domestic consumption last year, less that which was spent on foreign goods (imports) plus the amount spent on domestic goods by foreigners (exports). In Figure 9–8 exports are assumed to be equal to imports.

Investment decisions are based on the estimated profitability of individual projects and the level of the cost of capital, or the real rate of interest. In Figure 9–8 it is assumed that the level of investment spending in $t + 1$ is equal to the level of savings in the previous year. This need not always be the case, however.

The amounts spent by business firms on production for consumption and investment in plant and equipment are paid to the factors of production, land, labor, and capital. These payments become the income for year $t + 1$. With exports equal to imports and savings equal to investment, the level of income in $t + 1$ is the same as in t. Indeed, unless something happens to change the level of investment, or to cause an imbalance between exports and imports, income will remain indefinitely at $10 billion.

However, suppose something does happen to cause investment spending to increase from $2 billion to $3 billion in period $t + 2$—a reduction in interest rates or the receipt of new information that causes business firms to revise upward their estimates of the expected rates of return on their investment projects. The effect of this will be to increase the level of income to $11 billion in $t + 3$. If the split between savings and consumption remains the same, $8.8 billion will be spent on consumption in $t + 3$. This means that if the international balance of trade stays even, production for consumption will rise to $8.8 billion in $t + 4$. If investment spending stays constant at $3 billion, the level of $t + 4$ income will grow to $11.8 billion. This will lead to a further increase in consumption, followed by more production for consumption and more income. Each successive yearly increase in income is smaller than the last, however, and we gradually move toward a new, higher equilibrium level of national income.

An increase in the level of exports relative to imports will have a similar effect. This results in an increase in production for consumption, which increases the level of national income, which increases domestic consumption, which in-

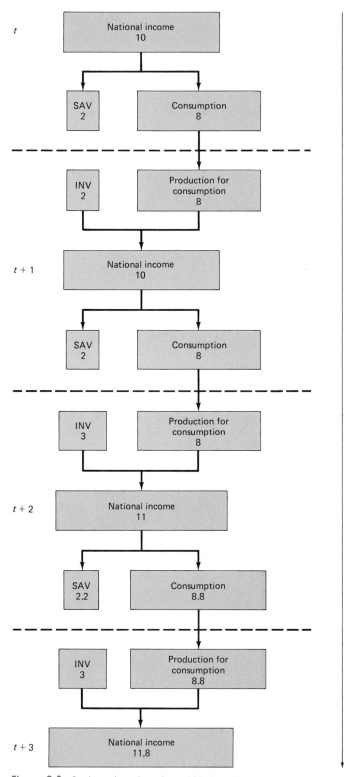

Figure 9-8 Savings, Investment, and National Income

creases production for consumption again. Once again, we move in progressively smaller steps toward a higher equilibrium level of national income.

In general, the following events will tend to push income upward:

1. An increase in the fraction of income consumed
2. An increase in the level of exports
3. An increase in investment spending

In the same sense, the following events will tend to push income downward:

1. A decrease in the fraction of income consumed
2. An increase in the level of imports
3. A decrease in investment spending

A change in the level of national income may lead to a change in the levels of real and nominal interest rates. Suppose, for example, that national income should increase. If production in the economy is near capacity, the increase in aggregate demand may be inflationary. If there is an increase in the current rate of inflation, this may lead to an increase in the expected rate of inflation for future periods. Given this, there will be an accompanying increase in the *inflation premium* in interest rates.

An increase in national income may also affect the real rate of interest as well. As you know, the real rate of interest is determined at the intersection of the supply and demand for money. An increase in national income may increase the transactions demand for money, because, unless the pattern of transacting changes, people will want to carry larger checking account balances to support their larger volume of spending. If the Fed doesn't support the increase in national income by expanding the money supply, people will attempt to generate their own increment in liquidity by selling securities (consols). This will drive down the price of securities and drive up the real rate of interest.

You see, there is an interconnection between interest rates and national income. Given our preceding discussion, we know that income can affect interest rates, but interest rates can affect income as well. An increase in the level of interest rates means a higher cost of capital and, therefore, a lower volume of spending on plant and equipment by business firms. An increase in the real rate of interest in the United States also means that the U.S. financial markets are more attractive to foreign investors. Foreign investors will buy dollars in order to purchase securities in the United States. This drives up the value of the dollar. A strong dollar makes U.S. goods more expensive to foreigners and makes foreign goods less expensive to U.S. domestic consumers. Thus, we would expect exports to decrease and imports to increase. Given the flows in Figure 9–8, we would expect U.S. firms to react by producing fewer consumption goods. This means a reduction in national income.

As we will see in the next section, to understand fully the impact of various "shocks" to the economic system, we must keep in mind these interrelationships between interest rates and national income.

THE EFFECT OF A CHANGE IN THE MONEY
SUPPLY ON REAL AND NOMINAL INTEREST RATES

What will be the ultimate impact on interest rates if the Fed increases the supply of money in the economy? The initial effect will be to create an imbalance in the portfolio positions of investors. People now have too much money in savings and checking accounts, relative to their investments in securities or consols. Presumably, before the injection of funds, they had struck an ideal balance in their portfolios. Now the balance is upset. They respond by attempting to restore it by buying consols in the financial markets. This drives up the market price of consols and drives down the real rate of interest. Because portfolio adjustments can be made very rapidly, this first adjustment of interest rates to the change in the money supply is almost instantaneous. When the money supply goes up, we expect interest rates to fall immediately in response to portfolio adjustments. This first adjustment is called the *liquidity effect*.

The liquidity effect can be seen in Figure 9–9. As the money supply increases from S to S^*, at the old real rate, $E(r_c)$, the supply of money is greater than the demand. As people attempt to get rid of the surplus money by buying consols, bond prices rise and the rate of interest falls to $E(r_c^*)$, closing the gap between supply and demand.

The lower rate of interest has two implications for the real (as opposed to the financial) sector of the economy. First, lower interest rates means a lower cost

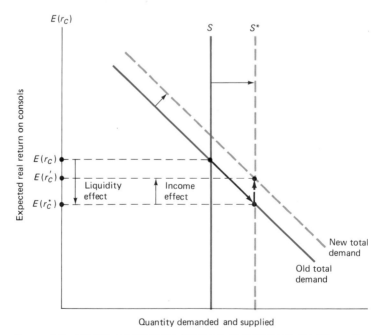

Figure 9-9 Liquidity and Income Effects of an Increase in the Money Supply

of capital, which means that spending on plant and equipment by business firms will increase. The increase in investment spending by firms will force income upward in the coming year. Second, the lower real rate of interest makes the U.S. financial markets less attractive to foreign investors. The demand for dollars to buy U.S. securities falls, and the value of the dollar falls as well. This makes it cheaper for foreigners to buy U.S. goods and more expensive for U.S. citizens to buy foreign goods. Exports will rise and imports will fall. This stimulates the production of consumption goods by U.S. firms. More spending on production means more income, so income is on the rise, propelled by a lower cost of capital and a more favorable balance of trade. Of course, the increase in national income will stimulate domestic consumption, which leads to further increases in production and still more income in periods to come. Income, in any case, will be on the increase.

In response, individuals will want to maintain larger checking account balances to support their larger levels of spending. If the Fed doesn't meet this demand with a second increase in the money supply, people will attempt to generate their own liquidity by selling off securities in the financial markets. As a result, the market price of consols falls, and the real rate of interest rises. At the higher rate of interest, they will be willing to hold a larger fraction of their portfolio in consols and a smaller fraction in savings accounts. Thus, although the total money supply (savings plus checking) remains the same, a larger fraction is held in the form of checking account balances.

This second adjustment in interest rates is depicted in Figures 9–2 and 9–9. In Figure 9–2 the increase in the level of national income to Y'' increases the transactions demand for money to T''. The increase in transactions demand shifts the total demand for money to the right in Figure 9–9. The result is a movement in interest rates from $E(r_c^*)$ back up to $E(r_c')$. This second interest rate adjustment is called the *income effect* of a change in the money supply. The income effect follows the liquidity effect, and it moves in the opposite direction.

A third effect reinforces the income effect: The *price effect* results from a change in expectations relating to the future rate of inflation. If the economy is operating near capacity, the increase in national income may be inflationary. If so, it may increase the expected *future* rate of inflation, which results in an increase in the inflation premium in the *nominal* interest rate. If this happens, the real rate of interest may be lower than it was before the monetary increase, but the nominal rate may well end up at a higher level. You may have read articles in the financial news about exchanges between congressional committees and the chairman of the Federal Reserve Board, relating to whether the Fed should expand the money supply to reduce interest rates. In the past, the chairman has argued that monetary expansion may well result in higher, as opposed to lower, interest rates. In assessing these exchanges, it may be said that Congress is thinking in terms of the liquidity effect, whereas the Fed is thinking ahead to the income and price effects.

The links in the chain of events connecting the initial increase in the money supply with the final increases in interest rates are given in the accompanying diagram.

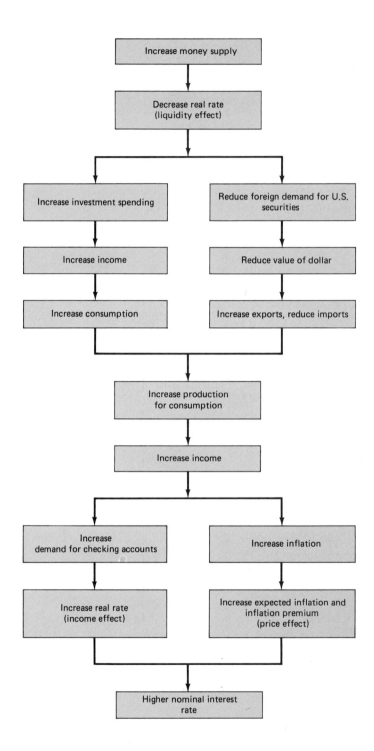

It is interesting to think about the timing of the liquidity, income, and price effects. The liquidity effect should appear very rapidly, because portfolio adjustments can be made very rapidly. On the other hand, the effect of the change in monetary policy on the real economy should take place more slowly. Firms must adjust their capital budgeting decisions to the change in the cost of capital resulting from the liquidity effect. Plans must be changed and projects initiated. All these things take time, so the upward pressure on interest rates, stemming from the resulting increase in national income, will take time as well.

At first thought, we might expect the income and price effects to appear many months after the appearance of the liquidity effect. However, suppose you are an intelligent investor who knows the whole process from beginning to end. The Fed has injected money into the system and interest rates have fallen with the liquidity effect. Are you going to sit around holding consols and waiting for the income and price effects to come a few months later? Why wait for the fall in bond prices when you can get out now? That's exactly what you would expect people to do: anticipate the income and price effects and sell before they come. If this happens, we will see the income and price effects well before we see the increases in national income and inflation actually take place. Empirical evidence seems to indicate that the financial markets are indeed acting in advance of the real economy. Although the lag between the liquidity and the income and price effects was as long as six months a few decades ago, more recent studies have indicated that the lag has now shortened to a month or two.[2]

THE EFFECT OF A CHANGE IN FISCAL POLICY

A Tax Cut

In Figure 9–10 government is added to our simple model of the economy. We have assumed that 20 percent of income is taxed and that consumers save 20 percent of their after-tax income and consume the rest. We also assume, initially, that savings is equal to investment, exports are equal to imports, and that government spending is equal to government revenue. In this case income in $t + 1$ is equal to income in t. We have assumed that there is a 50 percent tax cut in period $t + 1$. Government revenue falls from \$2 billion to \$1 billion. Government spending remains at \$2 billion, so there is a deficit in the budget of \$1 billion. What will be the impact of the tax cut on interest rates? Once again, there will be liquidity, income, and price effects.

The liquidity effect comes from the financing of the deficit. In our simple economy, the deficit is financed by selling consols in the financial markets. To see the impact of this, consider the schedule for the speculative demand for money

---

[2]See Gibson and Kaufman (1968), Gibson (1970), Melvin (1983), Mishkin (1981, 1982), and Brown and Santoni (1983).

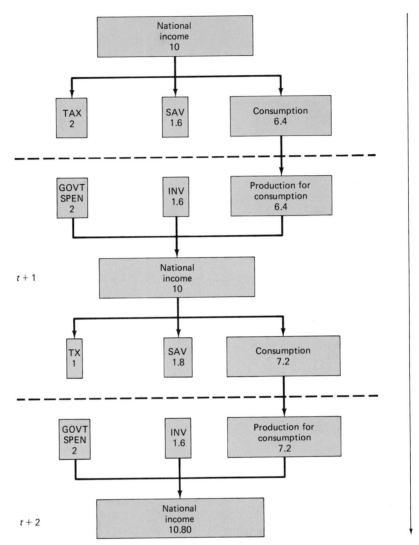

Figure 9-10 The Effect of a Tax Cut on National Income

in Figure 9–11. The initial speculative demand for money schedule is labeled *S*. It shows the *dollar* demand for savings accounts, given particular interest rates on consols. It is based on the assigned portfolio weights to consols and savings accounts. As we know, these portfolio weights are determined on the basis of the relative risk and expected return of the consol and the savings account. Given a dollar volume of consols outstanding, these *percentage* portfolio weights imply the desired *dollar* investments in savings accounts, plotted in Figure 9–11 as the speculative demand schedule. That is, if all investors desired to invest 40 percent of their portfolios in savings accounts, this would imply a $2 billion demand for savings accounts if there were $3 billion in consols outstanding. If

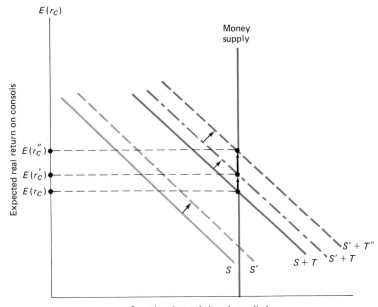

Figure 9-11   The Effect of a Tax Cut on the Real Rate of Interest

there were, instead, $6 billion in consols outstanding, the demand for savings accounts would rise to $4 billion.

Given the preceding discussion, we would expect that an increase in the supply of consols in the market will shift the speculative demand for money schedule to the right. At each real rate of interest on the consol, given their desired portfolio *weights,* investors will desire a larger dollar amount of savings accounts. The impact of this is to shift the total demand for money schedule to the right in Figure 9–11, increasing the real rate of interest from $E(r_c)$ to $E(r_c')$. This is the liquidity effect of the tax cut on interest rates, and it should be coincident with the financing of the deficit.

The tax cut will also increase consumption, because it increases after tax income. Since 80 percent of after-tax income is consumed, consumption will increase by $.8 billion, to $7.2 billion in $t + 1$; $.2 billion of the tax cut will be lost to savings. The increase in consumption will stimulate production for consumption in period $t + 2$. This will lead to a series of increases in income in $t + 2$ and beyond. The increases in income will be dampened somewhat by the increase in real interest rates stemming from the liquidity effect. The increase in the cost of capital will reduce investment spending, and as foreign investors move into the U.S. securities markets, the value of the dollar will rise, stimulating imports and reducing exports. However, there should be a net increase in the level of national income in any case.

As a result of the increase in income and spending, people will require larger balances in their checking accounts. The Fed isn't expanding the money supply, so people will "attempt" to generate the extra liquidity themselves by selling

Forecasting a Turnaround

It's 9:00 P.M. Streams of busy shoppers are making their way home through the streets of Chicago down below. Sy Lotsoff leans back in his chair on the thirty-second floor of the Civic Opera Building, contemplating the future—not his future but the future of the economy and interest rates in particular.

Sy is president of Lotsoff Capital Management, an investment management firm that runs the portfolios of pension plans and life insurance companies nationwide. He specializes in the management of fixed-income securities, and because of this he watches the movement in interest rates very closely. Rather than forecast what the *level* of rates is going to be in the future, Sy concentrates on direction. If you can get a jump on direction, you can make excess returns for your client, even if you are only accurate to within six months of forecasting the peak or trough.

To help him forecast the future direction of rates, Sy employs several macroeconomic models, which take as inputs such factors as the money supply, actual and estimated capital expenditures of business firms, consumer savings, and other factors that help him forecast loan demand like aggregate corporate cash flow (depreciation plus corporate profits).

In the past few weeks, Sy watched as things began falling into place. The economy was nearing the tail end of the boom part of the business cycle and entering the early slowdown phase. Retail sales were beginning to falter, and corporations were being forced to borrow to finance expanding inventory. Firms were finding that internally generated cash flows were inadequate to finance spending commitments made earlier in the boom, again forcing them into the markets for capital. Although not a particular problem this time around the cycle, inflation was reaching its peak. Sy could feel it. This was the time of maximum upward pressure on interest rates.

To Sy, this meant two things: He should begin to move his portfolios long, and he should begin to move them low. *Long* means long maturity, concentrating on

consols in the market. The price of consols will fall, and the real rate of interest will rise once again. This second increase in the real rate is again called an income effect. The income effect is graphed in Figure 9–11 by the second shift in the total demand for money curve. This time the curve shifts as a result of a change in the transactions demand for money. The real rate of interest ends up at $E(r_c'')$.

We may again have a price effect that is coincident with the income effect. If the increase in income that results from the tax cut is inflationary, it may increase expectations regarding future inflation and the inflationary premium in interest rates. In this case, the nominal rate would go up by even more than the real rate. Rather than cut taxes, we could have increased government spending.

those bonds with lower coupons selling at discounts under their face values. These are the bonds least likely to be called after the coming fall in interest rates. These are the bonds that will enjoy the greatest appreciation in their market prices. *Low* means lower quality, as low as issues rated BBB.

Sy moves low because, in addition to being the time of the interest rate peak, this is the time of the greatest spreads between the yields on the highest quality issues and the bonds of lesser quality. To a great extent the market anticipates the coming recession, lowering the prices of medium-grade issues relative to those of the highest quality. This is also the time of greatest financial stress. Lines of credit are being stretched, and commercial banks are forcing companies, especially those without unquestioned financial strength, to go out into the financial markets to obtain permanent financing. This not only helps to force rates up in general, but it also forces the rates on medium-grade issues up in particular, widening the spreads. By moving low and long, Sy maximizes the potential return that will come as the general level of rates begins to fall in the

coming months and as the spreads begin to narrow into their normal range.

Perhaps six months, perhaps eighteen months, after the coming recession has ended, the growth in loan demand will once again begin to accelerate after an extended flat, or down, period. Sy calls this the inflection point in the cycle. All the forces now signaling downturn will be reversed. Rates will have fallen and spreads will have narrowed as internal sources of financing open up, and financial markets anticipate substantial corporate profit improvement. This is the time that Sy shifts his posture from long and low to short and high.

Sy is seldom one to go to extremes. Even now he doesn't *know* that rates are reaching their peak. Because of this, his shifts in posture are often made slowly, prudently, depending on how confidently he feels he can locate himself in the business cycle. Sy's approach has been successful in the past. The average returns on his portfolios have exceeded the Lehman Brothers Bond Index returns in eight of the last ten years. If Sy's expectations prove correct, it will be nine out of eleven.

The effects on interest rates would have been very similar. We would have again seen the liquidity, income, and price effects. The main difference is that we would feel the full force of the increase in spending, while a fraction of the tax cut was lost to savings.

Monetizing the Deficit

In the previous example, it was assumed that the deficit was financed by selling consols to the public. The result of this is an immediate increase in the real rate of interest through the liquidity effect. The Treasury can avoid the liquidity effect by selling its securities to the Fed instead of to the public at large.[3] In this case there will be no increase in the supply of consols held by the public and no shift to the right in the speculative demand for money schedule, as we had in Figure 9–11. However, the Treasury will eventually spend the money it gets from selling securities to the Fed. When it does, new money will flow into the economy, resulting in an increase in the money supply. Once the money supply goes up, we release liquidity, income, and price effects, which has the net effect of putting upward pressure on the level of nominal interest rates. Thus, if the deficit is financed by selling securities to the Fed instead of to the public, we avoid the short-run problem of the liquidity effect's putting upward pressure on the real rate, but face the longer run problem of income and price effects' putting upward pressure on nominal rates.

THE RECENT EXTRAORDINARY BEHAVIOR OF THE REAL RATE OF INTEREST

The real rate of interest can be estimated, at any given point in time, by subtracting from the nominal rate an estimate of the expected rate of inflation over the life of the security. So, to compute the real rate of interest on a one-year treasury bill, you would subtract from its nominal interest rate an estimate of the expected rate of inflation for the next year. Based on such estimates, researchers have found that the real rate of interest is typically quite small, usually only 1 or 2 percent.[4] In 1981, however, there was a sharp upward jump in the real rate, in the range of 6 to 10 percent. Jumps like this had been seen before, but usually they extended for only a brief period, after which the real rate fell back to its normal range. This time the real rate remained extraordinarily high for several years. There are several possible explanations for this unusual behavior.

Tax Cuts and Budget Deficits

Beginning in 1981 the Reagan administration instituted a series of three substantial tax cuts. The cuts were initially intended to be matched with cuts in government spending. However, the administration found it unexpectedly difficult to cut back spending on social programs and, at the same time, propose sizable increases in defense spending. The result was an increase in government expenditures accompanied by a reduction in government revenue, as seen in Figure 9–12. There was an obvious increase in the size of the deficit. As we will see

---

[3]Technically speaking, the Treasury cannot, under existing law, sell securities directly to the Federal Reserve. Instead, the Fed can engage in open market purchases of securities in the secondary markets at the same time that the Treasury sells in the primary markets.

[4]See Ibbotson and Sinquefield (1982).

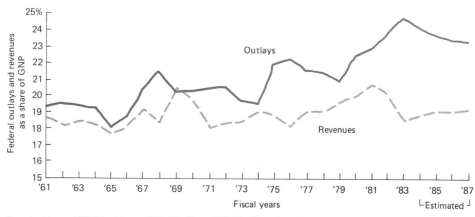

Kennedy-Johnson, 1961-64 • Johnson, 1965-68 • Nixon, 1969-72 • Nixon-Ford, 1973-76 • Carter, 1977-80 • Reagan, 1981-84 •

Figure 9-12 The Increase in the Size of the Budget Deficit

SOURCE: *Wall Street Journal*, Feb. 2, 1984. Reprinted by permission of *Wall Street Journal*, © Dow Jones & Company, Inc. 1984.

below, the Fed refused to monetize the deficit, and it had to be financed by selling securities to the public. In order to induce the public at large to accept the increased supply of securities, the Treasury had to sell them at a relatively high real rate of interest. This, of course, is the liquidity effect referred to in the discussion of tax cuts in the section on fiscal policy. In any case, the tax cut, and the resulting deficit, contributed greatly to the unusually high level for the real rate of interest for the period.

Tight Monetary Policy

As you can see in Figure 9–13, in November 1980 there was a sharp change in the long-run rate of growth in the money supply. Prior to November, the money supply had been growing at double-digit rates. From November 1980 through most of 1982, the rate of growth was held to less than 4 percent. The economy, however, continued to inflate at a rate far beyond this, at least throughout 1981. In this sense, the real money supply, adjusted for inflation, was falling throughout the period. The result of this is to induce a concurrent liquidity effect that puts upward pressure on the real rate of interest. This liquidity effect runs in the opposite direction from the one associated with an increase in the money supply.

Increase in Interest Rate Uncertainty

As previously discussed, in October 1979, the Fed announced that it was changing its policy from one that used the level of interest rates as a target to one that used the money supply as a target. Thus, instead of trying to control interest rates, the Fed was going to try to control the rate of growth in the money supply.

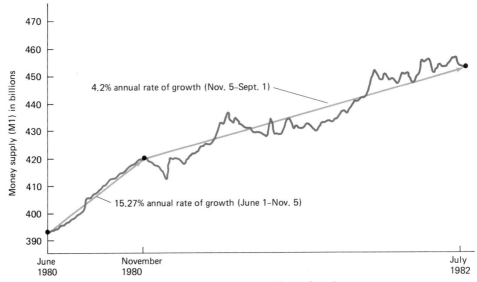

Figure 9-13   The Change in the Rate of Growth in the Money Supply

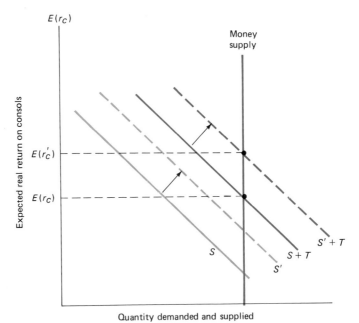

Figure 9-14   The Effect of an Increase in Interest Rate Risk on the Real
Rate of Interest

The effect of this change in policy is dramatically pictured in Figure 9–1. Shifting the target from interest rates to money appears to have had a destabilizing effect on the level of interest rates. Many believe that the sizable increase in the real rate of interest was due to the substantial increase in interest rate risk in the period.

An increase in interest rate risk will increase the risk of the consol relative to the savings account. Recall that the savings account is assumed to have no interest rate risk, only inflation risk. An increase in the risk of the consol relative to the savings account increases its relative disadvantage as an investment. Given a lower level for the expected real rate of return on the consol, investors will now want to invest a smaller percentage of their portfolio in consols. This translates into a reduced dollar demand for consols at each level for the real interest rate and a corresponding increase in the dollar demand for savings accounts. Consequently, an increase in interest rate risk results in a shift to the right in the speculative demand for money. The shift in the speculative demand shifts the total demand for money schedule to the right, as in Figure 9–14. The result is an increase in the real rate of interest to $E(r_c')$.

Summary

The nominal rate of interest can be divided into two parts, the real rate and the inflation premium. The real rate compensates investors for delaying consumption; the inflation premium compensates them for erosion in the purchasing power of the dollar payments they get from investing in the security.

The real rate of interest equilibrates the supply and demand for money. The supply of money is determined by the monetary policy of the Federal Reserve Board. The demand for money can be divided into transactions demand and speculative demand. Transactions demand is the demand for money as a medium of exchange. We have represented it as the demand for checking accounts. Transactions demand increases with the level of national income. Speculative demand is the demand for money as an investment alternative to securities (consols). We take the speculative demand for money to be the demand for savings accounts. The speculative demand for money is inversely related to the expected real return on the alternative investment, the consol.

If the demand for money is greater than the supply, people will attempt to generate their own liquidity by selling off securities. This selling pressure reduces the price of securities, increases the real rate of interest, and lowers the demand for money to the point where it is equal to the supply. If supply is greater than demand, people use the surplus liquidity to buy securities, and the opposite happens.

There is an interaction between the real rate of interest and the level of national income. An increase in the real rate of interest reduces the level of investment spending on plant and equipment by business firms and also creates an unfavorable balance of trade through its effect on the value of the dollar. Both factors exert downward pressure on the level of national income. On the other hand, an increase in national income exerts upward pressure on the real rate of interest. This is because higher levels of income mean greater demand for transactions balances. In attempting to get them, people will sell off securities, lowering the prices of securities and increasing their real expected rates of return.

A change in the money supply changes the rate of interest through the liquidity, income, and price effects. The liquidity effect comes from portfolio adjustments in response to the change in the level of liquidity induced by the Fed. The income effect results from the link among interest rates, investment spending, the balance of trade, and the level of national income. A change in the level of national income means a change in the transactions demand for money and a resulting change in the real rate of interest. If the change in national income affects the rate of inflation, a price effect may occur. The price effect is caused by a change in the inflation premium. It affects the magnitude of the nominal rate but not the real rate.

Forces that exert upward pressure on interest rates include autonomous increases in investment spending, a reduction in the savings rate by consumers, increases in the level of exports, reductions in the level of imports, increases in government spending, and tax cuts. Movements in the opposite direction by these factors exert downward pressure on interest rates.

QUESTIONS AND PROBLEMS

1. Contrast the nominal rate of interest with the real rate of interest.
2. Assume that there is no inflation in an economy and that if you put aside $100 today in a riskless investment, you will receive $105 back in one year. What are the real and nominal rates of interest? Next, assume the same information, except that prices are expected to rise generally by 4 percent over the year. What are the real and nominal rates of interest?
3. Suppose the transactions demand for money was described by

$$T = .3Y$$

where T = transactions demand and Y = national income.

a. What is this equation telling us?

b. If we are experiencing a decreased velocity of money, what sort of change would we expect in the equation?

c. Improvements in the workings of the economy's mechanism for payments would lead to what sort of change in the equation?

4. If your holdings of money as an investment yield a return that is less than the return from consols, why would people want to hold *any* money as an investment?

5. Explain why a lower rate on consols would be associated with a larger quantity of "speculative" money being demanded.

Refer to the following figure for questions 6 through 8.

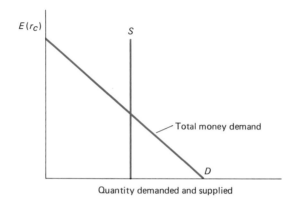

6. Indicate how the equilibrium interest rate on consols would be determined on the figure.

7. Indicate graphically the result of a decrease in the total demand for money. What is the implication for the interest rate on consols?

8. What would be a possible explanation for the decrease in total money demand indicated in question 7?

9. Suppose the Federal Reserve decreased the money supply and immediately thereafter the demand and supply of money were in disequilibrium.

a. What exactly do we mean by "disequilibrium" here?

b. Explain the forces that would be set in motion in this market to bring it back to equilibrium.

10. Suppose the Federal Reserve implemented a policy action that caused an increase in the real rate of interest.

a. Discuss how national income and the real interest rate itself will respond.

b. Differentiate between the income effect and the liquidity effect.

c. Could there be a price effect as well?

11. Suppose that the economy is in equilibrium, with businesses producing a total of $75 billion for consumption and $25 billion for investment in plant, equipment, and the like. The national income being generated is $100 billion. Individuals, in the aggregate, save one-fourth of their income. Assume that there is no government and the economy is closed with no imports or exports. Suppose now that businesses reduce investment to $20 billion.

   a. What is the implication for national income over the next three time periods? (Assume that the business investment remains at the $20 billion level.)

   b. Can you determine what the equilibrium level of national income would be if we followed the impact over a large number of time periods? (Business investment remains at $20 billion.)

12. Will the reduction in expenditures on investment posed in question 11 (plant, equipment) ultimately have an impact on the real rate of interest?

13. Explain the impact of a tax increase on the real rate of interest and the level of national income.

BIBLIOGRAPHY

BROWN, W. W., and G. J. SANTONI, "Monetary Growth and the Timing of Interest Rate Movements," *Federal Reserve Bank of St. Louis Review* (August–September 1983).

CAGAN, P., *The Channels of Monetary Effects on Interest Rates*. Washington, D.C.: National Bureau of Economic Research, 1972.

FRIEDMAN, M., "Factors Affecting the Level of Interest Rates," *Money Supply, Money Demand, and Macroeconomic Models*. Boston: Allyn & Bacon, 1972.

GIBSON, W. E., "Interest Rates and Monetary Policy," *Journal of Political Economy* (May–June 1970).

GIBSON, W. E., and G. E. KAUFMAN, "The Sensitivity of Interest Rates to Changes in Money and Income," *Journal of Political Economy* (May–June 1968).

IBBOTSON, R. G., and R. A. SINQUEFIELD, *Stocks, Bonds, Bills, and Inflation: The Past and the Future*. Charlottesville, Va.: Financial Analysts Research Foundation, 1982.

MELVIN, M., "The Vanishing Liquidity Effect of Money on Interest: Analysis and Implications for Policy," *Economics Inquiry* (April 1983).

MISHKIN, F. S., "Monetary Policy and Long Term Interest Rates: An Efficient Markets Approach," *Journal of Monetary Economics* (January 1981).

———, "Monetary Policy and Short Term Interest Rates: An Efficient Markets–Rational Expectations Approach," *Journal of Finance* (March 1982).

WALSH, C. E., "Interest Rate Volatility and Monetary Policy," *Journal of Money, Credit and Banking* (May 1984).

10 THE TERM STRUCTURE OF INTEREST RATES

Introduction

In the Capital Asset Pricing Model and the Arbitrage Pricing Theory, attention centers on the relationship between the risk of a security and the security's expected rate of return. In this chapter we are interested in the term structure of interest rates, or the relationship between the *term* to maturity of bond investments and their promised *yields* to maturity. The promised yield to maturity is the rate of return a bond investment would earn if held from the current time until its maturity date, and if there was no default on any of the promised payments. The term to maturity is the number of years until the last promised payment.

THE NATURE AND HISTORY OF THE TERM STRUCTURE

The term structure of interest rates is usually drawn for bonds of a uniform quality with respect to the probability of default and for bonds with a uniform degree of tax exposure. Thus, you might examine the term structure for treasury bonds, all of which are default free, are taxable at the federal level, and are tax exempt at the state level. The term structure is drawn for a given point in time. Figure 10–1 represents the term structure of interest rates for treasury bonds as

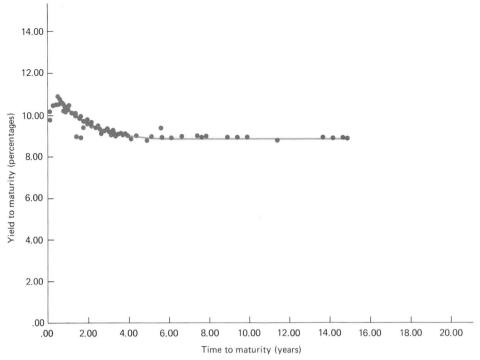

Figure 10-1 Term Structure, January 1, 1979

of January 1, 1979. Each point on the graph represents one treasury bond. The smoothed curve that has been drawn through the points represents the term structure, or the relationship between yield to maturity and term to maturity. At the beginning of 1979, the term structure was downward sloping, in the sense that short-term yields were higher than long-term yields.

The shape of the term structure changes dramatically as time goes by. This is readily apparent in the three-dimensional diagram of Figure 10–2. In this figure yield to maturity is plotted vertically and time is plotted horizontally. Note that term to maturity increases as you move toward the rear of the diagram. Thus, the broken line, in the lower right portion of the diagram, is the term structure for the month of January 1955. This term structure is upward sloping, with long-term yields above short-term yields. As is evident from the figure, upward sloping term structures are more common than downward sloping term structures. As we shall see later, this may reflect the presence of what we call "liquidity premiums" in expected bond returns, or it may simply reflect the fact that the market to some extent anticipated the upward trend in the general level of interest rates that occurred over the period. In any case, it is obvious that the term structure undergoes dramatic changes in shape over time.

If you go to work for a major bank and end up managing the bank's portfolio of government bonds, the term structure of interest rates will be a crucial piece of information you will be dealing with each day. In fact, your major objective

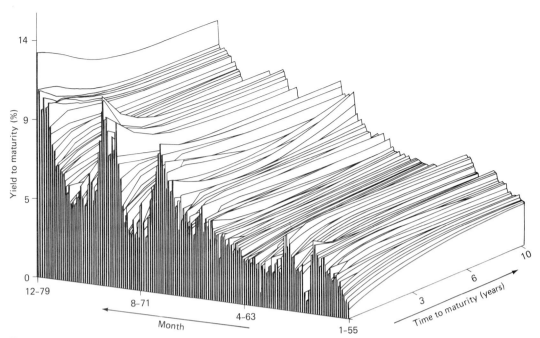

Figure 10-2 History of the Term Structure, January, 1955–December 1979

may be to place the bank's bond portfolio on an optimal point on the term structure. Suppose, for example, that you were dealing with the term structure of Figure 10–1. Given the general policy of a typical bank, you will confine your bond investments to bonds with terms to maturity no longer than five years. The main question at issue for you here is, "Should I shorten the average maturity of the bank's portfolio to pick up the additional increment in yield offered by the shortest term bonds?"

Although it appears from Figure 10–1 that as you move to shorter terms to maturity, you may increase your expected return, this is not necessarily the case, at least for your return for a given period of time into the future. As we shall see, a downward sloping term structure, such as the one in Figure 10–1, is usually consistent with a market expectation of a decline in interest rates. If interest rates decline, the prices of long-term bonds will rise. Although long-term bonds are priced to produce an *average* return to investors of approximately 9 percent over their periods to maturity, this is not necessarily the rate of return expected on the bonds in the *next year*. A one-year bond may be priced to yield a rate of return of 10 percent in the coming year, but, given the expected decline in interest rates and the accompanying capital gains, *long-term* bonds may be expected to produce a rate of return in excess of 10 percent, at least in the coming year.

To answer intelligently the question of where to position yourself on the term structure, you must first understand the forces that bend and twist the term structure into the various shapes that we see over time.

CHAPTER 10   The Term Structure of Interest Rates

As discussed, in drawing the term structure, you deal with bonds of a given investment quality and tax exposure. In Table 10–1 is a listing of a group of such bonds, treasury bonds, taken from the *Wall Street Journal*. The listing is for March 13, 1984. The first column, labeled "Rate," shows each bond's annual interest, or coupon, payment divided by the bond's principal, to be paid at maturity. The principal for these bonds is $1000, so a rate of 9 percent indicates an annual interest payment of $90. Actually, the interest is paid every six months in $45 increments. Interest is paid each year on the fifteenth day of the month in which the bond matures and on the fifteenth day of the month falling six months earlier.

The next two columns show the maturity date for each bond. First is the year in which the bond matures. If a range of years is given, this means that the bond matures on the last year but is callable as of the first year. After the year is the month in which the bond matures. The symbol "n" after the month indicates that the issue is a treasury note, as opposed to a treasury bond. Aside from the maturity when originally issued, there is really no important investment difference between notes and bonds.

In the fourth and fifth columns are the bid and asked prices for the bonds. Treasury bonds are bought and sold through dealers, who carry an inventory of each issue. The bid price is the price they are willing to pay in order to add bonds to their inventory. The asked price is the price you must pay in order to induce dealers to sell you a block of bonds from their inventory. The price is expressed as a percentage of the principal amount of the bond ($1000). It is important to note that the number following the decimal point in the quote is not really a decimal. The price is quoted in 32nds, so a bid price of 80.30 indicates that the price of the bond is 80 and 30/32 percent of $1000, or $809.375. The number in the sixth column is the change in the bid price from the previous day.

Table 10–1 Price Listing for U.S. Treasury Securities

Treasury Bonds and Notes

Rate	Mat. Date	Bid	Asked	Bid Chg.	Yld.	Rate	Mat. Date	Bid	Asked	Bid Chg.	Yld.
14s,	1985 Jun n	100.7	100.11+	.1	2.51	13¼s,	1986 May n	105.14	105.18+	.1	7.30
10s,	1985 Jun n	100.2	100.6		3.65	13s,	1986 Jun n	105.2	105.6		7.67
10⅝s,	1985 Jul n	100.12	100.16		6.04	14⅞s,	1986 Jun n	106.29	107.1 +	.1	7.65
8¼s,	1985 Aug n	100.5	100.9 +	.1	6.27	12⅝s,	1986 Jul p	104.31	105.3 −	.2	7.78
9⅝s,	1985 Aug n	100.12	100.16+	.1	6.21	8s,	1986 Aug n	100.8	100.12−	.4	7.66
10⅝s,	1985 Aug n	100.18	100.22		6.89	11⅛s,	1986 Aug n	103.24	103.28 −	.3	7.81
13⅛s,	1985 Aug n	100.29	101.1		6.23	12⅞s,	1986 Aug p	104.27	104.31−	.5	7.95
10⅞s,	1985 Sep n	100.31	101.3		6.75	11⅞s,	1986 Sep p	104.18	104.22−	.3	7.96
15⅞s,	1985 Sep n	102.11	102.15−	.1	6.70	12¼s,	1986 Sep n	104.31	105.3 −	.3	8.00
10½s,	1985 Oct n	101.3	101.7 +	.1	6.97	11⅝s,	1986 Oct p	104.15	104.19−	.3	8.01
9¾s,	1985 Nov n	100.30	101.2 +	.1	6.99	6⅛s,	1986 Nov	97.28	98.28−	.2	6.98
10½s,	1985 Nov n	101.9	101.13		7.24	10⅜s,	1986 Nov p	102.27	102.31−	.4	8.16
11¾s,	1985 Nov n	101.23	101.27+	.2	6.99	11s,	1986 Nov n	103.23	103.27−	.3	8.05
10⅞s,	1985 Dec n	101.25	101.29+	.2	7.15	13⅞s,	1986 Nov n	107.22	107.26−	.2	7.90
14⅛s,	1985 Dec n	103.17	103.21 +	.2	6.99	16⅛s,	1986 Nov n	110.21	110.25−	.3	7.88
10⅝s,	1986 Jan n	101.26	101.30+	.1	7.36	9⅞s,	1986 Dec p	102.10	102.14		8.15
10⅞s,	1986 Feb n	102.5	102.9 +	.1	7.47	10s,	1986 Dec n	102.16	102.20+	.1	8.14
13½s,	1986 Feb n	103.26	103.30		7.28	9¾s,	1987 Jan p	102.3	102.7		8.26
9⅞s,	1986 Feb n	101.11	101.15+	.1	7.55	9s,	1987 Feb n	101.1	101.5		8.24
14s,	1986 Mar n	104.26	104.30+	.1	7.40	10s,	1987 Feb p	102.13	102.17−	.2	8.37
11½s,	1986 Mar n	102.28	103 +	.2	7.49	10⅞s,	1987 Feb n	103.25	103.29+	.1	8.31
11¾s,	1986 Apr n	103.10	103.14+	.3	7.57	12¾s,	1987 Feb n	106.20	106.24−	1	8.31
7⅞s,	1986 May n	100.5	100.9 +	.4	7.55	10¼s,	1987 Mar n	102.30	103.2 +	.1	8.37
9¾s,	1986 May n	101.13	101.17+	.4	7.59	10¾s,	1987 Mar p	103.24	103.28+	.1	8 37
12⅝s,	1986 May n	104.11	104.15+	.4	7.65						

Riding the Yield Curve

The room is in the shape of a square, roughly the size of a baseball diamond. The eighty people who fill the room don't seem very active, but the atmosphere is electric. Substantial sums of money are being made or lost through trading in securities related to the government bond market. On any given day, more is usually made than lost.

We are at the Chicago-based division of a large government securities dealer. This company trades for its own account in U.S. government bonds, government agency securities, and options and futures contracts on these securities.

The floor rises on two sides from the middle of the room as a V. Four rows of desks move up the V on each side. Eight traders are positioned along each row. Before each trader is an array of monitors, some green, some black. Flashed on the monitors are prices for foreign currency futures, Government National Mortgage Association securities, treasury bonds, and other options and futures contracts. Some of the information on these monitors are quotations from one or more of the thirty-six primary government bond dealers in the United States. Each of these dealers is required to make a bid on all outstanding treasury securities. These dealers support the secondary market in government and agency securities. Approximately $40 billion to $50 billion is traded in this market daily, as compared to the approximately $2 billion that is traded in the stock market each day. Only the dealers have access to the quotations on the screen. None of the individual dealers knows which dealer actually stands behind the quote. This firm is one of the thirty-six dealers.

Rob Schumacher sits before one of the panels of monitors. Rob graduated with an MBA in finance from Northwestern University in 1976. He now rides the yield curve every day, trading in long- and short-term government securities. Among other things, he tries to forecast movements in the term structure of interest rates and then trades on the basis of his forecasts. The yield curve is currently upward sloping, and Rob expects it to flatten over the next day or so. One of the positions he has taken today is to go long in 26 million of five-year treasury bonds. He has financed the position by going short in 14 million three-year treasury bonds and 12 million four-year bonds. If short rates go up and long go down, the rates of return on the bonds he is short in will be less than the rate associated with his long position, and the difference will belong to his company.

Rob makes his prediction based on his own economic training, the past history of spreads between securities of Treasury and government agencies and movement of issues relative to the yield curve, and areas of supply, such as the Treasury financing schedule. He is trading the company's money, and this is not a job for a timid soul.

Prices begin to move on screens everywhere. A voice from the center of the room cries out, "Something is happening." People attempt to guess at what, but no one knows for sure. Rob studies his monitors steadily and intently.

A bell rings announcing the close of the market. The head of this division begins announcing the closing prices of several key issues. As prices are read off one by one, Rob breaks into a broad smile. He turns to his colleague and beams, "We got a great close." The firm is several hundred thousand to the good.

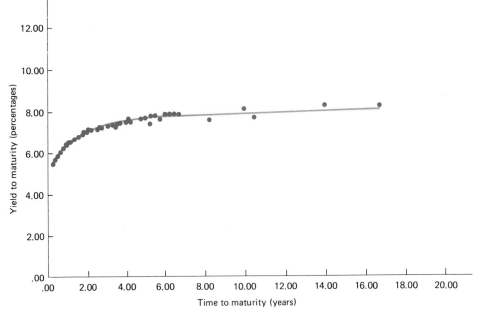

Figure 10-3 Term Structure: July 1, 1976

The number in the final column is the yield to maturity for each bond. As indicated above, the yield to maturity is the average annual rate of return you will get on the bond if you hold it until maturity.

The bonds in Table 10–1 are arranged in order of term to maturity. In Figure 10–3 we have plotted the yields and terms to maturity of treasury bonds taken from a different point in time, July 1, 1976. We have plotted yield to maturity on the vertical axis and term to maturity on the horizontal axis. The smoothed curve running through the scatter is our estimate of the term structure.

METHODS OF COMPUTING THE YIELD TO MATURITY

The yield to maturity is the average annual rate of return promised over the life of a bond. As discussed in the appendix to this chapter, there are three accepted methods of computing the average rate of return. Each method carries its own assumption about what you do with profits you earn on the investment along the way.

The Arithmetic Mean Yield to Maturity

The most straightforward method is to compute the *arithmetic mean* of the expected periodic future rates of return on the bond. Let's assume that we are dealing with periods equal to one year.

With this method, first estimate the rates of return you expect the bond to produce in each of the years of its life. The rate of return in any given year is equal to the sum of the annual interest payment and the change in the price of the bond in the course of the year, divided by the market price of the bond at the beginning of the year. To get the arithmetic mean yield to maturity, you sum up the expected returns on the bond in each of the coming years of its life and divide the sum by the number of years until maturity.

The arithmetic mean yield to maturity assumes that you keep the dollar investment in the bond constant over time. That is, at the end of each year, you set any profits aside. If you have a loss for the year, you restore the investment to its original dollar value by adding new funds. Given this assumption regarding the reinvestment of funds, the arithmetic mean yield to maturity gives you the expected average annual percentage increase in your (constant) capital investment in the bond. In their test of the Capital Asset Pricing Model, Black, Jensen, and Scholes employed the arithmetic mean to measure the returns on their ten stock portfolios.

The Geometric Mean Yield to Maturity

Another method is called the *geometric mean yield to maturity*. To compute the geometric mean, you add 1.00 to each of the expected future annual returns on the bond. Thus, if you expect the bond to produce a rate of return of 15 percent next year, you would convert that number to 1.15. Then you multiply all the converted returns together, and take the *n*th root of the product, where *n* is the number of years to maturity for the bond. After subtracting 1.00 from the root, you have the bond's geometric mean yield to maturity. The geometric mean yield assumes that you reinvest all profits back into the bond. That is, as interest is paid, you reinvest the interest payments by buying more of the bond. Moreover, you do not realize capital gains or restore capital losses. Under these assumptions, the geometric mean yield to maturity gives the average percentage increase in your wealth over the life of the bond.

The Internal Yield to Maturity

The numbers in the last column of Table 10–1 are called *internal yields to maturity*. To compute the internal yield to maturity, you find the rate of discount that will discount all the cash flows associated with the bond investment to a present value equal to the current market price of the bond. The cash flows, of course, are the interest and principal payments. The internal yield to maturity assumes that, as interest payments are received, they can be reinvested in the market at a rate of interest that will always be equal to the internal yield. This assumption is reasonable if the interest rate can be expected to remain at its present level. If interest rates are expected to decline, the internal yield is an overestimate of the true average percentage increase in your wealth that you can expect to get over the life of the bond. The internal yield assumes that interest payments received in the future will be reinvested at today's interest rates. If future interest rates are expected to be lower than those of today, this is an overly optimistic assumption.

In spite of the fact that it makes an assumption that at times can be unrealistic, the internal yield to maturity is the accepted standard of the industry. Nevertheless, you should recognize that other methods for computing the yield of a bond are available, and at times their assumptions may be more acceptable to you.

Because of its relative simplicity, in the discussion of the theories of the term structure that follows, we shall be working with a term structure of arithmetic mean yields to maturity. A more complete discussion of the three methods of computing yield to maturity is provided in the appendix to this chapter.

A BRIEF OVERVIEW OF THE THREE
THEORIES OF THE TERM STRUCTURE

At any given point in time, three factors influence the shape of the term structure:

1. The market's *expectations* regarding the future direction of interest rates

2. The presence of *liquidity premiums* in expected bond returns

3. Market *inefficiency* or impediments to the flow of funds from the long- (or short-) term end of the market to the short- (or long-) term end

There are three theories of the term structure. In each of the theories, one of the three factors takes center stage.

The *market expectations theory* contends that the term structure is influenced exclusively by the first factor. In this theory the yield to maturity of a five-year bond is simply the average of the yields expected on one-year bonds over the next five years.

The *liquidity preference theory* contends that the shape of the term structure is also affected by the presence of liquidity premiums. A *liquidity premium* is a type of risk premium. If investors don't regard long-term bonds and short-term bonds as perfect substitutes, they may require different returns from them over common intervals of time, much as they require different returns from high and low beta stocks. The liquidity preference theory contends that the shape of the term structure is affected not only by the market's expectations regarding future interest rates but also by the nature of the liquidity premiums between long- and short-term bonds.

The third theory, the *market segmentation theory,* is consistent with the notion of the market's inefficiency in the pricing of bonds. The theory contends that each maturity sector of the bond market can be viewed as being segmented from the others. It is segmented in the sense that there are impediments to the free flow of capital from one segment to another. Each segment of the market is said to be inhabited by a distinct group of investors that feels that they must invest in bonds of a given maturity, irrespective of opportunities for higher returns outside their preferred maturity range. If money happens to flow to the inhabitants of the long-term segment, they will buy long-term bonds, bidding their prices up and their yields down. The term structure will tend to be downward sloping not because of market expectations or risk premiums but merely because of the direction in which funds happen to be flowing.

THE MARKET EXPECTATIONS
THEORY OF THE TERM STRUCTURE

Under the market expectations theory,[1] the term structure is determined solely by the market's expectations regarding future interest rates. When we speak of future interest rates, we will be referring to the future expected yields to maturity on one-year bonds. The choice of a year as the basic interval of time is arbitrary; we could as easily discuss the theories in terms of monthly returns.

The numbers in the first six rows of the table in Figure 10–4 are expected yearly returns on bonds of various maturities. These are the returns we expect to get by investing in the bonds in the years indicated. The returns are computed by summing the interest payment and capital gain or loss for the bond for the year and dividing this sum by the market price of the bond at the beginning of the year.

As we move across the rows toward the right, we move to different bonds, each having a longer maturity than the next. As we move down the columns, we move farther and farther into the future. The first row represents the rates of return expected on the bonds in the current year. The second row represents the rates of return expected next year, and so on. The first column of numbers represents the market's expectation of future yearly rates of return on one-year bonds. Because these bonds mature at the end of each year, these one-year holding period returns are also the market's expectation of the yields to maturity on these bonds.

As we said, when we speak of the market's expectation for future interest rates, we are speaking of the numbers going down the first column of the table. In this particular case, the market expects interest rates to rise from their current level of 3 percent to 12 percent in three years and then fall back to 8 percent at the end of five years. These numbers, of course, have been arbitrarily assumed.

As the years pass, each bond moves to a cell in the table to its immediate lower left. Thus, a bond that is a two-year bond today will be a one-year bond in a year from now. Its expected yearly return moves, therefore, from the cell in the first row, second column, to the cell in the second row, first column. The paths taken by each of the bonds are given by the arrows in the table.

The arithmetic mean yield to maturity for any one of the bonds can be com-

---

[1]Fisher (1896) was the first to suggest that market expectations influence the shape of the term structure. The theory was later refined by Hicks (1939) and Lutz (1940).

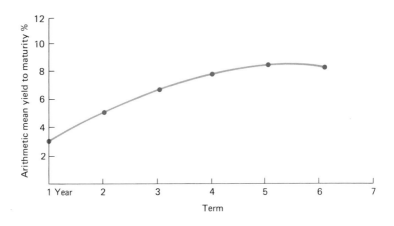

	1-yr bond	2-yr bond	3-yr bond	4-yr bond	5-yr bond	6-yr bond	
Now	3%	3	3	3	3	3	
1 year from now	7%	7	7	7	7	7	
2 years from now	10%	10	10	10	10	10	Expected annual rates of return
3 years from now	12%	12	12	12	12	12	
4 years from now	10%	10	10	10	10	10	
5 years from now	8%	8	8	8	8	8	
Arithmetic mean yield to maturity	3%	5	6.67	8	8.4	8.33	Yields to maturity
Geometric mean yield to maturity	3%	4.98	6.63	7.95	8.35	8.29	

Figure 10-4 Market Expectations Theory

puted by averaging its expected future rates of return from the current year until the time it matures. To compute the yield to maturity for a three-year bond, simply average the three returns in the three cells moving diagonally from first row, third column, to third row, first column. The current yield to maturity of a three-year bond is thus the average of 3, 7, and 10 percent, or 6.63 percent. The current arithmetic mean yields to maturity for each of the bonds is given in the seventh row of the table. The eighth row provides the geometric mean yields to maturity. Note that there is very little difference between the magnitude of the two types of yields.

The arithmetic mean yields to maturity are graphed in the term structure of Figure 10–4. For the most part, the shape of the term structure is upward sloping, reaching a peak for the yield to maturity of a five-year bond. Humped-shaped term structures like this one are consistent with a market expectation of one-year interest rates rising to a future peak and then falling.

The distinctive feature of the market expectations theory is that, for a given period of time, the market expects to get the same rate of return on all bonds, regardless of their term to maturity. Thus, in the table in Figure 10–4, the market expects a 3 percent rate of return on all of the bonds in the current year. Over the next two years, you can expect to get an average rate of return of 5 percent by buying a one-year bond today at 3 percent, holding it until maturity, and then buying another one-year bond a year from now at 7 percent. You can get the same 5 percent average return by holding a two-year bond until maturity or by buying a three-year bond and selling it after two years. Your average expected return on all of these investments is 5 percent over the next two years. This is true for any combination of bond investments over any given period of time.

Under the market expectations theory, we can say the yield to maturity on an n-year bond is equal to the average of the yields to maturity on one-year bonds for the next n years. This is true because all the numbers going across the rows are identical. Given this, the numbers going down the first column (future yields on one-year bonds) are identical to the numbers going down the diagonals (future rates of return expected on an n-year bond). However, this relation between the yield on an n-year bond and the future yields on one-year bonds over the next n years holds only for the market expectations theory.

The market will require the same rate of return on a three-year bond as it does on a one-year bond if it regards them as perfect substitutes. This will be the case if there is perfect certainty regarding the future returns on the bonds, if investors are risk neutral, or if it is the case that the risk associated with uncertainty in future interest rates can be diversified away or is perceived to be unimportant by investors as a whole. These are the conditions under which the market expectations theory of the term structure will hold. If these conditions don't hold, we may expect differentials in expected return, or risk premiums, to arise among bonds of different maturity. In the context of the term structure, these risk premiums are called liquidity premiums, and they are the focal point of the liquidity preference theory.

THE LIQUIDITY PREFERENCE
THEORY OF THE TERM STRUCTURE

The market may not regard a five-year bond as a perfect substitute for a one-year bond. Consider the probability distributions for rates of return on the bonds for the next year, as given by Figure 10–5. In dealing with treasury bonds, where there is no probability of default, the rate of return on the one-year bond is known with certainty. The distribution is drawn as a single spike with zero vari-

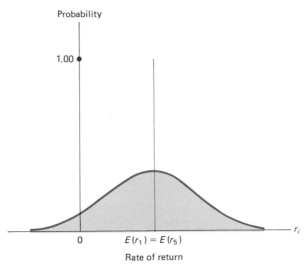

Probability

1.00

$E(r_1) = E(r_5)$

Rate of return

r_i

0

Figure 10-5 Probability Distributions for One- and Five-Year Bonds Under Market Expectations Theory

ance. In the course of the next year, however, the five-year bond has an uncertain rate of return. If interest rates should fall, the price of the bond will rise by the end of the year, and, based on both the interest payment and the capital gain, the return may be very large. On the other hand, if interest rates should rise, the price of the bond will fall. The capital loss may more than offset the interest payment, and the return for the year could well be negative. Thus, the probability distribution for the rate of return has a positive variance.

In Figure 10–5 both distributions have the same expected value, but if investors are risk averse, they may lower the current price of the five-year bond relative to the one-year bond to create a risk premium on the five-year issue, as in Figure 10–6. Given the presence of the premium, they may now be willing to invest in the five-year bond, even though it is perceived to have a greater degree of risk.

The liquidity preference theory allows for the possible existence of risk, or liquidity, premiums such as those in the term structure.[2] To see the effect they may have, consider the table in Figure 10–7. The market's expectations regarding future interest rates on one-year bonds are identical to those in Figure 10–4. However, now it is assumed that investors require an additional 2 percent premium in their expected return to invest in a two-year bond over what they require to invest in a one-year bond. Thus, although they expect to get 3 percent by holding a one-year bond for the current year, they expect to get 5 percent by holding a two-year bond in the same year. A three-year bond is assumed to command a 3 percent premium over the one-year bond. This same premium is assumed to hold for bonds with maturities in excess of three years. The structure

[2]Hicks (1932) was the first to argue that the market expectations theory was incomplete.

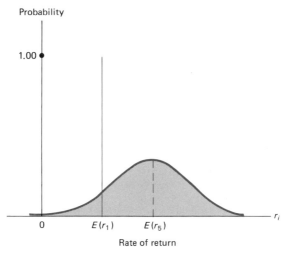

Figure 10-6 Probability Distributions for One- and Five-Year Bonds Under Liquidity Preference Theory

of liquidity premiums is assumed to remain constant in future years, although this is not a required assumption for the liquidity preference theory. A two-year bond is assumed to command the same premium in expected return in five years as it does today. This, of course, is an arbitrary assumption of the table.

The effect of liquidity premiums that increase in size with term to maturity is to make the term structure more upward sloping, if rates are expected to rise, or less downward sloping, if rates are expected to fall. In the table in Figure 10–7, the yield to maturity for a two-year bond is now the average of 5 and 7 percent (which is 6 percent) instead of the average of 3 and 7 percent (which is 5 percent). The broken curve of Figure 10–7 is reproduced from Figure 10–4. It shows the yield curve based on market expectations alone, without any liquidity premiums. The solid curve shows the term structure based on the expected interest rates in the table, including the liquidity premiums. The term structure has changed from being hump-shaped to being upward sloping through the six-year bond.

Not much is known about the nature of the liquidity premiums in the term structure. It is even possible to argue that for some investors, long-term bonds may be viewed as less risky than short-term bonds. The probability distributions of Figure 10–5 were drawn on the basis of a one-year horizon. Suppose, however, that you were concerned with how much money you were going to have at the end of five years instead of one year. Suppose also that the five-year bond is truly a five-year bond, in the sense that it is a pure discount issue with no interest payments until the payment in the fifth year. Over a five-year horizon, the probability distribution for the five-year bond is now a single spike with zero variance. However, the one-year bond can now be viewed as being risky. This is because we have to buy new one-year bonds at the end of each year. Although we know the one-year rate in effect now, we don't know what the one-year rate

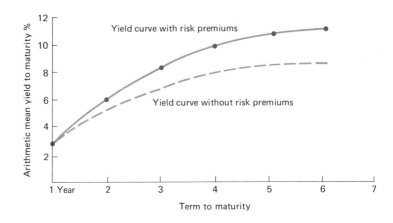

	1–yr bond	2–yr bond	3–yr bond	4–yr bond	5–yr bond	6–yr bond	
Now	3%	5	6	6	6	6	
1 year from now	7%	9	10	10	10	10	
2 years from now	10%	12	13	13	13	13	Expected annual rate of return
3 years from now	12%	14	15	15	15	15	
4 years from now	10%	12	13	13	13	13	
5 years from now	8%	10	11	11	11	11	
Arithmetic mean yield to maturity	3%	6	8.33	10	10.6	10.67	Yields to maturity
Geometric mean yield to maturity	3%	6	8.32	9.97	10.56	10.62	

Figure 10-7 Liquidity Preference Theory

will be a year from now, or the year after that, and so on. The probability distribution for investments in one-year bonds now has a variance, and investors with long-term horizons may require a premium to invest in short-term bonds.

To complicate matters further, the bond market is dominated by financial institutions with widely differing time horizons. Commercial banks have short-term liabilities in the form of deposits. These institutions minimize risk by matching these liabilities with short-term investments. On the other hand, pension funds and life insurance companies have long-term liabilities. If they are concerned at all about their survival, they would view long-term bonds as less risky than short-term bonds.

Furthermore, even if we agree that investors uniformly have short-term horizons, and therefore long-term bond return distributions have bigger variances, it isn't clear that the bigger variance would be regarded as an undesirable property. As we argue in the chapter on forward and futures contracts, long-term government bonds produce their greatest rates of return when interest rates are falling. Interest rates tend to fall in times of economic adversity. Thus, long-term bonds tend to pay off the most when investors are in greatest need of the funds. In this sense they act as insurance, and, when viewed in this light, their greater variance may be viewed as a desirable property.

Thus, we face ambiguity on two fronts. First, do long-term or short-term bonds have the larger variance of return? The answer to this question depends on the time horizons of investors. Second, if long-term bonds do indeed have the larger variance of return, do investors regard this as a desirable or undesirable property? The answer to this question depends on the perceived relationship between the level of interest rates and general economic activity.

The empirical evidence relating to the issue is also inconclusive. The best guess seems to be that there is approximately a 1 percent premium in going from the very shortest term bonds to bonds with maturities in excess of one year. Beyond one year there appears to be little evidence of additional liquidity premiums.

THE MARKET SEGMENTATION
THEORY OF THE TERM STRUCTURE

In essence, the market segmentation theory assumes that the market is populated by individual investors who are extremely risk averse and corporations and financial institutions for which survival is of paramount importance.[3] All seek to "immunize" their portfolios. As we learn in the next chapter, your portfolio is immunized if the effective maturity of your assets is matched up with the effective maturity of your liabilities.

This means that if you run a commercial bank, you will always buy short-term bonds because your liabilities are deposits, and their maturities are mostly short term. If you manage a pension fund, you will buy long-term bonds because you have contracted to pay long-term annuities over the retired lives of pensioners. If you were seeking to maximize the market value of the stock of the firm backing the pension fund, you might actively manage your bond portfolio, buying long-term bonds when you think interest rates are going to fall and moving short when you think a rise in rates is imminent. The market segmentation theory assumes, instead, that the survival of the institution is the objective function. To assure survival, you minimize risk, and this means matching the maturities of

[3]A leading advocate of the market segmentation theory is Culbertson (1957).

assets and liabilities, irrespective of the relatively attractive rates of return you may see in other maturities.

In Figure 10–8, the term structure is divided into two parts, a short-term segment and a long-term segment. For each segment there is a schedule of supply and demand for loanable funds. At the intersection of supply and demand, we establish the yield. The suppliers of loanable funds are those who invest in the securities. The demanders of loanable funds are those who issue the securities.

The suppliers in the short segment of the market are commercial banks and nonfinancial corporations. The nonfinancial corporations are investing their liquid balances until they need them to purchase raw materials, pay laborers, or make expenditures on plant and equipment. If you were working for the treasurers of these firms, you would invest these funds in the short-term end of the market. You may be thinking here of your own survival. If you invest these funds long, and rates go up, what will happen to your job if your investment decision results in a liquidity crisis for your firm?

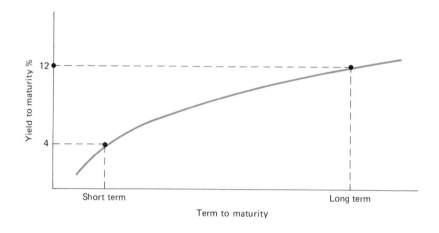

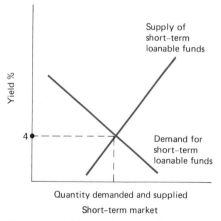

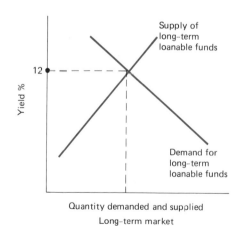

Figure 10-8 Market Segmentation Theory

The suppliers in the long-term segment include life insurance companies and pension funds. Life insurance companies sell their product on the basis of the assertion that they are financially as sound as a rock. To assure their policyholders that this is true, they minimize the risk of their investments. This, of course, includes matching the maturities of their assets and liabilities.

The demanders of funds include the Treasury of the United States and nonfinancial corporations seeking financing for their investments. Once again the market segmentation theory assumes that the financing strategies of the nonfinancial corporations are shaped by their desire to survive. Just as financial institutions seek to match the maturities of their investments with their liabilities, so do nonfinancial corporations match their liabilities with the maturities of their investments. If they are investing in an expansion of their inventory, they seek to finance their inventory expansion with short-term loans. On the other hand, if they are financing the construction of a major plant that is expected to produce cash flows for the corporation for many years to come, they can be expected to finance this type of investment with long-term debenture or mortgage bonds. In any case, the demand for long- and short-term loanable funds is said to be determined by the nature of the investment opportunities of corporations.

As we said earlier, the yield in each segment of the market is determined by the intersection of supply and demand. The supply schedule in each market shifts back and forth with the flow of funds into and out of the various types of financial institutions. If funds flow out of pension funds and into commercial banks, this puts upward pressure on long rates and downward pressure on short rates. The demand schedules shift with changes in the nature of investments being financed by corporations. At the beginning of the up side of the business cycle, the demand for long-term funds should increase, putting upward pressure on long-term interest rates. As the cycle matures and inventories begin to accumulate, demands for short-term loans to finance inventory expansion should increase, putting upward pressure on short-term rates. In this framework the term structure is shaped not by market expectations regarding the future direction of rates or by the structure of liquidity premiums but rather by the direction of fund flows from one financial institution to another and by the intensity and nature of economic investment by business firms.

In assessing this theory, it must be said that immunization is, in fact, widely practiced by financial institutions. However, it is doubtful that survival is the paramount objective of corporations and financial institutions. If these firms sought survival without any regard to maximizing the market value of their stock, they would soon find themselves targets for takeover by other firms that would gladly maximize their stock value and realize the capital gain.

Moreover, there are many individual investors here, and all over the world, who reject immunization in favor of wealth maximization. The market segmentation theory is a theory of market inefficiency. If the term structure is shaped without regard to the best available estimate of the future course of interest rates, then huge profit opportunities arise for the speculator who is free to invest in either end of the market. Suppose, for example, that based on the best available information, it is highly likely that interest rates were going to fall. In spite of this, because of the nature of fund flows and investment demands, the term structure is upward sloping. In this case, the expected rates of return to long-term bonds are going to be much higher than for their short-term counterparts. Speculators will move into long bonds to capture these attractive returns. In the process, they will drive the prices of long bonds up and their yields down. This pressure will continue until the expected returns on long-term bonds return to reasonable levels. This, of course, will happen only when the shape of the term structure conforms to the market's expectations.

Summarizing the discussion of the three theories, it may be reasonable to conclude that the term structure is shaped, for the most part, by the nature of the market's expectations regarding the future direction of interest rates. Liquidity premiums may play a role, but at this point, that role has not been clearly defined. At times, market imperfections and the pattern of capital flows through the marketplace may also play a role, causing the shape of the term structure to depart temporarily from that which is consistent with the best available estimate of the future direction of interest rates. When that happens, it is time for you, as a financial analyst, to act. In the process of acting, you may make a profit for your firm, or your own portfolio, and help force prices to conform to the best estimate of expected future interest rates.

DERIVING THE MARKET'S FORECAST OF FUTURE INTEREST RATES FROM THE TERM STRUCTURE

To the extent that the bond market is efficient in pricing securities so that price levels reflect the best available information, the term structure of interest rates will reflect the best estimate of the future course of interest rates. If you make an assumption about the structure of liquidity premiums, it is possible to extract from the term structure the market's forecast of future interest rates.

To see how this is done, consider Figure 10–9. The current yields to maturity on bonds with maturities from one to six years are provided in the seventh row of the table in the figure, and the term structure itself is plotted in the figure. What we would like to find is the market's forecast of future one-year interest rates going down the first column of the table.

One of these numbers is directly observable. The current yield to maturity of a one-year bond is 5 percent. Thus, you can write 5 percent in the first row of the first column. To get more numbers, we need to make an assumption about the structure of liquidity premiums. Let's assume that bonds with two or more years to maturity command a 1 percent premium in their yearly expected returns. This being the case, whereas investors expect to get a 5 percent return on a one-year bond in the first year, they will expect 6 percent on all bonds with two or more years to maturity. Thus, you can write 6 percent in all the remaining columns of the first row.

Now we can determine the numbers in the second row. The current yield to maturity of a two-year bond is 8 percent. We know this is the arithmetic mean

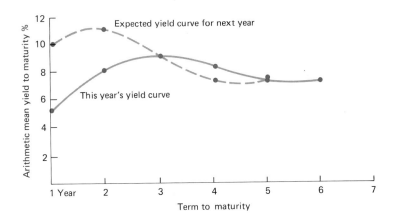

	1–yr bond	2–yr bond	3–yr bond	4–yr bond	5–yr bond	6–yr bond	
Now							
1 year from now							Expected annual rates of return
2 years from now							
3 years from now							
4 years from now							
5 years from now							
Arithmetic mean yield to maturity	5%	8%	9%	8%	7%	7%	Yields to maturity
Next years mean yield to maturity							

Figure 10-9 Extracting the Market's Forecast from Arithmetic Mean Yields

of the bond's expected returns in the first and second years. The bond is expected to produce a rate of return of 6 percent in the first year (first row, second column). Given an 8 percent mean, the market must be expecting a 10 percent rate of return in the second year (second row, first column). Given our assumption regarding the liquidity premiums, the market is expecting one-year interest rates to climb to 10 percent next year. If we assume the structure of liquidity premiums remains constant over time, we can now fill in the remaining numbers in the second row. Bonds with two or more years to maturity will command a 1 percent increment in their yearly expected return, so we can write in 11 percent for all the remaining numbers.

We can now find the market's expectation for the one-year rate of interest two years from now. The current yield to maturity on a three-year bond is 9 percent. This is the arithmetic mean of 6 percent, 11 percent, and the number in the first column, third row. That number must therefore be 10 percent.

The three remaining numbers in the first column can be computed in the same way. In making the computations, you will find the market expects one-year interest rates to fall to 4 percent in three years, continue falling to 2 percent in four years, and rise back to 6 percent in six years. This rather strange forecast results from the peculiar hump shape that we have assumed for the yield curve.

You can also find the market's expectation for the term structure of interest rates for next year and years beyond. To do this, just move forward one year and drop off the first row of the table. We know that the expected yield to maturity of a one-year bond is 10 percent (first column, second row). You can write this number in the first column of the last row of the table. To find the yield to maturity of a two-year bond next year, think of the remaining expected returns in its life. It is expected to produce an 11 percent return next year (second row, second column) and a 10 percent return in two years. The arithmetic mean of these two numbers is 10.5 percent, so this will be the yield to maturity of the bond next year. Write this number in the second column of the table. Continuing in this fashion, you can compute the market's expectation for the yield to maturity for a three-year bond to be 8.67 percent, for a four-year bond, 7.25 percent, and for a five-year bond, 7.2 percent. These numbers are plotted as the broken curve in Figure 10–9. The market expects short-term rates to rise, intermediate-term rates to settle somewhat, and long-term rates to rise a little.[4]

Summary

The term structure of interest rates relates the yields to maturity of bonds of a given quality to their terms to maturity. There are three theories concerning the forces that cause the term structure to change its shape as time goes by.

The *market expectations theory* contends that the term structure is shaped exclusively by the market's expectations regarding the future yields on one-year bonds. The market expectations theory is consistent with a world of certainty or a world populated by risk-neutral investors. If investors are risk averse, they may not regard bonds of different maturities as perfect substitutes. In this case, risk (or liquidity) premiums may arise in

[4]Technically speaking, this procedure requires an observed set of arithmetic mean yields to maturity. In actual practice, neither arithmetic mean nor geometric mean yield is directly observable. Using internal yields in place of either will only produce an approximation of the market's expectation of future interest rates. For an exact procedure to calculate market expectations from internal yields, see Haugen (1986), chapter 14.

the expected rates of return on bonds of different maturities. This is the case of the *liquidity preference theory.* Both the market expectations theory and the liquidity preference theory assume a relatively efficient and integrated market. On the other hand, the *market segmentation theory* assumes that the market can be divided into segmented or contained submarkets on the basis of maturity. The investors who populate each market are assumed to be unwilling to venture into other markets, irrespective of how attractive they perceive returns to be there. In this environment, the term structure is shaped by the flows of funds from one segmented market to another, and not on the basis of market expectations about future interest rates, or on the basis of the structure of liquidity premiums. In truth, the term structure is probably affected by all three forces, with market expectations the probable dominant force.

APPENDIX: AVERAGING MULTIPLE RATES OF RETURN

A rate of return expresses the percentage change in your wealth from one period to another. An average annual rate of return over several years expresses the average annual percentage change in wealth from the beginning of the first year to the end of the last. For example, you might ask, "If you start out with $100, and you end up with $220 after three years, then what's been your rate of return?" This is the same as asking, "What constant annual percentage change would increase your initial investment of $100 to $220 in the time of three years?" The answer to this question is 30 percent.

$$\$100 \times 1.30 = \$130 \qquad \$130 \times 1.30 = \$169 \qquad \$169 \times 1.30 = \$220$$

If we talk about a single period of time, the meaning of a rate of return is clear, but if we talk about multiple periods of time where you are getting amounts of money along the way, the concept of a rate of return becomes somewhat ambiguous.

First consider a single period of time. Let's suppose we're dealing with the cash flows of the investments given by the graph in Figure A10–1. Presume that we're talking about a stock, and you're investing $100 in the stock at the beginning of the period, so you have a negative cash flow of $100 at the beginning of the first year. At the end of the first year, the stock is worth $110 and you get a $40 dividend. Let's suppose you sell the stock at the end of the year. The total amount you receive is $150. You compute the rate of return by the equation at the bottom of the figure. The symbol r is the rate of return, equal to the dividend that you get on the stock plus any change of price, or capital gain or loss, divided by the market price of the stock at the beginning of the year—the price at which you bought the stock. Note that it is also equal to the dividend plus the ending stock value divided by the beginning value, less 1.

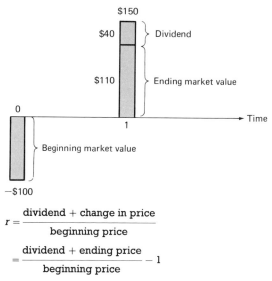

$$r = \frac{\text{dividend} + \text{change in price}}{\text{beginning price}}$$

$$= \frac{\text{dividend} + \text{ending price}}{\text{beginning price}} - 1$$

Figure A10-1 Single Period Return

Now consider the example in Figure A10–2. This is the case of a stock with a beginning market value of $100. At the end of one period you get a dividend of $30 from the stock. At the end of the second period you get another dividend of $20, and at the end of this period the stock is worth $120. So you've got an interim cash flow of $30, an ending value of $120, and an ending dividend of $20. What is the rate of return on this investment?

The problem here is that we need to make an assumption about what we are going to do with the $30 that we get at the end of the first period. The average rate of return that you get on the investment will depend on the nature of that assumption. There are three different ways of computing the average rate of return, each carrying a different assumption with respect to what we do with the money along the way. They are the arithmetic mean, the geometric mean, and the internal rate of return.

The arithmetic mean assumes that you keep the dollar amount invested constant, so if you invest $100 in the beginning, you always keep $100 invested in your portfolio. The geometric mean assumes that you reinvest all profits back into the stock, and those reinvestments earn the rates of return that the stock earns in subsequent periods. The internal rate of return assumes that you take any interim cash flows that are generated by the investment, and you reinvest those cash flows at the internal rate of return. Let's go through an illustration of each.

Consider the stock we were dealing with in Figure A10–2. We didn't discuss what the market price of the stock was at the end of the period, but let's assume it was $120. The price of the stock goes from $100 to $120, and then it remains at $120 through the end of the second period. The stock distributes a dividend of $30 at the end of period one and then $20 at the end of the second period.

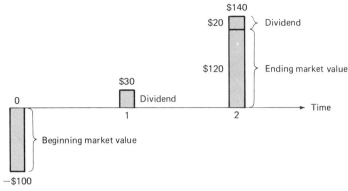

Figure A10-2 Multiperiod Return

If we compute the rate of return in each of the two years, we find them to be 50 and 16.7 percent, respectively.

$$(\$30 + \$20)/\$100 = 50\%$$
$$(\$20 + \$0)/\$120 = 16.7\%$$

How do you compute the average rate of return going across both periods? Keep in mind that this return should express the average percentage of increase in our wealth, going from the beginning of the first period to the end of the second. You have three choices in computing the average return.

The Arithmetic Mean

In computing the arithmetic mean, we take individual rates of return in each year, add them up, and divide by the number of years. In the example

$$(50\% + 16.7\%)/2 = 33.3\%$$

Remember, this computation assumes that the dollar amount invested is kept constant—in this case, at $100. You start with a $100 investment and you assume you keep $100 invested at the beginning of each year. So at the end of the first year, you have a stock worth $120 and you have a dividend of $30. You're going to have to put the dividend aside, and you're going to have to sell off $20 worth of stock and put that aside as well. So you set aside $50, and you leave invested in the stock your initial $100 capital commitment.

The stock then earns a 16.67 percent rate of return in the second period. If you've got $100 invested in the beginning of the second period, you're going to end up with $116.67 at the end of the period. You'll also have the $50 set aside. Your total income across the two periods will be $66.67. If you divide that by 2, your average annual income is $33.33. And because you've invested at all times $100, the average annual income represents an annual percentage increase in the amount invested of 33.3 percent.

Consider now a stock that doesn't pay any dividends. It starts out at the beginning of the first year at $100, doubles in price to $200, and then halves in price to $100. What's the rate of return? At first glance, it appears to be zero, but that's only because you're used to thinking in terms of reinvesting your money in the security. If this is true, you will end up with as much money as when you started. But with the arithmetic mean formula, you assume that you set aside profits and keep the dollar amount invested constant, and if you do that, your wealth will increase at an average annual rate of 25 percent. The rate of return in the first year is 100 percent. In the second it's -50 percent. So the average rate is 25 percent. Under what conditions will 25 percent represent your average return? It will if you set aside your profits at the end of each period. You leave $100 invested and you take the $100 gain at the end of the first year and set it aside. Now you've got $100 left invested in the stock. The stock produces a -50 percent rate of return for the second period, leaving you with $50. But you still have your $100 set aside. That gives you a total of $150 at the end of the second period—a total profit of $50 or $25 per year. This represents a rate of return on the amount you had invested ($100) of 25 percent per year.

The Geometric Mean

The second method of computing the average rate of return is called the geometric mean, which assumes that you let your profits ride and reinvest everything in the security. The formula for the geometric mean rate of return is

$$G_r = \{(1 + r_1)(1 + r_2) \ldots (1 + r_n)\}^{1/n} - 1$$
$$G_r = \{(1.5)(1.167)\}^{1/2} - 1 = 32.29\%$$

The geometric mean rate of return also represents your average percentage increase in wealth but under different assumptions relating to what you do with income produced during the life of the investment. This time you assume that all profits are reinvested in the investment. If you've got a capital gain, you leave it alone. If you get any dividends, you buy more stock. In this case you've got a $30 dividend at the end of the first period. At that time, the stock is selling for $120, so you can buy a quarter of a share for $30. Thus, going into the second period, you would own 1.25 shares. Each share produces $140 at the end of the second period. Each share will be worth $120, and each will distribute a dividend of $20. You own 1.25 shares, so your ending wealth will be equal to 1.25 times $140, or $175. What kind of an average percentage increase does that represent? That is, for what rate could you increase $100 twice in a row to get $175. The answer in this case is 32.29 percent.

$$\$100 \times 1.3229 = \$132.29 \qquad \$132.29 \times 1.3229 = \$175$$

The Internal Rate of Return

The internal rate of return can be defined as the rate of return that discounts the cash flows coming from an investment to a present value equal to the amount initially invested. In the example we are working with, you invest $100 at the beginning of the first period when you buy the stock. At the end of the first period, you get a $30 dividend, and at the end of the last period, if you sell the stock and keep the dividends, you have $140. So you have two positive cash flows, $30 and $140, following your initial negative cash flow, which was $100.

Time	0	1	2
Cash flow	−$100	$30	$140

To compute the internal rate of return, you find the rate of discount that will discount the positive cash flows equal to a present value that is equal to $100.

$$\text{Time} \qquad 0 \qquad\qquad 1 \qquad\qquad 2$$

$$\text{Present value} \qquad \$100 = \frac{\$30}{1+r} + \frac{\$140}{(1+r)^2}$$

The rate of discount can be found through trial and error. That is, you try a value for r and compute the present value. You then compare it to the amount on the left-hand side of the above equation. If it's not equal, you try a different r until you converge to equality between the right- and left-hand sides of the equation. In this case, the rate of discount that will discount those two flows to $100 is 34.27 percent.

$$\$100 = \frac{\$30}{1.3427} + \frac{\$140}{(1.3427)^2}$$

Again, the internal rate of return assumes that you take any interim money you get along the way and reinvest it at this particular rate of return. It assumes that there's some investment available that always yields that return. In the example, we get $30 at the end of the first period. If we put that in the investment and earn 34.27 percent on it, we would end up at the end of the last period with $40.28. If we added that to our $140, which we get as a holder of the stock at the end of the last period, that gives us an ending wealth of $180.28. Again, if $100 increases twice by a percentage amount equal to 34.27, it totals $180.28:

$$\$100 \times 1.3427 = \$134.27 \qquad \$134.27 \times 1.3427 = \$180.28$$

QUESTIONS AND PROBLEMS

Assume the following information for questions 1 through 3.

				Maturity
Year	0	1	2	3
Bond price	$970	$975	$985	$1000

Assume that the bond pays an annual coupon at the end of each year of $60. Assume that to receive the end-of-year coupon, you must have purchased the bond at the beginning of the year.

1. Compute the one-year rates of return on the bond for each of the periods represented in the data.

2. Compute the average multiperiod rate of return if you had purchased the bond at time 0 and sold it at time 2. Do this for each of the following methods of computing such a return:

   a. Arithmetic mean yield
   b. Geometric mean yield
   c. Internal yield

3. Compute the average multiperiod rate of return if you had purchased the bond at time 0 and held it until maturity (at time 3). Do this for each of the following methods of computing such a return:

   a. Arithmetic mean yield
   b. Geometric mean yield
   c. Internal yield

4. a. Which of the multiperiod methods for computing return has become the standard in bond markets?

   b. In what sense could this standard method be misleading to an investor?

5. Suppose you purchased a stock at year-end 1981 and sold it at year-end 1983. The year-end stock prices are shown below. The stock paid no dividends.

1981	1982	1983
$100	$112	$100

   a. Compute the average annual return according to the arithmetic mean method.
   b. Compute the average annual return according to the geometric mean method.
   c. Compute the average annual return according to the internal yield method.
   d. Compare the results and indicate which is more intuitively appealing in assessing the performance of your investment.

6. The text presented an equation used to fit a yield curve to a set of yield data as well as parameter estimates for this equation at July 1, 1976. Given this information, compute the approximate yields on one- and five-year U.S. government securities at July 1, 1976.

Refer to the following information for questions 7 through 10. Assume that the following represent points on the currently observed yield curve (assume these are arithmetic mean yields).

1-year bond	9.62%
2-year bond	9.12
3-year bond	8.72
4-year bond	8.42
5-year bond	8.17

7. Assuming the market expectations theory of the term structure, compute the market's expectations of one-year yields to occur

   a. One year in the future
   b. Two years in the future
   c. Three years in the future
   d. Four years in the future

8. Assuming the market expectations theory of the term structure, compute the market's expectations of

   a. The expected one-year return on a two-year bond, one year in the future
   b. The expected one-year return on a three-year bond, one year in the future

9. Assuming the market expectations theory of the term structure, compute the market's expectation of the term structure that will exist in one year.

10. Suppose that we assume there are liquidity premiums embedded in bonds with maturities greater than one year. In particular, suppose that there is a uniform 1 percent liquidity premium in all bonds with maturity greater than one year. Compute the market's expectations of one-year yields to occur

    a. one year in the future
    b. two years in the future
    c. three years in the future
    d. four years in the future

11. Assume the market expectations theory of the term structure and that the observed yields are geometric mean yields to maturity. Suppose the following points on the yield curve are observed currently:

1-year bond	9%
2-year bond	10
3-year bond	10.5

Compute the market's expectation of one-year bond yields expected to occur

    a. One year in the future
    b. Two years in the future

12. Why would a belief in the segmented markets theory of the term structure imply a belief in market inefficiency?

13. When you look at the yields to maturity on U.S. government securities plotted against time to maturity, the data do not plot exactly on a smooth curve. What would account for departures of the actual yields from a smooth curve?

BIBLIOGRAPHY

CULBERTSON, J. M., "The Term Structure of Interest Rates," *Quarterly Journal of Economics* (November 1957).

FISHER, I., "Appreciation and Interest," *Publications of the American Economic Association* (August 1896).

HAUGEN, R., *Modern Investment Theory*. Englewood Cliffs, N.J.: Prentice-Hall, 1986.

HICKS, J. R., *Value and Capital*. London: Oxford at the Clarendon Press, 1939.

LONG, J. B., "Stock Prices, Inflation and the Term Structure of Interest Rates," *Journal of Financial Economics* (July 1974).

LUTZ, F. A., "The Structure of Interest Rates," *Quarterly Journal of Economics* (November 1940).

MEISELMAN, D., *The Term Structure of Interest Rates*. Englewood Cliffs, N.J.: Prentice-Hall, 1962.

SCOTT, R., "An Arbitrage Model of the Term Structure of Interest Rates," *Journal of Financial Economics* (January 1978).

11 BOND PORTFOLIO MANAGEMENT

Introduction

In the chapters on portfolio management, we learned how to construct the efficient set. The efficient set contains portfolios of securities, not merely common stocks but bonds and other types of securities as well. In this chapter we talk about some issues and problems relating to the estimation of the risk and expected rates of return to bond investments.

The chapter is divided into two parts. In the section on aggressive bond portfolio management, our attention will center on how to estimate the expected rate of return and the risk of a bond investment over some specified planning period. Armed with estimates of these numbers, you can then maximize your return, given risk, using standard portfolio optimization techniques that address the stock, bond, and other components of your portfolio.

In the section on immunization, or defensive bond portfolio management, you will learn how to eliminate completely all sources of risk from a bond portfolio. If, for example, you are faced with the prospect of having to make a series of payments in the future, you will learn how to invest the present value of those payments to ensure that you have the required funds at the required times.

Throughout our discussion in this section, we will be assuming that we are dealing with relatively high-quality bonds. Speculative bonds, where default is a real factor, are priced by the market and can be treated by the portfolio investor much like common stock. Higher grade issues, on the other hand, are priced for the most part on the basis of the term structure of interest rates. Your estimate of the bond's expected rate of return, therefore, is based largely on your forecast of the term structure of interest rates at your horizon point, say, a month or a year from now.

Forecasting Expected Returns on Treasury Bonds

Suppose, as portfolio managers, we're faced with the task of estimating the expected returns on treasury bonds over the course of the next year. Our first step is to examine the current shape of the term structure. Suppose that we fit the term structure as in Figure 11–1. Notice that the individual treasury bonds are positioned above and below the curve. As discussed in Chapter 10, the bonds positioned above the curve have relatively large semiannual interest payments and are selling at prices at or above their principal values. Those positioned below the curve have smaller interest payments and usually sell at discounts below their principal values.

We shall refer to the ratio of the bond's yield to the yield of a bond of identical maturity taken from the curve as its *relative yield differential,* or RYD. The relative yield differential of any one of the bonds is given by the following equation:

$$RYD = Y / Y^*$$

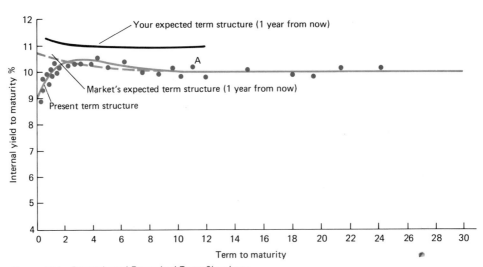

Figure 11-1 Present and Expected Term Structures

where Y^* is the yield to maturity from the term structure for a bond with the same number of years to maturity, and Y is the yield to maturity of the individual bond.

Our objective is to compute each bond's expected rate of return in the course of the next year. In general, the expected rate of return on a bond can be defined as

$$E(r) = \frac{E(\text{Interest payment} + \text{Ending price})}{\text{Current market price}} - 1$$

In the case of a treasury bond, we know the interest payment with certainty, so the formula can be written as

$$E(r) = \frac{\text{Interest payment} + E(\text{Ending price})}{\text{Current market price}} - 1$$

Our task is to estimate each bond's ending market price. The key to estimating the bond's ending market price is the estimation of its yield to maturity at the horizon point. Once we estimate the bond's ending yield to maturity, we can estimate the bond's ending price using equation (11–1). In the equation, the current time is assumed to be 0, and the bond is assumed to have currently n years to maturity. For simplicity, we have assumed that the bond's interest payments are paid annually, at the end of each year.

$$\text{Ending price} = \sum_{t=1}^{n-1} \frac{\text{Interest payment}}{(1 + Y_1)^t} + \frac{\text{Principal payment}}{(1 + Y_1)^{n-1}} \qquad (11\text{--}1)$$

where Y_1 is your estimate of the bond's internal yield to maturity at the end of the year.

Estimating the bond's yield at the end of the year requires a forecast of (a) the term structure and (b) a forecast of the bond's position relative to the term structure, or its relative yield differential. Let's begin with our forecast of the term structure.

We might start by asking what the market thinks the term structure of interest rates will look like next year. To extract the market's expectations from the term structure, we need to go through the process discussed in Chapter 10. Suppose we assume that there are no liquidity premiums in the term structure. Reading from the curve of Figure 11–1, we can develop the following schedule of internal yields to maturity:

Bond	Internal Yield
1 year	10.00%
2 years	10.37
3 years	10.45
4 years	10.41
5 years	10.33

Technically speaking, these are *internal* yields to maturity. In general, the differences between these yields and arithmetic yields to maturity will be small. To get a reasonably accurate *approximation* of what the market is thinking about next year's term structure, we will treat these as if they were arithmetic mean yields. Based on this assumption, and the procedure developed in Chapter 10, we find that the market expects the following series of one-year bond rates:

Time	1-Year Rate
Now	10.00%
Next year	10.74
2 years from now	10.61
3 years from now	10.29
4 years from now	10.01

Next year the one-year rate is therefore expected to be 10.74 percent. The yield to maturity on a two-year bond will be the average of 10.74 and 10.61 percent, or 10.67 percent. The yield to maturity on a three-year bond will be the average of 10.74, 10.61, and 10.29 percent, or 10.55 percent. Similar calculations can be made for bonds of other maturities.

Based on these calculations, the market's expectation for the term structure of internal yields to maturity is given by the broken curve in Figure 11–1. The market expects short-term rates to rise substantially and long-term rates to remain relatively constant.

You have to ask yourself whether this forecast is reasonable. If the forecast turns out to be accurate, all the bonds on the term structure will produce about the same rate of return in the course of the coming year. Equality in rates of return over given periods of time, of course, is consistent with the market expectations theory, and we have assumed away liquidity premiums in constructing the market's expectation of the term structure.

Suppose you have noticed that the Fed has dramatically increased its rate of growth in the money supply in recent months, and you have decided this is consistent with a permanent change in policy toward monetary expansion. Surveys have also indicated intentions on the part of consumers to lower their savings rate and on the part of business firms to increase their spending on plant and equipment later in the year. You anticipate the year-end incidence of income and price effects associated with the lower savings rate and monetary expansion and the liquidity effect of business firms attempting to finance their investments in the long-term market. You believe that short rates will be higher than the market expects, and you believe that long-term rates will rise to 11 percent. Your personal forecast of the term structure is given by the heavy solid line in Figure 11–1.

Having made your forecast of the term structure, to obtain consistent forecasts of the expected rate of return on each bond, you need to forecast the relative yield differential of each bond with respect to your term structure estimate. If you are willing to assume that these yield differentials remain constant over time, you can estimate each bond's year-end yield by multiplying the yield consistent with your personal forecast of the term structure by the bond's current relative yield differential.

For example, the bond labeled A in Figure 11–1 has a relative yield differential of 1.02. The bond is currently an eleven-year bond, but at the end of the year it will be a ten-year bond, and you have forecasted the general level of ten-year bond rates to be 11.0 percent. The forecast of the yield on this particular bond is thus 11.22 percent.

$$1.02 \times .1100 = .1122$$

You can obtain forecasts for each of the bonds on the term structure in the same fashion. Once you have estimates of each bond's individual yield to maturity, you can turn these into estimates of their year-end market prices by employing Equation (11–1). The year-end prices can then be used to estimate the expected returns for the year.

For example, suppose we are dealing with a three-year bond carrying a $100 annual interest payment. It is currently positioned above the yield curve and it has a relative yield differential of 1.05. Your forecast of the yield to maturity for a two-year bond is 10.67 percent. If the bond's relative yield differential persists, your forecast of its yield at the end of the year is

$$11.20\% = 1.05 \times 10.67\%$$

Given this estimated yield and Equation (11–1), we can estimate the price of the bond as

$$\$979.50 = \frac{\$100}{1.112} + \frac{\$100 + \$1000}{(1.112)^2}$$

If the bond is currently priced at $976.22, our expectation for its rate of return over the coming year is

$$10.57\% = \frac{\$100.00 + \$979.50}{\$976.22} - 1.00$$

Forecasting Expected Returns on Corporate Bonds

The expected returns on corporate bonds is a little more difficult to estimate. First, there is usually some probability of default on the bonds. If you assume that the probability of partial payments is zero, the expected value of the interest payment can be found as follows:

$$\text{Expected interest payment} = \begin{matrix}\text{Promised}\\\text{interest}\\\text{payment}\end{matrix} \times (1 - \text{Default probability})$$

Thus, if the promised payment is $100, and the probability of default is 2 percent, the expected interest payment is $98.

In estimating expected returns, you will be dealing with corporate bonds of a given quality, as estimated by the rating agencies. Thus, your estimates of AA utility bonds will be conducted separately from your estimates of BBB industrial bonds. For the higher quality issues, you can probably assign the same (small) probability of default to all the issues in the class. For lower quality issues, you may want to assign differential probabilities because, even though every bond in the class has the same rating, there is still a considerable range of quality within the rating class. After allowing for the tax effect of the size of the promised interest payment, you may want to accept the market's assessment of the chances for default and assign higher probabilities of default to bonds that are positioned above the term structure and lower probabilities to those positioned below.

Another difficulty associated with corporate bonds comes from the fact that the maturity of the bonds is, in the majority of cases, ambiguous. The firm usually holds an option to call the bond at a fixed price (or, more likely, prices that vary through time). If the market value of the bond rises above this call price, it is likely that the firm will exercise its option and retire the bond. The firm can usually exercise its option any time after a period of call protection, which begins immediately after the bond is originally issued.

In addition to call provisions, corporate bonds may have sinking fund provisions mandating that stated portions of the bond issue be retired each year. The corporate treasurer has the option of buying the bond in the market at prevailing market prices or calling some of the bonds in at a predetermined price. The identity of the specific bonds called in is determined by lottery. In any case, a corporate bond with ten years until maturity isn't really *expected* to be "alive" for ten years, the longest possible period of its life. Given the nature of its sinking fund and call provisions, the corporate bond's expected life may be considerably less than ten years.

The ambiguity regarding the life of corporate bonds causes potential problems. First, if you plot the bonds in terms of yield against their longest possible maturity, you're not going to get as good a fit as with treasury bonds because corporate bonds may be priced in terms of the time they are expected to be called, as opposed to the time they mature. Consider, for example, a corporate bond carrying a $150 coupon, originally issued when interest rates were at 15 percent. The bond has twenty years until maturity, but it is callable by the firm in two years at a price of $1150. Interest rates are currently at 10 percent, and if they stay there, the firm will certainly exercise its option to call. It is likely that the market will be pricing this bond as a two-year issue with a "principal" payment of $1150 (the call price). If the term structure is flat at 10 percent, the market price of the bond will be

$$\$1210.74 = \frac{\$150.00}{(1.10)} + \frac{\$150.00 + \$1150.00}{(1.10)^2}$$

Based on this price, the bond's internal yield to *maturity* is 12.4 percent. Plotted on this basis relative to its term to maturity, it would be positioned well above the curve fitting the term structure.

In fitting the term structure, you must take situations like this into account. Of course, not every case will be so clear-cut, so unless you can obtain perfectly accurate assessments of the market's *expected* maturity and yield to expected maturity, the fit you obtain will not be nearly as good as the one obtained for treasury bonds.

It's best to think of a callable bond as a portfolio of two securities. The portfolio consists of a positive position in the straight bond, without the call option attached, and a negative position in the call option, that is held by the firm that issued the bond. The market price of the bond that you read in the financial news is really the net value of these two individual securities. Consequently, if you compute the bond's yield to maturity based on this net value, you will get a confused picture of the straight bond's true yield.

The yield to maturity can be accurately computed by estimating the market value of the call option, and then adding this to the net value of the straight bond and the call option to find the value of the straight bond. The yield to maturity on the straight bond can then be found as the rate that will discount the stream of interest and principal payments to a present value equal to this estimated value.

We will be learning how to value options that are similar to those attached to corporate bonds in Chapters 12 and 13.

In estimating the bond's expected rate of return, you must estimate the net market value of the straight bond and the call option at the end of your planning period. The market value of the straight bond can be estimated using essentially the same procedure that you followed in estimating the ending market value for a treasury bond. The details involved in estimating the ending value for the call option are best saved for the next two chapters, but we can say at this point that the estimated value of the call will crucially depend on (1) your estimate of the ending value for the straight bond, and (2) your estimate of the variance of the daily rate of return to the straight bond.

Estimating the Risk of Bond Investments

To compute the efficient set, you need to estimate the covariance between the periodic returns on each bond and the rest of the securities in your population. In making the estimates, you can follow the same procedures you used for common stocks, but you need to keep one additional factor in mind. As time passes, the time to maturity of a bond becomes shorter and shorter. This is of little consequence if you are taking sample estimates of covariances over relatively short time intervals. However, if your sample extends over a considerable period, the nature of the bond may change dramatically from the beginning of the period to the end. Your covariance estimate reflects a composite picture of the risk of the bond as it goes from a relatively long-term bond at the beginning of the period to a relatively short-term bond at the end of the period.

To get more accurate estimates of the covariances, you may have to construct index bonds of various maturities. Suppose that your investment horizon is one month long. To construct an index bond representing a two-year treasury issue, you might fit the term structure for a series of months. You are interested in the series of rates of return produced by a bond that is a two-year bond at the beginning of each month and a one-year, eleven-month bond at the end of each month. Suppose, in the first month of your sample, that your fitted curve indicates that a two-year bond should have an internal yield of 12 percent. At the end of the month (or the beginning of the next), the curve indicates that a one-year, eleven-month bond should have an internal yield of 11.5 percent. If you make the working assumption that the bond was selling at a price equal to its face value at the end of the first month, you can compute its rate of return over the month by using the following procedure:

$$\text{Price (beginning of first month)} = \frac{\$120.00}{(1.12)^1} + \frac{\$120.00 + \$1000.00}{(1.12)^2}$$

$$= \$1000.00$$

$$\text{Price (beginning of second month)} = \frac{\$120.00}{(1.115)^{11/12}} + \frac{\$120.00 + \$1000.00}{(1.115)^{23/12}}$$

$$= \$1017.69$$

In the course of the month you will receive accrued interest of $10. Thus, the rate of return on the bond for the month is given by

$$r_t = \frac{\$10.00 + \$1017.69}{\$1000.00}$$

$$= 2.77\%$$

By performing this same operation for each of the months of the series in your sample, you can produce a series of rates of return on a bond that is a ten-year bond at the beginning of each of the months in the sample period. These rates of return can then be used to compute sample covariances with other bond returns (constructed in the same way) and stock investments.

Dividing the Portfolio Between Bonds and Stocks

The division of the portfolio between bonds and stocks should come naturally in the process of finding the efficient set. You input your estimates of expected returns on both stock and bond investments. Both estimates reflect your expectations of what will be happening to the general level of interest rates and the term structure in the various parts of the bond market (AAA industrial, AA utility, and so on). You also input your estimates of the covariances that exist between the different investments, bonds as well as stocks.

With these estimates, the computer can find the efficient set. If you forecast that the economy is recession bound, with business firms experiencing falling interest rates and deteriorating profitability, you will find that the efficient portfolios are weighted heavily in high-quality bonds. If, instead, you forecast that the economy will be emerging from a recession, with interest rates and corporate profits rising, your efficient portfolios may be more heavily invested in stocks and lower quality bonds.

In other words, the character of the efficient set reflects the character of your forecast of the economy, interest rates, the profitability of firms in general, and the relative performance of different companies. The optimal mix of bonds and stocks in your portfolio is then determined by the point of tangency between your indifference curve and the efficient set.

DEFENSIVE BOND PORTFOLIO
MANAGEMENT: INTEREST IMMUNIZATION

In the previous sections we talked about making forecasts of future interest rates and then positioning our portfolios to take best advantage of our forecast. This might be called *aggressive* bond portfolio management. In the sections that follow, we discuss *defensive* portfolio management. In managing the portfolio defensively, our objective is to reduce the risk of the portfolio to zero. A portfolio with zero risk is said to be *immunized*. Immunization is gaining increasing popularity with pension funds. Currently, billions of dollars in pension assets are immunized against changes in the rate of interest.

Pension funds promise to pay annuities to retired employees over their remaining lifetimes. A change in interest rates may threaten the fund's ability to fulfill its promise. If interest rates fall, interest income must be reinvested at lower rates. The wealth of the fund may not accumulate as fast as anticipated, and the fund may run short of money while it has remaining liabilities outstanding. The fund can protect against this risk by investing in very long-term bonds that produce most of their cash flows at points in time beyond the required payments to the pensioners. However, in doing this, the fund faces another risk. To make its promised payments, the fund must sell its bond investments in the market. If interest rates go up, the market value of its bonds may not be sufficient to produce the funds required to make the required payments. Thus, if you invest too short, you run the risk of having to reinvest the proceeds of your investments at inadequate rates. On the other hand, if you invest too long, you run the risk of having to liquidate your portfolio at inadequate market prices. When you immunize, you take a safe position between the two extremes.

To understand the concept of immunization, consider the pension fund in Figure 11-2 that has promised to pay the retired employees of the firm it represents annuities for the remainder of their lives. As time goes by, the employees gradually die, and the total amount of the payments gets smaller, finally reaching zero in twenty-three years.

If the pension fund is fully funded, it has sufficient invested assets to enable it to pay the liabilities in full at the current level of interest rates. Assume that interest rates are currently 10 percent and the present value of the stream of

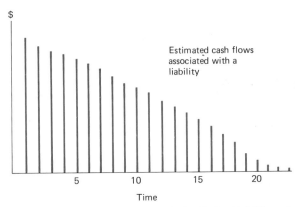

Figure 11-2 Cash Flows Associated with the Liabilities of a Pension Fund

payments at that rate is $10 million. Assume also that you invest this amount of money in short-term treasury bills. Suppose interest rates should fall. In this case the present value of the stream of payments goes up. The amount of money you need to have invested at the lower rate of interest is higher than it was before. However, the market value of your portfolio of treasury bills will have changed very little. The market prices of very short-term bonds are insensitive to changes in interest rates. You are in trouble. As portfolio manager, you have less money in your portfolio than you need to make all the expected payments to the retired workers.

Now assume, instead, that you invested the money in a twenty-three-year treasury bond. To make the payments along the way, you plan to sell off some of your holdings in the bond each year. Interest rates now go up. Being highly sensitive to changes in interest rates, the market value of your treasury bond falls dramatically in price. The present value of your liabilities falls also, but not as much as the fall in the value of your bond portfolio. The amount of money you have invested is once again less than the amount you need to make all the payments. You must sell many more bonds than expected to make the relatively large payments at the beginning of the stream. You are again in trouble. You will run out of bonds to sell while you still have more payments to make.

In each case your portfolio isn't immunized. There is no risk of default, because you have invested in treasury bonds. There is no inflation risk, because we have assumed that the pension isn't indexed with respect to inflation, so your liabilities are written in fixed dollar amounts. You still, however, are subject to *interest rate risk,* and this is what keeps getting you in trouble.

To immunize the portfolio against interest rate risk, you must invest so that its value fluctuates in accord with the present value of your liabilities. The easiest way to achieve this state is by *cash matching.* A cash-matched portfolio produces a stream of cash flows that match up exactly with the stream of liabilities. One way to cash match the liabilities of Figure 11–2 is to buy treasury bonds that have been stripped of their coupons or interest payments. You would buy enough one-year treasury bonds so that their total principal payments would equal your first pension payment coming at the end of one year. You would receive the money from the Treasury and pay it out to the retired workers on the same day. If you did the same thing with all the other payments in your liability stream, you would have cash matched your portfolio and you would now be immunized.

Cash matching is conceptually simple, but it has a major disadvantage. The problem is that, to cash match, you have to invest in many different bonds, some of which may be unattractive to you for tax reasons. Bonds having the same probability of default can still sell at differential pretax yields to maturity, based on the size of their annual interest payments. Bonds with relatively large coupons are typically positioned above the term structure, and those with small coupons are typically positioned below. This is because the low coupon bonds sell at prices that are discounted below their face values. As they approach maturity, their prices will rise to their face values. Thus investors in these bonds receive their return in the form of tax-sheltered capital gains as well as interest income. To make their after-tax yields commensurate with high coupon bonds, these bonds sell at lower pretax yields.

Pension funds pay no income taxes. For a pension fund, the pretax yield is also the after-tax yield. As a pension fund portfolio manager, it is in your interest to invest in bonds with the largest coupons or interest payments. These have the greatest tax exposure and the greatest pretax yields. Because you pay no taxes, you keep the entire yield. If you cash match, you must spread your investments over many different bonds, and you give up the opportunity to concentrate your investments in the two or three bonds on the term structure with the greatest tax exposure. This means that cash matching may cost you a great deal of money.

What we need is a means to achieve immunization while concentrating our investments in one or two securities. The total market value of these securities must rise or fall in step with the present value of our liabilities. Thus, we need a measure of the sensitivity of the values of our liabilities and assets to a change in interest rates. Duration is such a measure.

Macaulay's Duration

The formula for Macaulay's duration (1938) is given below for the case of a bond investment.

$$D = 1 \frac{\dfrac{C_1}{(1+Y)^1}}{V} + 2 \frac{\dfrac{C_2}{(1+Y)^2}}{V} + \ldots + n \frac{\dfrac{C_n + P_n}{(1+Y)^n}}{V}$$

where Y is the bond's internal yield, C is the annual coupon or interest payment to be paid in each year, P is the principal payment, n is the number of years until maturity, and V is the current market value of the bond. The formula assumes that interest is paid annually, with the first payment coming at the end of the first year. Each maturity date $(1, 2, \ldots, n)$ is multiplied by the ratio of the

Stalking the Big One

The decor of the room is absolutely impeccable. It reflects wealth and power. We are in the offices of National Investment Services of America (NISA), based in Milwaukee, Wisconsin.

Six people sit around an oval dining table, drinking coffee from fine china. Four of the six represent NISA. The other two are potential clients. NISA has been immunizing pension fund portfolios for several years now, using the Macaulay duration and the techniques discussed in this chapter. The techniques have worked effectively. At this point, in addition to extensive management of conventional stock and bond portfolios, NISA currently has approximately $500 million under immunization for several clients.

But this account is the big one. The client is one of the biggest firms in America. Its pension fund is approximately $7 *billion*. The portion of this that is being considered for immunization is approximately $2.5 billion. Four of those at the table are very tense; two are quite relaxed.

Each representative from NISA speaks in turn. Joe Gorman, president of the company, introduces his three colleagues. Mary Jo Dempsey runs the immunization program and trades in the bonds, when reimmunization is required. Tom Tushin markets the program on a nationwide basis. Professor Leif Grando works for the company as a consultant. He designed the program and has introduced modifications when required by NISA. These four have been through such sessions many times before, but this time is clearly different. The stakes are high—so high that when you open your mouth to speak, you wonder if it will be a lucid train of logic or garbled nonsense.

Gorman begins, and it is a lucid train of logic. The client already has an existing bond portfolio that is so large that moving completely out of it into an immunized portfolio is unfeasible. The size of the required trades would be so large as to upset prices in the market. To attack this problem, Gorman proposes the following solution. NISA would sell from existing bond holdings those issues for which the cash flows couldn't be forecast with precision. These would be callable bonds with large coupons, similar bonds with sinking funds, and bonds of doubtful quality.

Gorman explains that they are dealing with two types of risk. First, there is the risk that the cash flows associated with the liabilities and the assets of the pension fund will not actually be as expected. This is an actuarial risk for the liabilities and a default or call risk for the bonds. This risk will be minimized by retaining the proper investments in the bond portfolio—high-quality bonds for which there is little danger of premature retirement through call or execution of the sinking fund. Second, there is the risk of a change in interest rates. This will be eliminated through immunization.

After retaining the investments with relatively certain cash flows, these cash flows will be netted against the cash flows associated with the liabilities of the fund. The remaining net cash flow stream will have cash outflows in most months, but it can also have cash *inflows* in months where the cash inflows associated with the bonds retained are greater than the cash outflows associated with expected pension fund payments.

This *net* cash flow stream is to be immunized using NISA's conventional immunization techniques, with government bonds as a "cap" for the rest of the portfolio. If, on the basis of relative yield spreads or other considerations, part of the underlying corporate bond portfolio can be traded at a profit, the composition of the government bonds in the cap will be adjusted to keep the overall portfolio immunized.

Gorman goes into some of the more technical aspects of the program until both sides agree that the plan is a sound one.

Then the client voices the first challenge to the presentation. "But why immunize in the first place? The $2.5 billion will be completely riskless, but the rest of the portfolio will be invested in risky securities like common stock. On an overall basis, it will be as though we hadn't considered immunization."

NISA is ready for this question. Gorman's eyes lock with Grando's, and Grando begins the response.

"The beneficiaries of the pension fund can be divided into two groups, those who are still working and those who have already retired. It is difficult to estimate the benefits associated with the active workers, because they will be based on wages paid at retirement. If retirement comes in prosperity, the benefits will be large; if it comes in adversity, they will be small. To reduce the risk associated with the fund, the assets supporting these benefits should be invested in variable-income securities like common stock. To invest these funds in bonds would be to increase the risk of the fund rather than reduce it. The benefits for those who have already retired can be estimated much more precisely. These liabilities can be considered as fixed, and they can be either immunized or matched up with fixed-income securities. By dividing up the liabilities of the fund in this way, you address the problem of risk reduction in the fund in a more systematic, precise fashion."

"But why should we act to reduce the risk associated with the fund at all? Why shouldn't we manage the fund actively to squeeze out some extra profit?"

"That's a good question. Your stockholders won't care if you reduce the risk associated with your pension fund. They can readily change the risk of their portfolios in the capital market by buying or selling additional amounts of stocks or bonds. But management operates for the benefit of more than one constituent. In making decisions, for example, management must also consider the welfare of its employees. These people are interested in the firm's survival because they want to keep their jobs.

"Because of this, firms generally make decisions that will extend the expected life of the firm, when they can do so without penalizing the market value of their common stock. In making their investment decisions in the real sector of the economy, the firm can't hide from risk because the most risky projects may be those that will increase the price of their common stock. If management doesn't adopt these projects, someone else will buy up the stock of the firm and invest in them for them. But prices in the capital market are set on a highly competitive basis. There are no clearly profitable or unprofitable investments in the securities market. Thus, management can take low-risk positions there without materially affecting the price of its common stock. It can extend the expected life of the firm and so benefit its employees without penalizing its common stockholders. Immunization can be viewed as a precise way of reducing the risk associated with the pension fund."

The tension in the room begins to ease. Some goods points have been made. Doubts have been eliminated. NISA clearly has a long road to go on this account, but today it has taken a very big step toward landing the big one.

present value of the payment to be received to the total present value of all the payments.

Suppose we are dealing with a bond that carries a $100 annual coupon and has two years to maturity. The internal yield to maturity of the bond is 10 percent. The present value of the first annual coupon is

$$\$90.91 = \$100.00/(1.10)^1$$

The present value of the principal payment and the second annual coupon is

$$\$909.09 = \$1100.00/(1.10)^2$$

making the total present value of the bond

$$\$1000.00 = \$90.91 + \$909.09$$

In computing the duration, we think of the bond as a portfolio of two individual payments and compute the weighted average *maturity* of the portfolio much as we would the weighted average expected rate of *return* of a stock portfolio. For the stock portfolio we would weight each stock's expected return by the fraction of the total value of the portfolio attributed to each stock. We do the same thing here. We weight the maturity of each payment by the fraction of the total present value accounted for by each payment.

The fraction accounted for by the first payment is

$$\$90.91/\$1000.00 = .09091$$

The fraction accounted for by the second payment is

$$\$909.09/\$1000.00 = .90909$$

Thus, the weighted average maturity of the two payments, the duration, is given by

$$(.09091 \times 1 \text{ year}) + (.90909 \times 2 \text{ years}) = 1.9091 \text{ years} = D$$

Duration and Yield Elasticity

Duration not only measures the average length of the payment stream, it also approximates the elasticity of the value of the bond with respect to a change in one plus the bond's yield to maturity.

$$D \approx - \frac{\dfrac{V_1 - V_2}{(V_1 + V_2)/2}}{\dfrac{Y_1 - Y_2}{1 + (Y_1 + Y_2)/2}} = - \frac{\text{Percentage change in value}}{\begin{array}{c}\text{Percentage change in one}\\\text{plus internal yield}\end{array}}$$

Suppose that the internal yield of the two-year bond discussed above increased from 10 to 12 percent. In that case the market value of the bond would fall from $1000 to $966.20.

$$\$966.20 = \$100.00/1.12 + \$1100.00/(1.12)^2$$

The elasticity of the value of the bond with respect to the change in one plus the internal yield could then be computed as

$$\frac{\dfrac{\$966.20 - \$1000.00}{(\$966.20 + \$1000.00)/2}}{\dfrac{1.12 - 1.10}{(1.12 + 1.10)/2}} = -1.908$$

The elasticity is the percentage change in value accompanying each percentage change in one plus the yield. In computing an elasticity, the base used for computing the percentage change is the average of the beginning and ending values, rather than the beginning value alone. The negative sign in front of the elasticity indicates that there is an inverse relationship between value and yield.

Thus, given that a bond has a duration of nine years, if there is an increase in one plus its yield to maturity of 1 percent, there will be a decrease in its market value of approximately 9 percent. The approximation becomes better as the change in the yield becomes smaller. For infinitesimally small changes in yield, it is an exact relationship. Thus, duration is *approximately* equal to the negative of the *arc* elasticity and *exactly* equal to the negative of the *point* elasticity.

Duration provides us with a reasonably accurate measure of the response of the present value of a stream of payments to a change in the level of interest rates.[1] Keep in mind that the objective of immunization is to invest so that the market value of our investment portfolio goes up and down in accord with the present value of our liabilities. If this is the case, we will always have in the portfolio an amount equal to what we need to have in order to pay off our liabilities at the current level of interest rates. Because duration provides a measure of the response of both to interest rate changes, the basic objective of immunization is to equate the durations of assets and liabilities.

Immunizing a Single Payment Liability

Suppose you have a liability where you must make a single payment of $1931 in ten years. The rate of interest is currently 10 percent, and the term structure is flat. The present value of the liability is $745, as given by

$$\begin{array}{ll} \text{Present value} \\ \text{of liability} \end{array} = \frac{\$1931}{(1 + Y)^{10}} \qquad (11\text{--}2)$$

$$\$745 = \frac{\$1931}{(1.10)^{10}} \qquad (11\text{--}3a)$$

[1]Technically, the present value of two different streams of payments with the same Macaulay duration will respond identically to a change in interest rates if we start from a term structure that is flat and move to another term structure that is flat. There are other measures of duration that are consistent with other forms of interest rate changes. See, for example, Fisher and Weil (1979), Cox, Ingersoll, and Ross (1979), Brennan and Schwartz (1983), and Khang (1979).

Thus, you must invest $745 now to accumulate enough cash to pay off the liability in ten years. If interest rates remain at 10 percent, you will have enough cash to pay off the liability no matter what kind of bond you invest in now, as long as it is default free. However, unless you immunize, if interest rates should change between now and the time the liability is due, you may not have enough to pay the bill.

Because it is a single payment, the liability has a Macaulay duration equal to its maturity, ten years. To immunize, you must invest in a bond that also has a duration of ten years. At a 10 percent interest rate, a twenty-year bond carrying a $70 annual interest payment has a current market value of $745 and a duration of ten years. That is

$$\$745.00 = \frac{\$70}{(1.10)^1} + \frac{\$70}{(1.10)^2} + \ldots + \frac{\$70 + \$1000}{(1.10)^{20}} \qquad (11\text{–}3b)$$

$$10 = 1\frac{\dfrac{\$70}{(1.10)^1}}{\$745} + 2\frac{\dfrac{\$70}{(1.10)^2}}{\$745} + \ldots + 20\frac{\dfrac{\$70 + \$1000}{(1.10)^{20}}}{\$745}$$

The Effect of Interest Rate Changes on Present Values

If you invest in the bond represented in Equation (11–3b), you are immunized against a change in interest rates. To understand this, consider what happens to the present value of your required payment and the market value of the bond, as determined by substituting different interest rates into Equations (11–3a) and (11–3b), if interest rates go either up or down. The present value of the liability and the market value of the bond are given in the following table.

Interest Rate (Y)	Bond Value	Liability Value	
4%	$1409	$1305	
6%	$1115	$1078	
8%	$902	$895	
10%	$745	$745	Present levels
12%	$627	$622	
14%	$536	$521	
16%	$466	$438	

Note that at the current interest rate of 10 percent, the liability and the bond have the same value. However, if interest rates should either rise or fall, the value of the bond becomes larger than the value of the liability. This means that you have more funds invested in your bond portfolio than you need to be able to pay off the liability at each interest rate.[2]

[2]It's important to remember that these calculations assume that the shape of the term structure remains flat at all levels of the interest rate.

The Effect of Interest Rate Changes on Terminal Values

Moving from present values to terminal values, consider how much your bond investment will be worth in ten years when you have to pay off the liability. Table 11–1 shows the total value of your bond investment at the end of the tenth year under three assumed scenarios for interest rates. The first set of numbers assumes that interest rates remain constant at 10 percent. If they do, you will be able to invest each interest payment when received at 10 percent. The first payment received after one year, for example, can be reinvested for nine years at 10 percent, accumulating to a terminal value of $165 at the end of the tenth year. The second, reinvested for eight years, accumulates to $150, and so on. The total value of the accumulated interest payments is $1115. In addition to the interest payments, of course, you also will have a bond in your portfolio with ten years remaining until maturity. The market value of the bond at the end of the tenth year is given by the formula at the bottom of the table. At a 10 percent interest rate, the market value is $816. Thus, if you sell the bond and add the proceeds to your accumulated interest, you will have a total of $1931, exactly enough to pay off the liability.

Now suppose that instead of remaining constant, interest rates fall in the first year to 4 percent and remain at that level through the tenth year. In this case, something good and something bad happens. You're happy because the bond is

TABLE 11–1 Effect of Interest Rate Changes on Terminal Values

	Rates Stay at 10%	*Rates Fall to 4%*	*Rates Rise to 16%*
Accumulated value of interest payments received and reinvested at indicated interest rates	$70 \times (1.10)^9 = \$ 165$ $70 \times (1.10)^8 = 150$ $70 \times (1.10)^7 = 136$ $70 \times (1.10)^6 = 124$ $70 \times (1.10)^5 = 113$ $70 \times (1.10)^4 = 102$ $70 \times (1.10)^3 = 93$ $70 \times (1.10)^2 = 85$ $70 \times (1.10) = 77$ $70 \times 1 = 70$ Total $1115	$70 \times (1.04)^9 = \$100$ $70 \times (1.04)^8 = 96$ $70 \times (1.04)^7 = 92$ $70 \times (1.04)^6 = 89$ $70 \times (1.04)^5 = 85$ $70 \times (1.04)^4 = 82$ $70 \times (1.04)^3 = 79$ $70 \times (1.04)^2 = 76$ $70 \times (1.04) = 73$ $70 \times 1 = 70$ Total $842	$70 \times (1.16)^9 = \$ 266$ $70 \times (1.16)^8 = 229$ $70 \times (1.16)^7 = 198$ $70 \times (1.16)^6 = 171$ $70 \times (1.16)^5 = 147$ $70 \times (1.16)^4 = 127$ $70 \times (1.16)^3 = 109$ $70 \times (1.16)^2 = 94$ $70 \times (1.16) = 81$ $70 \times 1 = 70$ Total $1492
Market value of bond in the tenth year at indicated interest rate	$ 816	$1243	$ 565
Grand total	$1931	$2085	$2057
Less required payment	−$1931	−$1931	−$1931
Surplus	0	$ 154	$ 126

$$\text{Market value of bond in tenth year} = \frac{\$70}{(1 + Y)} + \frac{\$70}{(1 + Y)^2} + \cdots + \frac{\$70}{(1 + Y)^{10}} + \frac{\$1000}{(1 + Y)^{10}}$$

worth more in the tenth year than before ($1243). It's worth more because interest rates are lower, and consequently, market values are higher. On the other hand, you're sad because the annual interest payments must be reinvested at a lower rate and they accumulate to only $842. However, when you net out the good and bad things, you still have more money than you need to make the payment, with $154 remaining.

The same thing happens if interest rates rise to 16 percent instead of fall. You're happy because the annual interest payments can be reinvested at the higher 16 percent rate, accumulating to a sum of $1492. On the other hand, you're sad because at the higher interest rate the market value of your bond in the tenth year is only $565. Again, however, when you net the good and the bad, you find you have more money than you need to make the payment. You now have $126 remaining. You're protected against a swing in rates in either direction.

I know what you may be thinking: This works if interest rates rise or fall in the first year and then stay there, but what if rates go down to 4 percent, stay there until the tenth year, and then rise to 16 percent just before you have to sell the bond. If this happens, you're sad twice—and you're in trouble.

If you lost, you lost because you didn't stay immunized. When interest rates fell, the duration of your bond became longer. Remember that duration is the weighted average maturity of the stream of payments, where you are weighting by the relative contribution of each payment to the total present value. When interest rates fall, the present values of all the individual payments go up. However, the present values of the more distant payments go up by a greater percentage amount than do the present values of the payments coming soon. This means that the fraction of the total present value accounted for by the distant payments increases. Given this, the weighted average maturity becomes longer, and so does the duration.

While the duration of the bond became longer, the duration of the liability remained at ten years. This is because the liability consists of a single payment. Thus, its duration is always equal to its maturity, irrespective of the level of interest rates.

At 10 percent interest, your durations were matched; at 4 percent interest, the duration of your bond is too long. To remain immunized, you must sell the bond and reinvest the proceeds in another bond that has a duration of ten years. This means that you have to invest in a bond that has a maturity shorter than twenty years or an annual interest payment greater than $70. Given maturity, bonds with larger annual interest payments have shorter durations, because these bonds pay out more money in a shorter time period.

If you reimmunize with each change in interest rates, you can be assured you will have more than enough money to make the payment, provided you are willing to make one assumption. On the days that you must reimmunize, in moving from one bond or bond portfolio to another, you must be able to *maintain* the internal yield on your portfolio. That is, the new portfolio you're getting into must have an internal yield to maturity that is at least as large as the *current* internal yield of the old portfolio you're getting out of. This, of course, will be the case if the term structure is flat, which is the inherent assumption of the Macaulay duration. If the term structure isn't flat, you may have to slide down the term structure to a portfolio with a lower yield. If you consistently lose yield when you reimmunize your portfolio, you may run short of money when it comes time to pay the liability.

Fortunately, as we shall see later, more often than not you gain yield, as opposed to lose, upon reimmunization. This is because there are differentials in bond yields caused by taxes and other market imperfections. More often than not, you can put together a portfolio of bonds with the duration you need to be immunized and still maintain or increase the internal yield on your portfolio.

Computing the Duration and Internal Yield of a Bond Portfolio

The expected return and beta of a stock portfolio are simply weighted averages of the expected returns and betas of the stocks you put in the portfolio. This is because the expected returns for all the stocks are computed with reference to a common horizon interval. In our examples this interval was usually a month.

In the case of bond investments, each bond has a different maturity date, and you can't simply average the internal yields to maturity to get the internal yield of the portfolio. If you did, you'd be averaging apples and oranges. A 10 percent yield on a thirty-year treasury bond isn't comparable to a 20 percent yield on a thirty-day treasury bill. If you invested half your money in each, the yield on your portfolio wouldn't be 15 percent.

To understand this, consider two pure discount bonds, both of which pay no interest until maturity. Bond A pays $1100 and matures in one year. Bond B pays $1407 and matures in seven years. Both bonds are selling for the same market price, $1000. The yields on each portfolio can be computed as

$$Y_A = 10\% = (\$1100/\$1000)^1 - 1.00$$
$$Y_B = 5\% = (\$1407/\$1000)^{1/7} - 1.00$$

Suppose that you bought both bonds, investing half your money in each bond. Would the yield on your portfolio be 7.5 percent, the weighted average of the two yields?

The cash flows for your portfolio are shown in Figure 11–3. You have an immediate outflow of $2000 associated with buying the bonds. Then you get two positive cash flows, $1100 from bond A at the end of the first year and $1407 from bond B at the end of the seventh year. What is the internal rate of return to this portfolio?

The internal rate of return is the rate of discount that will discount the stream of payments associated with the portfolio to a present value equal to its market value. In the case of this portfolio, the internal yield is 5.634 percent.

$$\$2000 = \frac{\$1100}{(1.05634)} + \frac{\$1407}{(1.05634)^7}$$

To compute the internal yield to a portfolio, you must first set forth the cash flows associated with investing in the portfolio and then find the rate of discount that will equate the present value of the cash flows to the market value of the portfolio. In Figure 11–3 are the cash flows associated with a two-year bond paying a $100 coupon and a four-year bond paying a $200 coupon. The cash flows associated with a portfolio of the two bonds are depicted in the lower portion of the figure. In the first year you receive $300 worth of interest pay-

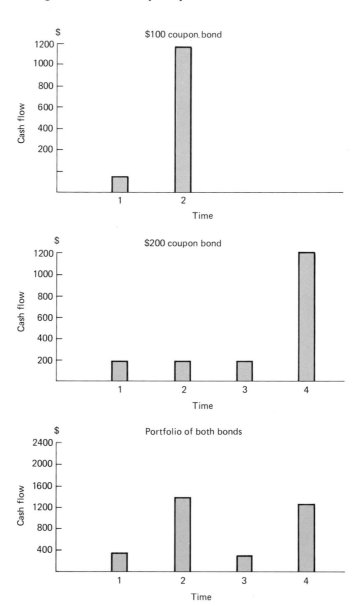

Figure 11-3 Cash Flows Associated with Two Bonds and a Portfolio

ments. In the second year you receive $300 in interest plus $1000 in principal. In the third year you receive $200 in interest, and finally in the fourth year $1200 in interest and principal. Once the cash flows have been set forth, it is an easy matter for a computer to calculate the portfolio's internal yield.

Once you have an internal yield, you can then compute the Macaulay duration, weighting the maturity of each payment by the fraction of the portfolio's total value accounted for by the present value of each payment given the internal yield.

You should remember that neither the internal yield nor the duration can be found by taking a simple weighted average of the components in the bond portfolio. This is a mistake commonly made by bond portfolio managers in the real world. They use internal yields on individual bonds; and quite often you will find them averaging internal yields and durations to obtain portfolio yields and durations.

Combination Lines for Internal Yield and Duration

Figure 11–4 shows the combination lines relating internal yield to duration for portfolios of five different bonds. Note that the combination line is concave when the bond with the shorter duration has the lower internal yield, as with the case of combining bonds E and D. The combination line is convex when the bond with the shorter duration has the higher yield, as with A and C. Sometimes it is the case that when you combine two bonds with the same duration but with different yields, the duration of the portfolio may be longer than that of either bond, as with bonds B and D. Only when the bonds have the same yield, as with A and B, do both duration and internal yield combine as a weighted average.

Immunizing a Multiple Payment Liability

Suppose you are managing a pension fund, and you face the stream of required cash payments that is depicted in Figure 11–5. The Macaulay duration of this stream depends on the rate of interest used to compute its present value. The higher the rate of interest, the lower the duration, because with higher rates the more distant payments account for a smaller fraction of the total present value. Thus, as depicted in Figure 11–6, at an interest rate of 10 percent, the duration might be seven years, and at an interest rate of 4 percent, the duration might be as high as ten years. The curve drawn in Figure 11–6 is called the *immunization curve*. It shows the duration of this particular stream of liabilities at various values for the interest rate. Each stream of liabilities has its own associated immunization curve.

To immunize your portfolio, you need to take a position on the immunization curve. In the case of Figure 11–6, if you invest in a bond with an internal yield of 10 percent and a duration of seven years, you are immunized. You are also

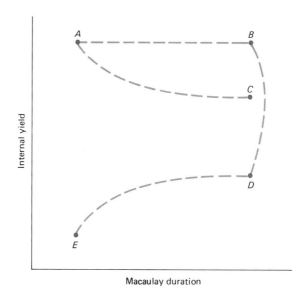

Figure 11-4 How Bonds Combine into Portfolios

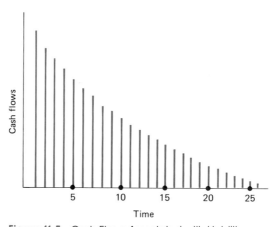

Figure 11-5 Cash Flows Associated with Liability

immunized if you invest in a bond with a 4 percent yield and a ten-year duration. Naturally, the present value of the liabilities is smaller at 10 percent than it is at 5 percent, so you would prefer 10 percent, because you have to invest less.

As portfolio manager, your objective is to climb as high on the immunization curve as you can. The scattered points plotted in Figure 11–6 represent the positions of individual bonds. You want to find the portfolio of bonds that will put you as high on the curve as possible. In this example you can achieve this by combining bonds A and B into a portfolio at point *P*.

Finding the highest yielding immunized portfolio must be done through a process of trial and error by a computer. Immunizing a single payment liability can

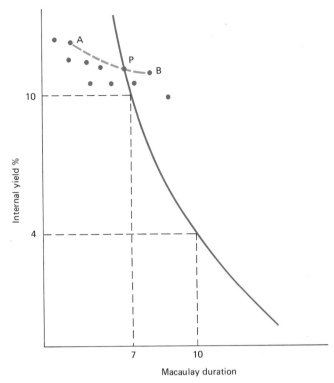

Figure 11-6 Immunizing with a Multiple Payment Liability

be done in the same way. The immunization curve for a single payment liability is, of course, a vertical line at a duration equal to the maturity of the liability.

A Test of Immunization

A test of the effectiveness of immunization was done by Patrick Lau (1983). Lau looks at the time period January 1955 through December 1979. He assumes that you face a single payment liability of $1 million due in eight years. You are allowed to invest in treasury bonds of various maturities. He begins his first experiment in January 1955. In this month he combines the pair of highest yielding bonds from either side of the immunization curve (a vertical line at an eight-year duration) into a portfolio with an eight-year Macaulay duration. He then computes the present value of $1 million at the yield of the portfolio and invests this amount in the portfolio. The market value of the portfolio is, thus, initially equal to the present value of the liability.

At the beginning of February 1955, he again combines the two highest yielding bonds from either side of the immunization curve, and he reimmunizes the portfolio. At the new portfolio yield, the market value of the portfolio may now be different from the present value of the liabilities. In any case, the process is

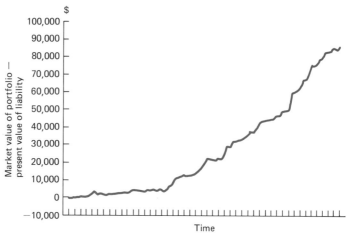

Figure 11-7 Difference Between Portfolio Value and Liability Value Through Time

continued through December 1963. At this point he compares the market value of the portfolio with the required payment for the liability ($1 million). The differences between the market value of the portfolio and the present value of the liability for each of the months between January 1955 and December 1963 are plotted in Figure 11-7. At the end of the eight-year period, you obviously have more money than is necessary to meet the payment.

Lau now repeats the experiment, this time beginning the whole process in February 1955. He keeps repeating until the end of his horizon date coincides with the last date of his study, December 1979. In all, he conducts 204 overlapping simulation experiments. Table 11-2 shows the results for all the experiments. The first and second columns indicate the mean values for the beginning and ending value of the portfolio. Surprisingly, in every one of the experiments the ending portfolio value exceeds the value of the liability payment ($1 million). The third and fourth columns show the results in terms of the expected internal yield to maturity on the initial portfolio and the actual realized yield over the course of each experiment. Note that, on average, the realized yield is higher than the expected yield by approximately 1.33 percentage points.

Table 11-2 Results of Lau Test

| | *Investment Horizon = 8 Years* | | | |
| | *1* | *2* | *3* | *4* |
	Initial Investment Value ($)	*Terminal Investment Value ($)*	*Realized Rate of Return (%)*	*Expected Rate of Return (%)*
Mean	703,420	1,106,600	5.90	4.57
Standard deviation	69,073	43,490	1.6761	1.3414
Minimum value	536,240	1,038,000	3.41	2.46
Maximum value	823,030	1,220,400	9.59	8.10

Summary

You can determine the ratio of bond to stock investments in your portfolio by finding the portfolios in the efficient set. The portfolios in the efficient set specify not only how many bonds and stocks to buy but also which individual bonds and stocks.

Bonds present some unique problems in estimating expected return and risk for purposes of portfolio analysis. Relatively high-quality bonds are priced relative to the term structure for other bonds in their risk and tax classification. To estimate their expected return, you must first forecast the term structure and then estimate the position of the bond relative to the term structure. This is a comparatively simple problem for treasury bonds. However, there are additional complications for corporate bonds. Corporate bonds are usually callable, and they have sinking fund provisions. This makes estimating their expected life problematic. It is, therefore, difficult to position the bonds relative to both today's term structure and the forecasted term structure at the horizon point.

It is also difficult to estimate the covariance between a bond and other investments in the portfolio. Covariances are usually estimated by sampling from a series of past returns. If the series of past returns is long, the bond will slowly mature during the series, and its nature will change from the beginning to the end. This problem can be overcome by estimating the returns on "indexed" bonds taken from points on the term structure of interest rates.

A portfolio is immunized if it is devoid of risk. Investors who interest immunize seek a guaranteed return over their horizon interval. One way to accomplish this is to cash match, that is, invest in a pure discount bond (or bonds) that matures at your horizon point (or points). The disadvantage of cash matching is that you are constrained to invest in bonds that might otherwise be unattractive to you, given your tax status. If you immunize using duration, on the other hand, you can invest in one or two of the bonds that are the most attractive to you in terms of after-tax return.

To immunize, you construct your portfolio of bonds such that its duration is equal to the duration of your liabilities. You must reimmunize with each change in interest rates, because as interest rates change, durations change as well. In immunizing with the Macaulay duration, you can be assured of meeting your required payments if, when you reimmunize from one portfolio to another, the new portfolio has an internal yield at least as large as the yield of the old portfolio.

1. What does it mean to say that a bond has a value less than one for its relative yield differential? What might account for such a differential?

2. Why is the maturity of some bonds ambiguous?

3. What problems are there in trying to derive information about the term structure of interest rates from data on corporate bond yields?

4. Suppose a bond with a face value of $1000 pays an annual coupon of $100. Interest rates are currently at 7 percent for all maturities of the same default risk. The bond has ten years until maturity, but is callable in two years at a price of $1075.

    a. If interest rates are expected to stay at 7 percent, would you expect the institution that issued the bond to call it in two years?

    b. Given your answer to part a, what would be the current market price of the bond?

    c. How would you compute the internal yield to maturity on this bond?

5. In view of discussion in earlier chapters about selecting optimal portfolios of securities, how should you reach a decision about the relative importance of bonds in a portfolio of various securities?

6. a. What does it mean to adopt a cash-matching management strategy?

    b. What is the objective of a cash-matching management strategy?

7. Assume the following characteristics for a particular bond:

    Face value = $1000

    Annual coupon payment = $60

    (First payment due in 1 year)

    Internal yield to maturity = 7%

    Term = 3 years

    a. Compute the Macaulay duration of the bond.

    b. Given your answer to part a, compute the approximate change in the bond's value if the internal yield fell to 6.5 percent. (You should use the duration in part a for this computation.)

    c. Now compute the actual change in the bond's value.

8. Consider a pure discount bond (no coupon payments) with a maturity of four years. The current internal yield to maturity is 9 percent. If the internal yield suddenly changes to 8.5 percent, how would the Macaulay duration respond to such a change?

9. You are faced with a liability requiring payment of $2000 one year from now and $2000 two years from now. You can invest in bonds with internal yields to maturity of 9 percent.

    a. Compute the Macaulay duration of this liability.

b. Suppose the yield suddenly changes to 10 percent. Use the duration computed in part a to approximate the dollar change in the present value of the liability.

10. What is immunization intended to accomplish? What is meant by reimmunization?

11. Explain the elasticity interpretation of the Macaulay duration.

12. Suppose we have matched the maturity and present value of a single payment liability with the same characteristics of a coupon bond. When we make the match, the yield curve is flat at 7 percent. Immediately after making the match, the yield curve shifts to 8 percent (still flat).

a. What would be the result of such a change?

b. Was the strategy appropriate to help you achieve an immunized position?

13. Assume that although the level of interest rates may change, the yield curve remains flat. You attempt to immunize at the beginning of some time horizon by matching the value and Macaulay duration of a single payment liability with the value and Macaulay duration of a bond portfolio. Will this match at the beginning of the horizon be sufficient to keep your portfolio immunized as time passes?

14. Suppose you purchase one of each of the following bonds:

	Annual Coupon	Face Value	Internal Yield	Years to Maturity
Bond 1	$85	$1000	10%	2
Bond 2	0	$1000	9%	1

a. Compute the internal yield of the portfolio of bonds.

b. Show how you would proceed to get the Macaulay duration of this portfolio.

15. The following are values for the indicated internal yields on a particular bond.

Present Value	Internal Yield (Y)
$979	8.0%
$950	9.0%

Compute the arc elasticity of the bond's value with respect to $(1 + Y)$. Define arc elasticity.

16. Suppose you put together the following portfolio:

a. Purchase one pure discount bond (no coupons) with a twenty-year maturity. Face value to be received at maturity is $1000.

b. Sell short 1.92 pure discount bonds having five years until maturity. Face value at maturity is $1000. Assume your short sale allows you the full use of the proceeds.

c. Invest $1127.49 in very short-term bonds (zero duration).

Assume the internal yield on all issues is 5 percent to start.

a. How much of your own money was required to put this portfolio together?

b. Compute the Macaulay duration of the assets in the portfolio and then of the liability (the short sale).

c. Suppose that the internal yield on all maturities rises to 6 percent. What is the value of the portfolio (asset value less liability value)?

d. Suppose that the internal yield on all maturities falls to 4 percent. What is the value of the portfolio (asset value less liability value)?

BIBLIOGRAPHY

BIERWAG, G. O., and G. KAUFMAN, "Coping with the Risk of Interest Rate Fluctuations: A Note," *Journal of Business* (July 1977a).

———, "Immunization, Duration, and the Term Structure of Interest Rates," *Journal of Financial and Quantitative Analysis* (December 1977b).

BRENNAN, M. J., and E. S. SCHWARTZ, "Conditional Predictions of Bond Prices and Returns," *Journal of Finance* (May 1980).

———, "Duration, Bond Pricing and Portfolio Management." In *Innovations in Bond Portfolio Management: Duration Analysis and Immunization.* Greenwich, Conn.: JAI Press, 1983.

COOK, T. Q., "Some Factors Affecting Long Term Yield Spreads in Recent Years," *Monthly Review,* Federal Reserve Bank of Richmond (September 1973).

COOPER, I., "Asset Values, Interest Rate Changes and Duration," *Journal of Financial and Quantitative Analysis* (December 1977).

COX, J. C., J. E. INGERSOLL, and S. ROSS, "Duration and the Measurement of Basis Risk," *Journal of Business* (January 1979).

DARST, D. M., *The Complete Bond Book.* New York: McGraw-Hill, 1981.

FISHER, I., and R. L. WEIL, "Coping with the Risk of Interest Rate Fluctuations," *Journal of Business* (January 1979).

HO, T. S. Y., and R. F. SINGER, "Bond Indenture Provisions and the Risk of Corporate Debt," *Journal of Financial Economics* (December 1982).

INGERSOLL, J. E., J. SKELTON, and R. L. WEIL. "Duration Forty Years Later," *Journal of Financial and Quantitative Analysis* (November 1978).

JAFFE, J. F., and G. MANDELKER, "Inflation and the Holding Period Returns on Bonds," *Journal of Financial and Quantitative Analysis* (December 1979).

KHANG, C., "Bond Immunization When Short Term Rates Fluctuate More Than Long Term Rates," *Journal of Financial and Quantitative Analysis* (December 1979).

LAU, P. W. P., "An Empirical Examination of Alternative Interest Rate Risk Immunization Strategies." Ph.D. dissertation, University of Wisconsin, 1983.

MACAULAY, F. R., *Some Theoretical Problems Suggested by the Movements of Interest Rates, Bond Yields, and Stock Prices in the United States Since 1856.* New York: NBER, 1938.

REDINGTON, F. M., "Review of the Principles of Life-Office Valuations," *Journal of the Institute of Actuaries* (no. 3, 1952).

VAN HORNE, J. C., *Financial Market Rates and Flows.* Englewood Cliffs, N.J.: Prentice-Hall, 1978.

12 EUROPEAN OPTION PRICING

Introduction

A stock call option is a contract giving its owner the right to buy shares of a stock at a stated *exercise price* on (and sometimes before) a stated *expiration date.* A put option is basically the same thing, but it gives its owner the right to *sell* the shares of stock at the exercise price. These contracts are truly *options,* in the sense that they do not obligate you to buy or sell. You may transact at the stated prices if it is in your interest to do so. It is in your interest to exercise a call option if, at expiration, the market price of the stock is greater than the exercise price in the options contract. It is in your interest to exercise a put option if the market price is below the exercise price at expiration.

There are two types of options. European options given their owners the right to exercise only at the expiration date. American options give their owners the right to exercise at any time on or before the expiration date.

An understanding of option pricing is extremely important because options can be used in many imaginative ways to create many attractive investment opportunities. In addition, as discussed in Chapter 13, securities that are commonly observed, such as callable bonds, can be viewed in principle as portfolios of options. In this sense, options are the building blocks of many financial securities, and an understanding of the pricing of options is vital to an understanding of the pricing of nearly all securities. In this chapter you will learn how to estimate the value of European options and how their prices behave in relation to the prices of the stocks they are written on. In Chapter 13 we talk about some issues in options pricing, the pricing of American options, and the development of investment strategies employing options.

The discussion of the pricing of European options proceeds in three stages. In each stage, the assumptions we make become progressively more realistic. First, we will assume that investors are risk neutral and that there is an equal probability of getting any stock value between two extremes at the expiration date. In this setting it is very easy to value an option. You can also get an intuitive feel for the basis of options pricing and the behavior of options prices relative to stock prices. In the second stage, we will admit risk-averse investors into the market, but with the assumption that there are only two possible prices for the stock at the expiration date. In this setting, it is easy to understand the important principle that an option must be priced so that, when used to construct a risk-free investment strategy, you earn the risk-free rate of return on your investment. We then take this important principle to the final stage, where we make the more realistic assumption that rates of return on the stock are normally distributed, and we value options under the Black-Scholes option pricing framework.

PRICING OPTIONS UNDER RISK NEUTRALITY AND UNIFORM PROBABILITY DISTRIBUTIONS

Valuing a Call Option

Consider a European call option written on a stock that pays no dividends and that expires at the end of one year. The probability distribution for the value of the stock at the end of the year is given in Figure 12–1. The distribution is assumed to be shaped like a rectangle, with equal probabilities for all stock values between an extreme low value ($10) and an extreme high value ($50).

Under risk neutrality, the market value of the stock at the beginning of the year is equal to its expected value at the end of the year, discounted at the risk-free rate, r_F. It is easy to compute the expected value for a rectangular uniform distribution, such as that of Figure 12–1. You simply add the extreme high and low values and divide by 2. In the case of Figure 12–1, the lowest possible value for the stock is $10 and the highest possible value is $50. The expected value falls half way, at $30. The market value of the stock is found by discounting the expected value by the risk-free rate, which we will assume to be 10 percent.

The market value for the stock is therefore $27.27:

$$\frac{(\$10.00 + \$50.00)/2}{1.10} = \$27.27$$

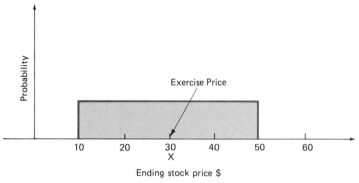

Figure 12-1   Probability Distribution for Stock

The current market value for the call option is also equal to its expected value at the end of the year discounted at the risk-free rate. The value of the call at the end of the year is equal to

Ending stock price − Exercise price, or 0.00

whichever is greater. Remember, we are dealing with an option, so if the ending stock price is less than the exercise price, you can always throw the contract away. You don't have to exercise it.

The probability distribution for the ending value of the option is given in Figure 12–2. We have assumed that the exercise price is $30. Given this, if the year-end stock price is less than $30, the option will be worthless. In Figure 12–1 we see that half the rectangle for the stock lies to the left of a $30 stock price. This means that the probability that the call option will be worthless at the end of the year is equal to .5. This probability is represented by the spike in Figure 12–2. It is also the case that the probability the option will be worth $1 is the same as the probability the stock will be worth $31. The probability for a $2 option value is the same as for a $32 stock value and so on. Thus, the probabilities in the part of the rectangle lying to the right of $30 in Figure 12–1 are the same as those lying to the right of the spike in Figure 12–2.

It is very easy to find the expected value of the ending *stock price*. It is only slightly more difficult to find the expected value of the year-end value of the *call option*. To compute the expected value, first calculate the expected value as though 100 percent of the probability was in the rectangle lying to the right of the spike. If this were true, the expected value would be the midpoint of the rectangle, which can be computed as

(High stock value − Exercise price)/2 = ($50 − $30)/2 = $10

Next, multiply this *conditional* expected value by the fraction of the total probability that is actually in the rectangle. We know that half the probability is represented by the spike, so the other half is in the rectangle. The fraction of the probability that is in the rectangle can be found by

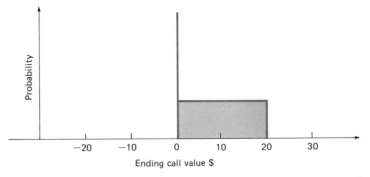

Figure 12-2 Probability Distribution for Call Option with Exercise Price = $30

(High stock value − Exercise price)/(High stock value − Low stock value)

($50 − $30)/($50 − $10) = .50

The product of this fraction and the conditional expected value is

$5 = .50 × $10

For those cases where the lowest possible value for the stock is greater than the exercise price, the expected year-end value for the option is computed as the difference between the expected stock price and the exercise price:

Expected value call option = Expected stock value − Exercise price

Inasmuch as we are assuming that investors are risk neutral, and therefore don't require risk premiums in expected rates of return, the market value of the option at the beginning of the year is equal to its expected year-end value, discounted at the risk-free rate:

$$\text{Market value call option} = \frac{\text{Expected value call option}}{(l + r_F)}$$

In the case of the probability distributions of Figures 12–1 and 12–2, the market value of the call is $4.55 if the risk-free rate is 10 percent.

$$\$4.55 = \frac{\$5.00}{1.10}$$

Valuing a Put Option

A put option is valued in nearly the same way as is a call option. The only difference is that a put option takes on value when the year-end value of the stock falls *below* the exercise price. Thus, the year-end value for the put is given by

$$\text{Exercise price} - \text{Ending stock price, or } 0.00$$

whichever is greater.

The probability distribution for the value of the put at the end of the year is given in Figure 12–3. Except for the fact that the horizontal axis is reversed, it is identical to the distribution for the value of the call, because the exercise price is again assumed to be equal to the expected value of the stock price.

The procedure for finding the expected year-end value for the put is nearly the same as the formula for the year-end expected value for the call. Again, calculate the expected value of the rectangle in Figure 12–3, assuming first that 100 percent of the probability is in the rectangle. The lowest possible value for the put option is $0, for those cases where the stock is worth more than $30. The highest possible value is $20, when the stock is worth $10. The expected value of the rectangle is therefore $10. The fraction of the total probability actually in the rectangle, or the probability of exercising the option at maturity, is .50. Taking the product, we find the expected value of the put option:

$$\text{Expected value of put option} = (\text{Exercise price} - \text{Low stock value})/2 \times$$
$$\text{Probability of exercise}$$
$$(\$30 - \$10)/2 \times .50 = \$5$$

Similar to the call, for the case where the exercise price is greater than the highest possible value for the stock, the expected value for the put is given by the exercise price less the expected stock price. The market value for the put at the beginning of the year is thus

$$\text{Market value put option} = \frac{\text{Expected value put option}}{(1 + r_F)}$$

which, for the distribution in Figure 12–1, is equal to

$$\$4.55 = \frac{\$5.00}{1.10}$$

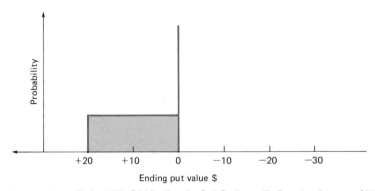

Figure 12-3 Probability Distribution for Put Option with Exercise Price = $30

The Relationship Between
Option Values and Stock Values

Suppose we change the market value of the stock that the options are written on. The market value will change if we change expectations about possible ending market prices for the stock. Assume that the market receives some good news about the stock, causing the probability distribution for ending stock values to shift to the right, as in Figure 12–4. The expected ending value for the stock is now $40

$$(\$60 + \$20)/2 = \$40$$

and the market value is now $36.37

$$\$40.00/1.10 = \$36.37$$

The change in the probability distribution for the stock induces changes in the probability distributions for the call and the put, as in Figures 12–5 and 12–6. Given that the exercise price remains the same at $30, the expected ending value for the call can again be found by first finding the conditional expected value of the rectangular distribution lying to the right of the spike. The midpoint, or expected value, of this distribution is $15. To find the expected value, multiply this conditional expected value by .75, which is the fraction of the total probability actually included in the rectangular part of the distribution. The expected ending value for the call is, thus, $11.25

$$\$15.00 \times .75 = \$11.25$$

and the market value of the call is $10.23

$$\$11.25/1.10 = \$10.23$$

The market value of the put is found in the same way. The put takes on value at the end of the year if the value of the stock falls *below* $30. In this case, a contract giving you the right to sell someone a share for $30 is valuable. The

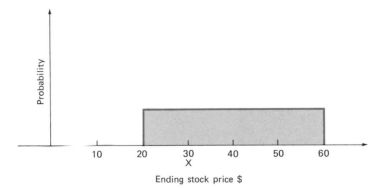

Figure 12-4 Probability Distribution for Stock

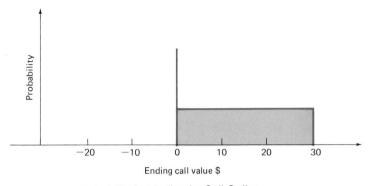

Figure 12-5 Probability Distribution for Call Option

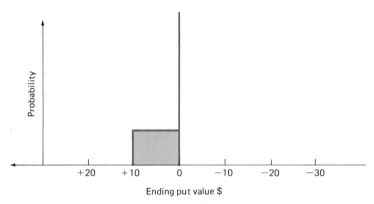

Figure 12-6 Probability Distribution for Put Option

probability of the stock being worth $30 or more is .75. This is the probability of the put being worth nothing at the end of the year. The lowest possible value for the stock is now $20. This means that the highest possible value for the put is now $10.

To find the expected ending value for the put, again find the conditional expected value for the rectangular part of the distribution and multiply it by the fraction of the total probability actually in the rectangle. The conditional expected value, or midpoint of the rectangle, is $5. The fraction of the total probability in the rectangle is .25, so the expected value is $1.25

$$\$5.00 \times .25 = \$1.25$$

and the market value is $1.14

$$\$1.25/1.10 = \$1.14$$

Thus, the increase in the price of the stock produces an increase in the price of the call and a decrease in the price of the put.

Other pairs of values for the put and the call can be found by shifting the expected value and market price of the stock to other values. In each case, we change only the midpoint of the rectangle and not the spread between the highest and lowest possible values. Put and call values corresponding to various stock values are given by the following schedule:

| | Market Value | |
Stock	Put	Call
$18.18	$10.23	$1.14
$27.27	$4.55	$4.55
$36.36	$1.14	$10.23
$45.45	$0.00	$18.18
$54.55	$0.00	$27.27
$63.64	$0.00	$36.36

This schedule is presented for the call and the put in Figures 12–7 and 12–8, respectively. Notice that as the stock price increases, the value of the call approaches a line with a slope equal to 1.00 emanating from the present value of the exercise price. The value of the call reaches the line when the distribution shifts to the right to such an extent that the lowest possible stock value exceeds the exercise price of $30. In Figure 12-8 we see that as the stock price decreases, the value of the put approaches a line with a slope equal to -1.00 emanating from the present value of the exercise price ($27.27). The put reaches the line when the highest possible value of the stock is less than the exercise price.

Based on Figures 12–7 and 12–8, we can make the following conclusions about the behavior of the options relative to the behavior of the stock:

1. The value of the call increases with the value of the stock, whereas the value of the put decreases with the value of the stock.

2. Unless the option is certain to be exercised, the absolute dollar change in the stock value is greater than the accompanying absolute dollar change in the option value.

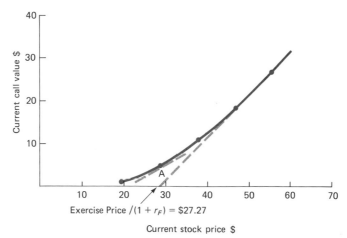

Figure 12-7 Relationship Between Prices for Stock and Call Options

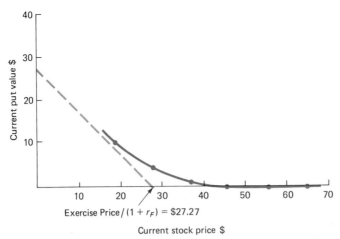

Exercise Price/$(1 + r_F)$ = $27.27

Current stock price $

Figure 12-8 Relationship Between Prices for Stock and Put Options

3. The *difference* between the absolute dollar changes for the stock and for the options become smaller as the options move from *out-of-the-money* to *in-the-money*. (A call option is said to be out-of-the-money if the stock price is less than the present value of the exercise price. It is said to be in-the-money if the stock price is greater than the present value of the exercise price. The opposite relationship holds for a put option.)

4. The absolute *percentage* changes in the options prices are greater than the accompanying absolute percentage changes in the stock price. (Looking at the schedule, we see that in going from $18.18 to $27.27, the stock price increased in value by 50 percent. This change induces a reduction in the value of the put of approximately 56 percent and an increase in the value of the call of almost 300 percent.)

5. The *difference* in the absolute percentage changes between the stock and the options again becomes smaller as the options move from being out of the money to being in the money. Thus, out-of-the-money options are inherently more volatile than their in-the-money counterparts.

Now consider the slope of a line drawn tangent to the curves in Figures 12–7 and 12–8 at any point, such as point *A* in Figure 12–7. The slope of the line is the ratio of the change in the value of the option accompanying a very small change in the value of the stock. This slope is equal to the probability of exercising the option at maturity. As the stock price goes up, the slope of the line approaches 1.00, as does the probability of exercising the option. Finally, when the lowest possible value for the stock price climbs above the exercise price, the probability of exercising the option is 100 percent, and the slope of the relationship between the value of the stock and the value of the option is 1.00.

The Effect of a Change in
Stock Variance on Option Values

Suppose the ending value for the stock is distributed as in Figure 12–4. There we found that the market value for the stock was $36.36, the market value for the put was $1.14, and the market value for the call was $10.23. Now assume that something happens to increase the uncertainty about the ending price of the stock. While before, the price at the end of the year was believed to fall somewhere between $20 and $60, now it is believed to fall between $10 and $70. The new distribution for the value of the stock is given in Figure 12–9. The expected value is still $40, and, given our assumption of investor risk neutrality, the market value will still be $36.36.

Although the price of the stock stays the same, the price of both the put and the call will go up. Consider the probability distribution for the ending value for the call. The conditional expected value for the rectangle is now $20. Two-thirds of the total probability is actually in the rectangle, so the expected value of the call is now $13.33. The market value is, therefore, $12.12, an increase in price of more than 18 percent. Why does the price of the call rise? The stock can go as high as $70 now. This means that the option can go as high as $40, as in Figure 12–10, whereas before its highest possible ending value was $30. Although it is true that the lowest possible stock price is now $10, as holder of the call option, you don't really care, because as soon as the stock falls below $30, your option is worthless in any case. The increase in the variance of the stock price has increased the up-side potential for your investment, while leaving the down-side potential unaffected. Granted the *probability* of a zero value for the option is now greater (33.3 percent instead of 25 percent); however, this is more than offset by the increase in the conditional expected value for the rectangle.

Now consider the probability distribution for the put in Figure 12–11. The conditional expected value for the rectangle is $10. One-third of the total probability is actually in the rectangle, so the expected value of the put is $3.33 and its market value is $3.03, an increase of nearly 200 percent. Again the increase in variance has increased the up-side potential for the investment.

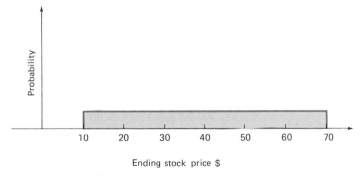

Figure 12-9   The Effect of an Increase in Variance on the Stock

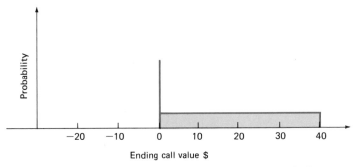

Figure 12-10   The Effect of an Increase in Variance on the Call

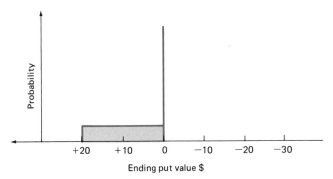

Figure 12-11   The Effect of an Increase in Variance on the Put

Based on our analysis thus far, we can draw two more conclusions about the behavior of stock options:

1. An increase in the variance of the stock will increase the market value of put and call options written on the stock.

2. Given a change in the variance of the underlying stock, the absolute percentage change in the price of out-of-the-money options will be greater than the absolute percentage change in the price of in-the-money options.

The variance of the stock price is actually a key factor in pricing options and developing investment strategies based on options. Although the variance of the price of a stock sometimes remains stationary for periods as long as months or even years, the variance can undergo abrupt, dramatic changes. When this happens, the value of the options written on the stock will change. Thus, recognizing changes in variance shortly after they occur and understanding the implications of these changes for the valuation of options are important facets of developing options investment strategies.

Summarizing our discussion so far, as the stock price increases, the value of a call will rise and the value of a put will fall. The absolute value of the slope of the relationship between the stock and option values tells you the probability of exercising the option. Options are more volatile in terms of percentage changes in market value than are stock investments, and out-of-the-money options are more volatile than in-the-money options. An increase in the variance of the underlying stock price will drive up the price of an option written on the stock. The resulting percentage change in the values of in-the-money options will be less than that for out-of-the-money options. Although these relationships have been derived in the context of a very simplistic framework, they hold under more complex pricing structures and actually characterize the way real options are priced.

We have obtained these relationships under the very special assumption that the distribution of the ending value for the stock is uniform, or rectangular. However, it is important to realize that these relationships generalize to a wide variety of different assumed shapes for the ending stock value. For example, as we will see later, in the case of the Black-Scholes model, a lognormal distribution is assumed for the ending value for the stock price. It is still the case that all the relationships discussed here hold for Black-Scholes option prices. We have also assumed that investors are risk neutral. In the next section, we release this assumption and discuss how to price an option to produce a risk-free return for someone who constructs a risk-free portfolio with it.

TWO-STATE OPTION PRICING

In this section we change our assumption concerning the nature of the distribution for the ending value for the stock. Rather than assume a uniform distribution, we will assume that, in the course of each period, there are two possible percentage changes in the stock price. If the options expire at the end of one period, then there are also two possible ending values for the stock price. At first, this may seem unrealistic, but remember that the length of the period can be made arbitrarily small. Given this, there can be an arbitrarily large number of periods before expiration. As the number of periods grows large, the probability distribution for the final value of the stock at the end of the last period approaches the shape of a lognormal distribution. There is evidence that an assumption of lognormality is reasonable for the ending stock value.

As the analysis in the previous section might indicate, options are among the riskiest securities in existence. If risk and risk premiums affect the values of any securities, it will play a substantial role in the pricing of these securities.

Researchers on option pricing were stymied for many years because they couldn't resolve the riddle of how options would be priced in the presence of risk-averse investors. One of the problems was the shape of the probability distribution for the ending value of the option. As you can infer from Figures 12–1, 12–2, and 12–3, even if the probability distribution for the ending value of the stock is normally distributed, the distribution for the ending value of the option is going to be skewed toward values above the expected value. This means that unless we make unrealistic assumptions about investor preferences, it may be inappropriate to price options on the basis of models like the Capital Asset Pricing Model.

In 1973, Fisher Black and Myron Scholes published a paper that resolved the riddle. Their insight was that options, in combination with the stocks they are written on, can be used to construct riskless investments. Given this, the options must sell at prices such that, when you construct such a riskless portfolio, you earn the risk-free rate of return on your own investment in the portfolio.

Consider, for example, the relationship between the put option and the stock in Figure 12–8. If the stock is priced at $27.27 (the present value of the exercise price), the slope of the relationship between the value of the put and the value of the stock will be − .50. This means that if the stock rises in price by $1, the value of the put option will fall by approximately 50¢. You can create a riskless portfolio by buying one share of stock and two put options. In this case, the fall in the price of the put options will completely offset the rise in the price of the stock.

Of course, with each change in the price of the stock, you move to a new point on the relationship, with a new slope, so you have to adjust slightly the number of puts you buy in relation to the number of shares of stock you hold. In any case, by adjusting your portfolio, you can maintain its riskless status over time (much in the manner of reimmunization, see Chapter 11). If the portfolio is riskless, it should produce the same rate of return as other riskless investments. Thus, the put options should sell at a price to make this the case.

Two-State Call Option Pricing over a Single Period

Suppose we have a European call option, with one year to expiration and an exercise price of $110. The current market price of the stock it is written on is $100. In the course of the next year, two rates of return on the stock are possible, − 10 percent and + 20 percent. Thus, the price of the stock can either fall to $90 or rise to $120. No dividends are expected to be paid on the stock. The risk-free rate of interest available in the bond market is 10 percent.

How can you hedge an investment in this option? There are two possible ways to make a hedged investment. Because the values of the call and the stock move in the same direction, you must buy one and sell the other. Thus, you can hedge by buying the stock and selling some options or by selling short the stock and buying some options.

Suppose you do the former. How many options must you sell for each share of stock you buy? To find out, consider the two possible ending values for the stock and the corresponding ending values for the option. If the stock turns out to have a market price of $120, based on its exercise price of $110, the option will be worth $10 at the end of the year. If the stock, instead, falls to $90, the option will be worthless. There is a $30 difference between the possible high and low values for the stock and a $10 difference for the option. Because the spread for the stock is three times as great as for the option, to create an exact offset in the value of your two positions, you must sell three options for every share of stock you buy. To compute the number of options sold for each share of stock bought, use the following formula:

$$\frac{\text{Number of call options sold}}{\text{for each stock bought}} = \frac{\text{High-low spread for stock}}{\text{High-low spread for option}}$$

$$3 = \frac{\$120 - \$90}{\$10 - \$00}$$

Consider the year-end value of your portfolio if you buy one share of stock and sell three options, which obligates you to sell three shares of stock to buyers of the options at a price of $110. If the stock falls to $90, you will have one share of stock worth $90. The holders of the options you sold will choose to throw them away at expiration because the price of the stock is below the exercise price. Thus, the total value of your portfolio will be $90.

On the other hand, if the stock rises to $120, you will have one share of stock worth $120, but the three people holding your options will choose to exercise them, because the market price is now above the exercise price at expiration. Each will come with $110, asking for a share of stock. You will have to go into the market three times to buy three shares for $120 each. You will lose $10 each time, for a total loss of $30. The net value of your portfolio is, thus, $90.

One share of stock	$120
Loss associated with exercise of three options	−$30
Net portfolio value	$90

Thus, your portfolio is worth $90, irrespective of whether the stock goes up or down. Because we have assumed that these are the only two things that can happen, the portfolio is a riskless investment, and as such, it should be expected to yield the riskless rate of return of 10 percent for the year. The portfolio's rate of return can be computed as follows:

$$r_P = \frac{\text{Year-end portfolio value}}{\text{Price of 1 share of stock} - 3 \times \text{Call option price}} - 1.00$$

$$10\% = \frac{\$90}{\$100 - 3 \times \text{Call option price}} - 1.00$$

We can now solve for the option price that will yield the risk-free rate to someone who follows this hedging strategy. If the options sell at a price of $6.06, the hedged portfolio requires an initial investment of $81.82 = $100 − 3 × $6.06. Because the ending value for the portfolio is known to be $90, this is consistent with a portfolio return of 10 percent:

$$\$90.00/\$81.82 - 1.00 = 10\%$$

You can also hedge by selling the stock short and buying options. Again, based on the relative spreads on the two investments, you must buy three options for each share of stock you sell short. Three options will cost you $18.18

at the price indicated above. You will receive $100 from short selling the stock, so you can invest the remaining $81.82 in risk-free bonds. Note that you don't have to invest any of *your* money in this portfolio. Because you don't invest any money, and because it is a riskless investment, the fair value for the payoff should be zero. If it is not, you could get something for nothing. If the options sell at $6.06, the ending value of this portfolio will be zero, whether the stock goes up or down.

If the stock rises to $120, you will own three options worth a total of $30. It will cost you $120 to buy the stock to cover the short sale, and the $81.82 you invest in risk-free bonds at the beginning of the year will be worth $90 at the end of the year. The total value of the portfolio is $90 + $30 − $120 = $00. You invest nothing in the portfolio, you take no risk, and you get nothing back. What could be fairer? If the stock falls to $90, the options will be worthless and you can use the $90 from investing in the risk-free bonds to cover the short sale. Again the portfolio is worthless. You put nothing in and you take nothing out.

Consider, however, what happens if the options sell at a price other than $6.06. What if they sold at a price of $10? In this case, the rate of return on the first hedged portfolio where you bought the stock and sold the options would be 28.57% = $90/($100 − $30). If this were true, the bottom would drop out from the bond market. Why invest in risk-free bonds for a return of 10 percent when you can hedge risklessly with options for a return of 28.57 percent? Investors would move into the options market, attempt to hedge by selling options, and force the price back down to $6.06. In fact, if we could sell riskless bonds to raise funds, we all could become infinitely wealthy, without taking any risk, by selling the bonds at an interest rate of 10 percent and using the funds to invest in the hedged option portfolio at 28.57 percent.

What would happen if the option sold at a price below $6.06, say, at $5? Now we can make money from nothing by using the other hedge. Sell the stock short, raising $100. Buy three options for a total cost of $15 and invest the remaining $85 in risk-free bonds. If the stock goes up, it will cost you $120 to cover the short sale, the options you own will be worth $30, and your investment in risk-free bonds will produce $93.50 at the end of the year. The portfolio will have a net value of $3.50, and it didn't cost you anything to get into it. On the other hand, if the stock goes down, it will cost you $90 to cover the short sale, the options will be worthless, and your bond investment will produce $93.50, a net gain of $3.50—again for no investment. Because this strategy requires no investment, you can make the net gain as large as you want, simply by selling more stock and buying more options. This operation is very similar to constructing the arbitrage portfolios in the Arbitrage Pricing Theory.

Strong economic forces keep the price of the option at $6.06. If the price goes above or below this, we can all become infinitely wealthy through arbitrage. In the face of these forces, $6.06 must be the only possible equilibrium price.

It can be argued that we, as individual investors, can't take advantage of these arbitrage opportunities because we aren't free to invest the proceeds of short sales. As a matter of fact, we must commit an amount of money as a margin to guarantee that we will be able to cover the short sale when necessary. There is also a margin required to sell puts and calls. However, it takes only one powerful investor to force the option to its equilibrium value. Large financial institutions employ arbitragers to hunt for opportunities to make money while making no commitment of capital and taking no risk. These large institutions can invest the proceeds of short sales in other investments, especially when they are riskless, and they are not restricted by margin requirements. These institutions can effectively police the options market, forcing the market value of the option to conform to the value that eliminates arbitrage opportunities.

Two-State Put Option Pricing over a Single Period

A put option can be priced in the same way as is a call option. Because the value of the put and the value of the stock move in opposite directions, in order to hedge, we need either to buy or sell them both.

Our relative position in the put and the stock is still determined on the basis of the relative spread between their high and low values. In the example discussed above, if the stock goes to $120, the put (an option to sell the stock at a price of $110) is worthless. If the stock falls to $90, the put is worth $20.

The number of puts you must buy for each share of stock you hold is given by the following equation:

$$\frac{\text{Number of put options bought}}{\text{for each stock bought}} = \frac{\text{High-low spread for stock}}{\text{High-low spread for put}}$$

$$1.50 = \frac{\$120 - \$90}{\$20 - \$00}$$

If you buy two shares of stock, you need to buy three puts to hedge. If the stock goes to $120, you have two shares of stock worth a total of $240 and three puts that are worth nothing. If the stock falls to $90, you have two shares of stock worth a total of $180 and three puts worth $20 each, for a total portfolio value of $240. Your portfolio is worth $240 in either case. It is riskless. As such, it should offer investors the risk-free rate of return. The rate of return on this portfolio is given by

$$r_F = \frac{\text{Year-end portfolio value}}{\text{Price of 2 shares of stock} + 3 \times \text{Put option price}} - 1.00$$

$$10\% = \frac{\$240}{(\$100 \times 2) + (3 \times \text{Put option price})} - 1.00$$

In this example, the equilibrium value for the put option is also $6.06. With this value, it will cost a total of $218.18 to invest in the portfolio. We know that the portfolio will pay off $220 if either rate of return on the stock appears. Given this, the rate of return to the portfolio is known to be 10 percent.

Once again, if the put sells at a price below $6.06, we can obtain a riskless rate of return in excess of 10 percent by buying puts in combination with an investment in the stock. If the put sells at a price below $6.06, we can all become infinitely wealthy, with no required investment, by selling puts and the stock short and using the proceeds to invest in riskless bonds. Strong economic forces are again present to keep the price of the put at its equilibrium level of $6.06.

Two-State Option Pricing over Multiple Periods

We can use the valuation principle of pricing to give a hedge the risk-free rate to value an option that expires in two years instead of one. Suppose that in each of the two years, the stock can either increase in value by 20 percent or decrease by 10 percent. This means that after one year the stock can move from its current price of $100 to either $120 or $90. If it goes to $120, it can move in the second year to either $144 (with another 20 percent increase) or to $108 (with a 10 percent decrease). If, on the other hand, the stock drops to $90 at the end of the first year, it can rise in the second year to $108 (with 20 percent increase) or fall again to $81 (a second 10 percent decrease). These possible values are indicated by the event tree in Figure 12–12.

Now assume we have a call option with an exercise price of $110 that expires at the end of the second year. The option values that correspond with the stock values are given by the tree in Figure 12–12. Consider first the possible values for the option at expiration at the end of the second year. Because the exercise price is $110, the option is worthless if the stock is priced at $108 or $81. It is worth $34 if the stock is priced at $144, however.

Consider, first, the possible values for the option at the end of the *first* year. If the stock has fallen to $90, it can rise in the second year to $108 or fall to $81. In either case, it will be below the call option's exercise price. Thus, if the stock falls to $90 in the first year, the option is dead, and its market value will be zero.

If, instead, the stock rises to $120 in the first year, the option has a positive value based on the chance that the stock will rise again to $144. We can compute the market value for the option in the same way we did for a one-year option.

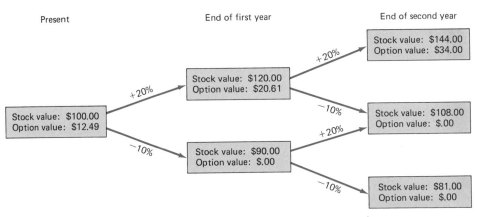

Figure 12-12 Two-State Option Pricing over Two Periods (Exercise Price = $110.00, $r_F = 10\%$)

The spread between the high and low values for the stock is $36. The corresponding spread for the option is $34. This means that for each share of stock we buy, we must sell 1.0588 options ($36/$34 = 1.0588). Let's operate on a big scale, buy 10,000 shares of stock and sell 10,588 options.

If the stock price rises at the end of the second year, our stockholdings will be worth $1,440,000. The options we sold will be exercised, and this will cost us $360,000. Thus, our portfolio will be worth the difference, or $1,080,000. This is also what our portfolio will be worth if the stock falls to $108, because in this case the options will not be exercised. We have a riskless portfolio that we know will be worth $1,080,000 at the end of the second year.

To build this portfolio at the beginning of the second year, we will have to pay $1,200,000 for the 10,000 shares of stock less what we can raise by selling the 10,588 call options. The call options must sell at a price to give us the riskless rate of return on this investment, which we will assume is still 10 percent. This equilibrium price is $20.61.

$$10\% = \frac{\$1,080,000}{\$1,200,000 - 10,588 \times \$20.61} - 1.00$$

Now let's move to the beginning of the first year. Based on our analysis thus far, we know that there are two possible values for the option at the end of the first period, $20.61 (if the stock rises to $120) and $0.00 (if the stock falls to $90). We can again create a riskless portfolio that has a known and certain value at the end of the first period by hedging. The spread between the high and low possible values for the stock is $30. The corresponding spread for the option is $20.61. To hedge, we must sell 1.4556 options for each share of stock we buy ($30.00/$20.61 = 1.4556). Let's buy 10,000 shares of stock and sell 14,556 options. If we do this and the stock goes up, we have a portfolio worth $900,000. Our long position in the stock is worth $1,200,000, and our short position in the options is worth $300,000 ($20.61 × 14,556). Our portfolio is also worth $900,000 if the stock falls to $90, because in this case the options are dead, and our short position has no value.

Because the portfolio is riskless, it should again produce the riskless rate of return. To build the portfolio at the beginning of the first period, we must invest an amount equal to $1 million worth of stock, less what we can get by selling 14,556 options. If we sell the options at a price of $12.49, building the portfolio will require an investment of $818,196, and the portfolio will procure a 10 percent rate of return in the first period:

$$10\% = \frac{\$900,000}{\$1,000,000 - 14,556 \times \$12.49} - 1.00$$

Thus, the equilibrium value for the two-year option is $12.49. Note that the only difference between this option and the one-year call option priced in the previous section is the term to expiration. The one-year option was based on the same stock and had the same exercise price. Yet the value of the one-year option was only $6.06. Just as with the variance of the underlying probability distribution for the stock, as the time to expiration for an option is increased, all other factors being held constant, the market value for the option is increased. The reason for this is that the up-side potential for the stock is increased. The fact that the down-side potential increases as well is unimportant because, once an option is dead, it is dead, and it makes no difference if the stock goes to $108, to $81, or for that matter to $0.

If we extended the analysis to a three-year case and beyond, we would find that the option again increases in value. Each successive increase would be smaller than the last, however. And as the term to expiration approached perpetuity, the value of the option would approach the value of the common stock, or $100.

In Figure 12–13 we move to a different example. Here we are dealing with a

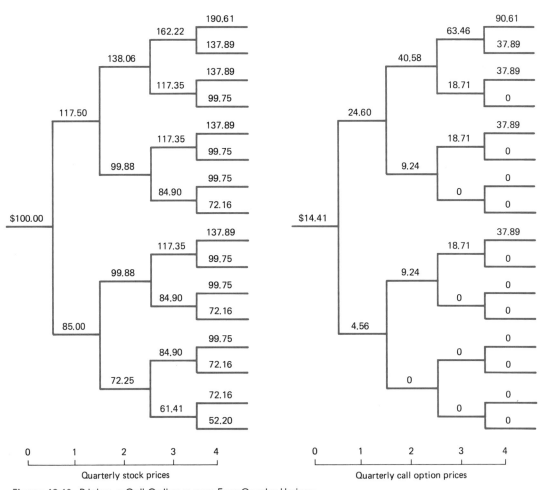

Figure 12-13 Pricing a Call Option over a Four-Quarter Horizon

SOURCE: R. J. Rendleman, Jr., and B. J. Bartter, "Two State Option Pricing," *Journal of Finance* (December 1979).

one-year call option, but we have reduced the period for the percentage changes on the stock to one quarter. In each quarter there are two possible percentage changes on the stock, +17.5 percent and −15 percent. To value the option, we need not specify the probabilities of getting either percentage change. However, let's assume they are equal. The distribution for the rate of return on the stock in any quarter is given in Figure 12–14a. As you can see in Figure 12–13, with this distribution for the quarterly return, there are five possible year-end values for the common stock. There are sixteen ending branches on the tree. There is an equal probability of reaching each branch. A stock value of $190.61 is represented on only one of the branches. The probability of getting this value, therefore, is 1/16. A stock price of $137 is represented on four of the branches. The probability to getting this price, therefore, is 1/4. The probability distribution for the ending value of the stock is given in Figure 12–14b. Note that the distribution for the year-end value for the stock looks much different from the distribution

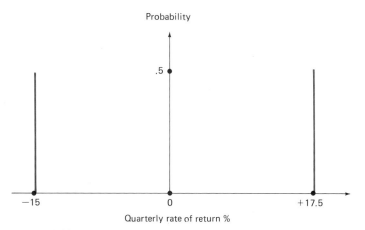

Figure 12-14a Probability Distribution for Quarterly Rates of Return on Stock

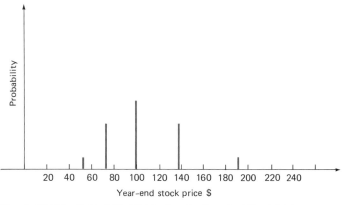

Figure 12-14b Probability Distribution for Year-End Stock Value

for the quarterly return: The distribution for the quarterly rate of return is symmetric; the distribution for the ending value for the stock is skewed to the right.

The corresponding values for a call option on the stock, with an exercise price of $100 and that expires at the end of the year, are given in Figure 12–13. The option prices are computed using the same technique employed in the previous sections. You start at the end of the tree, valuing the option at expiration and work backward. In each case, you value the option so that a riskless portfolio produces the riskless rate of return, which, in this example, is assumed to be 1.25 percent per quarter.

Note that to maintain your hedged position from quarter to quarter, you must keep adjusting your relative position in the stock and in the call. At the beginning of the first quarter, the spread for the stock is $32.50 and $20.04 for the option. Thus, you must sell 1.622 options for each share of stock you buy. If the stock goes up, its spread in the second quarter is $38.18. The option's spread is $31.34, so you must now sell 1.218 options for each share of stock you buy. And so, as you move along in time, you must keep adjusting your positions in the option and the stock to remain hedged.

Computer programs are readily available that value options based on the two-state multiperiod framework. The programs are available for use on personal computers, and they are currently used by professional traders to help formulate their investment strategies.

We are now very close to the framework assumed in the option pricing model of Black and Scholes (1973). In the example we're considering, we have assumed that the distribution of rates of return to the stock is constant through time and binomial (two-point) in form, which implies a distribution for the ending value of the stock of the form in Figure 12–14b. We have assumed that, in hedging, you adjust your position at the end of each quarter. And we value the option to give you the riskless rate of return on your hedged position.

Black and Scholes make two slightly different assumptions. First, they assume that the distribution for rates of return on the stock is normal or bell-shaped. Second, they reduce the time interval for the percentage changes from a quarter to an instant. Except for these changes, the principle for valuing the options is the same.

VALUING OPTIONS USING
THE BLACK-SCHOLES FRAMEWORK

As discussed earlier, Black and Scholes assume that the probability distribution for rates of return on the stock over an instant of time is normal, as in Figure 12–15a. Just as the distribution of rates of return in Figure 12–14a implied the distribution for ending stock values in Figure 12–14b, so the normal distribution in Figure 12–15a implies the lognormal distribution of stock prices at the expiration of the option in Figure 12–15b. The nature of a lognormal distribution is

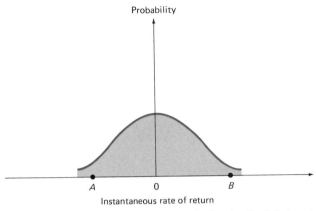

Figure 12-15a Normal Probability Distribution for Stock Rates of Return

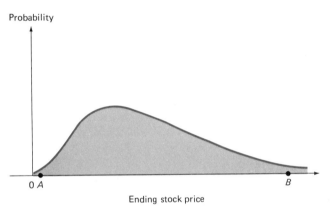

Figure 12-15b Lognormal Probability Distribution for Ending Stock Values

such that if you plotted the stock values on a log scale on the horizontal axis of the graph, the distribution would then take the shape of a normal distribution.

That the normal distribution of rates of return implies the lognormal distribution of ending stock prices can be better understood if you think of the following. Suppose the stock undergoes a long series of negative percentage changes such as that represented by point A in the normal distribution. This would imply that the stock price would approach a value near zero, such as point A in the lognormal distribution. If, on the other hand, the stock has a long series of positive percentage changes, such as that of point B in the normal distribution, its ending value would become extremely large, falling well to the *right* of point B in the lognormal distribution. Thus, even though the distribution for the percentage changes is symmetric, the distribution for the ending values is skewed to the right.

Black and Scholes value the option to give you the risk-free rate of return if you attempt to hedge with the option. As a hedger, you must continuously adjust your relative positions in the stock and the option, just as the hedger did on a quarterly basis in the example in Figure 12–13. In this example, your relative position is based on the relative spreads between the high and low values for the stock and the option. With a normal distribution for the rates of return, we can no longer base our position on these spreads. Instead, our position is based on the ratio of the dollar change in the value of the option that will accompany each dollar change in the value of the stock, much in the manner of the hedge we discussed in relation to Figure 12–7. If a 2¢ change in the stock price induces a 1¢ change in the options price, we hedge by selling two options for each share of stock we buy.

Based on this framework Black and Scholes have derived an equation for the market values of European put and call options. The equations are technically correct for options on stocks that do not pay dividends, but the model can be amended for dividend by subtracting from the stock price the present value of any dividends expected to be paid during the life of the option. Because the stock price can be expected to drop by approximately the amount of the dividend at the ex-dividend date, we allow for this up front by subtracting from the stock price the present value of the expected dividend.

The Black-Scholes formula is provided in the appendix to this chapter. Don't try to make intuitive sense of the formula. It is in a final, simplified mathematical form, and the economic intuition behind the formula can't be seen in this final form. Just remember that if the option sells at the Black-Scholes price and you hedge with it, continually adjusting your portfolio position over time, the rate of return on your hedged investment will be the riskless rate of return in the bond market.

The Black-Scholes option pricing formula has become the most widely used benchmark for pricing options in the industry. Prices based on the formula are published by financial services, and routines for computing the Black-Scholes value are readily available in modules for hand-held calculators. One reason for the model's popularity is that it isn't very demanding in terms of the estimates required to compute the value of an option.

The inputs to the model are

1. The current stock price
2. The exercise price
3. The risk-free rate
4. The number of years to expiration
5. The variance of the stock's rate of return

The current stock price and the yield on a treasury bill with a maturity date equal to the expiration date can be read from the financial news. The exercise price and term to expiration can be read from the option contract. The only challenging estimate is that of the variance or standard deviation of the instantaneous rate of return on the stock.

Estimating the Variance of a Stock's Return

Technically, the variance is that of the instantaneous rate of return on the stock. However, most people estimate the variance on the basis of sampling the stock's daily rate of return. You are trying to estimate the variance of the stock's return over the remaining life of the option. Thus, your sample should be over a period that immediately precedes the current date. If the variance remains constant over time, the longer the sample period, the more accurate the sample estimate. However, a stock's variance typically undergoes changes from time to time. In view of this, you will want to extend the sample period as far back as you are confident that there was no change in the underlying variance.

Consider Figure 12–16. Time is plotted on the horizontal axis. As you move to the right, you are moving farther into the past. The daily rate of return on the stock is plotted on the vertical axis. Based on the plot connecting daily rates of return, it appears there was a reduction in the stock's underlying variance that occurred approximately sixty trading days ago. Given this, you will want to estimate the variance using a sample of returns taken over the preceding sixty days.

The variance you get from this sample will be an estimate of the stock's daily variance. If you are using annualized numbers for t and r_F in the Black-Scholes formula, you will have to annualize your variance estimate as well. If you are willing to make the reasonable assumptions that successive changes in stock prices are uncorrelated, and that stock values continue to fluctuate even on days when we can't see the fluctuations because they aren't traded, the annualized variance can be obtained by multiplying the daily variance by 365.

After obtaining the annualized sample variance, you now have to ask yourself whether the future period, covering the remaining life of the option, is comparable to your sample period. Stock prices usually become more variable around earnings and dividend announcements, so if there was an announcement date in

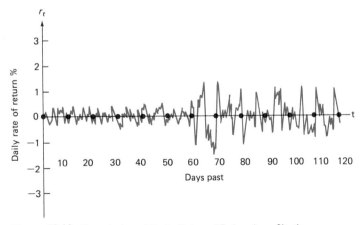

Figure 12-16   Time Series of Daily Rates of Return to a Stock

OUT ON THE STREET

A Run for His Money

In a split second the computer's evaluation of the spread flashes on the screen. Again, the implied market value of the spread, and the return based on the current value is simply incredible!

Jack Reynoldson is sitting in the offices of First Options of Chicago, a clearing firm on the Chicago Board Options Exchange (CBOE). Jack is a market maker on the CBOE. In the parlance of market makers, he is known as a neutral spreader. Neutral spreaders acquire options that are mispriced relative to theoretical values and hedge these options against other puts, calls, or stock. Jack's game is to buy the theoretically underpriced options and sell the theoretically overpriced options to create a position that is insensitive to small changes in the stock price. He then waits until the options revalue themselves. When the options become properly priced, Jack closes out his positions and takes his profits.

Jack is watching a television monitor furnished to him by the clearing firm. He holds a seat on the exchange and works for himself. Each time he makes a trade on the floor, he pays a small commission to the clearing firm. In return, the firm provides him with accounting and other services like this computer. The computer is programmed to value options based on several option pricing models, including the Black-Scholes model. The system provides model value estimates, including the expected variance of the underlying stock, the forecast for interest rates, and dividends that are expected to be paid out over the life of the option.

During the four years he has been trading options, Jack has found that the Black-Scholes model provides him with the best indicator of mispricing in the options market. In his opinion, the biases that exist in the model are small and 99.9 percent of the time have no impact on the spreads he designs and executes. In any case, any bias presents no problem to him, as long as it's consistent over time and he is aware of it. At times, though, he knows he has to be careful about the appropriateness of the assumptions of the model to the particular situation.

For instance, one of the assumptions of the model is that the distribution of returns on the stock is normal. At times it clearly is not. This is particularly true in a takeover situation. During these instances Jack knows that the options slip away from their Black-Scholes values, not because they are mispriced but because the model's assumptions are inappropriate for the situation. A good example is the case of Superior Oil. Superior was rumored to be a takeover candidate on several occasions. Each time the call options on the stock appeared to be overpriced on the basis of the Black-Scholes model. The options, however, were discounting the possibility of a huge one-time return on the stock, assuming the takeover went through. For those who bet that the rumors were inaccurate and that the model assumptions were correct, losses on short positions in calls appeared when the stock price jumped on the news that Mobil was indeed buying out Superior Oil. On an overall basis, however, the normality assumption is a reasonable one.

Jack can feel his adrenaline building

with each response from the terminal. He was attracted to this particular stock because of an unfavorable announcement regarding negotiations with the company's labor union. A strike seemed imminent. The announcement was made at 9:30 A.M., and the options promptly began changing in price, perhaps by too much. The out-of-the-money calls really took a dive. Seeing this, Jack thought he'd better check out the situation on the machine.

The computer is telling him that the market for the options is completely out of kilter. The puts are overpriced while the out-of-the-money calls are greatly underpriced. The only way you could justify the call prices is with an extremely low estimate of the stock's variance, far below the estimates provided him by the services. A strike seems like a sure thing at this point, but the length of the strike is another matter. If the strike is settled more quickly than expected, these call options could be worth more money. Factoring in uncertainty regarding the length of the strike into the variance estimate, the call options are clearly underpriced. The question now becomes how best to take advantage of the situation.

Jack now goes through the familiar process of designing the best spread through a sensitivity analysis. A key element in designing a spread is the option "delta." Delta is equivalent to 100 multiplied by $N(d_1)$ in the Black-Scholes equation. Each option contract (to buy or sell 100 shares of stock) can be thought of as the equivalent to holding a certain number of shares of stock. If a call option contract has a delta of 50, that means if

the stock goes up by $1, the option contract will rise in value by $50. To hedge, you must buy fifty shares of stock for each contract you sell.

The deltas on the deeply out-of-the-money options approximate 10. Because Jack feels these are the most underpriced, he will want to buy them. The question is, how to match them up to create the spread.

One candidate is the stock. Jack enters a spread into the computer in which he sells short 1000 shares of stock and buys 100 option contracts. Now he inputs estimates for the risk-free rate (in this case it's the ninety-day treasury bill rate) and the variance for the stock. The computer displays a theoretical price for the spread that is justified on the basis of the Black-Scholes model. The current market value is much less than what is generated on the basis of the theoretical values for the options. A good sign.

Now Jack tries to find out how sensitive the value of the spread is to changes in the values of the model's parameters. Suppose the stock's variance declines substantially from what the services are now estimating. If Jack exits from the spread under these conditions, he will have to buy the stock and sell the call options. The computer indicates, however, that even if the variance decline is substantial, the spread will still be profitable because of the relative cheapness of the calls. Similar analysis also indicates that its potential profitability is also insensitive to changes in interest rates.

Jack has never seen the market this far out of line. He now tries an alternative spread. This time he simultaneously buys the puts and the calls. Then he tries one where he buys fifty deeply out-of-the-money calls and sells twenty offsetting in-the-money calls. The process is repeated until Jack has tried nearly all possible combinations. He can't try everything, because he simply can't afford the time. He's not the only one looking at a screen like this one. Other spreaders are becoming aware of the situation. He's got to move fast. There are others who are looking to execute similar neutral spreads, acting to drive options prices closer in line with theoretical values.

While Jack still makes money on 70 percent of his spreads, the business isn't as profitable as it was two years ago, and certainly not as profitable as it was four years ago. Part of the problem is

machines like this one and the prevalence of all the options pricing services. To make money these days you've got to become faster on your feet and increasingly more sophisticated.

As it turns out, the first spread is the best one. Jack curses the waste of time under his breath. He turns off the machine and races to the street. The CBOE is just next door. Jack races through the doors of the CBOE and into the pit where the options are bought and sold.

Several other traders have preceded Jack in discovering that the market is out of whack. Fortunately, they haven't as yet had an impact on the deeply out-of-the-money call options. Jack executes his buy order and prepares to set up his short position. This one's going to be a winner for sure!

your sample period but none in the remaining period to expiration, you may have to adjust downward your estimate of the sample variance. Perhaps there is some ambiguity regarding the characteristics of a new product, the outcome of a serious litigation involving the firm, or the possibility of a takeover bid that will be resolved sometime during the life of the option. In these cases, the stock will make a significant move up or down when the ambiguity is resolved. In such situations you may want to adjust upward your sample estimate of the variance.

Using the Black-Scholes Formula to Find the Market's Estimate of the Stock's Variance

If you substitute the current market price of the option into the Black-Scholes formula, along with the specifics of the option contract and the risk-free rate, you can solve for the remaining unknown value in the equation, the variance of the rate of return on the stock. This value can't be solved for directly, but there are computer routines that can be used to solve for the implied variance through an iterative process. Thus, you can find the variance that is consistent with the current price of the option and the Black-Scholes option pricing framework.

Given the validity of the framework, the implied variance serves as an estimate of the variance that the market has in mind for the stock in setting the price for the option.

Because, as we discuss in Chapter 13, there is a possible problem of bias in the model, when pricing options that are significantly in or out of the money, it is best to compute the implied variance using an option where the underlying stock price is approximately equal to the present value of the exercise price. Figure 12–17 plots the implied variance on such an option over time. Superimposed on the diagram are the percentage changes in the price of the security underlying the option. Notice that as the variability of this series becomes smaller, the implied variance associated with the option becomes smaller as well. The market is apparently reassessing its estimate of the security's variance as it experiences lower variability in the return from day to day.

The Relationship Between Black-Scholes Put and Call Values and Underlying Stock Prices

In Figures 12–18a and 12–18b we have plotted the relationship between the value of a call and put, respectively, and the value of the stock options. Note that, once again, the values of the options approach a line with slope +1.00 (for a

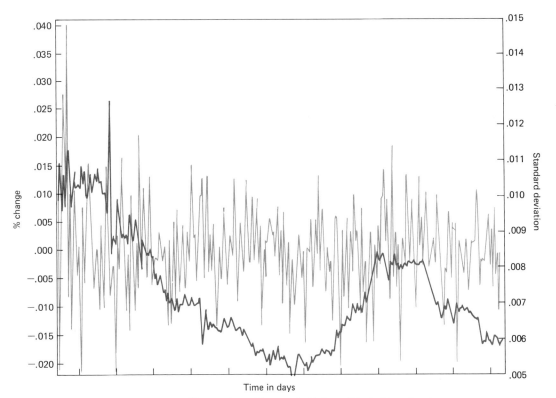

Figure 12-17 Implied Variance and Percentage Change in Value of Underlying Asset

Figure 12-18a Black-Scholes Relationship Between Stock Value and
European Call Value

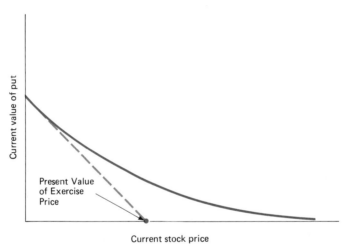

Figure 12-18b Black-Scholes Relationship Between Stock Value and
European Put Value

call) and −1.00 (for a put) emanating from the present value of the exercise price. Now the call option value approaches but never reaches the line. This is because the probability distribution isn't truncated on the left side as it was in the case of the rectangular uniform distribution. As a consequence, there is always some small probability of not exercising the option, no matter how large the present price of the stock becomes.

The negative of the slope of the line at any point, such as point *A*, reflects the probability of exercising the (put) call option. As the stock price becomes larger, so does the probability of exercise at maturity. The slope of the line also reflects the number of shares of stock you must buy for each call (put) option you sell (buy) in order to hedge at the current price of the stock. As the stock price changes, you move to a new point on the curve, with a new slope, and you must adjust your hedge position. If we increase the stock's variance, we move to a higher curve such as the broken curve in Figure 12–18a. Increasing the time to expiration also moves us to a higher curve.

Summary

A European option gives you the right to either buy or sell a stock at a specified exercise price on a specified expiration date. A call option gives you the right to buy the stock, and a put option gives you the right to sell it.

The value of a call (put) option increases (decreases) with the price of the stock. For both types of options, the dollar changes in the options are less than the corresponding dollar changes in the price of the stock, but the percentage changes are greater. In terms of percentage changes, out-of-the-money options are more variable than in-the-money options. The value of both the put and the call will increase with the variance of the stock they are written on.

In the presence of risk-averse investors, options can be valued to provide the risk-free rate of return to an investor who hedges with them. If the value of the option deviates from this equilibrium price, investors can become infinitely wealthy through riskless arbitrage portfolios that require no investment. Thus, there are strong economic forces that keep the options price in line with that which will produce a risk-free rate of return to a hedged investor.

The Black-Scholes model assumes that the probability distribution for the instantaneous rate of return to the stock underlying the option is constant over time and normally distributed. This implies that the probability distribution for the ending price of the stock at the expiration of the option is lognormal in shape. The model prices the option to provide the risk-free rate of return to hedgers that continually adjust their positions as the stock price changes over time. The Black-Scholes model is technically a model for European options. However, as discussed in Chapter 13, it can be used in some cases to value American options as well.

APPENDIX: THE BLACK-SCHOLES VALUES FOR CALL AND PUT OPTIONS

Call Option

Based on the Black-Scholes framework, the value of a European call option written on a stock that pays no dividends is given by the following equation:

$$V_C = V_S N(d_1) - \frac{X}{e^{r_F t}} N(d_2) \qquad (A12–1)$$

where V_S is the current market price for the stock, X is the exercise price for the option, r_F is the continuously compounded, riskless interest rate, and t is the number of years to expiration. The symbol e is the natural antilog of 1.00, or 2.718. When we raise this number to a power equal to the product of r_F and t, we convert it to a discount factor that discounts the exercise price to a present value, using continuous compounding. The term multiplied by $N(d_2)$ is, thus, the present value of the exercise price.

The numbers d_1 and d_2 are determined by the following formulas:

$$d_1 = \frac{\ln(V_S/X) + (r_F + {}^1\!/2\, \sigma^2_r)t}{\sigma_r \sqrt{t}} \qquad (A12–2)$$

$$d_2 = d_1 - \sigma_r \sqrt{t} \qquad (A12–3)$$

In the formula $\ln (\cdot)$ is the natural logarithm of the number in brackets. The term σ^2_r is the variance of the rate of return on the underlying stock. The numbers d_1 and d_2 can be taken to be deviations from the expected value of a unit normal distribution. A unit normal distribution is a special case of the normal distribution. It has an expected value of zero and a standard deviation of 1.00. Thus, a value for d of -1.5 would imply a deviation equal to 1.5 standard deviations below the expected value.

$N(d)$ is a probability operator. It tells you the probability of getting a deviation that is even further below the expected value than is d. In Figure A12–1, d is taken to be -1.00. We are thus one standard deviation below the expected value of a normal distribution. $N(d)$ is the probability remaining in the shaded area of the distribution. It is roughly 16 percent. Table A12–1 shows the values for $N(d)$ corresponding to various values for d. To illustrate the table, if d_1, computed on the basis of Equation (A12–2), is 0.00, then $N(d_1)$ is equal to .50. We are right on the unit normal distribution's expected value. The probability of falling below the expected value is 50 percent.

To compute the value of a call option using the Black-Scholes formula, first compute the values for d_1 and d_2 using Equations (A12–2) and (A12–3). Then find the values for $N(d_1)$ and $N(d_2)$ using Table A12–1. Finally, multiply $N(d_1)$ by the current stock price and $N(d_2)$ by the present value of the exercise price and net the two products.

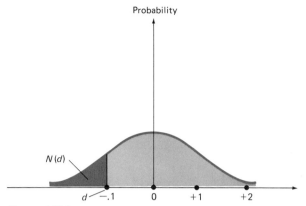

Probability

$N(d)$

d $-.1$ 0 $+1$ $+2$

Figure A12-1   Unit Normal Probability Distribution

Suppose we have a call option written on a stock with six months (.5 year) to expiration. The current stock price is $100, the exercise price is $100, the annualized standard deviation of the stock's instantaneous rate of return is 50 percent, and the riskless rate is 10 percent. The value for d_1 is given by

$$d_1 = .318 = \frac{\ln(\$100/\$100) + (.10 + 1/2 \times .25).5}{.5 \times .707}$$

Interpolating from Table A12–1, we see that $N(d_1)$ is .6236.

The value for d_2 is given by

$$d_2 = -.0355 = .318 - .50 \times .707$$

We can see from the table that the corresponding value for $N(d_2)$ is .4859.

The value for the call option is now computed using Equation (A12–1):

$$V_C = \$100 \times .6236 - \frac{\$100}{2.718^{.10 \times .5}} \times .4859 = \$16.14$$

Put Option

The Black-Scholes formula for the value for a put option is deceptively simple:

$$V_P = V_C + \frac{X}{e^{r_F t}} - V_S \qquad (A12–4)$$

The reason I say "deceptively" is because V_C is the Black-Scholes value of an identical call option written on the same stock. You add the present value of the exercise price to this value and then subtract the current stock price.

If the stock pays dividends, the expected value of the dividends paid before expiration must be subtracted from the stock price in A12–1, A12–2, and A12–4.

Table A12–1 Values for *d* and *N(d)*

d	N(d)	d	N(d)	d	N(d)
		−1.00	.1587	1.00	.8413
−2.95	.0016	−.95	.1711	1.05	.8531
−2.90	.0019	−.90	.1841	1.10	.8643
−2.85	.0022	−.85	.1977	1.15	.8749
−2.80	.0026	−.80	.2119	1.20	.8849
−2.75	.0030	−.75	.2266	1.25	.8944
−2.70	.0035	−.70	.2420	1.30	.9032
−2.65	.0040	−.65	.2578	1.35	.9115
−2.60	.0047	−.60	.2743	1.40	.9192
−2.55	.0054	−.55	.2912	1.45	.9265
−2.50	.0062	−.50	.3085	1.50	.9332
−2.45	.0071	−.45	.3264	1.55	.9394
−2.40	.0082	−.40	.3446	1.60	.9452
−2.35	.0094	−.35	.3632	1.65	.9505
−2.30	.0107	−.30	.3821	1.70	.9554
−2.25	.0122	−.25	.4013	1.75	.9599
−2.20	.0139	−.20	.4207	1.80	.9641
−2.15	.0158	−.15	.4404	1.85	.9678
−2.10	.0179	−.10	.4602	1.90	.9713
−2.05	.0202	−.05	.4801	1.95	.9744
−2.00	.0228	.00	.5000	2.00	.9773
−1.95	.0256	.05	.5199	2.05	.9798
−1.90	.0287	.10	.5398	2.10	.9821
−1.85	.0322	.15	.5596	2.15	.9842
−1.80	.0359	.20	.5793	2.20	.9861
−1.75	.0401	.25	.5987	2.25	.9878
−1.70	.0446	.30	.6179	2.30	.9893
−1.65	.0495	.35	.6368	2.35	.9906
−1.60	.0548	.40	.6554	2.40	.9918
−1.55	.0606	.45	.6736	2.45	.9929
−1.50	.0668	.50	.6915	2.50	.9938
−1.45	.0735	.55	.7088	2.55	.9946
−1.40	.0808	.60	.7257	2.60	.9953
−1.35	.0885	.65	.7422	2.65	.9960
−1.30	.0968	.70	.7580	2.70	.9965
−1.25	.1057	.75	.7734	2.75	.9970
−1.20	.1151	.80	.7881	2.80	.9974
−1.15	.1251	.85	.8023	2.85	.9978
−1.10	.1357	.90	.8159	2.90	.9981
−1.05	.1469	.95	.8289	2.95	.9984

QUESTIONS AND PROBLEMS

1. Suppose that the end-of-year price on a stock is uniformly distributed from a low of $0 to a high of $100. Assume that investors are risk neutral and that the rate of interest is zero. A call option exists on this stock, with an exercise price of $60.

a. Sketch the probability distribution of the ending stock price.

b. Sketch the probability distribution of the ending call option value.

c. What is the expected value of the ending call option value, conditional on the assumption that you know the ending stock price will be such that the option will not be worthless?

d. What should be the current market value of the option?

2. What does the assumption of risk neutrality imply about determination of the current market value of some risky asset (like a stock)?

Refer to the following information for questions 3 through 7. A given stock's end-of-year price is uniformly distributed from a low price of $75 to a high price of $175. Investors are risk neutral. The one-year interest rate is 6 percent.

3. What should be the current market price of the stock?

4. Assume a call option exists with an exercise price of $150 and one year to expiration.

a. What should be the current market price of the call?

b. What is the probability that the call will be exercised?

5. Assume a put option exists with an exercise price of $75 and one year to expiration.

a. What should be the current market price of the put?

b. What is the probability that the put will be exercised?

6. Suppose the stock price distribution now changes so that it is uniformly distributed from a low of $65 to a high of $165.

a. What would be the current price of the stock?

b. Compute the current price of the call from question 4 and note the change.

c. Compute the current price of the put from question 5 and note the change.

7. Starting from the original stock price distribution ($75 to $175), suppose the distribution "spreads out," now ranging from a low of $65 to a high of $185. The distribution is still uniform.

a. How would the current stock price compare with the price computed in question 3?

b. Compute the current price of the call from question 4 and note the change.

c. Compute the current price of the put from question 5 and note the change.

8. Consider the following statement: "When we are modeling the ending stock price with a uniform distribution and assuming risk neutrality, a change in

the variance of the stock price should be irrelevant in determining the value of a call or a put option." Is this statement true or false? Explain.

Refer to the following information for questions 9 and 10. A stock's current price is $160, and there are two possible prices that may occur next period: $150 or $175. No dividends will be paid. The interest rate on risk-free investments is 6 percent per period.

9. Assume that a European call option exists on this stock having an exercise price of $155.

   a. How could you form a portfolio based on the stock and the call so as to achieve a risk-free hedge?

   b. Compute the equilibrium market price of the call.

10. Assume that a European put option exists on this stock having an exercise price of $180.

   a. How could you form a portfolio based on the stock and the put so as to achieve a risk-free hedge?

   b. Compute the equilibrium market price of the put.

11. Assume the following information for a stock and a call option written on the stock.

$$\text{Exercise price} = \$40$$
$$\text{Current stock price} = \$30$$
$$\sigma_r^2 = .25$$
$$\text{Time to expiration, } t = .25 \text{ year}$$
$$\text{Risk-free rate} = .05$$

   a. Use the Black-Scholes procedure to determine the value of the call option.

   b. Change the time to expiration, t, to .5 and compute the call value again.

12. In using the Black-Scholes call options formula, what would be the impact on the call option value in each of the following situations?

   a. If σ_r rises, other things remaining the same

   b. If t falls, other things remaining the same

   c. If the current stock price rises, other things remaining the same

13. Consider the Black-Scholes call options formula and suppose that the price of the underlying stock gets very large, relative to the option's exercise price. As the stock price gets larger, what value would the option be approaching?

14. Describe how the Black-Scholes call options formula can be used to make an inference about the variance of the return on a stock.

BIBLIOGRAPHY

ATCHISON, M., R. DeMONG, and J. KLING, *New Financial Instruments: A Descriptive Guide*. The Financial Analysts Research Foundation, 1985.

BLACK, F., "Fact and Fantasy in the Use of Options," *Financial Analysts Journal* (July–August 1975).

BLACK, F., and M. SCHOLES, "The Pricing of Options and Corporate Liabilities," *Journal of Political Economy* (May–June 1973).

COX, J. C., S. A. ROSS, and M. RUBINSTEIN, "Option Pricing: A Simplified Approach," *Journal of Financial Economics* (March 1979).

GESKE, R., "The Valuation of Compound Options," *Journal of Financial Economics* (March 1979).

MERTON, R., "The Theory of Rational Option Pricing," *Bell Journal of Economics and Management Science* (Spring 1973).

RUBINSTEIN, M., "The Valuation of Uncertain Income Streams and the Pricing of Options," *Bell Journal of Economics* (Autumn 1976).

RUBINSTEIN, M., and J. R. COX, *Option Markets*. Englewood Cliffs, N.J.: Prentice-Hall, 1985.

SMITH, C. W., "Option Pricing: A Review," *Journal of Financial Economics* (December 1976).

13 ADDITIONAL ISSUES IN OPTION PRICING

Introduction

The previous chapter covered European options, which can be exercised only at maturity. In this chapter we explore some additional topics related to options. These topics include the parity relationship between the prices of put and call options written on the same stock, problems in pricing American options that pay dividends, bias in the pricing of options through the Black-Scholes model, and the use of options to take advantage of special situations. We shall also discover that conventional securities, like corporate bonds, can be viewed as portfolios of options, or option-like securities. In this sense, options can be viewed as the building blocks of complex financial contracts.

PUT-CALL PARITY

Consider a put and call option written on the same stock with the same exercise price and expiring at the same time. The difference between the prices on the put and the call must take on a specific parity relationship, or opportunities for unlimited arbitrage profit once again open up. If the options are in parity with respect to one another, the difference in their prices must be equal to the difference between the present value of their exercise price and the current market price of the stock.[1]

$$\text{Put price} - \text{Call price} = \frac{\text{Exercise price}}{(1 + r_F)^t} - \text{Stock price} \qquad (13\text{--}1)$$

where r_F is the risk-free rate of return, and t is the time to expiration of the options.

Suppose, first, that the difference between the put and call prices is greater than that of parity. In that case, we can manipulate Equation (13–1) to form the following inequality:

$$(1 + r_F)^t \times \underbrace{\{\text{Stock price} + \text{Put price} - \text{Call price}\}}_{\text{Amount invested}} > \text{Exercise price}$$

The inequality implies that there is an investment strategy we can use to make money while taking no risk and making no investment of our own funds. We will sell the stock short, sell the put, and buy the call. The net proceeds of this transaction are in the braced { } expression on the left-hand side of the inequality. If we invest these net proceeds in a riskless bond, the ending value of the investment will be greater than the exercise price of the options.

This is important because we are obligated under the short sale to return a share of stock to our broker. Because we own a call option, if, at expiration, the stock is selling above the exercise price, we can acquire a share at the exercise price using the call option. If the stock is selling at a price less than the exercise price, we will throw away our call option, but the person to whom we sold the put option will exercise and sell us a share of stock at a price equal to the exercise price. Consequently, no matter what happens to the price of the stock at time t, we are set up to cover the short sale at a cost equal to the exercise price.

Thus, we can get out of the transaction for the exercise price, but, based on the inequality, this will be less than the ending value of our bond investment that we made with the initial net proceeds of the transaction. We have invested no money of our own, we have taken no risk, yet we have made money. The amount of money we can make is limited only by the number of shares we can find to sell short.[2]

Once again, strong economic forces are present to keep the prices of puts and calls in parity with one another. There are special times, however, when these forces are blocked, allowing the prices to move out of parity. One example of such a case occurred in March 1981. A takeover bid was announced, directed by Brunswick Corporation. Prior to the bid, the price of the stock was $20. The

---

[1]The equation for put-call parity is applicable when no dividends are to be paid before the option expires. If a dividend is to be paid, the equation should be modified by adding the compounded future value of the dividend to the exercise price.

[2]This can be considered truly riskless arbitrage only for European options. In the case of American options, they can be exercised prior to maturity, in which case the proceeds from the riskless bond investment may be insufficient to cover the short sale.

takeover bid price was approximately $30. Put and call options existed on the stock that had approximately two months to expiration. No dividend was expected to be paid over these two months. The exercise price on both these options was $30. Based on the takeover bid, the stock price rose to $29. The put was selling at a price of $9 and the call at $1. The risk-free rate of interest at the time was approximately 15 percent, so the present value of the exercise price was $29.31. Thus, the put and call were out of parity.

$$\$9.00 - \$1.00 > \$29.31 - \$29.00$$

You would generate net proceeds of $37 by selling the put, buying the call, and short selling the stock. You could have invested these proceeds at 15 percent in the bond market for two months, producing a terminal value of $37.87. You know that at the end of two months you will be able to cover your short sale at a price of $30 through either the put or the call option. Therefore, you make a profit of $7.87.

As individual investors, you and I aren't free to invest the proceeds of short sales in the bond market, and there are also margin requirements for both the short sale and the sale of the put option. Even in the face of these problems, however, the transaction offers an extremely attractive rate of return and no risk. Moreover, large financial institutions face no constraints on short selling and have no margin requirements on a riskless transaction such as this. Yet the prices of the put and call remained out of parity for several weeks.

The explanation lies in a blockage that occurred to the arbitrage. Because there was a bid outstanding for the common stock, it became impossible to find anyone willing to lend shares to sell short. If you had shares and lent them to someone for purposes of a short sale, you wouldn't be able to tender them to the acquiring company at the premium price. Thus, the supply of shares available to short sellers dried up completely. In the absence of this form of discipline by the market, the prices of the put and the call drifted out of parity.

Now assume that the difference between the prices of the put and the call becomes *less* than that of the parity relationship. In this case, the inequality goes in the opposite direction:

$$(1 + r_F)^t \times \underbrace{\{\text{Stock price} + \text{Put price} - \text{Call price}\}}_{\text{Amount borrowed}} < \text{Exercise price}$$

We can now reverse the transaction. We buy the stock and the put and we sell the call. We raise the net proceeds required to do this by borrowing money in the bond market. The total amount on the left side of the inequality is the amount that we must pay off on our loan at the expiration date for the options. Given our position in the put and the call, we know that we will be able to sell the stock at the expiration date at an amount equal to the exercise price, which is greater than the required payment on our loan. The difference is our profit on the transaction. We make no investment of our own, we take no risk; yet, once again, we make a profit, which is limited only by the number of shares and options we can buy and sell at the disequilibrium prices. In the process of buying the put and selling the call, we will widen the gap between them until it conforms to the parity relationship. At that point, the profit from the arbitrage transactions is zero.

THE LOWER LIMITS TO THE VALUE OF A CALL OPTION

One floor underlies the value of a European call option, and two floors underlie the market value of any American call option. We will call the single floor that underlies a European option the soft floor. When the option drops below the soft floor, the option dominates the stock it is written on, as an investment. Thus, the market for the common stock evaporates. The value of an American option is supported by a hard floor as well as a soft floor. The hard floor is positioned below the soft floor. The consequences of an option dropping below the hard floor are even more dramatic; we can all create unlimited wealth through arbitrage. We should emphasize here that these floors are applicable to options on stocks that are not expected to pay dividends during the lives of the options.

The hard and soft floors are given in Figure 13–1 as the solid and broken 45-degree lines, respectively, emanating from the horizontal axis. The hard floor emanates from the exercise price, and the soft floor from the present value of the exercise price. The hard floor is equal to

$$\text{Stock price} - \text{Exercise price or 0, whichever is greater}$$

and the soft floor is equal to

$$\text{Stock price} - \text{Exercise price}/(1 + r_F)^t \text{ or 0, whichever is greater}$$

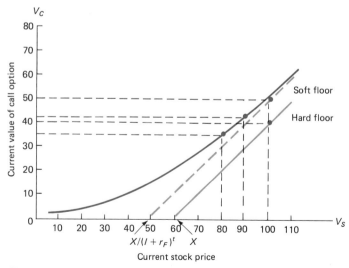

Figure 13-1 The Hard and Soft Floors

Market Forces Supporting the Hard Floor

In Figure 13–1 the exercise price of the option is $60, the present value of the exercise price is $50, and the current price of the stock is $100. Thus, given the present price of the stock, the hard floor is $40 and the soft floor is $50. Suppose the option sells below the hard floor at $38. You can now make money if you buy the option at $38 and then exercise and acquire a share of stock with it for an additional $60. The total cost of acquiring a share in this way is $98. Now you can turn around and sell the stock immediately for $100, making a profit of $2.

Why stop now when you can do it again? You can repeat this transaction as many times as you want, making $2 each time; and as you accumulate capital, you can increase the scale of the transaction, thus making more money each time around. In a short period of time, you, and people like you, will drive the price of the option above the hard floor.

When the option is below the hard floor, it makes sense to exercise it. You will exercise any options you own, and you will buy all the options that you can in order to exercise them. However, once the option is above the hard floor, except under special circumstances, no one will exercise unless the options are about to expire. Suppose, for example, that the option was priced at $42. If you exercise, it will cost you an additional $60 to buy the stock. If, instead, you sell the option, you can acquire the stock in the market at $100 by adding an additional $58 to the investment. Thus, if the option is above the hard floor, to invest in the stock, you sell the option and buy the stock rather than exercise the option.

Market Forces Supporting the Soft Floor

It can be shown that for call options, the hard floor is really redundant, because the market will not permit the stock to fall below the soft floor. Once the option falls below the soft floor, everyone will invest in the option rather than the stock. If, for example, the option were selling at $42, you could construct a portfolio with the option that would dominate an investment in the stock. The portfolio would consist of one option, purchased at a price of $42, and $50 invested in riskless bonds.

Because the present value of the exercise price of $60 is $50, we know that the $50 bond investment that matures at expiration will produce $60 at that time. You can use the $60 to exercise the option, should you choose to do so. If the stock is above $60 at expiration, you will exercise, and you will own a share of stock. If the stock is below $60 at expiration, you will throw your option away, but you will still have the $60 from your bond investment. Consequently, the lower limit on the value of your investment is $60.

If you bought the stock instead of this portfolio, there would be no lower limit on the value of your investment. Assuming there are no dividends paid on the stock, you are equally well off as is the options investor if the price of the stock is above \$60, but you are worse off if the price of the stock turns out to be below \$60. They have the \$60 from their bond investment; all you have is a share of stock worth less than \$60.

The options portfolio is clearly the better investment, but if the option is selling at a price below the soft floor, it is also cheaper to buy. At a \$42 options price, it costs \$92 to set up the portfolio of the option and bonds, but \$100 to buy a share of stock. The option is clearly the better buy. Everyone will recognize this, the market for the stock will evaporate, and everyone will move into the option, eventually driving its price above the soft floor. Because the portfolio of the option and the bonds is clearly the better investment, it commands a higher total price. This will be the case when the option sells at a price on the options pricing curve, *above* the soft floor.

We have discussed the hard and soft floors in terms of a call option. These floors also exist for put options. The hard floor is given by

Exercise price − Stock price or 0, whichever is greater

and the soft floor by

Exercise price$/(1 + r_F)^t$ − Stock price or 0, whichever is greater

In the case of an American put, the hard floor is above the soft floor, making the former the only floor of consequence.

When European and American Options Have Equal Value

Based on the discussion so far, we know that

1. An option will not be exercised prior to expiration unless it is priced below the hard floor.

2. The market will not permit the price of the option to fall below the hard floor (or even the soft floor, in the case of a call option).

The obvious conclusion is that American options normally will not be exercised before maturity. Although, as we will soon see, this conclusion doesn't hold for all American options, it does hold for American options on stocks that are not expected to pay dividends during the life of the option. For these options, because there is never an incentive to exercise prior to expiration, the right to exercise before expiration has no value. This means that identical American and European options written on the same stocks will have the same market value. Because the soft floor is not effective for put options, the probability of early exercise is greater for these.

The Black-Scholes equation is technically intended for the valuation of European options. However, given that the right to exercise early has no value, it can also be used to value American options that pay no dividends in the exercise period. The payment of a dividend in the exercise period complicates matters, however. As we will see in the next section, the expected payment of a dividend may provide an incentive for early exercise. If it does, then the right to exercise early has a value, and the Black-Scholes model may provide an inaccurate estimate of the value of the option.

HOW DIVIDEND PAYMENTS
MAY INDUCE PREMATURE EXERCISE

What if the stock in Figure 13–1 is going to pay a dividend of $20 to all stockholders of record at the end of today's trading? The price of the stock today is $100, because if you buy it today, you get the dividend of $20. If you wait until tomorrow to buy, however, you don't get the dividend. Consequently, tomorrow's price is expected to be $80.

The curved line approaching the soft floor call from above is the relationship that is expected to exist between the value of the option and the value of the stock. Thus, if the price of the stock is going to be $80 tomorrow, we can expect that the option will be priced at $35. Note that if you exercise the option today, it is worth $40 to you, because you can use it to buy a share of stock at $60, and if you buy the stock today, you get the dividend, which is worth $100 with the stock. Under these conditions, it makes sense for you to exercise your option prior to its expiration date, because you are $5 better off if you do. On the day that the stock goes ex-dividend, the market value of the options will be priced at $40, and they will all disappear by the end of the day.

Note that if the dividend were smaller, say, $10 instead of $20, it wouldn't trigger early exercise, at least in the case of the option in Figure 13–1. This is because we can expect the stock to be priced at $90 and the option to be priced at $42 tomorrow. It makes no sense for us to exercise the option for $40 today. The price of the option today will be approximately equal to $42, its expected price tomorrow. However, even a $10 dividend can trigger early exercise if the time between the dividend payment and the time to expiration was shorter. In this case, the present value of the exercise price would be closer to the exercise price, and the soft floor would be closer to the hard floor. Early exercise is triggered as soon as the expected value of the option after the ex-dividend day falls below the hard floor for the option today. This is more likely to happen the larger the dividend, the shorter the time between the ex-dividend date and the expiration date, and the smaller the variance of the stock price. (The larger the variance, the greater the distance between the curve and the soft floor.)

If you are valuing a call option where early exercise is a distinct possibility, you must be very cautious about using the Black-Scholes framework. This model should be used for valuing European options or for valuing American options where early exercise is unlikely. If early exercise is a distinct possibility, the right to exercise early has value, and the value of an American option rises above the value of a Black-Scholes European option.[3]

[3]In this case you may want to consider using option pricing by binomial approximation (see your software) or the alternative options pricing model for American options as developed by Roll (1977) and Geske (1979a). An explanation of the model can be found in Haugen (1986), Chapter 17 appendix.

AN ADDITIONAL BIAS IN THE BLACK-SCHOLES OPTIONS PRICE

The Black-Scholes model may have a propensity to overvalue out-of-the-money options and undervalue in-the-money options. This can be seen in the results of a study by MacBeth and Merville (1980) presented in Figure 13–2. On the vertical axis of the graph, the percentage difference between the actual market price of each option and the Black-Scholes price is plotted. On the horizontal axis, the percentage difference between the stock price and the present value of the exercise price is plotted. Each observation in the figure represents an option written on IBM stock. To be represented on the graph, the options must have at least ninety days to expiration. The variance estimate used in computing the Black-Scholes price is the implied variance for the IBM option that is closest to being in the money at the time the option value is computed.

For the option labeled *A,* the actual market price of the option was approximately 23 percent greater than the Black-Scholes value, at a time when the market price for IBM stock was 4 percent greater than the exercise price of this particular option.

Out-of-the-money options are positioned to the left of the vertical axis, and in-the-money options are positioned to the right. Note that in-the-money options

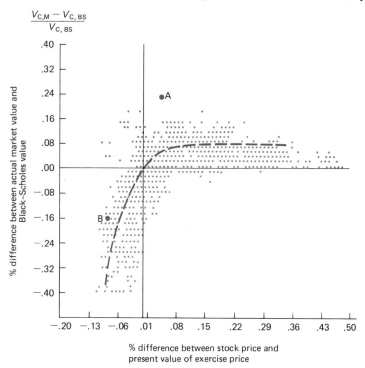

Figure 13-2 Bias in the Black-Scholes Model

source: James D. MacBeth and Larry J. Merville, "Tests of the Black-Scholes and Cox Call Option Valuation Models," *Journal of Finance* (May 1980).

CHAPTER 13   Additional Issues in Option Pricing

tend to be positioned above the horizontal axis, whereas out-of-the-money options are positioned below. If you compute the Black-Scholes value for an out-of-the-money option, the actual market price will likely be lower. The opposite will be true for an in-the-money option.[4]

We aren't detecting errors in pricing by the *market*. That is, there is no propensity for out-of-the-money options to rise to their "equilibrium" Black-Scholes values, and we also see no tendency for in-the-money options to fall back toward their "equilibrium" Black-Scholes values. This is because it is the Black-Scholes model that is in error, and not the market. The Black-Scholes value isn't the true equilibrium value for the option. Some aspect of the framework assumed in deriving the model apparently is misspecified, resulting in an error that is systematically related to the extent to which the option is in or is out of the money.

Thus, although the option positioned at point *B* is selling at a market price that is 16 percent below the value implied by the Black-Scholes equation, it would be wrong to conclude that this option was selling at a price below its true equilibrium value. In fact, given the extent to which other options, which are similarly out of the money, are overvalued by the Black-Scholes model, we might even conclude that this particular option is selling at a price that is *above* its true equilibrium value.

Others have found additional biases in the model. Using over-the-counter option data, Black and Scholes (1972) found that their model underpriced call options on low variance stocks and overpriced call options on high variance stocks. Geske and Roll (1984) found that the Black-Scholes model tended to underprice near maturity American call options.

If you are going to use an options pricing model like the Black-Scholes model as a yardstick to determine whether the market has over- or undervalued a particular option, you must do one of two things to allow for possible biases in your model:

1. You can estimate the bias in your model empirically and allow for it in determining the extent to which an option is mispriced.

2. Or you can revise your model, correcting the misspecification to eliminate the bias.

Estimating and Allowing for the Bias

If the bias is reasonably stable in form over time, you can estimate it by fitting a curve of best fit through the scatter of observations, such as in Figure 13–2. The curve can be fit with a computer using standard nonlinear regression routines. Having allowed for the bias in the model, you would now consider an option overvalued if it were positioned significantly above the curve and undervalued if it were significantly below the curve.

As discussed above, the bias can run in other directions as well. Thus, you

[4]This bias was also reported by Rubinstein (1981). However, the reverse bias was found in studies by Black (1975) and Emanuel and MacBeth (1981).

might want to obtain a statistical fit for the bias by running a multiple regression where the independent variables are percentages in or out of the money, term to maturity, and possibly even variance level.

Employing More General Options Pricing Models That Are Free of Bias Problems

The Black-Scholes model assumes that the variance of the rates of return to the underlying stock is constant throughout the life of the option. There are a number of empirical tests, however, that indicate a tendency for the variance of the rates of return to increase as the market value of a stock becomes smaller. This tendency makes some sense on a theoretical level, because a reduction in the market value of the common stock reflects an erosion in the firm's equity base. A reduction in the value of equity relative to the value of the firm's debt means an increase in the firm's financial leverage, and this, of course, means an increase in stockholder risk.

Cox (1975) has derived an alternative formula to that of Black and Scholes that assumes that stock returns are generated according to a process where the variance of returns becomes larger as the stock price becomes smaller. Once again, the model derives the option value required to produce a risk-free rate of return to an investor who hedges with the option. The Black-Scholes model can be viewed as a special case of the Cox model, where the variance is assumed to be independent of the stock price. To use the Black-Scholes model, you must estimate the variance of the stock's return. To use the Cox model, you must estimate both the variance and the propensity for the variance to change as the level of the stock price changes.

From available evidence, it appears that the Cox model is free of the bias problem that plagues the Black-Scholes model. The Cox model is believed to have little or no propensity to under- (or over-) value in- (or out-) of-the-money options. However, the Cox model is much more computationally complex than is the Black-Scholes model. A complete description of the Cox model is in MacBeth and Merville (1980).

Geske and Roll (1984) argue that the bias problems in the Black-Scholes model may result from the fact that a European model is being used to value American options. Roll (1977) and Geske (1979a) have developed an American options pricing model for stocks with dividend payments that are known with certainty. Although less complex than the Cox, this model is somewhat more complex than the Black-Scholes.

Don't be put off by the computational complexity of these models. When you use them, you will undoubtedly be employing high-speed computers in any case. Those who speculate in options are highly sophisticated. The Black-Scholes model is widely used by those who trade options. Even the more complex Cox model is used by some of the larger, more sophisticated trading firms. The race is on to find the model that most accurately describes the way options are priced, because those with the most accurate yardsticks can best discriminate between profitable and unprofitable options investments.

OUT ON THE STREET

Sliding Down the Capital Market Line

"But that's the point. Bonds have shown as much volatility as stocks in recent years. If you're going to reduce the risk of your portfolio, we think you've got to begin thinking about other markets. And we think the options market provides a viable alternative."

Peter Thayer is executive vice president of Gateway Investment Advisers, a money management firm located in Cincinnati, Ohio. Gateway specializes in the application of options to investment strategies. Pete is on the phone to a potential investor in Gateway Option Income Fund, which was established in December 1977. The fund is designed to provide its investors with high yield and low risk. It hopes to attain superior investment results over that which an investor can attain by combining investments in the overall market with investments in fixed-income securities.

Suppose you want your portfolio to have a beta of .5. Unless you want to go into the bond market or can sell short without restriction, you have to invest in common stocks with extremely low betas. This means concentrating your investments in regulated utility type stocks and exposing yourself to the residual variance associated with a portfolio with high industry concentration.

The Option Index Fund provides an alternative. Gateway invests in the population of nearly 400 optionable stocks. For each 100 shares of stock it buys, it sells one call options contract, at the money, on the same stock. The dollar movement in an at-the-money option is approximately half the dollar movement in the stock, so the beta of this partially hedged position will be approximately half the beta of the underlying common stock. Because the betas for the stocks in the overall portfolio are distributed around 1.00, the overall portfolio beta is usually between .4 and .6. This is accomplished for a widely diversified portfolio, without

OPTION STRATEGIES

The Straddle

Options can be put together into packages to take advantage of special situations. Suppose a firm is involved in antitrust litigation. The suit is to be settled in the next month, but the direction of the decision is completely unclear. If the company wins the suit, the price of the stock is likely to be worth $40; if it loses, the value will be $20. There is a 50 percent chance of the suit going either way, and the current market price of the stock is poised halfway between the two possible outcomes at $30.

the need to invest in fixed-income securities. This is particularly attractive to corporate investors, because, while they are taxed on interest income in its entirety, they get to include 85 percent of the dividend income from common stock investments for tax purposes.

Until passage of the new tax law in July 1984, there has been an additional tax advantage to investing in the fund for corporations. In selling the call options, Gateway, of course, raised money. The old law allowed the investment company to distribute these as ordinary dividends to corporations that could then take advantage of the 85 percent exclusion. Moreover, the biggest premiums are on at-the-money options.

As the prices of the individual common stocks move up and down, Gateway rolls out of its old out- or in-the-money positions and into a new at-the-money option. As the option moves away from being at the money, the beta for the combined position with the stock changes. For example, suppose the exercise price on the option was $100. If the stock price was $110, the beta for the combined position would be virtually 0.00, because the dollar change in each options contract would be approximately the same as the dollar change in each 100 shares of common stock. On the other hand, if the price of the stock moved to an out-of-the-money position, say, to $90, the beta would move toward the beta of the stock, because the dollar changes in the option would now be small relative to the dollar changes in the stock. Thus, Gateway must actively manage its positions to keep the betas halved. Considering the great liquidity in the options market, however, this presents no problem.

Gateway's mutual fund appeals to pension funds and corporate money managers who are looking for bond substitutes. It provides an effective way to slide down the capital market line for those who disdain making bond investments and paying taxes.

If you use options, it *may* be possible to construct a strategy whereby you make money regardless of the outcome. The strategy that is suitable for this particular situation is called a *straddle*. To construct a straddle, you buy an equal number of put and call options on the same stock that have the same exercise price and that mature on the same date. In this case, you'll want the expiration date on the options to be after the date the case is expected to be decided. The market value of the straddle as a function of the market value of the stock is shown in Figure 13–3.

In the figure we have presumed that the rate of interest is equal to zero, so the exercise prices *and* their present values are all equal to the current stock price, $30. The solid curves show the relationships between the put and call and the stock price. The broken curve shows the relationship between the value of

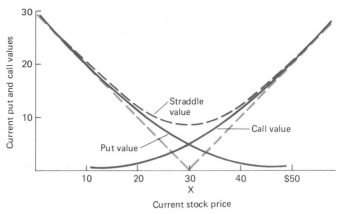

Figure 13-3 Current Market Value of the Straddle

the straddle and the stock price. Based on the Black-Scholes framework, when the term to expiration for the put and call are equal and when the present value of both exercise prices are equal to the current stock price, the put and call will have identical market values, in this case $4. Thus, the total value of the straddle is $8.

It seems that the value of the straddle will increase if the stock moves in either direction from its present position. This is true if the move takes place immediately. However, as time goes by and the expiration date of the options approaches, the value of the put will approach the difference between the exercise price and the stock price or 0, whichever is greater, and the value of the call will approach the difference between the stock price and the exercise price or 0, whichever is greater. Thus, at expiration, the value of the straddle will be positioned on one of the two 45-degree lines emanating from the exercise price. If the firm wins the case, the stock rises to $40 and the straddle is worth $10 at expiration (the value of the call). If the firm loses, the stock falls to $20, and the straddle is worth $10 at expiration (the value of the put). Because you paid $8 for the straddle initially, you win in either case.

There are two problems, however. First, there is always the possibility of the trial lingering on without a decision. If no decision is reached until after the expiration date, the price of the stock will remain at $30 at expiration, and the straddle will be worthless, resulting in the loss of your initial $8 investment.

Second, the market may fully recognize the firm's high variance situation in pricing the options. It may drive the price of the put and the call to $5, in which case you break even if the trial is decided before expiration. To make money, the price of the stock would have to move outside the $20 to $40 range. If it falls inside the range instead, you lose money on the straddle. Falling in or out of this range may well be an even bet. In determining whether the straddle is a good strategy, you must assess the extent to which the market has taken the firm's situation into account in pricing the options.

The Butterfly Spread

Another option strategy is the *butterfly spread*. You construct a butterfly spread when you believe that the possible outcomes for the stock price are in a narrower range than is implied in the pricing of the options by the market.

A butterfly spread can be constructed with call options written on the same stock and expiring at the same date but having three different exercise prices. Suppose the present price of the stock is $60. You buy one call option with an exercise price of $50 for a price we will assume is $13. You sell two calls with an exercise price of $60 for a market price of $5 each, and you buy one call with an exercise price of $70 for $1. The total cost of this investment is $4 = ($13 − 2 × $5 + $1).

The value of the butterfly spread at the expiration date for the options, as a function of the value of the stock at that time, is given in Figure 13–4. If the stock is worth $50 or less, all of the options are worthless. As the stock price goes from $50 to $60, the option with the $50 exercise price takes on value, rising from $0 to $10. Once the stock price increases in value beyond $60, the two options you sold with exercise prices of $60 take on value. Their value must be subtracted from the value of the $50 option, because your position in them is negative. Thus, if the stock price is $70, the $50 call you bought is worth $20, but the two $60 calls you sold are worth $10 each, so the total value of the package is $00. Once the stock price moves beyond $70, the $70 option you bought adds to the value of the package. Thus, at an $80 stock price, the $50 call is worth $30, the two $60 calls are worth a total of $40, and the $70 call is worth $10. Adding up the positive and negative positions, we again get a total value for the package of $00. No matter how far the stock price climbs above $70, the value of the butterfly spread will be $0.

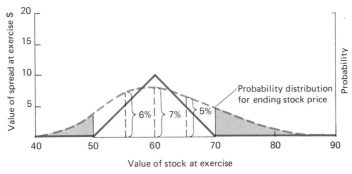

Figure 13-4   Ending Value of Butterfly Spread

The butterfly spread is a good investment if you believe the price of the stock will remain near its present value. If the stock price doesn't move, the ending value of the spread will be $10, and it cost you only $4 to set it up.

Computing the Expected
Return on an Option Strategy

To compute the expected rate of return on a strategy like the butterfly spread, you need to estimate the shape of the probability distribution for the value of the stock at the expiration date of the options. In Figure 13–4 we have super-imposed a probability distribution for the ending stock value. We assume the distribution for the rates of return to the stock is normal, so the resulting distribution for the ending value of the firm will be lognormal in shape.

From the distribution of the ending stock value, and the relationship between the ending spread value and stock value, we can construct the probability distribution for the ending spread value. First, consider the probability that the ending spread value will be $00. This is equal to the total probability in the shaded tails of the distribution for stock prices less than $50 and greater than $70. The sum of these probabilities is assumed to be equal to 20 percent, and this is graphed in Figure 13–5, which shows the probability distribution for the butterfly spread.

Other points in the distribution of Figure 13–5 can be obtained as follows. The probability of the stock being worth $60 is 7 percent. This is also the probability of the spread being worth its maximum value of $10. If the stock is worth either $55 or $65, the spread is worth $5. The probability of the stock being worth $55 is 6 percent, and the probability of its being worth $65 is 5 percent. The probability of the spread being worth $5 is the sum of these two probabilities, or 11 percent.

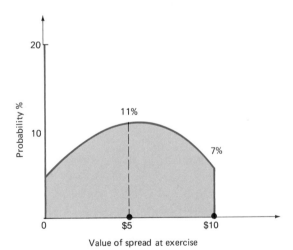

Figure 13-5 Probability Distribution for Ending Value of Butterfly Spread

We can repeat the same process for all other possible stock values and corresponding spread values and construct the probability distribution for the spread, as in Figure 13–4. Given the distribution, we can compute its expected value, which we will assume to be $5. The expected rate of return on the spread can now be found by dividing this expected value by the spread's cost, or $4:

$$20\% = \$5/\$4 - 1$$

This entire process can be easily computerized. If you supply the computer with estimates of the variance of each stock's return, then, based on an assumption of normality in the return distribution, it is easy to compute the probability distribution for the ending value for the stock. If desired, implied variance estimates can be computed using an options pricing model in conjunction with market prices of at-the-money options. You can also supply the computer with information on outstanding options on the stock, including their current market values. Based on this information, the computer can estimate the probability distributions for the ending values of every possible combination of options conceivable. Given the current prices for the options, it can find combinations that offer high expected rates of return at low risks and print out the most attractive strategies.

THE DEATH OF OUT-OF-THE-
MONEY OPTIONS AT MATURITY

As maturity approaches, the values of out-of-the-money options will approach zero. If you are holding these options you can expect to lose increasingly substantial *fractions* of the market value of the remaining investment as maturity closes in, even if the value of the underlying asset remains constant.

To see this, consider Figure 13–6. In the figure days to expiration are plotted on the horizontal axis. Plotted on the vertical axis is the expected rate of return on the (call or put) option, conditional on the fact that the price of the underlying asset (and its variance and the interest rate) remains constant. Four curves are plotted for options that are out of the money to varying degrees. For example, the lowest curve plots the expected returns for an option with an exercise price that is 10 percent greater (for a call option) or less (for a put option) than the market value of its underlying asset. All the computations are based on the Black-Scholes options pricing model.

Note that the options can be expected to produce substantial negative rates of return beginning approximately twenty days prior to expiration. Unless the underlying asset value increases, these can prove to be disastrous investments. With seven days to go before maturity, if you invest in an option that is 10 percent out of the money, you can expect to lose at least half your investment before the end of the day, unless the market value of the underlying asset increases. Of course, if the market value does increase, the value of the options

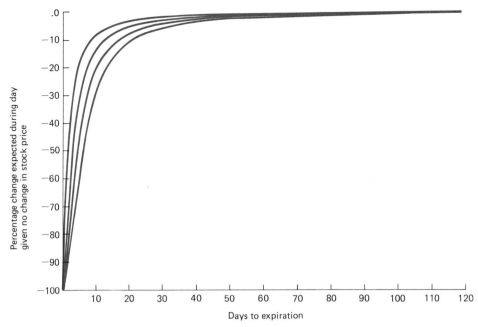

Figure 13-6 Expected Daily Return on Out-of-the-Money Options with Constant Underlying Asset Value

will show tremendous percentage price appreciation. The overall *expected* rate of return for an out-of-the-money call option may be positive, but it is truly a high-risk investment.

COMPLEX SECURITIES AS PORTFOLIOS OF OPTIONS

Common Stock as an Option

Toward the end of their paper on the valuation of options, Black and Scholes made the insightful point that the common stock of a levered firm is itself an options-like security. To see this, consider the simple case of a firm that has one bond issue outstanding. The bond issue is very simple in form. It matures in one year, calling for a single payment of principal and interest at that time that totals $50,000. There are no interim interest payments during the year.

Now consider the position of the stockholders. At the end of the year they have the choice of either paying $50,000 to the bondholders to retain control of the firm or, by not paying the $50,000, go into default and surrender ownership of the firm to the bondholders. In this sense, we can consider the stockholders as really owning an option to buy the firm from the bondholders at an exercise price of $50,000. The time to expiration for the option is equal to the time to maturity of the debt. Because the stockholders' claim is identical to that of an option holder, the stock should be priced in the market as though it was an option, with an exercise price of $50,000 and one year to expiration.

If the stock is priced as an option, it should be priced as in Figure 13–7. In the figure the total market value of all the assets of the firm is plotted on the horizontal axis. The 45-degree line emanating from the present value of the principal payment on the debt (which is $45,454, assuming a risk-free rate of 10 percent) is the same as the option's soft floor, emanating from the present value of the exercise price. The curved solid line shows the value of the common stock (the option) as it relates to the value of the firm. The slope of this line, once again, reflects the probability of exercising the option, which, of course, is the probability of making the payment on the debt. As the value of the firm rises above the promised debt payment, the probability of paying off the debt approaches 100 percent.

The 45-degree line emanating from the *origin* of the graph represents the total value of both the bonds and the stock. The total market value of both the bonds and the stock must sum to the total market value of the firm. Because this is true, the value of the bonds can be found by subtracting the value of the stock from this total value. Thus, if the total value of the firm is equal to $60,000, the value of the stock will be equal to $16,000, and the value of the bonds will be equal to $44,000. The bonds are selling at a price that is less than the present value of their promised payment, discounted at the risk-free rate, because there is some probability of default on the payment. As the total value of the firm's assets increases, however, the market value of the bonds approaches that of risk-free debt, $45,454.

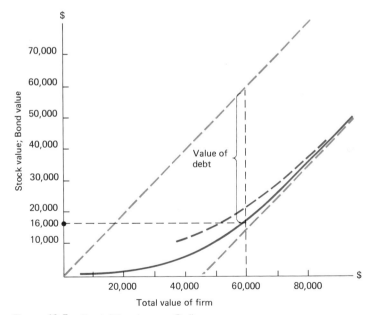

Figure 13-7   Stock Priced as an Option

OUT ON THE STREET

No Losses Possible

Peter Thayer hits the up button. The elevator door opens, and Pete steps in, sending the car to the eleventh floor of Carew Towers, in the heart of downtown Cincinnati.

Pete feels it. This is going to be a big day. Late yesterday afternoon they thought of an idea for a new product. Today the idea would be refined; tomorrow they would begin some preliminary marketing research.

Pete's firm, Gateway Investment Advisers, specializes in the creative use of options in investment management. Gateway firmly believes that innovative use of options of all types is the wave of the future. Today the volume of trading in options on stock market indices is huge. The most popular are put and call options to sell and buy the Standard and Poor's 100 index. Pete and his firm have used these options to create a product that has particular appeal to many financial and corporate investment managers.

It seems that these people are highly risk averse. To them, nothing seems worse than taking a loss on their investments. A modest gain is okay, but a loss can raise

serious questions—and put a career in jeopardy. On the other hand, a spectacular gain means favorable visibility and a possible promotion. The question is, "How can you avail yourself of the opportunity for spectacular gain without exposing yourself to the possibility of a loss?"

Gateway has the answer to that question. If a firm comes to Gateway with $1 million to invest, it takes most of the money and buys one-year treasury bills that pay off $1 million at maturity. This provides a floor to the ending value for the total portfolio. You have to exit with at least as much money as you came in with. At current interest rates, this leaves Gateway with approximately $100,000 to put at risk.

The remaining $100,000 is invested in either put options or call options written on the 100 index, depending on which way Gateway sees the market moving. To obtain maximum leverage, Gateway likes to invest in options that are slightly out of the money. However, Pete knows what can happen to out-of-the-money options as they close in toward maturity. Consequently, Gateway buys two-month options and one month later closes out its positions and once again moves into

---

Just as the common stock can be thought of as an option, the bonds can be thought of as the complement of an option. From this insight, we can gain a deeper understanding about the valuation of bonds. For example, it should be true that, holding all other factors constant, the default premium in the yield on a long-term bond should be greater than that of a short-term bond. We know that if you increase the term to expiration of an option, you increase its market value. Because you increase the market value of the option, you should decrease

three-month puts or calls, depending on its investment outlook.

If Gateway guesses right, the options can increase in value by as much as 300 percent in any given month. This means that the return on the overall portfolio can be as much as 30 percent in the month. If this happens, Gateway usually reinvests a portion of the profits in treasury bills, guaranteeing that the lowest possible return will now be a positive number. Of course, if the investment company guesses wrong three or four months in a row, there wouldn't be much left of the money put at risk, but there would still be no loss at the end of the year in the overall portfolio.

The general idea is to guess the market's future direction correctly more often than not. Gateway has been marketing this product for six months now, and it has been right in five of the six months. Of course, it doesn't expect that kind of success to continue indefinitely.

Yesterday, Gateway came up with a new idea to re-create the stock market using the money market and index options. It will create a mutual fund that encompasses three basic portfolios. The first portfolio is a basic money market fund. The second will be a combined investment in money market instruments and call options on the 100 index. The third will be a combined investment of money market securities and put options on the index. The option strategies will be designed so as to give the two option funds betas of $+3.00$ and -3.00, respectively.

Gateway feels that this type of investment should appeal to market timers. Once in the overall mutual fund, the timer could switch investments by telephone—if bullish into the high beta fund, if bearish into the negative beta fund, and if uncertain into the money market. Even operating on a relatively small scale, Gateway could tolerate that kind of switching, because it wouldn't have to be buying or selling individual common stocks. Index options on the 100 are so liquid that frequent trading presents no problem at all.

The investment performance of the three funds would be reported separately. That way one of the two extreme beta funds would always be one of the best performing funds in the country. Publicity is essential in marketing any product.

As the elevator doors open, Pete is already putting together the final details in his mind.

the market value of the option's complement, the bond. In Figure 13–7, if we increased the term to expiration or maturity for the bond, we move to the broken curve, which is positioned higher relative to the soft floor. This increases the percentage difference between the market value of the bond and corresponding risk-free debt.

Looking at bonds and stocks in this way also reveals some interesting conflicts of interest between bondholders and stockholders. Because stockholders have voting control, it is in the interest of management to maximize stockholder wealth. If the stock is priced as an option, management can increase its value by making investment and production decisions that increase the risk of the firm while maintaining its total market value. Thus, if the broken curve of Figure 13–7 reflects an increased level of variance for the firm, rather than an increased term to maturity, increasing risk can increase the market value of the stock from $16,000 to $20,000. This increase in stock value comes at the expense of the bondholders. There is now a greater probability of default on their debt, and there has been a transfer of wealth from bondholders to stockholders.

There is also an incentive for management to pay out large amounts of funds as dividends to stockholders. As you can see from Figure 13–7, because the slope of the options pricing curve is less than 1, paying $1 in dividends to the stockholders will reduce the total value of the firm by $1, but the value of the stock will fall by less than $1. The difference between the $1 payment and the reduction of the value of their stock again is reflected in a reduction in the value of the bonds. The payment of dividends results in a transfer of wealth from bondholders to stockholders.

Bondholders attempt to protect themselves from these tactics by including protective covenants in the bond indenture agreement. These provisions limit the amount of dividends paid to stockholders and attempt to control to some extent the investment and production decisions of management by at least specifying the purpose for which the proceeds of the bond issue will be used.

Bonds as Portfolios of Options and Option Complements

The previous discussion relates to a very simple debt security. Let's make the bond a little more complicated and see what this does to our conclusions.

Suppose we were dealing with a two-year bond that has an interest payment due at the end of the first year. The stockholders can now be viewed as holding an option to acquire *another* option to buy the firm from the bondholders at the maturity of the debt. If the stockholders pay the first interest payment, they acquire the option to buy the firm from the bondholders by making the final interest and principal payments at maturity. If they don't make the first interest payment, they lose all rights to the firm, and the bondholders take over. The stock can be viewed in this context as a compound option and the bond as the complement of a compound option. If we talk about a longer term bond, with a string of required interest payments, the option is merely compounded many times over.

Now consider a *callable* bond. The call provision gives the stockholders the option of buying the bond at a specific exercise, or call, price. The callable bond is a portfolio where you have taken a positive position in the complement of a compound option (this is the bond as a noncallable issue) and a negative position in a call option that is held by the stockholders. The market value of the callable bond is the net of its value as a noncallable issue and the market value of the call privilege held by the stockholders.

If we make the callable bond convertible, we simply add another option to the portfolio. Now the bond can be viewed as a portfolio of three securities: (a) a positive position in the complement of a compound option, (b) a negative position in the call option to buy the bond held by the stockholders, and (c) a positive position in another option to buy the stock of the firm at the conversion price. The market value of the bond will reflect the net value of this portfolio.

In this sense, options can be viewed as the structural building blocks of financial securities. The securities we see traded in the market place are really portfolios of options and option complements. Thus, an understanding of the behavior of options prices is crucial to a deep understanding of the behavior of the prices of all securities.

Summary

The difference between the market values of identical put and call options written on the same stock must be equal to the difference between the present value or the exercise price on the options and the market value of the common stock. If the put and call prices fail to have this parity relationship, arbitrage opportunities present themselves that offer unlimited wealth at no risk. Thus, there are very strong economic forces keeping put and call prices in parity.

There are two floors below which the value of the option cannot fall. The floors differ with respect to the strength of the economic forces supporting them. The hard floor is the difference between the stock price and the exercise price, or zero, whichever is greater. If the option falls below this floor, we all can gain unlimited wealth by repeatedly buying the option, exercising it, and selling the stock. The soft floor is the difference between the stock price and the present value of the exercise price, or zero, whichever is greater. If the option drops below this floor, an investment in the option dominates an investment in the stock, and the market for the stock evaporates. Because an option won't be exercised until it falls below the hard floor, options won't be exercised prematurely unless there is an expected sudden drop in the stock's price associated with a dividend payment. This implies equal value for European and American options on stocks that don't pay dividends.

The Black-Scholes model is subject to a bias problem, in that the model tends to overvalue options that are out of the money and undervalue options that are in the money. This problem can be resolved by either modeling the bias using a statistical procedure or by moving to a more general options pricing model that is free of the bias.

Options can be used to construct many interesting strategies that you can use to take advantage of special situations. For example, if you think a stock is going to make a significant move, but you aren't sure of the direction, you may want to buy a straddle, which is a put and call with the same exercise price and time to maturity. A butterfly spread may be a good investment for a stock you think is locked in its current position.

Many of the securities traded in the marketplace can be thought of as portfolios of options. Levered common stock, for example, can be thought of as an option to acquire the firm from the bondholders by making the required payments at maturity. Bonds can be viewed as the complements of options with other options attached.

QUESTIONS AND PROBLEMS

1. Suppose a put and a call exist on the same stock, each having an exercise price of $75 and each having the same expiration date. The current price of the stock is $68. The put's current price is $6.50 higher than the call's price. A riskless investment over the time until expiration will yield 3 percent. Given this information, are there any riskless profit opportunities available? Are the put and the call priced in an equilibrium relationship with one another?

Refer to the following information for questions 2 through 4. Suppose an American call option exists on a particular stock. The exercise price is $105. The present value of the exercise price is $100.

2. What is the hard floor price of the option if the underlying stock is priced at $160? Sketch a graph of the hard floor options prices against several stock prices.

3. Sketch a graph of soft floor prices against several stock prices.

4. At a stock price of $125, you notice the option selling for $18. Would this options price be an equilibrium price? Explain.

5. Suppose the stock price is $135. You notice the option is selling for $32. Would this options price be an equilibrium price? Explain.

6. Although the Black-Scholes call options formula was developed for European call options, could it be legitimately used to value American calls?

7. A stock is selling today for $150. If you are holding the stock today, you will receive a $15 dividend. Holding the stock tomorrow will no longer entitle you to the dividend. You are holding an American call option on the stock having an exercise price of $130. Suppose the anticipated options price is $12 when the stock price is $135. Would you hold on to your option or exercise it? Why?

8. What is the nature of the bias in Black-Scholes options pricing discovered empirically by MacBeth and Merville?

9. Contrast the assumption of the Black-Scholes model and the Cox model on the variance of the return on a stock.

10. Suppose you construct a strategy based on options on a stock that is currently selling for $100. The strategy is as follows:
    - Buy one call option having an exercise price of $95.
    - Sell two calls having an exercise price of $100.
    - Buy one call option having an exercise price of $105.

    All of the options are written on the same stock and all have the same expiration date.

    a. Compute the payoff (the dollars you receive) from this strategy at the expiration date for each of the following alternative stock prices: $90, $95, $98, $100, $102, $105, and $110.

    b. What additional information would be required to determine whether your strategy had been profitable?

    c. What is the name of this strategy?

11. a. What constitutes the price of a straddle?

    b. Suppose you sold a straddle. What would cause your sale to be a profitable one?

12. If you view common stockholders as if they are holding a call option on the firm, what bias might the stockholders have in selecting projects for the firm to undertake? Explain.

13. Consider a callable bond and view it (as in the text) as a portfolio of options-like instruments.

    a. In what sense have the bondholders sold a call option to the stock-holders?

    b. Can you speculate on the impact the call provision of the bond might have on desire by the stockholders to select risky investment projects?

BIBLIOGRAPHY

BLACK, F., "Fact and Fantasy in the Use of Options," *Financial Analysts Journal* (July–August 1975).

BLACK, F., and M. SCHOLES, "The Valuation of Option Contracts and a Test of Market Efficiency," *Journal of Finance* (May 1972).

COX, J., "Notes on Option Pricing I: Constant Elasticity of Diffusions," unpublished draft, Stanford University, September 1975.

COX, J., and S. ROSS, "The Valuation of Options Under Alternative Stochastic Processes," *Journal of Financial Economics* (January–March 1976).

EMANUEL D., and J. MACBETH, "Further Results on Constant Elasticity of Variance Call Option Models," *Journal of Financial and Quantitative Analysis* (November 1981).

GESKE, R., "A Note on an Analytic Valuation Formula for Unprotected American Call

Options on Stocks with Known Dividends," *Journal of Financial Economics* (December 1979a).

———, "The Valuation of Compound Options," *Journal of Financial Economics* (March 1979b).

GESKE, R., and R. ROLL, "On Valuing American Call Options with the Black-Scholes European Formula," *Journal of Finance* (June 1984).

GESKE, R., R. ROLL, and K. SHASTRI, "Over-the-Counter Option Market Dividend Protection and "Biases" in the Black-Scholes Model—A Note," *Journal of Finance* (September 1983).

HAUGEN, R., *Modern Investment Theory* Englewood Cliffs, N.J.: Prentice-Hall, 1986.

LATANÉ, H., and R. RENDLEMAN, "Standard Deviations of Stock Price Ratios Implied in Option Prices," *Journal of Finance* (May 1976).

MacBETH J., and L. MERVILLE, "An Empirical Examination of the Black-Scholes Call Option Pricing Model," *Journal of Finance* (December 1979).

———, "Tests of the Black-Scholes and Cox Option Valuation Models," *Journal of Finance* (May 1980).

ROLL, R., "An Analytic Valuation Formula for Unprotected American Call Options on Stocks with Known Dividends," *Journal of Financial Economics* (November 1977).

RUBINSTEIN, M., "Non-Parametric Tests of Alternative Option Pricing Models Using All Reported Quotes and Trades on the 30 Most Active CBOE Option Classes from August 23, 1976 through August 31, 1978," Berkeley Working Paper No. 117, October 1981.

STERK, W., "Tests of Two Models for Valuing Call Options on Stocks with Dividends," *Journal of Finance* (December 1982).

———, "Comparative Performance of the Black-Scholes and the Roll-Geske-Whaley Option Pricing Models," *Journal of Financial and Quantitative Analysis* (September 1983).

WHALEY, R., "On the Valuation of American Call Options on Stocks with Known Dividends," *Journal of Financial Economics* (June 1981).

———, "Valuation of American Call Options on Dividend Paying Stocks," *Journal of Financial Economics* (March 1982).

14 FINANCIAL FORWARD AND FUTURES CONTRACTS

Introduction

Forward and futures contracts have generated a great deal of interest in the last decade. The volume of futures contracts increased more than tenfold between 1968 and 1983. Moreover, in recent years, the most popular futures contracts have been *financial* futures, which are contracts to buy or sell financial securities, with treasury bond futures leading the way in terms of volume.

A forward or futures contract *obligates* you to buy or sell a specific commodity at a specific price on a specific delivery date. If you buy such a contract, you must buy the commodity at the stated time and price. If you sell the contract, you must sell the commodity at the stated time and price. If I sell you a contract, I must sell and you must buy according to the terms of the contract. As an example, you typically initiate the purchase of a residence by exchanging a forward contract with the seller. The buyer and the seller obligate themselves to purchase and sell the house at the closing date and at the stated price.

An *options* contract, on the other hand, gives you the *right* to buy or sell. With a *forward or futures* contract, you *must* buy or sell according to the terms of the contract, unless you liquidate the contract in the marketplace prior to expiration. The lower limit to the value of an options contract is zero, because you always have the right to throw it away. A forward contract, on the other hand, can have a negative value. If you have obligated yourself to buy a commodity at a price of $20, and the current price of the commodity has dropped to $10, the contract has a negative value of $10, if today is the expiration date.

In the discussion of options, our attention focused on the market value of the contract itself, given a fixed value for the exercise price. In the pricing of forward and futures contracts, the situation is turned around. By tradition, the *exercise price* (which is called the forward or futures price) is initially set so that the current market value of the contract is equal to zero. Thus, with respect to these contracts, given a fixed (zero) market value for the contract, we attempt to find the forward or futures price (the exercise price) that is consistent with this zero market value.

One significant difference between a forward and a futures contract is in the way your account is handled. With a forward contract, you obligate yourself to buy or sell a commodity, some time in the future, at a particular price. As we said, initially the forward price is set so that the current market value of the contract is zero, but this value can become positive or negative as time goes by. Suppose expectations about the future commodity price are revised upward so that new forward contracts issued today are issued at a higher forward price than yesterday. If you hold a contract to buy at the previous, lower forward price, the market value of your contract becomes positive. Forward contracts are always designed initially to have a zero value, but as expectations change, their value can become positive or negative.

The terms of a futures contract, on the other hand, are revised every day to maintain a zero market value for the contract. The aspect of the contract that is revised is the futures price. Suppose that initially you entered into a futures contract to sell a commodity for $10 in thirty days. The next day the futures price of identical contracts for sale in twenty-nine days is being negotiated at a futures price of $9. If your contract were a forward contract, it would take on a positive market value. As a futures contract, however, the futures price of your contract would be revised to $9, and you would have added to your account the difference between the futures price yesterday and today, multiplied by the number of commodities controlled by the futures contracts you have outstanding.

This process of revising the terms of the contract, and crediting or debiting your account accordingly, is called *marking to market*. The process of marking to market is an important difference between a forward and a futures contract. It does, obviously, create a difference in the cash flows to investors in forward and futures contracts. There are no cash flows to an investor in a forward contract until the settlement date. There are positive or negative cash flows from day to day associated with investing in a futures contract, as you mark to market in correspondence with changes in the prevailing futures price.

This subtle difference in the way your account is handled, and the associated difference in the cash flows, differentiate the two types of contracts in terms of the way they are priced. As we shall see, this difference may be especially important in the pricing of financial futures.

Futures contracts are also standardized in terms of their specifications, such as maturity date and the price at which the commodity is to be exchanged. In addition, a clearinghouse stands between the buyer and seller of the contract, guaranteeing to each that the commodity can be purchased or sold on the terms specified in the contract. Futures contracts are traded on organized exchanges, and the futures price is determined in a market setting. Consequently, positions in futures contracts can be easily liquidated prior to the maturity date of the contract. For example, if you have purchased futures contracts to sell a given amount of a commodity at a certain date, you can later relieve yourself of the obligation by selling futures contracts to sell the same amount of the commodity at the same date. This is an important relative advantage of futures contracts over forward contracts.

Forward contracts may not be standardized in their specifications. The terms of the contracts, including the forward price, are set by the parties to the contracts through negotiation. In some cases, as in the sale of a house, one or both of the parties may be required to put up funds or securities as a guarantee that they will meet the obligation of the forward contract. If you want to terminate the agreement prior to maturity, you must seek relief through negotiation from the other party to the contract. In this sense, forward contracts are less liquid than are futures contracts. On the other hand, the terms of the contract (the forward price, the maturity date, the grade or type of commodity acceptable for delivery, the place of delivery) can be more precisely tailored to the needs of the buyer and seller.

Remember that when we talk about the pricing of forward and futures contracts, we are talking about determining the *"exercise prices"* for the contracts. We are trying to determine the values for the forward or futures price that will make the current value of the contract equal to zero. Table 14–1 shows the open, high, low, and settling (closing) futures prices for U.S. treasury bonds. Also included in the table are the change in the futures price for the day, the yield to maturity based on the settling price, the change in the yield from the previous settling price, and the number of contracts currently outstanding. The prices are expressed as a percentage of principal value ($1000), with 75-13 indicating a price equal to 75 and 13/32 percent of $1000, or $754.06.

Table 14–1 Futures Prices for Treasury Bonds

Treasury Bonds (CBT) — $100,000; pts. 32nds of 100%

Mar	....	....	....	....		....	....		15,585
June	65–25	67–01	66–21	66–30	+	6	12.547	–	.036	116,569
Sept	66–07	66–15	66–03	66–12	+	6	12.655	–	.037	16,405
Dec	65–21	65–29	65–20	65–28	+	6	12.753	–	.037	6,578
Mar85	65–05	65–14	65–05	65–14	+	7	12.839	–	.044	6,079
June	64–24	65–02	64–24	65–01	+	5	12.920	–	.044	4,143
Sept	64–14	64–21	64–14	64–21	+	7	12.996	–	.044	1,130
Dec	64–08	64–11	64–06	64–11	+	7	13.059	–	.045	918
Mar86	64–02	64–02	64–02	64–02	+	7	13.117	–	.045	1,201
June	63–19	63–26	63–19	63–29	+	7	13.169	–	.045	1,909
Sept	63–14	63–19	63–13	63–19	+	7	13.214	–	.046	326
Dec	63–08	63–13	63–08	63–13	+	7	13.253	–	.046	2

SOURCE: Reprinted by permission of *Wall Street Journal,* © Dow Jones & Company, Inc., 1984. All rights reserved.

Each contract obligates you to buy or sell 100 U.S. treasury bonds at the stated price. If you buy or sell a contract, you must put up a margin of $2000. This isn't really an investment, as the margin can be put up in the form of U.S. treasury bills. As you mark to market, money will be added or subtracted from this account. Thus, you can control a portfolio of $100,000 in U.S. treasury bonds (in principal amount) with an initial "investment" of only $2000! The high degree of possible leverage helps to explain why forward and futures contracts have gained such a wide following.

THE DETERMINATION OF FORWARD PRICES

As explained, a forward contract obligates you to buy or sell a specific commodity at a specific time and at a specific price. It is fundamentally different from an options contract, which gives you the right to buy or sell. The difference between the two contracts is easily seen in Figure 14–1, which shows the values of forward contracts to buy or sell a commodity and the values of call and put options as they relate to the value of the commodity at the expiration date of each of the contracts. The lower limit to the value of the options is zero, and the forward contracts can take on a negative value. If you have contracted to buy a commodity at a price of $50, and at expiration the prevailing market price of the commodity is $30, you would be willing to pay someone $20 to assume the burden of the contract for you.

Note that, at expiration, the value of a forward contract to buy a commodity is equal to

$$\text{Commodity price} - \text{Forward price}$$

whereas the value of a forward contract to sell is equal to

$$\text{Forward price} - \text{Commodity price}$$

The Relationship Between the Forward Price and the Current Commodity Price

The forward price can be easily expressed in terms of the current commodity price and the risk-free rate of interest across the time period to expiration. If you sell a forward contract, you are assuring yourself of a dollar payment equal to the forward price at the expiration date. You can buy the commodity at its present market value, and you can receive the forward price for the commodity when you sell it at expiration. Because this is a riskless transaction, the following relationship must hold in the absence of carrying costs for the commodity:

$$\text{Current commodity price} = \frac{\text{Forward price}}{(1 + Y)^T}$$

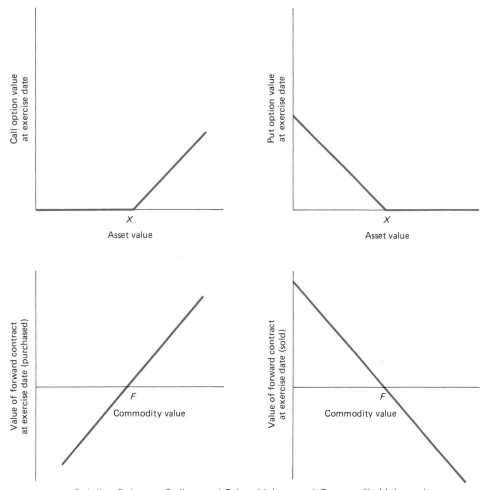

Figure 14-1 Relation Between Option and Future Values and Commodity Values at Expiration

where Y is the yield to maturity for a risk-free bond with a maturity equal to the term of the forward contract, T. Thus

$$\text{Forward price} = \text{Current commodity price} \times (1 + Y)^T$$

That is, the forward price is also equal to the *future value* of the current commodity price invested at the risk-free yield to maturity for the term of the contract.

To illustrate, consider a forward contract to sell risk-free bonds with fifteen years to maturity and annual interest payments of $150. The forward contract expires in one month. The fifteen-year bonds are currently selling at $1000 to yield 15 percent until maturity. Comparable risk-free bonds with one month until

Spreading Futures

Gregg Silver raises five fingers into the air, and as quickly as that, sells five contracts obligating him to sell $500,000 in U.S. treasury bonds in four months. Gregg is a floor trader on the Chicago Board of Trade. He trades from his own personal capital. This particular trade requires a margin of $10,000, $2000 for each $100,000 of U.S. treasury bonds controlled.

Gregg is standing in the U.S. treasury bond futures pit. The pit rises on all sides as a series of steps, similar to the amphitheaters in Greek times. The room is huge, approximately the size of a small city block. Other pits for other securities like U.S. treasury note futures are arranged in the room by rule and tradition at points to make the process of price discovery as smooth and orderly as possible. To an outsider, the milling about of the 1200 to 1500 traders seems like chaos. An experienced trader sees through the chaotic activity to the trading process refined through the years to facilitate the exchange of money for contracts and to make possible rapid price adjustments to new information.

Gregg wears a badge on his jacket with the letters "IYO" identifying him. Some of those around him wear loud ties or trading jackets with wild designs in an effort to attract attention, so that they may get their trades processed a little more quickly. In the pit a few seconds can mean thousands of dollars. Some of the largest traders have made or lost in excess of $1 million in a single day!

Trading can be tough on the nerves. Many believe that in most cases a trader's "life span" on the floor is limited to six years before he or she becomes emotionally burned out. Gregg knows that this is a misnomer, however. It is the losers who burn out. Successful traders trade well into their sixties and many into their seventies. As a point of fact, Gregg's great uncle traded until he was eighty-two years old, when it finally became too physically taxing.

Good traders have to have enough self-confidence to take risk, when warranted, in whatever form necessary. Yet they must have sufficient flexibility to quickly admit mistakes in judgment. They must take losses quickly rather than become intellectually wedded to an idea that can

maturity are selling at prices to yield a 1 percent monthly rate of return. The current forward price for the fifteen-year bonds must then be $1010:

$$\text{Forward price} = \text{Current commodity price} \times (1 + Y)^{1/12}$$
$$\$1010.00 \quad = \quad \$1000.00 \quad \times \quad 1.01$$

Suppose that we extend the maturity of the contract to two years. The forward price must now reflect the existing yield to maturity on risk-free, two-year bonds such that

ultimately become very expensive. The pit is no place for the insecure.

Gregg's trading horizon usually ranges from one to five days. His trading decisions are based on his knowledge of the domestic and international economy, Federal Reserve policy, and political events shaping up in Washington. Over the years he has also developed a sensitive feel for historical relationships between the yields on securities of different term and risk. When these relationships move out of line, he moves in to make money with a spread position.

A spread consists of a long and short position in two different issues. For example, today Gregg is going short in treasury bill futures and long in treasury bond futures. His position is based on his feeling that the economic outlook doesn't justify the extreme spread between the yields on long- and short-term securities. He feels that the yields on treasury bills will rise and that the yields on treasury bonds will fall over the next day or so. If so, he will make money on his position.

Gregg recalls a similar position taken earlier in the year. The first rumblings were coming out about problems with respect to payments on loans by third world countries. The spread between the yield on treasury bill futures and Eurodollar futures was then seventy-five basis points. (A basis point is 1/100th of 1 percent.) Typically, the spread hovers around fifty basis points. At the time, Gregg had a sinking feeling that this was going to become more serious and that all the information relating to the problem hadn't been fully disclosed.

If he was wrong, Gregg estimated that he would lose twenty-five basis points on his spread position. On the other hand, if he was right, the spread could widen to as much as 150 basis points. As it turned out, the spread widened by seventy-five basis points in a single week, eventually reaching as much as 220 basis points.

Unfortunately, not every position is as profitable as that one. On any given workday, traders never know whether they will pay or get paid. You can only make your decisions, execute them with confidence, and hope for the best. With this in mind, Gregg climbs from the treasury bond futures pit and makes his way toward the bond options pit.

$$\begin{matrix} \text{Current} \\ \text{commodity} \\ \text{price} \end{matrix} = \frac{C}{(1 + Y)^1} + \frac{C + \text{Forward price}}{(1 + Y)^2}$$

where Y is now the existing yield to maturity on risk-free, two-year bonds, and C is the annual interest payment on these bonds. The forward price must therefore be equal to

$$\text{Forward price} = \text{Current commodity price} \times (1 + Y)^2 - C \times (1 + Y) - C$$

Thus, in our example, if the annualized yield on two-year bonds is 13 percent, with a $150 annual interest payment and a $1000 current market price for the fifteen-year bonds, the forward price must be equal to

$$\$957.40 = \$1000 \times (1.13)^2 - \$150 \times (1.13) - \$150$$

The Relationship Between the Forward Price and the Expected Commodity Price

If you enter into a forward contract to buy a commodity at a stated price, you know for certain the price at which you are going to be able to buy the commodity. If the commodity is a treasury bond, you know that you will be able to buy the bond at the forward price, irrespective of what happens to interest rates between now and the time the contract matures. In effect, you have eliminated the risk of fluctuations in interest rates.

Suppose, initially, that you don't care about risk. You are risk neutral. The relationship between your utility, or well-being, and the total amount of your consumption of goods and services at the time the contract expires is presented in Figure 14–2. Note that if you are risk neutral, the relationship is linear. The additional increment in utility associated with an additional increment in consumption is the same, irrespective of the total amount of your consumption of goods and services.

If you are risk neutral and don't care about risk, you won't care about the fact that the contract eliminates the risk of interest rate fluctuations. If the sellers of the contract are also risk neutral, they won't care about the fact that the contract assures them of the price for which they will sell the bond. In this situation both the buyers and sellers of the contract will be willing to enter into the agreement to buy and sell, at expiration, at a forward price equal to their expectation for the value of the commodity at the time the contract expires.

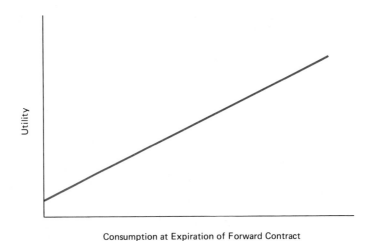

Consumption at Expiration of Forward Contract

Figure 14-2 Utility Function for Risk Neutral Investor

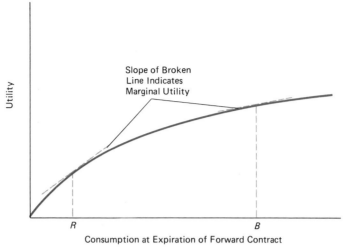

Figure 14-3 Utility Function for Risk Averse Investor

Under these conditions, the equation for the forward price is

Forward price = Expected commodity price

It is important to realize, however, that this relationship holds only for risk neutrality. If investors are, instead, risk averse, the relationship between their utility and the level of their total consumption of goods and services looks something like Figure 14–3. In this case, as total consumption goes up, utility goes up but at a decreasing rate. Suppose that at the time of expiration of the contract, we are in a recession, and total consumption is low, as in the case labeled *R*. In this situation, you need money badly, and an additional increment in consumption brings a substantial increase in your well-being or utility. In states like these, your *marginal utility* is high. On the other hand, suppose that we are in economic prosperity or boom when the contract expires. This might be a case like the one labeled *B* in Figure 14–3. In this case you've already got lots to eat, you're driving a new car, and although it might be nice to have a little more money, you don't really need it very much. In boom periods the additional utility (marginal utility) gained from additional amounts of consumption is low.

If you are risk averse you will care about whether a securities or financial contract pays off most in booms or recessions, because your need for additional increments of consumption is different in prosperity and hard times. Recall that at expiration the value of a forward contract can be positive or negative. You will like it if the contract tends to pay off the most when times are hard, because this is when you need the money the most. Although losses are never welcome, you will prefer it if the value of the contract tends to be negative in boom periods rather than in recessions, because a drainage of cash in times of prosperity isn't going to present you with a lot of problems. If the contract tends to pay off in this way, it acts like an insurance policy, stabilizing your overall level of consumption and reducing your risk. If, on the other hand, the contract pays off the most in booms and the least in recessions, it increases the uncertainty of your

Figure 14-4 Positive Correlation Between Commodity
Price and Total Consumption

overall level of consumption and generates risk in your overall portfolio, much
like a security with positive covariance–generated risk in the market portfolio in
the Capital Asset Pricing Model.

Because the payoff to the buyer of a forward contract is equal to the difference between the commodity price and the forward price (which is fixed), the
relationship between the commodity price and the aggregate level of consumption will determine whether the contract is insurance or risk generating to the
buyer. In Figure 14–4 the relationship between the commodity price and the
level of consumption for a representative investor is plotted. Each point in the
plot represents the level of consumption and the commodity price that existed
in a given period of time. If, as in Figure 14–4, the commodity price tends to go
up and down with aggregate consumption, the contract will pay off the most in
booms and the least in recessions, and it will be risk generating to the buyer. If,
as in Figure 14–5, the commodity price tends to move in the opposite direction

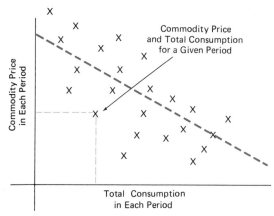

Figure 14-5 Negative Correlation Between Commodity Price and Total Consumption

362   **PART FIVE**   **The Valuation of Complex Securities**

from aggregate consumption, the contract will act as insurance to the buyer. Because the payoffs to the seller of the contract are the opposite of those to the buyer, the opposite will be true for the seller.

In the presence of risk-averse investors, the value for the forward price that the buyers and sellers will be willing to negotiate into the contract is given by

Forward price = Expected commodity price − Risk premium

The sign and magnitude of the risk premium is determined by the sign and magnitude of the covariance between the commodity price and the aggregate level of consumption. For most commodities the covariance is positive. Because the risk premium is subtracted from the forward price, in this case the forward price will be less than the expected commodity price. Viewed from the buyers' prospective, the contract generates risk in their portfolios, and they will be willing to enter the contract only at a forward price that is less than their expectation for the commodity price. Remember, the *lower* the forward price the better for the *buyer* of the contract. Because the payoffs to the sellers are the opposite of those for the buyers, the contract *reduces* risk in *their* portfolios. Because they view the contract as insurance, they will be willing to enter the contract at a forward price that is lower than their expected commodity price. Remember, the *higher* the forward price the better for the *seller* of the contract.

If the commodity happens to move in the *opposite* direction from the aggregate level of consumption, as in Figure 14–5, the contracts acts as insurance for the buyer and generates risk for the seller. In this case the forward price would be expected to be above the expected commodity price. If there is no relationship between the commodity price and the aggregate level of consumption, any risk in the contract is presumably diversifiable and, therefore, inconsequential, and the forward price is then equal to the expected commodity price.

If the forward price is less than the expected commodity price, we are said to be in a situation called "normal backwardation." If, on the other hand, the forward price is greater than the expected commodity price, we are in a situation called "contango." Whether we are in normal backwardation or contango depends on the properties of the commodity we are dealing with. Because the values of most commodities are positively correlated with the value of wealth in general, normal backwardation is the typical situation.

If investors are risk neutral, they have linear utility functions. This means that marginal utility is a constant and does not decrease as consumption increases. This also means that their need for money doesn't vary from recessions to booms. Thus, here we have the case where the forward price is equal to the expected commodity price.

The Consistency of the Two Expressions for the Forward Price

We now have two equations for the forward price, one in terms of the *current* commodity price and one in terms of the *expected* commodity price. It is easy to show that the two equations are mutually consistent, because if we equate them we can solve for an expression for the current commodity price that is quite reasonable. By equating our two equations for the forward price, we can solve for the following expression for the current commodity price:

$$\text{Current commodity price} = \frac{\text{Expected commodity price} - \text{Risk premium}}{(1 + Y)^T}$$

Thus, if we are dealing with a forward contract to buy a common stock, we can express the current stock price as the discounted (at the risk-free rate) value of the expected stock price at time T, less the risk premium associated with the stock investment.

Market Value of Previously Issued Forward Contracts

Although the forward price is initially set to make the market value of the contract equal to zero, as time passes and the forward prices for contemporary contracts change, the market value of the previously issued contract may become greater or less than zero. In Figure 14–6 the solid line represents the value at expiration of a contract previously purchased for a forward price of $30. The broken line represents the value at expiration for a contract purchased for the current forward price of $40. Both contracts expire at the same time. Note that the difference in the payoffs for the two contracts is a constant, $10, across all possible values for the ending commodity price.

Because the value of a contract written with the current forward price is zero, and because the difference in the payoffs between the two contracts is a known constant, the market value of the previously issued contract is equal to the discounted value of the constant difference in the payoffs. The difference is a known constant, so we discount at the risk-free rate. The value of the contract is given by

$$\frac{\text{Contemporary forward price} - \text{Original forward price}}{(1 + Y)^t} = \begin{array}{c} \text{Market value} \\ \text{of previous} \\ \text{forward} \\ \text{contract} \end{array}$$

where Y is the yield to maturity of a bond that matures at the expiration date of both forward contracts, and t is the time remaining to expiration of both contracts.

DETERMINATION OF FUTURES PRICES

As we learned, a major difference between a forward and a futures contract is in the way an account is handled. With a futures contract, the futures price is revised each day to make the current market price of the contract equal to zero.

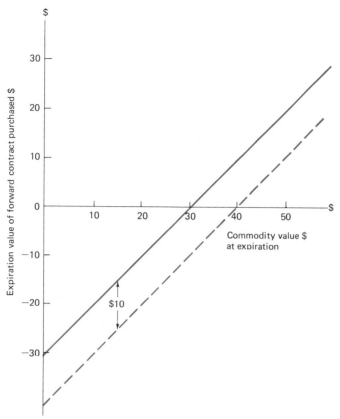

Figure 14-6 The Difference Between the Expiration Value of Two
Forward Contracts

If you bought the contract, and the futures price today is greater than the futures price yesterday, your account is credited with the difference multiplied by the number of commodities controlled by the contracts you have open. If the price is less, your account is debited in the same way.

Table 14–2 sets forth an assumed series of commodity, forward, and futures prices and the associated market values and cash flows accruing to the contracts in the course of a year. Both the forward and futures contracts are assumed to have one year to expiration at the beginning of the year. It is assumed that the futures account is marked to market at the end of each quarter, rather than on a daily basis, which is actually the case. The market value of the forward contract originally issued at the beginning of the year is computed using the equation for the market value of a previously issued forward contract, at an assumed interest rate of 10 percent. Notice that the market value of the futures contract is always equal to zero, because the futures price is adjusted to keep it that way.

The four rows at the bottom of the table show the cash flows accruing to

Table 14–2 Cash Flows from Forward and Futures Contracts

Time	Beginning of Year	End of First Quarter	End of Second Quarter	End of Third Quarter	End of Fourth Quarter
Commodity price	10	12	8	10	11
Current forward price	9	10	8	9	11
Current futures price	10	11	8	10	11
Market value of forward contract issued at beginning of year ($r_F = 10\%$)	0	.93	−.95	0	2
Market value of futures contract issued at beginning of year	0	0	0	0	0
Cash flow to buyer of forward contract at beginning of year	0	0	0	0	+2
Cash flow to seller of forward contract at beginning of year	0	0	0	0	−2
Cash flow to buyer of futures contract at beginning of year	0	+1	−3	+2	+1
Cash flow to seller of futures contract at beginning of year	0	−1	+3	−2	−1

buyers and sellers in each of the contracts. The cash flows associated with the two types of contracts are markedly different. If you bought a futures contract to buy one unit of the commodity, at the end of the first quarter $1 is credited to your account, because the prevailing futures price has increased by $1. You are free to take this money and reinvest it at prevailing interest rates. If, on the other hand, you sold a futures contract, your account is debited by $1. To maintain the balance in your account, you may have to borrow money at current interest rates.

The differences in the cash flows, associated with investing in a forward or futures contract, create a meaningful economic difference between the two contracts. This difference results in a divergence between the forward and futures price. The formula for the futures price contains (a) an additional term that is related to the profit or loss that can be expected to be generated from reinvestment of the cash flows from marking to market, and (b) a second additional term that is present because a futures contract pays off over shorter periods of time than does a forward contract.

The futures price can be written as

$$\frac{\text{Futures}}{\text{price}} = \frac{\text{Expected}}{\text{commodity price}} - \frac{\text{Risk}}{\text{premium}} + \frac{\text{Reinvestment}}{\text{premium}} + \frac{\text{Term}}{\text{premium}}$$

The nature of the risk premium is the same as that of the forward contract. The sign of the reinvestment premium depends on the relationship or the covariance between the commodity price and the level of interest rates. If the relationship is positive, as in Figure 14–7, the contract tends to pay off the most to a buyer when interest rates are high. This means that buyers will tend to have money added to their accounts when interest rates are high. Thus, they will be able to reinvest the profits from the contract at attractive terms. On the other hand, they will have money taken from their account when rates are low. They will also be able to borrow money to replace these amounts at favorable terms. This is an attractive feature of the contract to buyers, and it increases the expected value of the payoff to them. The reinvestment premium is positive when the covariance is positive, and buyers of the contract are willing to negotiate for a higher futures price. What is good for the buyer of the contract is, of course, bad for the seller. Sellers will refuse, therefore, to enter into the contract unless the futures price is also above their expectation for the commodity price.

As we said, the sign of the reinvestment premium depends on the relationship between the commodity price and the level of interest rates. If the relationship is positive, the reinvestment premium is positive. In the case of a futures contract to buy treasury bonds, the relationship is almost certainly negative. When interest rates go up, treasury bond prices go down. Thus, the sign of the reinvestment premium for treasury bonds is probably negative, driving down trea-

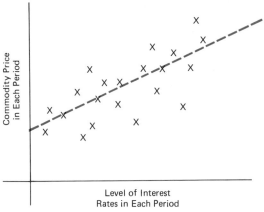

Figure 14-7   Positive Correlation Between Commodity
Price and Interest Rates

sury bond futures prices relative to expectations about the future value of treasury bonds. On the other hand, the reinvestment premium for a futures contract to buy gold can be argued to be positive. Gold prices are high in periods of inflation because gold acts as a reasonably good inflation hedge. Interest rates also tend to be high in periods of inflation. Thus, the buyers of a gold futures contract can expect to reinvest positive payoffs from the contract at high rates, and they can borrow to finance negative payoffs at low interest rates. Given this, the buyers would be willing to enter the contract at futures prices that are high relative to their expectations about the future price of gold.

Due to the process of marking to market, the term or duration of the payoffs of a futures contract is shorter than for a forward contract. If it is the case that positive liquidity premiums exist in the term structure, such that long-term contracts command higher expected rates of return, buyers of futures contracts would be willing to accept higher futures prices than they would forward prices. The futures contract has an advantage because it has a shorter effective term for its payoffs. Thus, the presence of positive liquidity premiums implies a positive term premium and a higher futures price relative to the expected commodity price. Unlike the risk and reinvestment premiums, the sign and magnitude of the term premium isn't very sensitive to the commodity underlying the futures contract.

Under the special case of risk neutrality, the equation for the futures price simplifies to

Futures price = Expected commodity price + Reinvestment premium

The risk premium disappears because risk-neutral investors don't care whether the contract acts as insurance or a risk-bearing security. The effect of entering into the contract on the risk of their overall portfolios is immaterial. The term premium disappears because there are no liquidity premiums in the term structure in a risk-neutral world. The reinvestment premium remains because the relationship between the commodity price and interest rates does affect the *expected value* of the payoffs for the contract. Risk-neutral investors may not care about the risk of the contract, but they do care about its expected value.

The Sign of the Premiums for Various Financial Futures

The magnitude of the term premium is essentially the same for all commodities. The magnitude of the reinvestment and risk premiums, however, may be expected to differ from commodity to commodity. Although there is little in the way of empirical evidence on this matter, we may conjecture about the signs of the two premiums for the various financial futures contracts.

Futures Contract	*Sign of Reinvestment Premium*	*Sign of Risk Premium*
Treasury bonds	(−)	(−)
Treasury bills	(−)	(−)
Stock indices	(−)	(?)

For futures contracts on high-quality fixed-income securities like treasury bonds and bills, the sign of the reinvestment premium is undeniably negative. There is an identity relationship between the prices of these securities and the level of interest rates that forces a negative covariance between interest rates and long-term bond prices. The risk premium is also likely to be negative. We learned in Chapter 9 that real and nominal interest rates are likely to be higher in times of economic prosperity than in recession. The real rate is driven up by liquidity and income effects, and the nominal rate is driven up even further by the price effect associated with inflation. Higher nominal rates mean lower prices for fixed-income securities. Bond prices are likely to be low in times of prosperity when your need for additional funds is low as well. Thus, the risk premium will be negative. Both premiums should be larger for bonds than for bills because the prices for bonds are much more volatile.

There is a great deal of ambiguity in signing the premium for common stock futures. Some empirical evidence supports the notion that stock prices and interest rates are negatively correlated. Based on this evidence, you might expect that the reinvestment premium for common stock futures is negative. The sign of the risk premium is more difficult. To the extent that investors revise their expectations for the profitability of firms downward in recession, this has a depressing effect on stock prices, and may have the effect of forcing stock prices

OUT ON THE STREET

A Forward or a Future?

Professor Leif Grando peers intently. He is seated directly across the table from Joe Gorman, the president of National Investment Services of America, an investment management firm based in Milwaukee, Wisconsin. The firm has grown rapidly to become one of the largest (based on total assets managed) investment management firms in the nation. Most of this growth has been based on the strength of the firm's interest immunization programs. The two are having lunch at the University Club on Lake Michigan in downtown Milwaukee. Gorman is studying a series of charts and tables that are before him on the table.

"Leif, I've asked you to lunch today because we've got a slight problem. As you know, for most of our pension fund clients we immunize their liability streams on the basis of a "core and cap" strategy. The client comes to us with a stream of required payments to be made to its retired employees and a portfolio of existing securities that it expects to produce investment income to make the required payments. Our job is to reconstruct the portfolio so as to be able to effectively guarantee that the income will always be sufficient to make the payments as required.

"With the core and cap strategy, the first thing that we do is sell from the client's investment portfolio those securities we feel are inappropriate for immunization. Basically, these are the securities that have payment streams that are risky in terms of their timing and magnitude. These would include variable-income securities such as common stocks, low-quality bond issues, and bond issues where the call provision plays a significant role in their pricing. Once these issues have been removed, we are left with what we call the "core portfolio." When we plot the payments expected to be received from the core portfolio as a function of time into the future, they may look like the pattern I have drawn in Figure A.

"The client's required liability payments usually take the pattern of Figure B. The client promises to pay each retired employee a constant dollar annuity for his or her remaining lifetime. Based on actuarial estimates of expected remaining lifetimes, the stream of payments is

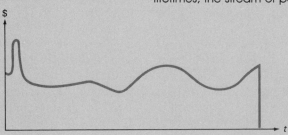

Figure A   The Payments Associated with the Core Portfolio

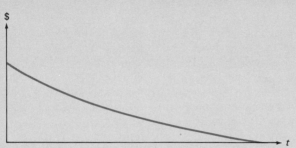

Figure B The Liability Stream

expected to become smaller as we move farther into the future.

"To get what we call "the cap," we subtract the payments in the core from the liability stream. For example, if in the first year we expect to receive $1 million from the core portfolio, and we have a $1.5 million required payment in the liability stream, we have a net required payment of $.5 million in the cap. The stream of payments associated with the cap are plotted in Figure C.

"After determining the best available yield, we compute the present value of the cap and invest this amount of money in a portfolio of government bonds that has a duration equal to the duration of the stream of payments in the cap. In this

way, the client's total portfolio is immunized."

Grando responds, "Yes, I'm very familiar with this strategy, but I don't see your problem."

"Well, take a close look at that large negative payment in the second year of Figure C. This results because the income produced by the core portfolio happens to be much larger in that year than the required payment to the pensioners. Now think of what happens to the duration of the portfolio as we enter the second year, receive the net payment, and reinvest it in the government bond portfolio. A dramatic change will occur in the pattern and the duration of the remaining payments in the cap. This means that we

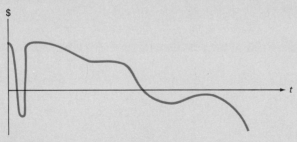

Figure C The Payments Associated with the Cap

must make a dramatic readjustment in the government bond portfolio in order to reimmunize. We like to avoid dramatic changes of this type whenever possible, because at times they can work against us."

Grando ponders the problem and then begins to smile. "I think I may have an answer to your problem. If you buy a forward or futures contract to buy, let's say ten-year bonds, for a total value equal to the amount of the negative payment, in effect you can exchange the negative payment in the second year for payments associated with the bonds you buy that come in the following ten years. The effect of this will be to change the nature of the cap to that in Figure D."

Gorman responds, "I see. You mean the cash flow coming in in the second year disappears because it is used to buy the ten-year bonds under the forward or futures contract, and the payments received from the bond investment reduce the magnitude of the positive payments required in each of the next ten years."

"Exactly, and now you immunize the new cap in accord with your standard procedures with no dramatic changes in required duration expected along the way."

"This sounds like the answer I've been looking for, but should we use a forward or futures contract to execute the strategy?"

"Well," replies Grando, "each contract has its own advantages and disadvantages. If you buy a futures

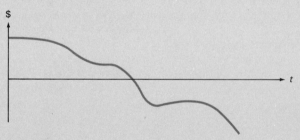

Figure D   The Cap Reflecting the Effect of the Forward or Futures Strategy

down, even in a period of low interest rates. Based on this argument, the sign of the risk premium may be negative, although this one is really very hard to call because of the propensity of the stock market to lead the economy.

The Significance of the Premiums to Investors and Financial Managers

As an investor, you have to take the three premiums into account in making your investment decisions. First, it obviously would be foolish to take the fu-

contract, you will have to buy contracts that have fixed maturity dates that extend in three-month intervals for a limited time into the future. You will also be marked to market every day, and that will create an uncertain pattern of cash flows during the next year in which you hold the contract. This, of course, will create uncertainty in the duration of your bond portfolio. Moreover, in a futures contract there is considerable uncertainty in the bond that you will ultimately receive for delivery. The seller of the futures contract that you buy can deliver a number of different qualifying bond issues. In fact, you may end up taking delivery on an issue that doesn't even exist at the present time but that may be issued by the Treasury during the coming year."

Grando adds, "On the other hand, if you decide to go with a forward contract, you will have to find someone who is willing to sell the contract to you on the terms that you want. I can give you a pretty good idea of what the forward price should be, but you and the party on the other side of the contract, perhaps your government bond dealer, are going to have to provide some assurances that each will ultimately be able to meet the obligation specified in the contract. The seller has to be sure that you will buy the

bonds at the stated price, and you have to be sure that he or she will sell the bonds to you. With a futures contract a clearinghouse stands between you and the seller, assuring the both of you that you will be able to complete the contract at the stated terms, if you desire."

Gorman responds, "Based on what you're saying, it appears that it's going to be much easier to get into, and for that matter, out of the transaction with the futures contract, but the strategy can be executed with much more precision, which is very important to us, with the forward contract. The forward contract can be tailored exactly to our needs, if we can find someone with complementary needs on the sell side."

"That's right. It's a matter of weighing the advantages against the disadvantages and selecting the contract that most fits your needs. I would suggest first trying to negotiate a forward contract that meets your particular needs, and if you find that infeasible, then go to the futures market."

Gorman's eyes shift to the waiter who has been patiently waiting to take their order. He quickly returns to Grando and asks, "The usual?" As Grando nods, Gorman responds, "I think we're both going to have the buffet today."

tures price as an estimate of the market's expected commodity price. The fact that the adjusted futures price for bonds is below the current level of bond prices doesn't necessarily imply that the market expects bond prices to fall. The premiums may, in fact, mask an expectation for a fall in interest rates. Second, you must recognize that the expected return on buying a futures contract may be negative for some commodities. This is the case because the contract has a propensity to reduce risk, but you still must weigh this propensity against the price you must pay for it, the risk premium, in making your investment decision.

There has been an explosive growth in the use of financial futures by financial institutions. These institutions typically use the futures market to hedge. If the expected commodity price is different from the futures price, there may be a cost or even a profit associated with hedging. If the securities markets are fully integrated, and risk is priced uniformly everywhere, the institution will not affect the market value of its stock by hedging (or speculating) with futures. If hedging with the futures contract truly reduces the risk of the institution's common stock, hedging will come at a commensurate cost that will reduce the expected return on the stock to the exact extent required to maintain its market value. Your institution may be interested in other things besides maximizing stock value, however. If it is interested in survival or maximizing profits, a knowledge of the costs and benefits of hedging with futures contracts will give you a crucial edge in helping your company to achieve its objectives.

THE SECURITY UNDERLYING A FUTURES CONTRACT TO BUY TREASURY BONDS

On March 21, 1984, the futures price on U.S. treasury bond contracts expiring in June closed at 66.08. If you bought such a contract, you agreed to buy 100 treasury bonds at 66.25 percent of their principal value ($1000 each). The person on the other side of the contract can actually deliver to you any one of a number of different treasury bonds. To be eligible for delivery, a bond must have at least fifteen years remaining until maturity or earliest call date. The price of 66.08 actually only applies to a bond that has a coupon rate of 8 percent. If a bond with a coupon rate different from 8 percent is delivered, you must buy the bond at an adjusted futures price. The adjusted futures price is determined on the basis of the following formula:

$$\text{Adjusted futures price} = \text{Unadjusted futures price} \times \frac{\sum_{t=1}^{n} \frac{C}{(1.04)^t} + \frac{\$1000}{(1.04)^n}}{\$1000.00}$$

where C is the semiannual coupon on the bond being delivered, and n is the number of semiannual interest payments until maturity. In choosing which bond to make delivery, the seller of the contract will compare the adjusted futures price with the current market price for the bonds. The seller will want to deliver the bond with the highest adjusted futures price relative to the prevailing market price.

In March 1984, the most popular bond for delivery was the U.S. treasury maturing on August 15, 2013, with a 12 percent coupon. The adjusted futures price for this bond is 94.11, and on March 21 the bond closed at a price of 95.31 in the cash market.

Can we say that the market expected interest rates to rise and the price of the bond to fall by June? We cannot. Given the presence of the various premiums in the equation for the futures price, the fact that the futures price is below today's bond price doesn't necessarily indicate that the expected bond price is lower than today's bond price. It may well be that the reinvestment premium is negative and is large (in absolute value) relative to the size of the other premiums, and interest rates were really expected to fall. The futures price doesn't give an unbiased estimate of the market's expected price even in the presence of risk neutrality.

Similar flexibility and corresponding adjustments in the futures price are present in the terms of delivery for other financial futures contracts. The buyers of such contracts should be aware of the terms and should anticipate delivery of the securities that are least favorable to them.

HEDGING WITH BOND FUTURES CONTRACTS

Suppose you are carrying a portfolio of long-term government bonds. You want to liquidate the portfolio at the end of the year, and you are concerned about possible fluctuations in the value of the portfolio between now and the end of the year. You can reduce the interest rate risk associated with the portfolio by entering into a contract to sell treasury bonds at a specific price through a treasury bond futures contract.

One problem with reducing risk in this way is, given the terms of the futures contract, the bond to be delivered under the contract may not correspond to the bonds that you have in your portfolio. However, you can adjust for this by adjusting your position in the futures contract relative to the total market value of your bond portfolio.

To be completely hedged, you want the dollar change in the market value of your bond portfolio to be the negative of the dollar change in your futures position. Because you are selling the futures contract, the changes will be of opposite signs, but you want them to be equal in absolute magnitude. Thus, you want the following relationship to hold:

$$\text{Dollar change in bond portfolio} = \text{Dollar change in futures position}$$

The dollar change in your bond portfolio accompanying a change in its average yield to maturity can be approximated by

$$\begin{array}{c}\text{Dollar change} \\ \text{in bond} \\ \text{portfolio}\end{array} \approx \underbrace{\begin{array}{c}\text{Portfolio} \\ \text{duration}\end{array} \times \begin{array}{c}\text{Change in one} \\ \text{plus portfolio} \\ \text{yield}\end{array}}_{\substack{\text{Percentage change in} \\ \text{bond portfolio}}} \times \begin{array}{c}\text{Market value} \\ \text{of bond} \\ \text{portfolio}\end{array}$$

The portfolio's duration is roughly equal to the absolute value of the ratio of the percentage change in the portfolio value relative to the percentage change in one plus the portfolio's yield to maturity. Thus, multiplying duration by the change in one plus the portfolio's yield, we get the percentage change in the portfolio's value.

Similarly, the dollar change in the futures position can be approximated by

$$
\begin{matrix}
\text{Dollar change} \\
\text{in futures} \\
\text{position}
\end{matrix}
\approx
\underbrace{
\begin{matrix}
\text{Duration of} \\
\text{bond underlying} \\
\text{contract}
\end{matrix}
\times
\begin{matrix}
\text{Change in one} \\
\text{plus underlying} \\
\text{bond yield}
\end{matrix}
}_{\substack{\text{Percentage change in market value} \\ \text{of bonds controlled by futures contract}}}
\times \text{Futures position}
$$

By equating the right-hand sides of both approximations and solving for the futures position, we get

$$
\frac{\text{Futures}}{\text{position}} \approx \text{Duration ratio} \times \text{Yield change ratio} \times \text{Portfolio value}
$$

The duration ratio is the ratio of the duration of the bond portfolio to the duration of the bond controlled by the futures contract. The yield change ratio is your expectation for the ratio of the change in one plus the yield on the portfolio to the change in one plus the yield for the bond controlled by the futures contract. Short-term bond yields are usually more volatile than are long-term bond yields. Thus, if the portfolio has a shorter duration than the bond expected to be delivered under the futures contract, the yield change ratio would be greater than one. The yield change ratio must be estimated by observing the relationship between the yield of your bond portfolio and the yield of the bond underlying the futures contract over past periods.

To illustrate, suppose that the duration of your bond portfolio is three years. The duration of the bond underlying the futures contract is five years, and your estimate of the yield change ratio is 1.30. (You estimate that fluctuations in one plus your portfolio yield are 30 percent greater than are fluctuations in one plus the yield of the bond underlying the futures contract.) The market value of your bond portfolio is $30,000,000. Your futures position should then be

$$
\$23,400,000 = .60 \times 1.30 \times \$30,000,000
$$

That is, you should sell a sufficient number of futures contracts such that you control $23,400,000 in bonds at market value.

USES OF STOCK INDEX FUTURES

Stock index futures contracts are written on major stock indices such as the New York Stock Exchange Index, the Standard and Poor's 500 Index, or the Value Line Index. These futures contracts can be used to manage the risk of any given stock portfolio. The first step in managing risk with futures contracts is to estimate the beta of your stock portfolio. The beta must be estimated with reference to the index that the futures contract is written on. For example, if you are going to be dealing with futures contracts written on the New York

Stock Exchange Index, you would estimate your portfolio beta by relating its returns to the NYSE Index.[1]

The beta will help you determine the position that you should take in the index futures. Your position is measured in index units. A unit of the NYSE Index is equal to 500 multiplied by the value of the index. Let's suppose the index is at $50. Then an index unit is $25,000. If your portfolio is currently worth $250,000, then we can say it is worth ten index units. We will now define the value H as

$$H = \frac{\text{Number of index units sold}}{\text{Current value of portfolio in index units}}$$

If you sold six index units, H would be equal to .6.

The effective beta factor of your portfolio, taking into account your position in the index futures, can be computed as

$$\beta_P^* = \beta_P - H$$

where β_P is the beta of your stock portfolio as computed with reference to the index. Based on this relationship, it is obvious that you can make the beta of your portfolio anything you want by adjusting your position in the index.

This method of adjusting risk may be desirable if you want to change the risk of your portfolio without changing the composition of your stock investments. You might, for example, be forecasting a low return for the market as a whole but also the appearance of positive residuals for some of the high beta stocks currently in the portfolio. By increasing the value of H, you can reduce the effective beta of your portfolio while maintaining your position in the high beta stocks.

Suppose you feel that you can earn excess rates of return by making better than average forecasts of company-specific events. You are good at doing this, but you feel that you have no particular ability to forecast the market. You don't want swings in the market to have an influence on your investment performance. If this is the case, you can render your portfolio insensitive to overall market movement by adjusting your position in index futures such that $H = \beta_P$.

Summary

Forward and futures contracts obligate you to buy or sell a specific commodity at a specific time at a specific price. The difference between the two contracts is in the way your account is handled. There are no cash flows associated with a forward contract until the expiration date, when the contract is worth (to a buyer) the difference between the market value of the commodity and the originally contracted forward price. A futures contract is revised each day, so the market value of the contract itself remains at zero through time. The futures price is revised each day to

[1]For a detailed discussion of risk management with futures contracts, see Figlewski and Kon (1982).

the contemporary futures price, which is set at a level to make the market value of the contract zero. Your account is credited each day with the difference between the futures price today and the futures price yesterday. Thus, you have positive or negative cash flows accruing to your account throughout the life of the contract.

The difference in the cash flows creates a difference in the value of the forward and futures price. With risk neutrality, the forward price is equal to the expected commodity price. With risk aversion, it is equal to the expected commodity price plus a premium that is dependent on the relationship between the price of the commodity and the aggregate level of consumption. If the relationship is negative, the contract pays off the most in times of economic adversity, when you need the money the most. In this case the contract is useful as a hedge, and you would be willing to buy the contract at a futures price that is higher than your expected commodity price.

With risk neutrality, the futures price is equal to the expected commodity price plus a premium that depends on the relationship between the commodity price and interest rates. If the commodity price tends to be high when interest rates are high, your account will be credited when rates are high, and you can reinvest the credits on favorable terms. Thus, a positive covariance between the commodity price and interest rates increases the expected value of the contract to you, and you would be willing to buy it at a futures price that is higher than your expected commodity price, even if you are risk neutral.

Under risk aversion, the futures price differs from the expected commodity price because of three premiums. The term premium is the same for all commodities and is a factor in determining the futures price if there are liquidity premiums in the term structure of interest rates. The reinvestment premium is related to the relationship between the commodity price and interest rates. Again, a positive relationship increases the expected value of the contract to a buyer. The third premium is the risk premium. This premium is similar to the premium in the forward price under risk aversion.

QUESTIONS AND PROBLEMS

1. Suppose the following prices represent the time series of futures prices for various months for wheat to be delivered in August of the same year (in price per bushel).

Month	Feb.	Mar.	Apr.	May	June	July	Aug.
Futures price	$3.20	$3.25	$3.35	$3.25	$3.25	$3.30	$3.40

Suppose that in February you sold a contract for 1000 bushels of August wheat.

a. What was the value of your contract at its inception?

b. If you are marked to market at the end of each month, what would your cash flow be for each of the months?

2. What is the basic difference between a forward contract and a futures contract? Of what importance is this difference in determining the contract prices?

3. Is the "forward price" the same thing as the "value of the forward contract"? Explain.

Refer to the following information for questions 4 through 6. A forward contract exists for a unit of two-year government securities with delivery to take place three years from now. Suppose the price of these securities three years from now is uniformly distributed from a low of $800 to a high of $1400. The one-year expected riskless rate of interest is 5 percent for all periods under consideration.

4. If investors are risk neutral, what should be the current forward price?

5. Suppose now that investors are risk averse and that the forward price is $1200. What do you know about the relationship between the market value of two-year government securities and aggregate consumption?

6. Continue to assume (as in question 5) that the current forward price (at time 0) is $1200. One year from now (at time 1) the forward price for the same item and same delivery date is $1000. Determine the time 1 value (to the buyer) of the contract that was agreed upon at time 0.

7. Explain why a long-term treasury bond might possess a hedging property that would be of value to individuals. What implication would this have for the relationship of long-term to short-term interest rates?

8. Suppose that utility is a linear function of consumption.

a. What does this imply about forward prices?

b. What does this imply about futures prices?

9. Suppose a particular commodity's price tends to be negatively correlated with consumption. What does this imply about the forward price for the commodity?

10. Suppose that the reinvestment premium from the formula for the futures price is positive. What impact does this have on the futures price? Explain the intuition behind this influence.

11. Suppose the pure expectations theory of the term structure is correct. Which of the "premiums" in the futures price is affected, and in what way?

BIBLIOGRAPHY

BLACK, F., "The Pricing of Commodity Contracts," *Journal of Financial Economics* (September 1976).

CORNELL, B., and M. REINGANUM, "Forward and Futures Prices: Evidence from the Forward Exchange Markets," *Journal of Finance* (December 1981).

Cox, J. C., J. E. Ingersoll, and S. A. Ross, "The Relation Between Forward and Futures Prices," *Journal of Financial Economics* (December 1981).

Figlewski, S., and S. Kon, "Portfolio Management with Stock Index Futures," *Financial Analysts Journal* (January–February 1982).

Garbade, K., and W. Silber, "Futures Contracts on Commodities with Multiple Varieties: An Analysis of Premiums and Discounts," *Journal of Business* (July 1983).

Grauer, F. L. A., and R. H. Litzenberger, "The Pricing of Commodity Futures Contracts, Nominal Bonds and Other Risky Assets Under Uncertainty," *Journal of Finance* (March 1979).

Jarrow, R. A., and G. S. Oldfield, "Forward Contracts and Futures Contracts," *Journal of Financial Economics* (December 1981).

Kilcollin, T. E., "Differences Systems in Financial Futures Markets," *Journal of Finance* (December 1982).

Leland, H., and M. Rubenstein, "Replicating Options with Positions in Stock and Cash," *Financial Analysts Journal* (July–August 1981).

Morgan, G. E., "Forward and Futures Pricing of Treasury Bills," *Journal of Banking and Finance* (December 1981).

Resnick, B. C., and E. Hennigar, "The Relationship Between Futures and Cash Prices for U.S. Treasury Bonds," *Journal of Futures Markets* (vol. 2, no. 3, 1983).

Richard, S. F., and M. Sundaresan, "A Continuous Time Equilibrium Model of Forward Prices and Futures Prices in a Multigood Economy," *Journal of Financial Economics* (December 1981).

Stevenson, R., and R. Bear, "Commodity Futures: Trends or Random Walks," *Journal of Finance* (March 1970).

Trainer, F. H., "The Uses of Treasury Bond Futures in Fixed Income Portfolio Management," *Financial Analysts Journal* (January–February 1983).

15 THE EFFECT OF TAXES ON INVESTMENT STRATEGY AND SECURITIES PRICES

Introduction

The government usually takes a share of the returns from an investment through federal, state, and local income taxes. One of the things we're going to learn in this chapter is how to maximize your after-tax return from an investment while reducing the share of investment income going to government.

While trying to minimize the tax bite, investors trade and thereby affect the relative prices of securities with differing degrees of tax exposure. The prices of securities with the greatest exposure to taxation are lowered relative to the prices of securities with tax-sheltered income. In the end, the ideal strategy isn't necessarily one of investing in those securities with the least tax exposure. These investments are likely to be more "expensive" than others, and you must weigh the "price" of sheltering your investment income against the increase in taxes associated with exposing it.

In this chapter we will discuss the structure of the new tax law and how it affects your investment strategy. We will also discuss how taxes may affect the pricing of securities. Because of the wide diversity of the treatment of taxes at the state and municipal levels, we will center most of our attention on the federal income tax.

In the United States, personal income is still taxed progressively at graduated rates of 14% and 28%. However, it is still the case that different individuals with the same level of taxable income may pay income taxes at different rates. Given your level of income, your tax rate may depend on your tax status. For each level of income, the tax rate for married couples may be less than for a single person.

What Investment Income Is Taxed?

Not all investment income is subject to taxation. The interest income from state and municipal bonds, for example, is exempt from the federal income tax. Income from capital gains on these bonds is not exempt, however. Although exempt from federal income taxation, state and municipal bond interest is subject to state and local income tax.

Interest income from bonds issued by the U.S. government is subject to taxation by the Internal Revenue Service, but it is exempt from taxation by state and local governments. Interest income from corporate bonds is subject to taxation at all levels by the federal, state, and local governments.

If you buy a bond that was *originally issued* at a price that is less than the principal payment, you must report as interest income each year the amortized difference between the principal and the original issue price. Suppose you buy a bond that promises a single principal payment with no annual interest payments. If the bond had five years to maturity when originally issued, had a principal value of $1000, and was sold for a price of $750 when originally issued, you must report interest income in an amount of $50 per year for each year that you own the bond. Thus, you must pay taxes on the interest even though you receive no cash payments from the bond.

The new tax law allows some individuals to invest a limited amount each year in an Individual Retirement Account (IRA). The amount invested can be deducted from your taxable income for the year. You can also defer taxation on any income earned on the investment until you withdraw the money at some future date. The funds can be invested in a wide variety of investments, including mutual funds, making the IRA an extremely attractive tax shelter for all investors.

Keogh Retirement Plans are similar to an IRA and are available in limited amount to those investors who have income from self-employment. You can invest limited annual amounts of self-employment income in a Keogh plan. The investment amount itself is deductible from taxable income, and investment income earned in the plan isn't taxable until withdrawn.

Tax-sheltered annuities are also available to certain individuals (such as those who are employed by nonprofit institutions). These individuals can invest limited amounts in a tax-sheltered annuity. Again, the contribution is deductible, and income earned on the investment is deferred until withdrawn. Tax-deferred annuities are available to educational and other nonprofit institutions. In a tax-deferred annuity, the investment itself is not deductible. However, income earned on the investment isn't taxed until withdrawn.

These tax shelters are really doubly advantageous for the following reasons. First, income, which would normally be taxed away, can be successively rein-vested to produce yet more income. This feature dramatically increases the earning power of the investment. Second, you will presumably withdraw funds from the account at retirement, when your annual income will be less than it is when you make the contributions. Thus, in addition to deferring payment of the tax, you eventually may be taxed at a lower rate.

Capital Gains and Losses

A capital gain or loss results from a change in the market value of your invest-ment. Capital gains and losses are taxed in the year that they are realized.

There are tax advantages in taking your investment income in the form of capital gains, as opposed to regular interest or dividend income. Taxation of capital gains can be deferred until the gain is realized. This gives you the oppor-tunity to earn more profits by reinvesting the income that would otherwise be taxed away. In effect, it's like getting an interest-free loan from the government in an amount equal to what would be the capital gains tax, if the gain were realized immediately. *Other things being equal,* if you pay taxes, you should have a preference for investments that produce their investment income in the form of capital gains, as opposed to periodic cash payments like interest or div-idends, which may be exposed to the full force of the income tax.

TAXES AND INVESTMENT STRATEGY

Computing After-Tax Rates of Return

To compute the after-tax rate of return on an investment, you must first estimate the cash flows associated with the investment, determine the tax status of these cash flows, and then estimate your expected tax rate at the time the cash flows are received. For example, suppose you are considering purchasing a riskless bond with n years until maturity that pays interest annually. The after-tax inter-nal yield to maturity on the bond can be found as the rate that will discount the after-tax cash flows on the bond to a present value equal to the bond's current market price. Thus, through a process of trial and error, you would solve for Y in the following formula:

$$V = \sum_{t=1}^{n} \frac{C - \tau_t C}{(1 + Y)^t} + \frac{P - \tau_n^*(P - V)}{(1 + Y)^n} \qquad (15\text{--}1)$$

where C is the annual interest payment, V is the current value of the bond, τ_t is your expected tax rate on marginal income at time t, and τ_t^* is your expected tax rate on capital gains or losses in the year that the bond matures. (τ_t and τ_t^* may be equal, or if you foresee changes in the tax law you may presume them different.)

As you move into the future, your tax rate on investment income may be expected to change because of changes in the expected level of your total *taxable* income or because of anticipated changes in the tax law. In each year we subtract from the interest payment that amount of the payment that will be paid to the government in taxes. P represents the principal payment on the bond. For conventional bonds, the bond is originally issued at a price equal to the principal payment. If interest rates subsequently go up, and you buy the bond at a price, V, that is less than P, you will have realized a capital gain, equal to $P - V$, when the bond matures. Your capital gains tax, equal to the gain multiplied by the estimated effective tax rate on capital gains at maturity, is subtracted from the principal payment at maturity.

To illustrate the computation, consider the following example. Assume that you foresee a future tax structure whereby you are in the 27 percent tax bracket for regular income. Your capital gains are also expected to be taxed at a 27 percent rate. You are considering the purchase of either of two U.S. government bonds. Both have two years to maturity. We will assume for simplicity that interest is paid annually at the end of each year. One of the bonds carries a $50 annual interest payment and sells at a price of $823.42. Its pretax internal yield to maturity is therefore 16 percent.

$$\$823.42 = \frac{\$50.00}{(1.16)} + \frac{\$1000.00 + \$50.00}{(1.16)^2}$$

The other bond carries an annual interest payment of $160 and sells at a price of $1000. Its pretax internal yield is also 16 percent.

$$\$1000.00 = \frac{\$160.00}{(1.16)} + \frac{\$1000.00 + \$160.00}{(1.16)^2}$$

If you were a tax-exempt institution, and didn't pay taxes, you would be indifferent to either bond. However, because you are in the 27 percent bracket, you are attracted to the $50 bond because it produces its income in the form of capital gains as well as interest. As the bond approaches its maturity, the price of the bond will rise from its current value of $823.42 to its principal value of $1000. The fact that some of the income from this investment is in the form of price appreciation is advantageous to you because you can defer payment of the tax on the capital gain.

The after-tax yield to maturity on the $50 bond can be computed according to Equation (15–1). It is equal to 11.82 percent.

$$\$823.42 = \frac{\$50 - \overbrace{(.27 \times \$50)}^{\substack{\text{Tax} \\ \text{on} \\ \text{interest,} \\ \text{first} \\ \text{year}}}}{(1.1182)}$$

$$+ \frac{\$50 - \overbrace{(.27 \times \$50)}^{\substack{\text{Tax} \\ \text{on} \\ \text{interest,} \\ \text{second} \\ \text{year}}} + \$1000 - .27 \times \overbrace{(\$1000 - \$823.42)}^{\substack{\text{Tax} \\ \text{on} \\ \text{capital gain,} \\ \text{second} \\ \text{year}}}}{(1.1182)^2}$$

On the other hand, the after-tax yield on the $160 bond is only 10.4 percent.

$$\$1000 = \frac{\$160 - \overbrace{(.27 \times \$160)}^{\substack{\text{Tax} \\ \text{on} \\ \text{interest,} \\ \text{first} \\ \text{year}}}}{(1.1168)} + \frac{\$160 - \overbrace{(.27 \times \$160)}^{\substack{\text{Tax} \\ \text{on} \\ \text{interest,} \\ \text{second} \\ \text{year}}} + \$1000}{(1.1168)^2}$$

Thus, although the pretax yields on the two issues are the same, the after-tax yield is smaller on the high coupon issue. Because the two investments are nearly identical in all other respects, it is in your interest to invest in the issue with the smaller interest payment. To determine the best investment, you would make your decision on the basis of a comparison of the *after-tax* yields.

The Locked-In Effect

As discussed, capital gains and losses are taxed and deducted, respectively, when realized rather than when accrued. Suppose you bought a bond some time in the past; interest rates have since fallen, and the bond is now selling at a price much higher than the price you originally paid. You are looking at an alternative bond that is selling at a very attractive yield. The problem is this. If you sell the bond that you own, you will realize the capital gain, and the government will take some of your invested funds. In other words, you won't be able to commit as much capital to the new bond as you now have invested in the old. Even if the new bond is more attractive than the old in terms of percentage yield, your total dollar return may be less. In effect, the accrued capital gain has "locked" you into the investment in the old bond in the sense that it has increased the propensity for you to stay with it.

Accrued capital losses do the opposite. They provide an incentive to sell and move into other investments, because if you sell, you can realize the capital loss and take it as a tax deduction.

How can you tell when it is in your interest to realize a capital loss by switching from one bond to another? When is it best to remain in a bond with an accrued gain, even though there are other, alternative bonds with more attractive yields?

In computing the after-tax yield in Equation (15–1), we found the rate that would discount the after-tax cash flows, that we would get if we bought the bond, to a present value equal to what we would have to give up in order to get the bond, its current market price. To compute the after-tax yield on a bond you already own, you make a similar computation. However, Equation (15–1) must be modified in two respects.

First, the capital gain or loss at maturity is computed on the basis of the *price that you paid for the bond when you bought it* rather than the bond's current market price. Second, in the original equation, we related the after-tax cash flows associated with buying the bond to what we had to give up in order to buy it. If you don't already own the bond, you have to give up the market price in order to acquire it. If you already own the bond, you relate the after-tax cash flows associated with keeping the bond to what you have to give up to keep it. To keep the bond, you're giving up the net proceeds associated with selling it. The proceeds are equal to the bond's current market value less any capital gains tax you must pay if you sell now, or if you have an accrued capital loss, any taxes you would save by deducting the loss immediately.

Thus, the after-tax yield to maturity for a bond you already own is computed by solving for Y in the following equation:

$$V - \tau_0^* (V - V_K) = \sum_{t=1}^{n} \frac{C - \tau_t C}{(1 + Y)^t} + \frac{P - \tau_n^*(P - V_K)}{(1 + Y)^n} \qquad (15\text{--}2)$$

where V_K is the price you originally paid for the bond. The second term on the left side of the equation represents the capital gains tax you must pay if you sell the bond now. The capital gain is computed as the difference between the current price of the bond and your original cost. There is a similar term in the numerator of the last term on the right side. This represents the capital gains tax you must pay if you hold the bond to maturity. The capital gain in this case is computed as the difference between the principal payment and your original cost.

If you have an accrued capital loss, you can use the same equation. In this case by holding the bond you are giving up, in addition to its value in the market, the tax deduction associated with realizing the accrued capital loss. We relate the sum of these two to the after-tax cash flows associated with keeping the bond in calculating the after-tax yield to maturity.

To illustrate the formula, suppose that there are two bonds that have two years to maturity and $100 annual interest payments. You bought one of the bonds many years ago at a price of $600. The price of this bond is now $918.71.

The price of the other bond, which you don't own, is being offered to you at the seemingly attractive price of $910.00. In this example, assume that you feel that there will be future upward revisions in tax rates and that capital gains will be taxed at a preferred rate in the future. Assume now that you *expect* in the *future* to be in a 35 percent tax bracket, and will be taxed in the *future* at the rate of only 17.5 percent on capital gains and losses, and that the after-tax internal yield on the bond you don't own is equal to 11.01 percent.

$$\$910 = \frac{\$100 - (.35 \times \$100)}{(1.1101)}$$
$$+ \frac{\$100 - (.35 \times \$100) + \$1000 - .175(\$1000 - \$910)}{(1.1101)^2}$$

The after-tax yield on the bond you do own is 13.29 percent.

$$\underbrace{\$918.71 - .27(\$918.71 - \$600.00)}_{\text{What you give up to keep the bond}} = \underbrace{\frac{\$100 - (.35 \times \$100)}{(1.1329)}}_{\text{What you get if you keep the bond}} + \frac{\$100 - (.35 \times \$100) + \$1000 - .175(\$1000 - \$600)}{(1.1329)^2}$$

What you give up to keep the bond

What you get if you keep the bond

Thus, even though someone who doesn't own either bond would prefer the bond with the lower price, because in all other respects the two bonds are identical, it is in your interest to hold on to the bond you already own. If you sell it to move into the other issue, you must pay tax on the gain that you have accrued. Thus, you must give to the government money that you could otherwise keep invested on your own account. By comparing after-tax yields computed in this way, you can determine when it is to your advantage to realize a gain or loss and move into another issue.

Dividend Clienteles

As you know, bonds that sell at discounted prices below their principal values have a tax advantage. Part of the return that these bonds produce for investors comes in the form of a capital gain, as the value of the bonds approaches the principal at maturity. Because capital gains can be deferred, the income from these types of bonds is, to some extent, tax sheltered.

A similar phenomenon exists in the stock market. A stock's total expected return can be broken down into two parts:

$$E(r) = \frac{E(D) + E(\Delta V)}{V} = \frac{E(D)}{V} + \frac{E(\Delta V)}{V} = \frac{\text{Dividend}}{\text{yield}} + \frac{\text{Expected}}{\text{growth}}$$

where ΔV is the change in the value of the stock during the period that you hold it.

In general, as stocks pay out a larger fraction of their earnings as dividends, and thereby retain less for future investments, they reduce the expected growth

OUT ON THE STREET

Stripping Dividends

"What's your pleasure, Buddy?" Peter Thayer slammed the taxi door and responded, "La Guardia, and push it. I've got forty-five minutes to make a flight." This was the tail end of a business trip on which Pete landed two new corporate accounts, both for the investment management service that specializes in providing dividend income in concentrated doses to corporate investors.

This is still another specialized service of Gateway Investment Advisers, the money management firm located in Cincinnati, Ohio. Gateway specializes in the creative use of options in investment management. In this case, it was using options to provide corporations with concentrated doses of dividend income from common stocks, without exposing them to the risks associated with the fluctuations in the prices of the common stocks.

Corporations typically have liquid funds that they must invest prior to making financial commitments, such as the payment of interest on their bond issues. Because the funds move in and out of the market rather quickly, the investments must be highly liquid. The problem is that most corporations are in a relatively high bracket for marginal income, and this takes a big bite on anything they can earn on their financial investments.

However, the tax law allows corporations to deduct a large percent of their dividend income from their taxable income. This creates a major incentive for them to invest in any security that distributes what the IRS will recognize as dividends. After all, the effective tax rate for them on this type of investment income is very small. Five or six years ago corporations had big preferred stock portfolios. However, many preferred stocks lacked real liquidity. Moreover, because they were the only investments around with low risk and dividend income, the corporate demand forced their prices up and expected returns down relative to other securities.

With Gateway's service, its corporate

in their stock price. Thus, by changing the fraction of earnings paid out as dividends, they alter the mix of return to their investors between dividends and capital gains. As we will see in the next section, just as discounted bonds sell at lower pretax yields than bonds that sell at premiums, investors may require higher rates of return on stocks that pay larger dividends and therefore have greater tax exposure.

There is some question as to whether this is really true, but if it is, it has been suggested that stocks may then have particular investor clienteles, where low-bracket investors invest in stocks with high dividend payouts, and high-bracket investors invest in stocks with low dividend payouts. This is directly parallel to the clienteles that exist in the bond market. High-bracket investors generally invest in municipal bonds, and low-bracket investors, like pension funds, which

clients can capture common stock dividends without worrying about capital gains or losses. Gateway's strategy is to buy common stocks that are about to go ex-dividend. At the same time it sells relatively deep in-the-money call options on the same stock. It also takes positive positions in put options to sell the Standard and Poor's 100 Index, to provide additional protection against a downward slide in stock market prices that may force its call options out of the money. After the stock goes "ex," Gateway holds it for the length of time required under the law to enable its corporate clients to avail themselves of the 85 percent exclusion. It then sells the stock, buys back its options, and moves into another stock that is about to go ex-dividend.

Prior to July 16, 1984, corporations were required to hold stocks for more than sixteen days to get the exclusion. Now they must hold them for forty-six days. This, however, is approximately the average length of the holding period for Gateway's dividend investments anyway. Even with the extended holding period, Gateway can produce up to eight quarterly dividends a year for the invested dollar instead of the normal four.

The market for this strategy has been huge. It is low risk. The beta factor for these portfolios is typically around .2. If the companies invest in Eurodollars or certificates of deposit, they can expect to earn (1 to 46 percent) of whatever these securities are yielding. The dividend strategy produces a higher pretax return, and they get to keep 93.1 percent of it. This adds up to double or triple the after-tax return for their corporate cash. Although it may sound odd for dividends to be moving from one corporation to another to be taxed again before final receipt by investors, they've got to invest their idle cash in something, and this minimizes the tax bite going to government.

Peter notices the red blur of what might have been a traffic light outside the window. "I know I said push it, but not all the way to the floor. Please!"

pay no income taxes at all, generally avoid municipals and invest in corporates and U.S. government issues.

The existence of clienteles in the stock market can be questioned, however, because there are mechanisms for investors to separate the dividend and capital gains components of a stock's total return and then invest exclusively in either one. If you want to invest exclusively in the dividend of a given stock, you need only do the following:

1. Buy a share of stock.

2. Buy a put option on the stock, with any arbitrary exercise price, X, that expires shortly after the ex-dividend date.

3. Sell a call option on the stock with an exercise price and expiration date equal to that of the put.

4. Borrow the present value of X and use the money to help finance the purchase of the share.

Now consider the proceeds of this strategy on the expiration date of the options. First, if the stock price, V_S, is greater than X

Stock value	V_S + dividend
Put value	0
Call value	$-(V_S - X)$
Debt value	$-X$
Total value	Dividend

On the other hand, if the stock value turns out to be less than X

Stock value	V_S + dividend
Put value	$X - V_S$
Call value	0
Debt value	$-X$
Total value	Dividend

As you can see, no matter what happens to the stock, you get the dividend as the only payoff from the strategy. If you want to invest in dividends, you need not restrict your investments to stocks with high dividend payouts. You can easily invest in low payout companies and strip the dividends from the stocks with the strategy. There is no need for any particular type of clientele in certain companies.

Although the transactions costs associated with adopting such a strategy may be large for the individual investor, financial institutions can employ the strategy on a large scale and then market the dividend fund to investors.

THE EFFECT OF TAXES ON SECURITIES PRICES

Because taxes may alter the trading strategies of individual investors, they may have an impact on the way securities are priced in the market. In this section we will look at the way taxes affect the pricing of dividends versus capital gains in the stock market, and the pricing of securities that are taxable, such as corporate bonds, relative to the pricing of securities that are tax exempt, such as municipal bonds.

The Effect of Dividends on Expected Stock Returns

Brennan (1973) introduced personal income taxes into the Capital Asset Pricing Model. He assumed that capital gains were taxed at a lower rate than dividends, investors could borrow and lend at a risk-free rate of interest, and dividends were known with certainty. Under these assumptions, Brennan derived the following analog to the securities market line in the no-tax CAPM:

$$E(r_J) = r_F + a_1\,\beta_J + a_2\,(d_J - r_F)$$

Risk-free   Risk   Tax exposure
rate   premium   premium

In the equation, you can interpret a_1 as the slope of the relationship between risk and expected rates of return, and a_2 as a coefficient relating the firm's dividend yield, d_J, to its expected rate of return. Firms with dividend yields (the ratio of the dividend to the market price) greater than the risk-free rate sell at a premium in their expected return, and firms with lower dividend yields sell at a discount in their return. In the Brennan model, the coefficient a_2 is a weighted average of the marginal tax rates of investors in the market, and it is a positive number.

Miller and Scholes (1978) have presented a counterargument to show that the fraction of its earnings a firm pays out as dividends should have no impact on the expected return of its common stock. Essentially, they argue that there are many ways investors can shelter dividends from taxes. We discussed some tax shelters at the beginning of this chapter. In addition to these, Miller and Scholes suggest the following.

If you have some taxable dividends from your stock investments, all you need is a tax deduction to shelter them. To get one, you need only borrow money and invest it in something like a tax deferred annuity. You won't be taxed on the income from the annuity, and you won't increase your risk if the income from the annuity is derived from risk-free investments. If you borrow (and invest) enough money so the interest on the debt is equal to the amount of your dividends, you can use the dividends to pay the interest and use the interest as a tax deduction to cover the dividends. In effect, you have transformed the dividends into a tax-deferred annuity. Because you can do this with any form of investment income, the tax exposure of investment income should matter little to you. If tax-exposed investments sell at lower prices, you can take advantage of these discounted prices while paying no taxes on the associated investment income.

In a more recent paper Litzenberger and Ramaswamy (L-R) (1982) empirically tested a slightly modified version of Brennan's model. They looked at a large sample of stocks in the period 1940 through 1980. In the sixty months prior to any given month of their test, they estimated the beta factors for all the stocks in their sample by relating the returns on each stock to the returns on their New York Stock Exchange market index. They then estimated the dividend for each stock for the month, using a statistical model that employs information that was available at the beginning of the month. Having estimated the dividend, they then computed each stock's dividend yield.

At this point, L-R examined the relationship between the dividend yields for different stocks and the returns produced in each month, after allowing for the effect of differences in beta on differences in security return. Do the stocks that have large dividend yields, and therefore great tax exposure, tend to be priced so as to produce larger returns before taxes? To answer this question. L-R examined the relationship between pretax return and dividend yield in each of the months covered by their study by fitting a linear line through the cross section of stocks in their sample. The slopes of each of these lines were then averaged, and the average turned out to be a positive number that is statistically significant. Thus, their study supports the view that stocks, like bonds, with greater tax exposure tend to sell at lower prices and greater expected pretax rates of return. Thus, their results support Brennan and are inconsistent with the tax avoidance argument of Miller and Scholes.

There remains a puzzling question: If dividends do affect the expected rate of return on stocks, why don't all firms act to reduce their costs of capital by lowering the amount of their dividends? Why, in fact, do dividends exist at all when you can deter payments with capital gains? Researchers in finance are actively seeking the answer to this question.

Relative Expected Returns on Taxable and Tax-Exempt Securities

It is clear that there is a differential expected return between securities that are fully exposed to taxes, such as corporate bonds, and securities that are exempt from taxes, such as municipal bonds. In his presidential address to the American Finance Association, Merton Miller (1977) introduced a model that helped to predict how large a differential should be expected. In the most simple form of his model, he assumes that investors can escape taxation on common stock returns through the various tax-avoidance mechanisms discussed earlier. Given that they can, common stock should sell at the same (risk-adjusted) expected rate of return as fully tax-exempt securities, such as municipal bonds. He assumes that corporate bonds are fully exposed to personal income taxes, and that the interest on these bonds is deductible for purposes of computing the corporate income tax.

Corporations can finance their investments by either selling common stock or corporate debt. The payments on the debt are deductible; the dividends on the stock are not. Given this, if the stock and the debt sell at the same (risk-adjusted) rate of return, firms will prefer to finance with debt. If τ_C is the corporate income tax rate, the firm corporate income tax rate, the firm can save $\tau_C r_C v_D$ dollars in taxes for each year the debt is outstanding, where r_C is the interest rate on the corporate debt. If the debt is perpetual, the present value of these tax savings is equal to $\tau_C r_C v_D / r_C$, or $\tau_C v_D$. Thus, for each dollar in debt issued by the firm, the market value of the firm goes up by τ_C cents.

The relationship between the value of the firm and the amount of debt outstanding under these assumptions is given in Figure 15–1. Note that it is in the interest of the firm to issue as much debt as possible, if it wishes to maximize its market value. In other words, if corporate debt sells at the same (risk-adjusted) expected rate of return as common stock and municipal bonds, corporations will flood the market with debt. Suppose debt sells at a higher (risk-adjusted) expected rate of return. In this case, the firm gets the benefit of the tax deduction but pays a penalty through the premium in the cost of debt. In this case the slope of the function in Figure 15–1 is reduced. Suppose that the differential in the (risk-adjusted) expected returns between corporate debt and stock

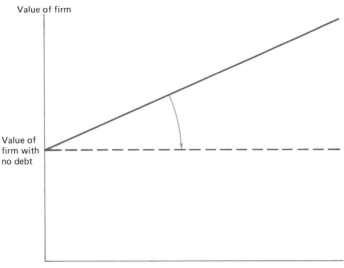

Figure 15-1 Debt and Firm Value: Miller

and municipal bonds becomes large enough to equate the after-tax returns for someone in the same bracket as the corporate tax rate. This will be the case when $r_C = r_S/(1 - \tau_C)$ where r_S is the (risk-adjusted) expected return on stock investments. Now the penalty through the differential premium exactly offsets the benefit of the tax deduction. In Figure 15–1 the slope of the function is now zero, as given by the broken line. If the differential in return becomes any bigger, the slope becomes negative.

Thus, if the (risk-adjusted) expected return on debt is greater than $r_S/(1 - \tau_C)$, the firm will want to issue no debt, because debt drives down the value of the firm. If it is less than $r_S/(1 - \tau_C)$, all firms will want to finance with all debt, because debt drives up the value of the firm. The supply curve for corporate debt is, therefore, perfectly horizontal at a (risk-adjusted) interest rate of $r_S/(1 - \tau_C)$, as given in Figure 15–3.

The equilibrium interest rate on corporate debt will be determined by the intersection of supply and demand. The demand curve is based on the needs of individual investors. Miller assumes that these investors are taxed at graduated rates. Because the interest payments on debt are taxable, investors will prefer municipal bonds and common stock, unless there is a (risk-adjusted) differential in the pretax expected return on corporate debt. If this differential is very small, only those investors in the very lowest brackets will prefer corporate debt as an investment. As the differential is increased, investors in the higher brackets will be enticed into the market for corporate debt. The demand curve is thus upward sloping, reflecting the fact that there will be a greater demand for corporate debt as its pretax interest rate is increased. (Most demand curves are *downward* sloping, because prices, and not interest rates, are plotted on the vertical axis.)

In Figure 15–3 the rising demand curve intersects the horizontal supply curve at a risk-adjusted interest rate that fully reflects the corporate tax rate. Miller *assumes* that the marginal corporate rate is less than the highest marginal personal tax rate. Firms will be indifferent to issuing debt or equity to finance their investments, because the amount of debt outstanding has no impact on the value of the firm, as can be seen by the broken line in Figure 15-1.

The Miller equilibrium has been modified by DeAngelo and Masulis (1980). DeAngelo and Masulis introduce other tax deductions, such as depreciation charges, into the model. In the presence of these, the firm may find that in any given year the interest payment is in whole or in part unnecessary, because earnings are small enough that depreciation charges are sufficient to reduce the tax liability to zero. As additional units of debt are issued by the firm, the probability increases that the earnings will be small enough to make the additional interest payments redundant as a tax deduction. Their expected value as a tax shelter decreases. As additional units of debt are issued, the value of the firm increases, but at a decreasing rate, as with the solid curve of Figure 15–2.

If we introduce a differential between the (risk-adjusted) expected return on debt and equity, each firm will issue debt until, for the last unit of debt issued, the diminishing benefit associated with the tax deduction is exactly equal to the penalty associated with the yield differential. As the yield differential becomes smaller, each firm will issue additional amounts of debt. Thus, in the context of this model, the supply curve for debt is downward sloping, as with the broken curve of Figure 15–3. The differential (risk-adjusted) expected return on corporate debt now reflects a break-even tax rate that is less than the corporate rate. The differential does bring down the curve of Figure 15–2, however. In the presence of the differential, the relationship between firm value and the amount of debt issued is given by the broken curve, and the optimal amount of debt for the firm is given by v^*_D.

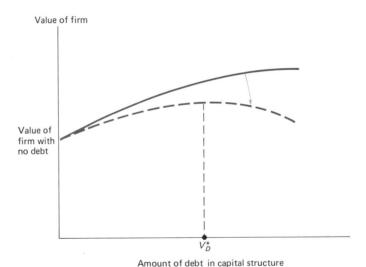

Figure 15-2 Debt and Firm Value: DeAngelo-Masulis

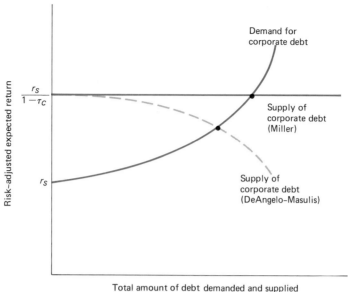

Figure 15-3 Equilibrium in the Market for Corporate Debt

DeAngelo and Masulis have assumed, of course, that redundant tax shelters can't be transferred from firm to firm through takeover or through some other mechanism allowed by law. They have also assumed that the mechanism for carrying over shelters to successive years is either limited or imperfect. In the actual tax law, it is both. No credit is given for interest that could have been earned on the money and the amount of the carryover is limited.

We can contrast the theories of Miller and DeAngelo-Masulis. In Miller, the tax rate that will make you indifferent between investing in municipal and corporate bonds is the *corporate* tax rate. Moreover, we would expect that this rate should be a constant over time. In DeAngelo-Masulis, the break-even rate is less than the corporate rate, and we would expect it to be variable over time, as the expected profits and available depreciation charges fluctuate. The evidence on which theory is correct is inconclusive. You will usually find the rate that equates the after-tax, promised yields to maturity on corporate bonds and municipal bonds, to be less than the corporate tax rate. On the other hand, you must be very cautious about drawing a conclusion from this, because of the following points:

1. There may be differential default probabilities between the corporate and municipal bonds, and the relative promised yields to maturity may not be a good indicator of relative expected yields.

2. There may be differential provisions related to callability and sinking funds.

3. The market may not expect the differential tax treatment between corporate and municipal bonds to persist indefinitely in the tax law. If they see a real possibility that all interest will become tax exempt in the next year, the prices of long-term corporate and municipal bonds will be very close, even if corporates are *currently* taxable.

Skelton (1979) has examined the differential between realized rates of return on corporate and municipal bonds and has found that the differential is close to the corporate rate, at least for short-term issues. This is consistent with the Miller model, but the available evidence on the issue, thus far, is incomplete.

Summary

Taxes have an impact on investment strategy and securities prices. You can avoid taxes on your investments by investing in tax-exempt securities, bonds that are selling at deep discounts, stocks that pay small dividends, or tax-deferred to tax-sheltered retirement plans. You can determine which investments will give you the most lucrative returns after taxes by computing their after-tax rates of return. In computing these returns, you must relate what you have to give up to get or keep the investments to what you expect to get after tax payments if you buy or keep them. In general, it is in your interest to realize capital losses for tax purposes and defer capital gains, at least until they are long term.

Taxes may affect the relative prices of common stocks. Capital gains are tax shelters because they can be deferred, and they are taxed at a lower rate than dividends. As a result, the stocks of firms that pay out large dividends may be viewed as less desirable by investors, and their pretax expected rates of return may be higher. Some have argued against this possibility because of the ease of sheltering dividends from taxes. The best available empirical evidence, however, indicates the possible presence of dividend effect in expected stock returns.

Taxes affect the relative yield differential between tax-exempt securities like municipal bonds and fully taxable securities like corporate bonds. In the presence of perfect capital markets, where redundant tax shelters like depreciation charges can't be marketed from firm to firm by takeover or other mechanisms allowed in the tax law, the differential between the rates on municipal and corporate bonds will reflect the corporate tax rate. In a less than perfect capital market where the interest tax shelter may go unused by anyone, the break-even rate may be less than the corporate rate.

QUESTIONS AND PROBLEMS

1. In what sense could a capital gain on an investment you have made in the past effectively "lock" you into that investment, even though other investments appear to have better prospects for the commitment of new money?

Assume the following information for questions 2 and 3. The data are for three bonds, each having one year until maturity and each having a principal payment due at maturity in the amount of $1000.

You purchased bond 1 several years ago for $850. Assume that you foresee your marginal tax rate on ordinary income will be 40 percent and your tax rate on capital gains will be 20 percent. Suppose you view the three bonds as having the same default risk.

	Annual Coupon Payment	*Current Market Price*
Bond 1	$50	$970
Bond 2	80	980
Bond 3	40	960

2. Would it be advantageous to sell bond 1 and reinvest the proceeds in one or both of the other bonds?

3. What if you were considering the investment of additional funds in one or more of the three bonds. Which would offer the best after-tax return?

Assume the following data for questions 4 through 6. Both of the bonds have two years until maturity and both have a principal payment at maturity of $1000. Assume that your marginal tax rate on ordinary income is expected to be 50 percent and the tax rate on capital gains is expected to be 25 percent.

	Annual Coupon Payment	*Pretax Internal Yield*
Bond A	$200	10%
Bond B	100	13

4. What are the current prices of the two bonds?

5. Suppose you were considering an investment of new funds in one of these bonds. Which one would give the better rate of return on an after-tax basis?

6. Suppose that you already owned bond A and had purchased it for $1500. You were now contemplating whether you should have your funds in that bond or direct them toward the purchase of bond B. Which one would bring a better return? (Assume capital gains are currently taxed at 25 percent.)

7. Suppose that you want to invest in just the dividend portion of a stock. A stock, a put, and a call exist with the following characteristics:

$$
\begin{aligned}
\text{Current stock price} &= \$100 \\
\text{Expected dividend} &= \$\ \ 2 \\
\text{Exercise price (on both the put and call)} &= \$\ 95
\end{aligned}
$$

Both the put and call options expire on the same date, immediately after the dividend is paid. The rate of interest for the period until the options' expiration date is 3 percent.

   a. Indicate what portfolio would ensure an ending payoff equal to the dividend payment.

   b. Demonstrate that the portfolio indicated in part a would give the dividend as a payoff under two alternative price assumptions for the stock at the expiration date: $90 or $110.

8. Suppose you have $1000 invested in a stock and, during the course of the year, you are paid $50 in dividends on the stock. If you can borrow at 8 percent, and if there is a tax-deferred annuity available for purchase, which pays 8 percent, can you contrive a way to shield your dividend payments from taxes?

9. What would be the logic in support of the idea that stocks paying higher dividend yields would also have an extra premium incorporated in their equilibrium returns? Why would some (like Miller and Scholes) argue that the dividend payout should have no bearing on the expected return?

10. Suppose a firm happened to be financed entirely with $200,000 of stock. The dividends it pays to stockholders represent the same risk-adjusted return as the firm would have to pay on debt. Suppose that this rate is 8 percent. Also, assume that the corporate income tax rate is a flat 50 percent.

   a. What would you recommend to the firm in terms of possible changes in its debt-equity structure?

   b. How much would the company save each year by implementing the strategy suggested in part a?

11. Suppose that the rates of return paid by firms on debt and equity have adjusted so that, from the firm's viewpoint, neither security is preferred to the other as a means of raising funds.

   a. If income from stock is considered to be tax exempt, what would be the relationship between the rate paid on debt and the rate paid on stock?

   b. What market scenario might account for this kind of relationship?

BIBLIOGRAPHY

BARNEA, A., R. HAUGEN, and L. SENBET, "An Equilibrium Analysis of Debt Financing Under Costly Tax Arbitrage and Agency Problems," *Journal of Finance* (June 1981).

BLACK, F., and M. SCHOLES, "The Effects of Dividend Yield and Dividend Policy on Common Stock Prices and Returns," *Journal of Financial Economics* (March 1974).

BRENNAN, M. J., "Taxes, Market Valuation and Corporate Financial Policy," *National Tax Journal* (Dec. 1973).

CONSTANTINIDIES, G. M., and M. S. SCHOLES, "Optimal Liquidation of Assets in the Presence of Personal Taxes: Implications for Asset Pricing," *Journal of Finance* (May 1980).

DEANGELO, H., and R. W. MASULIS, "Optimal Capital Structure Under Corporate and Personal Taxation," *Journal of Financial Economics* (March 1980).

DYL, E. A., "Capital Gains Taxation and Year-end Stock Price Behavior," *Journal of Finance* (March 1977).

EADES, K. M., P. J. HESS, and E. H. KIM, "On Interpreting Security Returns During the Ex-Dividend Period," *Journal of Financial Economics* (March 1984).

HESS, W., "The Ex-Dividend Behavior of Stock Returns: Further Evidence on Tax Effects," *Journal of Finance* (May 1982).

JORDAN, J. V., "Tax Effects in Term Structure Estimation," *Journal of Finance* (June 1984).

LITZENBERGER, R. H., and K. RAMASWAMY, K. "The Effects of Dividends on Common Stock Prices: Tax Effects or Information Effects," *Journal of Finance* (May 1982).

MILLER, M., "Debt and Taxes," *Journal of Finance* (May 1977).

MILLER, M., and M. SCHOLES, "Dividends and Taxes," *Journal of Financial Economics* (Dec. 1978).

SKELTON, J. F., "The Relative Pricing of Tax-Exempt and Taxable Debt," mimeo. University of California, Berkeley, November 1979.

TRZCINKA, C., "The Pricing of Tax-Exempt Bonds and the Miller Hypothesis," *Journal of Finance* (September 1982).

16 STOCK VALUATION

Introduction

In this chapter we will learn to estimate the intrinsic value of common stocks. In the chapters on asset pricing, our attention centered on the appropriate rate of return to require from a common stock investment. How does one go about measuring risk, and, given risk, what is the appropriate rate of return? This, however, is only one side of the coin in valuing a security. In addition to determining the appropriate capitalization rate, you must also estimate the investment income to be capitalized. In the case of common stocks, the income payments to be capitalized are dividends. In this chapter we will derive some models that can be used to value stocks, based on the expected flow of future dividends.

A FRAMEWORK FOR VALUING COMMON STOCKS

The only way a corporation can transfer wealth to its stockholders is through the payment of dividends. Because dividends are the only source of cash payments to a common stock investor, it follows that dividends are the single source of value for common stocks.

At this point you might object and point to the fact that most investors are far more concerned with capital gains than they are with dividends. After all, the principal determinant of the variability in a stock's return from year to year is the magnitude of the capital gains or losses. However, the changes that occur in the stock price can be attributed to changes in the market's expectations regarding the magnitude of dividends to be received beyond the current year.

The current market price for the stock can be written as a function of the market's expectation of the dividend to be received at the end of the year and the market price to be in effect at the end of the year.

$$V_0 = \frac{E(D_1) + E(V_1)}{1 + E(r)} \qquad (16\text{--}1)$$

where V_0 is the current stock price, $E(D_1)$ is the expected year-end dividend per share, $E(V_1)$ is the expected year-end price, and $E(r)$ is the market's required or expected rate of return on the stock. The expected rate of return is equal to the sum of the rate of return available on risk-free securities and the risk premium that is appropriate, given the risk of the individual stock.

However, if the expected rate of return on the stock is not expected to change, the expected price at the end of the year can similarly be written as

$$E(V_1) = \frac{E(D_2) + E(V_2)}{1 + E(r)} \qquad (16\text{--}2)$$

Substituting Equation (16–2) into (16–1), we get

$$V_0 = \frac{E(D_1)}{1 + E(r)} + \frac{E(D_2) + E(V_2)}{(1 + E(r))^2}$$

Now the stock value is seen to be determined by the dividend payments expected in the first two years. This same process can, of course, be continued through years 3, 4, and so on, resulting finally in

$$V_0 = \frac{E(D_1)}{1 + E(r)} + \frac{E(D_2)}{(1 + E(r))^2} + \cdots + \frac{E(D_N)}{(1 + E(r))^N} \qquad (16\text{--}3)$$

where N is the number of years remaining in the life of the firm.

Thus, even if investors are primarily concerned with capital gains, because the source of the capital gains is expected future dividends (or changes in expected future dividends), the current market price of the stock is based on the expected flow of dividends throughout the life of the firm.

Dividends Versus Earnings

It might seem more logical to capitalize the expected series of cash earnings per share to obtain a stock value. After all, stockholders have a claim on these cash earnings after payment of bond interest and other expenses. However, it must be remembered that the magnitude of future dividends is due, in part, to the reinvestment of some fraction of the current earnings. Thus, you can't have the one without reinvestment of a part of the other.

We can write Equation (16–3) in terms of earnings by making the following substitution for the expected dividend in any given year, t:

$$E(D_t) = E(\text{Earnings}_t - \text{Retained earnings}_t)$$

Once the role of retained earnings is recognized, the earnings and dividend approaches to stock valuation are completely equivalent.

The Constant Growth Model

If you are willing to assume that the dividend payments on a stock are going to grow at a constant rate in perpetuity, the stock valuation equation collapses to a very simple form. Suppose that the dividend paid yesterday is given by D_0. The value of the stock can be written as

$$V_0 = \frac{D_0(1 + E(g))}{(1 + E(r))} + \frac{D_0(1 + E(g))^2}{(1 + E(r))^2} + \cdots \text{ and so on}$$

Although this is a perpetual sum, it does reach a limit if the expected rate of growth is less than the required rate of return. The limit is equal to

$$V = \frac{D_0(1 + E(g))}{E(r) - E(g)} = \frac{E(D_1)}{E(r) - E(g)}$$

To illustrate, consider a stock that paid a dividend of a dollar yesterday, the expected growth in the dividend is a constant 10 percent, and the required rate of return is 20 percent. The expected series of dividends is

$$E(D_1) = \$1.00 \times 1.10 = \$1.10$$

$$E(D_2) = \$1.10 \times 1.10 = \$1.21$$

$$E(D_3) = \$1.21 \times 1.10 = \$1.33$$

and so on. The market value for the stock is given by

$$\frac{\$1.10}{.20 - .10} = \$11.00$$

Under the constant growth model, both price and dividends per share grow at the same rate through time. For example, in the case of the stock considered above, because the dividend expected to be paid at the end of the second year is equal to $1.21, the market price of the stock is expected to be equal to

$$\frac{\$1.21}{.20 - .10} = \$12.10$$

The change in price from $11.00 to $12.10 represents a rate of growth of 20 percent

$$\frac{\$12.10 - \$11.00}{\$11.00} = 20\%$$

which, of course, is consistent with the rate of growth in the dividend.

We should also note that, in the context of this model, the investor's expected return is equal to (a) the ratio of the next expected dividend to the market price plus (b) the constant expected growth rate in dividends and market price.

$$E(r) = \frac{\text{Expected year-end dividend}}{\text{Beginning of year market price}} + \text{Expected growth rate}$$

In the context of our example, this would be

$$20\% = \$1.10/\$11.00 + 10\%$$

Although the constant growth model is conceptually very simple, the assumption of a constant rate of growth in perpetuity is unacceptable, however, because a company growing at a constant, but above average, rate can be expected eventually to grow to encompass the entire economy. Thus, we need to make a more realistic assumption regarding future growth.

The Multistage Growth Model

Analysts frequently make the assumption that a firm's growth rate will change in a series of stages. The most simple variant is the two-stage growth model. Here we assume that the dividend will initially grow at an above or a below average rate for a number of years. At the end of this period, which is called the *growth horizon,* the growth rate reverts to that of an average or standard share. The length of the growth horizon depends on the length of time into the future you feel comfortable with your forecast of abnormal growth for the stock. Obviously, at some point in the future, things will seem so uncertain that you have no reason to believe that the stock can be distinguished in terms of its growth rate. Beyond this point the best assumption will be that the stock will grow at an average rate.

The *growth profile* for a two-stage model is presented in Figures 16–1 and 16–2. In both figures time into the future is plotted on the horizontal axis. However, in Figure 16–1 the expected growth rate for the dividend is plotted on the vertical axis, and in Figure 16–2 the dividend itself is plotted. In this example the dividend is initially expected to grow at an above average rate and then revert to the average rate at the end of the growth horizon (the end of year n).

The market value of the stock can be expressed as the present value of the dividend stream of Figure 16–2.

$$V = \frac{D_0\,(1 + E(G))}{(1 + E(r))} + \frac{D_0\,(1 + E(G))^2}{(1 + E(r))^2} + \ldots + \frac{D_0\,(1 + E(G))^n}{(1 + E(r))^n}$$
$$+ \frac{D_0\,(1 + E(G))^n(1 + E(g))}{(1 + E(r))^{n+1}} + \ldots \text{ and so on} \qquad (16\text{–}4)$$

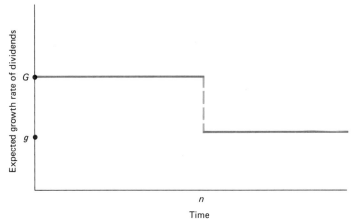

Figure 16-1   Expected Rate of Growth in Dividends

where $E(G)$ is the initial above or below average rate of growth, and $E(g)$ is the average or standard rate of growth. Although this is again a perpetual sum, if $E(g)$ is less than $E(r)$, the sum approaches a finite limit.

As was the case in ''Hunting for Bargains Out On the Street'' in Chapter 7, the required rate of return can be estimated using an asset pricing model such as the CAPM. The average growth rate can be estimated by observing the past growth rate for earnings and dividends per share associated with some broad stock market index such as the Standard and Poor's 500. The average, historic growth rate for the index can then be subjectively modified to account for any differences in the economic environment between the past and the future.

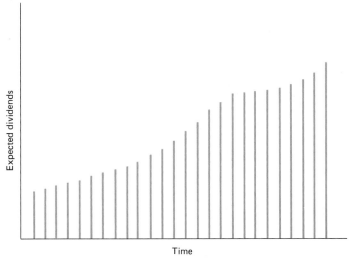

Figure 16-2   Expected Dividends

One important difference to consider is the rate of inflation. If you think the rate of inflation in the future is going to be greater than it was in the past period over which you measured the historic growth rate for the index, you may want to adjust upward your estimate for the average future rate of growth to account for this.

To illustrate the two-stage growth model, consider the following example. A stock has just paid a dividend of $1 per share. The dividend is expected to grow at a rate of 30 percent for the next six years. Thereafter the growth rate is expected to revert to the standard or average rate of 6 percent. The required expected rate of return on the stock is assumed to be 15 percent.

The following stream of dividends is expected to be paid from the stock at the end of each year:

$$\text{Year 1: } D_0 (1 + E(G))^1 \qquad\qquad = \$1.30$$
$$\text{Year 2: } D_0 (1 + E(G))^2 \qquad\qquad = \$1.69$$
$$\text{Year 3: } D_0 (1 + E(G))^3 \qquad\qquad = \$2.20$$
$$\text{Year 4: } D_0 (1 + E(G))^4 \qquad\qquad = \$2.86$$
$$\text{Year 5: } D_0 (1 + E(G))^5 \qquad\qquad = \$3.71$$
$$\text{Year 6: } D_0 (1 + E(G))^6 \qquad\qquad = \$4.83$$
$$\text{Year 7: } D_0 (1 + E(G))^6 (1 + E(g))^1 = \$5.12$$
$$\text{Year 8: } D (1 + E(G))^6 (1 + E(g))^2 = \$5.43$$
and so on

With a 15 percent discount rate, the present value of this stream of dividends is

$$\$1.30/1.15^1 = \$1.13$$
$$\$1.69/1.15^2 = \$1.28$$
$$\$2.20/1.15^3 = \$1.45$$
$$\$2.86/1.15^4 = \$1.64$$
$$\$3.72/1.15^5 = \$1.85$$
$$\$4.83/1.15^6 = \$2.09$$
$$\$5.12/1.15^7 = \$1.92$$
$$\$5.43/1.15^8 = \$1.78$$
and so on

Total present value $34.00

As we learned, in the context of the constant growth model, dividends and price per share can be expected to grow at identical constant rates. In the two-stage model, however, the growth rates in dividends and market price will differ until we reach the end of the growth horizon, when the growth in the dividend is expected to revert to that of an average share. In the period of the growth horizon, the growth rate in the stock price will fall between the initial expected growth in the dividend and the growth rate of an average share. The longer the period of the growth horizon, the closer will be the growth rate in the stock price relative to the initial growth rate in the dividend.

To illustrate this point, we can use Equation (16–4) to calculate the present value of the expected dividend stream for the stock in the above example, as we move forward in time through the growth horizon. To compute each future market price for the stock, we compute the present value of the remaining dividends at the assumed capitalization rate of 15 percent.

Beginning of Year	Present Value of Remaining Dividends	Growth Rate in Present Value
1	$34.00	—
2	$37.79	11.15%
3	$41.77	10.53%
4	$45.85	9.77%
5	$49.87	8.76%
6	$53.61	7.52%
7	$56.86	6.05%
8	$60.27	6.00%

The general pattern of expected growth in market price and dividends per share is given in Figure 16–3. The solid lines depict the relative growth pattern for a stock that is initially expected to grow at a relatively fast rate for a relatively long period. The broken lines depict the pattern for a stock that is initially expected to grow at a below average rate for a relatively short period.

Even when the growth rate in expected dividends is not constant through time, it will still be the case that we can break the expected return into two parts: (a) the ratio of the next expected dividend to current market price and (b) the expected growth in the market price during the year. For example, in the case of the stock considered above, at the beginning of year 1

Expected return = Year-end dividend/Beginning price + Growth in price
15%   = $1.30/$34.00   +   11.5%

Equation (16–4) and Figures 16–1 and 16–2 relate to a two-stage valuation model. When desirable, you can also employ three-stage models and beyond. These models are computationally easy to use, are readily available, and are widely employed in computer software packages.

PRICE-EARNINGS RATIOS

An indicator widely followed by investors in common stocks is the ratio of the current market price per share to the current earnings per share. The price-earnings ratio is computed on the basis of earnings available for distribution to common stockholders, that is, after deducting operating expenses, depreciation, taxes, and interest from net revenue.

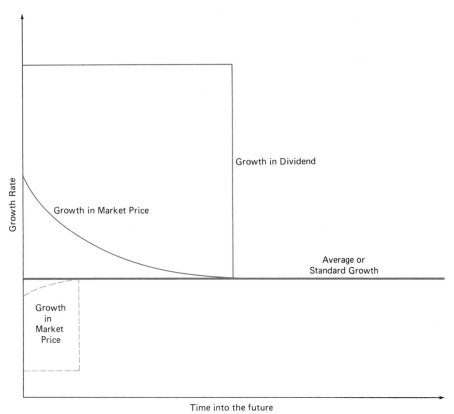

Figure 16-3 Relative Growth Rates in Dividends and Market Price

What Determines the Level of the Price-Earnings Ratio?

In the context of a two-stage growth valuation model, we can say that the current price-earnings ratio becomes larger, (a) the smaller is the stock's expected rate of return, $E(r)$, and (b) the larger is the stock's initial expected rate of growth, $E(G)$. It is also true that the price-earnings ratio becomes larger as the growth horizon becomes longer, when $E(G) > E(g)$, and the growth horizon becomes shorter, when $E(G) < E(g)$.

Given the expected stream of earnings and dividends, the lower the expected return required from the investment, the more investors will be willing to pay for the investment in terms of the current market price for the stock. Thus, holding other things constant, the lower the expected return, the greater the ratio of the current price to the current level of earnings per share.

If future earnings and dividends are expected to be larger than their current levels, the present value of these future dividends, the current market price, will also be large relative to the current dividend and earnings per share. Thus, given

Using a Three-Stage Model

The sun slipped slowly behind the southern leg, and Dan Coggin was cast in the shadow of the Gateway Arch. The other end of the shadow was about thirty feet away, and sunlight would be at least five minutes in returning to the park bench situated on the eastern side of the Mississippi River.

Dan felt the temperature drop perceptibly. It was early spring, warm for the season but still a bit chilly. Dan briefly considered moving, but rejected the thought. He was tired, had finished a long day, and he needed to relax awhile.

Dan had walked the three blocks to the park from Centerre Trust Company in St. Louis, where he works as the head of the quantitative analysis department of the investment division. Dan has been at Centerre for some time now. Through the years he has watched the firm progressively become more quantitative and systematic in its stock selection.

There's no question about when the move began. It started when Jim Wright was hired as research director in 1979. Before Jim's arrival, the analysts at Centerre pretty much picked stock subjectively. After hearing a story about some stock, they might decide that it would be a good idea to put some of it in the portfolio, and in it would go. One of the first things Jim decided to do was to develop a systematic approach for ranking stocks for possible purchase. Dan worked with Jim in getting the system running and in selling its merits to the rest of the firm.

The system they developed for valuing stocks is based on a dividend discount model (DDM) that forecasts dividend growth in three stages or phases. The first is called the *growth phase*. In this initial phase the firm behind the stock is introducing new products, gaining market share, and growing off a relatively small capital base. Eventually, however, the rate of product introduction begins to subside, the firm begins to stabilize its market share, and the rate of growth in earnings and dividends begins to slow. When this begins to happen, the stock moves into what is called the *transitional phase*. In the transitional phase the rate of growth in dividend income declines in a linear fashion to the basic level of growth for the general economy. When the growth rate actually reaches the basic level, the stock is then said to be in the *maturity phase* of its growth profile. The assumed growth profile for a given company might look like the accompanying figure.

Thus, in using the model, the analyst must estimate (a) the initial growth rate for the growth phase, (b) the length of the growth phase, and (c) the length of the transitional phase. The growth rate for the maturity phase is the same for all companies and isn't changed very often.

The length of the phases is determined by the individual analyst, on the basis of fundamental security analysis. Centerre has six security analysts, each assigned to follow about fifty stocks in a few industries. Firms like Apple Computer and Wang Labs might be considered to be rather early in their growth phase, whereas firms like Boise Cascade and Weyerhaeuser might be considered more transitional. The length of the growth phase does vary from

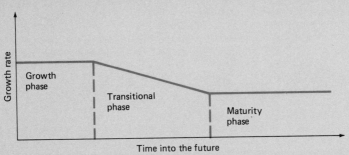

Growth Profile for the Three-Phase Model

stock to stock, but it averages about five or six years. The transitional phase might be ten years for a stock with low estimated growth in the growth phase to twenty years for a stock with high estimated growth in the growth phase.

The expected rate of growth in the growth phase is estimated on the basis of a standardized procedure. The analysts at Centeree use a variation of a standard security analytic model called the Du Pont Model. They fill in formalized input sheets with their forecasts of net sales, total assets, and pretax profits, and these, as well as other estimates, are funneled through the model to obtain an estimate of the net rate of return on equity capital. This net rate of return is then multiplied by an estimate of the fraction of earnings per share retained in the firm each year to come up with the final estimated rate of growth for the growth phase. In coming up with their estimates for the inputs to the model, Centerre's analysts examine the nature of the firm's product line, its competition, and the firm's history.

Dan feels that it is the quality control of the inputs to the model that differentiates

Centerre's success with dividend discounting from that of other investment management firms. In addition to using the Du Pont Model on a formal basis, the analysts' inputs are checked for consistency and accuracy of assumptions. They must also justify any changes made in these inputs in terms of changes in the fundamental outlook for the company. Other firms may use DDMs, but their analysts frequently "game" them and inevitably destroy their effectiveness. For example, if the analyst thinks for some reason that IBM is a good buy, he or she may simply increase the initial expected growth rate to 40 percent so that it comes out well under the DDM. In Dan's opinion, this is deadly. If you're going to use a DDM, you've got to use it systematically, with quality control, and not merely pay lip service to it.

Centerre's success in using the three-phase model is evident in the numbers provided in the accompanying table. In the table, each number represents the total rate of return on an equally weighted portfolio of common stocks. The returns include both dividends and capital gains,

OUT ON THE STREET

Results of Stock Selection Based on the Three-Phase Model

Quintile	1979	1980	1981	Year 1982	1983	1984	1985
1	35.07%	41.21%	12.12%	19.12%	34.18%	15.26%	38.91%
2	25.92%	29.19%	10.89%	12.81%	21.27%	5.50%	32.22%
3	18.49%	27.41%	1.25%	26.72%	25.00%	6.03%	35.83%
4	17.55%	38.43%	−5.59%	28.41%	24.55%	−4.20%	29.29%
5	20.06%	26.44%	−8.51%	35.54%	14.35%	−7.84%	23.43%
250 stocks	23.21%	31.86%	1.41%	24.53%	24.10%	3.27%	33.80%
S&P 500 Index	18.57%	32.55%	−4.97%	21.61%	22.54%	6.12%	31.59%

but do not incorporate taxes or transactions costs.

Starting with a population of roughly 250 large capitalization firms that Centerre believes to be of high quality and good growth potential, the analysts at Centerre ranked the firms on the basis of their betas, as estimated using historical returns over the five-year period previous to each individual month. The firms were then grouped by beta into five quintiles.

Then the expected rate of return was computed on each stock using the three-phase DDM and the market price of the stock at the beginning of the month. The expected return is computed as the rate that will discount the expected flow of dividends to a present value equal to the current market price for the stock. The stocks in each beta quintile were then ranked by expected rate of return and then grouped into expected return quintiles. The stocks in the highest expected return quintile from each beta grouping were assembled into an equally weighted portfolio. The same thing was done for the next highest quintile and so

on down to the lowest quintile. Thus, quintile 1 in the table is an equally weighted portfolio of the 20 percent of the stocks with the highest expected returns from each of the beta quintiles. Quintile 2 contains the 20 percent of the stocks with the next highest expected return and so on through quintile 5.

By following this procedure, we can expect that at the beginning of each month, each of the portfolios has approximately the same beta factor. Some firms adjust the percentages in each quintile, allowing fewer stocks in quintiles 1, 2, 4, and 5 and more in 3. This reflects a belief that most stocks are fairly valued by the market, with any under or over valuation falling in the extreme quintiles.

In any case, Centerre followed strict quintile ranking. The procedure of ranking into quintiles was repeated on the first business day of each month from January 1979 through December 1985.

It should be stressed that each portfolio was actually constructed at the time of the beginning of the first business day of each month using estimates of the initial growth rate, the length of the growth phase, and the length of the transition phase for each company. At the beginning of the next month the portfolios were rebalanced on the basis of new estimates turned in by the analysts. Thus, it actually took six years to produce the numbers in the table.

The ratios of ending to beginning values of an investment made in each quintile for the six-year period are given in the accompanying table.

Wealth Accumulation Based on the Three-Phase Model

Quintile	*Ratio Ending to Beginning Investment Value*
1	4.47
2	2.44
3	2.49
4	2.04
5	1.45
250 stocks	2.52
S&P 500 Index	2.10

The results are impressive. Even though it initially started as an experiment with no actual commitment of invested funds, the success of the strategy over the years attracted the attention of Centerre's portfolio managers. These managers increasingly began to rely on the dividend discount model. By 1984, most of the managers were heavily into the model,

and Centerre had constructed the P1 Fund, which was an actual equally weighted fund invested exactly according to the rules of the strategy.

It is interesting to consider the 1982 experience. In this year performance was *perversely* related to the quintile rankings. This can be attributed to a significant error in the general economic forecast made by Centerre for the year. At the beginning of the year, it was looking for a resurgence in the rate of inflation that never materialized. Normally errors made in a macroeconomic forecast tend to have a uniform effect on different stocks. Inflation, however, has a different impact on different companies. Oil and energy stocks, for example, are highly sensitive to inflation. Consequently, the error in the inflation forecast led the model to favor stocks that would be expected to respond well to increased inflation. When inflation failed to increase, these stocks failed to respond. By the end of the year, however, this error had been corrected.

Dan is well aware of the fact that the success of a DDM depends crucially on the ability of analysts to predict *relative* growth rates among companies. He is also well aware of the literature (discussed in Chapter 17) that purports that the pattern of earnings changes for companies as a random walk. Dan feels that the demonstrated success of properly formulated DDMs makes that research irrelevant to the practice of stock selection.

The sun begins to flash from the other side of the southern leg. It feels promisingly warm. Summer will soon be here.

the *length* of the period of abnormal growth expected by the market, the larger the abnormal *growth rate* expected, the larger will be future dividends (and their present value, the market price) relative to the current levels of dividends and earnings per share.

If the market expects the initial growth rate to be above average, the longer this growth rate is expected to persist, the larger will be future dividends (and their present value, the market price) relative to current earnings per share. Similarly, if the initial growth rate is expected to be below average, the smaller will be the level of future dividends relative to those of an average stock, and the smaller will be the price-earnings ratio relative to that of an average stock.

Changes That Can Be Expected in the Price-Earnings Ratio over Time

If both the growth of earnings and dividends and the stock's expected rate of return are expected to remain constant over time, the price-earnings ratio should also be expected to remain constant. If, instead, the growth rate is expected to change in a series of stages, the price-earnings ratio can be expected to change as time goes by, eventually ending up at the level of the price-earnings ratio for an average (growth rate) stock in the same risk class.

The pattern of change that can be expected in the case of a two-stage growth stock is presented in Figure 16–4. In the figure the price-earnings ratio is plotted

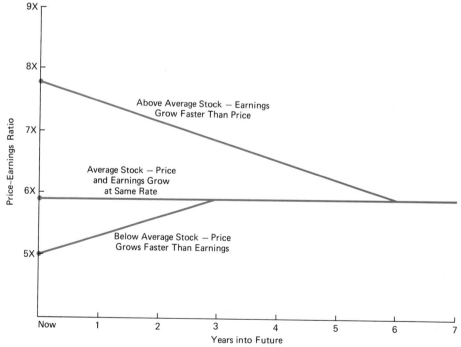

Figure 16-4 Expected Future Price-Earnings Ratios for Three Stocks

on the vertical axis and time into the future on the horizontal axis. The expected price-earnings ratios for three firms are plotted. In the case of the upper curve, the initial expected rate of growth is presumed to be 12 percent for six years. In the case of the stock represented by the lower curve, it is presumed to be 0 percent for three years. The horizontal line represents a stock that is expected to grow perpetually at the average rate, which is presumed to be 6 percent. For all three stocks, we have also presumed that 50 percent of earnings is paid out as dividends, and the expected rate of return is expected to be constant at 15 percent.

To obtain the curves in the figure, we begin with an initial value for the dividend, determine its future values based on the assumed growth rates, and double each value to obtain the corresponding future values for earnings per share. Then we determine the future values for the stock price using Equation (16–4). It is then easy to find the future values for the price-earnings ratios by dividing the future stock prices by the future earnings per share in each year.

Note that we can expect the price-earnings ratio to decline for the stock with abnormally high initial growth and for its abnormally low growth counterpart. The change in the price-earnings ratio isn't induced by changes that are occurring in investor expectations but merely by the evolution of each stock toward the status of that of an average share as time passes.

Summary

The market value of any corporate security must be based on the expected flow of cash from the firm to the investor. In the case of common stock, this transfer is always in the form of dividends. Thus, the market value of a common stock is based on the discounted value of expected dividends throughout the life of the firm.

A multistage growth model provides a convenient way to model the flow of future dividends. The model makes the assumption that the dividend will grow at above or below normal rates for assumed periods and then revert to the rate of growth of an average share after this growth horizon. Obviously, in using the model, you have to make a decision concerning the length of the growth horizon. For how long a period into the future do you want to forecast an above or below average rate of growth for the stock? We address this question in Chapter 17.

QUESTIONS AND PROBLEMS

1. Why would an investor, concerned primarily with capital gains, estimate a stock's current market price on the basis of expected future dividends?

2. Explain how the earnings and dividends approaches to stock valuation are equivalent.

3. Assume a stock has a current market price of $26.25 and is expected to grow at a perpetually constant rate of 5 percent. Current dividend is $1. What is the capitalization rate that justifies this price? State any necessary assumptions.

4. Explain what is meant by growth horizon in terms of the two-stage growth model.

5. In years 1 through n, a dividend is expected to grow to an annual rate of G. In years $n + 1$ and beyond, the dividends are expected to grow at an annual rate of g. The current dividend is D_0. In terms of D_0, $E(G)$, $E(g)$, and n, what is the expression for the expected dividend in year $n + 2$, (or $E(D_n + 2)$)?

6. What could cause a higher than average ratio of current stock value to current dividend, V_0/D_0? Will this ratio for a given stock persist as a permanent characteristic of that stock?

7. Consider the price-earnings ratio where the earnings are known and invariant (constant for the period under consideration) and the numerator, V_0, depends on the extent to which higher or lower future growth is discounted into the current price of the stock. What market forces can cause changes in the current market price of the stock?

BIBLIOGRAPHY

BAYLIS, R., and S. BHIRUD, "Growth Stock Analysis: A New Approach," *Financial Analysts Journal* (July–August 1973).

BEAVER, W., and D. MORSE, "What Determines Price-Earnings Ratios," *Financial Analysts Journal* (July–August 1978).

BERNSTEIN, P., "Growth Companies vs. Growth Stocks," *Harvard Business Review* (September–October 1956).

BIERMAN, H., D. DOWNES, and J. HASS, "Closed Form Price Models," *Journal of Financial and Quantitative Analysis* (June 1972).

BING, R., "Survey of Practitioners' Stock Evaluation Methods," *Financial Analysts Journal* (May–June 1971).

GOOD, W., "Valuation of Quality-Growth Stocks," *Financial Analysts Journal* (September–October 1972).

HOLT, C., "Influence of Growth Duration on Share Prices," *Journal of Finance* (September 1962).

KEENAN, M., "Models of Equity Valuation: The Great Serm Bubble," *Journal of Finance* (May 1970).

MALKIEL, B., "Equity Yields, Growth, and the Structure of Share Prices," *American Economic Review* (September 1970).

WILLIAMS, J., *The Theory of Investment Value*. Cambridge, Mass.: Harvard University Press, 1938.

17 ISSUES IN ESTIMATING FUTURE EARNINGS AND DIVIDENDS

Introduction

Unlike bond investments, which have payments that are fixed in time and magnitude, the dividends from stocks may become larger or smaller as time goes by. One of the jobs of the security analyst is to estimate the propensity for growth or decline in the expected dividend stream. In doing their jobs, analysts must come to grips with an important issue: How far into the future can the relative growth in earnings and dividends be forecast with any reasonable degree of accuracy? Can a prudent analyst really say that a given stock is going to grow at a faster or slower than average rate over the next decade or so? How much confidence can we place in such forecasts? How do the answers to these questions affect the way we value stocks or the development of our investment strategy? In this chapter we will begin seeking the answers to these questions.

PAYING IN ADVANCE FOR GROWTH

The market's expectations for the future relative rates of growth in earnings and dividends per share are discounted into current market prices per share. If investors think a stock's dividends are going to grow at a faster than average rate for a prolonged period of time, they will bid up the current price of the stock relative to the *current* level of dividends per share. The ratio of the stock's current market price to its current dividend per share will be greater than that for an average stock.

Thinking in terms of Equation (16–4), suppose we have two stocks with the same expected or required rate of return, $E(r)$. One of the stocks is expected to grow indefinitely at the average rate, $E(g)$, and the second stock is expected to grow at a rate, $E(G)$, that is higher than average over some growth horizon, n. In this case, if the initial dividend is the same for both stocks, the present value of the dividend stream for the second stock will be greater than that of the first. The ratio of the present value to its current dividend will also be greater. It is also true that if you buy the stock at a price equal to this higher present value, the higher than average expected growth must materialize in order for you to earn your minimum required rate of return, $E(r)$, on the investment. If it turns out that, instead, the stock grows at the average rate, the rate of return earned will be less than the minimum requirement.

In this sense you are *paying in advance* for the higher than average rate of growth that is expected to occur. The stock must achieve this greater than average level of performance just to provide you with a reasonable rate of return. If the stock's performance, in terms of dividend growth, turns out to be merely average, its rate of return to you as an investor is likely to be below average. This is true because the dividends you receive will be small relative to the price you paid, and because investors are likely to revise downward their expectations for future growth in the dividend stream, resulting in possible capital losses for your shares.

To illustrate the principle of paying in advance for growth, and the market's willingness to discount liberal expectations of future growth into current share prices, let's go back in time to the year 1960 and take a look at two stocks, Florida Power and Light and New England Electric System. Both stocks are regulated electric utilities and have similar risk characteristics, so they are likely to have similar expected or required rates of return. Their stock price histories are graphed in Figure 17–1. Each bar in the figure represents the range between the high and the low price for the month. The records for each company, in terms of earnings and dividends per share, are given in the accompanying table.

Year	Florida Power and Light Earnings	Dividends	New England Electric System Earnings	Dividends
1953	.77	.40	1.18	.90
1954	.88	.44	1.16	.90
1955	1.03	.50	1.24	.90
1956	1.30	.61	1.23	1.00
1957	1.49	.66	1.19	1.00
1958	1.76	.76	1.26	1.00
1959	1.93	.87	1.31	1.02
1960	2.11	.97	1.35	1.08
Growth Rate (1953-1960)	15%	13%	2%	3%

Florida Power & Light Company
Stock price

New England Electric System
Stock price

Figure 17-1 Stock Price History of Florida Power and Light and New England Electric System

SOURCE: *Moody's Handbook of Widely Held Common Stocks*, 3rd ed. (Moody's Investor's Services, Inc., 1969), pp. 214 and 388.

CHAPTER 17   Issues in Estimating Future Earnings and Dividends   417

Note that Florida Power and Light was distributing a smaller fraction of its earnings as dividends. The remaining earnings were retained and reinvested in the firm to provide a base for larger future earnings and dividends. This may account for the superior record of Florida Power and Light in terms of earnings and dividend growth through the year 1960.

Recognizing the greater potential for future growth, the market bid the current market price of Florida Power and Light up, relative to its current dividend. In 1960, the price reached $68 per share, which was approximately seventy times the current dividend. The market price of New England Electric System was as low as $20 per share in 1960, a multiple of only nineteen times its current dividend.

If we make assumptions about the expected rate of growth for an average or standard share and the market's expected or required rate of return for these two stocks, we can determine the future growth performance that will justify these prices.

The late 1950s was a period of little or no inflation. Extrapolating the rates of growth in earnings and dividends per share for the aggregate market indices that were occurring then into the future, a conservative estimate for the rate of growth in dividends for an average stock might be 2 percent.

In 1960, the yield to maturity on AAA public utility bonds was only 4.6 percent. The average rate of return to the market in general, over the period 1926 through 1960, was approximately 9 percent. We will take 8 percent as a reasonable estimate of the minimal required expected return for an investment in these two relatively low-risk common stocks. If we substitute into Equation (16–4) 8 percent for $E(r)$, 2 percent for $E(g)$, and $20 and $48 for the market prices of New England Electric and Florida Power and Light, respectively, we can find values for $E(G)$ and n that will make the present value of the future dividend stream equal to the two stock prices.

For example, in the case of Florida Power and Light, if you were to assume that the dividend was going to grow at a rate of 12 percent over the next twenty-five years, through 1985, the current market price for the stock could be justified. If the dividend were to grow at that rate, and you paid $48 for the stock, you would indeed get an 8 percent rate of return on your investment. If the rate of growth turned out to be more modest, your rate of return would also be more modest. Thus, the growth profile in Figure 17–2 would produce an 8 percent rate of return for an investor in the stock. Different combinations of $E(G)$ and n would also suffice. For example, a 20 percent rate of growth for ten years would also generate 8 percent.

The picture for New England Electric is much different. The growth rate in dividends need only be slightly greater than the assumed average rate of 2 percent to justify the current price. For example, if the dividend were to grow at 3 percent for twenty-five years, the rate of return produced for investors in the stock would be greater than 8 percent. Thus, the price is justified with the relatively modest growth profile in Figure 17–3.

As things turned out, Florida Power and Light did grow at a faster rate than New England Electric during the next twenty-five years. However, the differ-

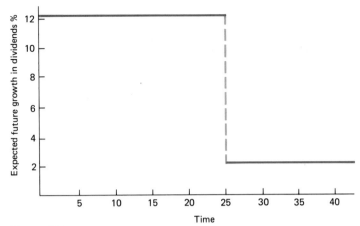

Figure 17-2 Future Growth Required to Produce an 8% Return for Florida Power and Light

ence wasn't nearly as great as would be implied by their relative stock prices in 1960. The earnings per share of Florida Power grew at approximately a 7 percent annually compounded rate, whereas the earnings of New England Electric grew at a 6 percent rate.

The cases of New England Electric and Florida Power and Light illustrate the point that the market has at times exhibited a willingness to discount growth rates in dividends that are *much* different from average, for *prolonged* periods of time, into the current prices for common shares. However, it can be argued, as we do below, that the attitude of professional security analysts toward growth, and their willingness to capitalize expected future growth into current stock prices, have undergone evolutionary changes over time.

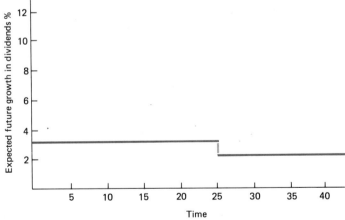

Figure 17-3 Future Growth Required to Produce an 8% Return for New England Electric System

OUT ON THE STREET

In First Place

It was well beyond time to leave for work, but going through the article one more time seemed irresistible. After all, it's not every day that you get favorable press in the *New York Post Magazine.* The *Post* had surveyed twenty professional security analysts, asking them which industries would outperform the market over the next six- to twelve-month period. Elaine Garzarelli was one of those analysts. As it turned out, the industries that she selected produced a 25 percent return for the period in the face of a 9 percent return for the market as a whole.

Elaine is the director of sector analysis at Shearson-Lehman Brothers in New York City. While working on her Ph.D. at New York University, she became interested in building econometric models to forecast industry earnings. Over the last ten years she progressively refined her techniques, steadily increasing the accuracy of her projections. At this point, Elaine can document the fact that her quantitative, econometric-based projections are considerably more accurate than the more subjective estimates of earnings per share made by the typical security analyst. For one thing, analysts usually go directly to the company and ask management what it thinks about the future prospects for the firm. These opinions are usually biased upward. Analysts can also become emotionally committed or opposed to a firm or industry, adding a further element of bias to their forecasts. Elaine's approach is more objective. She

forecasts earnings per share by industry for a period of up to twelve to eighteen months into the future. The reliability of forecasts beyond this point depends on your confidence in your general economic outlook, and beyond two to three years your confidence usually isn't very good.

Elaine makes forecasts for sixty industries as defined by Standard and Poor's. The forecast for each industry is based on a set of approximately fourteen statistical models. One of the models, for example, might be the product of a correlation, or regression, analysis where she is trying to explain the movement in sales for the steel industry over the last fifteen years. She might be correlating percentage changes in steel sales with factors like percentage changes in nonresidential construction, domestic auto sales, and producer durable equipment spending.

The correlation analysis reveals the relationship between changes in each of these variables, or factors, and changes in steel industry sales. Elaine has found that she can explain up to 90 percent of the changes in steel sales on the basis of the changes in her factors. Having identified the relationship, if she herself supplies or is given forecasts for each of the determining factors, she can calculate a forecast for future steel sales.

Similar relationships are modeled for other elements of the income statement, like labor and fixed costs. The models provide estimates of each element of the income statement, and after all costs have been subtracted from revenue, Elaine has a forecast of earnings in the steel industry. Elaine revises her models annually to account for any changes that may occur between the factors and the income statement element she is trying to forecast. She has found that, although the nature of the relationships may change, the identity of the factors themselves is relatively stable. For example the prime interest rate was an important factor in explaining changes in auto sales back in 1974, when it was 8 percent, and it still was an important factor in 1979, when she was using an 18 percent prime.

The models tell her the relationship between the factors and the various elements of the income statement for the industry. However, to implement each model, she needs forecasts of the future values of the factors themselves. She begins with the outlook for the general economy, moving then to an element like consumer durables, and gradually filtering down to the factors required for the forecast. In part, she relies on her own training as an economist, but she also looks to Sherson's economists and published surveys, such as for expected capital spending, from McGraw-Hill and the Commerce Department.

Elaine's basic, final product is a booklet entitled "Sector Analysis," published by Shearson and released to its clients once each month. In the booklet, Elaine classifies the sixty different industries into three categories: (a) those that will outperform the market in the next six to twelve months, (b) those that will move with the market, and (c) those that will underperform. In order to be placed in the

"outperform" classification, an industry must meet two qualifications. First, Elaine's forecast for the industry's earnings growth must exceed that which she is forecasting for the earnings growth for the Standard and Poor's 500 Stock Index. Second, the industry's average price-earnings ratio must be 5 percent under its normal relationship to the price-earnings ratio for the 500 Index. Meeting both above average prospects and undervaluation, the industry gets on the outperformance list.

In each of the last eight years, Elaine's forecasts have proved to be more accurate than Zack's Consensus published out of Chicago. Zack surveys eighty brokerage firms to get individual company forecasts. The individual company forecasts are then aggregated by industry, as defined by Standard and Poor's.

The accuracy of Elaine's forecasts is paying off. Recently *Institutional Investor* magazine surveyed approximately 3000 institutional clients asking them to vote on which professional analyst had given them the most reliable information over the last year. Based on the survey, the top analysts were named to the magazine's "All America Team." Elaine was not only named to this team, she placed first in the balloting.

Enough. Time is money. Looking through the window of her Greenwich Village apartment, she can see the window of her office at 2 World Trade Center. With luck, in five minutes she would be back in the thick of things.

GROWTH AND STOCK VALUATION:
A HISTORICAL PERSPECTIVE

In the early part of this century, security analysts were concerned with estimating the value of a company's earnings per share under "normalized" conditions. They tried to make adjustments in earnings numbers to account for differences in accounting techniques among companies, and they tried to allow for the presence of unusual or extraordinary conditions that might make the current number different from what might be expected in a "normal" year. Present-day analysts do this as well, but they also tend to spend a great deal of time trying to estimate the growth potential for different stocks.

In contrast, early financial analysts regarded growth as a "speculative," as opposed to an "investment," consideration in security valuation. Prudent analysts estimated as carefully as possible the level of current, normal earnings, and then they computed the intrinsic value of the stock through the product of earnings and a value-earnings multiple that was based, for the most part, on the quality of the issue. Quality, it should be said, had little or nothing to do with the potential for growth. This practice is consistent with the hypothesis that expected growth is completely unpredictable, that the growth profile for all stocks should be identical with $n = 0$. No stock could be predicted to grow at a below or above average rate for any period of time into the future.

This philosophy was challenged with the publication of a book in 1926 by Edgar Lawrence Smith entitled *Common Stocks as Long Term Investments*. Smith presented some numbers that showed the historical rates of return on common stock investments had been much greater than returns to bond investments. The differential could be argued to be too large to be attributable to the greater relative risk of common stocks. Instead, Smith argued, it was due to an error being made in stock valuation. Stocks were clearly different from bonds in that the income from a stock can be expected to grow. The analysts of the time were missing half the picture. Much of their effort should have been spent determining which stocks had the greatest potential for growth. These stocks should be assessed at greater intrinsic values.

Smith's book gained wide attention, and the race was on to find "growth stocks." Growth stock prices were bid up to extremely large multiples of current income. The valuation of common stocks had entered a new era, and appropriately enough the new valuation philosophy was called the "New Era Theory." The New Era Theory ended abruptly with the great stock market crash of October 1929.

In the midst of the Great Depression, in 1934, Benjamin Graham and David Dodd published a book, *Security Analysis*. In their book they attacked the New Era Theory and growth stock valuation. They argued for a return to former practice and continued to maintain their position in later years:

> . . . the analyst's philosophy must still compel him to base his investment
> valuation on an assumed earning power no larger than the company has

already achieved in some year of normal business. Investment values can be related only to demonstrated performance.[1]

Graham and Dodd felt that future growth was largely, if not completely, unpredictable. Stock valuation could be founded only on *demonstrated,* as opposed to *anticipated,* earning power. They were particularly opposed to estimating future earnings by extrapolating from historical trends: "Value based on a satisfactory trend must be wholly arbitrary and hence speculative, and hence inevitably subject to exaggeration and later collapse."[2]

But they also regarded as undependable estimates of relative future growth that were based on factors other than simple trend, such as the relative amount of earnings retained as dividends (as in New England Electric and Florida Power and Light).

> *if a business paid out only a small part of its earnings in dividends, the value of its stock should increase over a period of years; but it is by no means so certain that this increase will compensate the stockholders for the dividends withheld from them. An inductive study would undoubtedly show that the earning power of corporations does not in general expand proportionately with increases in accumulated surplus.* Assuming that the reported earnings were actually available for distribution, *then stockholders would certainly fare better in dollars and cents if they drew out practically all these earnings in dividends.*[3]

In the years after the publication of Graham and Dodd's book, analysts seemed to discard the emphasis on factoring growth into stock valuation. *Security Analysis* was a highly successful text and went through many editions. However, it began to fall out of favor in the late 1950s as the previously questioned theory purporting growth as a significant factor in the valuation of common stocks was dusted off and revived. Once again a paper was published by Fisher and Lorie (1964) showing that common stocks had far outstripped bonds in producing high rates of return. Sophisticated stock valuation models were developed by Myron Gordon (1962) and others in which future growth in earnings and dividends played a central role.

Coincident with these developments, however, the work of I. M. D. Little was published supporting the view that growth in earnings per share for the largest manufacturing firms in the United Kingdom was random and therefore

[1]Graham, Dodd, and Tatham (1951, pp. 422–423).

[2]Graham and Dodd (1934, p. 314).

[3]Graham and Dodd (1934, p. 330). The inductive study suggested by Graham and Dodd was actually conducted thirty-six years later by Baumol, Heim, Malkiel, and Quandt (1970). In this study the authors concluded:

> *Ploughback does generally appear to yield a positive return. . . . Nevertheless, as we have seen, the rate of return to firms relying on ploughback for their new investment is typically uncomfortably small. . . . All this raises serious questions about the workings of the economy and the efficiency of the investment process. Is it really true that earnings retention serves the interests of the stockholder? (pp. 354–355.)*

unpredictable. This work would later lead to further studies in the United States that were largely consistent with this point of view.

Thus, we have two opposing views. One says that relative growth rates between stocks are largely predictable. If this is true, stocks that are expected to grow at faster than average rates for prolonged periods of time should be assigned higher prices by the market. The other says that relative growth rates are largely unpredictable. If this is true, differences in ratios of market price to current normalized earnings per share should be due only to differences in risk. As time has gone by, those who value stocks in the market seem to have favored one view and then the other. If the nature of the economy is reasonably stable over time, it is likely that only one view is correct. In the sections that follow we examine the evidence relating to the issue and the implications for investment strategy.

THE ACCURACY OF PREDICTIONS OF GROWTH IN EARNINGS AND DIVIDENDS

Is Past Growth a Reliable Guide to Future Growth?

In 1962 a British professor named I. M. D. Little published the results of a study investigating the relationship between past and future rates of growth in earnings per share for British companies. Alluding to the resurgence of analysts' emphasis on growth in stock valuation that had occurred at the end of the 1950s, Little stated

My impression is that many stockbrokers, financial journalists, economists, and investors believe that past growth behavior is some sort of guide to future growth. This belief seems to have developed especially in the last few years.[4]

To test whether past growth was indeed a guide to future growth, Little related the rate of growth in earnings per share for a given period to the rate of growth in a subsequent period, as in Figure 17–4. Each observation in the figure represents a particular firm. The firm's rate of growth in one period is plotted on the horizontal axis, and its rate of growth in the next period is plotted vertically.

If growth rates were perfectly stable, replicating themselves from one period to the next, the points would plot as a 45-degree line emanating from the origin. Instead, in this example, the points plot as a scatter. The broken line of best fit has a slightly positive slope, indicating that a relatively high rate of growth in the first period would lead you to believe that the same firm has a better than even chance of growing at an above average rate in the second period. The goodness of fit about the line, or the correlation coefficient, provides an indica-

[4]I. M. D. Little (1962, p. 391).

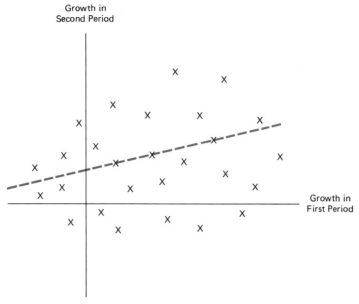

Figure 17-4 Possible Relationship Between Past and Future Growth

tion of the accuracy of a prediction of growth in the second period, based on a knowledge of growth in the first period. In this particular case, the correlation coefficient is rather low, so a prediction of future growth, based on growth in the first period, would not be very reliable.

Little ran a number of correlations of this type covering the decade of the 1950s. The correlations can be classified by the industry of the firms in the study and by the number of years in the first and second periods over which growth is measured. To illustrate the nature of the results, consider the group of correlation studies in which four years are included in both the first and second periods. A total of eighteen such correlations are run covering different industries and different years. Out of the eighteen, nine correlations are significantly negative, five are significantly positive, and four are not significantly different from zero. The average value for the correlation is .02.

Similar results are found when Little changed the number of years included in the first and second periods. Overall, if there was any relationship to be found at all between past and future growth, it was slightly *negative*. The firms that grew at a faster than average rate in the first period had a *slight* propensity to grow at a slower than average rate in the second period. Little also found little relationship between the rate of retention of earnings in one period and growth in future periods. Company size also appeared to have little to do with future growth.

Little's findings were disturbing. They drew much attention, and soon others attempted to see if the same conditions were true in the United States. Surprisingly, these early studies came to similar conclusions. The firms that grew at a faster than average rate in one period seemed to have only an even chance of growing faster than average in the next period.

Researchers pressed on, applying increasingly sophisticated procedures to model the time series of earnings per share. By analyzing the behavior of quarterly earnings per share over some past period, they tried to develop models that could predict the future value of earnings per share based on its past behavior. Although the models were reasonably successful in predicting for short periods, forecasts of the growth in earnings became highly inaccurate when the time horizon was extended beyond a single year.

Thus, in making a forecast of the long-term rate of growth in earnings and dividends per share, analysts would be ill-advised to base their forecasts on the historical record. In spite of this survey, studies (Cragg and Malkiel [1968]) showed that in making their forecasts, analysts started with the historical record and then made subjective modifications. The actual forecasts of growth made by professional analysts tend to be positively correlated with the past growth records of the same companies.

Given that the amount of useful information in the past record of growth is meager, the growth forecasts of analysts are likely to be inaccurate, unless the subjective modifications they make are based on more useful information. In the next section we determine whether this is, in fact, true.

The Accuracy of Growth Forecasts Made by Professional Analysts

In making their forecasts, analysts look to other information in addition to that contained in the past time series of earnings per share numbers. This includes information pertaining to the firm's industry, the outlook for interest rates, inflation, the value of the dollar, and innovations in products and techniques of production. They attempt to assess how each of these factors will affect the firm's profitability. In addition, during the course of the year, management often makes announcements regarding the outlook for the year-end profits for the firm. This information, and more, are factored into the analyst's forecasts for growth in the firm's earnings per share.

One would expect that, given their access to all this additional information, the forecasts of professional analysts should be considerably more accurate than those based on a statistical analysis of the past time series of earnings alone. This question was addressed in a study by Collins and Hopwood (1980), in which the accuracy of earnings forecasts made by the Value Line Investment Survey and by statistical models were compared. The Value Line Investment Survey is a well-known investment service that provides information, analysis, and forecasts of earnings and other numbers for their subscribers.

Value Line's sample consists of fifty firms with quarterly earnings data available from 1951 through 1974. Annual forecasts were obtained for the period 1970 through 1974. Several statistical models were employed as a basis of comparison. To assess the relative accuracy of the forecasts, the absolute value of the percentage difference between the forecast and the actual value for the earnings number reported at the end of the year is computed. This value is averaged for all the forecasts made by Value Line and by the statistical models. To adjust for the influence of extreme errors (such as a forecast of $1 when actual earnings turn out to be $.01) Collins and Hopwood make an adjusted comparison where they assign a percentage error of 300 percent to all errors greater than this value.

The results are given in the accompanying table by the quarter during the year in which the forecast of earnings per share for the same year is made. The results indicate that Value Line's forecasts are more accurate than the statistical models, although they are nearly identical when extreme outliers are eliminated from consideration. Much of the superiority is apparently due to the inability of the models to respond to economic events such as strikes that will have a known effect on earnings per share. Note also that the accuracy of Value Line's predictions begins to fade rapidly as the length of the period of the forecast is extended to a year.

	Unadjusted Average Absolute % Error	*Adjusted Average Absolute % Error*
First quarter		
Value Line	34	32
Statistical models	60	32
Second quarter		
Value Line	28	26
Statistical models	47	25
Third quarter		
Value Line	22	18
Statistical models	33	20
Fourth quarter		
Value Line	10	10
Statistical models	18	11

Another study, by Crichfield, Dyckman, and Lakonishok (1978), covers a more representative group of analysts. They assess the relative accuracy of forecasts published in the *Earnings Forecaster,* a biweekly publication of Standard and Poor that collects the forecasts of more than fifty investment firms. In any given issue there may be up to ten forecasts for any given single firm. The study covers forecasts for forty-six firms during the 113 months of January 1967, through May 1976.

As a basis of comparison, they use forecasts from five models, such as a prediction that next year's earnings will be identical to this year's. In each case they compute the difference between the forecast and the actual earnings number reported at the end of the year. In the case of the analysts, their individual forecasts are averaged, and the accuracy of the average is assessed. The errors are then squared and summed by month, relative to the actual report month. For example, the errors for all the average forecasts of the analysts, or a particular model, made three months prior to the month in which the actual earnings were reported would be summed together. To assess the accuracy of the analysts relative to any given model, they compute a ratio of the sum of the model's squared errors to the sum of the analysts' squared errors. If the ratio is greater than 1, the analysts' forecasts are more accurate.

The analysts' forecasts *are* more accurate when compared to four of the five forecasting models. However, with the exception of the model forecasting that next year's earnings will be the same as this year's, none of these models allows for seasonal patterns in earnings. The fifth model allows for such patterns. Predictions under this model are based on the following rules. Remember that we are trying to predict earnings for the current year, *during* the current year.

1. Predictions made during April, May, and June: This year's earnings will be equal to four times the earnings reported for this year's first quarter plus or minus the error you would have made using such a rule last year.

2. Predictions made during July, August, and September: Same as for April, May, and June, except you use the second quarter's earnings.

3. Predictions made in October, November, December, and the following January (earnings aren't usually reported until February or March of the following year): Same as for April, May, or June, except you use the third quarter's earnings.

The ratios of the model's squared errors to the analysts' squared errors are as follows:

Month	Ratio
April	.62
May	.68
June	.75
July	.85
August	.81
September	1.10
October	1.22
November	1.44
December	1.55
January	1.67

Early in the year, the simple model actually makes better forecasts than the average of the analysts. Only later in the year, when announcements are being made by management about expectations for the earnings numbers, do the forecasts made by the analysts become relatively more accurate.

Overall, we seem to be able to draw the following conclusion. It is very difficult to forecast the future growth in earnings based on a statistical analysis of the past earnings series. The accuracy of these forecasts diminishes rapidly as the term of the forecast extends beyond one year. Professional forecasters can rely on a wealth of additional information besides the past series of earnings numbers. In spite of this, the accuracy of their forecasts seems to be only marginally better. It seems that forecasting the relative rate of growth for a particular stock beyond one year is hazardous at best.

If forecasts for the long-term relative rates of growth for earning and dividends are inherently inaccurate, then you should be hesitant to make them. You should also be hesitant to pay for them in advance if they are discounted into the current price of a stock.

The price-earnings ratio offers a rough indication of the extent to which a prolonged period of abnormal growth is discounted into the current market price of a stock. If the market price is large, relative to an estimate of current normalized earnings, then either of the following is likely to be true: (a) The market expects earnings in the future to be considerably larger than it is today, or (b) the market is capitalizing the income stream at an unusually low rate. If a case cannot be made that the stock is of unusually low risk, then the former, and not the latter, is likely to be true. If you buy the stock you are paying in advance for a prolonged above average record of growth. If this above average performance materializes, the rate of return on your investment will not be above average but only reasonable. If the stock, instead, grows at an average rate, the return on your investment will be less than sufficient.

Available evidence points to the conclusion that forecasts of prolonged above or below average growth are highly unreliable. If you believe that this is true, you should approach a stock with a large ratio of price to normalized earnings with great caution. The price may be based on an optimistic forecast for growth, and there is good reason to believe that this forecast is unreliable. On the other hand, you should be attracted to stocks with small ratios of price to normalized earnings. These stocks are priced on a pessimistic forecast that is also unreliable. If both stocks have approximately an equal chance of growing at an above or below normal rate in the long run, the high price-earnings stock is overpriced, and its low price-earnings counterpart is a bargain.

If (a) high (low) price-earnings ratios are attributable to optimistic (pessimistic) forecasts of growth rather than to low (high) risk, and if (b) these forecasts tend to be overly optimistic (pessimistic), this leads to the following prediction: *After adjusting for differences in risk, stocks with high (low) price-earnings ratios should earn lower (higher) than average rates of return.* If these stocks truly have no better than an even chance of performing at an above or below average level over the long term, the market will show a tendency to revise both its expectations and the market prices for the shares as the optimistic or pessimistic forecasts fail to materialize in the earnings numbers. In fact, as we will learn in Chapter 20, some available evidence supports this prediction.

Summary

The appropriate answer to the question of the extent to which future growth in earnings and dividends should play a role in stock valuation isn't completely clear, and the issue can be said to be controversial. The prevailing philosophy of financial analysts regarding the issue has vacillated. At times the attention of analysts has centered on estimating the current level of normalized earnings. Stocks with similar current earnings and similar risks were assigned similar values. At other times attention has shifted to the future and to the expected rate of growth in normalized earnings. Then the stock with the larger expected growth in normalized earnings would be assigned a significantly larger value.

What should be the role of expected future growth in the valuation of common stocks? The answer to this question depends on the length of the period over which we can say that one stock will grow at a faster rate than another with any degree of accuracy. Based on presently available evidence, it appears that this period is relatively short, not much more than a year for a representative pair of stocks. If you believe that this is true, *and* that the market is pricing stocks on the basis of a longer forecasting period, then you should be inclined to move against the market's forecasts and, other factors being equal, invest in stocks with relatively low price-earnings ratios.

QUESTIONS AND PROBLEMS

1. An investor considers a stock undervalued. He or she buys it at a price higher than can be justified by current average expected growth, g, because the investor expects a higher future growth rate, G. Several other investors do the same, bidding up the market price of the stock, V_0. What can happen if the market turns out to be wrong in its evaluation of the stock?

2. In the text, two regulated utilities companies are used in an illustration of the application of a two-stage growth model. If the expected rate of growth for an average or standard share, $E(g)$, and the market's expected or required rate of return for the stocks, $E(r)$, can be estimated, and the market prices of the stocks, V_0, are given, an abnormal rate of growth, $E(G)$, for a number of years, n, that will justify the stock prices can be found. Set up an equation that a computer could use to solve for $E(G)$ and n, given $E(g)$, $E(r)$, and V_0. Assume that the abnormal rate of growth occurs over the years 1 through n, and thereafter the stocks growth reverts to the market average rate, $E(g)$.

3. What is meant by normalized earnings?

4. In the 1960s there were two opposing views regarding stock valuation. State these and their basic implications.

5. What comparisons did Little make to test his theory of stock valuation, and what were his overall findings?

6. How accurate are models of the time series of earnings per share in predicting the future value of earnings per share based on past information?

7. What are some subjective modifications used in an analyst's forecasts (as opposed to a statistician's) of growth in earnings per share?

8. Collins and Hopwood (1980) compared the accuracy in earnings forecasts made by Value Line Investment Survey with that of forecasts made by statistical models. What were their findings?

9. Crichfield, Dyckman, and Lakonishok (1978) compared the accuracy of analysts' forecasts with those of five forecasting models. What were their findings?

10. Comment on the following statement: "Forecasting the relative rate of growth for a particular stock beyond one year is hazardous at best."

11. Would it be an appropriate investment strategy always to buy growth stocks that have high P/E ratios? If not, suggest an alternative strategy.

BIBLIOGRAPHY

BAUMOL, W., P. HEIM, B. MALKIEL, and R. QUANDT, "Earnings Retention, New Capital, and the Growth of the Firm," *Review of Economics and Statistics* (November 1970).

COLLINS, W., and W. HOPWOOD, "A Multivariate Analysis of Annual Earnings Forecasts Generated from Quarterly Forecasts of Financial Analysts and Univariate Time Series Models," *Journal of Accounting Research* (Autumn 1980).

CRAGG, D., and B. MALKIEL, "Consensus and Accuracy of the Predictions of the Growth of Corporate Earnings," *Journal of Finance* (March 1968).

CRICHFIELD, T., T. DYCKMAN, and J. LAKONISHOK, "An Evaluation of Security Analysts Forecasts," *Accounting Review* (July 1978).

FISHER, L., and J. LORIE, "Rates of Return on Investments in Common Stock," *Journal of Business* (Jan. 1964).

GORDON, M. *The Investment, Financing and Valuation of the Corporation.* Homewood, Ill.: Irwin, 1962.

GRAHAM, B., and D. DODD, *Security Analysis.* New York: McGraw-Hill, 1934.

GRAHAM, B., and D. DODD, with C. TATHAM, *Security Analysis.* New York: McGraw-Hill, 1951.

LITTLE, I. M. D., "Higgledy Piggledy Growth," *Institute of Statistics Oxford* (November 1962).

LINTER, J., and M. GLAUBER, "Higgledy Piggledy Growth in America," in *Modern Developments in Investment Management,* ed. J. Lorie and R. Brealey. New York: Praeger, 1972.

18 INVESTING INTERNATIONALLY

Introduction

Although the capital market in the United States is the largest and most developed in the world, it is only one among many active markets for securities and investments. As an intelligent investor, you would do well to consider the many opportunities available in the international markets. To the extent that the returns on these securities are less than perfectly correlated with domestic investments, diversifying internationally may reduce the overall risk of your portfolio. Moreover, some foreign markets may be less efficient at pricing securities to reflect their intrinsic values than is the domestic capital market. Given this, if you can access information about the foreign companies and the foreign economy as quickly and efficiently as the local participants in the foreign market, you may be able to use your investment skills to greater advantage in the relatively less efficient market. In addition, even if the foreign market is as efficient as the domestic market, if there are differentials between the two markets in the level of the risk-free rate of return or the structure of risk premiums, these differentials may open up arbitrage opportunities that combine investments in both markets.

Given these potential advantages to international investing, in this chapter we will examine the scope of the world capital market, the properties of the distributions of rates of return to the securities of the world market, and some theories of international asset pricing.

SCOPE AND COMPOSITION
OF THE WORLD CAPITAL MARKET

As a basis of comparison, let's begin with the relative composition of the investable wealth in the United States. The pie diagram in Figure 18–1 shows the division of investable wealth by type of investment. Although residential real estate is the most important form of investable wealth, the diagram points out the important role of common stock, and particularly common stock on the New York Stock Exchange, in the U.S. capital market. Note also the relative importance of government debt over that of private or corporate debt.

In Figure 18–2 we move to world investable wealth from the viewpoint of a U.S. investor. That is, foreign durable goods and foreign real estate are not included in the diagram. Also, the diagram includes only a limited number of countries to the United States, Europe, Japan, Hong Kong, Singapore, Canada, Mexico, Australia, and South Africa.

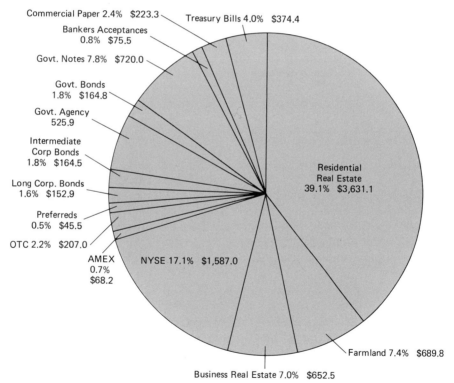

Figure 18-1 U.S. Investable Wealth Distribution

SOURCE: R. Ibbotson, L. Siegel, and K. Love, "World Wealth: Market Values and Returns," *Journal of Portfolio Management* (Fall 1985).

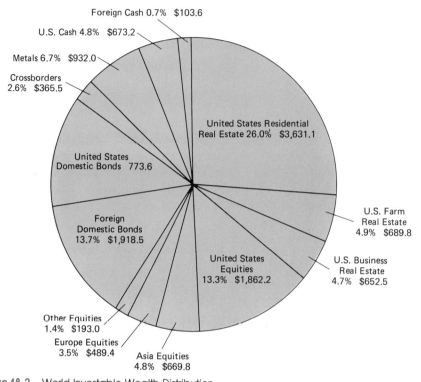

Figure 18-2 World Investable Wealth Distribution

source: R. Ibbotson, L. Siegel, and K. Love, "World Wealth: Market Values and Returns," *Journal of Portfolio Management* (Fall 1985).

In Figure 18–3 we add foreign real estate and durable goods to get a picture of the world wealth portfolio. Even this, however, falls far short of the world *market portfolio,* as the diagram doesn't include many of the countries of the world, nor does it include many types of wealth, such as human capital. Having considered this, it is obvious that the U.S. stock market makes up only a very small fraction of the world market portfolio. You should remember this in putting into perspective empirical tests of the Capital Asset Pricing Model. It is also obvious from the diagrams that the provincial investor is missing out on tremendous potential opportunities for diversification and profit.

Figure 18–4 plots the distribution of world investable wealth from 1959 through 1984. Notable trends are the displacement of equity securities with debt securities and the rise and fall of metals, such as gold and silver, in the late 1970s and early 1980s. The rise and fall pattern was due more to changes in the relative value of these metals than it was to changes in the quantity outstanding.

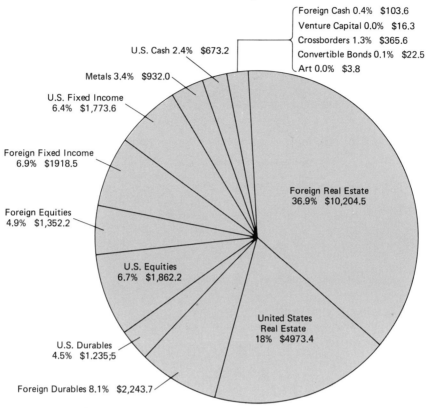

Total World Wealth
1984 = $27,681.5 Billion

Foreign Cash 0.4% $103.6
Venture Capital 0.0% $16.3
Crossborders 1.3% $365.6
Convertible Bonds 0.1% $22.5
Art 0.0% $3.8

U.S. Cash 2.4% $673.2

Metals 3.4% $932.0

U.S. Fixed Income
6.4% $1,773.6

Foreign Fixed Income
6.9% $1918.5

Foreign Equities
4.9% $1,352.2

Foreign Real Estate
36.9% $10,204.5

U.S. Equities
6.7% $1,862.2

United States
Real Estate
18% $4973.4

U.S. Durables
4.5% $1.235;5

Foreign Durables 8.1% $2,243.7

Figure 18-3   World Wealth Distribution

SOURCE: R. Ibbotson, L. Siegel, and K. Love, "World Wealth: Market Values and Returns," *Journal of Portfolio Management* (Fall 1985).

RETURNS TO DOMESTIC AND FOREIGN INVESTMENTS

Figure 18–5 plots the rates of return to U.S. and foreign equity securities from 1960 through 1984. The returns are those that would have been earned by a U.S. investor consuming in dollars. The two series have approximately the same means and standard deviations, and they are positively correlated with one another. (The correlation coefficient is .672.) A similar plot for total U.S. government and corporate bonds is presented in Figure 18–6. Although both series have approximately the same standard deviations, the average rate of return for the foreign bonds is somewhat greater. The correlation coefficient (.242) is substantially lower than that for equity securities. Note that the variance of both series increased substantially in the last fifteen years.

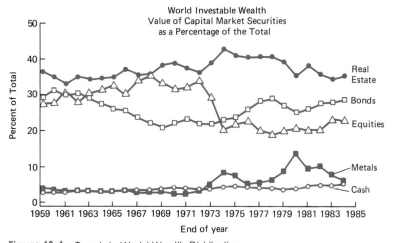

Figure 18-4 Trends in World Wealth Distribution

SOURCE: R. Ibbotson, L. Siegel, and K. Love, "World Wealth: Market Values and Returns," *Journal of Portfolio Management* (Fall 1985).

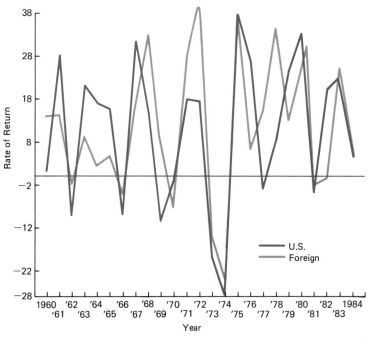

Figure 18-5 Equity Returns

SOURCE: R. Ibbotson, L. Siegel, and K. Love, "World Wealth: Market Values and Returns," *Journal of Portfolio Management* (Fall 1985).

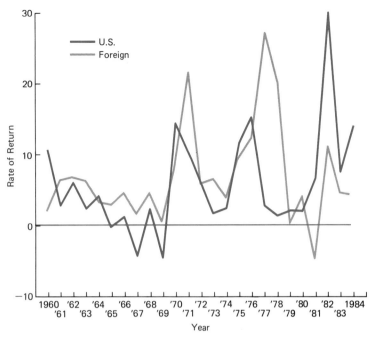

Figure 18-6 Bond Returns

SOURCE: R. Ibbotson, L. Siegel, and K. Love, "World Wealth: Market Values and Returns," *Journal of Portfolio Management* (Fall 1985).

Figure 18–7 shows returns to short-term money market instruments. In this case both series have approximately the same mean return, but the foreign series has substantially greater standard deviation. Note that the two series are almost completely uncorrelated. (The correlation coefficient is only .01.) Again, the variance of the series tends to increase in the more recent years. Finally, Figure 18–8 shows the series of rates of return to total investable wealth in U.S. and foreign markets. Although the series have about the same average rates of return, the foreign series has a substantially greater level of variance. The correlation coefficient between the two series is .53.

Table 18–1 provides a more complete matrix of correlation coefficients between various forms of investments in U.S. and foreign markets. Note that apart from the equity securities, the correlation coefficients are quite low. This would indicate that there are real benefits to diversification across the world investment portfolio. Table 18–2 shows the beta coefficients, coefficients of determination, and residual standard deviations for various types of investments, where the proxy used for the market porfolio is world wealth excluding metals. Note that world equity securities lead the way in terms of systematic risk and residual variance. U.S. wealth is somewhat below average in terms of systematic risk, and foreign wealth is somewhat above average.

Figure 18–9 plots the means and standard deviations of various types of foreign and domestic investments.

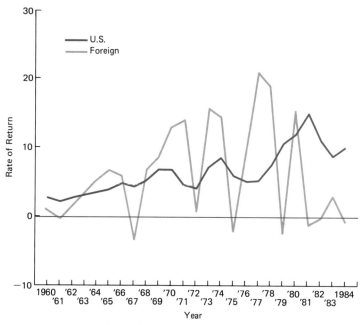

Figure 18-7 Money Market

SOURCE: R. Ibbotson, L. Siegel, and K. Love, "World Wealth: Market Values and Returns," *Journal of Portfolio Management* (Fall 1985).

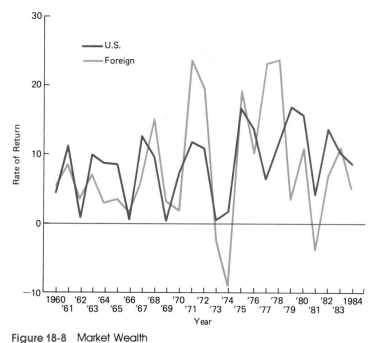

Figure 18-8 Market Wealth

SOURCE: R. Ibbotson, L. Siegel, and K. Love, "World Wealth: Market Values and Returns," *Journal of Portfolio Management* (Fall 1985).

438

Table 18–1 Correlation Coefficients Between Classes of Investments

	U.S. Total Equities	Foreign Total Equities	U.S. Total Government Bonds	U.S. Total Corporate Bonds	Foreign Domestic Corporate Bonds	Foreign Domestic Government Bonds	U.S. Total Real Estate	U.S. Total Cash	World Total Cash	Gold	Silver
U.S. Total Equities	1.000										
Foreign Total Equities	0.672	1.000									
U.S. Total Government Bonds	−0.006	−0.226	1.000								
U.S. Total Corporate Bonds	0.323	0.075	0.863	1.000							
Foreign Domestic Corporate Bonds	0.050	0.314	0.085	0.264	1.000						
Foreign Domestic Government Bonds	0.024	0.255	0.117	0.266	0.890	1.000					
U.S. Total Real Estate	0.054	0.129	−0.040	−0.123	0.164	0.303	1.000				
U.S. Total Cash	−0.079	−0.162	0.332	0.136	−0.265	−0.217	0.405	1.000			
World Total Cash	−0.238	−0.180	0.236	0.029	0.048	0.080	0.529	0.891	1.000		
Gold	−0.088	0.044	−0.206	−0.323	0.001	0.107	0.684	0.210	0.366	1.000	
Silver	0.116	−0.020	−0.109	−0.187	−0.286	−0.054	0.580	0.123	−0.014	0.438	1.000

SOURCE: R. Ibbotson, L. Siegel, and K. Love, "World Wealth: Market Values and Returns," *Journal of Portfolio Management* (Fall 1985).

Table 18–2 The Relationship Between Returns to Security Classes and the World Market Portfolio

Dependent Variable	Beta	Adjusted R^2	Standard Deviation of Residuals
World equities	2.32	0.804	7.19
World total bonds	0.67	0.362	5.39
World cash	0.04	−0.021	1.52
U.S. real estate	0.31	0.254	3.20
U.S. market wealth	0.85	0.893	1.86
Foreign market wealth	1.38	0.764	4.83

SOURCE: R. Ibbotson, L. Siegel, and K. Love, "World Wealth: Market Values and Returns," *Journal of Portfolio Management* (Fall 1985).

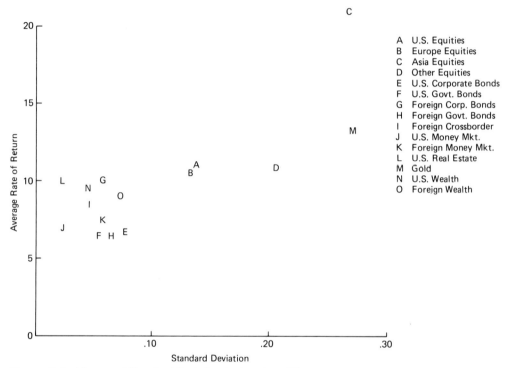

Figure 18-9 Mean and Standard Deviation by Investment Type

SOURCE: R. Ibbotson, L. Siegel, and K. Love, "World Wealth: Market Values and Returns," *Journal of Portfolio Management* (Fall 1985).

FOREIGN EXCHANGE RISK

When you invest in a security of a foreign country, you must first acquire that country's currency in the amount of the investment plus the transactions costs associated with buying it. Later, when you sell the security and receive proceeds in the currency of the foreign country, you must then exchange those proceeds for dollars.

Suppose you want to invest in a British security with a current market value of 1000. Assume that the current exchange rate is \$1.30 for each pound sterling. That means that it will cost you \$1300 to invest in the security. Now assume that, in the course of a year, the market value of the security doubles to 2000 in Britain. In the same time period, the exchange rate increases to 2 for each pound sterling. This means that you will be able to liquidate your investment in the British market and convert the proceeds in pounds sterling to \$4000. Your total profit on the transaction is \$2700 and your rate of return is \$2700/\$1300 = 308%.

Now suppose that, instead, the value of the dollar rose during the period, and the exchange rate went to \$1 for each pound sterling. This means that when you convert the proceeds of liquidating the investment to dollars, you will receive only \$2000. Your profit will be \$700, and your rate of return will be only 54 percent.

The total rate of return on the transaction, including the effect of fluctuating exchange rates, can be computed by multiplying one plus the rate of return to the security in the foreign country by the ratio of the exchange rate at the end and the beginning of the period. In our example one plus the rate of return to the security in the British market can be computed as

$$\frac{2000}{1000} = 2$$

In the first instance, where the dollar fell and the exchange rate went up, the total rate of return could be computed as

$$\left(2.00 \times \frac{2.00}{1.30}\right) - 1.00 = 308\%$$

$$\left(\begin{array}{c}\text{Return in} \\ \text{foreign} \\ \text{country}\end{array} \times \begin{array}{c}\text{Ratio} \\ \text{of exchange} \\ \text{rates}\end{array}\right) - 1.00 = \text{Total rate of return}$$

In the second instance, where the dollar rose and the exchange rate went down, the total rate of return is

$$\left(2.00 \times \frac{1.00}{1.30}\right) - 1.00 = 53\%$$

Obviously, fluctuations in foreign exchange rates can have a potentially large impact on the total rate of return to a foreign investment. We should note that the returns represented in Figures 18–5 through 18–8 reflect fluctuations in the foreign exchange rates between the U.S. dollar and the currencies of the respective foreign countries.

The risk of fluctuations in foreign exchange rates can be eliminated, however, through the sale of forward or futures contracts. Forward contracts can be purchased or sold through the Interbank Foreign Exchange Market and futures contracts can be purchased or sold through the International Monetary Market. In our example, you might contract, through a forward or futures contract, to sell British pounds sterling at the end of the year at the forward or futures price. As we found in Chapter 14, the forward and futures prices reflect the market's expectation for the future exchange rate plus a risk premium for the forward contract and risk, term, and reinvestment premiums for the futures contract.

Suppose the forward price reflects an exchange rate of 1.35. Then you know that the total rate of return to your investment will be given by

$$\left(r \times \frac{1.35}{1.30}\right) - 1.00 = \text{Total investment return}$$

where r is the rate of return to the security in the currency of the foreign country. This return is multiplied by a constant, which is the ratio of the exchange rate reflected in the forward price to the current exchange ratio. In this way the *risk* of fluctuations in foreign exchange rates is completely eliminated.

INTERNATIONAL RELATIONSHIPS BETWEEN EXPECTED RETURNS

International Capital Asset Pricing

If you assume that all goods, services, and assets are freely transferable across international borders, that investors think the same and focus on real returns, adjusted for the rate of inflation of a common market basket of goods and services, and if there is a common risk-free (in real terms) asset across different countries, then the expected rate of return to any capital asset will conform to the simple version of the Capital Asset Pricing Model.

$$E(r_J) = r_F + (E(r_M) - r_F)\beta_J$$

In the equation returns are expressed in real terms. In other words $E(r_J)$ is the expected change in the number of units of the common market basket of goods and services that you will be able to buy if you invest in asset J. Asset F is the international risk-free asset, and M is the worldwide market portfolio.

This very simple relationship between the relative expected returns to the investments of different countries will hold only under the very idealized conditions discussed above. Under more realistic conditions this simplified form of the international Capital Asset Pricing Model breaks down and we have much more complex forms of the model. For example, as we learned in Chapter 17, the introduction of taxes into a domestic asset pricing system results in an additional premium in the expected rate of return that relates to the relative tax exposure of an individual security. In an international setting, we have a multiplicity of tax systems across different countries that may result in an even more complex relationship between expected return and international tax exposure.

There are also barriers to the exchange of goods and services and the investment in capital goods and securities across different countries. These barriers may result in segmentation of the international markets similar to the market segmentation theory of the term structure of interest rates. One such barrier is exchange control or limits imposed on the amounts of investment income that foreign investors can repatriate from a particular foreign country to their home country. In addition to limits on the quantity of income that can be transferred, many countries may also impose taxes on income that is transferred across borders.

A second such barrier is differential costs of acquiring information between domestic and foreign investors. Domestic investors are likely to be more knowledgeable about channels of information and are also likely to be able to access information in a more timely manner. Perhaps the most significant barrier of all is the inability of domestic investors to access many markets in foreign countries. These would include the capital markets of emerging and developing countries and the markets for consumer durables and real estate in developed countries.

Interest Rate Parity

Aside from the form of the equilibrium relationship between expected rates of return to the risky securities of different countries, there are strong economic forces that keep the returns to the risk-free securities in a particular relationship to one another. This relationship is called *interest rate parity*.

Consider, for example, the relationship between the riskless rates of interest in Canada and the United States. If you, as a U.S. resident, buy Canadian risk-free bonds, you face an exchange rate risk. As we discussed, you can eliminate that risk by selling a forward contract to sell Canadian dollars at the prevailing forward price, in an amount equal to the payment on the risk-free bond at maturity. The rate of return on your transaction will be equal to the promised return on the bond (in Canadian dollars) multiplied by the ratio of the forward price for Canadian dollars and the current price of Canadian dollars.

$$\text{Net return} = \text{Riskless return in Canada} \times \frac{\text{Forward price Canadian dollar}}{\text{Current price Canadian dollar}}$$

In this equation both the net return and the return are computed as one plus the conventional returns.

Suppose the interest rate on Canadian bonds is 10 percent. The current price for a Canadian dollar is $.80. The forward price is $.82. The net return is then computed as

$$1.127 = 1.10 \times \frac{\$.82}{\$.80}$$

This is a riskless transaction, so the net return must be equal to one plus the rate of return available in the United States on riskless treasury securities. If the net return is greater than this, everyone in the United States would shun the domestic bond market for the more attractive riskless investments in Canada. If the net return is less than this, Canadian investors would be buying forward contracts to buy Canadian dollars and investing in the more lucrative riskless investments in the United States.

Thus, the net return must be equal to the riskless rate of interest in the United States. By equating the net return with the risk-free U.S. rate, we can solve for the following parity relationship between risk-free interest rates in the two countries:

$$\frac{\text{Riskless return in the U.S.}}{\text{Riskless return in Canada}} = \frac{\text{Forward price Canadian dollar}}{\text{Current price Canadian dollar}}$$

The Impact of Simultaneous Trading of an Asset in Different Countries

To an increasing extent, domestic securities are being traded simultaneously on the exchanges of foreign countries. For example, many common stocks of U.S. companies are traded on the stock exchanges of Great Britain, France, Japan, and other countries, as well as on the floor of the New York Stock Exchange. Arbitrageurs will ensure that the market values of the securities are nearly identical as among the exchanges in the different countries. At the same time, the prices of the stocks must conform to the asset pricing structure of each of the domestic countries. Suppose that the international capital markets are segmented and the individual asset pricing structures are distinctly different from one another. If we introduce numbers of securities that are traded in all markets, and at the same time force the market prices of each of these securities to be identical in each of the international markets, we introduce a powerful force promoting the integration of the international capital asset pricing structure.

Thus, even in the presence of the barriers to market integration discussed earlier, given that arbitrageurs will force equality in the prices of individual issues traded on multiple securities exchanges, the presence of localized price pressure of these issues to conform to the domestic pricing structure (or pressure on the domestic pricing structure to conform to the prices of the individual issues) may eventually force an integration of the international asset pricing system.

Summary

The international capital market may offer the astute investor many opportunities for expanded opportunities for diversification and profit. Given that the correlation between many types of international securities is low, adding international investments to your portfolio may result in significant reductions in overall portfolio risk. Given that some foreign markets are less efficient than the capital market in the United States, or given a less than fully integrated international asset pricing system, international investing may also expand your opportunities for increasing your expected rate of return.

As an international investor, you face the added risk of possible fluctuations in international exchange rates. This risk can be eliminated by selling forward contracts to sell the currency of the foreign investment at the points in time that the investment is expected to produce cash flows.

Under very idealized conditions the world capital asset pricing system will conform to the simple form of the Capital Asset Pricing Model, where the returns are expressed in real terms. In a more complex world, with different consumption baskets and tax systems, the asset pricing relationships become much more complex. Indeed, barriers exist that may promote segmented asset pricing structures between countries. In spite of this, there are certain parity relationships that can be argued to exist between countries. One of these is interest rate parity. If riskless interest rates in two countries are in parity with one another, the ratio of the interest rate in the domestic country to the foreign country will be equal to the ratio of the forward exchange rate to the current exchange rate. In the absence of this parity relationship, the investors of one of the two countries will find it to their advantage to invest in the riskless securities of the foreign country, eliminating exchange rate risk with the foreign contract.

QUESTIONS AND PROBLEMS

1. In the context of Figures 18–2 and 18–3, what is the difference between the concepts of "total world wealth" and "world investable wealth"?

2. Define the term exchange rate risk. Would this risk be the same for all investors in different countries? Would you expect exchange rate risk to have increased or decreased in recent years as the volatility of interest rates has increased?

3. What impact does the correlation between exchange rates and the rates of return to securities in foreign countries have on exchange rate risk?

4. How might one cope with exchange rate risk through the use of forward and futures contracts to buy and sell foreign exchange? What might be the relative advantages and disadvantages of these two forms of contracts in this respect?

5. Suppose that you, as a U.S. investor, buy 200 shares of a Canadian stock that pays no dividends and is valued at $85 at the beginning of the year (in Canadian dollars) and sells at $105 at the end of the year. During the course of the year the value of the Canadian dollar falls from $.85 to $.80. Assuming you liquidate your investment at the end of the year, compute the net rate of return on the transaction.

6. Compute your net rate of return, assuming that you partly eliminated exchange rate risk by selling a forward contract to sell $20,000 Canadian dollars at an exchange rate of $.86 at the end of the year.

7. Suppose that the one-year risk-free interest rate in the United States is 14 percent, and the risk-free rate in Canada is 16 percent. If the current rate of exchange of U.S. for Canadian dollars is $.80, what would you expect the forward price to be on a contract to sell Canadian dollars in one year? What would the forward price be on a corresponding contract to sell U.S. dollars? Would you expect identical prices on corresponding futures contracts? Why, or why not?

8. Describe some of the barriers to the free flow of capital across national borders. What impact might these barriers have on relative securities prices and expected rates of return? What implications might this have on investment strategy?

BIBLIOGRAPHY

ALIBER, R. Z., "The Interest Rate Parity Theorum: A Reinterpretation," *Journal of Political Economy* (November–December 1973).

BERGSTRUM, G. L., "A New Route to Higher Returns and Lower Risks," *Journal of Portfolio Management* (Fall 1975).

BLACK, F., "The Ins and Outs of Foreign Investment," *Financial Analysts Journal* (May–June 1978).

CORNELL, B., "Spot Rates, Forward Rates, and Market Efficiency," *Journal of Financial Economics* (August 1977).

GRAUER, F., R. LITZENBERGER, and R. STEHLE, "Sharing Rules and Equilibrium in an International Capital Market Under Uncertainty," *Journal of Financial Economics* (June 1976).

GRUBEL, G. G., and K. FADNER, "The Interdependence of International Equity Markets," *Journal of Finance* (March 1971).

IBBOTSON, R., L. SIEGEL, and K. LOVE, "World Wealth: Market Values and Returns," *Journal of Portfolio Management* (Fall 1985).

JACQUILLAT, B., and B. SOLNIK, "Multinationals Are Poor Tools for Diversification," *Journal of Portfolio Management* (Winter 1978).

LEVY, H., and M. SARNAT, "International Diversification of Investment Portfolios," *American Economic Review* (September 1970).

SENBET, L., "International Capital Market Equilibrium and Multi-National Firm Financing and Investment Policies," *Journal of Financial and Quantitative Analysis* (September 1979).

SOLNIK, B., "An Equilibrium Model of the International Capital Market," *Journal of Economic Theory* (August 1974a).

———, "Why Not Diversify Internationally Rather than Domestically?" *Financial Analysts Journal* (July–August 1974b).

19 MARKET EFFICIENCY: THE CONCEPT

Introduction

The Capital Asset Pricing Model and the Arbitrage Pricing Theory allegedly describe the *structure* of the prices of financial assets. They tell us how we can expect prices and expected rates of return on securities to differ when the securities differ with respect to their risk characteristics.

In contrast, when we talk about *market efficiency,* we are interested not in the form of the structural relationship between risk and expected return but rather in the precision with which the market prices securities in relation to its structure, whatever that structure may be. If new information becomes known about a particular company, how quickly do market participants find out about the information and buy or sell the securities of the company on the basis of the information? How quickly do the prices of the securities adjust to reflect the new information? If prices respond to all relevant new information in a rapid fashion, we can say that the market is relatively efficient. If, instead, the information disseminates rather slowly throughout the market, and if investors take time in analyzing the information and reacting, and possibly overreacting, to it, prices may deviate from values based on a careful analysis of all available relevant information. Such a market could be characterized as relatively inefficient.

You might ask, because on average investors are clearly not fully informed about all securities, and perhaps not about even a single security, how could the market reach a state where the prices of all securities fully reflect all information that is both relevant and available? The answer to this question is that prices are not established by the *consensus* of all investors. Prices are set by those marginal investors who actively trade in the stock. An advocate of the notion that the stock market is relatively efficient would argue that there exists an army of intelligent, well-informed security analysts, arbitrageurs, and traders who literally spend their lives hunting for securities that are mispriced, based on currently available information. These professionals are armed with computers, and they subscribe to data base management services that are tied into their computers. They have at their fingertips up-to-date information on thousands of companies, and they process that information using state-of-the-art analytical techniques. These people can access, assimilate, and act on information very quickly. In their intense search for mispriced securities, professional investors may police the market so efficiently that they drive the prices of all issues to fully reflect all information that is knowable about the company, its industry, or the general economy.

Whether or not this is the case is a controversial question. Until recently, the weight of the evidence supported the notion that the market was relatively efficient in pricing securities. However, recently released studies have cast some doubt on the validity of the efficient market hypothesis. In this chapter we will discuss the concept of market efficiency, its importance as an issue, and the characteristics of an efficient market. Some of the evidence on both sides of the issue is examined in Chapter 20.

FORMS OF THE EFFICIENT MARKET HYPOTHESIS

The issue is not black or white; the market is neither strictly efficient nor strictly inefficient. The question is one of *degree:* Just how efficient is the market?

One way to measure the efficiency of the market is to ask what types of information, encompassed by the total set of all available information, is reflected in securities prices. The outer circle of Figure 19–1 represents all information relevant to the valuation of a particular stock that is currently knowable. This includes publicly available information about the company, its industry, and the domestic and world economy. It also includes information that is privately held by select groups of individuals. Within the outer circle is a second circle that represents that part of the information set that has been publicly announced and is therefore publicly available. The information outside this set is, therefore, inside or private information. Within the second circle there is yet a third circle that represents a subset of the information that is publicly available. This third circle contains any information relevant to the valuation of the stock that can be learned by analyzing the history of the market price of the stock. For example,

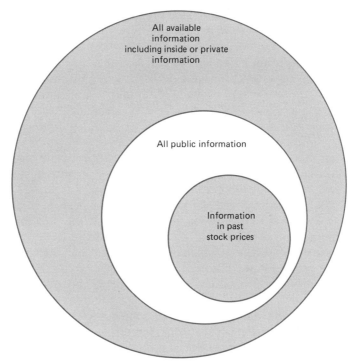

Figure 19-1 Subsets of Available Information for a Given Stock

has the stock been rising or falling, and does this have any implications for the future?

There are three forms of the efficient market hypothesis. Under each, different types of information are assumed to be reflected in securities prices.[1]

Under the *weak* form of the efficient market hypothesis, stock prices are assumed to reflect any information that may be contained in the *past history of the stock price* itself. For example, suppose there exists a seasonal pattern in stock prices such that stock prices fall on the last trading day of the year and then rise on the first trading day of the following year. Under the weak form of the hypothesis, the market will come to recognize this and price the phenomenon away. Anticipating the rise in price on the first day of the year, traders will attempt to get in at the very start of trading on the first day. Their attempts to get in will cause the increase in price to occur in the first minutes of the first day. Intelligent traders will then recognize that to beat the rest of the market, they will have to get in late in the last day of the previous year when stock prices have historically fallen. Their attempts to buy late in the day will act to support prices and reduce the extent of the fall on the last trading day of the year.

---

[1]The three forms of the efficient market hypothesis were first suggested by Fama (1970).

This process of attempting to get in earlier and earlier will, of course, continue until the entire year-end pattern of a dip and rally is eliminated from the price series. Other, more complex patterns in the price series will be detected and eliminated in similar fashion, until it becomes impossible to predict the future course of the series by analyzing its past behavior. Once this state has been reached, the weak form of the efficient market hypothesis will be satisfied.

Under the *semistrong* form of the efficient, market hypothesis, *all publicly available information* is presumed to be reflected in securities prices. This includes information in the stock price series as well as information in the firm's accounting reports, the reports of competing firms, announced information relating to the state of the economy, and any other publicly available information relevant to the valuation of the firm.

The *strong* form of the efficient market hypothesis takes the notion of market efficiency to the ultimate extreme. If you believe in this form, you believe that *all information* is reflected in stock prices. This includes private, or inside, information as well as that which is publicly available. Under this form, those who acquire inside information act on it, buying or selling the stock. Their actions affect the price of the stock, and the price quickly adjusts to reflect the inside information.

As you move from the weak form of the hypothesis to the strong form, various types of investment analysis become ineffective in discriminating between profitable and unprofitable investments. If the weak form is valid, technical analysis, or charting, becomes ineffective. A chartist plots movements in the price of the stock over time. When the stock price movements take certain patterns, this implies to the chartist that the stock may take off in a particular direction in the future. In effect, the chartist is using various techniques to analyze the past series of stock prices in order to predict the future of the series. If the weak form is in effect, there is no information in the past series that is useful in predicting the future. Any information that was there has been analyzed by thousands of watchful chartists everywhere. They have acted on what they found, and the stock price has settled to a level that reflects all the useful information embedded in past stock prices. To find under- or overvalued stocks, you have to resort to some other form of analysis that is based on information other than the past price series.

If the semistrong form of the efficient market hypothesis is in effect, no form of analysis will help you attain superior returns as long as the analysis is based on publicly available information. This means, for example, that an analysis of the firm's accounting statements is now ineffective in discriminating between profitable and unprofitable investments. These statements have already been analyzed by thousands of other analysts before you. The other analysts have acted on what they found, and the current price of the stock now reflects all the relevant information that can be found in the accounting statements. The same is true for all other sources of public information. Traditional security analysis as well as technical analysis is now useless as a weapon to beat the market. You have to report to attempts to uncover, or purchase, private information if you are going to distinguish yourself as an investor.

All is lost if the market is strong-form efficient. Under this form those who acquire inside information act on it, and they quickly force the price to reflect the information. Allegedly, the initial acquisition of new pieces of this information is largely a matter of chance, and because stock prices already reflect the existing inventory of inside information, efforts to seek out inside information to beat the market are ill-advised. Under this ultimate form of the hypothesis, the professional investor truly has a zero market value, because no form of search or processing of information will consistently produce superior returns.

THE SIGNIFICANCE OF THE EFFICIENT MARKET HYPOTHESIS

Why should you care if the market is efficient?

If you are gong to take a job in the securities industry, this is a crucial issue for you. If your fellow analysts have been so proficient at doing their jobs that mispriced securities are, for all intents and purposes, nonexistent, it may be impossible for you to be effective in doing what you are hired to do. You may well be hired to find mispriced securities so that you can produce an additional increment of return on the portfolios that you are managing. If the market is truly efficient, in making it that way, professional investors have performed a valuable service for society.

The investment decisions of the managers of business firms are based to a large extent on signals they get from the capital market. If the market is efficient, the cost of obtaining capital will accurately reflect the prospects for each firm. This means that the firms with the most attractive investment opportunities will be able to obtain capital at a fair price that reflects their true potential. The "right" investments will be made, and society will be better off. To the extent that professional security analysts played a role in making it this way, they have served society well, and the total benefit of their services may be very large.

The *marginal* benefit of any one analyst is another matter, however. If the market is efficient, any one financial institution can fire all its analysts without affecting its expected investment performance. Rather than doing analysis, the institution can select its investments at random, knowing that each security selected has been priced correctly by the remaining analysts. In an efficient market, the *total* product of professional investors may be positive, but the *marginal* product of any one analyst is close to zero. Unfortunately, the amount that any one firm is willing to pay an analyst is based on the marginal product. Thus, unless you can convince people that the market is inefficient, you will make very little money as a security analyst. If the market is truly efficient, and you happen to land a job as an analyst, your success in your profession will be a matter of chance. Your expected probability of beating the market in any one year will be 50 percent, and there is nothing that you, personally, can do to improve these odds.

Suppose that you, instead, take a job as a corporate financial manager. Of what significance is market efficiency to you then?

Companies frequently repurchase their own stock because they feel that it has been undervalued by the market. If the market is strong-form efficient, this rationale is untenable. The stock is never undervalued by the market. If you, as manager, disagree with the valuation, it may be because your estimate of the company's prospects are overly optimistic. Perhaps you have neglected to consider carefully the implications of some macroeconomic variable, such as the future course of interest rates, on the future prospects and valuation of your firm.

Frequently, investment projects are postponed, or financing is done with debt rather than with equity, because management feels that the entire stock market is depressed. If by the term "depressed" management means that stock prices have fallen below their intrinsic value based on available public information, this rationale is also inappropriate if the market is semistrong-form efficient. In a semistrong-form efficient market, stock prices are never "depressed," in the sense that their values are less than the present value of the best estimate, based on available information, of the future stream of dividends. In an efficient market, the cost of equity capital to the firm is both fair and reasonable in bear, as well as bull, markets. Future prospects may not appear as good in bear markets, but in an efficient market, the prospects on which stock prices are set are based on rational analysis of all publicly available information.

In an efficient market, you can also question the rationale for including complexities like call provisions in bond indentures. A call provision gives the firm a call option to buy the bonds back from the bondholders at a specific price. This call option held by the firm has an implicit market value. The market value of a callable bond will be less than the market value of a comparable noncallable bond by the market value of this call option.

If the only rationale for including the call provision is to provide the firm with the opportunity to reissue the bond at a lower interest cost should interest rates fall, this rationale should be questioned, if the market is taken to be efficient. In an efficient market, the callable bond will be priced as the difference between the market value of an identical noncallable issue and the market value of the call option held by the stockholders. Both market values will be based on the best available forecast of the future course of interest rates. Given that the firm's forecast can't be better than the best forecast available, the firm is no better off by including the call provision in the bond indenture than it would be by selling the bond as a noncallable issue. You can look at it this way: If the call option is priced correctly by the market, the firm should be indifferent toward buying it (including it in the bond indenture) or not buying it.

You will frequently see advertisements by firms announcing that the firm has achieved a remarkable growth record in earnings and dividends. These advertisements often appear in financial publications such as the *Wall Street Journal*. If these advertisements were placed to cast a favorable light on the firm's common stock so as to support its market price, the money to purchase the ad was unwisely spent, given that the market is semistrong-form efficient. The information contained in the ad has already been publicly disclosed, fully analyzed by the army of professional analysts, and it is already reflected in the stock price. If the market is efficient, the ad will have absolutely no impact on the market value of the common stock.

Managers sometimes express concern over the effect that a change in accounting procedure will have on reported earnings per share. If the market is semi-strong-form efficient, they should not be concerned. Informed, rational analysts will adjust for different accounting procedures used by different firms and assess prospects based on standardized numbers. The adjustment in accounting technique will have no effect on the opinions of these analysts or on the price of the firm's common stock.

As you can see, the issue of market efficiency has some important practical implications, even if you don't become one of the members of the army of professionals who allegedly enforce market efficiency. Many important business decisions are based on rationales that implicitly assume the securities markets' price inefficiency. In this chapter and the next, we will investigate the accuracy of this assumption.

RISK AND EXPECTED RETURN IN AN EFFICIENT MARKET

The efficient market hypothesis doesn't assume or imply any particular theory relating to the structure of stock prices. However, because we are familiar with it, in this particular discussion we assume that all investors invest in mean-variance efficient portfolios and that the structure of stock prices is that of the simple form of the Capital Asset Pricing Model.

Let's assume first that the strong form of the efficient market hypothesis is in effect, which means that securities prices reflect all the information that is available and relevant to valuation. Suppose that you are Superanalyst, and you gather all the information that is relevant to the valuation of the securities of each firm. For each firm you process and analyze the information using state-of-the-art techniques to estimate the expected return and the beta factor for each security in the market. If you did this, and the market were strong-form efficient, your plot might look like that in Figure 19–2. Note that securities are priced so that each, based on an analysis of all available information, has an expected rate of return that is consistent with its risk level and the CAPM. Viewed from the perspective of the total information set, the risk-return relationship is perfectly crisp and clean. Given the CAPM structure of securities prices, the market is pricing efficiently with respect to that structure.

Now suppose you make the same estimates of risk and expected return, but this time you confine your analysis to publicly available information. Your estimates of beta, for example, are based on sampling from the past series of rates of return to the securities and the market index, as well as such company char-

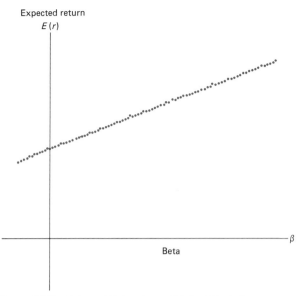

Figure 19-2 Risk and Return in an Efficient Market

acteristics as leverage, size, and earnings stability. Again, you employ state-of-the-art techniques of analysis, but the information you feed into the techniques is all publicly available information. Your plot may now look something like that of Figure 19–3. The relationship between your estimates of risk and expected return is no longer crisp and clean. Securities are positioned above and below the security market line.

If you did a creditable job of estimating risk and expected return based on publicly available information, it would appear to you that securities like the one labeled A were undervalued; their expected rates of return are excessive, given their level of risk. Securities like B appear overvalued; their expected rates of return are inadequate. The market appears to be inefficient to you. Given the results of your analysis, you might even think that you deserve to be paid an impressive salary, because it seems obvious that you can easily discriminate between profitable and unprofitable investments.

In reality, however, securities A and B are not mispriced. You are the one who is inefficient, and not the market. The reason you think the market is inefficient is because you are basing your analysis on an incomplete set of information. In fact, both A and B have expected returns that are fair and reasonable if you examine them from the perspective of both private as well as public information. You might be surprised to discover that if you put together a portfolio of "undervalued" securities like A, the average realized returns on this portfolio are no more likely to be greater than average than a portfolio of "overvalued" securities like B. If your salary is based on your realised performance, it is not likely to remain impressive for long.

Now let's shift gears and assume that the market is only semistrong-form efficient. In this case, if you do your analysis based on publicly available information alone, your plot will look like Figure 19–2. However, if you are able to acquire private or inside information, your plot would appear as in Figure 19–3. Now you really have identified over- and undervalued securities, and you do deserve to make a lot of money as an analyst. Portfolios of stocks like A are, in fact, likely to outperform other portfolios in their risk class.

If we could locate Superanalyst, we could obtain plots like these and resolve the issue of how efficient the market is. Unfortunately, that person doesn't exist, so we have to settle the issue some other way. As it turns out, an efficient market exhibits certain behavioral traits or characteristics. We can examine the behavior of the real market to see if it conforms to these characteristics. If it doesn't, we can conclude that the market is inefficient. If the market is efficient, it should exhibit the following characteristics:

1. Securities prices should respond quickly and accurately to the receipt of new information that is relevant to valuation.

2. The change in securities prices from one period to the next should be random in the sense that the change in price that takes place today should be unrelated to the change in price that occurred yesterday or any other day in the past.

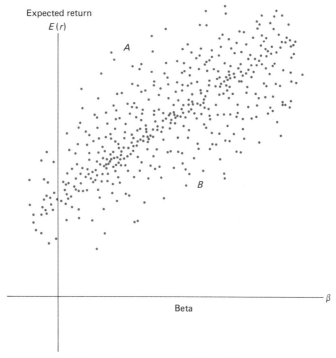

Figure 19-3 Risk and Return in an Inefficient Market

3. It should be impossible to discriminate between profitable (in the sense that the returns are greater than what you would normally expect to see, given the risk) and unprofitable investments in a future period based on any of the characteristics of these investments that can be known in the current period. It should be impossible, for example, for us to construct a trading rule that utilizes information available at time t that enables us to predict the most profitable investments of $t + 1$.

4. If we separate investors who are knowledgeable from those who are not, we should discover that we are unable to find a significant difference between the average investment performance of the two groups. Moreover, it should be the case that differences in the performance of individual investors within each group should be insignificant. In other words, differences in performance between groups and within groups should be due to chance, and not something systematic and permanent, like differences in ability to find information not already reflected in stock prices.

QUICK AND ACCURATE
RESPONSE TO NEW INFORMATION

Every day a rich flow of bits and pieces of information pours into the market. The information pertains to general economic conditions, weather, strikes, shortages of raw materials, international tension, and product demand. This information is relevant to security valuation, and it affects the prices of securities.

If the market is efficient, securities prices should respond to the information as soon as it is received. Naturally, the response can't be instantaneous, but the gap between the receipt of the information and the reaction of the price should reflect the best available procedures and techniques for receiving and processing the information. The reaction of market prices should also be unbiased. The initial reaction should accurately reflect the true implications of the information on the value of the security. There should be no need for a subsequent correction, for example, of an overreaction to a piece of information.

Figure 19–4 presents three possible scenarios for the reaction of a stock market price to the receipt of a single piece of information. This is an idealized example, for we assume that in all the days plotted on the horizontal axis only a single piece of information is received that is relevant to the valuation of the stock. The information is received on the day labeled 0. The information is positive and increases the best available estimate of the value of the stock from $30 to $33.

Consider the solid line. This represents the path taken by the stock in an efficient market. In this case there is an immediate increase in the value of the stock to $33 on the day that the information is received. No further changes take place in the value of the stock, because we have assumed that no additional new information is received by the market.

Now consider the broken line. This line depicts the path that the stock might take in an inefficient market. The story behind the path might go as follows: The

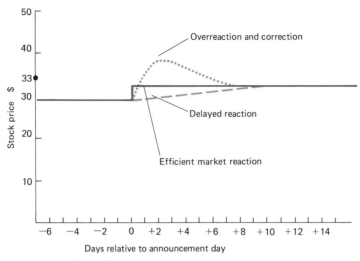

Figure 19-4 Stock Price Reaction to New Information in an Efficient and Inefficient Market

information is released. It is acquired by the national offices of several large brokerage houses. They wire the information to their local offices and begin analyzing the implications of the information for the companies and the stocks affected. Local brokers receive the information and begin making their own, less sophisticated analyses. They may inform their more important clients about the information without drawing firm conclusions. A few people might initiate trading in the stock, driving the price up slightly in the first day. After a lag of one or more days, the analysts employed by the investment institutions release reports showing that the information warrants a significant upward revision in the intrinsic value of the stock. Brokers inform their clients that the stock is undervalued at its current price. Decisions are made as to whether the stock should be purchased, and if so, how the money should be raised. Orders flow into the market in the course of the next several days, causing the stock to rise gradually to its new intrinsic value of $33.

The dotted line represents still another scenario that is consistent with an inefficient market. In this case those investors who are the most optimistic about the implications of the information on the value of the stock either get the information first or are prepared to act on it first. They are of the impression that the new intrinsic value of the stock is above $33, and their buying activity begins driving the stock above that level. The best estimate of the new value is, of course, $33, and eventually this view prevails. More sophisticated investors begin selling the stock, causing a correction in the price back down to the $33 level.

If the market is truly efficient, neither of the last two scenarios should be evident in the real market. If we were to observe the reaction of stock prices to the release of quarterly earnings reports, for example, there should be no evidence of a lag in the reaction or a tendency to overreact and then subsequently correct.

OUT ON THE STREET

The Flow of Information

The light turns red. Mark Fedinia brings his new Porsche to a halt on Twenty-second Street in New York City. Mark is on his way to work at Shaw Data Systems, a firm specializing in the collection and dispensing of financial information via computers. Shaw has about 200 clients managing about $150 billion to $200 billion in assets.

Mark is just completing a Ph.D. in finance. In addition to this, however, he has his own small firm, Almark Enterprises, specializing in computerized financial services. Recently, he moved to New York to work with Bill Burnett, president of Shaw, on some special projects.

Shaw's basic service is an accounting system for portfolio managers. A large investment or trust company might manage hundreds, or even thousands, of individual portfolios. Without a computerized system, it would be difficult, if not impossible, to keep track of all the portfolios. With Shaw's system, the company inputs its daily trades to Shaw. Shaw accounts for commissions, cash and stock dividends, and splits and keeps track of base positions for purposes of computing accrued capital gains and losses. It also provides a profile of each portfolio in terms of industry concentration and diversification on the basis of economic sector, such as consumer durable or defense.

Many of Shaw's clients use Shaw's accounting system in conjunction with a portfolio optimization routine that creates efficient sets on the basis of the Single Index Model, such as the one offered by Wilshire. The current weights for each portfolio are fed from the accounting system into the optimization program. The optimization program makes buy and sell recommendations, which are executed.

RANDOM CHANGES IN STOCK PRICES

If the market is efficient, the change in the price of a security that is taking place today should be completely unrelated to the change in price that took place yesterday or any other day in the past.[2] The crucial condition that must hold is

[2]That random movements in stock prices are consistent with an efficient market was proven by Samuelson (1965). It should be noted that this is only *strictly* true in a market where equilibrium expected rates of return are also serially uncorrelated. An increase in the value of a levered firm today will reduce its debt to equity ratio. This may result in a lower required and expected rate of return tomorrow. Thus we may have a slight tendency for negative correlation in stock returns, even in an efficient market. In most multiperiod equilibrium models, you would expect to find some serial correlation in equilibrium prices and expected rates of return. Within the context of these models, it is technically correct to say that market efficiency is consistent with the case where future deviations from equilibrium rates of return can't be predicted on the basis of past deviations from equilibrium rates of return.

The trades are then fed back to the accounting service, and the structure of the new portfolio is displayed, showing diversification by category, industry, and asset type.

Shaw's system is designed for portfolio managers who usually have relatively long-term horizons. Similar systems, called work stations, are also available for traders who usually have much shorter horizons. A work station usually works from an IBM personal computer that is linked to a mainframe. Flashed on the screen is the trader's portfolio with current trade-by-trade prices, including other information such as recent earnings reports.

In addition to its accounting system, Shaw also dispenses many forms of financial information to its clients. It employs Merrill-Lynch and IBES to supply it with forecasts of quarterly earnings for approximately 2000 companies. Shaw supplies its clients with this information, as well as comprehensive balance sheet and income statement information supplied by the Value Line Investment Survey.

Other information is also available from sources other than Shaw. The Dow Jones News Retrieval will tell you anything that has happened about a particular stock on a given day with only a fifteen-minute delay. Services like Goldman and Sachs make macroeconomic forecasts and updated buy and sell recommendations on individual issues. Money management companies can access these forecasts by tying into them via computers.

The problem with the information system as it exists, however, is that a given management company needs a set of terminals each tied to a different service. What is needed is an information intermediary that ties together different services by channeling them through its system. In this way the various services can be integrated as well.

that the *expected* change in the price on any given day must be unrelated to the past series of changes that have already taken place.

Momentum, for example, is a characteristic that is inconsistent with an efficient market. If, once started on a downward slide, stock prices develop a propensity to continue sliding, the expected change in price today would, in fact, be related to the price changes that have occurred in the past. Given a series of past negative price changes, we would lower our expectation for the expected price change that we are going to see for today.

Why should securities prices move randomly from one day to the next in an efficient market?

If the market is efficient, today's stock price should already reflect all the information that is both relevant to the valuation of the stock and knowable. By "knowable," we mean all information that has been announced and that which can be predicted, based on past announcements. The only information not reflected in the stock price is that which hasn't been received and can't be predicted to be received. This kind of information, by its very nature, must come into the market in an unpredictable, random fashion. As the market price responds instantly and accurately to its receipt, the price itself changes in a random, unpredictable fashion over time.

You might think at this point that some important economic series have definite seasonal or cyclical patterns. Gross national product is an example of such a series. If GNP exhibits a cyclical pattern, and stock prices instantly respond to announced changes in GNP, why don't stock prices exhibit a mimicking cyclical pattern? The answer is that stock prices don't respond to *changes* in GNP; they respond to errors in the market's *forecast* of the change in GNP. In an efficient market, the cyclical pattern will be recognized, identified, and modeled. Stock prices are set on the basis of the best possible forecast of the next GNP number. Suppose that the best available estimate of the next change in GNP is +$10 billion. There will be no reaction to the announced change in GNP, unless it turns out to be different from the forecast of +$10 billion implicit in stock prices. The market will react only to errors in its forecast. These errors themselves must be random. If they are not, they can be modeled statistically and incorporated into an improved forecast. If the market is employing the best available forecast in setting the prices, the errors will be random, and the response of prices to the errors will be random as well.

Consider the three scenarios in Figure 19–4. In the case of the broken curve, the change in price that is occuring on day +2 can be functionally related to the change in price that took place the day before. The stock price is rising on day +2, *because* the stock price reaction was incomplete on day +1. The two changes are connected. If it takes a matter of days for the market to complete its reaction to new information, a positive price change today should increase our expected value for the price change that will take place tomorrow. Tomorrow, we will expect to see a continuation of the reaction that began today.

In the same sense, in our case of the dotted curve, the stock price is falling in days +3, +4, and +5 *because* it overreacted in days +1 and +2. These changes are not independent; they are, in fact, connected causally. In the presence of such reversal patterns, a series of large positive price changes should cause us to lower our expectation for the price change that will take place tomorrow.

Now consider the solid path, which is consistent with market efficiency. A single impulse of information induces a single instantaneous price change in the stock. No further changes will take place until the next unpredictable impulse of information. The next change is totally unrelated to the change that took place at day 0. Prices change in a series of unrelated, unpredictable steps.

FAILURE OF SIMULATED TRADING STRATEGIES

If the market is efficient, there should be no way to discriminate between profitable and unprofitable investments based on information that is currently available. A profitable investment is one that is expected to produce a rate of return that is higher than it should be, given an appropriate benchmark.

One way to test for market efficiency is to test whether a specific trading rule, or investment strategy, would have produced profitable rates of return in the past. Suppose, for example, you think that the market is slow to react to the announcement of new information, like the release of the firm's earnings reports. In this case, your investment strategy might be always to invest in the top ten companies that have reported the highest dollar increases in earnings per share for the year. To test your hypothesis, you go back to a past period of time and try to simulate the results of investing on the basis of this trading rule. The question is, Would this strategy have produced profitable returns in the past? If the market is truly efficient, all strategies should fail in this regard.

Your first problem in testing any strategy is defining what you mean by a profitable rate of return. By ''profitable,'' you must mean that the expected, or realized, rate of return is greater than what the investment should have, given some benchmark. If you chose the Capital Asset Pricing Model as a benchmark, the expected rate of return should be the rate given by the beta factor of the investment and securities market line. If you chose the Arbitrage Pricing Theory as a benchmark, the expected rate of return should be that given by the risk-free rate and the sum of the products of the factor betas of the investment and the factor prices. Your test of the performance of the trading rule, in this sense, can be viewed as a joint test of two hypotheses:

1. You have chosen the correct benchmark to measure profitability.

2. The market is efficient relative to the information employed by your trading rule.

In constructing your simulation experiment, you have to be careful about a number of potential pitfalls. First, you must be sure you are formulating your investment strategy on the basis of information that is actually available at the time you buy or sell the securities. If your strategy is to invest in the stocks that have the greatest dollar increases in earnings per share for the previous year, in simulating the results of executing this strategy in the past, you must be sure you have the earnings number for the year at the time that you assume you buy the stock. If you ''buy'' the stock at the beginning of 1976 on the basis of the difference in the 1975 and 1974 earnings numbers, you are biasing your test in favor of the trading rule. This is because the final quarter of 1975 earnings typically is not reported until February 1976. Because you are investing in the ten firms with the greatest growth in earnings per share, the final quarter for each of the firms was probably unexpectedly good. Even in an efficient market, the reaction to the final quarter wouldn't occur until after the beginning of the year. By buying all the stocks at the beginning of 1976, your simulated portfolio will enjoy the increase in market value that you know is coming in the vicinity of the earnings release date. Your trading rule will show profitable returns, not because of a lag in market reaction to new information but rather because your simulation assumed you had access to information (the final quarter's earnings) that may have been available to no one at the time you executed your strategy. The appropriate way to test this rule would be to buy the stocks only after you could determine which ten actually had the greatest earnings growth. This is when the *last* candidate actually reports its earnings number.

In testing the profitability of your investment strategy it is also important to consider the costs involved in finding and processing the required information, as well as the differential costs involved in transacting in the market. In a passive investment strategy, you would invest at the very beginning of the period and hold on to your investments until the very end. In the strategy just discussed, you would completely reconstruct the portfolio at the end of every year or at the end of every quarter. In selling your investments of the previous period and buying your investments of the next period, you would not only incur round-trip commissions but you would also be subject to the capital gains tax, possibly the short-term capital gains tax. The extra commissions and extra taxes may serve to neutralize completely the performance of your trading rule.

You also have to determine whether any extra return produced by your strategy is due to chance or to your having successfully exploited some systematic inefficiency in pricing by the market. To do this, you must determine whether the magnitude of the extra return is significant in a statistical sense.

The issue whether the extra return is merely compensation for bearing extra risk must also be addressed. This gets back to the question of selecting the appropriate benchmark. Even if you have employed information that was actually available at the time you made your investments, even if you have factored in the additional costs associated with transacting and taxes, and even if you still find a statistically significant increment of extra return associated with your trading rule, you must be prepared to defend what you mean by "extra." Have you selected the right pricing model? Have you selected the proper market indices? Have you measured risk correctly?

After allowing for all these factors, if you can find trading rules that are capable of producing superior returns, you have found evidence that the market is inefficient with respect to the information employed by those trading rules.

MEDIOCRITY IN THE
PERFORMANCE OF INFORMED INVESTORS

If securities prices don't reflect all available information, those investors who are fully informed should be able to construct portfolios that produce superior returns. If the true market pricing structure is that of the Capital Asset Pricing Model, and if securities prices reflect publicly available information alone, traders who possess private information should see investments positioned relative to the securities market line as in Figure 19–3. They should be able to construct portfolios that are also positioned above the securities market line. If we use the CAPM-based risk-adjusted performance measures to assess their performance, we should find that their performance is superior to that of other investors.

If, on the other hand, the market is efficient, no investment is truly positioned above or below the securities market line. If you see an investment in such a position, it is because you are estimating its expected return and risk on the basis of less than the complete set of available information. You may construct a portfolio composed of securities that you *think* are above the securities market line, but because their true expected returns are all positioned on the line, your investment performance will be indistinguishable from that of any other investor. It should also be true that, within the group of professional investors, there should be no significant differences in their performance. Even if some are more intelligent or have more resources than others, if securities prices reflect all relevant information, intelligence and capital will be ineffective in searching for undervalued securities.

Thus, we can assess the efficiency of the market by first separating those investors who are likely to be most informed and then measuring their investment performance. If these investors exhibit records of superior performance, they must be investing on the basis of information that is both relevant and not reflected in securities prices.

Professional investors are likely to be most informed. They are trained in security and portfolio analysis, and they spend their working days searching for and analyzing information. Thus, in attempting to resolve the question of market efficiency, we should determine whether professionals as a group are distinguished in terms of their performance, and whether we can find significant differences in the performance of individual professional investors.

Once again our test is based on a joint hypothesis. We must first select the appropriate benchmark. This means we must make a hypothesis about the nature of the pricing structure. If we assume the CAPM we may measure performance relative to an estimate of the securities market line. Having made this assumption, we can then test the hypothesis that the market is efficient.

You may already have an opinion about this aspect of the investigation. You may have listened to many professional investors on talk shows on television, or have read books written by investors who have amazing records of performance. If we take these records as being accurate, how can the market possibly be efficient?

Literally millions of people invest in the securities markets. Suppose we take all these people, put them in a gigantic stadium, and have them flip coins. We will declare flipping a head as winning and flipping a tail as losing. Even if each is flipping a fair coin, we will find individual "flippers" with unbelievable records of success and failure. There will be some who flip more than twenty heads in a row. These individuals, convinced of their superior flipping ability, will go on television to tell others of their amazing success. Those who flip twenty tails in a row will hide in shame. Because all the head flippers will surface to expose themselves, it will appear as though winning is not a mere matter of chance. To determine whether it is, we would have to do a careful statistical analysis of the performance of the flippers. This is what we intend to do with respect to the performance of professional investors.

Summary

In a perfectly efficient market, securities prices reflect all information that is knowable and relevant. There are no undervalued or overvalued securities. Whatever the pricing structure of the market may be, the market is priced perfectly with respect to that structure.

There are degrees of market efficiency, each specifying the type of information that is reflected in securities prices. If the market is *weak-form* efficient, then securities prices reflect any information pertaining to the security's future expected return that can be obtained by examining the security's past price history. If the weak form holds, technical analysis, or charting, will be ineffective. If the market is *semistrong-form* efficient, securities prices reflect all publicly available information. Among other things, this includes the firm's accounting statements and announced statistics pertaining to the general economy. If the semistrong form holds, both technical and fundamental security analysis are ineffective. To beat the market, the analyst must seek out private information. The extreme case is the *strong form* of the efficient market hypothesis. Here all information that is knowable is reflected in securities prices. If this is true, no form of analysis will be effective in discriminating profitable from unprofitable investments.

To determine whether the market is, in fact, efficient, we must examine its behavior. An efficient market will exhibit the following behavioral characteristics:

1. Securities prices should respond quickly and accurately to the receipt of new information that is relevant to valuation.

2. The change in securities prices from one period to the next should be random.

3. It should be impossible to discriminate between profitable and unprofitable investments in a future period based on any of the characteristics of these investments that can be known in the current period.

4. If we separate investors who are knowledgeable from those who are not, we should discover that we are unable to find a significant difference between the average investment performance of the two groups. Moreover, it should be the case that differences in the performance of individual investors within each group would be insignificant.

In Chapter 20 we examine the extent to which the real market exhibits these characteristics.

1. A rationale frequently given for the issuance of callable debt by a firm is that the firm would like to be able to save money if interest rates should fall. The call provision in the debt allows the firm to call in the debt and then issue new debt at a lower interest rate. If markets are efficient, what is the fallacy in this argument?

2. Suppose you discovered a systematic relationship between the price-earnings ratios of stocks and the performance of stocks. In other words, knowledge of a firm's price-earnings ratio proved helpful in predicting which stocks would show superior performance. Would this evidence be consistent with any of three versions of the efficient market hypothesis?

3. If the market adheres to the strong form of the efficient market hypothesis, what is the implication for the usefulness of gathering and analyzing data about companies? What sort of logical paradox seems to result?

4. If you believe that the market is efficient with respect to one of the information sets mentioned in the chapter, does this necessarily imply that you believe the market is inefficient with respect to one of the other information sets? Explain.

5. For each of the following kinds of information, indicate which form of the efficient market hypothesis is correct, if that information is reflected in securities prices.

   a. Government-released data on the money supply

   b. A corporate quarterly earnings report

   c. A public release of information from the Securities and Exchange Commission on insider trading

   d. Confidential discussions of a corporate board of directors on dividend policy

   e. A history of a bond's prices

6. Suppose there is a consistent seasonal movement in stock prices. Why might this be inconsistent with the efficient market hypothesis?

7. Consider the following statement: In an efficient market, today's price will have no systematic relationship to tomorrow's price. Is this true or false? Explain.

8. Refer to Figure 19–4 and the solid line depicting the efficient market scenario. Plots of actual stock prices show substantially more variability than this idealized plot. What is being assumed in Figure 19–4 that accounts for this difference?

9. What does it mean to use the Capital Asset Pricing Model as a benchmark to test a trading strategy?

10. Suppose you follow and compare two recommended trading strategies over several years. One strategy results in significantly higher average return.

Does this necessarily imply that the higher return strategy is a superior strategy? Explain.

11. Can you think of any readily available sources of data on the investment performance of professional investment analysts?

12. Tests of market efficiency are often referred to as "joint tests" of two hypotheses. Explain the meaning of this. Further, try to speculate on the difficulty this poses for tests of market efficiency.

13. Suppose you know several individuals who devised and implemented several trading rules or strategies, based on publicly available information. They show you their returns, which are much higher than what would have been obtainable by investing in a broad market index. Would this information alone cast doubt on the efficiency of the market?

BIBLIOGRAPHY

BARON, D. P., "Information, Investment Behavior, and Efficient Portfolios," *Journal of Financial and Quantitative Analysis* (September 1974).

BLACK, F., "Random Walk and Portfolio Management," *Financial Analysts Journal* (March–April 1971).

BREALEY, R. A., *An Introduction to Risk and Return from Common Stocks*. Cambridge, Mass.: MIT Press, 1969.

FAMA, E. F., "Efficient Capital Markets: A Review of Theory and Empirical Work," *Journal of Finance* (May 1970).

GRANGER, C. W. J., "The Random Walk Misunderstood?" *Financial Analysts Journal* (May–June 1970).

GROSSMAN, S. J., "On the Efficiency of Competitive Stock Markets Where Traders Have Diverse Information," *Journal of Finance* (May 1976).

GROSSMAN, S. J., and J. E. STIGLITZ, "On the Impossibility of Informationally Efficient Markets," *American Economic Review* (June 1980).

JAFFE, J. F., and R. L. WINKLER, "Optimal Speculation Against an Efficient Market," *Journal of Finance* (March 1976).

LAFFER, A. B., and R. D. RANSON, "Some Practical Applications of the Efficient Market Concept," *Financial Mangement* (Summer 1979).

MALKIEL, B. G., and P. B. FINSTENBERG, "A Winning Strategy for an Efficient Market," *Journal of Portfolio Mangement* (Summer 1978).

PIPER, T. R., and W. E. FRUHAN, "Is Your Stock Worth Its Market Price?" *Harvard Business Review* (May–June 1981).

SAMUELSON, P. A., "Proof That Properly Anticipated Prices Fluctuate Randomly," *Industrial Management Review* (Spring 1965).

VERRECCHIA, R. E., "Consensus Beliefs, Information Acquisition and Market Information Efficiency," *American Economic Review* (December 1980).

20 MARKET EFFICIENCY: THE EVIDENCE

Introduction

In Chapter 19 we learned that an efficient securities market exhibits four characteristics.

1. Securities prices respond rapidly and accurately to new information received by the market.

2. The changes in securities prices from one period to the next should be random so that the change in price that will occur tommorrow can't be predicted on the basis of changes that occurred today or any other day in the past.

3. Trading rules fail to produce superior returns after adjusting for risk, taxes, and transactions costs in simulation experiments.

4. Professional investors fail to produce superior returns individually or as a group.

In this chapter we will examine some of the studies that have addressed the question of whether the market exhibits these traits. We will look at evidence on both sides of the issue.

DO SECURITIES PRICES RESPOND RAPIDLY AND ACCURATELY TO THE RECEIPT OF NEW INFORMATION?

Measuring Stock Price Response

A large number of studies has been directed at examining the nature of the market's reaction to such events as the announcement of earnings, dividends, stock splits, merger announcements, and large block purchases and sales in the secondary market. In most of these studies, an effort is made to estimate the stock's excess returns in the vicinity of the event. The excess return in a given period is defined as the difference between the stock's actual return for the period and what one would expect the stock to produce, given the stock's characteristic line and the performance of the market for the period.

The first step in the process is to estimate the stock's characteristic line. This is usually done by sampling in a period other than the one surrounding the event. If you are going to examine the stock price response to the event on a day-by-day basis, you would estimate the characteristic line using daily rates of return. For example, if we call the day of the event day 0, and we are going to examine the response of the stock from ten days before to ten days after the event, we might estimate the characteristic line in the period from seventy days before to eleven days before (-70 to -11). Doing this, we fit the characteristic line as in Figure 20–1.

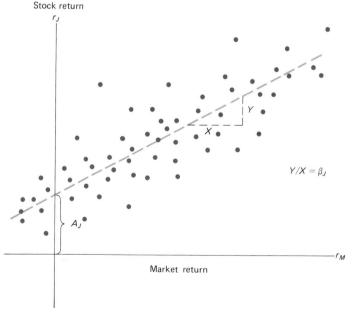

Figure 20-1 Estimating the Characteristic Line

The characteristic line gives us an expectation of what the stock's return should be on a particular day, given that the market has produced a particular rate of return. The expected rate of return on the stock, conditional on the appearance of a particular rate of return to the market on day t, is given by

$$\text{Expected stock return given market return} = \hat{A}_J + \hat{\beta}_J r_{M,t}$$

Because we are interested in the response of the stock to the event, we are interested in determining if the stock's returns in the vicinity of the event are above or below what we would expect to see, in light of the performance of the market. Thus, our measure of response on a given day is the difference between the stock's actual rate of return and its expected return, given the market rate of return. You may recognize this as the stock's residual or shock term, $\epsilon_{J,t}$.

$$\epsilon_{J,t} = \text{Actual stock return} - \text{Expected stock return given market return}$$

To measure the stock's overall reaction to the event, we might accumulate the responses over various periods going from day -10 to day $+10$. For example, the accumulated response in going from day -10 to day 0 would be given by

$$\text{Accumulated response through day } 0 = \sum_{t=-10}^{0} \epsilon_{J,t} = E_{J,0}$$

Individual stocks are subject to the flow of many types of information, some of which will push the stock up and some of which will push the stock down. Thus, the response to the particular event of interest may be masked by the responses to the other pieces of information. To handle this problem, we collect a large sample of stocks that have in common the incidence of a particular event, such as the announcement of a takeover bid on their common stock. The takeover bids may come at different calendar times for the different stocks, but for each stock we compute the accumulated response relative to day 0, the day the takeover bid is announced. For any given day t relative to day 0, the accumulated response is averaged over all M stocks in the sample to obtain what is called the cumulative average excess return:

$$\frac{\sum_{J=1}^{M} E_{J,t}}{M} = \begin{array}{l}\text{Cumulative average} \\ \text{excess return}\end{array}$$

Because the only thing that the stocks in the sample have in common is the event, the other factors that are influencing their prices should cancel out in the averaging. The movement in the cumulative average excess return as we approach the announcement of the event should give an indication of the average speed and accuracy of the response of stock prices to the particular event of interest.

Suppose the event is the announcement of information that should increase the market value of the stock. If the market is semistrong-form efficient, the cumulative average excess return should exhibit the pattern depicted in Figure 20–2. It should have a value that is not significantly different from zero, until we

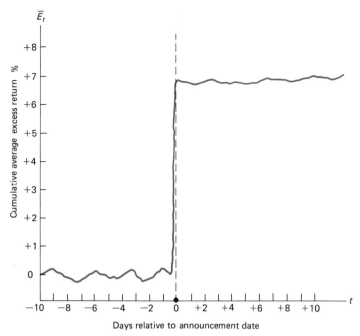

Figure 20-2 Stock Price Response to New Information in a Semi-strong-Form Efficient Market

reach the day of the announcement. On that day most of the stocks in the sample should experience a positive value for ϵ. (Some may not because of the incidence of a different negative piece of information on the day of the announcement.) The value for the cumulative average excess return should not change after the announcement. If the reaction to the event is completed on the announcement day, and if the firms in the sample have nothing in common other than the event, on any day after the announcement, approximately half the firms in the sample should have positive residuals and half should have negative residuals. If this is true, the value for the cumulative average excess return should not be expected to change from day to day.

If the market is strong-form efficient, and if information related to the event leaks out prior to the announcement, a different pattern should emerge, as that in Figure 20–3. The value for the cumulative average residual should gradually increase in the days prior to the announcement. There should be a substantial increase in the cumulative average residual on the day of the announcement (reflecting the response of those stocks for which information didn't leak), and there should be no further change in the cumulative average residual after the announcement.

Don't misinterpret the gradual increase in the cumulative average residual prior to the announcement. It doesn't necessarily reflect (a) a gradual response to the leakage of inside information for any one stock or (b) an incomplete response to the leakage of inside information. The only thing the stocks in the

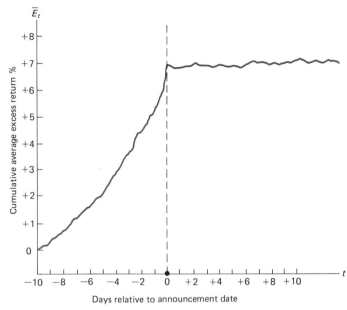

Figure 20-3 Stock Price Response to New Information in a Strong-Form Efficient Market

sample have in common is the public announcement of the event at day 0. For any one stock the inside information could have leaked out at any time prior to the public announcement date. Even though it may be the case that each stock responds fully and completely on the day of the leakage, in averaging over different stocks with different leakage dates, the average response may appear to be gradual.

The Response of Stock Prices to the Announcement of a Stock Split

Fama, Fisher, Jensen, and Roll (1969) were the first to employ the methodology discussed in the previous section. They used monthly data to study the reaction of stock prices to the event of a stock split. They studied most of the splits that occurred on the New York Stock Exchange between 1929 and 1959.

Why should the stock price react to a split when the split does nothing more than divide up the corporate pie into more pieces? If the stock splits two for one, shouldn't the price of each share halve? Why should there be any effect on the rate of return, adjusted for the split?

As it turns out, splits act as a leading indicator of an increase in the dividend for the stock. In approximately 80 percent of the cases, a stock split is followed by an increase in the dividend. An increase in the dividend is of significance to the stockholders for the following reason. Management has a reluctance to cut dividends. Thus, it won't increase the dividend unless it is convinced there has been a permanent increase in the profitability of the firm to support the increased dividend payment. An increase in the dividend serves as a signal from management that it perceives that the earning power of the firm has been permanently enhanced. Inasmuch as a stock split serves as a leading indicator—there is an 80 percent chance for a dividend increase—it should induce a response in the stock price that reflects this probability.

Figures 20–4, 20–5, and 20–6 show the results of the Fama et al. study. The results for the entire sample are depicted in Figure 20–4. Note that the cumulative average excess return begins climbing as much as twenty-nine months before the month of the split, which is month 0. The direction of causation here isn't running from the split to the stock price, however. Rather it is more likely the case that the split itself results from the run-up in the stock price in the months prior to its occurrence. The sizable jump in the cumulative average excess return immediately before the split month may reflect a reaction to the split. The public announcement of the split may fall within these months for some stocks, and leakages of inside information may also be occurring here.

In any case, the reaction to the split seems to be complete by the month of its occurrence. There is no propensity for the split stocks to rise or fall, as a group, in the months after. There is no evidence of an incomplete reaction or overreaction to the event.

Figure 20–5 represents the 80 percent of the sample cases where the dividend increase actually occurs. When the split is announced, the stock prices rise to

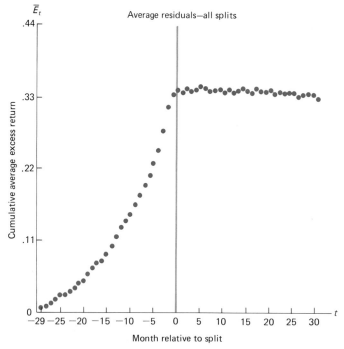

Figure 20-4 Price Reaction for All Splits

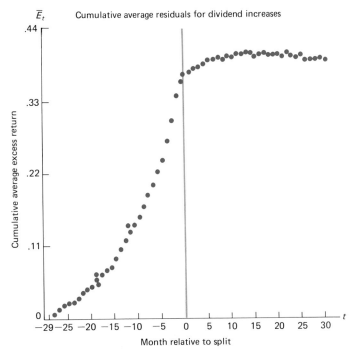

Figure 20-5   Price Reaction for Dividend Increases

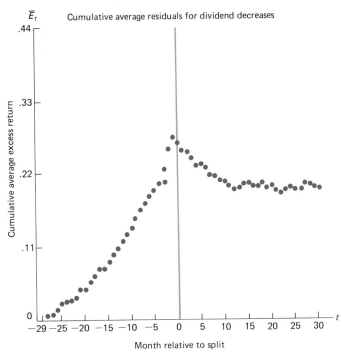

Figure 20-6   Price Reaction for No Dividend

reflect the 80 percent probability of the dividend increase. When the increase occurs, the odds, of course, increase to 100 percent, and the stock price rises accordingly.

Figure 20–6 shows the results for the 20 percent of the cases that had no accompanying dividend increase. Taking the split as a leading indicator, the prices of these stocks rose to reflect the 80 percent probability of a forthcoming dividend increase. When the dividend increase fails to appear, the cumulative average residual falls back to its presplit level.

Overall, the pattern seems to be consistent with that of a rational, efficient market that reacts rapidly and correctly to the announcement of a stock split. Admittedly, it is difficult to measure the speed of the reaction here, because we are using monthly returns and because the responses are lined up relative to the split month rather than the announcement month for the split. As mentioned, however, this is a pioneering study, and these shortcomings are addressed in later work, as we shall see below.

The Reaction of Stock Prices to Quarterly Earnings Reports

Many studies have been done of the price reaction to the earnings announcement event. The most comprehensive is that by Rendleman, Jones, and Latané (RJL) (1982).

RJL separated firms into ten groups according to the nature of their earnings report in a given quarter. To group the firms, they first estimated what the earnings per share would be, according to a statistical analysis of the firm's quarterly earnings numbers in the past. They then compared the actual earnings reported with the statistical estimate. If actual earnings were more than two standard deviations above their estimate, the firm was put in group 10. If the actual number was between 1.50 and 2.00 standard deviations above the mean, the firm was put in group 9. This process continued through group 1, which is composed of those firms that reported earnings more than two standard deviations below the estimated value.

The cumulative average excess returns for each of the groups in the days surrounding the announcement of earnings are depicted in Figure 20–7. The stock prices appear to begin reacting to the earnings numbers up to twenty days before the announcement is made. This is probably accounted for by leakages of inside information. There is also evidence of a sizable reaction in the immediate vicinity of the event. So far, all this is consistent with market efficiency. However, in those cases where the earnings number is extremely good or extremely bad, there appears to be a delayed reaction that continues up to ninety days after the announcement. Based on the figure, if you bought the stocks in group 10 on the day of the announcement, you would earn an additional increment in return of up to 8 percent that could be attributable to the earnings announcement. Group 1 shows a similar result in the opposite direction.

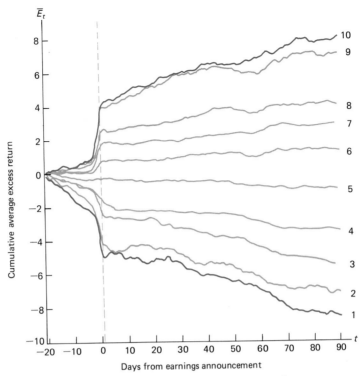

Figure 20-7 Price Reaction to Quarterly Earnings Report

These results indicate that there appears to be *some* inside information impounded in stock prices. The stock price, however, doesn't fully react to the *public* announcement of the earnings report until a full ninety days after the report is released. The results are, therefore, inconsistent with even the semistrong form of the efficient market hypothesis.

In fairness to the supporters of market efficiency, it must be said that most of the studies of market reaction to various events are consistent with market efficiency. However, because the RJL study is carefully done and the most comprehensive to date, it must be said that the best evidence indicates that the market's reaction, at least to the announcement of quarterly earnings, is less than efficient.

ARE CHANGES IN STOCK PRICES RANDOM?

If the securities market is efficient, current prices should reflect all information, and they should change only in response to *new* information, the receipt of which can't be predicted in advance. This type of information, by its very nature, comes to the market in a random, unpredictable manner. As securities prices respond instantly and accurately to its receipt, they themselves should change randomly over time.

Studies of Serial Correlation

What do we mean by random? Technically speaking, if securities prices followed a pure random walk, the probability distribution for the change in price would remain perfectly constant over time. All that is required for consistency with market efficiency, however, is that the best estimate of the expected change in the price for tomorrow be unrelated to the changes that have occurred in the price of the stock at any time in the past. This condition is violated in Figure 20–8, where the percentage changes that occur on any one day in the price of a stock are plotted on the horizontal axis and the changes that occur on the next day are plotted on the vertical axis. Each point in the figure represents a single observation for a pair of days. The broken line running through the scatter is the line of best fit.

Note that the scatter has a positive slope, indicating that when yesterday's change has been large, there is a propensity for today's change to be large as well. Thus, if yesterday's change was equal to that of point A, the probability distribution for today's change would be the one labeled A. If, on the other hand, yesterday's change was that of point B, the probability distribution for

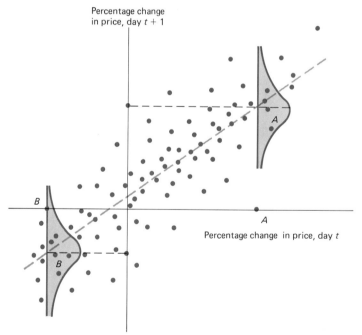

Figure 20-8   Correlation Between Successive Price Changes in an Inefficient Market

today's change would be the one labeled *B*. As you can see, the *expected* change for today is, in this case, positively related to the magnitude of yesterday's price change.

This can be contrasted with Figure 20–9. In this case, successive changes in price are uncorrelated. The expected change for today is totally unrelated to what happened to the price yesterday. If the market is efficient, we should obtain results like that of Figure 20–9 when we correlate percentage changes in any given stock. This should be true not only for successive percentage changes but also for changes lagged any number of periods. The change in price today should be unrelated to the change that took place yesterday, the day before, or any other day in the past.

Figure 20–10 depicts the relationship between successive percentage changes in a stock index for the months of 1982 and 1983. Figure 20–11 shows a similar relationship, where the percentage changes are separated by one month. In both cases, the correlation coefficient is not significantly different from zero. This result is typical of the results that have been found in many studies of many different stocks. Studies have been done on monthly, weekly, daily, and even interday returns on stocks that are both listed and traded on the over-the-counter exchange. In these studies, as the trading interval becomes smaller, the correlation coefficients for some stocks become significantly different from zero, usually for successive percentage changes. However, even when a statistically significant relationship is detected, it is seldom significant in an *economic* sense. That is, even if you were aware of it, and you attempted to trade on the basis of it, brokerage commissions would make your expected profits negative.

The evidence from studies that have attempted to model series of stock prices using standard statistical techniques seems to point in the direction that, unless you are a floor trader and pay no commissions, you would do well to look to sources other than the history of stock prices to make money in the market.

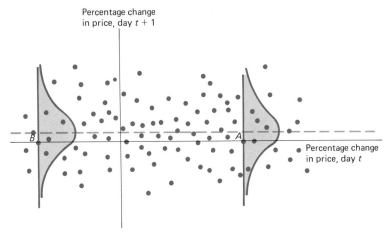

Figure 20-9   Correlation Between Successive Price Changes in an Efficient Market

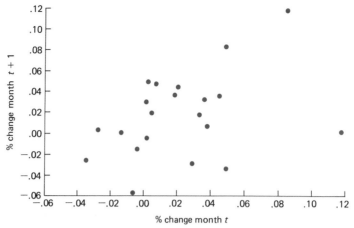

Figure 20-10 Relationship Between Successive Monthly Percentage
Changes in a Stock Index

The Day of the Week Effect

Two independent studies, conducted by French (1980) and by Gibbons and Hess (1981), found evidence consistent with the hypothesis that there are significant differences in the expected percentage changes for stocks depending on the day of the week that trading is conducted. The results of the Gibbons and Hess study are summarized in Figure 20–12.

Each bar in the figure represents the mean percentage change in the Standard and Poor's Index of 500 stocks for each of the five trading days of the week. The study covers more that 4000 trading days from 1962 through 1968. The expected percentage change on Mondays appears to be negative, and the expected

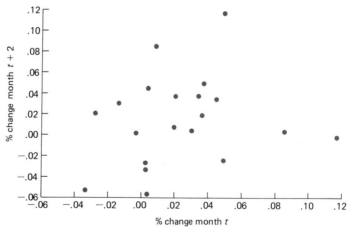

Figure 20-11 Relationship Between Lagged Monthly Changes in a
Stock Index

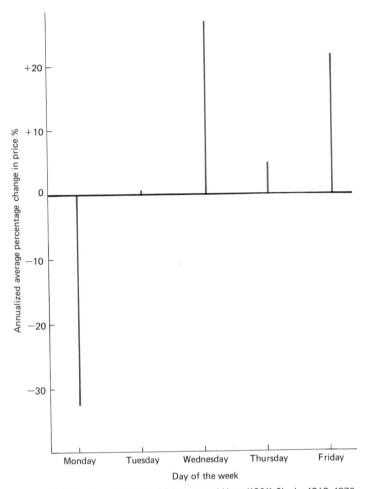

Figure 20-12 Results of the Gibbons and Hess (1981) Study, 1962–1978

percentage changes on Wednesdays and Fridays appear to be larger than on Tuesdays and Thursdays. Although there appears to be a *statistically* significant difference between some of the mean returns for the different days, the differences again are not economically significant if you have to pay commissions. Unless you are a floor trader, if you attempted to buy stocks near the end of trading every Monday and then sell them near the end of trading every Friday, you would find your broker to be the only person making money from your efforts.

You may want to consider the day of the week effect, however, in timing your purchases and sales. If you are planning to buy some stock at the beginning of the week, you may want to postpone your purchases until the opening of the market on Tuesday and thereby take advantage of the expected decline in prices on Monday. Transactions costs are immaterial to this strategy because they have to be paid on either day.

The January Effect

There is something unusual about the first few trading days in January in the stock market. Rozeff and Kinney (1976) were the first to notice that the average rate of return to stocks in January was higher than in any other month. In the period from 1904 to 1974, the average rate of return to an index of the stock market was 3.48 percent. The average rate of return for all months was only .68 percent. This difference between January and the other months is also present in various subperiods within the total period. For example, in the period 1929 through 1940 January's average return was 6.63 percent, compared with an average return for all other months of .19 percent.

This interesting result was confirmed by Brown, Kleidon, and Marsh (1983) and Keim (1983). In fact, in the study by Keim, he shows that a large proportion of the January effect is contained in the first five trading days of January. Note also that the January effect is most pronounced for the smallest companies. Figure 20–13 is taken from the study by Brown et al. (1983). The figure plots average monthly rates of return on five portfolios in each of the twelve months of the year. The companies in the sample are ranked by size and then grouped into portfolios, where the largest 20 percent are put into the first portfolio, and so on. The portfolios' average monthly rate of return is plotted on the vertical axis. Months of the year are plotted on the horizontal axis moving toward the east-southeast. Company size, from the largest to the smallest, is plotted on the horizontal axis moving toward the northeast.

There is a general propensity for small firms to produce larger returns, but this propensity is by far the most pronounced in January. These results are consistent with the hypothesis that, for some reason, funds flow into the equity mar-

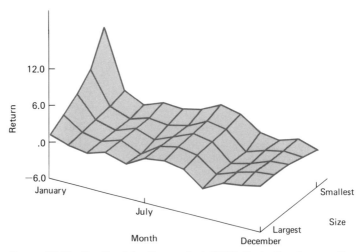

Figure 20-13 Results of the Brown et al. (1983) Study: The January Effect for Different Company Size Groupings

kets in the beginning of the month of January. This flow of funds is most easily absorbed by the larger firms, which have more active markets for their stock. The prices of the smaller firms are affected more dramatically, because the markets for their shares are relatively thin.

Is the January effect confined to the U.S. stock market? Apparently it is not. It seems to happen all over the world. Table 20–1 is taken from a study by Gultekin and Gultekin (1983). The numbers in the table are average monthly rates of return for each month of the year. Notice that the average rates of return are unusually high in January for nearly every country represented. These rates of return don't include dividends, and some are based on market indices that can be questioned as being representative. Nevertheless, the January effect appears to be a worldwide phenomenon.

A recent study by Tinic and West (1984) shows an even more surprising result for the month of January. Tinic and West examined the relationship between the monthly returns on common stocks and their betas to see if the relationship between risk and return was different in January than in the other months of the year. They found that it is indeed. It seems that January is the only month of the year where there exists a positive trade-off between the beta of a stock and its realized rates of return. In the month of January you expect to see high beta stocks of return. In the month of January you expect to see high beta stocks producing higher than average rates of return. However, in any other month, there is no evidence of a cross-sectional relationship between beta and realized return.

As we learned in our discussion of the CAPM, the slope of the relationship between average return and beta reflects the risk premium earned on the market index. Tinic and West found that the average monthly risk premium for their market index in the month of January was 3.02 percent during the period 1935 through 1982. The risk premium earned for the rest of the months of the year was only .36 percent, and statistically, this number is not significantly different from zero.

The evidence from Tinic and West is consistent with the situation of Figure 20–14, where market returns are plotted on the horizontal axis and stock returns on the vertical axis. The solid lines in the figure are the characteristic lines of stocks with different beta factors. It appears that in the month of January the expected return to the market lies to the right of the common point of intersection of the characteristic lines. Given that it does, the expected returns for the individual stocks in this month will be positively related to the slopes of the characteristic lines or the beta factors. In the other months of the year, the market's expected return appears to lie at the coordinates of the common point of intersection. Given that it does, all stocks would have the same expected rate of return, and you would see no cross-sectional relationship between beta and realized rate of return.

What force might cause funds to flow into nearly all the equity markets of the world at the same time, producing an abnormally high rate of return in the month of January? At this point, we really don't know, but at least three possible explanations can be offered.

Table 20–1 Mean Monthly Returns by Country, January 1959 to December 1979

Country	Jan.	Feb.	Mar.	Apr.	May	June	July	Aug.	Sept.	Oct.	Nov.	Dec.
Australia	2.649	−0.581	0.506	0.841	0.973	0.428	0.662	−0.365	−2.387	2.130	−0.848	3.993
Austria	0.743	0.890	0.239	−0.414	0.067	0.213	1.237	0.899	0.021	−0.224	0.651	1.233
Belgium	3.215	1.085	0.395	1.482	−1.355	−0.840	1.441	−1.166	−1.866	−0.688	0.415	−0.089
Canada	2.900	0.068	0.789	0.408	−0.963	−0.300	0.689	0.600	−0.061	−0.820	1.435	2.611
Denmark	3.041	−0.407	−1.191	0.584	0.448	0.383	0.506	−0.138	−1.297	0.264	−0.900	2.037
France	3.722	−0.176	1.983	0.936	−0.656	−1.902	1.529	1.028	−1.214	−0.719	0.433	0.152
Germany	3.099	−0.142	1.048	0.605	−0.016	−0.948	1.559	2.243	−1.681	−0.936	1.356	0.092
Italy	2.229	0.865	0.737	0.723	−1.303	−0.411	−0.573	2.346	−0.724	−1.292	0.255	−0.171
Japan	3.529	1.128	1.877	0.301	0.975	2.059	−0.321	−0.829	−0.133	−0.976	1.646	1.798
Netherlands	3.762	0.474	1.298	1.387	−0.982	1.436	0.492	−0.283	−1.911	0.246	−0.102	1.308
Norway	4.336	−1.176	−0.627	2.363	0.291	1.953	3.010	0.366	−1.559	−0.508	0.419	−0.320
Singapore	10.591	−0.418	2.093	−2.315	4.015	0.307	−0.487	−0.375	−0.954	2.350	−1.966	5.227
Spain	2.241	1.294	0.321	1.588	−1.873	0.062	0.794	1.290	−1.641	0.189	−0.436	−0.009
Sweden	3.996	0.383	1.006	0.879	−0.795	−0.246	2.409	−1.098	−1.335	−0.673	−0.179	0.823
Switzerland	4.585	−0.747	0.395	0.858	−1.267	−0.020	0.647	1.746	−1.536	−0.194	0.985	1.266
United Kingdom	3.406	0.687	1.248	3.129	−1.212	−1.689	−1.112	1.883	−0.239	0.798	−0.608	2.063
United States	1.041	−0.410	1.266	0.959	−1.384	0.560	0.139	0.338	−0.795	0.780	1.027	1.419

SOURCE: M. N. Gultekin and B. N. Gultekin, "Stock Market Seasonality: International Evidence," *Journal of Financial Economics* (Dec. 1983).

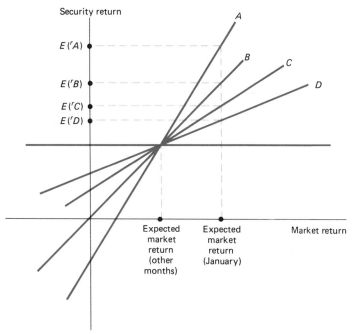

Figure 20-14 Possible Explanation for Tinic and West Results

We may be seeing a tax effect. Investors who have accrued tax losses may choose to realize them for tax purposes and then move back into the market at the beginning of the next tax year. If investors are rational, they will lock in their tax losses as they accrue during the year. This explains why we don't see a December effect in the opposite direction.

There are some problems with this explanation, however. First, why delay repurchase of another stock until the beginning of the next tax year? Why not just ask your broker to sell your tax loss stock and move the funds into another, nearly identical, issue on the same trading day? Brokers have lists of such paired issues for just this purpose. Why should tax loss selling in one year create an inflow of funds in the next? There is no tax advantage associated with waiting until the next tax year to buy. Second, many of the countries in Table 20–1 that show a January effect either do not tax capital gains or do not end their tax years in January. In fairness, it must be admitted that the January effect in these countries could conceivably be caused by foreign traders whose capital gains are taxed on the basis of realization by year end. Moreover, a recently published study by Schultz (1985) finds no evidence of a January effect in the United States before the 1917 income tax act.

A recent study by De Bondt and Thaler (1985) provides some support for the tax loss selling explanation for the January effect. They took a large group of stocks and ranked them on the basis of market performance over a sixty-month period. They examined the stocks that were distinctive in terms of very good or very bad market performance. Then they examined the average cumulative between the returns for the stocks and the returns for a market index for both groups in the period after the sixty-month evaluation period. For each stock the postevaluation period begins in January. Figure 20–15 plots the cumulative average excess return for both groups. It is easy to pick out January from the time series. In each subsequent January there is a jump in the cumulative average excess return. Note, also, that in the months of November and December there is a persistent decline in the cumulative average difference in return, at least for the stocks that performed poorly in the evaluation period.

The stocks in each group have only one thing in common, distinctive performance in the sixty-month evaluation period. At the beginning of the post-evaluation period, investors holding the stocks in the poor performing group are likely to have had accrued capital losses. It appears from the evidence that these stocks experienced year-end selling pressure as investors realized these losses for tax purposes. After this pressure the stocks then rallied in price in the month of January. This tendency persisted, although at a diminishing rate, over the next five years, as at the end of each year. The strength of the January rally following the November–December decline may suggest that the January effect may be attributed to more than tax loss selling.

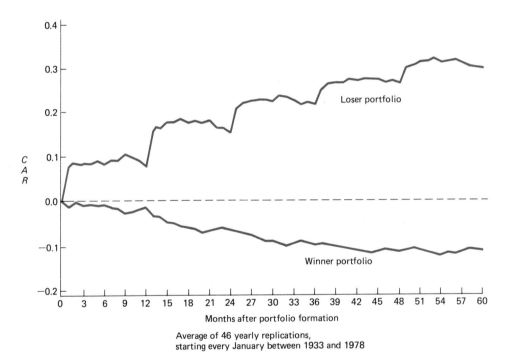

Months after portfolio formation

Average of 46 yearly replications,
starting every January between 1933 and 1978

Figure 20-15 Cumulative Average Residuals for Winner and Loser Portfolios of Thirty-Five Stocks, One to Sixty Months After Portfolio Formation; Length of Formation Period: Five Years

SOURCE: W. De Bondt, and R. Thaler, "Does the Stock Market Overreact to New Information?" *Journal of Finance* (July 1985), p. 803.

A second conjecture on a possible cause for the January effect was suggested to me by a group of professional traders. They allege that the January effect may be the result of the nature of the compensation system in the securities industry. Managers are typically rewarded at the end of the year with a Christmas bonus, the size of which is determined by the rate of return earned by the manager during the year. They suggest that it is not atypical for managers to behave in the following way.

Managers put the funds under their control at risk at the beginning of the year. If, at any time during the year, their portfolio produces a *satisfactory* level of dollar return, they lock in the return, and their bonus, by moving the portfolio out of the equity market and into low-risk investments. The point in time where a satisfactory bonus is achieved is, of course, different for different managers, which explains why there is no negative price reaction toward the end of the year associated with the January effect. At the beginning of January, the game begins again, and managers, en masse, move their managed funds back into equities.

A similar story can be told for unlucky portfolio managers who experience unusually bad returns during the year. There may be a level of negative performance at which their jobs are in jeopardy. As the managers approach this level, they might find it in their interests to shift the portfolio to low-risk investments until the end of the year, when their performance for the year is evaluated. After the evaluation they return to the risky segments of the market once again. Under this scenario, the January effect is caused by a conflict of interest between an agent (the manager) and a principal (the investor), which in turn results from the nature of the agent's compensation.

Portfolio window dressing may serve as a third explanation for the January effect. Professionally managed portfolios are usually subjected to scrutiny at the end of each year, when managers release details on the composition of their portfolios. Given that a "snapshot picture" is taken of their portfolios once a year, it may be in the interests of managers to "dress up" their portfolios by moving into more conservative investments before the picture is taken. Then, after the year-end picture is taken and released, the managers move into the higher risk segments of the market, forcing the prices of these issues up in the first few trading days in January.

At this point, all we can do is guess about possible causes for the January effect. We can say, however, that the effect is inconsistent with the efficient market hypothesis. Whatever its cause, an efficient market should be able to absorb a seasonal inflow of funds without a significant impact on price levels. Given the January effect, we can't say that the expected percentage change in the prices of stocks is independent of their past behavior. Given the past behavior of stocks, if yesterday was New Year's Day, the expected value for the daily percentage change shifts to the right for the next few trading days. The magnitude of this change is not insignificant.

Figure 20–16, taken from Keim (1983), shows the average *daily* abnormal return (adjusted for beta risk) during the month of January for ten equally weighted portfolios that are constructed on the basis of ranking stocks by market value at

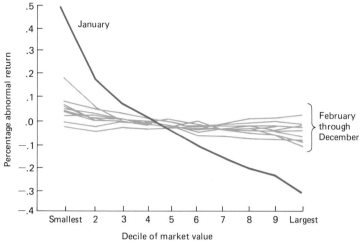

Figure 20-16 Average Daily Abnormal Return, by Month and Company
Size

SOURCE: D. B. Keim, "Size-Related Anomalies and Stock Return Seasonality:
Further Empirical Evidence," *Journal of Financial Economics* (June 1983).

the beginning of each month. The period covered is 1963 through 1979. For the
smallest companies, the abnormal return is large enough to overcome the transactions costs associated with moving into these companies at the beginning of
January and out at the end. This evidence contradicts even the weak form of the
efficient market hypothesis.

DO TRADING RULES FAIL UNDER SIMULATION?

In an efficient market, each security sells at a price and an expected return that
are reasonable and appropriate, given its risk, based on the *best* available estimate of the probability distribution of the future cash flows that will accrue to
the firm. If your analysis leads you to conclude that the expected return is unreasonable, it is because you are either using an inappropriate benchmark for a
"reasonable" return, or you are basing your analysis on insufficient information,
and, therefore, you don't have the best estimates.

In such a market, all strategies or trading rules that attempt to separate profitable from unprofitable investments should fail, because, based on the true underlying probability distributions, there are no such investments. This should be
true now, and it should have been true for any arbitrary point in the past, so
long as the trading rule is based on information that was available at the past
point in time and the market was efficient then as well as now.

Have trading rules surfaced that seem capable of consistently beating the market in past periods of time? We have to be careful here, because it is in the
interest of those who find such rules to hide them rather than publicize them.

With this caveat aside, it must be said that in the case of the vast majority of the trading rules that have been publicized as successful strategies, the tests have been later shown to employ defective methodology, biasing the results in favor of the rule, or the superior performance fails to reappear when the rule is tested in alternative time periods.

The Price-Earnings Anomaly

A trading rule based on the ratio of the market price of a stock to its earnings per share seems to have produced statistically significant excess returns after allowing for such factors as transactions costs and taxes. In following this strategy, you buy stocks that have inordinately low price-earnings ratios and you avoid stocks with inordinately high price-earnings ratios.

The idea behind the rule is that there is a large body of empirical evidence pointing to the conclusion that earnings per share follows a random pattern over time. It seems that even if you use the best available statistical techniques to model the time series of earnings per share numbers, the models are virtually useless in predicting the growth in earnings per share more than a few *quarters* into the future. In addition, studies by Brown and Rozeff (1978) and Cragg and Malkiel (1968) indicate that the forecasting ability of professional investors is highly questionable. Forecasting relative growth rates in earnings per share seems to be a hazardous business indeed.

In spite of this, the market seems to price stocks as though it can make useful forecasts of relative rates of growth in earnings per share for many years into the future. At times, stocks sell at prices that are more than thirty times what would be a reasonable estimate of the earnings per share number for the following year. Other stocks sell at prices that are less than two times current earnings. This is due to the price being set on the basis of the expectation that the growth rate in earnings for the high price-earnings stock will be well above the growth rate for the low price-earnings stock for a long time to come. On the basis of the evidence discussed, pricing the stocks on such an expectation would seem to be a mistake.

If the market has a propensity to make such a mistake, the way to exploit it is to buy those stocks that the market is most pessimistic about and avoid those issues that are most favorably regarded. This "contrarian" view has been espoused for some time by many people, but it recently has been popularized in a book written by Dreman (1982). If you are a contrarian, you are attracted to stocks with low price-earnings ratios.

Have portfolios with low price-earnings ratios tended to produce abnormally high rates of return in the past? There have been many studies directed at answering this question, but most have suffered from fatal flaws, which have been pointed out by others. The most conspicuous flaw in studies of the contrarian strategy is the method by which a sample of firms is chosen for the simulation. Typically a group of firms is chosen, all of which have survived the entire period of the study. Can you see the problem in picking the sample in this way? If you

Pieces Greater Than the Whole

The ice was really beginning to build up now. Traffic was literally crawling. The usual ninety-minute commute would probably double today to three hours.

Terry Langetieg was driving one of the several hundred thousand cars slowly making their way from New Jersey to Manhattan. The ice storm stood between him and the beginning of his working day at Salomon Brothers at One New York Plaza. It would have been great to get there on time today. The firm is conducting a major marketing operation of a new CMO. In this case the entire "Z Bond" piece was being marketed to Japanese investors in Tokyo. Increasingly, Salomon was finding international clientele with specialized investment needs. The firm met these needs, in some cases by splitting existing U.S. securities into component parts and marketing the parts to investors in the United States and throughout the world.

Take the CMO, for example—or collateralized mortgage obligation. Salomon, and later First Boston, were the first to enter the market for this new security, and in the past two years the volume of new issues has risen from literally nothing to $30 billion per year.

The CMO is basically a twist on the Ginnie Mae passthrough. The Ginnie Mae is notorious for uncertainty about the magnitude of its payments and the sensitivity of its market value to changes in interest rates. The Ginnie Mae is backed by a pool of conventional mortgages. The payments on these mortgages are passed through to the holder of the Ginnie Mae. If mortgage rates fall and prepayments on the underlying mortgages are greater than expected, the cash flows associated with the Ginnie Mae will also be greater than expected in the early years of the security's life. Because conventional mortgages are also relatively long term, the value of the Ginnie Mae will also be relatively sensitive to interest rate changes, a property that is undesirable to some investors.

With the CMO, the Ginnie Mae is

actually invested in a portfolio of stocks, all of which had extremely low ratios of price to earnings, what would you be most concerned about? Because the market is apparently very pessimistic about the prospects for these companies, you probably would be concerned that the market might be right, about some of them at least, and they would go into bankruptcy. However, if, in picking your sample, you choose firms for the study only if they survive the entire period, you have eliminated the major potential problem with the trading rule through the way you have constructed your sample. The test is now biased in favor of the rule.

effectively divided into pieces and then marketed to separate segments of the market. To market a CMO, you acquire a pool of Ginnie Mae securities and divide the pool into as many as eight classes, based on priority of receipt of interest and principal payments. For example the fast pay "Tranche" receives the highest priority. Its interest and principal payments will be entirely paid up within three years. Although interest is accruing to the remaining classes, no cash payments will be made to the second class until all payments to the Tranche have been fully paid. Then payments will begin on the second priority issue and so on through the lowest priority issue, which is called the Z Bond. The Tranche has some of the investment characteristics of a three-year treasury note, but it usually carries a fifty basis point premium in its yield over the treasury issue. The Z Bond is almost like a Zero coupon bond; no payments are made on this bond until all the payments are received on the pieces with greater priority.

The Z Bond is attractive to groups of investors like pension funds that have an aversion to buying corporate callable bonds, where the call option is a real threat in terms of the truncation of the cash flows associated with the investment. The Z Bond also seems to be attractive to many investors in Japan. That's what's behind today's major marketing operation.

Salomon initially found that the value of the pie's individual pieces was greater than the value of the pie as a whole. That is, the individual securities like the Tranche and the Z Bond could be marketed for a sum greater than the total value of the underlying pool of Ginnie Maes. This unexpected bonus disappeared, however, in the second year of the market history for the security. Now Salomon makes its money underwriting and market making in CMOs. Saloman and First Boston underwrite 80 percent of the new issues and make a secondary market for 100 percent of the trading in existing issues.

The traffic grinds to a complete stop. This is going to take even longer than he thought. Looks like a nerve-racking four-hour trip to the island.

There is one study that has overcome this problem as well as some others. Basu (1977) studied the performance of portfolios formed on the basis of price-earnings ratios between April 1957 and March 1971. He began with a representative sample of firms that were in existence in March 1957. No attempt was made to ensure that the stocks in this sample survived the time period covered by the study. At the beginning of each month, he ranked the stocks on the basis of their price-earnings ratio. The 20 percent of the stocks with the highest price-earnings ratios went into group A, the 20 percent with the next highest go into group B, and so on, through group E with the lowest price-earnings ratios. The

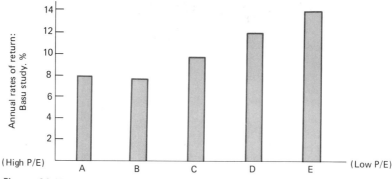

Figure 20-17 Annual Rates of Return: Basu Study

portfolios were re-formed in this way at the beginning of each year, and the performance of each of the portfolios was then evaluated over the time period covered by the study.

The basic results of the study are presented in Figures 20–17 through 20–20. The rates of return to each of the portfolios is presented in Figure 20–17. Note that the rates tend to become progressively larger as you move from the high price-earnings ratio portfolios to the low price-earnings ratio portfolios. The Jensen Index of performance is presented in Figure 20–18. Recall that the Jensen Index is the difference between the portfolio's return and the return you would expect it to have if it were positioned on the securities market line. In Figure 20–18 the securities market line was estimated using the average risk-free rate in the bond market. Basu obtained similar results when he used an estimate of the average rate of return on the zero beta portfolio. In any case, risk-adjusted performance improves as you move from the left to the right. The Treynor and Sharpe indices for the portfolios are given in Figures 20–19 and 20–20. Recall

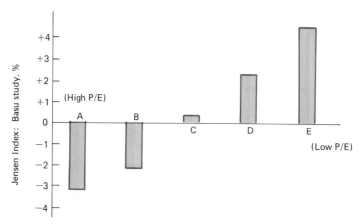

Figure 20-18 Jensen Index: Basu Study

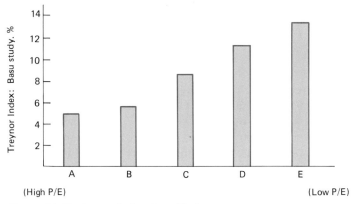

Figure 20-19 Treynor Index: Basu Study

that both are ratios of the risk premium earned on the portfolio to the risk of the portfolio. The Treynor Index uses beta to measure risk; the Sharpe Index uses standard deviation of return. With both indices, performance improves as price-earnings ratio is reduced.

In other parts of his study, Basu allowed for the differential transactions costs associated with re-forming the portfolios annually. He also allowed for the differential tax payments associated with realizing capital gains annually. Even in the face of these adjustments he found a statistically significant difference in the performance of an investor who holds a low price-earnings ratio portfolio from an investor who bought and then held the entire sample of stocks throughout the study period. Unless Basu's results can be refuted, they seem to contradict the semistrong form of the efficient market hypothesis.

In two papers published from dissertations written at the University of Chicago, Banz (1981) and Reinganum (1981) argue that the price-earnings ratio

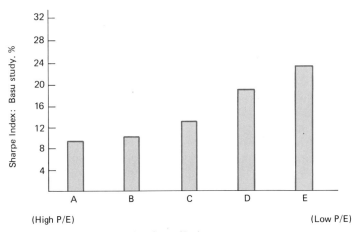

Figure 20-20 Sharpe Index: Basu Study

anomaly analyzed by Basu is really masquerading for a size effect that itself is not inconsistent with market efficiency. They argue that small firms have an element of risk that isn't captured by the risk measures in Basu's risk-adjusted performance ratings. Less information is known about small firms, and thus investors are likely to be less confident about their estimates of both risk and expected return. Thus, if a large company and a small company have identical betas, based on sample estimates of past returns, if you have additional information reinforcing your estimates for the large company, you may be more confident in your estimates of risk and expected return. Your lack of confidence in the estimates for the small company adds an extra dimension of risk that may increase the return you require to invest in the stock.

It can also be argued that, on a percentage basis, it costs more to buy and sell the shares of small companies. Among other things, the market for the shares of small companies is thinner. If you buy the stock from a dealer in the over-the-counter market, the spread between the bid and the asked prices will be greater. If you buy the stock on an exchange, trading a large block of stock may have an impact on the market price.

Based on the added dimension of risk and the higher costs of transacting, investors may require a higher rate of return on the stock of small companies. If this is true, it may explain why stocks with low price-earnings ratios produce abnormally large rates of return. The stocks of small companies tend to have low price-earnings ratios. Given this, portfolios consisting of low price-earnings stocks will also consist of stocks issued by smaller than average companies. Is the price-earnings effect due to the market's tendency to be overly optimistic or pessimistic? Or is it because low price-earnings stocks tend to be small, and the market *requires* a higher rate of return on smaller firms?

In a later paper, Basu (1983) attempted to address this criticism. Figure 21–21 plots the Jensen indices for twenty-five portfolios. The portfolios are formed by first ranking the stocks in the sample on the basis of the size of the firm and then on the basis of the total market value of the common stock. The firms are grouped into quintiles, where the 20 percent of the firms with the smallest total market value go into the first quintile, the next 20 percent into the second quintile, and so on, through the fifth quintile. Then, within each quintile the firms are ranked by price-earnings ratios and formed into five portfolios. The 20 percent of the firms with the smallest price-earnings ratio go into portfolio E, the next 20 percent into D, and so on, through A. In all, we form twenty-five portfolios widely dissimilar with respect to both size and price-earnings ratio. By examining the performance of these firms, we can get some insight into whether we are observing a size or a price-earnings effect.

The Jensen indices in Figure 20–21 show that there appears to be both a price-earnings and a size effect present. As you move across the horizontal axis of the graph, you move from the smallest group of firms to the largest group. Notice that as size is increased, performance tends to deteriorate. An advocate of the size effect would argue that *this* deterioration doesn't reflect market inefficiency, but rather the fact that Basu is measuring risk on the basis of beta alone and not adjusting for the differential costs of transacting in small and large companies.

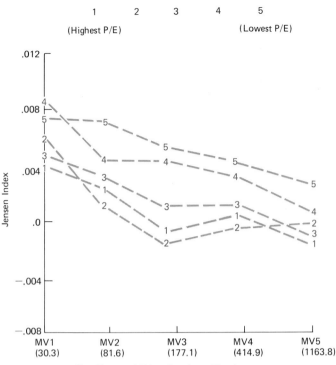

Figure 20-21 The Size and Price-Earnings Effect

Within each size grouping, however, the portfolios with the smallest price-earnings ratios have the highest risk-adjusted performance. Because the companies in the group are more or less uniform with respect to size, the differences in performance are likely to be attributable to differences in price-earnings ratio. This being the case, this evidence is inconsistent with the semistrong form of the efficient market hypothesis.

The Overreaction Anomaly

The plot in Figure 20–15 is actually part of the results of a study by De Bondt and Thaler (1985) that tested the hypothesis that the stock market overreacts to information. The hypothesis derives from studies of human behavior in the literature of psychology. Given these results, one might suspect a propensity for stock prices to overreact to releases of positive and negative information about firms. If this is indeed the case, then those stocks that have performed the best in the past should show a propensity to exhibit subnormal performance in future periods as the market corrects its initial overreaction. The reverse should also be true. The poorest performing stocks of the past should exhibit above average performance in the future.

De Bondt and Thaler tested their hypothesis by ranking stocks by their market performance over sixty-month periods. They measured performance in several different ways, including raw rate of return and cumulative average excess return. They then centered their attention on the stocks that performed extremely well and extremely badly and considered the performance of the stocks in the sixty months subsequent to the initial evaluation period. Once again performance was measured in several different ways with little effect on the final results. The plot of Figure 20–15 shows the cumulative difference between the rates of return for the stocks and the rates of return for a market index for the two groups of stocks. The results support the hypothesis in that the poorest performing stocks in the initial evaluation period outperform the market in the postevaluation period, and the opposite is true for the best performing stocks.

In interpreting these results, however, we should keep several points in mind:

1. Nearly all of the excess and deficient returns for the poor performers and superior performers, respectively, are earned in the month of January.

2. Given the empirical results of Tinic and West (1984), we know that risk premiums on stocks are realized exclusively in the month of January.

3. Given their relative market performance in the initial evaluation period, there is reason to suspect that the poor performers are of above average risk and the superior performers are of below average risk *at the end of the initial evaluation periods*.

4. Given points 2 and 3, we would expect the poor performers to produce a higher than average rate of return in January and the good performers to produce a lower than average return in January, not because of market inefficiency but because of their relative risk.

In fairness to De Bondt and Thaler, they found very similar results after adjusting the postevaluation returns for risk. (Risk, however, is measured by the beta factors for the stocks as estimated over the *entire* initial evaluation period. We would expect that the beta would be smaller [larger] for the superior [poor] performers at the end of the period than it is over the entire period.) They also examined the characteristics of the firms in the two groups and found that they can't be distinguished on the basis of leverage or size. Although De Bondt and Thaler's results probably don't constitute the final answer to the issue, they are nevertheless very intriguing.

ARE PROFESSIONAL INVESTORS DISTINCTIVE IN TERMS OF THEIR PERFORMANCE?

In the presence of the Capital Asset Pricing Model and a strong-form efficient market, all securities would appear to be positioned on the securities market line when estimates of beta and expected return are based on state-of-the-art analysis of all knowable information. If a security appears to you to be positioned otherwise, it is only because you are basing your estimates on less than the full set of information. Because no security is truly positioned above or below the securities market line, it is impossible to construct a portfolio that is so positioned, and if we take sample estimates of portfolio expected return and beta based on past returns, any deviation in the estimated position of the portfolio from the securities market line should be statistically insignificant.

For any given group of investors, errors in our sample estimates of expected return and beta should produce a clustering of estimated portfolio positions above and below the securities market line. However, on average, the portfolios should be positioned on the line, and the number of individual deviations from the line that are deemed to be statistically significant should be consistent with the level of confidence used in determining significance. For example, suppose we accept a deviation as being statistically significant if there is at most a 5 percent probability it is due to chance. Then, if all the deviations are actually due to chance (as they would be in an efficient market), you should find that approximately 5 percent of the portfolios have significant deviations.

Jensen (1969) examined the performance of 115 mutual funds in the period 1955 to 1964. The managers of these funds are usually highly trained and have access to broad sources of investment information. If the market is inefficient, we would expect this group of investors to capture abnormally high returns.

Jensen estimated the position of the security market line for the period using the Standard and Poor's Index of 500 stocks as a proxy for the market portfolio. The S&P is positioned in Figure 20–22 at point M. The beta factor for the S&P is, of course, 1.00, since its returns, when related to themselves, line up on a 45-degree line emanating from the origin of a graph like that in Figure 20–24, where portfolio return is plotted vertically and market index return horizontally. The risk-free investment is positioned at point r_F in Figure 20–22. This is the rate of interest available in the U.S. government bond market during the period. The security market line is estimated as a straight line drawn through points r_F and M.

Jensen measured the performance of each mutual fund by the vertical distance between the position of each fund in Figure 20–22 and the security market line. This benchmark is, of course, the Jensen Index, and we are assuming that securities are priced according to the version of the Capital Asset Pricing Model where investors are allowed to borrow and lend at the risk-free rate of interest. Note that you could have invested in the S&P 500 index portfolio during this period without doing any security analysis whatsoever. By combining this portfolio with a positive or negative investment in the risk-free bond, you could have attained any of the positions on this security market line. Thus, the security market line represents those positions that were available to those of us who were investing with little or no information. In assessing the performance of the mutual funds, we compare these positions with the positions actually attained by managers who presumably had access to a considerable fraction of the full information set.

The individual points in Figure 20–22 represent the positions of individual mutual funds. Funds with different investment objectives are represented by different symbols explained in the key to the figure. In moving from the top to the bottom of the key, you move from funds that invest in growth-oriented stocks, to funds that invest in income-oriented stocks, to funds that balance their in-

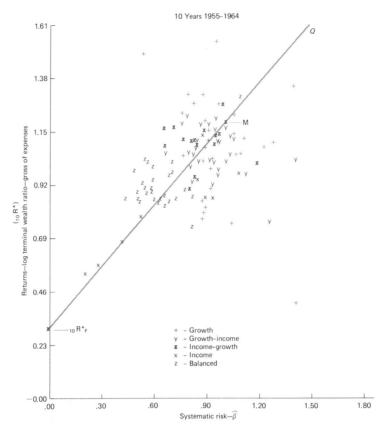

Figure 20-22 Jensen Index for Mutual Funds, Net of Expenses

vestments in stocks and fixed-income securities. In Figure 20–22 the funds are positioned according to the actual rates of return received by the investors in the funds. That is, the returns are net of the expenses incurred by the funds.

Jensen computed a beta factor for each fund by regressing its rates of return in the ten-year period on the returns to the S&P index portfolio. Each fund was then plotted according to its beta and its average return. Note that there are more funds positioned below the security market line than above it. In fact, in averaging the Jensen Index across all the funds, you find that, as a group, the mutual funds are *underperforming* by approximately 1 percent per year. That is, given the overall risk (beta) of the mutual funds, a naive investor, operating on the basis of little or no information, could have invested some money in the risk-free bond and the rest in the index portfolio and beaten the mutual funds by approximately 1 percent per year!

This finding is consistent with the hypothesis that all the efforts expended by mutual funds to find undervalued stocks were in vain. These efforts came at a cost: Analysts and staff salaries had to be paid; expenses associated with office space, advertising, data acquisition, and commissions also had to be paid. To determine whether these expenses were the source of the underperformance,

Jensen added the money spent on these items back into the funds' rates of return and recomputed the betas and average rates of return. The positions of the funds, gross of all expenses, are plotted in Figure 20–23. There are now an approximately equal number of funds above and below the line. If you were to average the positions of all the funds, you would find that the group as a whole is now positioned almost exactly on the security market line. This is, of course, consistent with the hypothesis that the source of the underperformance is, indeed, the expenditures of funds associated with the management of the funds.

Jensen concluded that mutual funds, as a group, are not distinctive in their investment performance from investors who have little or no access to information.[1] Are there, however, *individual* managers within the industry that have distinguished themselves in terms of their performance? Put another way, are the deviations from the security market line in Figures 20–22 and 20–23 due to sampling error or to the funds' actual *expected* rates of return being positioned above (or below) the security market line? Perhaps there are managers who

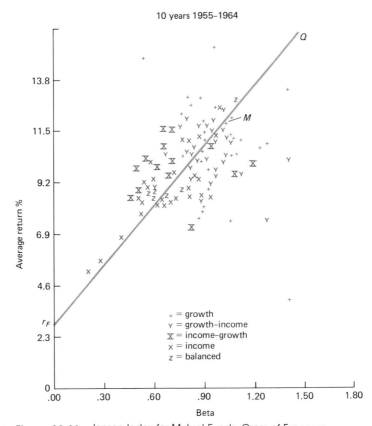

Figure 20-23   Jensen Index for Mutual Funds, Gross of Expenses

[1]Technically speaking, Jensen's test assumes that mutual fund returns are independent. This is clearly not the case, as most of the funds have securities in common.

CHAPTER 20   Market Efficiency: The Evidence   497

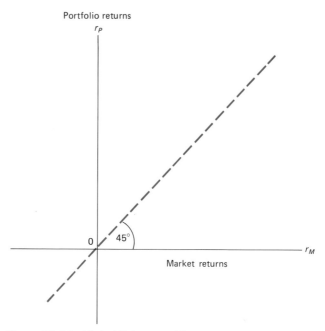

Portfolio returns
r_P

0 45°

r_M

Market returns

Figure 20-24 Market Returns and Portfolio Returns

are consistently superior and others who are consistently inferior, and they are canceling each other in the averaging so that the group as a whole appears neutral.

In an effort to investigate this possibility, Jensen analyzed each fund individually to determine whether its Jensen Index is significantly different from zero in a statistical sense. To do this he divided each index by its standard error to obtain a T statistic. Given the magnitude of the Jensen Index, the greater the *residual variance* in the fund's year-to-year return, the greater will be the standard error, and the lower will be the T statistic. Given the number of years of returns observed for each fund, if the T statistic has an absolute value greater than approximately 2.2, we can say there is less than a 5 percent probability that the fund has achieved a nonzero Jensen Index on the basis of chance (or sampling error) alone.

The distribution of T statistics for the net returns for the funds is given in Figure 20–25. The observations in the shaded areas on each side of the distribution can be considered to be statistically significant. Jensen found only one fund that came close to having a statistically significant *positive* Jensen Index and a large number of funds for which the index is significantly negative. Apparently, the negative funds are doing something consistently wrong, so that, given their risk levels, their expected returns are positioned below the security market line.

An advocate of market efficiency might argue that what the funds are doing wrong is expending large sums of money on security analysis. To determine

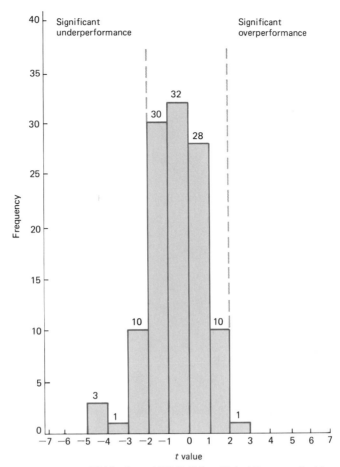

Figure 20-25 Distribution of "T" Statistics: Net of Expenses for Mutual Funds in Jensen Study

SOURCE: M. C. Jensen, "The Performance of Mutual Funds in the Period 1945–1964," *Journal of Finance* (May 1968).

whether this is true, Jensen again added back to their returns the amounts spent to manage the portfolios and recalculated all the T statistics. The distribution of T values *gross* is presented in Figure 20–26. Now there are only a few funds that exhibit T values that are significant in either the positive or negative direction. The number that are significant is, in fact, approximately equal to the number we would expect to see on the basis of chance alone. Because we are using a 5 percent test of significance, we would expect to see 5 percent of the sample of 115 funds showing significant T values, even if relative investment performance is totally a matter of luck.

Because these managers presumably have access to all forms of information, these results are consistent with the strong form of the efficient market hypothesis. This seems strange because we already have seen evidence that contradicts

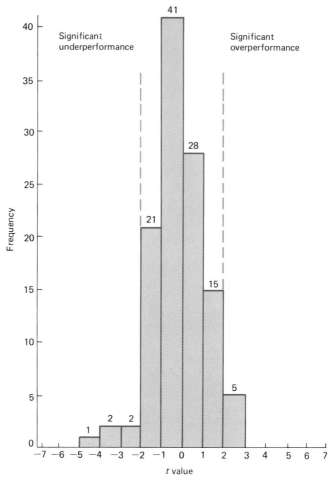

Figure 20-26 Distribution of "T" Statistics: Gross of Expenses for Mutual Funds in Jensen Study

SOURCE: M. C. Jensen, "The Performance of Mutual Funds in the Period 1945–1964," *Journal of Finance* (May 1968).

even the semistrong and weak forms. There are at least two explanations for this apparent contradiction in the evidence.

First, the mutual funds are rather large financial institutions. Even if the individual analysts are capable of discriminating between profitable and unprofitable investments, it may take a considerable period of time for these opinions to work their way down to actual changes in the portfolio position of the fund. The individual analysts may find themselves frustrated by the bureaucratic procedures involved in the funds' portfolio management process to the point where their analysis has little or no impact on the performance of the fund.

Second, it may be that the mutual funds are distinctive in their performance, but our benchmarks for measuring performance are too crude to detect their superiority. Several weaknesses in the various risk-adjusted performance measures were discussed in the chapter on portfolio performance. Additionally, another potential problem may explain why Jensen is unable to find many individual funds with statistically significant performance.

Most mutual funds try to forecast the future direction of the market. If they believe the return to the market is going to be high, they might take an aggressive position and invest in stocks that will respond vigorously to the coming bull market. In taking such a position, they might plunge into the stock market such that the characteristic line of the portfolio looks like that of the solid line labeled "bull" in Figure 20–27. When they are in such a position, they might experience periodic returns like those labeled with "o's" in the figure. If, on the other hand, they believe the return to the market is going to be low, they might move their funds into low beta stocks and fixed-income securities like bonds. When in this position, the fund's characteristic line might look like the solid line labeled "bear." The "x's" surrounding this line represent the fund's periodic return experience when it is in such a defensive position.

Now suppose you fail to recognize that the fund is actually shifting from one position to another. You simply regress all the fund's periodic returns on the

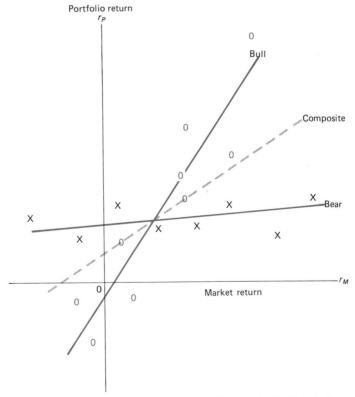

Figure 20-27 Obtaining a Composite Estimate of a Portfolio's Characteristic Line

returns to your market index. You will obtain a composite estimate of the fund's characteristic line that may look like the broken line in Figure 20-27. Note that the fund will appear to have much more residual variance than it actually has when in either an aggressive or a defensive position.

If you overestimate the fund's residual variance, you will also overestimate the standard error of its Jensen Index. Since the T statistic is the index itself divided by its standard error, you will obtain a downward biased estimate of the T statistic. This may explain why Jensen found that most of the T values in his sample were very low.

A study by Kon and Jen (1979) attempted to correct this problem. They employed a statistical analysis that enabled them to determine whether a sample of observations was associated with one or more characteristic lines, to estimate the characteristic line or lines, and to separate the observations on the basis of their associated characteristic lines. They then could estimate the Jensen Index on the basis of each individual characteristic line to determine whether the managers of the funds are able to select investments with abnormal returns, *when in a particular (aggressive or defensive) position.*

Kon and Jen found that for most of the funds there was a high probability that the returns could be associated with more than one characteristic line. After separating the observations coming from each characteristic line, they found that a large fraction of the Jensen indices were statistically significant. In computing the value for the index, they employed both the risk-free rate in the bond market and an estimate of the average rate of return on the zero beta portfolio. In both cases, they found many more significant T values than you would expect on the basis of chance. Their evidence is consistent with the hypothesis that some managers can be distinguished from others on the basis of talent in selecting profitable investments. This can be true only if the market is less than perfectly efficient.

In the face of the inadequacies of available measures of performance, it is difficult to draw definitive conclusions about the relative performance of professional investors. At this point, it appears that we can only say that no persuasive evidence exists one way or another, that professional investors have been distinctive in their performance.

Summary

In this chapter we have examined some of the evidence on whether the actual market exhibits four behavioral traits that are consistent with market efficiency.

In an efficient market, securities prices should respond instantly and accurately to the receipt of new information. There have been many studies of the response of stock prices to such events as stock splits, dividend announcements, takeover bids, block purchases and sales, and corporate earnings reports. Most of these studies have indicated that stock prices do, in fact, respond quickly and accurately to the receipt of new information. There has been convincing, contradictory evidence reported, however. A study of the response of stock prices to quarterly earnings reports indicates that there is a ninety-day lag in the response of stock prices to earnings reports that can be considered unusually favorable or unfavorable. The magnitude of the continuing response after the report is large enough to overcome the costs of transacting to take advantage of the lag. This study is carefully done and uses a sample of observations encompassing the samples used in all previous studies that produced results consistent with the efficient market hypothesis.

In an efficient market, the expected change in securities prices in any future period should be unrelated to the exhibited behavior of the security in any previous period. Again, most of the studies that have employed standard statistical procedures to search for systematic patterns in the series of stock prices have found little evidence that you can predict future price changes on the basis of past changes. However, recent evidence indicates a definite seasonal pattern in stock prices. The expected rate of return to the market apparently shifts substantially to the right in the month of January. At this point, we can only conjecture as to why this happens, but the evidence that it does happen in the United States, and throughout most of the world, is overwhelming.

In an efficient market, all trading rules should fail under simulation. Many trading rules have been tested and most have failed. At least one, however, has convincingly produced abnormal returns in simulations based on historical data. If the market tends to be overly optimistic and pessimistic in forecasting the earnings and dividends of firms, you can take advantage of this error by investing in stocks with low price-earnings ratios and avoiding stocks with high price-earnings ratios. Low price-earnings ratio portfolios have produced superior returns in the past, even after allowing for such factors as transactions costs, risk adjustment, statistical significance, and differential taxes. Some have argued that the price-earnings effect is really a small firm effect in disguise. However, the most recent evidence indicates that *both* effects are probably present in stock returns.

If the market is efficient, professional investors should not exhibit distinctive performance. Again, nearly all the studies of professional investment performance indicate that they do not. However, the available risk-adjustment performance measures are subject to a number of problems. One of these problems is a failure to separate returns produced by the funds when they are in aggressive and defensive positions. Failure to allow for this will tend to inflate the standard errors associated with the performance indices and reduce their apparent significance. At least one study that attempts to compensate for this has reported evidence consistent with the notion that fund managers can be distinguished on the basis of their skill in selecting undervalued issues. This is inconsistent with an efficient market, because in such a market there should be no undervalued issues.

Overall, the best evidence points to the following conclusion. The market isn't *strictly* efficient with respect to any of the so-called levels of efficiency. The study by Kon and Jen is inconsistent with strong-form efficiency. The price-earnings ratio phenomenon is inconsistent with semistrong-form efficiency, and the January effect is inconsistent with even weak-form efficiency. But the weight of the evidence indicates that a great deal of the information available at all levels is, at any given time, reflected in stock prices. The market may not be easily beaten, but it appears to be beatable—at least if you are willing to work at it.
Good luck!

QUESTIONS AND PROBLEMS

Assume the following equation of a characteristic line for stock A for questions 1 through 3.

$$E(r_A \mid r_M) = .01 + .9 \, r_M$$

Suppose the following represents the actual observations on r_A and r_M at several points prior to and including some event. The event occurred at time 0.

t	r_M	r_A
−3	.003	.0127
−2	.005	.0140
−1	.010	.0200
0	.008	.0192
+1	.0075	.01525
+2	.012	.02130
+3	.006	.0144

1. Compute the residuals from the characteristic line, that is, the portion of the stock's return that is not statistically associated with the market's return. Plot these residuals against values for r_M.

2. The values in the table represent only a few of the observations used to fit the characteristic line. What will the average residual be for all of the residuals?

3. Suppose the event was a change in the dividend. How would you use data like those given to proceed with an event study along the lines of the Fama, Fisher, Jensen, and Roll (FFJR) study?

4. From an examination of the evidence provided by FFJR, could you infer that a trading rule based on split announcements would allow you to make abnormal profits? Explain.

5. FFJR interpret their results as evidence in support of efficient markets. Do the results appear to provide support for one particular form of the efficient market hypothesis?

6. The FFJR study focuses on stock market reaction to stock splits. Since a stock split does not increase the fraction of a company held by an investor, one could argue that investors should be unconcerned with stock splits. Why, then, might a stock split be considered to be an important event for investors?

7. Rendleman, Jones, and Latané (RJL) focus on stock market reaction to earnings data. What is the specific event around which RJL take their measurements? What evidence is provided on the different forms of the efficient market hypothesis?

8. What is the January effect in stock prices? Would this result be consistent with any of the forms of the efficient market hypothesis?

9. One explanation of the January effect has to do with sales and purchases related to the tax year.

   a. Present the tax effect hypothesis.

   b. Studies have shown the January effect to occur internationally, even in countries where the tax year does not start in January. Speculate on a plausible reason for this.

10. In trying to test for the relationship between low price-earnings ratios and stock performance

   a. What is the problem with simply observing the performance of a group of low P/E stocks that had existed from beginning to end over a period of time?

   b. How did Basu's 1977 study overcome the problem in part a, and what did he find?

11. What is the phenomenon of the size effect in stock performance, and why did some researchers claim that this effect was the real factor in Basu's "low P/E ratio effect"? Further, how does the size effect show up in the studies of seasonality?

12. What did Jensen find, pertaining to the performance of mutual fund managers

   a. When expenses of the fund were deducted from returns?

   b. When expenses of the fund were not deducted from returns?

BIBLIOGRAPHY

ALEXANDER, S. S., "Price Movement in Speculative Markets: Trends or Random Walk," *Industrial Management Review* (May 1965).

ALLVINE, F. C., and D. E. O'NEILL, "Stock Market Returns and the Presidential Elec-tion Cycle: Implications for Market Efficiency," *Financial Analysts Journal* (September–October 1980).

BAESEL, J., G. SHOWS, and E. THORP, "Can Joe Granville Time the Market?" *Journal of Portfolio Management* (Spring 1982).

BANZ, R. W., "The Relationship Between Return and Market Value of Common Stocks," *Journal of Financial Economics* (March 1981).

BAR-YOSEF, S., and L. D. BROWN, "A Reexamination of Stock Splits Using Moving Betas," *Journal of Finance* (September 1977).

BASEL, J., and G. R. STEIN, "The Value of Information: Inferences from the Profitability of Insider Tradings," *Journal of Financial and Quantitative Analysis* (September 1979).

BASU, S., "The Investment Performance of Common Stocks in Relation to Their Price-Earnings Ratios," *Journal of Finance* (June 1977).

———, "The Relationship Between Earnings' Yield, Market Value and Return for NYSE Common Stocks," *Journal of Financial Economics* (June 1983).

BEAVER, W. H., "Market Efficiency," *Accounting Review* (January 1981).

BERNSTEIN, P. L., "Efficiency and Opportunity," *Journal of Portfolio Management* (Fall 1977).

BRENNER, M., "The Effect of Model Misspecification on Tests of the Efficient Market Hypothesis," *Journal of Finance* (March 1977).

BROWN, L., and M. ROZEFF, "The Superiority of Analysts' Forecasts as a Measure of Expectations: Evidence from the Earnings," *Journal of Finance* (March 1978).

BROWN, P., A. W. KLEIDON, and T. A. MARSH, "New Evidence on the Nature of Size Related Anomalies in Stock Prices," *Journal of Financial Economics* (June 1983).

COOTNER, P. H., *The Random Character of Stock Market Prices*. Cambridge, Mass.: MIT Press, 1964.

CRAGG, D., and B. MALKIEL, "Consensus and Accuracy of the Predictions of the Growth of Corporate Earnings," *Journal of Finance* (March 1968).

DANN, L. Y., D. MAYERS, and R. J. RAAB, "Trading Rules, Large Blocks, and the Speed of Price Adjustment," *Journal of Financial Economics* (January 1977).

DE BONDT, W., and R. THALER, "Does the Stock Market Overreact to New Information?" Working paper, University of Wisconsin, Madison, 1985.

DREMAN, D., *The New Contrarian Investment Strategy*. New York: Random House, 1982.

EMMANUEL, D. M., "Note on Filter Rules and Stock Market Trading," *Economic Record* (December 1980).

FAMA, E. F., "The Behavior of Stock Market Prices," *Journal of Business* (January 1965).

FAMA, E. F., L. FISHER, M. C. JENSEN, and R. ROLL, "The Adjustment of Stock Prices to New Information," *International Economic Review* (February 1969).

FINNERTY, J. E., "Insiders and Market Efficiency," *Journal of Finance* (September 1976a).

———, "Insiders' Activity and Inside Information," *Journal of Financial and Quantitative Analysis* (June 1976b).

FRENCH, K., "Stuck Returns and the Weekend Effect," *Journal of Financial Economics* (March 1980).

GIBBONS, M. R., and P. HESS, "Day of the Week Effects and Asset Returns," *Journal of Business* (October 1981).

GULTEKIN, M. N., and B. N. GULTEKIN, "Stock Market Seasonality: International Evidence," *Journal of Financial Economics* (December, 1983).

JENSEN, M. C., "The Pricing of Capital Assets and the Evaluation of Investment Performance," *Journal of Business* (April 1969).

JENSEN, M. C., and G. A. BENNINGTON, "Random Walks and Technical Theories: Some Additional Evidence," *Journal of Finance* (May 1970).

KATZ, S., "The Price Adjustment Process of Bonds to Rating Reclassifications: A Test of Bond Market Efficiency," *Journal of Finance* (May 1974).

KEIM, D. B., "Size-Related Anomalies and Stock Return Seasonality: Further Empirical Evidence," *Journal of Financial Economics* (June 1983).

KERR, H. S., "The Battle of Insider Trading vs. Market Efficiency," *Journal of Portfolio Management* (Summer 1980).

KON, S. J., and F. C. JEN, "Investment Performance of Mutual Funds: An Empirical Investigation of Timing, Selectivity and Market Efficiency," *Journal of Business* (April 1979).

LORIE, J., and V. NEIDERHOFFER, "Predictive and Statistical Properties of Insider Trading," *Journal of Law and Economics* (April 1978).

REINGANUM, M. R., "Misspecification of Capital Asset Pricing: Empirical Anomalies Based on Earnings Yields and Market Values," *Journal of Financial Economics* (March 1981).

RENDLEMAN, R. J., and C. E. CARABINI, "Efficiency of the Treasury Bill Futures Market," *Journal of Finance* (September 1979).

RENDLEMAN, R. J., C. P. JONES, and H. A. LATANÉ, "Empirical Anomalies Based on Unexpected Earnings and the Importance of Risk Adjustments," *Journal of Financial Economics* (November 1982).

ROBERTS, H. V., "Stock Market Patterns and Financial Analysis: Methodological Suggestions," *Journal of Finance* (March 1959).

ROZEFF, M. S., and W. R. KINNEY, "Capital Market Seasonality: The Case of Stock Returns," *Journal of Financial Economics* (Nov. 1976).

SCHULTZ, P., "Transactions Costs and the Small Firm Effect: A Comment," *Journal of Financial Economics* (June 1983).

———,"Personal Income Taxes and the January Effect: Small Firm Stock Returns Before the War Revenue Act of 1917: A Note," *Journal of Finance* (March 1985).

SCHWERT, G. W., "Adjustment of Stock Prices to Information About Inflation," *Journal of Finance* (March 1981).

———, "Size and Stock Returns, and Other Empirical Regularities," *Journal of Financial Economics* (June 1983).

STEVENSON, R. A., and M. ROZEFF, "Are the Backwaters of the Market Efficient?" *Journal of Portfolio Management* (Spring 1979).

STOLL, H. R., and R. E. WHALEY, "Transactions Costs and the Small Firm Effect," *Journal of Financial Economics* (June 1983).

TINIC, S. M., and R. WEST, "Risk and Return: January vs. the Rest of the Year," *Journal of Financial Economics* (December 1984).

GLOSSARY

American Call Option A contract giving the holder the right to buy a specified number of shares of stock at a given price on or before a given date.

American Put Option A contract giving the holder the right to sell a specified number of shares of stock at a given price on or before a given date.

Arbitrage Pricing Theory A theory purporting to describe the structure of securities prices. The theory assumes that stock returns are produced as they would be under a multi-index model. The theory describes the relationship between expected returns on securities, given that there are no opportunities to create wealth through riskless arbitrage investments.

Arithmetic Mean Yield The simple average of periodic rates of return. The arithmetic mean yield relates the ending to beginning wealth associated with an investment, if it is assumed that the dollar amount invested is kept constant at the beginning of each period.

At-the-Money Option A put or call option, where the current price of the underlying asset is approximately equal to the present value of the exercise price.

Beta Factor The slope of a security's characteristic line. The expected change in the security's rate of return divided by the accompanying change in the rate of return to the market portfolio.

Black-Scholes Option Pricing Model A model to value European put or call options that assumes the distribution for the instantaneous rate of return on the underlying asset is normal and constant over time. The model provides an options price that produces the risk-free rate of return to those investors who use the option to create a risk-free hedged position.

Broker An individual who acts as an agent to execute a trade for an investor.

Butterfly Spread A spread position using call options, where you buy options with relatively large and small exercise prices and sell options with intermediate exercise prices. The spread position pays off when the value of the underlying asset falls within a certain range.

Callable Bond A bond that can be redeemed by the issuer at a stated price (or prices, which change over time), usually beginning after a period of call protection.

Capital Asset Pricing Model A theory that purports to describe the structure of securities prices, where all investors in the economic system are presumed to hold efficient portfolios in expected return-variance space.

Capital Market Line A line showing the portfolio positions of individual investors in expected return-standard deviation space in the Capital Asset Pricing Model.

Cash Matching A form of interest immunization, where the timing of the cash flows associated with bond investments is matched with the timing of the required payments associated with the liability being funded.

Characteristic Line A line showing the relationship between the rates of return to a security or portfolio and the corresponding rates of return to the market portfolio.

Clearinghouse An organization associated with an organized exchange for trading options or futures contracts. The clearinghouse stands as a guarantor between you and the other party to the options or futures contract.

Closed-End Investment Company Similar to a mutual fund, except that shares in the fund are traded by investors in the secondary market. In the case of a mutual fund, you buy and sell shares directly from and to the fund. In the case of a closed-end investment company, you buy them from other investors who happen to own them and want to sell.

Coefficient of Determination The fraction of the variability in one variable that can be associated with the variability in another.

Combination Line A line showing what happens to the expected rate of return and standard deviation to a portfolio of two securities as the portfolio weights in the securities are changed from one value to another.

Commercial Paper Short-term promissory note issued by a corporation.

Conditional Expected Return The expected rate of return on a security or portfolio assuming the occurrence of a particular event, such as the rate of return produced by the market portfolio.

Consol A perpetual bond with a constant periodic interest payment and no maturity date.

Convertible Bond A bond giving its holder the option of exchanging the bond for a stated number of common shares of the issuing firm.

Correlation Coefficient Statistic describing the goodness of fit about a linear relationship between two variables. The correlation coefficient is equal to the covariance between the variables, divided by the product of their standard deviations.

Coupon The interest payment on a bond.

Covariance Statistic roughly describing the relationship between two variables. If the convariance is positive, when one of the variables takes on a value above its expected value, the other has a propensity to do the same. If the covariance is negative, the deviations tend to be of opposite sign.

Cox Option Pricing Model A model to price European put and call options that makes nearly the same assumptions as does the Black-Scholes model. This model, however, allows for the magnitude of the variance in the returns for the underlying asset to be a function of the level of the value of the asset. The Black-Scholes model is a special case of this model.

Critical Line Line drawn in terms of portfolio weights showing the weights for portfolios in the minimum variance set.

Cumulative Average Excess Return A measure of the cumulative response of securities prices to some economic event. The cumulative average rate of return between two points in time is the sum of the average residuals experienced by a sample of securities in each of the subperiods between the two points.

Cumulative Preferred Stock A security with a fixed periodic claim that must be paid before dividends can be paid on the common stock. If the payment is skipped it must be later paid in full before common dividend payments can be made.

Dealer An individual who maintains inventories of particular securities and trades from them, profiting from the difference in the prices at which he or she is willing to buy or sell from the inventory.

Debenture Bond A bond that is unsecured by real property.

Dividend Clientele The shareholders of a given company who are presumed by some to group themselves according to marginal tax rate, where the high-bracket investors buy stocks with low dividend yields, and low-bracket investors buy stocks with high dividend yields.

Duration Weighted average maturity of a stream of payments, where the maturity of each payment is weighted by the fraction of the total value of the stream that is accounted for by the payment. Duration is also a measure of the responsiveness of market value to a change in interest rates that assumes parallel shifts occur in a flat term structure.

Efficient Set The set of portfolios of a given population of securities that offer the maximum possible expected return for a given level of risk.

Elasticity of Yield to Maturity Percentage change in the value of a security accompanying the percentage change in one plus its yield to maturity. The yield elasticity is equal to the negative of some duration measures.

Equipment Trust Certificate Fixed-income security that is secured by a particular, designated piece of property that is both mobile and salable, such as a railroad car.

European Call (Put) Option. Contract giving the holder the right to buy (sell) a specified number of shares of a given stock on, but not before, a given date.

Exercise Price The price at which you have the right to buy (sell) a security under a call (put) options contract.

Expected Rate of Return Sum of the product of the possible rates of return on an investment and their associated probabilities.

Expected Return Plane Linear plane showing portfolio expected return corresponding to assumed values for the portfolio weights.

Factor Beta The slope of the linear relationship between the rates of return to a given security and some economic factor that induces correlation between the returns to different securities.

Factor Price The slope of the relationship between the expected return on a given security and its factor price in the Arbitrage Pricing Theory.

Fixed-Income Security A security with a defined, limited-dollar claim.

Floor Broker Individual who buys and sells securities on the floor of an organized exchange.

Forward Contract A contract that obligates you to buy (if you buy the contract) or sell (if you sell the contract) a given commodity at a given price (the forward price) at a given point in time. There are no cash flows associated with your account in a forward contract.

Fundamental Beta An estimate of the beta factor for an individual security that employs information about the nature of the company issuing the security (earnings stability, financial leverage, and the like), in addition to the past relationship between the security's returns and the market portfolio.

Futures Contract The same as a forward contract except that the price at which you contract to buy or sell is amended from period to period so as to keep the current market value of the contract at zero. The process of debiting or crediting your account to compensate for the amendments is called *marking to market*.

General Obligation Municipal Bond A bond backed by the full faith and credit of the issuing state or municipality.

Geometric Mean Yield The *n*th root less one of the product of one plus *n* periodic rates of return. The geometric mean relates the beginning to the ending wealth over the periods, if it is assumed that all income from the security is reinvested back into the security.

Global Minimum Variance Portfolio The lowest variance portfolio achievable, given a population of securities.

Hard Floor Floor underlying the market value of an option that is equal to the greater of zero or the difference between the underlying asset value and the option's exercise price.

Income Effect of a Change in the Money Supply Change in real rate of interest moving in the same direction as the change in money supply resulting from the change in transactions demand associated with the monetary-induced change in national income.

Indifference Curve Curve tracing portfolios defined in expected return-standard deviation space that a given investor faces with indifference.

Inflation Premium The difference between the nominal and real rates of interest. The inflation premium compensates investors for the loss of purchasing power due to inflation. It is equal to the expected average rate of inflation over the term of the investment for which the interest rate is computed.

Interest Immunization An investment strategy that ensures a portfolio will generate sufficient cash flows to meet a series of cash payments having the same present value as the portfolio.

Internal Yield The rate that will discount the cash flows associated with an investment to a present value that is equal to the present market value of the investment. The internal rate of return relates beginning to ending wealth levels, if you assume that cash flows can be reinvested at the internal yield when received.

In-the-Money Option A call (put) option where the underlying asset value is greater (less) than the present value of its exercise price.

Iso-Standard Deviation Ellipses Ellipses showing the combinations of portfolio weights on three stocks that produce portfolios, all of which have a given level of standard deviation.

January Effect Market anomaly whereby stock prices throughout most of the world have a propensity to rise sharply during the initial part of the month of January.

Jensen Index Risk-adjusted measure of portfolio performance equal to the difference between a portfolio's realized or expected rate of return and the return that it should have, given its risk and its designated position on the securities market line.

Liquidity Effect of a Change in the Money Supply The initial effect of a change in the money supply on the real rate of interest, moving rates in the opposite direction from the change in money, and caused by the adjustment of portfolio positions of investors in response to the change in the supply of money.

Liquidity Preference Theory of the Term Structure Theory that purports to explain the shape of the term structure on the basis of market expectations of future

interest rates and on the basis of risk, or liquidity, premiums that may be present in the expected rates of return to bonds of various maturities.

Liquidity Premium The difference between the expected rate of return over a given period of time on two bonds identical in every respect except maturity.

Locked-in Effect Propensity for investors to hold on to securities on which they have accrued capital gains in order to avoid realizing them for tax purposes.

Macro Event An economic event that has a broad impact on large numbers of individual common stocks and the market as a whole.

Marginal Probability Distribution Distribution that shows the probabilities of getting various rates of return on a particular investment.

Market Efficiency The extent to which the market prices securities so as to reflect available information pertaining to their valuation.

Market Expectations Theory of the Term Structure Theory that purports to explain the shape of the term structure on the basis of market expectations of future interest rates alone. Risk or liquidity premiums in expected returns on investments of different maturities are assumed away.

Market Portfolio The ultimate market index, containing a common fraction of the total market value of every capital investment in the economic system.

Market Segmentation Theory of the Term Structure Theory that purports to explain the shape of the term structure on the basis of flows of funds among the long-, intermediate-, and short-term maturity segments of the market. Each segment is viewed as compartmentalized, and the yield in each segment is determined by the supply and demand for loanable funds in the segment.

Markowitz Model Procedure for finding minimum variance portfolios that employs the general formula for portfolio variance.

Micro Event An economic event that affects only one individual firm.

Minimum Variance Set Set of portfolios that has the lowest possible variance achievable for the population of stocks, given their expected rates of return.

Minimum Variance, Zero Beta Portfolio The one portfolio in the minimum variance set that is completely uncorrelated with the market index.

Mortgage Bond A bond secured by the pledge of a specific property.

Multi-Index Model Model purporting to explain the covariances that exist between securities on the basis of unexpected changes over time in two or more indices, such as the market, the money supply, or the growth rate in industrial production.

Municipal Bond A bond issued by a state or municipality, the interest income of which is usually exempt from taxation at the federal level.

Mutual Fund A portfolio of securities owned collectively by a group of investors. Shares in the fund are bought and sold directly from the fund.

Nominal Interest Rate Interest rate relating the market value of an investment to its expected (or realized) future cash flows, unadjusted for the expected (or realized) rate of inflation. The nominal rate is composed of the real rate and the inflation premium, or the expected rate of inflation over the life of the investment.

Normal Probability Distribution Symmetric, bell-shaped distribution that can be completely described on the basis of its expected value and its variance.

Out-of-the-Money Option A call (put) option where the market value of its underlying asset is below (above) the present value of its exercise price.

Over-the-Counter Market A trading network of thousands of dealers in particular securities.

Portfolio Insurance Investment strategy in which you take simultaneous positions in a risky portfolio and a synthetic put option constructed by shifting funds from the risky portfolio to a safe asset on the basis of the Black-Scholes Option Pricing Model.

Portfolio Weight The fraction of your money that you invest in a particular security in the portfolio.

Preferred Stock A security with a defined, fixed, periodic claim on the income from a firm. The claim isn't mandatory, but it must be paid before dividends are paid on the firm's common stock.

Price Effect of a Change in the Money Supply The effect of a change in the supply of money on the inflation premium in the nominal rate of interest.

Primary Security Security issued to finance a real economic investment.

Private Placement A security issued to a small number of investors. The terms of the offering are typically tailored to the needs of the investors.

Pure Discount Bond Bond promising a single fixed payment at maturity with no interim interest payments.

Put-Call Parity Relationship between the market values of puts and calls written on the same stock, with the same exercise price and time to maturity, that prevents the opportunity for making pure arbitrage profits by taking simultaneous positions in the put, the call, and the underlying stock.

Random Walk Property of a time series where the probability distribution for the future changes in the series is constant and unrelated to changes in the series that have occurred in the past.

Real Rate of Interest The rate of return on an investment adjusted for changes in purchasing power. The real rate compensates investors for delaying consumption.

Reinvestment Premium Premium in a futures price associated with the relationship between the expected day-to-day payoffs on the contract and the level of interest rates.

Residual The vertical distance between the actual rate of return produced by a security and the return consistent with the return to the market index and the security's characteristic line.

Residual Variance Propensity for a security to deviate from its characteristic line. The probability weighted sum of the squared residuals.

Revenue Bond A bond, usually issued by a state or municipality, that isn't backed by the full faith and credit of the issuer. Rather, the interest and principal are to be paid from funds derived from a particular designated source, such as revenue from a toll bridge.

Risk-Adjusted Performance Measure Measure of performance that purports to be unaffected by the risk of the portfolio or the performance of the market.

Risk Premium Premium in and expected rate of return or futures price to compensate investors for the risk associated with the investment or contract.

Sample Estimate An estimate of a population value for the underlying probability distribution, obtained from observing, or sampling, a series of rates of return to an investment or investments.

Secondary Security A security, such as a futures contract, issued by one financial investor and sold to another. The net supply of secondary securities is zero.

Security Market Line Line showing the relationship between the expected returns and betas for all portfolios and securities under the Capital Asset Pricing Model.

Semistrong Form Efficient Market Hypothesis Securities prices fully reflect all information that has been made publicly available.

Sharpe Index Risk-adjusted performance measure reflecting both breadth and depth of performance and equal to the risk premium earned on the portfolio divided by its standard deviation.

Short Sale Act of selling securities you don't own. You borrow shares from someone, sell them, repurchase them at a later date, and return them to the lender of the shares.

Single Index Model Model that purports to explain the covariance that exists between the returns on different securities on the basis of the relationship between the returns and a single index, usually the market.

Sinking Fund A provision in a bond indenture that calls for the periodic retirement of fractions of the outstanding issue. The retirement can be made by purchase of the bond itself, or other similar bonds, in the open market or by redeeming the bonds at a specified call price, at the issuer's option.

Small Firm Effect Market anomaly whereby small companies exhibit a propensity to produce rates of return that are larger than those predicted on the basis of the Capital Asset Pricing Model.

Soft Floor Floor underlying the value of a call option, equal to the greater of zero or the difference between the market value of the underlying asset and the present value of the option's exercise price.

Specialist Individual on the floor of an organized exchange who keeps an inventory of one or more stocks and trades with floor brokers out of that inventory.

Speculative Demand for Money The demand for money as an alternative investment, usually reflected in the amounts of money kept in savings accounts.

Standard Deviation The square root of the variance. A statistic describing the propensity to deviate from the expected value.

Straddle Simultaneous long positions in put and call options written on the same stock with the same exercise price and time to expiration.

Striking Price See exercise price.

Strong Form Efficient Market Hypothesis Securities prices fully reflect all information that is knowable, including inside information.

Systematic Risk That part of a securities variance that can't be diversified away. In the context of the Capital Asset Pricing Model, systematic risk is equal to the square of the product of the beta and the market's standard deviation.

Tax Anticipation Note A note secured by taxes already due but not yet paid.

Term Premium Premium in a futures price associated with the fact that the process of marking to market shortens the effective duration of term of the obligation.

Term Structure of Interest Rates The relationship between yield to maturity and term to maturity for securities of a given risk and tax status.

Transactions Demand for Money The demand for money as a medium of exchange, usually kept in checking account balances.

Treasury Bill Security issued by the U.S. Treasury with a maximum maturity of one year and promising a single payment of interest and principal at maturity.

Treasury Bond Security issued by the U.S. Treasury with no maximum maturity and promising semiannual interest payments and return of principal at maturity.

Treasury Note Security issued by the U.S. Treasury having a maximum maturity of seven years and promising semiannual interest payments and return of principal at maturity.

Treynor Index Risk-adjusted performance measure reflecting depth, but not breadth, of performance and equal to the risk premium earned by the portfolio divided by its beta factor.

Two-State Options Pricing Model Model valuing put and call options that assumes, in any given period of time, two rates of return are possible for the underlying asset. The model values the option so as to give anyone hedging with it the risk-free rate of return.

Uniform Probability Distribution Rectangular distribution relating to the ending value for an asset, whereby all values between an extreme high and low value are equally probable.

Unit Normal Distribution Normal probability distribution having an unexpected value of 0 and a standard deviation equal to 1.

Utility of Wealth Function The relationship between your well-being and the amount of wealth you have at any given point in time.

Variance Propensity to deviate from the expected value. The probability weighted squared deviations from the expected value.

Velocity of Money Number of dollars of national income supported by each dollar in the money supply. A measure of the speed with which money turns over in the economy.

Warrant A contract giving the holder the right to buy a specified number of shares of a given asset at a given price on or before a given point in time. The difference between a warrant and a call option is that the former is a primary security, while the latter is a secondary security.

Weak Efficient Market Hypothesis Securities prices fully reflect any information concerning the future of the price series that can be obtained by analyzing the past behavior of the series.

Yield Curve See term structure of interest rates.

INDEX